T0214269

Lecture Notes in Computer Science 12056

Founding Editors

Gerhard Goos
Karlsruhe Institute of Technology, Karlsruhe, Germany
Juris Hartmanis
Cornell University, Ithaca, NY, USA

Editorial Board Members

Elisa Bertino
Purdue University, West Lafayette, IN, USA
Wen Gao
Peking University, Beijing, China
Bernhard Steffen
TU Dortmund University, Dortmund, Germany
Gerhard Woeginger
RWTH Aachen, Aachen, Germany
Moti Yung
Columbia University, New York, NY, USA

More information about this series at http://www.springer.com/series/7410

Abdelmalek Benzekri · Michel Barbeau ·
Guang Gong · Romain Laborde ·
Joaquin Garcia-Alfaro (Eds.)

Foundations and Practice of Security

12th International Symposium, FPS 2019
Toulouse, France, November 5–7, 2019
Revised Selected Papers

 Springer

Editors
Abdelmalek Benzekri
Université Paul Sabatier (CNRS IRIT)
Toulouse, France

Michel Barbeau ⓘ
Carleton University
Ottawa, ON, Canada

Guang Gong
University of Waterloo
Waterloo, ON, Canada

Romain Laborde
Université Paul Sabatier (CNRS IRIT)
Toulouse, France

Joaquin Garcia-Alfaro ⓘ
Telecom SudParis, IMT
Palaiseau, France

ISSN 0302-9743   ISSN 1611-3349   (electronic)
Lecture Notes in Computer Science
ISBN 978-3-030-45370-1   ISBN 978-3-030-45371-8   (eBook)
https://doi.org/10.1007/978-3-030-45371-8

LNCS Sublibrary: SL4 – Security and Cryptology

© Springer Nature Switzerland AG 2020
This work is subject to copyright. All rights are reserved by the Publisher, whether the whole or part of the material is concerned, specifically the rights of translation, reprinting, reuse of illustrations, recitation, broadcasting, reproduction on microfilms or in any other physical way, and transmission or information storage and retrieval, electronic adaptation, computer software, or by similar or dissimilar methodology now known or hereafter developed.
The use of general descriptive names, registered names, trademarks, service marks, etc. in this publication does not imply, even in the absence of a specific statement, that such names are exempt from the relevant protective laws and regulations and therefore free for general use.
The publisher, the authors and the editors are safe to assume that the advice and information in this book are believed to be true and accurate at the date of publication. Neither the publisher nor the authors or the editors give a warranty, expressed or implied, with respect to the material contained herein or for any errors or omissions that may have been made. The publisher remains neutral with regard to jurisdictional claims in published maps and institutional affiliations.

This Springer imprint is published by the registered company Springer Nature Switzerland AG
The registered company address is: Gewerbestrasse 11, 6330 Cham, Switzerland

Preface

This volume contains the papers presented at the 12th International Symposium on Foundations and Practice of Security (FPS 2019), which was held at Crowne Plaza, Toulouse, France, during November 5–7, 2019. The symposium received 50 submissions from countries all over the world. At least two reviews were made for each paper. The Program Committee selected 19 full papers and 9 short papers that cover diverse security research themes including attack prevention, trustworthiness, access control models, cryptography, or blockchain. A strong focus was on artificial intelligence and machine learning approaches with three sessions dedicated to this topic. The Best Paper Award of FPS 2019 was granted to the contribution "PAC: Privacy-preserving Arrhythmia Classification with Neural Networks" presented by Mohamad Mansouri, Beyza Bozdemir, Melek Önen, and Orhan Ermis.

Three excellent invited talks completed the program. Sokratis Katsikas from University of Science and Technology (Norway) and Open University of Cyprus (Cyprus) presented the challenges of securing Industrial Internet of Things, David W. Chadwick from University of Kent (UK) explained the evolution of Identity Management, and Soumaya Cherkaoui from Université de Cherbrooke (Canada) highlighted the challenges and opportunities related to securing 5G Internet of Vehicles. Finally, we introduced this year a new session dedicated to collaborative projects. Adrien Bécue from Airbus Defense and Space presented CyberFactory#1 and Abdelmalek Benzekri from Université Paul Sabatier (France) outlined Cybersec4Europe.

We would like to thank all the authors who submitted their research results allowing for such a great program. The selection was a challenging task and we sincerely thank all the Program Committee members, as well as the external reviewers, who volunteered to read and discuss the papers. We greatly thank the Local Organizing Committee: Marie-Angele Albouy, Abdelmalek Benzekri, François Barrère, Romain Laborde, Benoit Morgan, Florence Sedes, A. Samer Wazan, and Wafa Abdelghani; and the publications and publicity chair, Joaquin Garcia-Alfaro. We would also like to express our gratitude to all the attendees. Last, but by no means least, we want to thank all the sponsors for making the event possible.

To conclude, we would like to dedicate this FPS 2019 edition to François Barrère who left us much too young. François demonstrated during his career not only sound and thorough scientific qualities, but above all, he developed incomparable human qualities. May he rest in peace.

We hope the articles contained in this proceedings volume will be valuable for your professional activities in the area.

December 2019

Abdelmalek Benzekri
Michel Barbeau
Guang Gong
Romain Laborde

Organization

General Chairs

Abdelmalek Benzekri   Université Paul Sabatier, IRIT, France
Michel Barbeau   Carleton University, Canada

Program Committee Chairs

Guang Gong   University of Waterloo, Canada
Romain Laborde   Université Paul Sabatier, IRIT, France

Publications Chair

Joaquin Garcia-Alfaro   Télécom SudParis, France

Local Organizing Committee

Wafa Abdelghani   Université Paul Sabatier, IRIT, France
Marie-Angele Albouy   Université Paul Sabatier, IRIT, France
Abdelmalek Benzekri   Université Paul Sabatier, IRIT, France
François Barrère   Université Paul Sabatier, IRIT, France
Romain Laborde   Université Paul Sabatier, IRIT, France
Benoit Morgan   INPT, ENSEEEIHT, IRIT, France
Florence Sedes   Université Paul Sabatier, IRIT, France
Ahmad Samer Wazan   Université Paul Sabatier, IRIT, France

Program Committee

Diala Abi Haidar   Dar Al-Hekma University, Saudi Arabia
Kamel Adi   University of Quebec in Outaouais, Canada
Esma Aïmeur   Université de Montréal, Canada
Michel Barbeau   Carleton University, Canada
Mostafa Belkasmi   Mohammed V University in Rabat, Morocco
Abdelmalek Benzekri   Université Paul Sabatier, France
Guillaume Bonfante   Université de Lorraine, LORIA, France
Driss Bouzidi   Mohammed V University in Rabat, Morocco
Jordi Castellà-Roca   Universitat Rovira i Virgili, Spain
Ana Cavalli   Télécom SudParis, France
Frédéric Cuppens   IMT Atlantique, France
Nora Cuppens-Boulahia   IMT Atlantique, France
Mila Dalla Preda   University of Verona, Italy
Jean-Luc Danger   Télécom Paris, France

Vanesa Daza	Universitat Pompeu Fabra, Spain
Mourad Debbabi	Concordia University, Canada
Roberto Di Pietro	Hamad Bin Khalifa University, Qatar
Josep Domingo-Ferrer	Universitat Rovira i Virgili, Spain
Nicola Dragoni	Technical University of Denmark, Denmark
Eric Freyssinet	LORIA, France
Sebastien Gambs	Université du Québec à Montréal, Canada
Joaquin Garcia-Alfaro	Télécom SudParis, France
Guang Gong	University of Waterloo, Canada
Abdelwahab Hamou-Lhadj	Concordia University, Canada
Jordi Herrera-Joancomarti	Universitat Autònoma de Barcelona, Spain
Bruce Kapron	University of Victoria, Canada
Raphaël Khoury	Université du Québec à Chicoutimi, Canada
Hyoungshick Kim	Sungkyunkwan University, South Korea
Evangelos Kranakis	Carleton University, Canada
Igor Kotenko	SPIIRAS, Russia
Romain Laborde	Université Paul Sabatier, France
Pascal Lafourcade	Université Clermont Auvergne, France
Luigi Logrippo	University of Quebec in Outaouais, Canada
Suryadipta Majumdar	University at Albany, USA
Jean-Yves Marion	Université de Lorraine, LORIA, France
Ali Miri	Ryerson University, Canada
Benoit Morgan	INP Toulouse, France
Paliath Narendran	University at Albany, USA
Guillermo Navarro-Arribas	Autonomous University of Barcelona, Spain
Jun Pang	University of Luxembourg, Luxembourg
Milan Petkovic	Philips Research, The Netherlands
Marie-Laure Potet	Université Grenoble Alpes, VERIMAG, France
Silvio Ranise	Fondazione Bruno Kessler, Italy
Indrakshi Ray	Colorado State University, USA
Jean-Marc Robert	École de technologie supérieure, Canada
Michaël Rusinowitch	LORIA, Inria Nancy, France
Reyhaneh Safavi-Naini	University of Calgary, Canada
Kazuo Sakiyama	The University of Electro-Communications, Japan
Paria Shirani	Concordia University, Canada
Chamseddine Talhi	École de Technologie Supérieure, Canada
Nadia Tawbi	Université Laval, Canada
Alexandre Viejo	Universitat Rovira i Virgili, Spain
Edgar Weippl	SBA Research, Austria
Nicola Zannone	Eindhoven University of Technology, The Netherlands
Nur Zincir-Heywood	Dalhousie University, Canada

Additional Reviewers

Kevin Atighehchi
Olivier Blazy
Salimeh Dashti
Michele De Donno
Alberto Giaretta
Yoshikazu Hanatani
Yota Katsikouli

Vinh Hoa La
Marius Lombard-Platet
Wissam Mallouli
Cristina Onete
Bagus Santoso
Mariana Segovia
Eunil Seo

Steering Committee

Frédéric Cuppens	IMT Atlantique, France
Nora Cuppens-Boulahia	IMT Atlantique, France
Mourad Debbabi	University of Concordia, Canada
Joaquin Garcia-Alfaro	Télécom SudParis, France
Evangelos Kranakis	Carleton University, Canada
Pascal Lafourcade	Université d'Auvergne, France
Jean-Yves Marion	Mines de Nancy, France
Ali Miri	Ryerson University, Canada
Rei Safavi-Naini	Calgary University, Canada
Nadia Tawbi	Université Laval, Canada

Contents

Machine Learning Approaches

PAC: Privacy-Preserving Arrhythmia Classification with Neural Networks

Mohamad Mansouri, Beyza Bozdemir$^{(\boxtimes)}$, Melek Önen, and Orhan Ermis

EURECOM, Sophia Antipolis, France
{Mohamad.Mansouri,Beyza.Bozdemir,Melek.Onen,Orhan.Ermis}@eurecom.fr

Abstract. In this paper, we propose to study privacy concerns raised by the analysis of Electro CardioGram (ECG) data for arrhythmia classification. We propose a solution named PAC that combines the use of Neural Networks (NN) with secure two-party computation in order to enable an efficient NN prediction of arrhythmia without discovering the actual ECG data. To achieve a good trade-off between privacy, accuracy, and efficiency, we first build a dedicated NN model which consists of two fully connected layers and one activation layer as a square function. The solution is implemented with the ABY framework. PAC also supports classifications in batches. Experimental results show an accuracy of 96.34% which outperforms existing solutions.

Keywords: Privacy · Neural networks · Arrhythmia classification

1 Introduction

Artificial intelligence and machine learning have gained a renewed popularity thanks to the recent advances in information technology such as the Internet of Things that help collect, share, and process data, easily. This powerful technology helps make better decisions and accurate predictions in many domains including finance, healthcare, etc. In particular, Neural Networks (NN) can support pharmacists and doctors to analyse patients' data and quickly diagnose a particular disease such as heart arrhythmia. Nowadays, this disease can be detected at early stages with the help of smart wearable devices such as Apple Watch 4[1] that can record electric heart activities using Electro-Cardiograms (ECG) data. Nevertheless, we are experiencing severe data breaches and these cause crucial damages. A recent research[2] concludes that in 2018, the global average cost of a data breach is 3.86 million dollars and the healthcare sector is the first sector facing huge costs. ECG data is considered as very sensitive. Therefore, there is an urgent need for tools enabling the protection of such data while still being able to launch predictive analytics and hence improve individuals' lives. These

---

[1] https://www.apple.com/lae/apple-watch-series-4/health/.
[2] https://www.ibm.com/security/data-breach.

© Springer Nature Switzerland AG 2020
A. Benzekri et al. (Eds.): FPS 2019, LNCS 12056, pp. 3–19, 2020.
https://doi.org/10.1007/978-3-030-45371-8_1

tools will also help stakeholders be compliant with the General Data Protection Regulations (GDPR)[3].

In this work, we aim at addressing privacy concerns raised by the analysis of the ECG data for arrhythmia classification. Our goal is to enable service providers (data processors) perform classification without discovering the input (the ECG data). On the other hand, we also look into the problem from the service providers' point of view as they care about keeping the design of their services confidential from the users (data subjects or data controllers). Users using these systems/solutions should not be able to discover the details about the underlying system (such as the Neural Network model). The challenge often manifests as a choice between the privacy of the user and the secrecy of the system parameters. We propose to reconcile both parties, namely the service providers and the users and combine the use of neural networks with secure two-party computation (2PC). Since 2PC protocols cannot efficiently support all kinds of operations, we propose to revisit the underlying neural network operations and design a new, customized neural network model that can be executed to classify arrhythmia accurately, and this, without disclosing neither the input ECG data to the service provider nor the neural network parameters to the users.

With this aim, we reduce the input size of neural network by employing Principal Component Analysis (PCA) [6]. The proposed methodology is illustrated with a case study whereby some arrhythmia dataset from the PhysioBank database[4] is used. With this dataset, we show that the newly designed model only involves 2 layers with 54 hidden neurons. The resulting model is implemented in a realistic environment and uses the ABY framework [11] for 2PC. Experimental results show that the most optimal resulting model reaches an accuracy level of 96.34%. Our solution helps predict the class of one heartbeat in 1 s, approximately. In order to improve the performance of the solution even further, we propose to make predictions in batches and thus help the analyser (the doctor) receive the prediction of a set of heartbeats for a given period (e.g., 30 s). We show that by using the Single Instruction Multiple Data (SIMD) packing method offered by ABY, the computational overhead is significantly reduced.

In the next section, we introduce the problem of arrhythmia classification and identify the main challenges to ensure the privacy of the ECG data at the same time. Section 3 focuses on the case study and presents the newly proposed privacy-preserving variant of the neural network that we name PAC together with experimental results. In Sect. 4, we describe the additional optimisation method which consists of executing predictions in batches. Finally, we review the state of the art in Sect. 5.

---

[3] https://eur-lex.europa.eu/eli/reg/2016/679/oj.
[4] https://www.physionet.org/physiobank/database/mitdb/.

2   Problem Statement

As defined in [22], cardiac arrhythmias are abnormal heart rhythms, which cause the heart to beat too fast (tachycardia) or too slow (bradycardia) and to pump blood less effectively. These irregularities can be detected and classified by analyzing the Electro-Cardiogram (ECG) signals of a heart. Doctors classify arrhythmia to several types according to such behaviors of the heart.

In this work, we focus on the classification of heartbeats extracted from ECG signals into different classes of arrhythmia using machine learning techniques. In order to design an efficient arrhythmia classifier, we propose to use Neural Networks (NN). ECG signals representing patients' heartbeats can be considered as sensitive information. Thus, we aim at finding a solution where a service provider can execute the classification model without leaking and even discovering information about the input data. On the other hand, the classification model can also be considered as confidential against users, namely parties who will send their queries for classification. This model itself can also have some business value and therefore be protected. For this respect, we assume that the model should be unknown to the parties sending queries.

Performing some operations over data while these are kept confidential requires the use of advanced cryptographic tools such as homomorphic encryption [5,13,14,31] or secure multi-party computation [23,25]. While the integration of such tools offers better privacy guarantees, they unfortunately introduce some non-negligible overhead in terms of computation and communication. Furthermore, these tools may not always be compatible with the complex NN operations. Hence, we propose to follow a privacy-by-design approach and consider privacy requirements at the design phase of the neural network. We have identified the following three main challenges when building a neural network model customized for the use of privacy enhancing technologies:

- **Large size of the NN:** The size of the neural network directly depends on the size of the input and output vectors, the number of layers, and the number of neurons in the model. These parameters have a significant impact on the complexity of the model. Hence, the size of the neural network has to be optimized when designing privacy-preserving variants. Such an optimization, on the other hand, should not have an impact on the actual accuracy of the model.
- **Complex NN operations:** A neural network involves various operations executed by each neuron during the classification phase. These include sophisticated operations such as sigmoid or hyperbolic tangent that may not be easily and efficiently supported by existing cryptographic tools. Hence, the underlying operations should be optimized and sometimes even transformed when designing the privacy-preserving variant of the neural network classification model.
- **Real numbers instead of integers:** Most of the operations in the neural network are executed over real numbers whereas cryptographic tools usually support integers. Therefore, there is a need for either supporting floating point

numbers or approximating them to integers. Such an approximation should nevertheless not have a significant impact on the accuracy of the model.

To summarize, when designing a neural network model customized for the use of privacy enhancing technologies, one should address the trade-off between privacy, performance, and accuracy. The dedicated model should involve an optimized number of "simple" operations that advanced cryptographic tools can support while reaching a good accuracy level.

3 Privacy-Preserving Neural Network Arrhythmia Classifier - A Case Study with PhysioBank

In this section, we describe the privacy-by-design approach in details and use a publicly available database, namely the PhysioBank database, to build a concrete model as an example and evaluate the accuracy and performance of the newly developed model.

3.1 Solution Idea

In order to address the three main challenges identified in the previous section, we propose to build a neural network model from scratch. This approach is illustrated with a case study where a publicly available arrhythmia dataset is used. The design of the NN model is combined with secure two-party computation (2PC) which enables two parties to jointly compute a function over their private inputs without revealing any extra information about these inputs than what is leaked by the result of the computation. This setting is well motivated and captures many different applications to ensure privacy protection[5]. We propose to use ABY [11], a mixed-protocol framework that efficiently combines the use of Arithmetic shares, Boolean shares, and Yao's garbled circuits.

As for the design of the appropriate model, we propose to define a small neural network with two fully connected (FC) layers, one activation layer, and one softmax layer. This architecture seems sufficient to achieve a good accuracy level (see next section). The number of intermediate neurons can be optimized based on several simulations evaluating the accuracy of a model for each case. Additionally, to reduce the number of input neurons, we propose to apply Principal Component Analysis (PCA) [6] and filter out the most significant inputs. Furthermore, because of the complexity of the activation functions, we propose to use the square function, only. This operation can be supported by 2PC more efficiently. The design of the new model customized for the use of 2PC should not result in a significant decrease on the accuracy of the classification.

All operations within the newly designed neural network model will be executed through a client-server system, whereby the client who could be considered as the patient (Data Subject) or the hospital (Data Controller) holds the input

---

[5] Lectures 1&2: Introduction to Secure Computation, Yao's and GMW Protocols, Secure Computation Course at Berkeley University.

vector and the server (Data Processor) holds the model's parameters. The underlying protocol should therefore ensure (i) the **secrecy of the input** supplied by the client which means that the client would like to get the prediction results without leaking any information about the heartbeat signal; (ii) the **secrecy of the model parameters** supplied by the server while assuming that the client knows the architecture of the model, only; (iii) the **secrecy of the prediction results** with respect to the server.

3.2   The Optimized Neural Network Model

In order to ensure data privacy during the arrhythmia classification phase, a dedicated neural network model should be computed. Because the use of cryptographic primitives adds a non-negligible overhead, the complexity of the model should be optimized as much as possible. Hence, the primary goal while building a new prediction model, is to optimize the number of neurons at each layer while keeping an adequate accuracy level. As mentioned in the previous section, the cryptographic tool that we chose to ensure data privacy is 2PC [23] whereby the client holds the input vector, and the server has the NN prediction model which consists of the weight matrices and bias vectors. Similarly to [12] and [7], nonlinear operations such as the activation functions should be replaced with more efficient operations such as low degree polynomials. In this section, we describe our approach with a case study using the MIT-BIH arrhythmia dataset from the PhysioBank database. The resulting neural network model is presented with an incremental approach.

We first extract heartbeats from the Electro-Cardiogram (ECG) signals. Each heartbeat is composed of 180 samples with 90 samples before the R-peak, 1 sample for the R-peak, and, 89 samples after the R-peak. Once heartbeats were extracted, we have performed various filtering operations to create an appropriate dataset to build the neural network model. The PhysioBank database is shown in Table 1 and contains 23 different annotations for the extracted heartbeats. We have decided to only consider 16 out of 23 annotations representing meaningful arrhythmia classes that have significant number of instances in the dataset. Secondly, we realized that normal beats were dominating the dataset (67.3%) and hence resulting in an unbalanced dataset for model training purposes. We have reduced the number of normal beats in order for the model to predict anomalies more accurately while keeping this number sufficiently large so that it reflects reality. Moreover, we have used the over-sampling method to enforce the learning of low frequent classes such as class "e". Table 1 provides details about the final dataset we are actually using. We have removed some heartbeats from the dataset since the classes of V, ", —, Q do not represent any arrhythmia class, and also [,], S are rare. This dataset is further split such that 80% of the heartbeats are used to train the network and 20% of the heartbeats are used as a test dataset. We propose a model with 2 fully connected (FC) layers, one activation function, and a final softmax function that would provide the resulting arrhythmia class.

Table 1. Heartbeats for Arrhythmia classification and frequency in datasets

Arrhythmia class	Symbol	Our dataset		PhysioBank dataset	
		#	%	#	%
Normal beat	N	14985	34.02%	59926	66.593%
Left bundle branch block beat	L	6450	14.64%	6450	7.168%
Right bundle branch block beat	R	5794	13.15%	5794	6.439%
Premature ventricular contraction	V	5712	12.97%	5712	6.347%
Paced beat	/	5608	12.73%	5608	6.232%
Atrial premature beat	A	2042	4.64%	2042	2.269%
Rhythm change	+	1005	2.28%	1005	1.117%
Fusion of paced and normal beat	f	786	1.78%	786	0.873%
Fusion of ventricular and normal beat	F	647	1.47%	647	0.719%
Ventricular flutter wave	!	378	0.86%	378	0.42%
Nodal (junctional) escape beat	j	184	0.42%	184	0.204%
Non-conducted P-wave (blocked APB)	x	155	0.35%	155	0.172%
Aberrated atrial premature beat	a	123	0.28%	123	0.137%
Ventricular escape beat	E	85	0.19%	85	0.094%
Nodal (junctional) premature beat	J	68	0.15%	68	0.076%
Atrial escape beat	e	26	0.06%	13	0.014%
Signal quality change	V	NA	NA	508	0.565%
Comment annotation	"	NA	NA	352	0.391%
Isolated QRS-like artifact	—	NA	NA	112	0.124%
Unclassifiable beat	Q	NA	NA	29	0.032%
Start of ventricular flutter/fibrillation	[	NA	NA	5	0.006%
End of ventricular flutter/fibrillation	]	NA	NA	5	0.006%
Premature or ectopic supraventricular beat	S	NA	NA	2	0.002%

We now aim at optimizing the number of neurons in each layer. The number of neurons in the **output layer** corresponds to the number of arrhythmia classes. As shown in Table 1, we decide to take the first 16 out of the 23 arrhythmia classes in the studied dataset. Hence, the number of neurons in the output layer is set to 16.

In order to choose the appropriate number of neurons within the **hidden FC layer**, we have evaluated the accuracy of models on the validation dataset whereby the number of neurons varies from 2 to 100. We not only evaluate the overall accuracy but compute the confusion matrix that indicates the accuracy with respect to each arrhythmia class. We observe that 38 is a good choice as this implies less complexity in the model as well as its corresponding confusion matrix shows better fairness toward less frequent classes (see [26] for more details). The accuracy of our model is 96.51%. We represent the model's performance on the test dataset with the confusion matrix as illustrated in Fig. 1.

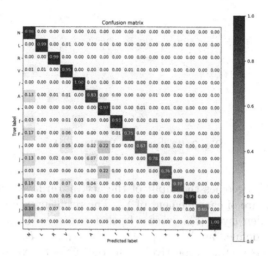

Fig. 1. Confusion matrix of the model for each class in the test dataset

The other parameter that affects the complexity of the NN model is the size of the **input vector**. This inherently reduces the dimension of the first matrix used for the FC layer. The main tool to adequately reduce the number of neurons of the input layer is the principal component analysis technique (PCA) [20]. PCA uses orthogonal linear transformations to find a projection of all input data (ECG heartbeats) into k dimensions which are defined as the principal components. Hence, PCA outputs the k features with the largest variance. The first k eigenvectors of the covariance matrix (of the dataset) are the target dimensions. The efficiency of using PCA for the ECG analysis domain has also been proved in [6]. It also helps reduce the noise in the ECG signals and hence improve the accuracy of the model. This is due to the fact that dimensions with low variance noise are automatically discarded. To identify the appropriate number of eigenvalues we run a simulation with 100 hidden neurons and change the value of the input size n starting from $n = 180$. The same simulation is executed using the square operation as for the activation function. From this analysis, we choose to set the input size to 16, mainly because the resulting prediction model provides good accuracy with acceptable complexity. Hence, the number of neurons of the input layer is now set to 16 (please see [26] for more details).

The Resulting Model: To summarize, the developed model, compatible with the use of 2PC, consists of 2-FC layer involving matrix multiplication, one activation layer implementing a square function and one softmax function. The architecture of the proposed neural network model is shown in Fig. 2.

The first layer consists of a fully connected layer and its main operations are: $Y'_h = X^T.W_h + B_h$. In this equation, X represents the input vector (PCA transform of a heartbeat). This input vector X of size 16 is multiplied with the weight matrix of the hidden layer, W_h, of size 16×38. This intermediate result is further added to the bias vector of the hidden layer, B_h, of size 38. The

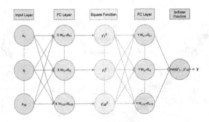

Fig. 2. The proposed NN model

resulting vector Y_h' becomes the input of the activation layer which consists of computing the square of each element of Y_h'. The resulting vector Y_h is the final output of the hidden layer. This vector further becomes the input for another FC layer which is defined as: $Y' = Y_h^T.W_o + B_o$. W_o and B_o denote the weight matrix and the bias vector, respectively. The output is the vector Y' of size 16. Finally, a softmax function is executed over the components y_j' of Y'. The aim of this function is to mainly identify the actual predicted class (the one that shows the greatest probability). The result y is the index of one of the 16 arrhythmia classes.

In total, the prediction phase consists of: $16 \times 38 + 38 \times 16 + 38 = 1254$ multiplications, $15 \times 38 + 38 + 37 \times 16 + 16 = 1216$ additions, 16 exponentiations, 16 divisions and 1 argmax operation.

Discussion on Principle Component Analysis: As previously mentioned, the NN model is revised and designed from scratch in order to be compatible with 2PC and remain as efficient as possible. To improve the performance of the classification phase, the size of the input is reduced using the Principle component analysis (PCA) method. PCA is a statistical method which identifies patterns, highlights similarity between elements within the dataset and finally reduces the dimension of the feature space. More formally, let S be a dataset and x_i be an element of it with dimension d. The first step of PCA (executed by the server) consists of computing the mean μ of all the elements x_i. Then, the covariance matrix A of S is computed. The eigenvectors and corresponding eigenvalues of matrix A are further evaluated and the first k eigenvectors with the largest eigenvalues are selected. In this particular case, where the dataset consists of 44048 heartbeats of 180 samples, the server obtains he 180×16 matrix of the most relevant eigenvectors. This matrix along with the vector μ is sent to the client who reduces the dimension of its input to 16 by first by subtracting his signal with the mean vector and further multiplying the result with the received matrix.

The use of the PCA transformation at the client side can result in some information leakage. The leakage resulting from the use of PCA mainly are the mean of the dataset and the 180×16 covariance matrix. We argue that the mean of all the signals in the training dataset does not carry any valuable information since the labels of the training signals are not included in the computation of the mean. On the other hand, the matrix of 16 eigenvectors does not correspond to the entire matrix of eigenvectors. Additionally, without the knowledge of the eigenvalues there exist an infinite number of inverse transformations back to the original covariance matrix. Therefore, one cannot discover the training dataset and hence the model from this reduced and transformed matrix.

On the other hand, we can also choose not to leak such information while designing the privacy-preserving NN classification. In this case, we either do not use PCA (which causes high bandwidth and computational cost) or include the PCA steps to the 2PC solution (additional overhead but less costly at the first FC layer). Accordingly, in this work, we propose the following three design approaches for PAC (as shown in Fig. 3) and evaluate the performance for each of them:

- Model 1: PCA is not integrated to 2PC (original and most efficient solution implies some leakage),
- Model 2: PCA is integrated to 2PC (less efficient but no leakage),
- Model 3: PCA is not used (worse performance but no leakage).

SIMD Circuits: In addition to reducing the size of the neural network and decreasing the cost of the underlying operations, we also take advantage of Single Instruction Multiple Data (SIMD) circuits which allow the packing of multiple data elements and the execution of operations in parallel. We use this technique to perform the matrix multiplications and additions more efficiently. In more details, since the number of hidden neurons is 38, the client creates the SIMD version of its input X (of size 16) repeated 38 times (i.e. the size of the share is $38 * 16 = 608$). Similarly, the server creates a SIMD version of the weight matrices W_h (of size 16×38) and W_o (of size 38×16) by flattening them to two vectors of 608 elements. Once these versions obtained, one single SIMD multiplication gate can be used to perform element-wise multiplication. The server also creates a SIMD version of the bias vectors and adds them to the vector resulting from the previous SIMD matrix multiplication. The square activation function can also be computed using one SIMD multiplication gate. To implement the argmax function, we transform the SIMD share of the previous layer to a non-SIMD share (i.e., the SIMD share is composed of 1 wire holding all the 16 values of Y' while the non-SIMD share is composed of 16 wires each wire will hold one value of Y').

Moreover, we propose a secure computation of PCA in Model 2. As previously described, the computation of the PCA can eventually introduce a limited leakage of the training dataset. Therefore, in Model 2, we propose to introduce the computation of the PCA vector into the 2PC. The two parties will first collaboratively compute PCA of the signal (using the confidential mean and the 16 eigenvectors) and further perform classification similarly to Model 1. This PCA computation layer adds 181 SIMD addition gates and 1 SIMD multiplication gate.

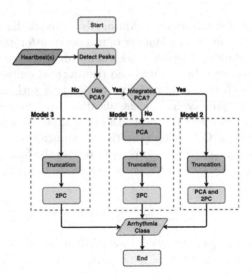

Fig. 3. PAC overview

3.3   PAC: Detailed Description

As previously mentioned, we propose to use 2PC to obtain the privacy-preserving variant of the arrhythmia prediction model, i.e., PAC. Since the underlying model involves several different operations (such as additions, multiplications and comparisons), we propose to use the ABY framework which supports all basic operations in a flexible manner using Arithmetic, Boolean or Yao's circuits. ABY supports Single Instruction Multiple Data (SIMD) gates. Furthermore, the current ABY implementation[6] also supports floating point representation if Boolean circuits are used. Hence, we first implement the privacy-preserving model using Boolean circuits. Nevertheless, floating point representation and the use of Boolean circuits appear to be inefficient. We therefore propose some improvements using fixed point representations that may result in some truncations of the inputs or intermediate values in the circuit. Additionally, since operations executed over Boolean shares are much more expensive than those executed over arithmetic shares, we propose to replace Boolean gates with arithmetic gates as much as possible, hence improve the system. Due to the space limitation, we have not included the model using Boolean circuits and refer to [26] for more details.

As the multiplication of two fixed-point numbers can yield numbers with a number of bits higher than the two initial numbers, hence to an overflow, these numbers need to be truncated and/or rounded in order to ensure that all intermediate values can be represented in 64 bits. We mainly propose two truncation methods: The first method consists of applying truncation at intermediate stages in the circuit and hence try to continuously keep a good accuracy level whereas

---

[6] https://github.com/encryptogroup/ABY.

the second method truncates the inputs before the prediction process starts, only. In this section, we only present the second truncation method since it shows better performance gains. The description of the first truncation method is given in the full version of the paper [26]. In this truncation approach, only the inputs to the circuits are truncated and this before the actual execution of the circuit. In order to avoid overflows, we multiply X, W_o and W_h by 10^3, B_h by 10^6 and B_o by 10^{15} and truncate the fractional part afterwards. We observe that this method is as safe as the maximum number a signed 64-bit integer variable can take is $9.223372037 \times 10^{18}$ and the upper bound for the values of Y' is 9,223 and the lower bound is $-9,223$. We observe that the risk of overflow is very low.

Thanks to this new approach, the actual circuit only consists of arithmetic gates except at the last stage where an argmax operation needs to be executed. We have tested the accuracy of the new model using the test dataset and we have achieved an accuracy of 96.34% which is very close to the accuracy of the original model (96.51%). The confusion matrix of the new model shows the same accuracies as presented in the original model (see Fig. 1).

To evaluate the computational and communication overhead of the model in a real setting, experiments were carried out by a computer which has four 3.60 GHz Intel Core i7-7700 processors, 32 GB of RAM acting as the server and a laptop which has two 1.70 GHz Intel Core i5-4210U processors, 4 GB of RAM acting as the client. On the other hand, the client and the server communicate through a local area network (LAN). The client is connected to the LAN through a wireless access point. A simulation of the bandwidth and the latency of the connection between the client and the server showed the values of 39 Mbit/sec for the bandwidth and 3.36 ms for the latency. Furthermore, we run the client and the server on two separate processes communicating through the localhost of the same computer, specifically the one with the four 3.60 GHz Intel Cores to evaluate the performance of the model without considering the limitation of the bandwidth. In ABY, we set the security parameter to 128 bits.

Table 2 shows the performance results in terms of prediction time and bandwidth consumption for the original Boolean circuits as well as for the 3 models implementing arithmetic circuits, mainly. Moreover, we have repeated all evaluations on a local set-up, i.e., the localhost on one machine, to give an insight about the overhead incurred by the low bandwidth (please see the full version for details). The prediction time of one heartbeat is measured as the total time adding to the BaseOT time.

We have also evaluated the performance of the prediction model without using any privacy enhancing technologies and making use of Tensorflow[7]. It takes 7.29 ms to predict one heartbeat in cleartext while this value becomes 117,859 ms with PAC (without any truncation). Nevertheless, from Table 2, we observe some significant performance gain in terms of computational and communication cost by employing the truncation method. Compared to the model built with Boolean circuits, the Total time with the second truncation method is reduced by a factor of 108.

---

[7] https://www.tensorflow.org/.

Table 2. Performance results for each model

Proposed NN models	Boolean circuits	Truncation v1		Truncation v2			
	Model 1	Model 1	Model 2	Model 1 without ARGMAX	Model 1	Model 2	Model 3
Circuit							
Gates	553925	35477	36418	128	34329	34696	34660
Depth	4513	160	168	5	146	147	146
Time (ms)							
Total[a]	117571.82	1218.613	2776.862	735.357	1082.804	2641.846	4723.203
Init	0.046	0.076	0.071	0.056	0.062	0.037	0.033
CircuitGen	0.046	0.074	0.062	0.067	0.078	0.055	0.047
Network[a]	272.867	268.39	94.142	248.92	51.391	89.46	34.221
BaseOTs	288.047	309.288	310.06	311.387	291.705	294.698	298.294
Setup[a]	107481.557	851.397	2373.818	714.511	817.807	2354.391	4409.689
OTExtension	106645.796	847.424	2369.377	714.278	816.069	2351.584	4407.521
Garbling	812.573	2.502	3.268	0.002	1.405	1.851	1.252
Online	10090.26	367.21	403.042	20.844	264.995	287.453	313.512
Data transfer (Sent/Rcv, in KB)							
Total	319269/309573	2629/2252	7113/6651	1910/1900	2171/2095	6560/6461	12266/12139
BaseOTs	48/48	48/48	48/48	48/48	48/48	48/48	48/48
Setup	305915/304815	2240/2227	6591/6579	1881/1881	2086/2071	6406/6391	12025/12010
OTExtension	301095/304815	2057/2227	6377/6579	1881/1881	2053/2071	6373/6391	11992/12010
Garbling	4819/0	183/0	214/0	0/0	33/0	33/0	33/0
Online	13354/4757	389/25	522/72	29/19	85/24	154/70	240/129

[a]The Total time corresponds to the Setup time and the Online time. The Network time represents the time for the connection to be established. The Setup time corresponds to the OTExtension time and the Garbling time.

Model 2 still provides better results than Model 3 of which is built without the use of the PCA method: The time and bandwidth consumption of Model 3 is larger with a factor of 1.8 than Model 2. We have also implemented Model 2 without the argmax layer (the output is a vector of 16-value where its argmax can be computed locally by the client) to show the size and performance of the arithmetic circuit without introducing any Boolean gates. Finally, the time performance presented in the table is highly affected by the low bandwidth of the communication channel between the client and the server. The time performance difference can be easily seen by comparing the results in Table 2 with the one in Table 5 in the full paper which represent the result of when the client and the server resides on the same machine and so no bandwidth limitation can affect the result. We observe that the time consumption of the model evaluated locally on the same machine can reach 39.785 ms which is 27 times less than the remotely evaluated model. This limitation comes from the core of the 2PC protocol which suffers from high bandwidth consumption. We believe this problem can be easily solved by a decent connection between the client and the server.

4   PAC in Batches

In this section, we propose to perform arrhythmia predictions in batches, namely, with several heartbeat inputs. This can be justified as the classification of a single heartbeat may not be sufficient to diagnose the disease for a patient and the doctor may need to receive the classification of the n consecutive heartbeats.

We also realize that, the online time becomes relatively short when the proposed design is used and that 21.2% (82.2% in case of evaluation on the same machine) of the Total time corresponds to the BaseOT phase. This phase is only processed once the two parties initiate the protocol. Hence, the overall time may again be decreased by performing predictions in batches (i.e., performing prediction of many ECG signals at once) using the SIMD technique, once again.

Indeed, the client may first record N signals, prepare the inputs, and further store them in a matrix $S(N)$ (see the full paper [26]). This matrix is further flattened into a vector of $16.N$ elements. Similarly, the server transforms the weight matrix vectors W_h and W_o and obtains vectors of $16.38.N$ elements. The server also creates the bias vectors $B_h(N)$ and $B_o(N)$ of size $38.N$ and $16.N$, respectively (see their representations in the original paper) by expanding the two original bias vectors B_h and B_o, respectively.

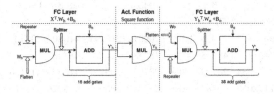

Fig. 4. Arithmetic circuit representation of the model with Truncation v2

The Arithmetic circuit of the NN model is implemented as described in Fig. 4 whereby only the structure of the inputs and output differ (i.e. SIMD vectors result in larger size). The number of SIMD multiplications does not change since all values are regrouped in one SIMD share and the multiplication is further performed. The number of SIMD additions also remains the same.

Finally, the Boolean circuit which represents the argmax layer is also performed with SIMD gates. Values of each class in each individual output in the vector $Y(N)$ are grouped in separate SIMD vectors. The same comparison and multiplexers gates described before are used but this time the inputs are SIMD shares of the Boolean circuit is the vector $y(N)$ whereby each value represents the index of the class of the corresponding individual.

We have run experiments with different batch sizes using the local and remote setups. The results are given in Table 3 for the remote setup (see Table 6 in the full paper [26] for the local setup). We can observe that the number of gates y slightly increases with respect to the number of heartbeats, which is much better than performing prediction on signals individually which will cost $y = 34329\,N$ gates. Also, the depth is constant regardless of the number of input heartbeats the model predicts.

We observe that the Total time still increases linearly with the number of signals but with a much better rate. More specifically, the batches model can

Table 3. Performance results for the multi-signal model

	# Input signals				
	1	10	100	200	400
Circuit					
Gates	33741	39552	40918	42422	45426
Depth	148	148	148	148	148
Time (ms)					
Total	1084.713	8002.287	77867.26	160114.6	314311
Init	0.061	0.09	0.062	0.059	0.058
CircuitGen	0.041	0.043	0.052	0.053	0.066
Network	7.115	7.681	7.513	5.34	4.307
BaseOTs	290.672	294.094	293.867	300.302	285.169
Setup	814.036	7575.32	75821.76	155921.4	306985
OTExtension	808.49	7509.797	75149.46	154673.2	304616
Garbling	5.056	62.455	650.642	1214.046	2310
Online	270.673	426.961	2045.492	4193.194	7325.77
Bandwidth (Rcv/Sent in KB)					
Total	2095/2167	21010/21652	209912/216247	419805/432465	839588/864898
BaseOTs	48/48	48/48	48/48	48/48	48/48
Setup	2071/2084	20782/20936	207647/209107	415276/418186	830533/836342
OTExtension	2071/2053	20782/20612	207647/205947	415276/411876	830532/823732
Garbling	0/31	0/315	0/3159	0/6309	0/12609
Online	24/83	227/716	2264/7139	4528/14278	9055/28555

decrease the time consumption with a percentage of 27% (70% in case of local evaluation) compared to performing prediction on signals one by one which takes $t = 1082.8\,\mathrm{N}\,\mathrm{ms}$ ($t = 39.7\,\mathrm{N}$ in case of local evaluation). Finally, the BaseOT time is approximately 290 ms and remains constant regardless to the number of input signals the model predicts. This is, again, much better than performing prediction on signals, one by one, where the BaseOT time bt costs $bt = 290\,\mathrm{ms}$. Table 3 also shows that the bandwidth grows linear with the number of signals.

To summarize, prediction in batches does improve performance in terms of computational cost but the size of the batch should be bounded according to bandwidth limitations.

5   Related Work

Existing privacy-preserving neural network classification techniques mostly focus on Convolutional Neural Networks (CNN) with the goal of classifying images and achieve data privacy using homomorphic encryption [4,7,9,12,15,16,18,19,34], secure multi-party computation [1,8,10,24,27,28,32,33,36], both techniques [3, 21,30], or, trusted hardware [17,29,35]. Similarly to our work, these methods aim at reducing the complexity of the underlying neural networks. However, the application scenarios (image classification with CNNs) significantly differ from ours (arrhythmia classification) and their models are more complex and not easily comparable to our solutions.

The closest study to our work is [2] which specifically focuses on privacy-preserving arrhythmia classification with neural networks. Authors in [2] use 2PC combined with a partially homomorphic encryption [31]. Their protocol is executed between the client who protects the input vector and the server who stores the model. Similarly to our model, their neural network is also composed of two layers: one hidden layer with SATLIN (a symmetric saturating linear) as an activation function and the output layer implementing the argmax function to decide on the arrhythmia class. Although this work uses the same dataset from the PhysioBank datasets as we do, authors achieve an accuracy of 86.3% whereas PAC reaches 96.43% for the classification of each heartbeat. Furthermore, while our model seems slightly more complex than the one in [2] ($38 + 16 = 54$ neurons instead of $6 + 6 = 12$ neurons), it shows better accuracy and performance results: The communication channel used in [2] is set to 1 Gbit/sec which is much larger than our bandwidth estimation (39 Mbit/sec). Authors evaluated the timing complexity to be about 7 s whereas our solution predicts one heartbeat in 1 s within a more realistic scenario (less performance in the client-side and lower bandwidth). This may be considered acceptable in applications wherein heartbeats are classified at the same pace at which they are produced. Additionally, the accuracy of the predicted heartbeat is higher and further, the number of output neurons is set to 16, PAC detects more arrhythmia classes. Moreover, the solution in [2] combines the use of homomorphic encryption with garbled circuits. The use of both techniques renders the prediction protocol more time consuming compared to PAC whereby mostly arithmetic circuits are used. Finally, while both solutions use packing at the encryption stage and thus allow for prediction in batches, our solution additionally parallelizes each operation in the model (using the SIMD packing method, once again) and hence optimizes the timing complexity.

6   Conclusion

In this paper, we have presented PAC, a methodology for designing Privacy-preserving Arrhythmia Classification that keeps users' ECG data confidential against service providers and the neural network model confidential against users. As a case study, we have designed a new model based on the PhysioBank dataset. The proposed model involves a customized two-layer neural network with 54 neurons. This model was built from scratch in order to be compatible with 2PC. The solution is implemented with the ABY framework which required the truncation of input values and model parameters. The second truncation method combined with Arithmetic circuits consists of multiplying the input values with 10^3 and shows significant improvement in terms of performance and accuracy. PAC achieves an accuracy of 96.34% and experimental results show that the prediction of one heartbeat takes approximately 1 s in real world scenarios. We show that more savings can be achieved with the use of SIMD for performing predictions in batches.

Acknowledgments. This work was partly supported by the PAPAYA project funded by the European Union's Horizon 2020 Research and Innovation Programme, under Grant Agreement no. 786767.

References

1. Ball, M., Carmer, B., Malkin, T., Rosulek, M., Schimanski, N.: Garbled neural networks are practical. Cryptology ePrint Archive, Report 2019/338 (2019). https://eprint.iacr.org/2019/338
2. Barni, M., Failla, P., Lazzeretti, R., Sadeghi, A.R., Schneider, T.: Privacy-preserving ECG classification with branching programs and neural networks. IEEE (TIFS) (2011)
3. Barni, M., Orlandi, C., Piva, A.: A privacy-preserving protocol for neural-network-based computation. In: MM&Sec. ACM (2006)
4. Bourse, F., Minelli, M., Minihold, M., Paillier, P.: Fast homomorphic evaluation of deep discretized neural networks. In: Shacham, H., Boldyreva, A. (eds.) CRYPTO 2018. LNCS, vol. 10993, pp. 483–512. Springer, Cham (2018). https://doi.org/10.1007/978-3-319-96878-0_17
5. Brakerski, Z., Gentry, C., Vaikuntanathan, V.: (Leveled) fully homomorphic encryption without bootstrapping. In: ITCS (2012)
6. Castells, F., Laguna, P., Sörnmo, L., Bollmann, A., Roig, J.M.: Principal component analysis in ECG signal processing. EURASIP J. Adv. Signal Process. **2007**(1), 1–21 (2007). https://doi.org/10.1155/2007/74580
7. Chabanne, H., de Wargny, A., Milgram, J., Morel, C., Prouff, E.: Privacy-preserving classification on deep neural networks (2017)
8. Chandran, N., Gupta, D., Rastogi, A., Sharma, R., Tripathi, S.: EzPC: programmable, efficient, and scalable secure two-party computation for machine learning. In: IEEE EuroS&P (2019)
9. Chou, E., Beal, J., Levy, D., Yeung, S., Haque, A., Fei-Fei, L.: Faster CryptoNets: leveraging sparsity for real-world encrypted inference (2018). http://arxiv.org/abs/1811.09953
10. Dahl, M., et al.: Private machine learning in tensorflow using secure computation (2018). http://arxiv.org/abs/1810.08130
11. Demmler, D., Schneider, T., Zohner, M.: ABY - a framework for efficient mixed-protocol secure two-party computation. In: NDSS (2015)
12. Dowlin, N., Gilad-Bachrach, R., Laine, K., Lauter, K., Naehrig, M., Wernsing, J.: CryptoNets: applying neural networks to encrypted data with high throughput and accuracy. In: ICML (2016)
13. Gentry, C.: Fully homomorphic encryption using ideal lattices. In: ACM STOC (2009)
14. Gentry, C.: A fully homomorphic encryption scheme (2009)
15. Hesamifard, E., Takabi, H., Ghasemi, M.: CryptoDL: deep neural networks over encrypted data (2017). http://arxiv.org/abs/1711.05189
16. Hesamifard, E., Takabi, H., Ghasemi, M., Wright, R.N.: Privacy-preserving machine learning as a service. In: PoPETs (2018)

17. Hunt, T., Song, C., Shokri, R., Shmatikov, V., Witchel, E.: Chiron: privacy-preserving machine learning as a service (2018). http://arxiv.org/abs/1803.05961
18. Ibarrondo, A., Önen, M.: FHE-compatible batch normalization for privacy preserving deep learning. In: Garcia-Alfaro, J., Herrera-Joancomartí, J., Livraga, G., Rios, R. (eds.) DPM/CBT -2018. LNCS, vol. 11025, pp. 389–404. Springer, Cham (2018). https://doi.org/10.1007/978-3-030-00305-0_27
19. Jiang, X., Kim, M., Lauter, K.E., Song, Y.: Secure outsourced matrix computation and application to neural networks. In: ACM CCS (2018)
20. Jolliffe, I.T.: Principal Component Analysis. Springer, New York (2002). https://doi.org/10.1007/b98835
21. Juvekar, C., Vaikuntanathan, V., Chandrakasan, A.: GAZELLE: a low latency framework for secure neural network inference. In: USENIX Security (2018)
22. Kass, R.E., Clancy, C.E.: Basis and Treatment of Cardiac Arrhythmias. Springer, Heidelberg (2006). https://doi.org/10.1007/3-540-29715-4
23. Lindell, Y.: Secure multiparty computation for privacy-preserving data mining (2008)
24. Liu, J., Juuti, M., Lu, Y., Asokan, N.: Oblivious neural network predictions via MiniONN transformations. In: ACM CCS (2017)
25. Malkhi, D., Nisan, N., Pinkas, B., Sella, Y.: Fairplay - secure two-party computation system. In: USENIX Security (2004)
26. Mansouri, M., Bozdemir, B., Önen, M., Ermis, O.: PAC: privacy-preserving arrhythmia classification with neural networks (2018). http://www.eurecom.fr/fr/publication/5998/download/sec-publi-5998.pdf
27. Mohassel, P., Zhang, Y.: SecureML: a system for scalable privacy-preserving machine learning. In: IEEE S&P (2017)
28. Mohassel, P., Rindal, P.: Aby^3: a mixed protocol framework for machine learning. In: ACM CCS (2018)
29. Ohrimenko, O., Schuster, F., Fournet, C., Mehta, A., Nowozin, S., Vaswani, K., Costa, M.: Oblivious multi-party machine learning on trusted processors. In: USENIX Security (2016)
30. Orlandi, C., Piva, A., Barni, M.: Oblivious neural network computing via homomorphic encryption. EURASIP **2007**, 037343 (2007)
31. Paillier, P.: Public-key cryptosystems based on composite degree residuosity classes. In: Stern, J. (ed.) EUROCRYPT 1999. LNCS, vol. 1592, pp. 223–238. Springer, Heidelberg (1999). https://doi.org/10.1007/3-540-48910-X_16
32. Riazi, M.S., Weinert, C., Tkachenko, O., Songhori, E.M., Schneider, T., Koushanfar, F.: Chameleon: a hybrid secure computation framework for machine learning applications. In: AsiaCCS (2018)
33. Rouhani, B.D., Riazi, M.S., Koushanfar, F.: DeepSecure: scalable provably-secure deep learning. In: DAC (2018)
34. Sanyal, A., Kusner, M.J., Gascón, A., Kanade, V.: TAPAS: tricks to accelerate (encrypted) prediction as a service (2018). http://arxiv.org/abs/1806.03461
35. Tramèr, F., Boneh, D.: Slalom: fast, verifiable and private execution of neural networks in trusted hardware. In: ICLR (2019)
36. Wagh, S., Gupta, D., Chandran, N.: SecureNN: efficient and private neural network training. In: PETS (2019)

Ransomware Network Traffic Analysis for Pre-encryption Alert

Routa Moussaileb[1,2](✉), Nora Cuppens[1](✉), Jean-Louis Lanet[2](✉), and Hélène Le Bouder[1](✉)

[1] IMT Atlantique, SRCD, Cesson-Sévigné, France
{routa.moussaileb,nora.cuppens,helene.le-bouder}@imt-atlantique.fr
[2] Inria, LHS-PEC, Rennes, France
ruta.moussaileb@irisa.fr, jean-louis.lanet@inria.fr

Abstract. Cyber Security researchers are in an ongoing battle against ransomware attacks. Some exploits begin with social engineering methods to install payloads on victims' computers, followed by a communication with command and control servers for data exchange. To scale down these attacks, scientists should shed light on the danger of those rising intrusions to prevent permanent data loss. To join this arm race against malware, we propose in this paper an analysis of various ransomware families based on the collected system and network logs from a computer. We delve into malicious network traffic generated by these samples to perform a packet level detection. Our goal is to reconstruct ransomware's full activity to check if its network communication is distinguishable from benign traffic. Then, we examine if the first packet sent occurs before data's encryption to alert the administrators or afterwards. We aim to define the first occurrence of the alert raised by malicious network traffic and where it takes place in a ransomware workflow. Logs collected are available at http://serveur2.seres.rennes.telecom-bretagne.eu/data/RansomwareData/.

Keywords: Ransomware · Network traffic · Machine learning

1 Introduction

Ransomware attacks represent a widespread phenomenon of this decade. None of the operating systems or electronic devices are spared. This pandemic affected more than 200 000 computers at the beginning of 2017 [34].

There is no doubt that ransomware is spreading at a high rate infecting not only governmental organizations but also end users and hospitals. Its timeline represents a lucrative business that combines intelligence of the attacker and the fear of the victims for the loss of his/her files.

© Springer Nature Switzerland AG 2020
A. Benzekri et al. (Eds.): FPS 2019, LNCS 12056, pp. 20–38, 2020.
https://doi.org/10.1007/978-3-030-45371-8_2

Motivation. Our motivation to join the malware battle specifically ransomware is its frequency. In fact, one attack occurs every 40 s (October 2016) infecting various sectors like education, entertainment, financial services, healthcare, etc. Unfortunately, these sectors are not immune to such attacks or extortion techniques (Deutsche Bahn, Honda, Renault, etc.) [2].

Even though previous operating system targets were essentially Windows computers, nowadays a wider range of infected equipment and OS is noticed: MacOS, IoT devices and Cellphones (Android OS) [35,41]. Previous work has been carried out knowing the signature of the ransomware on the file system that is the encryption of all victims' files. It is an obvious footprint representing solely that malicious software. In fact, data distribution diverges between an encrypted and a non-encrypted file. Thus, any statistical tool (Shannon Entropy, Chi Squared, ...) applied on these elements displays distinct results enabling an accurate detection. As follows, an emerging ransomware can neither go unnoticed in these conditions nor easily be detected. Our work does not represent a real-time based solution, but rather a study on ransomware families to potentially extract an additional signature besides the obvious encryption phase.

Contribution. The objective of this paper is to find a way to spot the same traceability, however, based on network analysis. The main contributions of this paper are summarized as follows:

1. Providing a mechanism for data filtering based on open source tools.
2. Creating ransomware models via machine learning on network flows.
3. Evaluating ransom notes and encrypted files to check whether the detection occurred at a time t inferior at the start of the encryption.

Outline. The paper is structured as follows. Ransomware's description is presented in Sect. 2. Ransomware state of the art is defined in Sect. 3. Data collection, filtering and detection mechanisms of ransomware are developed in Sect. 4. The results of the experiments are outlined in Sect. 5. Finally, the conclusion is drawn in Sect. 6.

2   Context

2.1   Ransomware

Ransomware is a specific type of malware that encrypts users' files or locks the screen where access to data is only granted if a ransom is paid. The payment is accomplished via Bitcoin or any other cryptocurrency. Another ransomware type such as Doxware operates in a distinct way: you can accept paying the ransom or you can provide information about two of your friends for cyber criminals. Ransomware's stages are outlined below:

1. **Infection** process by spam emails, self-propagation.
2. **Encryption** process (AES, RSA...) of specific file types (.doc, .xls, .jpg, .pdf).
3. **Deletion** of original files and Microsoft Shadow Volumes.
4. **Ransom Request** key exchanged for money.

Since 1989 (first known malware extortion attack), researchers have been aware of these attacks. Concurrently, cyber criminals have been improving their techniques for better gain. A glimpse of the recent attacks is presented below. Cyber attackers are shifting their focus to large companies for more fruitful hunts. For instance, National Health Service (NHS) England, and Telefonica have been infected with WanaCrypt0r [3].

Various categories of malware exist. Each one of them presents specific characteristics [22]. For example in 2012, the attacker of Reveton ransomware displayed a fraudulent message to the user. It declared that he/she has been illegally using some software or acquiring illegal documents/movies. In addition to that, to pressure the victim to pay, the attacker displays the IP address of the victim and an actual footage from his/her webcam representing scare tactics [4].

Another wave of ransomware named "CryptoLocker" emerged in 2013 using 2048-bit RSA for encrypting a whitelist of files. As a result, data is unrecoverable since decryption would take decades. This pandemic did not end here. It goes on with diverse attacks like CryptoWall, WannaCry, Petya and Bad Rabbit that infect currently just computers. However, Fusob that appeared in 2015–2016 targeted mobile devices. The most recent cyberattack struck Baltimore city on the 7th of May 2019. Multiple services were shutdown due to this ransomware attack [1].

Targeted files may vary from a ransomware to another. A fine sample that encompasses the majority of these extensions is: .odt, .docx, .xlsx, .pptx, .mdb, .jpeg, .gif, .bmp, .exif, .txt, etc. [32].

2.2   Ransomware Timeline

The timeline shown in Fig. 1 presents a glimpse of ransomware families initial release dates and their targeted systems. It will be used in Sect. 5 as a comparison means between the release date and the network activity observed throughout the collected data of various samples. Thus, the question remains, based on previous observations can we predict what will happen in ransomware's universe, or prevent a plausible attack.

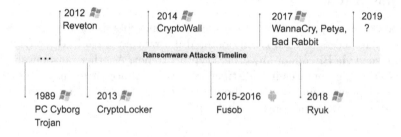

Fig. 1. Ransomware families debut timeline [17].

3   Ransomware Detection State of the Art

In the worst case scenario, if no noticeable characteristics alerted the user, encryption process will begin. To eradicate malicious threats, a myriad of solutions are available in the current literature [8, 19, 37, 40].

Some researchers delve into investigating ransomware's signals on the filesystem for instance API calls or relevant system calls [14, 24]; or they rely on metrics collected from encrypted files such as entropy [23, 36, 42]. However, some researchers delve into the study of network activity for ransomware detection [9, 12, 13]. Therefore, the analysis presented in the literature could be divided in two parts: host and network based ransomware detection.

3.1   Host Based Ransomware Detection

Previous work conducted in the literature emphasizes that each malware, even though is sometimes obfuscated, can present different patterns enabling researchers its detection at an early stage. Indeed, ransomware metrics have distinct values compared to benign processes such as I/O Request Packets Sequence, API Calls Flow Graph, and in our case, acquired system and network logs from ransomware execution.

Gomez Hernandez *et al.* illustrate in their work (RLocker) a ransomware early detection mechanism that could prevent its operations [20]. One of RLocker advantages is the detection of zero day's ransomware attacks. It is achieved by deploying a honeyfile structure to lure ransomware, which will block any process that passes through it, or try to modify it. However, previous requirements are crucial for the success of such operation. Nevertheless, RLocker has a limitation: it could be bypassed if a process passes randomly through the files without intercepting the lure folders. A similar limitation related to files traversals could be noticed in Moussaileb *et al.* work for early mitigation mechanisms [28]. Even though their solution, solely based on file system exploration, is effective (up to 100% detection rate), their detection would be delayed if a ransomware uses multithreading for simultaneously traversing and encrypting the filesystem (some encrypted files are inevitable in this case).

Most of the current detection mechanisms of ransomware rely on an obvious signature of the latter: the encryption process that occurs [16, 23–25, 36, 42]. In fact, many alerts based on monitoring the system activity are reported. For example, studying bits distribution, whether performing machine learning algorithms on various dlls or on functions called referring to a cryptographic context [14, 25]. This means that the encryption process is already taking place and losses are inevitable. All the solutions mentioned previously are viable for ransomware detection. Yet, some file losses occur and they are solely based on system activity when the malware is executing its payload.

A set of indicators can represent viably ransomware behavior as presented in CryptoLock by Scaife *et al.* [36]. Shannon entropy was one of their main metrics since encrypted or compressed files have high entropy. In their solution, few files are lost. Another statistical technique was adopted by Mbol *et al.* for ransomware detection [27]. Their focus was on JPEG files since they initially have high entropy. In order to distinguish between an encrypted image and a clear one, Kullback Leibler divergence was used and 128 KB up to 512 KB of JPEG files were analyzed. A high detection rate was achieved by their solution: 99.95%. A similar approach is used by Palisse *et al.*, however, using the goodness-of-fit test to distinguish between encrypted and non encrypted files achieving 99.3% true positive rate [30].

Wolf described in his latest work [39] multiple ransomware detection approaches. It includes a comparison of the metadata of a file before and after encryption is used. A high similarity indicates that little changes were made to the file thus indicating the absence of encryption.

3.2 Network Based Ransomware Detection

A victim's computer is like a zombie machine (compromised computer under remote direction) under ransomware instructions. It needs to communicate with the C&C system for information exchange such as the key needed for encrypting victims' files. Therefore, an additional step is taken into consideration to check if the communication between those two entities based on network activity is sufficient to detect malware attacks before the payload's fully execution and file losses. Some recent search topics switched from host to network analysis.

For example, Ganame *et al.* stated that to have a better coping mechanism with existent cyber threats researchers should move from signature to behavioral based detection [18]. Thus, they developed a data breach system that is able to identify zero-day malware: WannaCry. Its main advantage lays in its capacity to block the source of compromise preventing further ransomware propagation.

Cabaj *et al.* presented in their work clear characteristics of CryptoWall and Locky families [13]. They both communicate with the server via HTTP POST requests. Despite providing valuable insight on these two distinct families, very little information can be retrieved for instance from Shade ransomware since all its traffic is encrypted. In addition to that, other type of ransomware for example Bitman and Teslacrypt have some samples that communicate with the C&C (Command and Control) via GET requests only as shown in our experiments (for example 2e7f7cc9a815efd0a6590042ce27f6da Teslacrypt ransowmare). Thus, these ransomware samples can go unnoticed.

Alhawi *et al.* are able to detect Windows ransomware while only tracing the network traffic achieving a 97.1% detection rate [9]. Yet, no indication is provided as to whether the detection occurred before or after the encryption process. Moreover, conversation flow is used for the classification. In other words, N suspicious records are required to detect an anomaly or ransomware attack.

Our work is an extension of Alhawi *et al.* [9]. The same approach based on machine learning to flag malicious ransomware communication is used. However, our analysis is performed on packet inspection rather than the conversation flow. We take one step further in the analysis to localize this traffic in the ransomware workflow: When does it occur? Is it sufficient to separate benign vs ransomware activity?

We extend the current work sphere by analyzing packet flows rather than conversation flows. We are aware of the challenges encountered by using machine learning for network intrusion detection (lack of training data, data variability, malware polymorphism, adversarial training, ...) [10,31,38], we take them into consideration and we adopt the Machine Learning method as a means for classification.

4 Proposed Methodology

We develop in the current paper a proof of concept that can be implemented in a driver as a future work to avoid being detected by a ransomware process.

We endeavor to thwart ransomware nefarious behavior by analyzing the network traces. The malware analysis routine consists in executing the ransomware and gathering the needed information: system logs for reconstructing the malware session and displaying the timestamp of the first encryption process and network logs for traffic classification. Then, the machine learning process enables a classification between malicious and benign records. Finally, an evaluation is made to check whether the detection of malicious traffic occurs before the encryption process or afterwards. To accomplish this task, our proposed mechanism is divided into 3 main parts: Data Collection, Session Reconstruction & Data Filtering and Analysis & Model Development. It will be thoroughly explained in the following sections. All the steps are summarized in **Ransomware Network Alert** Algorithm.

Algorithm Ransomware Network Alert RNA

1: **procedure** RANSOMWARE NETWORK ALERT
2:     $R\_ \leftarrow \{R\_$: Ransomware Related $\}$
3:     def session_reconstruction(PML file, R_Hash):
4:     $process\_name \leftarrow \{$pname:R_Hash.exe$\}$
5:     $R\_pid \leftarrow \{$get PID / pname=R_Hash.exe$\}$
6:     **for** pid $\in$ PID.PML **do**
7:         **if** Parent(pid) $\in$ R_pid **then**
8:             $R\_children \leftarrow pid$
9:     $R\_session \leftarrow \{$Filter(PML File) / R_pid & R_children$\}$
10:
11:     def getR_Network_Activity(R_session, PCAP File):
12:     $R\_Network\_Activity \leftarrow \{$Filter R_session$\}$
13:     $R\_IP\_@ \leftarrow \{$get R_IP @ src-dst$\}$
14:     $R\_Ports \leftarrow \{$get R_Ports src-dst$\}$
15:     $R\_Net\_Act \leftarrow \{$Filter(Pcap File) / R_IP_@ & Ports $\}$
16:
17:     Construct R_Model
18:     **if** evaluate(Net_Act) $\in$ R_Model **then**
19:         return R_Alert
20:     return Benign_Activity

4.1   Data Collection

The ransomware is downloaded and executed on the pc of the victim (our bare metal platform) for 2 up to 3 min which is the time required until the encryption note or encrypted files pop up on the file system. Moreover, the time constraint is also due to the encryption process involved in the ransomware infection that could also encrypt the collected information.

The Wireshark and Process Monitor executables are launched on Windows OS 7 32 bits as in [21]. Each one of them has an independent task for collecting the following information: Wireshark collects the information about network activity whereas Process Monitor gathers the whole system activity (including network information).

Log formats are present below:

- PCAP (Packet Capture) File: Data created by Wireshark that contains the network packet data generated during a live network capture (source and destination IP address, ports, data exchanged, length of the data, . . .). It can be analyzed later on for network intrusion detection purposes.
- PML (Process Monitor Log) File: File created by Process Monitor and contains the log of system activities (process name, process id (PID), path, . . .).

The information from Process Monitor and Wireshark is acquired to perform a network analysis. Needed data is collected from an automated bare metal malware analysis platform built from scratch using Clonezilla Server [15].

A crawler downloads a ransomware from two databases Virus Share (https:// virusshare.com) and Malwaredb.Malekal (http://malwaredb.malekal.com) (currently down), then it is executed on Windows 7 32 bits machines for a period of 2 to 3 min. A dump corresponding to this malware behavior is saved for further post mortem analysis. For scalability reasons, parallel machines are used to perform the tests as well as an improved disk image distribution.

Dataset. All the methods and parsers are developed using Python and shell script. The analysis is performed on an Ubuntu 16.02 machine.

1054 ransomware were executed on Windows7 OS (Table 1). **Howbeit, 100 ransomware executables are kept for the machine learning phase since they were active** (encrypted the files of the victim). Even though only 100 samples are used for experiments but the machine learning is performed on packets. For example for 12 Bitman samples, we extracted 714 network records. Whereas if we consider the network flow as shown in [9] we get only 62 malicious records to evaluate.

Stratosphere IPS dataset is used for normal captures only [5]. In fact, it contains recent normal traffic captured since 2013 until 2017. An additional information is the description of the behavior captured making the labeling process feasible. Moreover, in the project's malware section, it contains ransomware packet capture: it is a mean of comparison between the ransomware traces provided by their dataset and our own generated in a bare metal platform explained in the following sections.

Table 1. An overview of the active ransomware families (total of 100 active samples from 1054 tested), ranked in descending order according to their samples number.

Family	Samples	Number of working samples
Teslacrypt	334	11
Yakes	252	2
Shade	139	56
Cerber	95	11
Deshacop	62	2
Zerber	57	5
TorrenLocker	38	0
Bitman	27	12
Razy	26	0
Locky	24	1
NotPetya	0	0

4.2 Session Reconstruction and Data Filtering

The Process Monitor format contains crucial information for reconstructing the malware session and activity. However, the initial log file contains megabytes of data. It represents the full activity on a computer: gathered information from all running processes. An initial filtering is required to extract all the information of the ransomware session.

In the following section, we describe the preprocessing (filtering) of the collected data to gather solely ransomware activity.

Let $\mathbb{P}$ be the ensemble of all the Processes running in Windows.

Let p_name, p_pid, p_ppid be respectively the name, the PID (process identifier) and the PPID (parent process identifier) of a specific process p.

Ransomware executable names are associated with their MD5 or SHA-256 hash. They represent a unique identifier, that is known prior to the execution of the ransomware for testing purposes (*line 4 of Algorithm Ransomware Network Alert*). To extract the information from the PML file, an initial lookup is made on all the processes that have a name constituted of the concatenation of the (Ransomware_MD5Hash or Ransomware_SHA256) and (.exe) a filename extension representing an executable file on Windows. The operator + denotes the concatenation operation.

$Ransomware\_name = Ransomware\_MD5Hash + .exe$
$Ransomware\_name = Ransomware\_SHA256 + .exe$

Consequently, an association of the name of the running process with the corresponding process identifier (PID) is achievable. It is a unique decimal number that represents this particular object (*line 5 of Algorithm Ransomware Network Alert*). The collection of all the PIDs associated to the ransomware is achieved.

$$R\_pid = \{\forall p \in \mathbb{P} \ / \ p\_name = Ransomware\_name\}$$

However, any process running on Windows creates different children as threads or new processes to accomplish its tasks or parallelize the workload. In ransomware's case, one thread is created for listing the files, another one for encryption. For this reason, the tree/graph of the current processes is essential since it displays the relation among all of them (*line 8 of Algorithm Ransomware Network Alert*).

$$R\_Children\_pid = \{\forall p \in \mathbb{P} \ / \ p\_ppid = R\_pid\}$$

At this stage, the identifier of the ransomware process and all the sub processes that it created are at our disposal. The relation between all processes is represented by a directed graph defined as followed $G = (N, E)$ where: N is the set of nodes containing the PID, E is the set of edges, dashed arrows are representing benign processes, red arrows are representing ransomware processes.

Figure 2 displays a sub-tree of some subprocesses running on the machines. The red arrow marks the beginning of TeslaCrypt's execution. It is clear that TeslaCrypt malware creates many processes to accomplish its tasks, even though having a benign parent and siblings. Therefore, it is essential to build this "relation" graph (*line 9 of Algorithm Ransomware Network Alert*).

$$R\_Activity = \{\forall p \in \mathbb{P} \ / \ p\_pid = R\_pid \mid R\_Children\_pid\}$$

Thus, an initial filtering on the PML log file can be performed. It is divided into a malicious log that consists of all the actions performed by the ransomware and the second file that implies only benign records (*line 10 of Algorithm Ransomware Network Alert*). The information gathered in the PML file is used to extract only the network communication from PCAP logs.

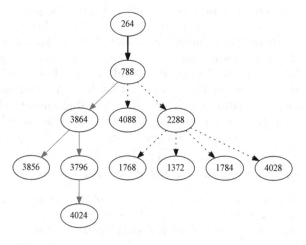

Fig. 2. TeslaCrypt Process IDs Tree: Red Arrow. (Color figure online)

Ransomware Network Session Reconstruction

Since there is a gap between the data provided by the PML and PCAP file, a mapping is needed to collect an exhaustive information from ransomware's network activity.

The network activity that exists in *R_Activity* acquired in the previous section is basic. It englobes only source and destination IP addresses, port numbers and the length of the packet found in the PML File, whereas additional features can be extracted from a PCAP file such as TCP window size, checksum, header length, etc.

We proceed by capturing the IP addresses and port numbers (*line 13 & 14 of Algorithm Ransomware Network Alert*) used during *R_Activity* for the communication with a third party (for example the C&C), then we filter the PCAP File based on the data obtained previously (*line 15 of Algorithm Ransomware Network Alert*).

Table 2 displays the different features found in a PML file (Table 2a) with the basic network elements (for instance IP addresses and ports) while detailed and additional characteristics (TCP checksum, flags, windows size) can be extracted from a PCAP file (Table 2b).

Table 2. TeslaCrypt network information extracted from:

(a) PML File.

Features	Record #1	Record #2
Time of Day	1/24/2019 5:46	1/24/2019 5:46
Process Name	htiyxhpnayrf.exe	htiyxhpnayrf.exe
PID	3916	3916
Operation	TCP Connect	TCP Send
Path	tivy-PC:49179 to cr1.toservers.com	tivy-PC:49179 to cr1.toservers.com
Event Class	Network	Network
Detail	Length: 0, rcvwin: 66240, seqnum: 0, ...	Length: 896, startime: 768, endtime: 770, seqnum: 0, connid: 0

(b) PCAP File.

Features	Record #3
IP Src	10.1.1.9
IP Dst	198.12.157.163
TCP Srcport	49209
TCP Dstport	80
TCP Checksum	0x00006ee0
TCP Flags	0x00000002
TCP Hdr_len	32
TCP Window_size	8192
TCP Len	0
TCP Nxtseq	0

4.3   Supervised Machine Learning

The goal of this machine learning step is to develop a model for ransomware detection via network traffic analysis. Point anomaly represents a suspicious record at a given time t: when a specific data instance deviates from the normal pattern. Whereas, collective anomaly represents a collection of similar events that are abnormal [7]. For example, point anomaly can be flagging Record#1 from Table 2a since it is not similar to benign records. Therefore, it is used for the machine learning process to flag any malicious network communication established by the ransomware. Its main advantage compared to collective anomaly is an early detection of ransomware presence rather than having to analyze n packets to expose the malicious behavior.

The supervised approach is effective since labeling the data is possible in our system. Thus, it enables us to detect other variants of ransomware based on an extrapolation of the data acquired throughout our experiments (line 17). Most of the research done in the literature on network intrusion detection via machine learning uses the following algorithms: decision trees, k-nearest neighbors and random forests [11,29,33]. Therefore, they will be adopted to detect ransomware behavior as a deviation from normal traffic. To perform this classification, Scikit-learn, a free software machine learning library, is used.

Our analysis addresses point anomaly subdivided in two, whether TCP or UDP protocol is used. In fact, each packet is different than the other and presents few common features such as IP addresses and ports.

Whereas, for the collective anomaly, the conversation flow is used. Each row in the list displays the statistical values for exactly one conversation (ports, addresses, duration and packets exchanged). This work has been already covered in the literature in [9].

Benign traffic is downloaded from Stratosphere IPS, an open source dataset used to reproduce the experiments [5]. It contains sufficient captures for our analysis.

Since the overall database of malware collection contains 100 active ransomware, we used the percentage split method (70/30) for the training and test set for each family. It splits our dataset into random train and test subsets. The first one contains 70% of the data while the second one 30%.

The separation between TCP and UDP training is made since the number of UDP communication outweighs the TCP ones thus making our dataset unbalanced.

For network log extraction as a CSV file from the PCAP, many features provided by the Wireshark community exist. Filtering the PCAP file is possible by extracting 243 fields from the TCP protocol or 29 from the UDP protocol (e.g., https://www.wireshark.org/docs/dfref/t/tcp.html). Nonetheless, many fields have non existent values for all the records, therefore, they were removed.

The features used for training UDP workflow are:
IP and Port source/destination, Protocol, UDP checksum and length.

The features used for training TCP workflow are:
frame.len, ip.src, ip.dst, ip.proto, _ws.col.Protocol, tcp.srcport, tcp.dstport, tcp.ack, tcp.analysis.ack_rtt, tcp.analysis.acks_frame, tcp.analysis.bytes_in _flight, tcp.analysis.initial_rtt, tcp.analysis.push_bytes_sent, tcp.checksum, tcp. flags, tcp.hdr_len, tcp.len, tcp.nxtseq, tcp.window_size, tcp.window_size_ scalefactor.

Data Preprocessing can have a significant impact on the performance of various ML algorithms [26]. It handles, among other things, missing values and categorical variables. In fact, an intervention is needed since classification models can not handle these elements on their own. In our samples, empty values are replaced by zero, as for the IP addresses and flags they are transformed into integers. Overall, the whole dataset consists of solely numerical values.

5   Experimental Results

UDP Results

For the Cerber and Zerber samples, we achieve a 100% detection rate using any of the Decision Trees, Random Forest or K Nearest Neighbors. In fact, the difference is explicit. More than 16000 UDP packets are sent through incremental IP addresses having the same length in a matter of seconds. Additionally, the same information is being conveyed to all those different servers or zombies. The protocol used is solely UDP, very rare in a user normal environment, and is blocked in some companies. Moreover, it is comparable to a Denial of Service (DOS) attack due to the important number of contacted servers via UDP that is not common in normal behavior in just few seconds.

The Udhisapi.dll module provides support in hosting compliant Universal Plug and Play (UPnP devices). We believe that it can be used as a method of discovering and communicating with Universal Plug and Play devices across the network, such as other personal computers, printers, mobile devices... that broaden the attack vectors for ransomware.

TCP Results

The results of the other samples are presented in Tables 3, 4, 5, 6 and 7.

Table 3. Bitman classifiers performance metrics.

Supervised learning algorithm	True positive rate	True negative rate	False positive rate	False negative rate	Training time (seconds)
K nearest neighbor (n = 2)	99.56	98.13	1.86	043	0.004
Decision tree	100	100	0	0	0.01
Random forest	100	99.79	0.2	0	0.03

Table 4. Cerber classifiers performance metrics.

Supervised learning algorithm	True positive rate	True negative rate	False positive rate	False negative rate	Training time (seconds)
K nearest neighbor (n = 2)	100	99.97	0.02	0	0.13
Decision Tree	100	100	0	0	0.16
Random Forest	100	100	0	0	0.24

Table 5. Shade classifiers performance metrics.

Supervised learning algorithm	True positive rate	True negative rate	False positive rate	False negative rate	Training time (seconds)
K nearest neighbor (n = 2)	100	99.99	1.4*10e-2	0	3.76
Decision tree	100	100	0	0	1.02
Random forest	100	100	0	0	1.57

Table 6. TeslaCrypt classifiers performance metrics.

Supervised learning algorithm	True positive rate	True negative rate	False positive rate	False negative rate	Training time (seconds)
K nearest neighbor (n = 2)	99.31	97.88	2.11	0.68	0.004
Decision tree	99.31	99.34	0.65	0.68	0.009
Random forest	100	100	0	0	0.035

Table 7. Zerber classifiers performance metrics.

Supervised learning algorithm	True positive rate	True negative rate	False positive rate	False negative rate	Training time (seconds)
K nearest neighbor (n = 2)	100	100	0	0	1.59
Decision tree	100	100	0	0	0.15
Random forest	100	100	0	0	0.32

Table 8. Zero day classifiers performance metrics.

Supervised learning algorithm	True positive rate	True negative rate	False positive rate	False negative rate	Training time (seconds)
K nearest neighbor (n = 2)	38.35	98.11	1.88	61.64	8.02
Decision tree	98.46	100	0	1.53	0.54
Random forest	95.7	100	0	4.29	0.7

Decision Trees provided the best results in terms of (true—false) (positive—negative) rate and training time. They spare potential overfitting problems by using random forest. As for the K nearest neighbors, since IP addresses are huge numbers (could go up to 4 billion), they have a higher weight than TCP flags (maximum value 32).

The experiments prove that machine learning classifiers are able to flag ransomware network traffic for both UDP and TCP records as in signature based detection.

A benchmark comparison is possible with the proposed work in [9]. In fact, the authors perform machine learning algorithms on protocols regardless if they were TCP or UDP based. However, we separate them since UDP records outweigh TCP ones, thus, this separation will enable us to have a balanced dataset. In addition, raw features are used such as described in Sect. 4.3. It means that any record or communication can be flagged without delaying the alert mechanism that relies on having n malicious conversation flows. Decision trees lead to more accurate results (98.46% vs 97.10% in [9]).

5.1 Zero Day Ransomware Detection

The experiments conducted are divided into two parts. Signature based ransomware detection explained in the aforementioned sections where the training and the testing is performed on samples from a specific ransomware RA, RB, ..., RN (see Fig. 3, Part a).

Yet, to detect zero day attacks, an administrator should test on new variants of ransomware. To implement this task, training is carried out on malware samples that appeared earlier or in the beginning of 2016. As for the tests, they will be executed on different ransomware families excluded from the training set (see Fig. 3, Part b).

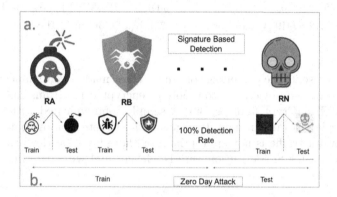

Fig. 3. ML on ransomware families.

Since a similarity is noticed between some Zerber and Cerber samples, in addition to TeslaCrypt and Bitman, we split our training and test set as followed:

- Training set families: TeslaCrypt, Cerber, Shade (our own dataset),
- Test set families: Spora (15), GlobeImposter (2), Jaff (8), Matrix (3) (downloaded from www.malware-traffic-analysis.net).

Since test samples did not figure in the training set, we have 98.46 % as true positive rate and 100% as a true negative rate (Table 8). They still represent a high value since the strategy of requests sent between the victim and the C&C is shared among the majority of ransomware families.

5.2 ALERT Time

Checking if encrypted files with ransom notes exist or not is crucial, in other words, if the detection occurs before the beginning of the encryption process or at the end. Consequently, it is essential to recapture the time of the last packet sent and the start of ransom notes. For example, after Cerber's network communication, it creates 9 different threads and immediately after that, the encryption process takes place. It leaves some nanoseconds for the prevention mechanism to take a decision (blocking or killing the process, freezing the pc) before any file loss. Table 9 shows that the first alert, a network UDP send request, appeared before the ransom note #DECRYPT MY FILES#.html.

Table 9. Snippet of Cerber PML File, hash: 534da47881eba8a6d3cf676e6c89d1be.

Time of day	Operation	Path
15:45:09,81792	UDP send	orfeas-PC:54673 → 85.93.63.255:6892
15:45:12,89509	CreateFile	C:\...\#DECRYPT MY FILES#.html
15:45:12,89919	CreateFile	C:\Py27\Lib\...\t56G_mZZIH.cerber

Table 10 presents the percentage of samples that made a communication with the server before an obvious ransom note or encrypted file (RansomAlert). For Bitman and TeslaCrypt families, only 1 sample communicated with the C&C before it displays a ransom note. It means that the detection mechanism based only on network traffic is not appropriate for those families. Howbeit, network traffic detection for Shade ransomware is efficient and will spare file losses for victims.

Table 10. Encryption alert.

Ransomware family	$t_{Communication} < t_{RansomAlert}$	Percentage
Bitman	1	8.33% (1/12)
Cerber	7	100% (7/7)
Shade	55	100% (55/55)
TeslaCrypt	1	7.69% (1/11)
Yakes	0	0% (0/2)
Zerber	2	66.67% (2/3)

Since each sample provides a distinct ransom note or a specific file extension representing the ransomware, all the PML files are analyzed manually to extract the required information.

An example of Bitman ransom Notes is given below:

– Recovery+ysddu.png,
– +-HELP-RECOVER-+bjkkl-+.png,
– _ReCoVeRy_+ioigp.png,
– help_recover_instructions+drl.txt,
– +-HELP-RECOVER-+wnonv-+.png.

Some Cerber samples killed Process Monitor process several times during their execution, so the PML file retrieved is corrupted. Therefore, a difference is found between the number of active samples in Table 1. To scale down any possible error, we did not consider those 10 truncated samples in the Alert Analysis because the acquired data was incomplete.

5.3 Results Overview

Based on the timeline mentioned in the context (Fig. 1) and on the network traffic, ransomware have evolved throughout the years and are polymorphic. They used to communicate via non encrypted HTTP traffic (TCP requests), then other families moved to GET requests. Shade ransomware for example uses only TLS protocol for its communication. In addition to that, it was one the pioneers for IPv6 communication. In 2016, UDP communication emerged. Based on the data gathered, new variants of ransomware can be detected if the divergence between new samples and existent ones are low. However, many cases are covered in our work. Attackers will have to work on covert channels for exfiltrating information or keep encrypted communication similar to benign application.

Tests are also performed on 18 samples from Cerber, Zerber, TeslaCrypt and Bitman without any Internet connection. The encryption still took place. Nonetheless, we know that the keys were generated locally, enabling us to retrieve them via a simple hook to Windows Crypto API or is hard-coded in ransomware's executable, highly unlikely. Two identical ransomware samples are found in Bitman/TeslaCrypt and two others in Cerber/Zerber. It denotes a resemblance between those families. For example, 2d2c589941dd477acc60f6b8433c3562 MD5 hash is flagged as Bitman by 7 anti-virus companies and as TeslaCrypt by 8 other anti-virus companies [6]. They are kept for signature based detection (no duplicate records in the same family since it appears just once), but removed from zero day analysis.

6 Conclusion

In this work, we are able to detect ransomware through network traffic monitoring. We conclude that the majority of ransomware behave similarly. We found some common patterns among various families. To get a precise ransomware detection, we use machine learning techniques.

To sum up, network alerts represent a first suspicion means informing the user of the presence of a potential ransomware. However, some drawbacks exist. This first alarm can take place after the creation of encrypted files or ransom notes as we noticed in some families. In addition, few elements are needed for a classification, we have underfitting problems (Zerber samples), prone to adversarial attacks. Besides, only Decision Trees among the tested algorithms provided high detection rates for zero day attacks. For all the reasons mentioned above, Network Alerts should be backed up with system data to provide a general detection mechanism, working on all types of ransomware. As for our future work, we will gather additional information from the file system to present a multi-layer alert strategy to detect ransomware's payload as early as possible. In this work, we chose multiple malware samples and executed them. We should examine the puzzle of infection mechanism such as spam email to detect ransomware download process before its installation on the victim's computer. Furthermore, merely 10% of the samples have encrypted files, that means we have only 10% active ransomware. We will check if it is due to evasion mechanisms (Sysinternal Tools, Wireshark,...) or if the ransomware database is outdated (C&C servers are down).

References

1. Baltimore ransomware attack. https://www.bbc.com/news/technology-48423954
2. Kaspersky Press Release. https://www.kaspersky.com/about/press-releases/2016_attacks-on-business-now-equal-one-every-40-seconds
3. Malwarebytes Blog. https://blog.malwarebytes.com/
4. Reveton Attack. https://krebsonsecurity.com/2012/08/inside-a-reveton-ransomware-operation/
5. Stratosphere IPS. https://www.stratosphereips.org/l
6. Virus Total. https://www.virustotal.com
7. Ahmed, M., Mahmood, A.N., Hu, J.: A survey of network anomaly detection techniques. J. Netw. Comput. Appl. **60**, 19–31 (2016)
8. Al-rimy, B.A.S., Maarof, M.A., Shaid, S.Z.M.: Ransomware threat success factors, taxonomy, and countermeasures: a survey and research directions. Comput. Secur. **74**, 144–166 (2018)
9. Alhawi, O.M.K., Baldwin, J., Dehghantanha, A.: Leveraging machine learning techniques for windows ransomware network traffic detection. In: Dehghantanha, A., Conti, M., Dargahi, T. (eds.) Cyber Threat Intelligence. AIS, vol. 70, pp. 93–106. Springer, Cham (2018). https://doi.org/10.1007/978-3-319-73951-9_5
10. Amit, I., Matherly, J., Hewlett, W., Xu, Z., Meshi, Y., Weinberger, Y.: Machine learning in cyber-security-problems, challenges and data sets. arXiv preprint arXiv:1812.07858 (2018)
11. Buczak, A.L., Guven, E.: A survey of data mining and machine learning methods for cyber security intrusion detection. IEEE Commun. Surv. Tutor. **18**(2), 1153–1176 (2016)
12. Cabaj, K., Gawkowski, P., Grochowski, K., Osojca, D.: Network activity analysis of cryptowall ransomware. Przegl. Elektrotechniczny **91**(11), 201–204 (2015)

13. Cabaj, K., Gregorczyk, M., Mazurczyk, W.: Software-defined networking-based crypto ransomware detection using HTTP traffic characteristics. Comput. Electr. Eng. **66**, 353–368 (2018)
14. Chen, Z.G., Kang, H.S., Yin, S.N., Kim, S.R.: Automatic ransomware detection and analysis based on dynamic API calls flow graph. In: Proceedings of the International Conference on Research in Adaptive and Convergent Systems, pp. 196–201. ACM (2017)
15. Clonezilla: The Free and Open Source Software for Disk Imaging and Cloning. http://clonezilla.org/
16. Continella, A., et al.: ShieldFS: a self-healing, ransomware-aware filesystem. In: Proceedings of the 32nd Annual Conference on Computer Security Applications, pp. 336–347. ACM (2016)
17. F-Secure: Evaluating the customer journey of crypto-ransomware and the paradox behind it. Technical report, July 2016
18. Ganame, K., Allaire, M.A., Zagdene, G., Boudar, O.: Network behavioral analysis for zero-day malware detection – a case study. In: Traore, I., Woungang, I., Awad, A. (eds.) ISDDC 2017. LNCS, vol. 10618, pp. 169–181. Springer, Cham (2017). https://doi.org/10.1007/978-3-319-69155-8_13
19. Genç, Z.A., Lenzini, G., Ryan, P.Y.A.: Next generation cryptographic ransomware. In: Gruschka, N. (ed.) NordSec 2018. LNCS, vol. 11252, pp. 385–401. Springer, Cham (2018). https://doi.org/10.1007/978-3-030-03638-6_24
20. Gómez-Hernández, J., Álvarez-González, L., García-Teodoro, P.: R-locker: thwarting ransomware action through a honeyfile-based approach. Comput. Secur. **73**, 389–398 (2018)
21. Homayoun, S., Dehghantanha, A., Ahmadzadeh, M., Hashemi, S., Khayami, R.: Know abnormal, find evil: frequent pattern mining for ransomware threat hunting and intelligence. IEEE Trans. Emerg. Top. Comput. (2017)
22. Idika, N., Mathur, A.P.: A survey of malware detection techniques. Purdue University, p. 48 (2007)
23. Kharaz, A., Arshad, S., Mulliner, C., Robertson, W., Kirda, E.: UNVEIL: a large-scale, automated approach to detecting ransomware. In: 25th USENIX Security Symposium (USENIX Security 2016), pp. 757–772. USENIX Association, Austin (2016). https://www.usenix.org/conference/usenixsecurity16/technical-sessions/presentation/kharaz
24. Kharraz, A., Robertson, W., Balzarotti, D., Bilge, L., Kirda, E.: Cutting the gordian knot: a look under the hood of ransomware attacks. In: Almgren, M., Gulisano, V., Maggi, F. (eds.) DIMVA 2015. LNCS, vol. 9148, pp. 3–24. Springer, Cham (2015). https://doi.org/10.1007/978-3-319-20550-2_1
25. Kolodenker, E., Koch, W., Stringhini, G., Egele, M.: Paybreak: defense against cryptographic ransomware. In: Proceedings of the 2017 ACM on Asia Conference on Computer and Communications Security, pp. 599–611. ACM (2017)
26. Kotsiantis, S., Kanellopoulos, D., Pintelas, P.: Data preprocessing for supervised leaning. Int. J. Comput. Sci. **1**(2), 111–117 (2006)
27. Mbol, F., Robert, J.-M., Sadighian, A.: An efficient approach to detect Torrent-Locker ransomware in computer systems. In: Foresti, S., Persiano, G. (eds.) CANS 2016. LNCS, vol. 10052, pp. 532–541. Springer, Cham (2016). https://doi.org/10.1007/978-3-319-48965-0_32
28. Moussaileb, R., Bouget, B., Palisse, A., Le Bouder, H., Cuppens, N., Lanet, J.L.: Ransomware's early mitigation mechanisms. In: Proceedings of the 13th International Conference on Availability, Reliability and Security, p. 2. ACM (2018)

29. Muniyandi, A.P., Rajeswari, R., Rajaram, R.: Network anomaly detection by cascading k-means clustering and c4. 5 decision tree algorithm. Procedia Eng. **30**, 174–182 (2012)
30. Palisse, A., Durand, A., Le Bouder, H., Le Guernic, C., Lanet, J.-L.: Data aware defense (DaD): towards a generic and practical ransomware countermeasure. In: Lipmaa, H., Mitrokotsa, A., Matulevičius, R. (eds.) NordSec 2017. LNCS, vol. 10674, pp. 192–208. Springer, Cham (2017). https://doi.org/10.1007/978-3-319-70290-2_12
31. Papernot, N., McDaniel, P., Sinha, A., Wellman, M.: Towards the science of security and privacy in machine learning. arXiv preprint arXiv:1611.03814 (2016)
32. Rajput, T.S.: Evolving threat agents: ransomware and their variants. Int. J. Comput. Appl. **164**(7), 28–34 (2017)
33. Revathi, S., Malathi, A.: A detailed analysis on NSL-KDD dataset using various machine learning techniques for intrusion detection. Int. J. Eng. Res. Technol. (IJERT) **2**(12), 1848–1853 (2013)
34. Sahi, S.K.: A study of wannacry ransomware attack. Int. J. Eng. Res. Comput. Sci. Eng. **4**(9), 5–7 (2017)
35. Salvi, M.H.U., Kerkar, M.R.V.: Ransomware: a cyber extortion. Asian J. Converg. Technol. (AJCT) **2** (2016)
36. Scaife, N., Carter, H., Traynor, P., Butler, K.R.: Cryptolock (and drop it): stopping ransomware attacks on user data. In: 2016 IEEE 36th International Conference on Distributed Computing Systems (ICDCS), pp. 303–312. IEEE (2016)
37. Sgandurra, D., Muñoz-González, L., Mohsen, R., Lupu, E.C.: Automated dynamic analysis of ransomware: benefits, limitations and use for detection. arXiv preprint arXiv:1609.03020 (2016)
38. Sommer, R., Paxson, V.: Outside the closed world: On using machine learning for network intrusion detection. In: 2010 IEEE Symposium on Security and Privacy, pp. 305–316. IEEE (2010)
39. Wolf, J.: Ransomware detection
40. Yang, T., Yang, Y., Qian, K., Lo, D.C.T., Qian, Y., Tao, L.: Automated detection and analysis for android ransomware. In: 2015 IEEE 17th International Conference on High Performance Computing and Communications, 2015 IEEE 7th International Symposium on Cyberspace Safety and Security, and 2015 IEEE 12th International Conference on Embedded Software and Systems, pp. 1338–1343. IEEE (2015)
41. Yaqoob, I., et al.: The rise of ransomware and emerging security challenges in the internet of things. Comput. Netw. **129**, 444–458 (2017)
42. Young, A.L., Yung, M.M.: An implementation of cryptoviral extortion using Microsoft's crypto API (2005)

Using Machine Learning to Detect Anomalies in Embedded Networks in Heavy Vehicles

Hossein Shirazi⬛, Indrakshi Ray$^{(\boxtimes)}$, and Charles Anderson$^{(\boxtimes)}$

Colorado State University, Fort Collins, CO 80526, USA
{shirazi,iray,chuck.anderson}@colostate.edu

Abstract. Modern automobiles have more than 70 electronic control units (ECUs) and 100 million lines of code to improve safety, fuel economy, performance, durability, user experience, and to reduce emissions. Automobiles are becoming increasingly interconnected with the outside world. Consequently, modern day automobiles are becoming more prone to cyber security attacks. Towards this end, we present an approach that uses machine learning to detect abnormal behavior, including malicious ones, on embedded networks in heavy vehicles. Our modular algorithm uses machine learning approaches on the internal network traffic in heavy vehicles to generate warning alarms in real-time. We tested our hypothesis on five separate data logs that characterize the operations of heavy vehicles having different specifications under varying driving conditions. We report a malicious detection rate of 98–99% and a mean accuracy rate of 96–99% across all experiments using five-fold cross-validation. Our analysis also shows that with a small subset of hand-crafted features, the complex dynamic behavior of heavy vehicle ECUs can be predicted and classified as normal or abnormal.

Keywords: Anomaly detection · SAE-J1939 · Heavy vehicle security

1 Introduction

In the last few decades, complex electronic systems have been incorporated into vehicles in order to improve performance, efficiency, safety, and usability. In modern-day vehicles, mechanical systems rely heavily on advanced electrical and computational systems that include network, software, and hardware. Consequently, modern day vehicles have become vulnerable to both physical and cyber attacks. In the near future with the advancement of wireless fleet management technology, we anticipate that cyber attacks would increase and have catastrophic consequences.

Checkoway *et al.* analyzed multiple attack vectors in vehicles and showed that Electronic Control Units (ECUs) have a potential of being compromised [1]. A compromised ECU can be used by an attacker to inject malicious messages into the in-vehicle network through a physical connection. Subsequently, researchers

© Springer Nature Switzerland AG 2020
A. Benzekri et al. (Eds.): FPS 2019, LNCS 12056, pp. 39–55, 2020.
https://doi.org/10.1007/978-3-030-45371-8_3

remotely compromised an ECU and injected messages to stop a Jeep Cherokee running on a highway [2]. This triggered a recall of 1.4 million vehicles [3]. Attacks can be launched by devices connected to the physical bus or through a remote connection.

Our research focuses on embedded networks of heavy vehicles. Heavy vehicles are expensive and they constitute a critical infrastructure of a nation. In order to allow interoperability of various components manufactured by different Original Equipment Manufacturers (OEMs), heavy vehicles use a standardized protocol known as SAE-J1939 implemented over a Controller Area Network (CAN) bus, which allows ECUs to communicate with each other. The use of standardized protocols makes heavy vehicles susceptible to attacks, as the code for deciphering messages is easily accessible. The damage inflicted by heavy vehicles can also be catastrophic. Consequently, heavy vehicles are a much higher target for attackers compared to cars [4].

Two different categories have been introduced as countermeasures against these attacks: *proactive* and *reactive*. *Proactive* mechanisms protect against malicious injections and are implemented through Message Authentication Code (MAC). While message authentication ensures a certain level of security in Internet applications, there are limitations of applying it to the heavy-vehicle domain. First, there is limited space for embedding the MAC in the messages. Second, the messages are required to be processed in real-time, which may not be feasible [3]. Third, applying this approach requires modification of lower-level protocols.

Multiple Intrusion Detection Systems (IDS)s have been proposed as implementations of *reactive* approaches in the literature [3,5–7]. Similar to other network defense mechanisms, current IDS systems monitor exchanged messages and detect any abnormal behavior, but there are certain limitations. The CAN bus is a broadcast communication network, and it cannot verify the sender of messages. Consequently, it is extremely difficult for state-of-the-art IDS systems to detect hijacked ECUs. Moreover, to the best of our knowledge, there is no defense mechanism that attempts to detect malicious message injection in the messages that adhere to the SAE-J1939 standard. Such message injections can compromise the *integrity* and the *availability* of the system.

In this work, we address some of the limitations stated above. We scope our work to detect the injection of messages which adhere to the SAE-J1939 standard. In the context of this work, we use the term heavy vehicle as one that uses the SAE-J1939 standard. Our proposed approach uses machine learning to detect abnormal traffic in the embedded network. A few reasons motivated our choice. The most important reason is the high-dimensional nature of the data, and its complicated non-linear relationship to the operational state of the vehicle. High-dimensional data is often difficult to understand. For instance, a single packet in heavy vehicles has many dimensions. Thus, the data is quite difficult to analyze or understand. Furthermore, there is a space-time correlation among the data that needs to be modeled. There are not many computational models besides machine learning that can analyze this complex temporal data.

The use of SAE-J1939 makes it possible to convert raw transmitted messages on the CAN bus to specific parameters of the vehicle. Thus, we define a machine learning model based on low-level vehicular PARAmeters. While each message contains information about the current state of the vehicle, it does not give any information about the previous state. To solve this limitation, we added the history of previous values to each parameter value to leverage the learning model. In addition, some statistical derivative features have been added to give even deeper insights about the model.

A vehicle's parameters are categorized in particular groups in the SAE-J1939 protocol, for example, frequency and sender. Thus, we created multiple models based on each parameter group, referred to as Parameter Group Number (PGN) in the standard. The learning algorithms create a behavioral profile for each PGN that will be used later to compare with its current behavior to detect any deviation from the regular pattern. We used a wide range of learning algorithms to train models and studied the performance of each algorithm.

Multiple challenges had to be addressed in our solution. The first challenge is that behavior varies across vehicles. While the SAE-J1939 standard is common to all the vehicles, the parts, models, embedded ECUs, and software are all different. As a solution, we applied general purpose machine learning algorithms. Machine learning classifiers can learn local features of interest in a collection of data. The feature set has been enriched by adding derived statistical features. We believe this is sufficient to accurately predict whether or not a given SAE-J1939 message is normal.

The next challenge is deciding the number of previous messages that need to be considered for creating a behavioral profile. If this number is too small, even standard infrequent patterns will be classified as abnormal. If this number is too large, abnormal behavior will not be distinguishable from the normal behavior pattern. We make this trade-off based on some experiments.

The other challenge relates to the computational intensity of the learning model. Machine learning models, in general, are computationally expensive, taking a long time to produce a prediction while also using a lot of resources. In an operational heavy vehicle, the ECUs generate messages every hundred milliseconds; our proposed approach is required to have a response time in that range. Furthermore, the experimental setup and hardware need to be applicable for an in-vehicle configuration. To address this challenge, we ran experiments on light-weight Raspberry Pi Zero computers. We report our results in the experiments section.

Key Contributions. This paper makes the following contributions:

- Developing profiles of PGNs by employing machine learning techniques to analyze high-dimensional data generated by the ECUs.
- Detecting abnormal messages by employing machine learning techniques and generating real-time alarms;
- Our proposed method produces significant accuracy in different experiments in the range of 98–99% which asserts our initial hypothesis.

The rest of the paper is organized as follows: Sect. 2 discusses background and existing defense mechanisms. Section 3 models the adversaries capabilities, attack scenarios, and simulation. Section 4 details architecture design of our proposed approach, which is evaluated in Sect. 5. Finally, we conclude the paper in Sect. 6.

2   Related Works

2.1   Background on CAN and SAE-J1939

Controller Area Network. Development of the Controller Area Network (CAN) started at Robert Bosch GmbH and was released in 1986 [8]. CAN employs a two wired differential bus, which supports speeds of up to 1 Mbit/s [9]. The initial version, CAN 1.0, used 11 bits for the identifier fields, which has since been upgraded to 29 bits in CAN 2.0 called an extended version. The protocol establishes a priority mechanism to prevent message collision on a shared bus; a lower value of the identifier specifies a higher priority for the sender [9]. CAN 1.0 was proposed in a time that neither the Internet nor concepts of *virus* and *worm* were prevalent [6] and security was not a concern. This is evident in the fact that the CAN protocol alone does not address any security concerns.

SAE-J1939 Standard. The CAN bus forms the lower layer of a vehicle's network. SAE-J1939 comprises the higher level layer of a heavy vehicle's network. The SAE-J1939 protocol allows ECUs from multiple vendors to communicate. SAE-J1939 defines five layers in the seven-layer OSI network model including the CAN ISO 11898 specification and uses only extended frames with a 29-bit identifier for the physical and data-link layers. *Protocol Data Unit (PDU)* is a block of information transferred over the internal network. Each *PDU* in the SAE-J1939 protocol consists of seven fields: *priority (P), extended data page (EDP), data page (DP), PDU format (PF), PDU specific (PS)* (which can be a destination address, group extension, or proprietary), *source address (SA)*, and *data field*. There is also a reserved field *Reserved(R)* with one bit length for further usage. These fields are all packed in one data frame and sent over the physical media to other network devices [10]. The combination of the *PF* and the *PS* fields derives two important parameters: Parameter Group Number (PGN) and Destination Address (DA). PGN is used to group similar vehicular parameters together in one single message frame. Each of these parameters is named Suspect Parameter Number (SPNs). Each SPN defines how the application layer can interpret some portion of the data field using the Digital Annex [11]. DA specifies destination of the message.

2.2   Introduced Defense Mechanism

Many concepts from the IT networks, such as securing the network, cryptography, proposed attacks and defense mechanisms, have been adapted for the internal network of automobiles. The proposed countermeasures can be classified into *proactive* and *reactive* mechanisms [12].

Proactive Mechanism. Proactive mechanisms focus on improving protocols, applications, systems, *etc.* to prevent the occurrence of any attacks. These mechanisms are not foolproof [12], but can be remarkably effective. The CAN and SAE-J1939 protocols do not support authentication and encryption so a wide range of attacks can be launched on them. Towards this end, Murvay *et al.* [9] proposed a mechanism to include message authentication on the protocol and evaluated the overall overhead on network communication. In addition, they evaluated their enhancement from a computational point of view and showed that low-end automotive-grade controllers are capable of symmetric cryptography and high-end cores can handle asymmetric (public-private cryptography) algorithms. However, even with an authentication mechanism on the CAN bus, the maximum payload length is only 8 bytes, so the available space for an encrypted Message Authentication Code (MAC) is very limited [3]. Multiple solutions have been proposed to address this limitation. These include sending MAC in multiple data frames, using multiple CRC fields, or exploiting an out-of-bound channel for message authentication [3,13–15]. Although proactive mechanisms are capable of preventing attacks, they would require changing the protocols, applications, and/or hardware. These types of solutions are unrealistic as they do not take into account vehicles that are currently operational.

Reactive Mechanism. Reactive mechanisms detect an attack or an impending attack and reduce its impact on the victim's vehicle at the earliest and provides a response mechanism to either block the attack or alert other systems [12] while trying to minimize the number of *false-alarms*[1].

The physical signal characteristics have been recently used to fingerprint ECUs connected to the CAN bus using voltage or time. Murvay *et al.* [16] have authenticated messages on the CAN bus using physical characteristics of ECUs. The approach requires measuring the voltage, filtering the signals, and calculating mean square errors to uniquely identify ECUs. The signals from different ECUs showed minor variations in, for example, how fast rising edge is set up or how stable a signal is. Although these characteristics remain unchanged over a period of several months, there are certain limitations. Examples include results varying with changes in temperature [17]. Furthermore, their method was evaluated on the low-speed bus with trivial ECUs, not on the high-speed bus with critical ECUs. In addition, the authors did not consider collision situations that would impact the identification mechanism [18].

Cho *et al.* [3] proposed a time-based IDS. The clock offsets and skews of asynchronous nodes depend solely on their local clocks, thus being distinct from others. Their method detects anomalies based on clock skew of different ECUs connected to the bus. The approach measured intervals of periodic messages for different ECUs to measure unique clock skews for each ECU. However, this method can be defeated in certain ways. For example, if an adversary can match the clock skews of a tampered device with that of the actual one, this approach does not work [19]. Moreover, this approach does not work for non-periodic messages.

---

[1] A false-alarm occurs when an alert is not due to an actual attack.

Machine learning algorithms are widely used for levels higher than the physical layer. Learning algorithms have the ability to learn patterns and detect any deviation outside of an accepted threshold. Hence, these algorithms have been widely employed to create detection mechanisms. Kang *et al.* [5] proposed an intrusion detection model that discriminates between regular and abnormal packets in an embedded vehicles network by using a Deep Neural Network (DNN). They generate features directly from a bit-stream over the network by counting the occurrence of '1' in the binary data field of messages. Consequently, the features have no semantics associated with them. For simulating the anomalies, they showed a wrong value of the Tire Pressure Monitoring System (TPMS) on the panel and achieved an accuracy of 99%. As this algorithm tested only one type of attack, it is unclear how this mechanism will detect more complex attacks. Furthermore, it authenticates targeted fields with other current field values but does not take into account previous values of the fields. An attack message that is consistent with other feature values can bypass this algorithm.

Chockalingam *et al.* [6] investigated the use of different machine learning algorithms in detecting anomalies in CAN packets or packet sequences and compared the algorithms. They used Long Short-Term Memory (LSTM) to consider the sequence of inputs for labeling the dataset. While they did not report the accuracy, the Area Under Curve (AUC) for Receiver Operating Characteristic (ROC) curve varies from 82% to 100% in different situations.

Narayanan *et al.* [7] introduced OBD Secure-Alert which detects abnormal behavior in vehicles as a plug-n-play device on the vehicle. They used Hidden Markov Model (HMM) to decide whether a vector is normal or not. HMM considers just a single previous vector so Narayanan *et al.* added more previous messages to each learning vector.

Mukherjee *et al.* [20] used a Report Precedence Graph-based (RPG) which describes how graphs modeling the state transitions can be used to distinguish between safety and security-critical events in real-time.

3   Threat Model

3.1   Adversary Capabilities

Attackers can compromise in-vehicle ECUs physically or remotely using known attack surfaces or exploiting new vulnerabilities. For example, they can exploit telematic devices to gain remote access to the CAN bus.

In this study, we assume that an adversary has access to the CAN bus. In addition, we assume that the adversary receives all messages on the CAN bus and is capable of generating SAE-J1939 compatible messages with the desired frequency, and has full control of all fields including the priority and data. Message priority helps the adversary to set a higher priority for their messages and block messages with lower priorities on the bus. This violates both the availability of some functionalities and the integrity of the system.

3.2   Attack Scenarios

We discuss the following attack scenarios that are feasible given the adversary capabilities. Certain attacks target vulnerabilities on the CAN level and are applicable to both regular and heavy vehicles. One of the most commonly studied attacks against the CAN network is a DoS attack. In this attack, the adversary will send unauthorized messages with the highest priority and frequency to dominate the bus. Thus, sending or receiving messages will be delayed or even impossible.

In a different attack, an adversary may monitor the CAN bus and target a specific action of the vehicle. Whenever the adversary sees a message related to that particular action, it sends a counter message to make the previous action ineffective. Hoppe et al. [21] implemented an application that monitors the bus, and every time there is a message to open the window, a counter message is sent to make the requested action ineffective. Such an attack is also plausible in a heavy vehicle because of easy access to the message documentation in the SAE-J1939.

Recently, however, attacks have been designed to take advantage of the SAE-J1939 protocol that are only applicable to heavy vehicles. Burakova et al. in [22] proposed the first special attack against heavy vehicles in 2016.

The adversary we modeled can inject SAE-J1939 crafted messages through a compromised ECU. ECUs frequently report an associated vehicular parameter. For example, the engine's ECU reports the value of RPM every 100 ms. In an attack scenario, an adversary can send incorrect parameter values, like RPM, with a higher priority to override original messages. In this case, an attacker can either dominate the original engine's ECUs with a higher priority message or can send an incorrect value for a specific parameter after seeing it on the bus.

For example, in the so-called fuzzing attack, the attacker changes the values of a specific parameter with random values and injects generated messages into the bus. In CyberTruck Challenge 2018[2], we conducted this attack on a real heavy vehicle. In that experiment, we successfully overwrote speed and RPM values on the CAN bus using SAE-J1939. We showed a speed of 50 mph on the dashboard even when the truck was stationary[3].

There is not any attack data publicly available to be used as a benchmark. Thus, we simulated new attack messages and injected them into the logged file to check whether our detection mechanism could find them. During our proposed attack, we maliciously changed the vehicle's parameters (such as current speed) multiple times.

Figure 1 shows one example of an attack where we changed the vehicles reported speed. It depicts the actual speed values of the vehicle and maliciously injected values. This attack in practice may violate the integrity of the system, can severely damage the vehicle, and give the driver incorrect information which may lead to an accident. While this experiment shows the manipulation

---

[2] https://www.cybertruckchallenge.org/.
[3] Due to a Non-Disclosure Agreement (NDA), we cannot release the make and model of the vehicle.

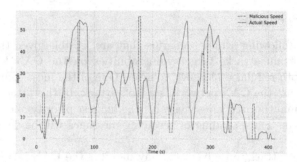

Fig. 1. Test data for speed where the speed value has been maliciously manipulated with other random values.

of speed, this attack is not simply limited to speed; we have tested a wide range of parameters and report our results in Sect. 5.

4   Proposed Defense Mechanism

4.1   Feature Engineering and Fingerprinting

The performance of machine learning is very much dependent on the choice of our features and how we represent them. In our proposed model, we define three types of features: `SPN values`, `History values`, and `Derivative features`.

SPN Values: Features based on SPN values are obtained by deciphering the sniffed messages on the CAN bus. We convert the raw messages to the SPN values.

History of Values: The value of each SPN depends on both the current vehicle's parameters and their previous values. Note that the classifier would need to use previous samples to make a more precise decision. Towards this end, we include n previous SPN values of each vector to overcome this challenge. As such, each vector will now have values of the current state and will also include the last n reported values for each SPN. We consider consecutive packets, *i.e.* $p_i \rightarrow p_{i-1} \rightarrow p_{i-2} \rightarrow p_{i-3} \rightarrow p_{i-4}$, where p_i denotes the current value, and p_{i-j} denotes previous values for $j >= 1$.

Derivative Features: To give more insight into how each SPN value changes over the last n history windows, we added multiple derivative features to the vector. For each *measured* SPN, we added *average, standard deviation*, and *slope* of the last n values to the feature set. In addition, we added history for these derived features as well. For example, the feature vector includes the current slope and the last n values of the slope as well. These new derivative features help the classifiers to better model the current behavior of ECUs and the change of the parameters over time; this leads to more precise predictions.

The other feature that we added was distance. We observed the changes between two consecutive messages of each PGN would be limited. This observation can be mathematically represented by the Euclidean distance between two feature vectors. If p and q are two consecutive vectors with the size of n, the Euclidean distance will be calculated by the formula given below which is used as a feature: $d(p, q) = \sqrt{(p_1 - q_1)^2 + (p_2 - q_2)^2 + ... + (p_n - q_n)^2}$.

4.2 Detection Mechanism Architecture

The architecture of the proposed detection mechanism consists of four separate modules: BusSniffer, Message Decoder, AttackDetector, and AlarmGenerator. Figure 2 highlights the architecture of the proposed detection mechanism.

BusSniffer connects to the CAN bus using an access point like the OBD-II port. This port connects directly to the CAN bus and captures all transmitted messages.

Message Decoder utilizes the SAE-J1939 standard to convert the raw messages on the bus to the SPN values and creates an initial vector of the vehicle's parameters. This module adds other meta-data fields including time-stamp, length of the data field, source address, destination address, and previously defined features such as derivative features and history of feature values.

AttackDetector consists of two phases: *Training* and *Detecting*. The *training* phase requires preparing a dataset of regular and abnormal messages for every PGN. Multiple classifiers can be trained on the dataset, and the classifier that performs the best will be subsequently used. The *training* phase may take a long time; however, the trained classifiers can be used countless times without needing to re-train. Note that this phase can be done offline and outside of the vehicle before installing it.

In the *detection* phase, whenever a new vector comes in, the AttackDetector fetches it's PGN value and sends it to the designated classifier object, which tests whether it is a normal vector or not. If the classifier detects an abnormal message, it will trigger the AlarmGenerator module.

AlarmGenerator is responsible for preparing appropriate alarm messages using SAE-J1939 and transmits it over the CAN bus. The message will be generated in the form of a *Broadcast* message, and all connected nodes will be aware of this abnormal situation. This can also include turning on a warning light on the dashboard to notify the driver.

4.3 Detection Algorithm

Algorithm 1 discusses the steps to decide whether a transmitted message on the bus is normal or not. In the first step, the BusSniffer module adds messages to the processing queue named mess. Then, each added message is decoded to give the SPN values and aggregated for the derivative features. Based on the PGN, the appropriate classifier object will be fetched and used to predict whether the current message is normal or not. If it is abnormal, it will be sent to the AlarmGenerator module.

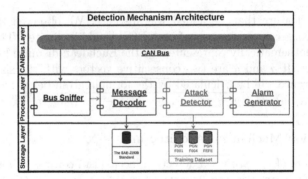

Fig. 2. Architecture of proposed detection mechanism.

Machine Learning Classifiers. We used seven classifiers: Decision Tree (DT), Gaussian Naïve Bayes (GNB), Gradient Boosting (GB), K-Nearest-Neighbors (KNN), Random Forrest (RF) and Support Vector Machine (SVM) with two kernels: Linear (SVCL(l)) and Gaussian (SVCR(r)). We trained the learning models and tested them in a five-fold cross-validation approach to avoid overfitting each classifier.

Result: Detecting Abnormal
$mess\_queue \leftarrow sniff\_bus()$;
while $mess\_queue \neq \{\}$ **do**
    $mess \leftarrow mess\_queue.pop()$;
    $vector \leftarrow decipher(mess)$;
    $add\_history \leftarrow add\_history\_length(mess)$;
    $fprint \leftarrow add\_derived\_features(added\_history)$;
    $cls \leftarrow get\_classifier\_Obj(fprint.PGN)$;
    $predict \leftarrow cls.predict(fprint)$;
    if $predict == Abnormal$ **then**
       | $Generate\_Alarm(fprint)$
    else
       | $Continue$;
    end
end

Algorithm 1. Detecting Abnormal Messages

5   Experiments and Evaluations

5.1   Creating Datasets from Previously Recorded Messages

We ran our experiments and modeled the problem using the log data. We use five previously captured CAN bus log messages that were generated at the University of Tulsa[4]. For security reasons, however, we cannot release information about the model or manufacturer of the vehicles. We describe the driving conditions and log files which we have used.

Since the learning algorithms need adequate data to learn the pattern, we had to select PGNs which had at least 500 messages in the log file. After we created the final dataset, we only used a maximum of 5000 instances for training and testing purposes as an upper-bound.

In the first step, we convert each log file into multiple datasets where each one includes vectors of only one PGN. We then inject abnormal messages with an injection ratio of 50% with a history length of 10 for the following experiments. It is safe to assume that the rate of malicious messages during any real attack would be less than 50%. As such, without loss of generality, we used a higher injection ration to circumvent difficulties in training models with imbalanced datasets. In this experimental context, the training phase has a chance to learn from more malicious messages, however, in real attack far less malicious messages would be present. These choices do not affect the validity or generality of our approach. Table 1 summarizes experiment descriptions, number of used PGNs, and experiment duration.

Table 1. Specification of each log file including log name, number of selected PGNs, experiment duration, and description of experiment.

Log	PGN	Time(s)	Description
DS1	10	411	The truck was driven around a block
			Three events of the vehicle braking suddenly (hard brake)
DS2	2	60	Log file does not have much data
			One hard braking event
DS3	10	270	We had 10 log files from 10 different driving conditions
			Selected one log file and used it to create in the DS3
			Used the DS3 dataset as a benchmark
			Highest recorded speed was 55 mph, followed by a hard brake
DS4	7	729	Vehicle was stopped for most of experiment
			Had a hard brake at the 400th second
DS5	9	2500	Vehicle was stopped during this experiment
			Had an active engine

5.2   Summarized Performance of Model

We selected the best classifier for each dataset and all of its log-PGN pairs. The number of messages related to each PGN was not equal in each dataset; as such

---

[4] The data is available at http://tucrrc.utulsa.edu/J1939Database.html.

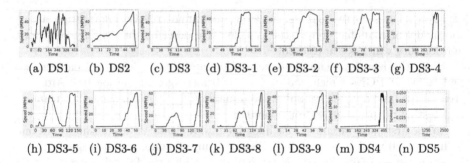

Fig. 3. Wheel-based speed from different driving conditions.

we calculated the weighted average of scores based on the portion of instances of each PGN in the dataset to normalize the average. To display this fact, in the DS2 log file, we have two PGNs: $F004_{16}$ and $FEF0_{16}$ which constitute 83.96% and 16.04% percent of the messages respectively. We normalized learning scores based on the percentage of messages in the log file and report the results in Fig. 4. The total scores show good results. True Positive Rate (TPR) is more than 98% in all cases and total accuracy (ACC) is at least 99% (excluding DS2, which scored a 96%).

5.3   Different Driving Scenarios

The vehicle's parameters are constantly being changed by either external (*e.g.* road, weather, and driver's habits) or internal (*e.g.* increasing speed or torque) factors. These may degrade the accuracy of the model. To check whether these conditions can have any effect on the efficacy of the model, we gathered 9 log files from different driving scenarios of the vehicle from DS3. Figure 3 shows the wheel-based speed for each driving condition. We repeated the previous experiment for each of the 9 log files and then calculated the weighted average of the machine learning scores identical to Sect. 5.2. If the internal or external parameters can affect the model, it should be captured in this model. We compared the performance of the model in all nine other driving scenarios with initial DS3 results and looked for any differences.

The first column in the Fig. 5 shows the result from the original DS3 scores, and the rest show the other nine driving conditions. Among ten different driving conditions, including the DS3 initial test, we do not see any significant variation in learning scores and we get consistently high scores in different driving conditions. This deduces that the proposed model works well for different driving conditions.

5.4   Performance Across Multiple Classifiers

Although all of the previously discussed experiments were repeated across multiple machine learning classifiers, we selected and reported the best one. In this experiment, we compared the performance of the different classifiers, We used Decision Tree (DT) with a max depth of 5, Gradient Boosting (GB), Gaussian Naïve Bayes (GNB), Random Forrest (RF), and SVM with two different kernels: *Linear* and *Gaussian (rbf)*.

Figure 6 compares the average performance of the classifiers in different datasets for two learning scores: TPR and ACC. The most striking results to emerge from Fig. 6 is that both GB and RF give the highest TPR on average for all of the datasets with more than 99%, which is significantly high. In other words, GB and RF detected more than 99% of injected malicious messages correctly. We achieved this detection rate along with an incredibly high accuracy rate simultaneously.

GB gives the best performance on average, and if there is a need for selecting one single classifier, it would be the best choice among the ones that we studied. Looking at two different kernels of SVM confirm that both perform almost identically in all cases. As a linear kernel gives us a very high accuracy, it deduces that data is linearly separable. Another benefit of this kernel is that it is much less complex than Gaussian (rbf) so linear kernel is a better choice.

For SVM with a linear classifier, the TPR and ACC are very close to 96.75% and 97.46% respectively. GNB and KNN do not generate good results and are not suitable for this problem. KNN is more suitable for clustering problems but the results show it does not work for this problem at all.

5.5   Timing Analysis

We want to detect any abnormal behavior in a real-time manner when the vehicle is moving. We need to demonstrate that our approach is efficient and can be installed on the vehicle. We selected Raspberry Pi Zero as a light-weight computer powered by a +5.1V micro USB supply and performed experiments on it. This device can read the CAN data via a connection to the OBD-II port.

Based on our proposed model, we can train the dataset before and save the trained model on the Raspberry Pi for online detection; therefore, we report the testing time only. For each dataset that includes multiple PGNs, we trained multiple classifiers for each PGN. Then we extracted the average testing time for each classifier-PGN. As the model can predict the next message in parallel (based on multiple trained classifiers), the longest testing time of each classifier-PGN will be the total testing time for each input. Consequently, we used the maximum testing time of classifier-PGNs in each dataset.

Figure 7 depicts testing time in a base-10 logarithmic scale in microseconds. DT has the best testing time among all classifiers. This classifier responds in less than six microseconds for all of the datasets. GB is the second best classifier which responds between 70–80 μs followed by GNB which takes around 200 μs. KNN did not perform well at all; it takes at least 16 ms for the best results. This is due to the way that this classifier predicts input samples and finds the k-closest to the input and labels it. This timing analysis shows that the best performing classifiers also act fast-enough to be employed in the heavy vehicle and run experiments in real-time.

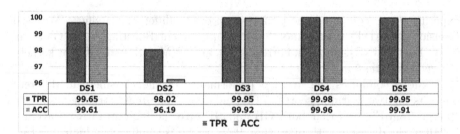

Fig. 4. The weighted average scores for each data log file

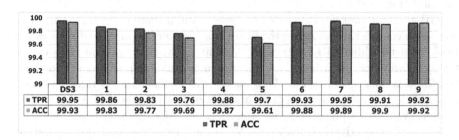

Fig. 5. TPR and ACC scores for different driving scenarios

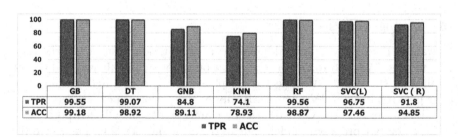

Fig. 6. TPR and ACC scorse for multiple classifiers on different datasets

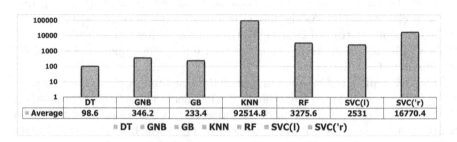

Fig. 7. Average computation time for each dataset for different classifiers

Table 2. Comparing discussed defense mechanisms from different perspectives

Authors	Description	ACC	Type	Techniques
Murvay et al. [9]	-Including message authentication to the protocol -Evaluated communication and computational overhead -It needs changes in existing technologies -Not useful for current vehicles	100%	Proactive	Message authentication
Cho et al. [3]	-Proposed an clock-based IDS -Detects based on clock skew of periodic messages	99.5%	Reactive	ML
Kang et al. [5]	-Intrusion detection technique using a DNN. -Packets are trained to extract features -Features have no semantic associated with them -May not be applicable for online detection due to the performance issue	99%	Reactive	ML
Chockalingam et al. [6]	-Studied at two different types of anomalies -Using LSTM helps to consider a sequence of inputs	82% to 100.0	Reactive	ML
Narayanan et al. [7]	-Introduced OBD Secure-Alert -Detecting abnormal behavior as a plug-n-play device -Added previous messages to each instance for detection	100%	Reactive	ML
Mukherjee et al. [20]	-Used a RPG anomaly detection technique -Visualized temporal relationships of human actions and functions and implemented by ECUs -Find out malicious intrusions in real time	N/A	Reactive	Precedence graph
Our Work	-Fingerprinting behaviour of embedded devices -Identifying regular behaviour of devices -Detecting anomalies using machine learning techniques -Carrying out experiments on five large datasets	96–99%	Reactive	ML

The lowest transmission rate of the message defined in the SAE-J1939 is 10 ms. Other messages are also not being generated faster than that rate. Our proposed mechanism can detect anomalies in order of 200 to 300 μs for two of our best classifiers. Thus, our algorithm detects anomalies 40–50 times faster than transmission rates for messages on the bus.

Table 2 compares five different approaches in the literature. Some of the previous research leveraged machine learning techniques to find anomalies in an online [23] or offline manner [5,6] in the vehicle. [9] introduced prevention approaches which include introducing message authentication to the protocol. [20] suggested a graph-based approach that detects malicious messages in real time. We also added the results of this study to Table 2 where logs taken from vehicle driving have been injected with abnormal messages.

6   Conclusion and Future Work

The identification of normal behavior of embedded devices is a substantial step towards detecting any abnormal activities. However, as our detection mechanism shows, it is possible to fingerprint the behavior of embedded devices in the vehicles with high accuracy. In future, we want to combine SPN values from multiple PGNs into one single machine learning vector instead of looking at each PGN separately. To achieve this goal, we need to consider the time-series analysis and different types of classifiers.

In future, we plan to explore the use of unsupervised machine learning as labeled data may not be available. In our study, for four out of five datasets, the rate of false positives is less than 0.05%, which is significantly low. We plan to lower this even further.

Acknowledgement. We thank Landon Zweigle for reading through the manuscript. This work was supported in part by NSF Award Number CNS 1715458.

References

1. Checkoway, S., et al.: Comprehensive experimental analyses of automotive attack surfaces. In: USENIX Security Symposium (2011)
2. Miller, C., Valasek, C.: Remote exploitation of an unaltered passenger vehicle (2015)
3. Cho, K.-T., Shin, K.G.: Fingerprinting electronic control units for vehicle intrusion detection. In: USENIX Security Symposium (2016)
4. Wolf, M., Lambert, R.: Hacking trucks-cybersecurity risks and effective cybersecurity protection for heavy duty vehicles (2017)
5. Kang, M.-J., Kang, J.-W.: A novel intrusion detection method using deep neural network for in-vehicle network security. In: Vehicular Technology Conference (2016)
6. Chockalingam, V., Larson, I., Lin, D., Nofzinger, S.: Detecting attacks on the CAN protocol with machine learning. In: Annual EECS 588 Security Symposium (2016)
7. Narayanan, S.N., Mittal, S., Joshi, A.: OBD_SecureAlert: an anomaly detection system for vehicles. In: International Conference on Smart Computing (2016)
8. Bosch, R., et al.: CAN specification version 2.0 (1991)
9. Murvay, P.-S., Groza, B.: Security shortcomings and countermeasures for the SAE J1939 commercial vehicle bus protocol (2018)

10. SAE J1931, Data Link Layer (2016)
11. SAE J1939, Digital Annex (2015)
12. Mirkovic, J., Reiher, P.: A taxonomy of DDoS attack and DDoS defense mechanisms (2004)
13. Szilagyi, C.J.: Low cost multicast network authentication for embedded control systems. Ph.D. thesis (2012)
14. Nilsson, D.K., Larson, U.E., Jonsson, E.: Efficient in-vehicle delayed data authentication based on compound message authentication codes. In: Vehicular Technology Conference (2008)
15. Van Herrewege, A., Singelee, D., Verbauwhede, I.: CANAuth-a simple, backward compatible broadcast authentication protocol for CAN bus. In: Workshop on Lightweight Cryptography (2011)
16. Murvay, P.-S., Groza, B.: Source identification using signal characteristics in controller area networks. In: Signal Processing Letters (2014)
17. Choi, W., Joo, K., Jo, H.J., Park, M.C., Lee, D.H.: Voltageids: low-level communication characteristics for automotive intrusion detection system. Trans. Inf. Forensics Secur. **13**, 2114–2129 (2018)
18. Choi, W., Jo, H.J., Woo, S., Chun, J.Y., Park, J., Lee, D.H.: Identifying ECUs using inimitable characteristics of signals in controller area networks. Trans. Veh. Technol. **67**, 4757–4770 (2018)
19. Taylor, A., Leblanc, S., Japkowicz, N.: Anomaly detection in automobile control network data with long short-term memory networks. In: International Conference on Data Science and Advanced Analytics (2016)
20. Mukherjee, S., Walker, J., Ray, I., Daily, J.: A precedence graph-based approach to detect message injection attacks in J-1939 based networks. In: International Conference on Privacy, Security and Trust (2017)
21. Hoppe, T., Kiltz, S., Dittmann, J.: Security threats to automotive CAN networks – practical examples and selected short-term countermeasures. In: Harrison, M.D., Sujan, M.-A. (eds.) SAFECOMP 2008. LNCS, vol. 5219, pp. 235–248. Springer, Heidelberg (2008). https://doi.org/10.1007/978-3-540-87698-4_21
22. Burakova, Y., Hass, B., Millar, L., Weimerskirch, A.: Truck hacking: an experimental analysis of the SAE J1939 standard. In: Workshop on Offensive Technologies (2016)
23. John, G.H., Langley, P.: Estimating continuous distributions in Bayesian classifiers. In: Uncertainty in Artificial Intelligence (1995)

Selection and Performance Analysis of CICIDS2017 Features Importance

Bruno Reis[ID], Eva Maia[(⊠)][ID], and Isabel Praça[ID]

GECAD - Research Group on Intelligent Engineering
and Computing for Advanced Innovation and Development,
School of Engineering of the Polytechnic of Porto (ISEP), Porto, Portugal
{missr,egm,icp}@isep.ipp.pt

Abstract. During the last decade network infrastructures have been in
a constant evolution. And, at the same time, attacks and attack vectors
become increasingly sophisticated. Hence, networks contain a lot of different features that can be used to identify attacks. Machine learning
are particularly useful at dealing with large and varied datasets, which
are crucial to develop an accurate intrusion detection system. Thus, the
huge challenge that intrusion detection represents can be supported by
machine learning techniques. In this work, several feature selection and
ensemble methods are applied to the recent CICIDS2017 dataset in order
to develop valid models to detect intrusions as soon as they occur. Using
permutation importance the original 69 features in the dataset have been
reduced to only 10 features, which allows the reduction of models execution time, and leads to faster intrusion detection systems. The reduced
dataset was evaluated using Random Forest algorithm, and the obtained
results show that the optimized dataset maintains a high detection rate
performance.

Keywords: Machine learning · Intrusion Detection System (IDS) ·
Ensemble learning · Random Forest · Decision trees · Feature
selection · CICIDS2017

1 Introduction

Due to the exponential growth of information systems in the last decades and the
resulting attention given to information security, has emerged the need to create
systems capable of identifying and dealing with external and internal threats.
Intrusion Detection Systems (IDSs) have been one of those systems whose aim
is to analyse traffic and report on eventual unnatural occurrences [17]. Most
IDSs detect intrusions through the analysis of either network logs and traffic
information (network-based), as considered in this work, or operating system logs
(host-based) which constitute most of the activity of an infrastructure. These

This work has received funding from European Union's H2020 research and innovation
programme under SAFECARE Project, grant agreement no. 787002.

© Springer Nature Switzerland AG 2020
A. Benzekri et al. (Eds.): FPS 2019, LNCS 12056, pp. 56–71, 2020.
https://doi.org/10.1007/978-3-030-45371-8_4

logs can be used to improve the system after a malicious occurrence by recording attack patterns that can later be used to identify similar attacks [26].

Besides types of IDS, another important concept is the anomaly-based detection and misuse or signature-based detection. Signature-based detection focuses on the analysis of network traffic, trying to identify sequences of bytes and packets that could be associated with threats and attacks. Therefore, the creation of signatures is dependent of the previous knowledge on the type of traffic (benign and non-benign) expected in a given network [20]. This process has, however, two major limitations: they are unable to detect zero-day or novelty attacks, i.e. previously unknown threats; and threats capable of changing and evolving as is the case with metamorphic malware (malware capable of reprogramming itself when propagated) and polymorphic malware (malware that uses encryption to avoid detection and capable of self-mutation) are also hard to identify [25].

In the case of anomaly-based detection, a normal activity profile is created, which can later be used to cross-reference against eventual network or host activity to find anomalies. The most prominent advantage of anomaly-based detection in comparison to signature-based is its potential to detect novelty attacks. Despite these benefits, anomaly-based detection is more prone to false positives (considering normal traffic as an attack), costing the operator time and money, than misuse detection. Finally, it is also important to mention that false negatives (considering attacks as normal traffic) are a problem in both approaches and need to be carefully observed when developing an IDS, since these error types pose a greater danger to the whole infrastructure [26]. Therefore, in this work we will focus mainly on misuse-based detection and the effect of feature reduction on the performance of methods intended for intrusion detection.

The CICIDS 2017 dataset is a very recent dataset that contains updated attack scenarios. Thus, we decided to analyse this dataset in order to develop valid models to detect intrusions as soon as they occur. Due to the large amount of features present in this dataset, preprocessing techniques and several feature selection approaches, such as permutation importance, are applied to the dataset in order to reduce the number of features without non-significant performance loss. Supervised ensemble learning algorithms are used to compare the feature selection methods and set the optimal number of features to ten. Finally, to evaluate the performance of the reduced dataset, the Random Forest algorithm is used.

The rest of the paper is organized as follows: in the Sect. 2 we introduce some ensemble learning techniques and its applications to intrusion detection field; the recent CICIDS2017 dataset is detailed in Sect. 3; different feature selection methods are described in Sect. 4; then, an analysis of the results of these methods are presented in Sect. 5. In Sect. 6 is evaluated the performance of the reduced dataset; and, finally, conclusions and future work are presented in Sect. 7.

2   Ensemble Learning and Intrusion Detection

Polikar defines ensemble learning as: "the process by which multiple models, such as classifiers or experts, are strategically generated and combined to solve a particular computational intelligence problem. Ensemble learning is primarily used to improve the performance of a model or reduce the likelihood of an unfortunate selection of a poor one." [29]. Thus, ensemble is just a collection of different models predictions which come together to give a final prediction, since different models working to the same aim should perform better than any single model alone.

Ensemble models are particularly adept at dealing with large datasets due to the ability to partition the data to train different classifiers with different samples and combining their results [30]. Diversity is also import since it allows classifiers to correct each other's errors. These features are very important in the context of the intrusion detection, since they allow the improvement of the intrusion detection attempts, reducing at the same time the number of misclassification. Below, we will describe two of the most popular ensemble methods - Random Forest and Gradient Boosting Machines - and its usage in intrusion detection systems. We also present the Decision Tree algorithm since it is the base of both Random Forest and Gradient Boosting Machines.

2.1 Decision Trees

A decision tree is a very simple algorithm that offers a very good trade-off between performance and interpretability, favoring the latter. It is a top-down algorithm that can be used to partition the predictor space into smaller non-overlapping regions with recourse to some splitting criteria [19]. The partitioning is done continuously by choosing the split-point and the feature that attain the best fit (maximize or reduce some metric in that specific division) [15].

In order to replace the Snort IDS system, Kruegel and Toth [24] proposed a decision tree model using the ID3 algorithm. This system grouped all the available rules in a large set and then divided them by similar characteristics/features. After this division, the authors trained a decision tree on the newly grouped data which was then used on the DARPA'98 dataset as a misuse detection mechanism showing an average speed improvement of 40% over the Snort rule-based system and an even steeper improvement when used with more rules. To reduce false positives the author [13] proposes a 3-phase model using a Support Vector Machine (SVM) a decision tree and a Naïve Bayes classifier. The proposed model starts by separating benign from malign traffic in the first phase using an SVM. After that, in the second phase, classification traffic identified as malign is sent to the tree model (J48) which is supposed to filter known attacks from unknown attacks, using the assumption that unknown attacks won't have a corresponding leaf on the tree. Unknown traffic is then forwarded to a Naïve Bayes classifier whose job is to model the probabilities of similarity with known attacks for further analysis by experts. This process is costly due to its sequential nature and the bottleneck caused by the tree model. Despite this drawback, the author was able to obtain an accuracy of 99.61% and an FPR of 1.57% in the KDD'99 dataset, with that said the model was trained with an old dataset which makes it hard to generalize results for more up-to-date data.

2.2 Random Forest

Random Forest is, probably, the most popular ensemble method. Despite it was presented independently by both Ho [16] in 1995, and Amit and Geman [2] in 1998, only in 2001 it became popular after Breiman publication [5].

Random Forest, together with decisions trees are some of the most studied ensemble techniques in intrusion detection literature especially in misuse-based intrusion detection, due to their supervised nature. This popularity can be attributed to 4 reasons [31]: (1) low computational complexity; (2) robustness to imbalanced data; (3) embedded feature selection; and (4) ability to deal with different features representations (continuous, discrete) as well as missing values. In 2013, Yin et al. [36] proposed an intrusion detection method based on the use of two Random Forest models for classification. The first model is trained using all the available data, both benign and malign (multiple classes) and the second model is trained using only malign data. The models are then employed in parallel, using the first model for an initial evaluation where uncertain classifications (less than 50% of the tree votes) are redirected to the other model for a second evaluation. This solution obtained higher results than a stand-alone Random Forest, with a precision and recall of 93% and 94%, respectively. Another work done by Bilge et al. [3] proposed the use of Random Forests to analyse large scale NetFlow data in order to identify botnet servers. The algorithm is used as a first filter and is followed by cross-examination of IP white-lists and black-lists to further reduce false positives. The authors tested the solution with data coming from 2 different networks totaling more than a billion flows. As expected, the results were lower when compared with artificial datasets, obtaining a ROC AUC (Area under ROC curve) of only 0.6 at best. Finally, Kim and Kim [23] proposed a 3 phased hybrid solution using Random Forests for misuse detection and Self-organizing Map (SOM) for anomaly detection. The first phase consisted of the use of hierarchical clustering together with factor analysis to extract the most relevant features. These features, in the second phase, were then given to the Random Forest classifier which detected known attacks. Afterward, in the last phase, the remaining traffic (benign) was sent to the SOM model which used outlier detection to detect unknown traffic. In the evaluation process, the authors opted, like many others, to use the detection rate together with False Positive Rate (FPR) on the NSL-KDD dataset [6], reaching 96.1% DR and 8.6% FPR. Despite the high detection rate, FPRs this high are often unacceptable in a real network context due to the associated human costs of verifying false positives.

2.3 Gradient Boosting Machines

Gradient Boosting Machines [12], introduced by Friedman in 2000, are a boosting algorithm that incrementally creates decision trees. In each iteration, a decision tree is trained from the residuals (difference between observed value and predicted value) of the previous learner. Then, the accumulation of predicted results of all learners is the final result.

XGBoost [8] and LightGBM [21] are both implementations of gradient boosting machines. These methods are especially relevant due to their heavy optimization which makes them very good candidates for regression and classification problems alike. Both these methods improve on two fundamental principles of gradient boosting, firstly they grow the decision trees differently preferring a leaf-wise growth to a level-wise growth and secondly they use different optimization techniques to find the best splits, such as histogram-based methods, ignoring sparse inputs, subsampling based on gradient value and feature bundling [22].

Despite being created in the early 2000s Gradient Boosting was not widely used until around 2015 with the appearance of XGBoost and later LightGBM. These methods improved on the original algorithm and made gradient boosting a state-of-the-art technique capable of competing with neural networks in some fields. Although gradient boosting has had recent success, it is still largely unexplored in intrusion detection. The authors in [11] applied XGBoost to the NSL-KDD dataset to measure the accuracy of the algorithm and obtained a value of 98.7% which outclasses all other classifiers. However, this value should be taken with a grain of salt since accuracy is usually not a good metric to use in unbalanced datasets due to its bias towards the majority class. Another group of authors [14] proposed a gradient boosted tree solution for intrusion detection in Vehicular Ad-hoc networks (VANETs), that consisted in the use of the model to detect RREQ flooding attacks together with evolutionary optimization for feature selection. The model is then trained and tested using synthetic data created for the purpose of testing RREQ flooding attacks. The attained results were high with 99.8% accuracy, 99.83% recall, 99.78 True negative rate (TNR) and 1 AUC.

2.4   Performance Metrics

There are several metrics that can be used in classification problems. Examples of these metrics are Accuracy, Receiver Operating Curve (ROC), Recall, Precision, and specificity. These metrics are not always applicable, especially in the case of intrusion detection where we are faced with problems with high class imbalance and sometimes of multiclass nature.

Accuracy is a very common metric in classification problems, and it aims to show the proportion of correctly classified samples in the full scope of the classification:

$$Accuracy = \frac{Number\ of\ correct\ predictions}{Total\ number\ of\ predictions}.$$

This metric is usually a good indicator of classifier performance. However, in the case of imbalanced data, as in the intrusion detection datasets, this measure is flawed since it favors the majority class (Benign traffic). Thus, this means that if the dataset was 90% benign traffic and the classifier failed to detect every attack but detected all normal traffic, it would still have an accuracy of 90%, which would only serve to mask the true performance of the model.

Precision is the ratio between the number of correct positives (TP) and the total number of positives (TP+FP),i.e., $Precision = \frac{TP}{TP+FP}$.

In the case of intrusion detection, it would be the ratio between the number of correctly predicted attacks and the total amount of instances predicted as attacks. Precision is usually better than accuracy because it is not biased towards the majority class.

Recall is the ratio of correctly predicted positive samples (TP) to the total number of positive samples (TP+FN), i.e., $Recall = \frac{TP}{TP+FN}$. In intrusion detection, it would be the ratio between the number of correctly predicted attacks and the total number of attacks.

Sometimes it is necessary to use a single metric where both recall and precision can be incorporated. F1-score is this metric. It can be described as the harmonic mean between precision and recall, i.e., F1-score $= \frac{2 \times Precision \times Recall}{Precision + Recall}$. The F1-score is a good measure when it is desired that both metrics to have similar values. However, in some cases, when there is the need to optimize one over the other, it is often not the best metric to optimize.

3   CICIDS2017 Dataset

Data are the most valuable asset to develop an efficient intrusion detection system. It is essential to have varied data sets with the most relevant features and real data, from updated types of attacks to real hardware and software scenarios [4]. In the literature, one can find many public available datasets that are intended to resemble real data traffic, such as KDD-99 [6], DARPA 98/99 [35] and ISCX2012 [33]. However, due to the continuous evolution of attack strategies, data sets need to be updated periodically to cover the current trends of attacks.

In this work we will use the most recent dataset CICIDS2017 [9], which was created to overcome the issues of existing datasets. This dataset is available in eight different (csv) files, containing five days of normal and intrusive traffic. Each file contains a labeled flow of network traffic corresponding to a certain period of time, that results of the network traffic analysis using CICFlowMeter software [10]. A total number of 79 features were extracted based on the information present on pcap file, such as time stamp, source and destination IPs, source and destination ports, protocols and attack [32].

CICIDS2017 dataset covers several attack scenarios based on the most common attack families: brute force attack, heartbledd attack, botnet, DoS attack, DDoS attack, web attack and infiltration attack [32]. Table 1 shows the attacks that are present in each csv file. Note that FTP-Patator and SSH-Patator are attacks that correspond to brute force attacks. PortScan is a tool that supports the infiltration attack. By merging all the csv files, it is observed that the dataset has 2830751 records.

Despite the CICIDS2017 dataset fulfills all the criteria of a true intrusion detection dataset, it also contains weaknesses: the division of the dataset in eight different files can be an issue, since processing individual files are a tedious and

Table 1. CICIDS2017 dataset files description

File name	Day	Attacks found
Monday-WorkingHours. pcap_ISCX.csv	Monday	Benign (Normal Activity)
Tuesday-WorkingHours. pcap_ISCX.csv	Tuesday	Benign, FTP-Patator, SSH-Patator
Wednesday-workingHours. pcap_ISCX.csv	Wednesday	Benign, DoS GoldenEye, DoS Hulk, DoS Slowhttptest, DoS slowloris, Heartbleed
Thursday-WorkingHours-Morning-WebAttacks. pcap_ISCX.csv	Thursday	Benign, Web Attack - Brute Force, Web Attack - Sql Injection, Web Attack - XSS
Thursday-WorkingHours-Afternoon-Infilteration.pcap_ISCX.csv	Thursday	Benign, Infiltration
Friday-WorkingHours-, Morning.pcap_ISCX.csv	Friday	Benign, Bot
Friday-WorkingHours-Afternoon-PortScan.pcap_ISCX.csv	Friday	Benign, PortScan
Friday-WorkingHours-Afternoon-DoS.pcap_ISCX.csv	Friday	Benign, DDoS

inefficient task; after combining all files, the size of the combined dataset becomes huge, which becomes a shortcoming due to loading and processing overhead; and the distribution of attacks present in the dataset is strongly tilted to benign, which means that the data set is prone to high class imbalances [27].

3.1 Preprocessing

CICIDS2017 dataset, as most of the datasets, contains some undesirable elements that must be removed to obtain an appropriate dataset. As already referred, the dataset was constructed using CICFlowMeter software, which collects specific network features that have no impact on model results such as flags that are never used. Thus, eight different features (*Bwd PSH Flags*, *Bwd URG Flags*, *Fwd Avg Bytes/Bulk*, *Fwd Avg Packets/Bulk*, *Fwd Avg Bulk Rate*, *Bwd Avg Bytes/Bulk*, *Bwd Avg Packets/Bulk* and *Bwd Avg Bulk Rate*) have been removed since all records had these values set to 0. The *Fwd_Header_Length* feature has also been removed, since it appears twice in the list. Therefore, the final dataset has only 70 features which helped in reducing the memory footprint of the dataset.

Another important step in the preprocessing phase was the removal of the records containing invalid values, such as the records where the duration of the flow was 0 due to rounding which caused the values dependent on time to become undefined (NaN,Inf), and the records with redundant information (mostly duplicated benign data points), since they can affect the performance of the model . After all these removals, the dataset has 2498185 records.

Despite ensemble learning techniques are capable of handling large datasets, we have decided to sample the dataset for training and testing purposes, since it is more efficient and cost-effective than surveying the entire dataset. Thus, 30% of the data were chosen using a stratified sampling method, i.e., the new dataset had the same proportion of attacks and benign traffic as the complete dataset. Nevertheless, this proportional cut affected attacks with less representation such as heartbleed, infiltration and SQL injections, which had less than 40 instances each. To solve this problem it was decided to include, all 3 attacks in the new dataset. Still, it is important to emphasize that this addition changed the original distribution of traffic, and can create an undesired bias in the data. Lastly, before starting the training phase, the new dataset was partitioned in train (77%) and test (23%) sets using again a stratified sampling strategy.

4   Feature Selection

Feature engineering and feature selection are prominent problems in fields such as medical analysis, image recognition, natural language processing and intrusion detection. Networks often contain thousands of features that can be used to identify attacks, from base features like packet size, destination port and protocol to more convoluted and less interpretable predictors like Inter-Arrival Time (IAT), or the number of bytes in a sliding window protocol [18]. This means that even trained professionals have difficulties in observing patterns in data that may lead to anomalous situations like potential attacks. Feature selection is especially powerful in these situations since it can use statistical and computational methods to determine the importance of a certain predictor in the detection of anomalous traffic. This leads to a better and more interpretable model that can be explained to a specialist, who can then use this information to improve the intrusion detection process [1,7].

There are several feature selection methods in literature, such as feature importance, variance tests or even chi-squared tests. In this paper, since we work more with tree-based methods, we have decided to use feature importance as the main feature selection method. In what follows, we will describe three different feature selection methods and analyse its application to our dataset.

4.1   Gini Importance

Gini impurity (or Gini index) is a metric used in decision trees to determine how to split the data in smaller groups. It measures how often a randomly chosen element from a set would be incorrectly labeled if it was randomly labeled according to the distribution of labels in the subset. Thus, the Gini impurity reflects the impurity level of a set of information: when the records are equally distributed among all classes, then the gini index reaches the maximum value $(1 - 1/n)$; if all records belong to one class then gini index reaches the minimum value zero [37].

Gini importance (also known by mean decrease in impurity) is one of the most common mechanisms for computing the feature importance, since it is easy to use and is available out of the box in most tree-based methods, such as Random Forests and gradient boosting. The Gini importance of a feature measures the effectiveness of this feature by reducing uncertainty or variance in creating decision trees [28]. Thus, each time a split occurs in a tree using a specific feature, the gini impurity is added to the total value of its importance. Thus, the features present in more splits, as well as those that result in greater impurity reduction, will have more importance.

Despite the popularity of this method due to its ease of use, it suffers from some inaccuracies when variables vary in their scale of measurement and their number of categories [34].

In this work, to perform the feature selection using this technique, a Light-GBM model was applied to the training data using a 10-fold cross-validation and the results of the ten models were then averaged to obtain the mean gini importance. A sample of the first 15 features selected by the algorithm can be seen in the Fig. 1.

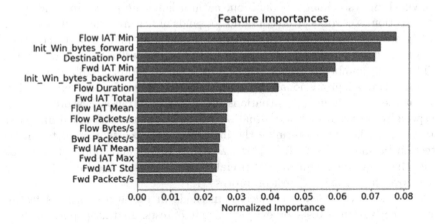

Fig. 1. Feature selection using gini importance.

As can be observed by the results presented in Fig. 1 the destination port strongly influences the outcome of the classification. In addition, the prominent presence of inter-arrival time (IAT) and its correlated features allow us to conclude that the IAT has a big influence in the detection of attacks. This can be explained by the analysis of peaks and valleys in the IAT that can, on some occasions, correspond to anomalous behavior. Another trend that can be observed is the presence of features that represent the flow direction: with 7 of the 15 features being in this direction, while only 2 of 15 are in the opposite direction.

Finally, the importance is well distributed throughout the dataset which means that, according to this technique, 38 features are needed to reach a cumulative importance of 90%.

4.2 Permutation Importance

Permutation importance measures the importance of a feature after the training of a model. It assumes that a particular feature is important if shuffling its values cause a considerable reduction in performance, in other words, if randomizing the order of a given column (feature) values results in less accurate predictions, then that feature has a positive importance equal to the reduction in performance. This type of importance is especially appealing because of two factors: first it can be done with a trained model, using the test set to verify the impact that the shuffling has in the prediction; and it can be used for most types of algorithms because it treats the algorithm as a black box.

Figure 2 shows the 15 most important features after the permutation importance calculation, using the same dataset and model used for Gini importance method. It can be observed that only a few features have meaningful importance. Using this technique, 10 features represent around 99% of the cumulative importance. Nonetheless, with this approach some of the relevant features are according with Gini approach: *Destination Port*, *Fwd IAT Min*, *Flow IAT Min* and *Init_Win_bytes_forward Init_Win_bytes_backward*, which reinforces the idea that these features are meaningful information for attacks prediction.

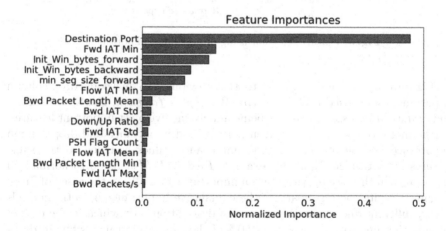

Fig. 2. Feature selection using permutation importance.

4.3 Drop-Column Importance

Despite being similar to permutation importance drop-column importance requires the retraining of the model since a model trained with a certain number of features cannot be tested with a different number of features. As a result, when employing drop-column importance one should account not only for the supposed benefits of more accurate feature selection but also for the accrued computation cost. However, if we can ignore the computation cost of retraining a model, drop-column importance is one of the most accurate feature importance techniques. As in the permutation importance approach, first it is calculated a baseline performance score with the complete dataset, then an entirely column, that corresponds to a feature, is dropped, the resulting dataset is retrained, and the performance score is recalculated. The feature importance is the difference between the baseline and the score from the model missing that feature [28].

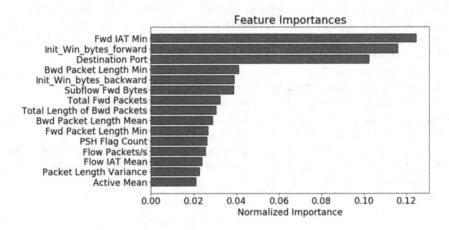

Fig. 3. Feature selection using drop-column importance.

Figure 3 shows that similarly to the previous two methods drop-column importance chose *Fwd IAT Min*, *Init_Win_bytes_forward*, *Destination Port* and *Init_Win_bytes_backward* as being among the five most important features. Furthermore, the similarity between permutation importance and drop-column importance can be observed in the importance values assigned to the same features by both algorithms, for example *Fwd IAT Min* has 0.15 normalized importance in the case of permutation importance and 0.12 in the cased of drop-column. Despite these similarities the cumulative importance of both methods is very different due to the importance of destination port which in the case of permutation importance represents 50% of the total importance while in drop-column it's only representative of 5%.

The comparison of these three methods strengthened the knowledge that the most important features are *Fwd IAT Min*, *Init_Win_bytes_forward*, *Destination Port* and *Init_Win_bytes_backward*. We can also conclude that the inter-arrival time is a meaningful predictor per the first and second methods presented. Moreover, the selection seems to indicate that the difference between features chosen by Gini and permutation importance is not as pronounced as would be expected, given the difference in paradigm. Additionally, it is still possible to notice a large discrepancy between the importance of *Destination Port* when comparing drop-column and permutation importance methods, which could be attributed to the different data used to create the measures - training set used for drop-column and testing set used for permutation importance.

5   Feature Selection Methods Analysis

Feature selection aims to identify and remove unneeded, irrelevant and redundant features from a dataset in order to reduce the complexity of the predictive model, but without compromising its accuracy. In the previous section we have studied three different feature selection techniques. Now, we need to compare its performance to decide which features are the most meaningful. Decision Tree and Random Forest algorithms were used, along with the different features suggested by the feature selection approaches, for performance evaluation. The tests were performed by iteratively removing resources and evaluating the F1-score and training time for each iteration.

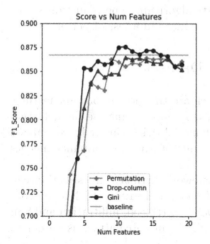 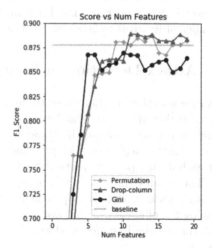

Fig. 4. Comparison of feature selection methods using Decision Trees.

Fig. 5. Comparison of feature selection methods using Random Forests.

The results of the different feature selection methods using the Decision Tree algorithm are represented in Fig. 4. The performance metric used was the F1-score since it allowed us to balance the precision and recall in the comparison to the feature selection methods. It is possible to observe that after the 7 features the performance of all methods stabilizes. Additionally, the performance of gini importance seems to be slightly better than that of the other methods. Overall, all importance methods perform reasonably with eight or more features, even surpassing the baseline performance (69 features) features with gini being more favorable due to the ease of use and the reduced cost. Thus, these results suggest that it is possible to use a number of features between 7 and 20, instead of the original 69, due to the substantial reduction in training time without any loss of performance. The success of gini can, however, be less pronounce in a scenario where more intricate relationships between variables are observed such as when using more complicated models like Random Forests.

Random Forests were also used to compare the previous feature selection methods. The results can be observed in Fig. 5. Similarly, to the previous example, the F1-score stabilizes with eight or more features. In this case the gini importance is clearly inferior to the other methods this could be, as explained earlier, due to the inability of gini importance to select meaningful features when the relationships between them are more convoluted. In this case, and mainly because of the computational cost, permutation importance would be preferable as a middle term between the high cost of running drop-column importance and the inaccuracies of gini importance. These observations, together with the previous analysis, suggest that permutation importance is the preferable approach if we give an emphasis to Random Forest performance.

After the selection of the most relevant feature importance method, we have decided to compare the impact of different number of features in the performance of attack detection using the Random Forests algorithm. The reduction in the number of features to 20 or even 10, would not incur in a loss of performance.

6   Attack Detection in Reduced Dataset

Feature selection has helped us to define which are the most important features for detecting attacks on the dataset. Thus, it is important analyse the detection rates, using for example the Random Forest model, with this reduced dataset (with only ten features). Table 2 shows the results of three performance metrics for each attack present in the dataset.

The results show that the proposed framework with feature selection can detect attacks with 93% of precision, 91% of recall and 91.9% of F1-score, confirming the efficiency of the process. The DDoS, heartbleed, infiltration and SSh Patator are the best detected attacks. The Web Bruteforce attack is harder to detect.

By analyzing the false positive and false negative rate (see Table 2) it is possible to observe that most errors are false negatives with close to zero false positives. More specifically there is only a 0.09 false negative rate (FNR) when using 10 features versus the 0.081 FNR when using 69 features with the FPR being unchanged at zero. Additionally, if we only account for attacks confused as benign traffic the numbers decrease further with 0.043 FNR at 10 features and 0.036 at 69 features. As with recall DDoS, DoS GoldenEye, DoS Hulk, FTP Patator, Heartbleed, infiltration, PortScan and SSH Patator were all identified with high accuracy and Bot Net, Web bruteforce, Web Sql Injections and Web XSS were all identified with poor accuracy with bruteforce being the worst at 0.554 FNR.

Table 2. Performance evaluation of the dataset considering 10 and 69 features

	Precision		Recall		F1-score		False negatives		False positives	
	RF - 69	RF - 10	RF - 69	RF - 10	RF - 69	RF - 10	RF - 69	RF - 10	RF - 69	RF - 10
Benign	0.999	0.999	0.999	0.999	0.999	0.999	0.001	0.001	0.003	0.003
Bot	0.826	0.828	0.807	0.785	0.816	0.806	0.193	0.215	0.000	0.000
DDoS	1.000	1.000	0.999	0.999	0.999	0.999	0.001	0.001	0.000	0.000
DoS Slowhttptest	0.994	0.983	0.993	0.983	0.993	0.983	0.007	0.017	0.000	0.000
DoS GoldenEye	0.996	0.997	0.996	0.993	0.996	0.994	0.004	0.007	0.000	0.000
Dos Hulk	0.999	0.998	0.998	0.998	0.998	0.998	0.002	0.002	0.000	0.000
DoS Slowloris	0.993	0.982	0.995	0.986	0.994	0.984	0.005	0.014	0.000	0.000
FTP Patator	1.000	1.000	1.000	0.998	1.000	0.999	0.000	0.002	0.000	0.000
Heartbleed	1.000	1.000	1.000	1.000	1.000	1.000	0.000	0.000	0.000	0.000
Infiltration	0.875	1.000	0.875	1.000	0.875	1.000	0.125	0.000	0.000	0.000
PortScan	0.992	0.992	0.996	0.997	0.994	0.994	0.004	0.003	0.000	0.000
SSH Patator	1.000	1.000	1.000	1.000	1.000	1.000	0.000	0.000	0.000	0.000
Web Bruteforce	0.608	0.577	0.446	0.446	0.515	0.503	0.554	0.554	0.000	0.000
Web SqlInjection	1.000	1.000	1.000	0.800	1.000	0.888	0.000	0.200	0.000	0.000
Web XSS	0.676	0.683	0.767	0.760	0.719	0.719	0.233	0.240	0.000	0.000
AVERAGE	0.926	0.931	0.919	0.910	0.921	0.919	0.081/0.036	0.090/0.043	0.000	0.000

7   Conclusion

In this paper we presented a detailed selection and subsequent performance analysis of the most significant features of the CICIDS2017 dataset by comparing three different feature selection methods: gini importance, permutation importance and Drop-column importance. When compared using both a decision tree and a Random Forest permutation importance came out as the best method by being a good middle ground between the computational cost of gini importance and the accuracy of drop-column. Additionally all these methods prioritize features related to the inter-arrival time, the initial windows of the TCP protocol and destination port and more specifically the following 5 features: *Destination Port, Fwd IAT Min, Init_Win_bytes_forward, Init_Win_bytes_backward* and *FlowIATMin*.

Furthermore, two datasets were compared, one using the original 69 features and the other using only 10 selected features. This comparison demonstrated a negligible difference in both F1-score (0.2%) and false positive rate ($\sim$0) and a difference of 0.007 in false negative rate. Finally, when comparing performance on a attack by attack basis some attacks were identified as having consistently reduced detection rate, namely Bot Nets, Web bruteforce, Web Sql Injections and Web XSS.

As a future work we pretend to use different feature selection techniques, or even different methods, to understand if they could be better suited for intrusion detection such as genetic algorithms, ant colony or variance tests. Moreover, as an incremental comparison, we intend to use rank aggregation techniques to select the best features from various methods while comparing the aggregated collection to the features selected by each individual method.

References

1. Al-Jarrah, O.Y., Siddiqui, A., Elsalamouny, M., Yoo, P.D., Muhaidat, S., Kim, K.: Machine-learning-based feature selection techniques for large-scale network intrusion detection. In: 2014 IEEE 34th International Conference on Distributed Computing Systems Workshops (ICDCSW). pp. 177–181, June 2014
2. Amit, Y., Geman, D.: Shape quantization and recognition with randomized trees. Neural Comput. **9**, 1545–1588 (1997)
3. Bilge, L., Balzarotti, D., Robertson, W., Kirda, E., Kruegel, C.: Disclosure: detecting botnet command and control servers through large-scale netflow analysis, pp. 129–138, December 2012
4. Boukhamla, A., Coronel, J.: Cicids 2017 dataset: performance improvements and validation as a robust intrusion detection system testbed. Int. J. Inf. Comput. Secur. (2018)
5. Breiman, L.: Random forests. Mach. Learn. **45**(1), 5–32 (2001)
6. University of California Irvine: Kdd cup 1999 data, March 2018. http://kdd.ics.uci.edu/databases/kddcup99/kddcup99.html
7. Chebrolu, S., Abraham, A., Thomas, J.P.: Feature deduction and ensemble design of intrusion detection systems. Comput. Secur. **24**(4), 295–307 (2005)
8. Chen, T., Guestrin, C.: XGBoost: a scalable tree boosting system, pp. 785–794, August 2016
9. Cyber Intelligence (CI) for Cybersecurity: Intrusion detection evaluation dataset (cicids2017), March 2018. https://www.unb.ca/cic/datasets/ids-2017.html
10. Cyber Intelligence (CI) for Cybersecurity: Network traffic flow analyzer, March 2018. http://www.netflowmeter.ca/netflowmeter.html
11. Dhaliwal, S.S., Nahid, A.A., Abbas, R.: Effective intrusion detection system using XGBoost. Information **9**(7), 149 (2018)
12. Friedman, J.: Greedy function approximation: a gradient boosting machine. Ann. Stat. **29**, 1189–1232 (2000)
13. Goeschel, K.: Reducing false positives in intrusion detection systems using data-mining techniques utilizing support vector machines, decision trees, and naive Bayes for off-line analysis, pp. 1–6, March 2016
14. Gulati, P.: Intrusion detection system using gradient boosted trees for VANETs. Int. J. Res. Appl. Sci. Eng. Technol. 482–488 (2017)
15. Hastie, T.: The Elements of Statistical Learning: Data Mining, Inference, and Prediction. Springer, Heidelberg (2009). https://doi.org/10.1007/BF02985802
16. Ho, T.K.: The random subspace method for constructing decision forests. IEEE Trans. Pattern Anal. Mach. Intell. **20**(8), 832–844 (1998)
17. Hodo, E., Bellekens, X., Hamilton, A., Tachtatzis, C., Atkinson, R.: Shallow and deep networks intrusion detection system: a taxonomy and survey. Workingpaper, January 2017
18. Iglesias, F., Zseby, T.: Analysis of network traffic features for anomaly detection. Mach. Learn. **101**(1), 59–84 (2015)
19. James, G., Witten, D., Hastie, T., Tibshirani, R.: An Introduction to Statistical Learning: With Applications in R. Springer, Heidelberg (2014). https://doi.org/10.1007/978-1-4614-7138-7

20. Jyothsna, V., Rama Prasad, V.V., Munivara Prasad, K.: A review of anomaly based intrusion detection systems. Int. J. Comput. Appl. **28**, 26–35 (2011)
21. Ke, G.,et al.: LightGBM: a highly efficient gradient boosting decision tree. In: Advances in Neural Information Processing Systems, vol. 30, December 2017
22. keitakurita: LightGBM and XGBoost explained, October 1999. http:// mlexplained.com/2018/01/05/lightgbm-and-xgboost-explained/
23. Kim, E., Kim, S.: A novel hierarchical detection method for enhancing anomaly detection efficiency, pp. 1018–1022, December 2015
24. Kruegel, C., Toth, T.: Using decision trees to improve signature-based intrusion detection. In: Vigna, G., Kruegel, C., Jonsson, E. (eds.) RAID 2003. LNCS, vol. 2820, pp. 173–191. Springer, Heidelberg (2003). https://doi.org/10.1007/978-3-540-45248-5_10
25. Mandayam Comar, P., Liu, L., Saha, S., Tan, P.N., Nucci, A.: Combining supervised and unsupervised learning for zero-day malware detection, pp. 2022–2030, April 2013
26. Mukkamala, S., Sung, A., Abraham, A.: Cyber security challenges: designing efficient intrusion detection systems and antivirus tools, January 2005
27. Panigrahi, R., Borah, S.: A detailed analysis of cicids2017 dataset for designing intrusion detection systems. Int. J. Eng. Technol. **7**(3.24), 479–482 (2018)
28. Parr, T., Turgutlu, K., Csiszar, C., Howard, J.: Beware default random forest importances, March 2018. https://explained.ai/rf-importance/
29. Polikar, R.: Ensemble learning. Scholarpedia **4**(1), 2776 (2009). revision #186077
30. Polikar, R.: Ensemble based systems in decision making. IEEE Circ. Syst. Mag. **6**, 21–45 (2006)
31. Resende, P.A.A., Drummond, A.C.: A survey of random forest based methods for intrusion detection systems. ACM Comput. Surv. **51**(3), 48:1–48:36 (2018)
32. Sharafaldin, I., Lashkari, A.H., Ghorbani, A.A.: Toward generating a new intrusion detection dataset and intrusion traffic characterization. In: Proceedings of the 4th International Conference on Information Systems Security and Privacy, Vol. 1, ICISSP, pp. 108–116. INSTICC, SciTePress (2018)
33. Shiravi, A., Shiravi, H., Tavallaee, M., Ghorbani, A.: Toward developing a systematic approach to generate benchmark datasets for intrusion detection. Comput. Secur. **31**, 357–374 (2012)
34. Strobl, C., Boulesteix, A.L., Zeileis, A., Hothorn, T.: Bias in random forest variable importance measures: Illustrations, sources and a solution. BMC Bioinform. **8**(1), 25 (2007)
35. Haines, J.W., Lippmann, R.P., Fried, D.J., Zissman, M.A., Tran, E.: 1999 DARPA intrusion detection evaluation: design and procedures, p. 188, February 2001
36. Yin, M., Yao, D., Luo, J., Liu, X., Ma, J.: Network backbone anomaly detection using double random forests based on non-extensive entropy feature extraction, pp. 80–84, July 2013
37. Zhi, T., Luo, H., Liu, Y.: A gini impurity based interest flooding attack defence mechanism in NDN. IEEE Commun. Lett. **22**(3), 1 (2018)

Semantic Representation Based on Deep Learning for Spam Detection

Nadjate Saidani[✉], Kamel Adi, and Mohand Said Allili

Department of Computer Science and Engineering,
University de Quebec en Outaouais, Gatineau, Canada
{sain06,Kamel.Adi,MohandSaid.allili}@uqo.ca

Abstract. This paper addresses the email spam filtering problem by proposing an approach based on two levels text semantic analysis. In the first level, a deep learning technique, based on Word2Vec is used to categorize emails by specific domains (e.g., health, education, finance, etc.). This enables a separate conceptual view for spams in each domain. In the second level, we extract a set of latent topics from email contents and represent them by rules to summarize the email content into compact topics discriminating spam from legitimate emails in an efficient way. The experimental study shows promising results in term of the precision of the spam detection.

Keywords: Spam detection · Embedding word · Domain-specific analysis · Semantic features · Deep learning · Classification

1 Introduction

The use of email boxes has been considered as the most popular means of communication for decades. However, email's popularity causes a big problem which is the sends of unsolicited emails called spams. Spam accounts for billions of emails sent every day which makes more than 50% of all sent emails in 2017 [5]. Even though the proposed solutions for spam detection in the literature have come a long way, spam still represents a real problem for IT infrastructure security.

Email spams come in different types targeting various domains (e.g., health, education, finance, etc.). The most common spam emails are disguised marketing campaigns for business promotions. It can be promotion of weight loss programs, credit card offers and any other popular product. Since spam emails usually have advertisement content which is distinct from legitimate emails, several spam detection models using semantic features have been proposed. For instance, authors in [8] proposed the Word Sense Disambiguation model (WSD) to extract semantic information from spam emails. Authors in [15] used the enhanced Topic-based Vector Space Model (eTVSM) using a semantic ontology to deal with synonyms. In [13] the authors used the Latent Semantic Indexing model (LSI) to discover thematic relationships between documents and words.

© Springer Nature Switzerland AG 2020
A. Benzekri et al. (Eds.): FPS 2019, LNCS 12056, pp. 72–81, 2020.
https://doi.org/10.1007/978-3-030-45371-8_5

Several other works using semantic features have been reviewed in [2]. However, most of these methods use holistic and general-purpose semantic features which are extracted independently of the type of email content (email domain). None of these methods apply these semantic models to specific domains for spam detection. In fact, it has been determined that the separation of domains to detect spam help to distinguish common features in terms of vocabulary and underlying semantics that can drastically change from one domain to another [14].

This paper is an extension of our previous work in [14] called here TBSR-SD (Text-Based Semantic Representation for Spam Detection). In that work we considered semantic information at two levels. In the first level, we used Bag-of-Words (BoW) model to categorize emails into subject domains (e.g., finance, medicine, etc.), which enables targeting each domain-specific semantics for spam detection. In the second level, semantic features are extracted for spam detection in each domain. We applied the CN2-SD algorithm [9] for an automatic extraction of semantic features. The features are represented in the form of rules which are a conjunction of words where each rule describes some semantic meaning in the text. In this paper, we use in both levels more elaborated semantic features based on deep learning and semantic ontology. In the first level, we use a deep learning approach based on Word2Vec model [10] to categorize email documents by domains. In the second level, we use eTVSM [15], based on semantic ontology, to extract the most dominant topics in the email content. The resulting topics are then used as input data of the CN2-SD algorithm for the extraction of the semantic features. These features, encoded as rules, are a conjunction of topics rather than words. Each rule has a binary outcome and acts by itself as a weak classifier for spam detection. Experiments on a large corpus of emails have shown that the combination of the whole rules produces a strong classifier enabling robust and accurate spam detection.

The rest of this paper is organized as follows: Sect. 2 gives a brief overview of related work. Sections 3 and 4 detail the proposed approach for an efficient spam detection. Section 5 discusses the evaluation results. Finally, Sect. 6 presents the conclusion and some directions for future work.

2   Related Work

In this section, we review some works related to email spam detection, mainly those based on the semantic content analysis. Many researchers explored the use of the Latent Semantic Indexing (LSI) model to study its effectiveness for the detection of spam emails [13]. This method uses singular value decomposition to reduce the dimensionality of the term's space into a latent semantic space. The underlying idea is that the LSI model tends to discover relationships between documents and the words they contain by producing a set of concepts relating words appearing in similar contexts. Other similar and popular models, as topic representation models, have been proposed such as probabilistic Latent Semantic Analysis (pLSA) [7] and Latent Dirichlet Allocation [1]. These models represent documents as a set of topic distributions and the topics as a set of words distributions. The authors in [8] used word's semantics for spam filtering by introducing a Word Sense Disambiguation (WSD) as a preprocessing step. Basically, WSD determines the different meaning of an ambiguous word according to its context. The authors in [15] proposed the enhanced Topic based Vector Space Model (eTVSM) based on ontologies to represent email documents as a vector space of topics. The proposed method shows that using word synonyms created from WordNet Ontology yields good results for document similarity.

The authors in [3] studied the use of sentiment analysis in a Bayesian spam filters. In their work, the authors assume that the semantics of a spam message should be shaped with a positive meaning. Some works using deep learning for spam detection have been proposed. For instance, in [19] the authors use the Doc2Vec model to obtain a vector representation of twits and use it as input features of standard machine learning algorithm in order to build a spam/ham classifier. Similarly, authors of [12] proposed to use the Word2Vec model to encode document words in a vector space and use this encoding in a multinomial naive Bayes algorithm. This vector representation allows to overcome the drawback of the conditional independence assumption of naive Bayes algorithm since words appearing in a similar context tend to be closer in the generated vector space.

These methods show the importance of using semantic information to improve spam detection. However, they do not extract higher level semantic concepts of emails which can be helpful for discriminating legitimate from spam emails. In fact, they do not take into consideration the type of email content (email domain) where different semantic content can arise. Our work tackles this problem by using two semantic levels. In the first level, we categorize email documents by domain according to their contents using embedding words approach. In the second level, we apply in each domain eTVSM and CN2-SD algorithms to generate a set of semantic features. The semantic features are ten used to train machine learning algorithms for spam detection.

3   Email Categorization by Domains

To build our model for spam detection, we start by categorizing email documents into the most targeted domains by spammers [4,6,16]. We have considered six domains: Computer, Adult, Education, Finance, Health and Others. The category 'Others' is used to ensure the completeness of the domain space. To assign emails to these domains, we train a supervised classifier on labeled data after operating a text preprocessing and applying Word2Vec word embedding [10] on email contents.

Preprocessing. The preprocessing step allows to convert an input text document to a vector of words. We consider five preprocessing steps to be applied for the input text document: keywords recognition, word with separate letters recognition, segmentation, stop-word removal and stemming. Keywords recognition allows automatic identification of keywords and abbreviations from predefined categories. Word with separate letters recognition enables to recognize words containing letters separated by blank spaces. Segmentation permits to segment email content into a set of words. Stop-word removal deletes most common words in a text (e.g., articles, prepositions, etc.). Stemming allows the transformation of words into their roots. See [14] for more details.

Word2Vec Word Embedding. Word2Vec is one of the most popular approaches to learn word embedding using neural networks. The approach converts words into corresponding vectors in such a way that the semantically similar vectors should be close to each other in an N-dimensional space (N refers to the dimensions of the vector). The powerful concept behind word2vec is that word vectors that are close to each other in the vector space represent words that are not only of the same meaning but of the same context as well.

Word2Vec is proposed in [10]. Google's Word2Vec is trained on Google News Corpus, which has more than 3 Million running words. The approach comprises two training models: Continuous Bag of Words model (CBOW) and Skip-Gram (SG). The CBOW predicts the target word using context information and the SG predicts each context word using the target word.

We choose to use Word2Vec representation to categorize email documents by domain because it has several advantages over BoW schemes. Word2Vec retains the semantic meaning of different words in a document without losing context information. Another advantage of using the Word2Vec model is the small size of the embedding vector it generates. Each dimension in the embedding vector contains information about one aspect of the word. We do not need huge sparse vectors, unlike the BoW-based approaches.

Figure 1 illustrates the steps used to classify email documents by domain. The model takes as input a set of text documents $D = \{d_1, \cdots, d_n\}$ where each document d_i is represented as a vector of words $d_i = \{w_1, \cdots, w_m\}$. The word vectors are then mapped into numerical vectors using Word2Vec. For the words not mapped in word2vec embeddings, spell checking is applied to check the word spelling by using the function Microsoft Word spell checker. If no suggestion of correction is proposed for a given word, a lookup for a similar word is executed. This task is performed in WordNet; it returns a similar word that is semantically related to a given word. Word2vec is again applied to find the word embedding vector corresponding to the similar word. If no similar word is found for a given word in WordNet, the word is deleted. The use of spell check software and WordNet dictionary allows to assign a semantically related vector representation of an unknown word rather than deleting it or assigning it to a random unrelated word vectors. In this step we have used a pre-trained vectors from Google's Word2Vec to convert the email documents into a vector form. We specifically induce 300-dimensional vectors by using the SG model. The SG is considered as an efficient method for learning high quality word embeddings from large-scale unstructured text data like email documents [18].

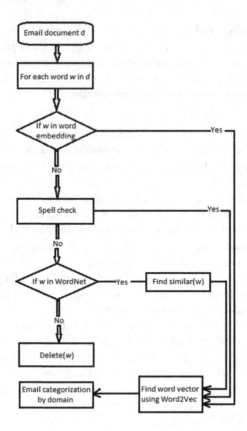

Fig. 1. Outline of the different steps used for email categorization by domain.

Categorization. To evaluate the performance of the obtained word embeddings from the previous step, various classification algorithms are applied to categorize email documents by domains. Word embeddings are used to generate the document embeddings t_i by averaging all word embeddings in the given document d_i as follows:

$$t_i = \frac{1}{|d_i|} \sum_{w \in d_i} T(w) \tag{1}$$

where $T(w)$ is the Word2Vec embedding of the word w.

The obtained results are then used to train a set of classification algorithms to categorize email documents by domain. For email categorization by domain, we compared the following classification algorithms: naive Bayes, K-nearest neighbor (Knn) and Support Vector Machine (SVM) and identify the best classifier giving the most precise email categorization.

4   Domain-Specific Semantic Feature Extraction

This level aims at extracting hidden semantic features for representing email content. Our final goal is to create a domain-specific semantic representation for an efficient detection of spams. In this regard, we consider two main models, eTVSM and CN2-SD. The model eTVSM is used to represent email documents as a vector of topics in each domain. CN2-SD is applied to represent the returned vectors as a set of rules which are used as input semantic features to build specialized classifiers for detecting domain-specific spams.

The eTVSM is an extension of the Topic-based Vector Space Model (TVSM). The basic premise of TVSM is that documents are represented by a vector of topics rather than terms. Therefore, each term vector is weighted and its direction represents term relevance according to fundamental topics. However, this model does not allow the expression of some linguistic phenomena like hyponymy, metonymy, etc. In contrast, the eTVSM model addresses this problem by using domain ontology to represent different relationships between various terms of each domain [11]. The use of an ontology provides a richer natural language retrieval model that is able to accommodate synonyms, homonyms and other linguistic phenomena [15].

In order to apply eTVSM to our database and represent email documents as operational vector space we fellow the steps used in [15]. We used the Themis[1] implementation which is an in-database data-structure. This data-structure is optimized for storing email documents and performing document similarity measurements based on the eTVSM [11]. In addition, Wordnet ontology is used to enhance the eTVSM Model.

The resultant vector representations of the email documents by eTVSM are used in our work by CN2-SD using a procedure proposed in [14] to generate a set of semantic features represented as a set of rules. Each rule has a binary outcome and acts by itself as a weak classifier for spam detection. The rationale behind applying CN2-SD is to check if a combination of one or more topics in a single semantic feature can help distinguish junk mail from legitimate mail. The obtained semantic features are then used to build specialized classifiers for detecting domain-specific spams such as naive Bayes, Knn and SVM.

5   Experimental Results

To evaluate our approach, we used two public datasets of both spam and ham emails and messages from discussion forums. The public datasets are Enron[2] and Ling-spam[3]. The discussion forums were necessary to fill the lack of legitimate messages, belonging to the six chosen domains in the public datasets Enron and Ling-spam. The collected dataset was categorized manually by domains according to the text content. We used a total of 8188 emails distributed over the six pre-selected

---

[1] https://code.google.com/archive/p/ir-themis/.

[2] https://www.cs.cmu.edu/./enron/.

[3] http://csmining.org/index.php/lingspam-datasets.html.

categories: Health, Adult Finance, Education, Computer and Others. Each category includes both spam and ham emails. The overall collection includes 4706 ham emails and 3482 spam emails. The evaluation was carried out by a 10-fold cross-validation, with standard accuracy metric, for both semantic levels.

Table 1. Quantitative evaluation of machine-learning classifiers for email categorization by domains.

Classifier	Accuracy
Knn	92.4%
naive Bayes	88.2%
SVM	96.2%

Table 1 shows the evaluation results for the first semantic level using Word2Vec model to categorize emails documents by domains. Based on the obtained results from the used classifiers, we see that Support Vector Machine (SVM) has given the highest accuracy value 96.2%. We see also that the K-nearest neighbor (Knn) classifier is quite effective and gives a value of 92.4%. In contrast, naive Bayes has the lowest accuracy as compared to other classifiers with 88.2%.

Table 2. Quantitative evaluation of machine-learning classifiers using eTVSM for spam detection in specific domains.

	Classifier	Accuracy
Computer	Knn	90.1%
	naive Bayes	97.9%
	SVM	89.3%
Adult	Knn	97.6%
	naive Bayes	97.8%
	SVM	90.4%
Education	Knn	96.6%
	naive Bayes	98.9%
	SVM	92.3%
Finance	Knn	95.4%
	naive Bayes	97.8%
	SVM	91.5%
Health	Knn	97.6%
	naive Bayes	98.5%
	SVM	94.9%
Others	Knn	91.6%
	naive Bayes	95.9%
	SVM	86.7%
Average	Knn	94.8%
	naive Bayes	97.8%
	SVM	90.9%

Table 2 shows the results of email spam classification in specific domains using semantic model eTVSM. Bayesian Classifier performs better than the other applied classifiers. It has given almost in all domains an accuracy of more than 97% which allows an average accuracy of 97.8% for the overall model.

As an overall evaluation of our approach, we have compared its performance with other semantic-based approaches of the literature and we have selected three methods: eTVSM, Doc2Vec and TBSR-SD. The obtained results are shown in Table 3. As we can see, our method outperforms eTVSM, TBSR-SD and Doc2Vec since we obtained the highest score with 97.8% of accuracy. It is clear that our approach gets advantages from specialization of the semantic-domains and domain oriented classifiers compared to the general-classifiers approach of eTVSM and Doc2Vec. Moreover, the high performance of our classifier compared to the TBSR-SD classifier can be explained by the fact that the used Word2Vec embeddings for domain classification allows to overcome the drawback of feature independence of the BoW model used in the TBSR-SD method. Furthermore, in the second level, TBSR-SD uses independent words as input data for the CN2-SD to generate rules, whereas our approach uses a set of topics produced to generate the rules which carry more semantic content than using words.

Table 3. Comparative evaluation with other methods.

Model	Classifier	Accuracy
eTVSM [15]	Knn	93.4%
	naive Bayes	97.6%
	SVM	97.6%
TBSR-SD [14]	Knn	95.5%
	naive Bayes	97.6%
	SVM	93.2%
Doc2Vec [19]	Knn	75.3%
	naive Bayes	65.8%
	SVM	84.6%
Our approach	Knn	94.8%
	naive Bayes	97.8%
	SVM	90.9%

6   Conclusion

We proposed a new approach using semantic-based model to detect spam emails in specific domains. For this purpose, we use two semantic level analysis. The first level categorizes email documents by domains using Word2Vec word embedding. The ultimate goal of this level is to obtain the global subject of the email content to allow the extraction of relevant semantic features related to a domain. The second level uses the eTVSM model to represent the email documents as a vector of topics and the CN2-SD to create semantic features. The semantic features are then used to train machine learning algorithms for spam detection. The experimental results showed that the application of the topic extraction model in specific domains allows an efficient detection of spam emails. For future work, we aim to increase the capacity of the classifiers prediction using more elaborated semantic features like WSD and LDA. Furthermore, to keep the filtering system running in an efficient way over time, we plan to create a dynamic learning system allowing continuous updating of rules based on the user feedbacks.

References

1. Bíró, I., Szabó, J., Benczúr, A.A.: Latent dirichlet allocation in web spam filtering. In: Proceedings of the 4th International Workshop on Adversarial Information Retrieval on the Web, pp. 29–32. ACM (2008)
2. Caruana, G., Li, M.: A survey of emerging approaches to spam filtering. ACM Comput. Surv. (CSUR) **44**(2), 1–27 (2012)
3. Ezpeleta, E., Zurutuza, U., Gómez Hidalgo, J.M.: Does sentiment analysis help in bayesian spam filtering? In: Martínez-Álvarez, F., Troncoso, A., Quintián, H., Corchado, E. (eds.) HAIS 2016. LNCS (LNAI), vol. 9648, pp. 79–90. Springer, Cham (2016). https://doi.org/10.1007/978-3-319-32034-2_7
4. Gudkova, D., Vergelis, M., et al.: Spam and phishing in Q2 2016. Kaspersky Lab, pp. 1–22 (2016)
5. Gudkova, D., Vergelis, M., et al.: Spam and phishing in Q2 2017. Securelsit, Spam and phishing reports (2017). https://securelist.com/spam-and-phishing-in-q2-2017/81537/
6. Gudkova, D., Vergelis, M., Demidova, N.: Spam and phishing in Q2 2015. Kaspersky Lab, pp. 1–19 (2015)
7. Hofmann, T.: Probabilistic latent semantic analysis. In: Proceedings of the Fifteenth Conference on Uncertainty in Artificial Intelligence, pp. 289–296. Morgan Kaufmann Publishers Inc. (1999)
8. Laorden, C., Santos, I., et al.: Word sense disambiguation for spam filtering. Electron. Commer. Res. Appl. **11**(3), 290–298 (2012)
9. Lavrac, N., Kavsek, B., Flach, P., Todorovski, L.: Subgroup discovery with CN2-SD. J. Mach. Learn. Res. **5**(2), 153–188 (2004)
10. Mikolov, T., Sutskever, I., et al.: Distributed representations of words and phrases and their compositionality. In: Advances in Neural Information Processing Systems, pp. 3111–3119 (2013)
11. Polyvyanyy, A., Kuropka, D.: A quantitative evaluation of the enhanced topic-based vector space model (2007)
12. Kadam, S., Gala, A., Gehlot, P., Kurup, A., Ghag, K.: Word embedding based multinomial naive bayes algorithm for spam filtering. In: 2018 Fourth International Conference on Computing Communication Control and Automation (ICCUBEA), pp. 1–5. IEEE (2018)
13. Renuka, K.D., Visalakshi, P.: Latent semantic indexing based SVM model for email spam classification, vol. 73, no. 6, pp. 437–442 (2014)
14. Saidani, N., Adi, K., Allili, M.S.: A supervised approach for spam detection using text-based semantic representation. In: Aïmeur, E., Ruhi, U., Weiss, M. (eds.) MCETECH 2017. LNBIP, vol. 289, pp. 136–148. Springer, Cham (2017). https://doi.org/10.1007/978-3-319-59041-7_8

15. Santos, I., Laorden, C., Sanz, B., Bringas, P.G.: Enhanced topic-based vector space model for semantics aware spam filtering. Exp. Syst. Appl. **39**(1), 437–444 (2012)
16. Symantec. Internet Security Threat Report, vol. 21, pp. 1–77 (2016)
17. Tang, G., Pei, J., Luk, W.-S.: Email mining: tasks, common techniques, and tools. Knowl. Inf. Syst. **41**(1), 1–31 (2013). https://doi.org/10.1007/s10115-013-0658-2
18. Wang, P., Xu, J.: Semantic clustering and convolutional neural network for short text categorization. In: Proceedings of the 53rd Annual Meeting of the Association for Computational Linguistics and the 7th International Joint Conference on Natural Language Processing, vol. 2, pp. 352–357 (2015)
19. Wu, T., Liu, S., Zhang, J., Xiang, Y.: Twitter spam detection based on deep learning. In: Proceedings of the Australasian Computer Science Week Multiconference, pp. 1–8. ACM (2017)

Interpreting Machine Learning Malware Detectors Which Leverage N-gram Analysis

William Briguglio and Sherif Saad[✉]

School of Computer Science, University of Windsor, Windsor, Canada
{briguglw,shsaad}@uwindsor.ca

Abstract. In cyberattack detection and prevention systems, cybersecurity analysts always prefer solutions that are as interpretable and understandable as rule-based or signature-based detection. This is because of the need to tune and optimize these solutions to mitigate and control the effect of false positives and false negatives. Interpreting machine learning models is a new and open challenge. However, it is expected that an interpretable machine learning solution will be domain specific. For instance, interpretable solutions for machine learning models in healthcare are different than solutions in malware detection. This is because the models are complex, and most of them work as a black-box. Recently, the increased ability for malware authors to bypass antimalware systems has forced security specialists to look to machine learning for creating robust detection systems. If these systems are to be relied on in the industry, then, among other challenges, they must also explain their predictions. The objective of this paper is to evaluate the current state-of-the-art ML models interpretability techniques when applied to ML-based malware detectors. We demonstrate interpretability techniques in practice and evaluate the effectiveness of existing interpretability techniques in the malware analysis domain.

Keywords: Cybersecurity · Machine learning · Malware detection · N-gram · Malware detector interpretability · Model robustness · Model reliability

1 Introduction

Adopting sophisticated machine learning techniques for malware detection or other cyber attack detection and prevention systems in a production environment is a challenge. This is because most of the time it is not possible to understand how machine learning systems make their detection decisions. In the malware detection domain, machine learning models can be trained to distinguish between benign binaries and malware, or between different malware families. The advantage of using machine learning models is that they are less sensitive to minute changes in malware binaries and can therefore detect unseen samples

© Springer Nature Switzerland AG 2020
A. Benzekri et al. (Eds.): FPS 2019, LNCS 12056, pp. 82–97, 2020.
https://doi.org/10.1007/978-3-030-45371-8_6

so long as they are designed and trained to detect characteristics common across seen and unseen samples. Furthermore, they're learnt relationships can be used to determine relevant features for a classification, limiting the amount of data malware analyst must sift through to determine the functionality of a malicious binary. However, there are several drawbacks that must be addressed before their full potential can be realized in the malware detection domain. Firstly, due to the quick evolving nature of malware, the models must be made efficient to train and update frequently when new malware families are discovered. Secondly, it is possible to create specially crafted "adversarial samples" which take advantage of peculiarities in the models learnt relationships to bypass the detector with relatively inconsequential changes to the binary. Finally, given the high degree of risk involved with classification errors, the models must provide a reason for their decisions in order to improve performance and increase trust in the model and its predictions. This last point is the focus of this paper.

The process of providing reasons for a machine learning model's predictions is known as interpretation. Interpretation in this setting should provide several key benefits. Firstly, due to the high cost of classification error, a low false positive and false negative rate is a must, and therefore these systems must be robust. A model is said to be robust if small changes in input do not cause large changes in output such as a different classification Second, the high risk necessitates a high degree of model confidence. Therefore, interpretation must provide evidence that the model has learnt something which can be corroborated with industry knowledge. This also goes hand in hand with the first requirement as an interpretation which can show a model is robust can improve model confidence as well. Additionally, the interpretation should aid malware analysts in down stream tasks such as determining the functionality of a malware binary.

Machine learning interpretation can be broadly separated into two categories. One is model agnostic techniques which are independent of the type of model which they are interpreting and rely solely on the input and output of the model. The other, which we will be using in this paper, are model specific techniques, which use specific elements of the model such as learnt weights or decision rules in order to provide an interpretation of a prediction. Interpretations themselves can be divided into global and local interpretations. Global interpretations provide an interpretation that is applicable across the entire feature space. Meanwhile local interpretations apply to only a single example or a small subset of the feature space. Some interpretation techniques provide only one type of interpretation while others provide both.

In this paper we explore the interpretability of machine learning based malware classifiers in relation to the goals of model robustness, confidence in model predictions, and aiding the process of determining the functionality of a malware sample. We train a logistic regression model, random forest, and a neural network on a Microsoft data set containing the hexadecimal representations of malware binaries belonging to several different malware families. We then apply model specific interpretation techniques to provide both a global and local interpretation of each of the models. The objective of this paper is to demonstrate interpretability techniques in practice on machine learning based malware detectors. We also try to evaluate the effectiveness of existing interpretability techniques in the malware analysis domain in terms of their usefulness to malware analysts in a practical setting. To the best of our knowledge, this is the only work which explores the application of machine learning interpretability techniques in the malware analysis domain.

2   Literature Review

In the last decade, with the increasingly massive data sets machine learning algorithms are being used on, and the growing complexity of the algorithms, the prediction process of these algorithms has become so non-intuitive that traditional analysis techniques no longer suffice. Analysis being necessary for a number of practical and legal concerns has caused research to now shift towards machine learning interpretability.

Molnar [11] put together a summary of machine learning interpretation methods in which he outlines a basic approach for the interpretation of Linear Regression models (of course the same approach can be applied to linear SVM's, Shirataki et al. [18]) where a feature's contribution to a prediction is the product of its value and weight. For logistic regression he shows that when the jth feature value is incremented by 1, then the quotient of the predicted odds of the sample belonging to the positive class after the increase over the predicted odds of the sample belonging to the positive class before the increase is equal to e^{β_j}, where β_j is the weight of feature j. Alternatively, this means that a unit increase in feature j results in the predicted odds increasing by $((e^{\beta_j} - 1) * 100)\%$. He goes on to discuss the seemingly trivial interpretation of decision trees as the conjunction of the conditions described in the nodes along a predictions path to a leaf node. Similarly, for rule list models, an "explanation" is simply re-stating the rule or combination of rules which lead to a decision.

However, the evaluation of a model's complexity is closely tied with its explanation's comprehensibility, especially for rule set models, linear models, and tree models. Given the following complexity definitions, the explanation approaches discussed above could be too complex for highly dimensional datasets. Ribeiro et al. [15] define the complexity of a linear model as the number of non-zero weights and the complexity of a decision tree as the depth of the tree. Meanwhile, Otero and Freitas [12] defined the complexity of a list of rules as the average number of conditions evaluated to classify a set of test data. They referred to this as the "prediction-explanation size".

There has also been work done on the interpretability of neural networks (NNs) such as the Layer-wise Relevance Propagation introduced in [3] as a set of constraints. The constraints ensure that the total relevance is preserved from one layer to another as well as that the relevance of each node is equal to the sum of relevance contributions from its input nodes which in turn is equal to the sum of relevance contributions to its output nodes. Any decomposition function following these constraints is considered a type of Layer-wise Relevance Propagation. In [19], Shrikumar et al. propose DeepLIFT which attributes to each node a contribution to the difference in prediction from a reference prediction by back propagating the difference in predication scaled by the difference in intermediate and initial inputs.

Moving on to model agnostic methods, Friedman in [6] used Partial Dependence Plots (PDP) to show the marginal effect a feature has in a predictive model. Similarly, Goldstein et al. [8] used Individual Conditional Expectation (ICE) plots to show a curve for each sample in the data set where one or two features are free variables while the rest of the features remain fixed. Since ICE plots and PDPs do not work well with strongly correlated features, Apley et al. [2] proposed Accumulated Local Effects plots to display the average local effect a feature has on predictions.

The H-statistic was used by Friedman and Popescu in [7] ((equations 44–46) to provide a statistical estimate of the interaction strength between features by measuring the fraction of variance not captured by the effects of single variables. Feature Importance was measured by Breiman [4] as the increase in model error after a feature's values are permuted (a.k.a. permutation importance).

Ribeiro et al. in [15] defined a version of the surrogate method which can explain individual predictions using an approach called Local Interpretable Model-agnostic Explanations (LIME) which trains an interpretable classifier by heavily weighing samples nearer to a sample of interest. Peltola [13] extended this work with KL-LIME, which generated local interpretable probabilistic models for Bayesian predictive models (although the method can also be applied to non-Bayesian probabilistic models) by minimizing the Kullback-Leibler divergence of the predictive model and the interpretable model. This has the added benefit of providing explanations that account for model uncertainty. Strumbelj et al. [20] detailed how to describe the contributions made by each feature to a prediction for a specific instance using Shapely Values, a concept adopted from coalitional game theory.

Finally, there are Example-Based methods such as the method put forward by Wachter et al. in [21] which produce interpretations by finding counter-factual examples which are samples with a significant difference in prediction, whose features are relatively similar to the sample of interest, by minimizing a loss function. The found sample is then used to explain what small changes would cause the original prediction to change meaningfully. There is also the MMD-critic algorithm by Kim et al. [9] which finds Prototypes (well represented examples) and Criticisms (poorly represented examples) in the dataset. To find examples in the training data which have a strong effect on a trained linear regression model (i.e. influential instances) Cook [5] proposed Cook's distance, a measure of the difference in predictions made by a linear regression model (however the measure can be generalized to any model) trained with and without an instance of interest. Koh and Liang [10] put forward a method for estimating the influence of a specific instance without retraining the model as long as the model has a twice differentiable loss function.

3   Method

Training and classification were done on a data set of 10,896 malware files belonging to 9 different malware families.[1] The data set is discussed in [16]. Each sample consists of the hexadecimal representation of the malware's binary content. The class details are summed up in Table 1.

Table 1. Class distribution in data set

Class no.	Family	Sample count	Type
1	Ramnit	1541	Worm
2	Lollipop	2478	Adware
3	Kelihos_ver3	2942	Backdoor
4	Vundo	475	Trojan
5	Simda	42	Backdoor
6	Tracur	751	TrojanDownloader
7	Kelihos_ver1	398	Backdoor
8	Obfuscator.ACY	1228	Obfuscated malware
9	Gatak	1013	Backdoor

Based on other work on the same data set, we decided to use n-grams as features. N-grams are sequences of words of length n which occur in a body of text. However, in our case the n-grams are sequences of bytes of length n which occur in a binary. The length of n-gram we settled on was 6 because they were shown to preform well in [14], however our approach can work with n-grams of arbitrary length. We extracted the 6-gram features from the hex representations of the malware files by obtaining the entire list of 6-grams present in the data set, and the number of files each 6-gram appeared in. This resulted in over 2,536,629,413 candidate features. Next, any 6-gram which did not appear in at least 100 files was removed from consideration, bringing the feature set size down to 817,785. This was done because [14] also showed that selection by frequency is an effective way to reduce the initial feature set size and a computationally cheap approach was needed considering the number of features.

Next, feature vectors were created for each of the malware samples so that a more sophisticated feature selection method can be preformed. This was done by searching for the selected 6-gram feature in a binary and setting the corresponding value in that binary's feature vector to 1 if the binary did contain the 6-gram, and 0 otherwise. To select the features for the logistic regression model, Chi^2 was used because it can detect if a categorical feature is independent of a predicted categorical variable (in this case our class) and is therefore irrelevant

---

[1] The data set was downloaded from https://www.kaggle.com/c/malware-classifi cation/data.

to our classifier. For the neural network and random forest, Mutual Information (MI) was used because it can detect the more complex dependencies between a feature and a sample's classification which can be taken advantage of by a neural network or random forest. Since the feature set was still very large, the Chi^2 and MI scores had to be calculated in batches. This was done by splitting the data set into 20 batches, each with the same distribution of classes, and averaging out the resulting scores for each feature. Next, the features with Chi^2 scores above 330 or MI scores above 0.415 were selected. This brought the feature set size down to 8867 in the case of the logistic regression model and to 9980 in the case of the neural network and random forest. The feature set size was determined based off other work using n-grams to classify the same data set. We did not attempt to find an optimal feature set size as our primary focus was model interpretation.

Next, the models were trained on their respective feature sets. To find the best parameters for the logistic regression model and train the model, grid search with 5-fold cross validation was used, yielding C = 10 and tolerance = 0.0001. The value of C inversely determines the strength of regularization, that is, smaller values of C cause more feature weights in the classifier to be set to 0, a value of 0 corresponds to no regularization, and values above 0 encourage the classifier to use more features. Tolerance determines the minimum change in error, from one iteration of the optimization algorithm to the next, that causes the algorithm to terminate training. Similarly for random forest, finding the best parameters and training was done with grid search with 5-fold cross validation as well. The number of trees found to preform best was 300 and the and the minimum samples per leaf found to preform best was 0.01% of the total number of samples. The grid search with cross validation, logistic regression model, and the random forest model were implemented using the scikit python library.

For the neural network the data was split into a training and a test set each with the same class distribution. This was done because the extra parameters in a neural network require a larger data set to learn more abstract patterns and splitting it up into many folds might have stifled this process. The neural network consisted of an input layer with one neuron per feature, an output layer with one neuron per class using the sigmoid activation function, and a hidden layer consisting of 40 neurons using the tanh activation function. 40 neurons was chosen because that number was found to preform the best after testing with various other configurations. There were also no bias units to aid in interpretation. The neural network was implemented using the Keras python library.

After training and testing the three models, the logistic regression model was interpreted by examining the weights used by the classifier. The random forest was interpreted by examining the feature importance as well as using the treeInterpreter python library [17] to obtain feature contributions to a particular prediction. In the case of the Neural network, the iNNvestigate python library by [1] was used to preform LRP to get the relevances of each node in the model for interpretation. The balanced accuracy on the left out fold was 96.19% for the logistic regression model and 96.97% for the random forest. The balanced accuracy on the test set was 94.22% for the neural network. A discussion of the model interpretations follows in the next section.

4   Interpretation

Logistic Regression Model Interpretation. The logistic regression model uses a one-vs-rest classification scheme whereby for each class, a constituent model is trained to classify a sample as either that class, or not that class, and therefore we are actually dealing with nine separate logistic regression models each making binary classifications. For this reason we cannot preform the typical global interpretation of the overall multi-class model by examining the weights since the weights should be different for each of the binary models. However, we can gain insight of the importance of each feature by averaging these weights across the 9 constituent binary models. For this we take the average of the absolute values of the weights. This is because if a feature contributes positively for one constituent binary classifier and negatively for another, then the weights would cancel each other out during averaging which would falsely give the impression that the feature was not important in the overall multi-class model. Table 2 shows the largest 15 averages of the absolute feature weights.

Table 2. Max 15 absolute weights of the logistic regression model averaged across all 9 binary sub-classifiers

Avg. abs. weight	Feature
1.3151053659364556	0000000066C7
1.3480135328294032	008B4C240C89
1.4629237676020752	8BEC83EC10C7
1.4846778818947817	00000000EB07
1.5276044995023308	B80000000050
1.540535475655897	500147657453
1.5605614219830626	006800004000
1.6494330450079937	89852CFDFFFF
1.685741868293823	0033C58945FC
1.7235671007282005	8B91C8000000
1.781357432072784	034C6F61644C
1.8232074423648363	8BEC6A006A00
2.071327588344743	00E404000000
2.15007904223129	0083C4088B4D
2.1561672884172056	C78530FDFFFF

Looking at the Table 2, we can see that three 6-grams are relatively heavily weighted, 00E404000000, 0083C4088B4D, and C78530FDFFFF. Recall from

Sect. 2 that for logistic regression, when the jth feature value is incremented by a value of 1, then the predicted odds increase by $((e^{\beta_j} - 1) * 100)\%$, where β_j is the learnt weight of the jth feature. In our case we are using binary feature values where a 1 indicates the presence of a 6-gram and 0 indicates its absence, so we interpret the weights as follows. When the 6-gram corresponding to the jth feature is present, the predicted odds increase by $((e^{\beta_j} - 1) * 100)\%$. One may be tempted to apply this to the weights in Table 2, but these are averaged *absolute* weights across all 9 constituent binary classifiers. Further, negative weights do not cause a decrease in the predicted odds that is proportional to a positive weight with the same absolute value due to the shape of the function $f(x) = e^x - 1$. Therefore, it would be inaccurate to say the average absolute effect of some 6-gram corresponds to a $(e^{avg_j} - 1)\%$ change in the predicted odds, where avg_j is the average absolute weight of feature j. Thus a global interpretation of a multi-class one-vs-rest logistic regression model using n-grams in confined to vague statements about which n-grams are important based solely off their average absolute weights, which is not very useful in a practical setting.

Table 3. Max 15 weights for Kelihos_ver3 binary sub-classifier

Weight	Feature
0.6438606978376447	000607476574
0.6438606978376447	000C07476574
0.6438606978376447	060747657444
0.6438606978376447	074765744443
0.6438606978376447	0C0747657444
0.6438606978376447	930644697370
1.3719246726968015	00000083FEFF
1.5114878196031336	E8000000895D
2.1067800174989904	0F85CC010000
2.3123117293223405	0A0100008B45
2.9041700918303084	000F859D0000
3.174276823535364	000F84700100
3.5334477027408613	0083C4088B4D
3.7941081330633857	034C6F61644C
4.391600387291376	00008B5DE43B

Next we will examine the max weights for a constituent binary model. This will allow us to make conclusions on what features the model uses to detect a specific class of malware in the data set. Furthermore, we will be able to determine exactly the change in predicted odds that the presence of an n-gram causes. For the sake of brevity, we will examine just the binary model for class 3, corresponding to the Kelihos_ver3 family of malware, as all three models performed well for this class but the same process can be followed for the other constituent binary models corresponding to other classes. Table 3 shows the max 15 weights of the classifier for class 3.

In Table 3 we can see three 6-grams have relatively large weights. This means these n-grams are most strongly associated with class 3 and in this case, since we are looking at only the weights for a single binary classifier, we can use our interpretation from above. That is, when the 6-gram corresponding to the jth feature is present, the predicted odds increase by $((e^{\beta_j} - 1) * 100)\%$. For example we can say the presence of 00008B5DE43B, increases the predicted odds of a sample belonging to class 3 by $((e^{4.3916} - 1) * 100)\% = 7977\%$. At first glance this number may seem excessive but in order to make good sense of it we must also determine what the predicted odds of a sample belonging to class 3 are when this 6-grams are not present, using a reference sample. For this we use a zero-vector corresponding to a sample where none of the 6-grams used as features are present. Since the dot product of a zero vector and the weight vector is zero, we only need to take the sigmoid of the intercept of the binary model for class 3 to determine the predicted probability of the reference vector belonging to class 3. The intercept is -4.2843, thus the predicted probability of the reference sample belonging to class 3 is sigmoid $(-4.28426) = 0.01360$. Next we must convert this to odds with $0.01360/(1 - 0.01360) = 0.01378$. This means a sample with no feature 6-grams present except 00008B5DE43B increases the odds from 0.01378 by 7977% to $0.01378 + (0.01378 * 79.77) = 1.11301$ predicted odds, or a 0.5267 predicted probability, of belonging to class 3. Thus we see that because of the intercept, the large weight of this feature does not necessarily guarantee a classification into class 3.

We can get a better idea of the robustness of the model by checking the number of 6-grams which play a significant role in the classification of a sample into class 3. This is because robustness is a measure of how tolerant a model is to small changes in input. Therefore, if the number of 6-grams which play a significant role is large, then a large number of changes in input will be required for a change in classification, thus giving us confidence in the model's robustness. However, if the number of significant features is low then only a small number of changes in input will be required for a change in classification, changes that may be easy and inconsequential for malware authors to make. Thus the robustness of the model would be called into question. In our case, 20 features have weights greater than or equal to about 0.59. 6-grams with weights above this number increase the predicted odds by $((e^{0.59} - 1) * 100)\% \approx 80\%$. Since the predicted odds of the reference example belonging to class 3 is 0.01378, this means about 11 such features can cause a sample to be classified as class 3 with about 90% predicted probability. This may indicate that the model is putting too much emphasis on just a few highly weighted 6-grams. To test this we can reclassify samples belong to class 3 with the highest weighted 6-grams set to 0. In our case, we set the nine highest weighted features to 0 for all samples. This required 22863 changes to the feature array, and the result was only 24 more misclassifications, 17 of which belonged to class 3, which has 2942 samples. Here, we encounter a specification issue. Currently, there is no formally defined metric to measure robustness quantitatively and once there is, a threshold for acceptable robustness will be application specific. We leave a definition of a robustness metric to future work, however, given that robustness is defined in terms of a model's tolerance to changes in input, and that tolerance to changes of insignificant features is irrelevant, we can be confident that this approach can give us an idea of our model's robustness. The models robustness becomes more clear when compared with other models. For example, if setting the same number of features to 0 in another model resulted in more or less misclassification, then we can say that model is less or more robust respectively than our logistic regression model Therefore, we can confidently say our approach gave an idea of model robustness for class 3. One can increase the model's robustness by further training the classifier with samples which have the highly weighted 6-grams removed. This would force the classifier to learn a more diverse set of features which correspond to class 3, meaning that more changes would be required to change a prediction to or from class 3. Thus by observing the important features, we can improve the models robustness to small changes in the input. A similar strategy can be followed for the most negatively weighted features. If there are features with too large negative weights, then a detector can be fooled by intentionally adding these 6-grams. Further training the classifier by adding the large negative weighted 6-grams to samples labeled class 3 will force the classifier to learn not to negate positively weighted features with one or a small set of 6-grams. Therefore we can conclude that examining the weights in the manner we have done here can be useful for debugging logistic regression models leveraging n-grams. This interpretation is still global in that it encompasses the entire feature space, however, it must be repeated for each class. On the upside though, the global interpretation doubles as a local interpretation as the relationship between the presence of an n-gram and the change in the predicted odds holds across the entire data set for each sample.

Furthermore, this method for finding important n-grams features can be helpful in a practical setting as it can be used to aid malware analysts in down stream tasks. A malware binary's functionality can be more easily determined by implementing a method which automatically disassembles binaries and highlights the code which corresponds to the most heavily weighted n-grams that are present in the binary. This approach can also improve confidence in the model if the highlighted code's functionality is corroborated with industry knowledge. Both these advantages require another interpretation step of mapping feature values from the feature space to the domain space (i.e. mapping n-grams to the corresponding code) which is not the focus of this paper. The downside to this interpretation approach is that it is specific to logistic regression models only, and unlike models such as neural networks or decisions tress, logistic regression models are not easily capable of learning more complex relationships between features and target values.

Random Forest Interpretation. In the case of the random forest, interpretation is more difficult. It is easy in a more general sense, in that we can get the

Table 4. Max feature 15 importances for random forest

Feature importance	Feature
0.006877917709695	726573730000
0.007047751117095	7450726F6341
0.00723117607771	647265737300
0.007262894349522	558BEC83EC08
0.007377076296786	0064A1000000
0.007401045194749	727475616C41
0.007815881804511	A10000000050
0.008221953575956	75616C416C6C
0.008652467124996	634164647265
0.008657476622364	8A040388840D
0.008840768087294	69727475616C
0.008879491127129	89F5034C2404
0.00898170788833	7475616C416C
0.008987620418762	008A840D2F06
0.009011931204589	060000E2EFB9

feature importance scores, shown below in Table 4, and use these to determine what features are generally most important, but getting a more fine grained interpretation is a challenge as the random forest is an ensemble of often hundreds of different decision trees.

Table 4 gives us a great idea of the model robustness. Since the total feature importance is always equal to 1, we can be sure that the model isn't relying on just a small number of features to make predictions because the 15 most important features only accounts for 0.9% of the total importance. Additionally, the feature importance steadily declines without one feature or a small group of features overshadowing the rest. Unfortunately, general statements about robustness which do not provide much utility to the malware analyst in a practical setting are the most we can say with a global interpretation. However considering a single example can give us more information, albeit only locally.

Interpretation of a Single Sample with Random Forest. With random forest, a local interpretation of a single example is difficult as a classification decision is the result of a vote amongst many different decision trees. However, here we find the tree with the highest predicted probability that a specific example belongs to its actual class. Then we use the tree interpreter library [17] to break down the contributions of each 6-gram feature. In our case we followed this procedure for sample 4WM7aZDLCmlosUBiqKOx and found that the 6-gram 002500000031 and the bias contributed 97.3% of the total feature importance. One may be tempted to think this means the model is relying on only a single feature however this is just one tree out of many which have heavily varying structures. Thus, changing this feature may not cause many of the other tree's predictions to change, such is the advantage of using random forests over single decisions trees. The significance of the resulting feature contribution is two fold. Firstly, the model designer can find the code corresponding to 002500000031 in the assembly code and determine weather the functionality of the code corroborates industry knowledge. If it does, then this can be used with other examples to improve model confidence. Secondly, by finding 6-grams in the constituent decision trees of the random forest model which are significant to a prediction, a process can be automated to disassemble the input file and highlight the code that corresponds to these significant 6-grams, aiding in malware analysis. The downside to this approach is that the random forest is made up of many different decision trees, many of which should all be predicting the correct class, so an automated process which collects significant 6-grams from these constituent trees and highlights the corresponding code may provide an overwhelming number of results. This is because well over a hundred trees will be contributing at least a few 6-grams, meaning that potentially 100's of snippets of code will be highlighted to the analyst. Once again we are faced with the problem of mapping the feature values to the domain, however this should not be too tall a task and we leave this challenge to future work.

Neural Network Model Interpretation. For our global interpretation of the Neural Network model, we used LRP to determine the most relevant input

Table 5. Max Average Absolute Relevances

Avg. abs. relevance	Feature
0.4204155570273673	24000000008B
0.438576163384531	**75616C416C6C**
0.4604056179848827	000400000000
0.6358686047042836	00FFFFFFFFFF
0.6414918343055965	**008A840D2F06**
0.6961477693970937	**060000E2EFB9**
0.7207968499760279	**8A040388840D**
0.7391062783969391	000001000000
0.7655264716760353	040000000000
0.7695977668414099	**89F5034C2404**
0.8623695409436033	416C6C6F6300
0.8762457266039623	6C6C6F630000
0.8811945910382549	**69727475616C**
1.1011308772023591	000000000400
1.129173981900078	0000000000FF

Bolded 6-grams also present in Table 4

Table 6. Max Avg Relevances for Class 3

Avg relevance	Feature
0.07849652902147494	**060747657444**
0.0858714786617495	8B0000006700
0.08840799934653523	07497357696E
0.09155762345728868	**0C0747657444**
0.09213969967088875	F10448656170
0.09360746295067239	00F0F0280000
0.09471450612061977	00F104486561
0.10572475395119978	C3008BFF558B
0.10603324133390207	009306446973
0.11341626335133194	**000C07476574**
0.11451772113662628	C38BFF558BEC
0.12097247805393918	**930644697370**
0.14448647700726405	04546C734765
0.1895982317973578	064469737061
0.24520372442763907	**034C6F61644C**

Bolded 6-grams also present in Table 3

nodes for classification. LRP was preformed in this experiment using iNNvestigate python library by [1]. First we found the relevances of the input nodes
for each sample and then we averaged the absolute values of these relevances
for the entire data set. This was done because one input node may be positively contributing to one output nodes prediction while negatively contributing
to another, causing the input nodes relevances to cancel out during averaging
and giving false impressions about the feature set. Table 5 shows the largest 15
averages of the absolute relevances.

In Table 5 we can see two values had significantly higher relevances than
the rest, 000000000400 and 0000000000FF, and are therefore important for the
models classification. Additionally, we can see many of the features which appear
here are also in the top 15 most important 6-grams for the random forest. This
result partially validates our technique for finding important 6-gram features in
a neural network which to the best of our knowledge is a novel use of LRP in
this domain. This gives us a general idea of the importance of features used by
the model but, just like in the case of the other two models, we are still confined
to vague general statements about a feature's importance. However, this time it
is due to the complexity of the model.

Next we will examine the max relevances for a particular class. In this case
we average the relevances for each node across all samples which were correctly
classified as class 3. Table 6 shows the max 15 average relevances for class 3.

In Table 6 we can see five of the features which appear here are also in the top
15 highest weighted 6-grams for the binary logistic regression classifier for class
3. This result also partially validates our technique for finding important 6-gram
features in a neural network for a single class. In this case we are still confined
to general statements about a features importance for a specific class. However,
we can get an idea of the model's robustness by setting the features with the
highest average relevances for class 3 to 0 for all correctly classified samples in
class 3. If the model relies heavily on only the presence of these 6-grams, then the
class accuracy will drop drastically, however if we have a similar class accuracy
as before, then it is unlikely that the features with a lesser average relevance
would have a larger effect on the class accuracy and therefore we can somewhat
confidently say the model is robust for this class. In our experiment the top 4
highest average relevance features were all set to 0 and it resulted in no further
misclassifications. Therefore we can say our model is somewhat robust for class
3. This result is somewhat helpful in a practical setting as a malware analyst can
use this technique to ensure the robustness of their model, but not much else.

Interpretation of a Single Sample with Neural Network

Next we'll further explore the neural network's predictions for samples belonging
to class 3 by taking the test sample with the highest predicted probability of
belonging to class 3, sample 4WM7aZDLCmlosUBiqKOx, and examining relevances for this sample in order to provide a local interpretation. In doing so we
can see what the internal nodes are learning. First we determine the internal
node relevances for this sample. The library used for this experiment did not

have a built in method to determine the relevances of internal layer nodes so we created a second neural network that was a duplicate of the last two layers of the original neural network. We then obtained the value of the second layer nodes before the activation function is applied when classifying this sample. That is, if W^1 is the weight matrix for the connections between layer 1 and layer 2, and X^1 is the outputs of layer 1, then we obtained $X^1 \cdot W^1$. We then inputted $X^1 \cdot W^1$ into our second neural network and preformed LRP to get the relevances of the first layer of our second neural network which are equivalent to the relevances of the hidden layer in our original neural network. The most relevant node by a substantial margin was the 40th node in the hidden layer with a relevance of 0.61 and an activation of -0.99996614. Since this node is in layer 2 we will denote it with n_{40}^2. Next we created a third neural network that had two layers. The first was identical to layer 1 of our original neural network, the second was just the single node, n_{40}^2, from the original neural network, and the weight matrix for the connections from layer 1 to layer 2 of this new network is $W_{(40)}^1$ were $W_{(i)}^1$ is the 9980-dimensional weight vector for connections from layer 1 to the ith node in layer 2 of the original neural network. In this way we were able to obtain the relevances of the input layer to only the activation of n_{40}^2 in the hidden layer. Table 6 shows the max 10 node relevances for the activation of n_{40}^2 in the hidden layer.

Table 7. Layer 1 nodes relevance to n_{40}^2

Activation	Relevance	Feature
1.0	0.025721772	007300000061
1.0	0.027428055	230000001900
1.0	0.02751717	2F0000002300
1.0	0.029254071	270000003300
1.0	0.030343212	00870000009D
1.0	0.03163522	002F00000025
1.0	0.031697582	040000C00000
1.0	0.03176714	002300000019
1.0	0.032007236	00C0000000D0
1.0	0.034308888	007701476574

In Table 7 we can see that many of the 6-grams have similar relevance's which slowly decrease. This corroborates our results when examining class 3 as a whole since the similar relevances across many input nodes indicates that many features are responsible for a classification which is to be expected when a model is robust to changes in the input data. One can automate the process of preforming LRP on specific examples to find relevant input nodes, both for the entire model and for a specific internal node possibly showing what the internal node is learning.

From there highlighting the disassembled code which corresponds to the most relevant nodes can help malware analyst either determine the functionality of the file or show that the model has learnt something which corresponds to industry knowledge, thus improving confidence in the model.

5 Conclusion

In this paper we demonstrated techniques for the interpretation of malware detectors which leverage n-grams as features. We've shown that it is possible to interpret a neural network, a logistic regression model, and a random forest, with the objectives of debugging and creating robust models, improving model confidence, and aiding malware analysts in downstream tasks. For the logistic regression model, examining the weights was all that was needed to meet these goals. However, although straight forward to interpret, the model was less expressive then the other two considered. The random forest required slightly more work for analysis but it was also possible to get a meaningful local interpretation that helped with the above stated goals. The downside here was that the random forest interpretation must consider many of constituent trees to be thorough, which can be time consuming and result in too much data. The neural network interpretation was much more intensive but by using layer-wise relevance propagation it was possible to determine the relevance or significance of different n-grams across the data set, across a specific class, and for a single example or for a single node. Thus, we were able to provide a global and local interpretation which was somewhat useful in a practical setting since by using these relevances it was then possible to get an idea of the robustness of the model and build confidence or aid in downstream analysis of samples.

Over all it was possible to satisfy our interpretation objectives for each model but the ubiquitous trade off between the interpretability and the expressivity of the model was still present. Additionally, n-grams in and of themselves seem slightly problematic as it is not easy to determine what a n-gram corresponds to on its own, without considering a single example for context. So providing a global interpretation of a n-gram in order to show what the model has learnt is difficult. To this end it would be advantageous to include human readable features as well or other features which can be easily interpreted in a manner that doesn't require examining a real specific example. For future work we will focus on evaluating model agnostic techniques and enabling explanations in specific domain applications such as malware detection.

References

1. Alber, M., et al.: Innvestigate neural networks! (2018)
2. Apley, D.W., Zhu, J.: Visualizing the effects of predictor variables in black box supervised learning models (2016)
3. Bach, S., et al.: On pixel-wise explanations for non-linear classifier decisions by layer-wise relevance propagation. PLoS ONE (2015)

4. Breiman, L.: Random forests. Mach. Learn. **45**(1), 5–32 (2001). https://doi.org/10.1023/A:1010933404324
5. Cook, R.D.: Detection of influential observation in linear regression. Technometrics **19**(1), 15–18 (1977). https://doi.org/10.1080/00401706.1977.10489493
6. Friedman, J.H.: Greedy function approximation: a gradient boosting machine. Ann. Stat. **29**(5), 1189–1232 (2001). https://doi.org/10.1214/aos/1013203451
7. Friedman, J.H., Popescu, B.E.: Predictive learning via rule ensembles. Ann. Appl. Stat. **2**(3), 916–954 (2008). https://doi.org/10.1214/07-AOAS148
8. Goldstein, A., Kapelner, A., Bleich, J., Pitkin, E.: Peeking inside the black box: visualizing statistical learning with plots of individual conditional expectation. J. Comput. Graph. Stat. **24**, 44–65 (2013). https://doi.org/10.1080/10618600.2014.907095
9. Kim, B., Khanna, R., Koyejo, O.: Examples are not enough, learn to criticize! criticism for interpretability. In: Proceedings of the 30th International Conference on Neural Information Processing Systems, NIPS 2016, pp. 2288–2296. Curran Associates Inc., USA (2016). http://dl.acm.org/citation.cfm?id=3157096.3157352
10. Koh, P.W., Liang, P.: Understanding black-box predictions via influence functions. In: Proceedings of the 34th International Conference on Machine Learning, ICML 2017, vol. 70, pp. 1885–1894. JMLR.org (2017). http://dl.acm.org/citation.cfm?id=3305381.3305576
11. Molnar, C.: Interpretable Machine Learning. GitHub (2019). https://christophm.github.io/interpretable-ml-book/
12. Otero, F.E., Freitas, A.A.: Improving the interpretability of classification rules discovered by an ant colony algorithm. In: Proceedings of the 15th Annual Conference on Genetic and Evolutionary Computation, GECCO 2013, pp. 73–80. ACM, New York (2013). https://doi.org/10.1145/2463372.2463382
13. Peltola, T.: Local interpretable model-agnostic explanations of Bayesian predictive models via Kullback-Leibler projections. arXiv:1810.02678 (2018)
14. Raff, E., et al.: An investigation of byte n-gram features for malware classification. J. Comput. Virol. Hacking Tech. **14**(1), 1–20 (2016). https://doi.org/10.1007/s11416-016-0283-1
15. Ribeiro, M.T., Singh, S., Guestrin, C.: "Why should i trust you?": explaining the predictions of any classifier. In: Proceedings of the 22nd ACM SIGKDD International Conference on Knowledge Discovery and Data Mining, KDD 2016, pp. 1135–1144. ACM, New York (2016). https://doi.org/10.1145/2939672.2939778
16. Ronen, R., Radu, M., Feuerstein, C., Yom-Tov, E., Ahmadi, M.: Microsoft malware classification challenge (2018)
17. Saabas, A.: Treeinterpreter (2015). https://github.com/andosa/treeinterpreter
18. Shirataki, S., Yamaguchi, S.: A study on interpretability of decision of machine learning. In: 2017 IEEE International Conference on Big Data (Big Data), pp. 4830–4831, December 2017. https://doi.org/10.1109/BigData.2017.8258557
19. Shrikumar, A., Greenside, P., Kundaje, A.: Learning important features through propagating activation differences. arXiv:1704.02685 (2017)
20. Strumbelj, E., Kononenko, I.: An efficient explanation of individual classifications using game theory. J. Mach. Learn. Res. **11**, 1–18 (2010). http://dl.acm.org/citation.cfm?id=1756006.1756007
21. Wachter, S., Mittelstadt, B.D., Russell, C.: Counterfactual explanations without opening the black box: automated decisions and the GDPR. arXiv:1711.00399 (2017)

Labelled Network Capture Generation
for Anomaly Detection

Maël Nogues[1]([✉]), David Brosset[1,2], Hanan Hindy[3], Xavier Bellekens[4],
and Yvon Kermarrec[1,5]

[1] Chair of Naval Cyber Defence, École Navale - CC 600, 29240 Brest Cedex 9, France
`mael.nogues@ecole-navale.fr`
[2] Naval Academy Research Institute, École Navale - CC 600,
29240 Brest Cedex 9, France
[3] Division of Cyber-Security, Abertay University, Dundee, UK
[4] Department of Electronic and Electrical Engineering, University of Strathclyde,
Glasgow, UK
[5] Institut Mines-Télécom Atlantique, Lab-STICC CNRS UMR 6285,
29238 Brest, France

Abstract. In the race to simplify man-machine interactions and maintenance processes, hardware is increasingly interconnected. With more connected devices than ever, in our homes and workplaces, the attack surface is increasing tremendously. To detect this growing flow of cyber-attacks, machine learning based intrusion detection systems are being deployed at an unprecedented pace. In turn, these require a constant feed of data to learn and differentiate normal traffic from abnormal traffic. Unfortunately, there is a lack of learning datasets available. In this paper, we present a software platform generating fully labelled datasets for data analysis and anomaly detection.

Keywords: Network traffic generation · Data analysis · Intrusion detection systems · Cyber security · Network security

1 Introduction

As our lives are ever more connected, from our smartphones to our homes, the attack surface increases exponentially. These attacks generally influence the working state of the systems, often triggering their detection. To describe cyber-attacks, models defining the paths they take to reach their target through different networks are often used. However, to train and test these attack recognition models, real or simulated data is needed. The data, generally consisting of network capture, must be sufficiently documented and reflect the reality of network exchanges. Leading to the classification of well-formatted datasets with defined classes for each flow through the scenarios of these captures.

Funded and supported by École Navale, IMT Atlantique, Naval Group, Thales and ENSTA Bretagne.

© Springer Nature Switzerland AG 2020
A. Benzekri et al. (Eds.): FPS 2019, LNCS 12056, pp. 98–113, 2020.
https://doi.org/10.1007/978-3-030-45371-8_7

Network captures available on the Internet are often provided without complementary information other than the context in which they were generated. Therefore, the exact content of these network captures is absent. Hence, users can only infer the classifications of the packets they contain.

Moreover, network captures are often transformed into CSV formatted datasets for intrusion detection systems. The most used dataset according to the taxonomy presented by Hindy et al. [4] is the KDD'99 dataset, generated for the information discovery and data mining tool competition [2] of KDD-CUP 1999. However, this dataset remains generic, does not contain IP addresses and lacks lot of key information defining an attack path and threat vectors. In addition, dating back to 1999, the dataset contains attacks that are outdated and not complex enough to reflect modern attacks. Al Tobi and Duncan also identified a number of errors in the dataset in [1]. The main concern raised in their manuscript is the dissimilarity between the number of attacks initially published by DARPA and KDD'99.

To this end, this paper presents a software platform to generate network traffic scenarios using a combination of real and/or virtual hosts. The platform automatically generates network capture in a reliable manner, with the property to identify and tag packets to the corresponding action.

The remainder of the paper is organized as follows; Sect. 2 presents a survey of network traffic generation tools and associated network captures. The platform to generate network captures is presented in Sect. 3. Section 4 provides a description and analysis of the results obtained and finally Sect. 5 concludes the paper and presents future work.

2   Background

This section describes related work as well as different captures and existing network traces available on the Internet.

2.1   Network Capture Generation

To the best knowledge of the authors, there is no software able to generate labelled packet captures based on specific scenarios. However, there exists network simulators and packet generators. Neither the simulators nor the packet generators are able to generate scenarios for the networks they emulate. Hence, this work is complementary to existing solutions and provides a large range of solutions to increase the flexibility and accuracy of dataset generation for machine learning based intrusion detection systems.

Three software for generating network traffic in different ways have been analysed, Swing [12], Sourcesonoff [11] and the network traffic generation tool of "Realistic Global Cyber Environment" [5]. In this subsection, their different features and network traffic generation are reviewed.

Swing. Vishwanath *et al.* presented Swing, a network generator based on traffic captures [12]. Swing allows you to explore different options, recreating the capture through different parameters. Swing can be used to generate network captures for network capacity planning, broadband router design, queue management rule design, or bandwidth estimation. Despite the flexibility that allows exploring network parameters, scenarios are not explicitly defined.

Sourcesonoff. This software is focused on accurate traffic generation and includes multiple protocols. The software is based on ON/OFF sources that allow the random generation of packets while following a well-defined distribution. It is developed in C and contains several different distributions to vary the generations of packets. The uniform distribution is based on the Linux functions *drand48()* and *random()*, with corrections to ensure perfect uniformity across all intervals. The Normal or Gaussian distribution is calculated using the Box-Muller transformation. Knuth's algorithm is used for Poisson distribution. Pareto, Weibull and Exponential distributions use a uniform distribution transformation. An additional pseudo-distribution is available: the Constant distribution. In this case, all generated values are equal to a user-defined constant. This method allows the user to generate more predictive behaviour. Factor multiplication allows users to convert randomly generated values into bytes and nanoseconds. Distributions can be limited by user-defined minimum and maximum values. Once converted, the data is used for communication in the network. The data flows can be parameterised by the user to refine the behaviour of the software for its use. Different sets of sources can work at the same time to produce more traffic consistent with the traffic seen on the Internet. Each set of sources will then be associated with its own distribution and parameters to allow greater control over the data generated to the user.

Traffic Generation for the *Realistic Global Cyber Environment*. The traffic generation tool that has been developed for the *Realistic Global Cyber Environment* (RGCE) is an Internet traffic simulation tool. It allows control of the traffic generation from a central point of the network while generating packets on different machines through this same network. This tool allows the generation of tailored traffic. RGCE use a complete simulation approach of network clients consisting of a hierarchical network of nodes forming a tree in which each node represents a client on the network.

The nodes are divided into several levels, each of which has a different role. The root node is the *King*, serving as a bridge between the network and the user interface of the tool. The user interface works through a web server.

The *Slavemaster* nodes represent network routers. They know the entire subnet and can be chained to create a tree of arbitrary depth. When they receive a message from the root node, if the message is destined for the *Slavemaster* it is then broadcast to all its children nodes, however, if the message is destined to one of its sub-nodes, then it sends the message in the direction of that sub-node.

The *Botmaster* nodes are the leaves of the tree. They represent the host machines of the system and can execute one or more *Bots* allowing to generate traffic on the network. *Botmasters* receive messages from the network traffic generation *Bots* and their status, passing them to the root node (*King*) to update the user interface. The *Bots*, meanwhile, are responsible for generating network traffic. Each *Bot* is responsible for generating a particular type of traffic (e.g., *HTTPBot* generates HTTP traffic). If a *Bot* encounters an error, it sends a notification to its *Botmaster* to send to the *King* to update the user interface.

2.2 Online Network Captures

Network captures can be found online, mostly provided as raw captures or processed such as *KDD'99*. However, network captures almost never come with well-defined protocols allowing users to understand the scenarios at hand and the action taken by the generators. This subsection explores two processed packet capture, the *KDD'99* dataset and the *UNSW-NB15* dataset. For the purpose of this manuscript, all network captures that does not come with a scenario describing its generation has an equivalent value. It seems then reasonable to limit ourselves to the most commonly used.

KDD'99. KDD'99 is a dataset provided by the University of California Irvine (UCI) for the third international knowledge discovery contest and data mining tools. The goal of the competition was to build a network intrusion detection system, based on a predictive model capable of distinguishing between "bad" connections, called intrusions or attacks, and "good" connections, called normal. The dataset contains a standard set of data to audit, including a number of simulated intrusions in a military network environment.

A list of the different attacks contained in this dataset is presented in Table 1.

Table 1. Attack list of the dataset from *KDD'99*

Type	dos	u2r	r2l	probe
Attacks	back	buffer_overflow	ftp_write	ipsweep
	land	loadmodule	guess_passwd	nmap
	neptune	perl	imap	portsweep
	pod	rootkit	multihop	satan
	smurf		phf	
	teardrop		spy	
			warezclient	
			warezmaster	

This dataset contains attacks of several different types that are:

– Denial of Service (DoS) Attack: An attack in which the attacker makes a computing resource or memory busy or full disabling him from handling legitimate requests, or denying legitimate users access to a machine.

- Privilege Elevation Attack (U2R): is an exploit class in which the attacker first accesses a normal user account on the system (e.g. through a dictionary attack, or social engineering) and exploits one or more vulnerabilities of the system to gain privileged access (root) on the system.
- Local Network Infiltration Attack (R2L): Occurs when an attacker has the ability to send packets to a machine on the network, but does not have an account on that machine, exploiting a vulnerability to obtain a local access as a user of a machine.
- Network Discovery Attack (Probe): is an attempt to collect information on a computer network for the purpose of circumventing security checks.

As aforementioned, KDD'99 no longer represents the current scene of cyber attacks found on the Internet. It remains , however, one of the most used datasets for detection of intrusions [4].

The features that have been chosen for *KDD'99* are presented in the Table 2 [1].

Table 2. Features of *KDD'99* [1]

1	2	3	4	5	6	7	8	9	10	11	12	13	14	15	16	17	18	19	20	21	22	23	24	25	26	27	28	29	30	31	32	33	34	35	36	37	38	39	40	41
duration	protocol_type	service	flag	src_bytes	dst_bytes	land	wrong_fragment	urgent	hot	num_failed_logins	logged_in	num_compromised	root_shell	su_attempted	num_root	num_file_creations	num_shells	num_access_files	num_outbound_cmds	is_host_login	is_guest_login	count	srv_count	serror_rate	srv_serror_rate	rerror_rate	srv_rerror_rate	same_srv_rate	diff_srv_rate	srv_diff_host_rate	dst_host_count	dst_host_srv_count	dst_host_same_srv_rate	dst_host_diff_srv_rate	dst_host_same_src_port_rate	dst_host_srv_diff_host_rate	dst_host_serror_rate	dst_host_srv_serror_rate	dst_host_rerror_rate	dst_host_srv_rerror_rate
Basic features (Total : 9)									Content features (Total : 13)													Time-based features (Total : 9)									Connection-based features (Total : 10)									

The *KDD'99* dataset is a transformation of a network trace generated by DARPA in 1998. This transformation was performed using the intrusion detection system *Bro* and deletes 5 essential information[1] to be able to link the records obtained from their sources in the trace of DARPA. In this transformation, ICMP packets are treated differently than other packets. Indeed, each ICMP packet is treated as an entire connection (so-called *stateless*) whereas the UDP and TCP connections consist of a sequence of packets exchanged between 2 machines (called *stateful*).

Many of *KDD'99*'s critics come from the network trace from which it was made, DARPA. Indeed, this network trace has a large number of attacks that are detectable using only the *time to live* (TTL) field in the headers of the packets. This over-representation of an attack characteristic can cause intrusion detection patterns, trained with this dataset, to increase detection bias.

---

[1] The start time of the connection, the source IP address, the source port, the destination IP address and the destination port.

According to Al Tobi and Duncan [1] the processing of *KDD'99* has introduced additional errors. For example, the resulting dataset contains more TCP traffic, less ICMP traffic, and less UDP traffic than the *DARPA* network trace from which it is made.

To solve some of *KDD'99* issues, Tavallaee et. al. present a new dataset based on *KDD'99*, called *NSL-KDD* [10], in their article [9].

UNSW-NB15. The Australian Centre for Cyber Security (ACCS) has generated a new dataset named *UNSW-NB15* presented in [6], simulating a modern environment allowing to generate network traffic resembling a modern traffic and containing a large variety of recent attacks, especially low-profile intrusions that may be difficult to detect and that do not exist in the *KDD'99* dataset.

The *UNSW-NB15* dataset was created using the *IXIA PerfectStormOne* tool, owned by the ACCS Cyber Range, using CVE services to retrieve information about the latest types of attacks used and discovered in cyberspace. CVE services are a kind of public dictionary of security vulnerabilities disclosed on various systems and applications that are accessible via the Internet. With this tool, researchers were able to generate more than 100 GB of data usable by intrusion detection systems. This data was retrieved by the network trace capture tool *tcpdump* deployed on one of the routers used in the network exchanges generation.

The configuration of the IXIA PerfectStorm tool for generating the *UNSW-NB15* dataset is detailed in Fig. 1.

For this dataset, the tool virtualises three servers. Servers 1 and 3 are set to generate basic network traffic, while Server 2 generates malicious and abnormal activity in the network. The servers are connected to the user machines via two routers. These routers are connected to a firewall that is configured to pass traffic from one router to another, whether normal or abnormal. Then they recovered the traffic generated by the *IXIA PerfectStormOne* tool thanks to *tcpdump*, installed on router 1, to save the data in an exploitable format. Finally, the *IXIA PerfectStormOne* tool is used here to generate and corrupt normal traffic with recent attacks thanks to its link with online CVE services.

This dataset thus proposes nine different types of attacks, representing the different methods of attacks existing in the cyberspace.

A study was conducted to evaluate the performance of the dataset *UNSW-NB15* [7]. In this study, the dataset was divided into two parts, one for learning and the other for testing classifications. These two parts were evaluated statistically, on the correlation of characteristics and finally on the complexity of the dataset. The results were then compared to those of the *KDD'99* dataset, particularly in terms of accuracy complexity and false alarm rate. The results of the evaluation show that the *KDD'99* dataset shows better results in false alarm rates. This is due to the lack of diversity of attacks and the over-representation of certain data characteristics in these attacks. In conclusion, the *UNSW-NB15* dataset is more complex than the *KDD'99* dataset because of the different types of modern attacks it uses.

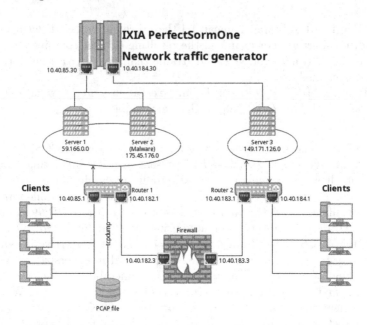

Fig. 1. Configuration of the *IXIA PerfectStormOne* tool for the dataset generation (inspired by [6])

Moustafa and Slay have thus been able to generate a synthetic network dataset, modern enough to answer current network analysis issues as shown by Moustafa et al. in the article [8], thanks to the tool *IXIA PerfectStromOne* using these nine types of attacks and by translating the network traces obtained in 49 characteristics that were extracted using tools of network activity audits such as *Argus* and intrusion detection systems such as *Bro*. They have shown that the *KDD'99* and *NSL-KDD* datasets do not represent modern network traffic that contains modern, low-impact attacks on network traces.

3 Network Captures Generation Platform

The goal of the platform presented within this manuscript is to allow the creation of replicable network captures based on pre-defined scenarios, from which one can easily extract sets of training data for IDS or for research.

For now this platform is still a proof of concept that aims to show that it is possible to create training datasets that are already labelled, for IDS and research, almost completely automatically. And that the generated datasets are easily reproducible thanks to their adjunct scenario file.

Figure 2 presents a schema of the operating principle of the platform.

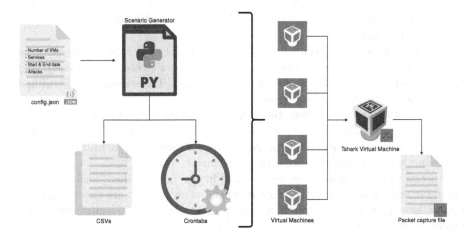

Fig. 2. Creations of the packet captures through the platform

3.1   Design and Implementation

This section describes the operating principles of the network capture generation platform from a software design perspective.

Description. The platform is based on a python implementation of the model developed, abstracting the concepts to be represented in the network (i.e., the virtual machines, the actions they perform, their services, the host machines, and their behaviours).

This platform allows to randomly generate scenarios of normal uses of a network using parameters specified by the user. Making it possible to create experiments with their protocols very simply. Once generated, the scenarios are transposed to the real and virtual hosts for the deployment and dataset generation phase. The deployed hosts are configured to be assigned to a crontab generated by the algorithm adding it to the list of devices to be listened to for the network capture.

After the capture, the platform transforms the PCAP file to a CSV before adding the labels to the newly generated dataset. The labels are added automatically thanks to the crontab files generated by the platform that can be correlated to the packets in the CSV file. This automatic labelling of the generated dataset is the main contribution of this manuscript as it allows for the production of ready to use datasets for data analysis or data mining without the hassle of labelling datasets manually. These datasets could also be used for training anomaly detection models.

Modelling of the Program. For the network capture generation platform, the network model used in this platform presents networks as a number of machines (virtualised in this implementation) and VLANs that allows for the creation of a complex network.

The virtual machines were modelled with their IP and MAC addresses, the enabled services, their behaviours (to simulate a user's choice of actions), and the actions they will perform during the generation. The services are identified with a name and relate to commands.

The actions are made from the commands available in the services, these commands have a list of different parameters in which the actions choose the final command to execute, the actions also have a time stamp defining when the command will be executed during the experiment.

Special virtual machines are also defined in the model, called "hacker". These virtual machines are different from the others as no services are executed, however, a list of commands with parameters are used to attack the legitimate virtual machines in the network.

Generating the Scenarios. The program uses a configuration file in JSON format. Listing 1.1 provides an example of the configuration, to define the services available for virtual machines, the number of virtual machines per configuration group, the number of configuration group changes, the prefix of the IP addresses to be used (e.g. "192.168.10."), the start date of the experiment, the end date of the experiment, the maximum number of actions per machine virtual, and attack commands available to the attacker.

By varying these parameters, the behaviour of the machines can be modified on the simulated network and thus the network traces that are recovered during the experiments.

```
1  {
2    "network": {
3      "number_of_vms": 2,
4      "number_of_changes": 1,
5      "prefixe": "192.168.10.",
6      "services": [{
7        "name": "sshd",
8        "commands": [{
9          "name": "ssh",
10         "parameters": ["tester@&ip"]
11       }]
12     }]
13   },
14   "experiment": {
15     "start_date": "2018-08-02 13:00",
16     "end_date": "2018-08-02 17:00",
17     "max_actions_per_vm": 500
18   },
19   "hacker": {
20     "attacks": [{
21       "name": "nmap",
22       "parameters": ["-T0 -sV --top-ports 5 &ip"]
```

```
23        }]
24     }
25  }
```

Listing 1.1. Configuration file example

To generate random behaviours of virtual machines, a list of virtual machines are generated (with their IP and MAC addresses, and their available services). From this list, configuration groups are created. Hosts in a configuration group are available at the same time during the experiment. The configuration group further allows defining the interactions between the machines, randomly choose the services to contact and the time of contact.

The definition of the configuration group is essential to the working of the platform. A misconfiguration in the file would essentially render the trace ineffective, hence, limitations were implemented to ensure appropriate hosts are contacted at appropriate times.

3.2   Generating the Attacks

This section describes the existing attack tools and algorithms. The attacks used by the attacker during the experiments are also presented in this section.

Attacks. To test the resilience of networks, a large number of tools exist. Nmap is undoubtedly the best-known tool for network discovery. Nmap has many possibilities to identify enabled services on a computer and identify open ports. Combined with the Nmap Scripting Engine (NSE), many vulnerabilities can be exploited directly by Nmap.

Other tools such as Metasploit were also used in this study. Metasploit is a framework for the development and execution of exploits and can execute attacks against remote machines. Metasploit features a commercial version, as well as, various other projects related to the framework. Among the most important, the Opcode database and The shellcode archive.

The platform also uses OpenVAS, which is a framework of different services and vulnerability scanning tools focusing on effective vulnerability management. The framework is used to execute a set of scheduled attacks on one or more machines and draw a detailed report of the vulnerabilities of the machines tested.

Malicious User. The generation of cyber attacks, in the network capture, is achieved through the integration of a virtual machine executing a set of attacks on the simulated network. The attacker host has a pre-defined IP and MAC address and is generated last.

The attacker's behaviour uses predefined commands from a list of attacks provided in the configuration file. These attacks are executed by the attacker's virtual machine, targeting randomly selected virtual machines from the list of all the virtual machines on the network.

The commands available for the attacker are those included by default on the Kali Linux distribution that is used as a base operating system. In particular, the commands used by the attacker are defined in the *config.json* configuration file.

4   Experiments

To test the network experiment generation platform, 3 experiments were conducted with different attacker behaviors:

- An attacker scans the entire network on all ports.
- An attacker scans the network looking for an SSH server and then connects to it by forcing the password of the root user.
- A very cautious attacker uses long interval settings to scan without raising suspicion of intrusion detection systems.

Several categorizations of attackers exist in the scientific literature. The taxonomy, proposed by SLN Hald and JM Pedersen, presents 8 different types of attackers namely; Script Kiddies, Cyber-Punks, Insiders, Petty thieves, Gray Hats, Professional Criminals, Hacktivists and Nation states [3]. According to this taxonomy, the first attacker of the list is the equivalent of a Script Kiddie, the second attacker is the equivalent of a Petty thieve and the last striker is seen as a Professional criminal.

A Windows 10 version 1803 machine with an i7-4720HQ processor and 20 GB of RAM was used to host these experiments. As this platform is a proof of concept, the test network was kept simple with 1 network in which 5 virtual machines, one being the attacker, were communicating.

Virtual machines in the test network are Arch Linux virtual machines, up to date at the time of the experiments. They include SSH, FTP, and HTTP services through the openssh, inetutils, and apache packages. The machine listening to the network is an Arch Linux virtual machine that is also up to date and contains the wireshark-cli package to use the tshark command to retrieve the packets transmitted over the network. Finally, the attacking machine is the virtual machine provided by the Kali Linux website for the VirtualBox platform.

The network capture files contains 22 different IP addresses including the 16 IP addresses belonging to the virtual machines that make up the observed network, the IP address of the machine running the network capture, the IP address of the machine running the attacks on the network, the 2 broadcast IP addresses (255.255.255.255/24 and 0.0.0.0/24) and 2 operating IP addresses (224.0.0.252/24 and 224.0.0.22/24).

The most used ports by the network machines are ports 21, 22 and 80 corresponding to the ports used by the services chosen to use for this experiment (FTP, SSH and Apache). Port 5355 is also used as it corresponds to the LLMNR protocol allowing for name resolution on the local network.

4.1   Experiment 1: Script Kiddie

During the experiment with the attacker repeatedly scanning the entire network, a total of 1,724,531 packets were collected over a period of 4 h. The average size of these packets is 69 bytes. Such a low average packet size is due to the network scan as discovery packets are fairly small.

A total of 790 034 packets exchanged between the hacker and other machines (IP address 192.168.10.48/24). It, therefore, represents more than 48% of the packet exchanges of the network capture.

Figure 3 presents the normal traffic compared to the attacker's traffic.

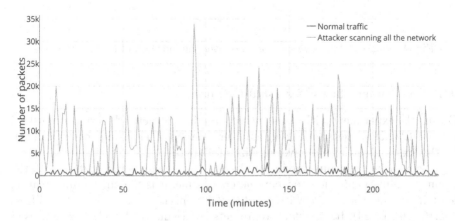

Fig. 3. Number of packages per minute over the duration of the experiments

4.2   Experiment 2: Petty Thief

During the experiment with the attacker repeatedly scanning the network for a machine with port 22 open, a total of 514,308 packets were collected over a period of 4 h. The average size of the packets obtained during this experiment is of 123 bytes.

The attacking machine did numerous recognition through Nmap. It is the one that communicates the most within the network trace with a total of 146 936 packets exchanged (IP address 192.168.10.210/24). It, therefore, represents more than 34% of the packet exchanges of the network capture.

The attacker, while focusing on a particular service, participates less in the network trace as it only represents 34% of the trace whereas in the previous experience it represented 48%.

This attacker could also represent a beginner using scripts, but with a specific goal that is to connect in ssh on machines whose port 22 is open. Figure 4 presents the normal traffic compared to the attacker's traffic.

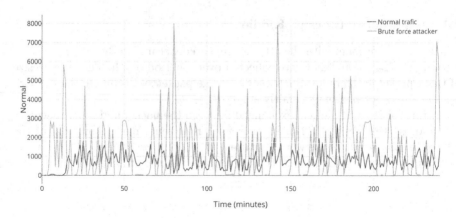

Fig. 4. Number of packages per minute over the duration of the experiments

4.3 Experiment 3: Professional Criminal

During the experiment with the attacker scanning the network very cautiously, a total of 123,626 packets were collected over a period of 4 h. The packets obtained by this experiment have an average size of 99 bytes.

The attacking machine having made very cautiously its recognition with the command Nmap and the good parameters of time, it is the one communicating least in the network trace with a total of 832 packets exchanged (IP address 192.168.10.147/24). It, therefore, represents less than 1% of packet exchanges of the network capture.

When these results are compared with the previous ones, it is noticed that the cautious attacker is much quieter than the others. This attacker could go unnoticed if it wasn't known that he was in the network trying to discover the computers that are accessible. Indeed, with a participation of 1% in the network trace, this attack could appear as a machine little talkative to an external observer. He therefore represents an attacker who knows exactly what he is doing and who is very organized. Figure 5 presents the normal traffic compared to the attacker's traffic.

4.4 Results Analysis

To fully understand the impact of the different behaviors of attackers on the generated data, Fig. 6 explores the difference in the number of packets exchanged per minute at the same time of the different experiments.

It can be pointed out that the attacker scanning the entire network generates a lot more packets than the other two attackers. Packets are grouped into peaks of activity, synonymous with wild recognition and noisy attack.

Attacker scanning cautiously does not change the packet line of its network trace, remaining relatively flat. This shows that this attack technique is rather

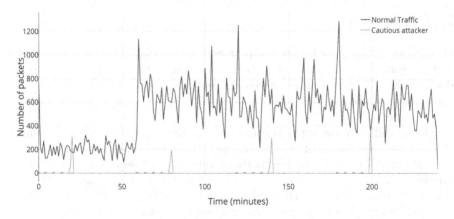

Fig. 5. Number of packages per minute over the duration of the experiments

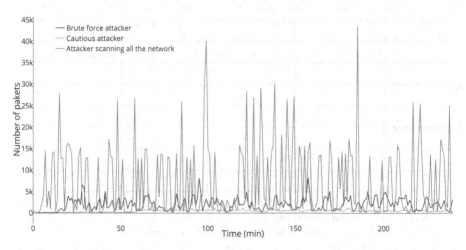

Fig. 6. Number of packages per minute over the duration of the experiments

difficult to spot in a network trace because it does not stand out from the rest of the supposedly normal traffic.

The different experiments performed show that the network traffic generation platform allows the creation of specific attacker's comportment which can be used to generate any kind of specific threats to get datasets representing them.

This approach of the generation allows for an easy automation of the transformation process, from network capture files to a readable format for any machine learning algorithm, as it is possible to relate all packets from the network capture files to its sources from the files containing the scenarios, generated by the platform.

5   Conclusion

The results obtained show that the proposed solution is able to generate pertinent network datasets. Traffic is clearly identified, unlike many datasets available. The tool developed makes it easy and quick to configure complex scenarios. The traces produced by the tool are also realistic as they are generated from fully fleshed systems.

The modelling of the types of attackers is achieved through relatively simple actions. The randomness of the scenario generation makes the attacker's actions disparate and could therefore affects the quality of the generated network traces, however, several differences can be observed in the network traces when the behaviour of the attacker is changed making the solution modular and flexible.

Future work include the move from a purely random behaviour to a simulated behaviour, managed by a multi-agent system, for example. The network trace generation platform could also be improved by integrating communication functions with other machines and virtual machine management functions to simplify the use of the virtual machine solution, enabling load balancing on several machines of the different virtual machines as well as manage the configuration of the different virtual machines necessary for the experiment requested automatically.

References

1. Al Tobi, A.M., Duncan, I.: KDD 1999 generation faults: a review and analysis. J. Cyber Secur. Technol., 1–37 (2018). https://doi.org/10.1080/23742917.2018.1518061, https://www.tandfonline.com/doi/full/10.1080/23742917.2018.1518061
2. Bay, S.D., Hettich, S.: UCI KDD Cup 1999. University of California, Irvine, School of Information and Computer Sciences (1999). https://archive.ics.uci.edu/ml/machine-learning-databases/kddcup99-mld/kddcup99.html
3. Hald, S.L.N., Pedersen, J.M.: An updated taxonomy for characterizing hackers according to their threat properties. In: 2012 14th International Conference on Advanced Communication Technology, pp. 81–86. IEEE (2012)
4. Hindy, H., et al.: A taxonomy and survey of intrusion detection system design techniques, network threats and datasets. arXiv:1806.03517 [cs], June 2018
5. Kokkonen, T., Hämäläinen, T., Silokunnas, M., Siltanen, J., Zolotukhin, M., Neijonen, M.: Analysis of approaches to internet traffic generation for cyber security research and exercise. In: Balandin, S., Andreev, S., Koucheryavy, Y. (eds.) ruSMART 2015. LNCS, vol. 9247, pp. 254–267. Springer, Cham (2015). https://doi.org/10.1007/978-3-319-23126-6_23
6. Moustafa, N., Slay, J.: UNSW-NB15: a comprehensive data set for network intrusion detection systems (UNSW-NB15 network data set). In: 2015 Military Communications and Information Systems Conference (MilCIS), pp. 1–6. IEEE, Canberra, November 2015. https://doi.org/10.1109/MilCIS.2015.7348942, http://ieeexplore.ieee.org/document/7348942/

7. Moustafa, N., Slay, J.: The evaluation of network anomaly detection systems: statistical analysis of the UNSW-NB15 data set and the comparison with the KDD99 data set. Inf. Secur. J.: Glob. Perspect. **25**(1–3), 18–31 (2016). https://doi.org/10.1080/19393555.2015.1125974, http://www.tandfonline.com/doi/full/10.1080/19393555.2015.1125974

8. Moustafa, N., Slay, J., Creech, G.: Novel geometric area analysis technique for anomaly detection using trapezoidal area estimation on large-scale networks. IEEE Trans. Big Data, 1 (2017). https://doi.org/10.1109/TBDATA.2017.2715166, http://ieeexplore.ieee.org/document/7948715/

9. Tavallaee, M., Bagheri, E., Lu, W., Ghorbani, A.A.: A detailed analysis of the KDD CUP 99 data set. In: 2009 IEEE Symposium on Computational Intelligence for Security and Defense Applications, pp. 1–6. IEEE, Ottawa, July 2009. https://doi.org/10.1109/CISDA.2009.5356528, http://ieeexplore.ieee.org/document/5356528/

10. Tavallaee, M., Bagheri, E., Lu, W., Ghorbani, A.A.: NSL-KDD—Datasets—Research—Canadian Institute for Cybersecurity—UNB, July 2009. https://www.unb.ca/cic/datasets/nsl.html

11. Varet, A., Larrieu, N.: How to generate realistic network traffic? In: IEEE COMPSAC 2014, 38th Annual International Computers, Software & Applications Conference, Västerås, Sweden (2014). https://hal-enac.archives-ouvertes.fr/hal-00973913

12. Vishwanath, K., Vahdat, A.: Swing: realistic and responsive network traffic generation. IEEE/ACM Trans. Netw. **17**(3), 712–725 (2009). https://doi.org/10.1109/TNET.2009.2020830. http://ieeexplore.ieee.org/document/4914755/

Attack Prevention and Trustworthiness

Lempel-Ziv Compression with Randomized Input-Output for Anti-compression Side-Channel Attacks Under HTTPS/TLS

Meng Yang[✉] and Guang Gong[✉]

Department of Electrical and Computer Engineering, University of Waterloo,
Waterloo, ON N2L 3G1, Canada
{m36yang,ggong}@uwaterloo.ca

Abstract. Security experts confront new attacks on TLS/SSL every
year. Ever since the compression side-channel attacks CRIME and
BREACH were presented during security conferences in 2012 and 2013,
online users connecting to HTTP servers that run TLS version 1.2 are
susceptible of being impersonated. We set up three Randomized Lempel-
Ziv Models, which are built on Lempel-Ziv77, to confront this attack. Our
three models change the deterministic characteristic of the compression
algorithm: each compression with the same input gives output of different lengths. We implemented SSL/TLS protocol and the Lempel-Ziv77
compression algorithm, and used them as a base for our simulations
of compression side-channel attack. After performing the simulations, all
three models successfully prevented the attack. However, we demonstrate
that our randomized models can still be broken by a stronger version of
compression side-channel attack that we created. But this latter attack
has a greater time complexity and is easily detectable. Finally, from
the results, we conclude that our models couldn't compress as well as
Lempel-Ziv77, but they can be used against compression side-channel
attacks.

Keywords: Lempel-Ziv compression · Encryption · Compression
side-channel attack · Randomization · TLS

1 Introduction

The Internet is growing bigger and bigger everyday. Along with Facebook's new
drone project that will allow more people to connect online, more information
will travel on the network. We would like this information to travel in a fast
and secure way. Data compression is used to make the information travel faster,
and data encryption is used to make sure the information is confidential. The
TLS communication protocol is used to ensure secure communications between

M. Yang—Currently working with Google.

© Springer Nature Switzerland AG 2020
A. Benzekri et al. (Eds.): FPS 2019, LNCS 12056, pp. 117–136, 2020.
https://doi.org/10.1007/978-3-030-45371-8_8

two nodes and to facilitate data exchange with compression. It also provides authentication with certificates, keeps confidentiality with encryption, and grants integrity with message digest. For compression, TLS uses either DEFLATE algorithm or Lempel-Ziv-Stat algorithm [1].

Currently, servers are using version 1.2 of TLS, which supports both encryption and compression. However, combining these two algorithms has security flaws. Attackers could open the content of the encrypted HTTP header and use the authentication token within the cookie to impersonate a user. To perform this attack, the attacker needs to create multiple forged strings, and append each one to the plaintext that get compress-then-encrypted, then needs to look for the encrypted text among them with the shortest length to recover a secret within the plaintext one character at a time. The type of attack that does not directly use brute force algorithms to retrieve the content of an encrypted message is called side-channel attack. For our case, the side-channel attack that exploits leakage from output's lengths of compression algorithms is called *compression side-channel attack*.

The compression side-channel attack was studied in a paper at the beginning of year 2002 [2]. The authors of the paper explain how an adversary could use the length the outputs of the compressed-then-encrypted text to retrieve a secret within the message. In recent years, two compression side-channel attacks were presented to public and demonstrated during the security conferences: CRIME (Compression Redundancy Infoleak Made Easy) in 2012 [3]; and BREACH (Browser Reconnaissance and Exfiltration via Adaptive Compression of Hypertext) in 2013 [4]. The presenters could successfully recover a secret string hidden inside HTTP message. TLS took a big hit and plans to shutdown all compression methods completely in its next version 1.3 [1]. The SSL Pulse survey [5] reported there is only 1 percent of the site that supports TLS compression in their June 2019 report.

Removing compression has a big impact on the network traffic due to large packets that are traveling without being compressed. In this paper, we propose three schemes where compression could be re-enabled before encryption without risk of compromising security. The three schemes randomly modify the inputs or randomly repeats the outputs of the compression algorithm:

1. Weak Cipher With Lempel-Ziv: the plaintext passes through a weak cipher before being compressed.
2. Lempel-Ziv With Control: the outputs of the compression are randomly repeated.
3. Lempel-Ziv With Control and Feedback: the outputs of the compression are randomly repeated, then decompressed and compressed again.

To test our schemes, we implemented the compression side-channel attack algorithm and performed simulations on them. We examine the results in terms of security, compression ratio, and runtime. Even though the attack was successfully prevented, we noticed the increase in time complexity of the algorithm, and increase in compression ratio. Since the attack is countered, we would like to test the limit of our schemes. We augmented the attack, named strong compression side-channel attack. This attack builds on top of the compression side-channel attack, and repeatedly sends and collects length of many outputs and uses the shortest average size of the lengths to decrypt the secret within encrypted message. After running the strong compression side-channel attack simulations, our three schemes resists the attack to a certain degree. The attack eventually breached all our schemes given a large amount of time. The time complexity is extremely large such that the new attack is infeasible given the lifetime of the secret.

Schemes are not limited only to randomly repeating inputs or outputs around the compression algorithm. We propose another scheme called PermuLZ, which will be discussed in detail in a separate paper. In the latter scheme, the plaintext is fragmented into smaller pieces then rearranged randomly before going through compression. This scheme could counter the attack, but it could have a longer time complexity and a decrease in compression ratio as trade-off.

2   Preliminaries

In this section, we describe the Lempel-Ziv compression algorithm family, component functions used in our schemes, and define the notations used in this paper.

2.1   Compression Algorithms

We use the following notations throughout the paper:

- $A||B$ concatenates two binary strings A and B
- ζ represents an alphabet or character.
- Σ is a set containing all possible ζ.
- M is the plaintext.
- C is the ciphertext.
- $argmin_x y$ is a function returning the argument x that associates to the smallest value y.

Lempel-Ziv Family

Lempel-Ziv 77. The Lempel-Ziv compression algorithm, shown in Algorithm 1, was created by Abraham Lempel and Jacob Ziv. They published the first version of the algorithm in 1977, called Lempel-Ziv77. This compression algorithm focuses on replacing strings that repeats in the file with a reference tuple. The reference is a length-distance tuple, which indicates the location of the pattern and its length. The tuple also contains the next character after the pattern.

Algorithm 1. LEMPEL-ZIV77($file$)

```
1:  current_position ← start of file
2:  outputs_list ← empty list
3:  while current_position not reach end of file do
4:      move sliding_window
5:      longest_str ← find longest matching string for current_pos in sliding_window
6:      pos ← relative starting position of longest_str from current_pos
7:      len ← length of longest_str
8:      next_char ← next character after longest_str in sliding_window
9:      append (pos, len, next_char) to outputs_list
10:     current_position ← current_position + j
11: end while
12: return outputs_list
```

Lempel-Ziv77 Example. When applying the Lempel-Ziv77 algorithm to "abcabcd", we would get "abc(−3, 3, 'd')" since the second "abc" happened previously. The second appearance is replaced by "(−3, 3, 'd')", where the first number, −3, is the relative location to its first occurence, and the second number, 3, is the length. This latter tuple would get converted into two bytes. Thus, for the text "abcabcd", Lempel-Ziv77 would give a compression ratio of $\frac{5}{7}$, since the original text has length of 7 bytes, and Lempel-Ziv77 outputs has length 5 bytes. When decompressing "(−3, 3, 'd')", the two numbers, −3 and 3, inside the tuple will be expanded. First, we move back three characters to point to the letter "a", then copy the next three characters indicated by the second number. Thus, the tuple "(0, 3, 'd')" gets replaced by "abcd".

Lempel-Ziv78. In the year that followed, 1978, the same authors published their second compression algorithm named Lempel-Ziv78, which is an extension of Lempel-Ziv77 [6]. In this version, the length of the repeated pattern is removed in the reference tuple. The repeated pattern gets replaced only by "(location, next character)" pair. The length is omitted since it can be calculated from start location and position of the next character.

Huffman Coding. Huffman Coding is another compression algorithm which is often used together with Lempel-Ziv77. This algorithm gives each character a new encoding. The compression happens when the characters get replaced. The most frequent characters has an encoding of fewer bits, and the least frequently used characters get an encoding of many bits.

DEFLATE and Gzip. Both DEFLATE and gzip are popular compression algorithms used by HTTP [7]. When the compression is done using DEFLATE algorithm, the plain-text is first compressed by Lempel-Ziv77, then the outputs are compressed again by Huffman encoding [8]. The gzip compression algorithm first compresses the plain-text with DEFLATE algorithm, then adds a header and a footer to the output of the compression. The header contains information about the file, such as the timestamp and compression flags, and the footer is a CRC-32 checksum generated from the compressed message [9].

2.2   Pseudo-Random Sequence Generator

De Bruijn Sequences. The sequence is named after the mathematician Nicolaas Govert de Bruijn. Given an order n, the sequence outputs a cyclic sequence of bits where every substring of length n is unique [10].

WG-8 Cipher. The WG-8 cipher is a light-weight cipher that outputs a sequence with 2-level auto-correlation. The keystream sequences outputs have many randomness properties, such as a period of $2^{160} - 1$, balanced 0's and 1's, two level auto correlation sequence, ideal t-tuple distribution, and large linear span of $2^{33.32}$ [11].

Mersenne Twister. Mersenne Twister generator was created in year 1997 by Matsumoto and Nishimura [12]. This pseudo-random number generator is based on a Mersenne Prime number, which is a prime number that can be written in this format: $2^n - 1$ where n is also a prime. The period of Mersenne Twister is equal to the prime number. It is a quick pseudo-random number generator and has better randomness properties than other fast generators. Generally, Mersenne Twister picks $2^{19937} - 1$ as its prime. It has good randomness properties such as period of $2^{19937} - 1$, and it passes Diehard tests.

2.3   Encryption Algorithm

AES Cipher. AES-128 is a block cipher. In HTTP or TLS protocol, compression is used before applying AES encryption. It takes a key of either 128, 196, 256 bits, and an input block of the same length, then outputs encrypted block of that length [13]. Other ciphers are used in HTTPS or TLS [1], but we used AES to demonstrate our results.

3   Anti-compression Side-Channel Attack

In this section, we first analyse the compression side-channel attack (CSCA), then propose three models to deter the attack, and finally present the results of the attack performing simulations against our models.

3.1   Compression Side-Channel Attack

To learn how to fight against the attack, we must first understand the attack. Here below, we present the compression side-channel attack algorithm, along with an example, and we also provide a theoretical proof of the leakage of compression and encryption combination.

Algorithm 2. CSCA($http\_request$)

```
 1: header ← HTTP header from http_request
 2: known_prefix ← secret's prefix from adversary
 3: guess_secret ← empty string of length  L  set by adversary
 4: for i = 0 to i = secret_length do
 5:     L ← empty list
 6:     for each ζ ∈ Σ do
 7:         guess_secret[i] ← ζ
 8:         g_ζ ← known_prefix||guess_secret[i]
 9:         M_ζ ← header||g_ζ
10:         C_ζ ← Enc(LZ77(M_ζ))
11:         C_ζ gets sent over network
12:         l_ζ ← length(C_ζ)
13:         L.insert(l_ζ)
14:     end for
15:     guess_secret[i] ← {ζ|ζ = argmin_ζ{l_ζ ∈ L}}
16: end for
17: return  guess_secret
```

Analysis of Compression Side-Channel Attack. The following algorithm, Algorithm 2, shows the execution steps of a compression side-channel attack.

We assume that the client's computer is already infected by a malware that can only manipulate HTTP requests before they get sent. We are also assuming that the adversary can only inspect and retrieve the lengths of encrypted TCP packages on the network. Additionally, we assume that the victim already made connection to a server, and has established an authentication token that is located inside the header of HTTP request.

Before the victim client sends another HTTP request to the server, the request is first held onto by the malware, and the whole HTTP header is retrieved in line 1. The adversary has already examined the format of the HTTP header and the cookie within in line 2, and knows the prefix string that prepends the secret. The prefix string has been already given to the malware. The malware first initiates an empty string, $guess\_secret$, that will eventually become the real secret at the end of the algorithm on line 3. The malware uses $guess\_secret$ to retrieve the real secret token within the HTTP header. It knows in advance that the length of the secret is constant. It constructs a string g as a concatenation of $known\_prefix$ and $guess\_secret$, and it will append g to the HTTP header. The $guess\_secret$ is constructed in a particular way. The malware tries to guess each character, one at a time, from left to right. For each i-th character in the $guess\_secret$, the malware sets it to be one of the possible characters, ζ, from the alphabet set Σ, shown in line 7. Once a character is set in $guess\_secret$, the latter is appended to $known\_prefix$, which becomes g and is then appended to the HTTP $header$ in lines 8–9. This new header, M, is compressed and encrypted, then gets sent to the server by the client in lines 10–11.

Since the message will be going through the network, its length l can be retrieved by sniffer at line 12. The lengths l_ζ for each ζ is then saved in a list L for later analysis, shown in line 13. After collecting all the lengths, the attacker analyses them and retrieve the message with the shortest length, since the length of the encrypted header with wrong guesses is longer than the length of encrypted header with the correct guess. The forged $guess\_secret[i]$ inside this message corresponds to the correct character at i inside the real secret. In other words, ζ that corresponds to the message with shortest length in L is the correct i character inside the real token, shown in line 15.

Once all the characters are recovered one by one, *guess_secret* will match the real secret token within *header*, and the adversary can use this token, *guess_secret*, to impersonate the victim.

Compression Side-Channel Attack Example. The following example explains how we simulated a compression side-channel attack on the following HTTP header. Lempel-Ziv77 was the compression algorithm used. This HTTP header below is the raw HTTP header from accessing the website https://www. google.com. We will use the compression side-channel attack to retrieve the authentication token: "rAJMNHlc ... Xle" hidden by encryption.

```
Alt-Svc: quic=":443"; ma=2592000; v="34,
33,32,31,30,29,28,27,26,25"
...
Set-Cookie: NID=79=rAJMNHlcYMf6Vg3FxMIPE
kxRcLStbWDVxb7Dng9puqepumjZJ5nsRnOQbiORO
MILZp8u-jHt2fExUTLMgVgb3MUYwdxbp2V7vb4YP
OLKxhHfx5e8bUekI4_Eo4NupdYpTDvsGqDfhgbG3
kWFw2y_yaNuQAhND4ULUizCoOEysyzvinM6Y6zba
5MOfVj9zhbnltLCVAcoiY15CeF7opB_DZ5vedm2d
bouqXle;
expires=Thu, 08-Dec-2016 21:59:58 GMT;
path=/; domain=.google.ca; HttpOnly
X-Firefox-Spdy: h2
...
```

In the first step, we retrieve the header and examine the secret's *known_prefix*, which is NID=79=. Then we create a forge string, g, which has the prefix NID=79=, and we add a guessing character from the alphabet, $\Sigma = a, b, \cdots, z, A, \cdots Z$. So, the first forged string g takes the first letter of the alphabet as guess: $g \leftarrow$ NID=79=a. Then, we appends g to the end of the header. Before the header gets sent, it gets compressed by Lempel-Ziv77 and encrypted by TLS. The content of the message is hidden, but the lengths of the cipher-text is not. After collecting the length l, we try the second letter b as guess: $g \leftarrow$ NID=79=b. After trying all the alphabets, we can collect the length of each ciphertext containing a different guess. By collecting all the lengths, we could determine that the ciphertext with the shortest length corresponds to the message containing the forged string with guess r. Thus, we can deduce that the first letter of the secret is r. These steps are repeated for guessing the second letter of the secret, which would be A, and we repeat for all 225 characters. Then, the whole secret token "rAJMNHlc ... Xle" is recovered.

Analysis of Lempel-Ziv Against Compression Side-Channel Attack. We now analyse compression side-channel attack and prove that an adversary can use it to retrieve any secrets within a encrypted message given that he knows the secret prefix.

Let S be the header concatenated together with the forged string:

$$S = s_0 s_1 \cdots P s_t s_{t+1} \cdots s_{t+T} \cdots G\hat{x}$$

where s_i are characters, P is a string that represents the secret's known prefix, s_t to s_{t+T} represents the real secret of length T, G is the known prefix appended by correct guessed characters, which is added by adversary, and $\hat{x}$ is the next character currently being guessed. We segment the file S into a list of sequence of strings, Q_is.

$$S = s_0 s_1 \cdots P s_t s_{t+1} \cdots s_{t+T} \cdots G\hat{x} = Q_0 Q_1 \cdots Q_m$$

After the plaintext goes through compression, some sequence Q_i would be replaced by a Lempel-Ziv77 compression output $r_i = (position, length, next\_char)$ since it happened before.

$$LZ77(S) = LZ77(s_0 s_1 \cdots s_n) = LZ77(Q_0 Q_1 \cdots Q_m)$$
$$= R = r_0 r_1 \cdots r_l$$

We define length of the compressed file $l = \|R\|$ as the number of Lempel-Ziv77 outputs. For the attack to be successful, the length of the compressed file with incorrect guess must be longer than the file with correct guess: $l_{\hat{x} \neq s_t} > l_{\hat{x} = s_t}$. We will prove this case below.

Property 1. $l_{\hat{x} \neq s_t} = l_{\hat{x} = s_t} + 1$, where l is size of R.

Proof. The prefix, P, and the first character of the secret, s_t, can be segmented in two ways.

1. $P s_t \in Q_u$: both P and s_t are found in the same segment Q_u.
2. $P \in Q_u$ and $s_t \in Q_{u+1}$: P is found in Q_u and s_p is found in Q_{u+1}.

The prefix and first character will be repeated in the forged string, which then will become an Lempel-Ziv output tuple r_i after compression. We can eliminate the second case, since because if only the segment that contains P is referenced, then s_t is included in the Lempel-Ziv output as the *next_character*. Thus, we can say that the prefix and the first character are in the same segment: $P s_t \in Q_u$. Now we show that the length of the the message with the incorrect guess is larger than one with correct guess. After compression, the input file S becomes compressed file R.

– If the guess is correct, $\hat{x} = s_t$, then $G\hat{x}$ is compressed to only one output r_{l_1}, that references Q_u. The compressed file R would have this output at the end: $R = r_1 r_2 \cdots r_{l_1}$.

– If the guess is incorrect, $\hat{x} \neq s_t$, then only the G is compressed since it matches the prefix P in Q_u. The output of compressing the prefix P is also r_{l_1} (call this r'_{l_1}) but with a smaller value for *length*, and the guessing character $\hat{x}$ is the *next_character*. However, the Lempel-Ziv77 algorithm also prints a terminal output r_{l_2} that has a new line as the *next_character* to mark the end of the algorithm.

The length of the compression result for the message with the correct guess is $l_{\hat{x}_0=s_t} = \|R_{correct}\|$ where $R_{correct} = r_0 r_1 \cdots r_{l_1}$. The length of the result with incorrect guess is $l_{\hat{x}_0=s_t} = \|R_{incorrect}\|$ where $R_{incorrect} = r_0 r_1 \cdots r'_{l_1} r_{l_2}$. This clearly shows that the length has increased by one block, thus, $l_{\hat{x}_0 \neq s_t} = l_{\hat{x}_0=s_t}+1$. To summarize, the length of the compressed file with incorrect guess is indeed longer than the file with correct guess: $l_{\hat{x} \neq s_t} > l_{\hat{x}=s_t}$.

3.2 Adding Randomization to Lempel-Ziv77

In the following, we explain our motivation behind increasing the randomness of Lempel-Ziv compression, then, we propose three methods built around Lempel-Ziv77 compression algorithm before applying encryption to stand against compression side-channel attack. The goal of each of the methods below is to make the compressed message's length not deterministic. With those models, the length of the message containing the forged token with the correct guess is not shorter than length of the message containing the forged token with the incorrect guess.

Length Analysis of Randomized LZ. Previously, we showed that an adversary can recover a secret from a cookie inside a web browser. We will show how we can prevent this attack by adding randomness to LZ. Our goal is to prevent the attacker from guessing $\hat{x}_0$. By varying the entropy of the plain-text or by randomly padding the outputs of LZ compression, we can achieve $l_{\hat{x}_0 \neq s_t} \geq l_{\hat{x}_0=s_t}$.

With a pseudo-random sequence generator, we can use the output bits as a control to change the entropy of the plaintext and the result of the compression won't be obsolete: the result with the correct guess could be larger than the result with an incorrect guess. Alternatively, we could vary with control the results of the Lempel-Ziv compression. This will provide us the same effect: $l_{\hat{x}_0 \neq s_t} \geq l_{\hat{x}_0=s_t}$.

Remark. Shannon's entropy is defined to be the number of bits needed to represent the information. By this definition, since compression removed all the redundancy, the entropy of the compressed text must be smaller than the entropy of the original plaintext. The information that could not be compressed is shared between the plaintext and the compressed plaintext, and this information is mutual information. If we add randomization to the compression algorithm, the entropy of the compressed text would not decrease as much, thus, increasing the mutual information, making the length of the compressed text unpredictable. This unpredictability will hinder the attacker from doing a compressed side-channel attack.

Model Elements. Before defining our models, we first look at some implementations that are used in the models.

Pseudorandom Sequence Generator (PRSG). Our three schemes below use the same pseudorandom sequence generator, PRSG, which generates a sequence of 0's and 1's. In our simulation, PRSG is constructed based on the random number generator in Python 2.7 that uses the Mersenne Twister algorithm to generate a floating number in the range of 0 to 1 exclusively. The floating numbers has 53-bit precision floats and a period of $2^{19937} - 1$. Note that Mersenne twister is not cryptographic secure [12]. However, in real world applications, it should use de Bruijn Generator or WG-8 (see Sect. 2.2).

Weighted Generator. We implemented a weighted pseudo-random number generator that generates an uneven number of 0s and 1s. Specifially, the PRNG outputs 10% 1's and 90% 0's. Since the Mersenne Twister random number generator from Python can output a random floating number between 0 and 1, we take this floating number to determine whether to output 0 or 1. If the number is bigger than a given *ratio*, 0.1 for example, then our generator outputs 0, and 1 otherwise.

The ratio must not stay 10% for each compression. It must vary or else the stronger compression side-channel attack works. We modify the ratio before compressing each file. First, our custom PRNG takes the original *ratio* (10%) specified by the user during initialization. Then, the *ratio* would get adjusted between *ratio* − 0.01 and *ratio* + 0.01, with probability of a Gaussian distribution. For our case with 10% as the base ratio, this will vary in the range of 9% to 11% in a Gaussian fashion. This Gaussian variation is done using the Python `random.gauss` function: another floating number is generated between 0 and 1 with Gaussian distribution with a mean of 0.5 and a standard deviation of 0.25, then its value decreases by 0.5 to make it between −0.5 and 0.5, and then multiplied by 0.02 to make its value between −0.01 and 0.01, finally this number gets added to our original 10% to get a variation of 0.01%.

Weak Stream Cipher. We are using a weak stream cipher to increase the entropy of a file without modifying it too much. It uses our custom PRNG as bit-stream input. It then performs XOR operation with the input file. The original message is only transformed by little due to uneven distribution of 0's and 1's.

Lempel-Ziv77. The Lempel-Ziv77 compression algorithm is implemented in Python 2.7. Just as described in Algorithm 1, a sliding window is created before the current character, and for each character, the algorithm would look for the longest sequence that matches within the sliding window.

Randomized Lempel-Ziv Models. By adding a pseudo-random number generator, we designed three models to add randomness to a simple Lempel-Ziv77.

Scheme 1: Weak Cipher with Lempel-Ziv77. For this method, we first process the text by passing it through a weak stream cipher before applying compression, shown in Sect. 3.2. Since each message will have a different entropy, they will all compress differently. So the transmitted message that has the shortest length may not contain the forged token with the correct guess since its entropy may be higher than a message with an incorrect guess due to the addition of the weak cipher.

The weak cipher is based on our PRSG. We changed the ratio from 10% to 1.308% because we want 10% of the characters inside the plain-text to be changed. The 1.308% came from $1 - \sqrt[8]{0.9}$, because each character are 8 bits and we want the 8 bits to be all 0's 90% of the time. Note in [2], the authors also proposed to use weak cipher as one of the countermeasures to the compression side-channel attacks, but neither analysis nor experiments are given (Fig. 1).

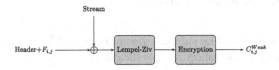

Fig. 1. Diagram of weak cipher with Lempel-Ziv

Scheme 2: Lempel-Ziv with Control. The idea behind Lempel-Ziv With Control, LZWC, Fig. 2, is to repeat some of the output tuples of Lempel-ZIv in order to mask the real length of the compressed output. A random stream of bits, r, will be needed. Each of the outputs of Lempel-ZIv will be matched with a bit in the stream r: when the bit is 1, then the output will be duplicated, or else nothing happens.

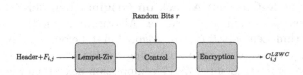

Fig. 2. Diagram of Lempel-Ziv with control

Scheme 3: Lempel-Ziv with Control and Feedback. This method aims to add even more randomness around the Lempel-Ziv compression step to prevent compression side-channel information leakage, Fig. 3. First, the plain-text is passed through a Lempel-Ziv77 compression algorithm. Then, some of its results are duplicated the same way as LZWC did. Afterwards, the result would get decompressed, then compressed again with Lempel-Ziv77.

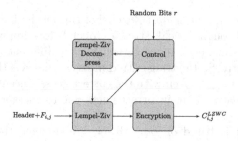

Fig. 3. Diagram of Lempel-Ziv with control and feedback

3.3   Simulation Results for Randomized LZ Models

We programmed our three compression schemes in Python2.7 and tested them against compression side-channel attacks.

Testing Environment. The simulated compression side-channel attack is run on our server that has the following specifications.

Processors	80
CPU	Intel(R) E7-L8867 @ 2.13 GHz
RAM	529105932 kB

The attack alongside the schemes are implemented in Python 2.7. The HTTP header used to do the tests is the same as above, but with different secrets. We ran the attack on 6 different header files, each one with a different secret.

Compression Side-Channel Attack on Original Lempel-Ziv77. We ran the compression side-channel attack, i.e. Algorithm 2, on the original compression algorithm Lempel-Ziv77, i.e. Algorithm 1 before encryption. Just as described abo, a forged token with a guessing character was added to the plaintext, which goes through Lempel-Ziv77 compression next; then the attack measures the length of the compressed texts and selects the shortest one to be the correct character. We were able to decode the secret within all the header files in a short amount of time.

Compression Side-Channel Attack on Lempel-Ziv77 with Randomization. The same attack was tested on plain-texts which went through Lempel-Ziv77 compression algorithm with addition of randomization. As expected, all three compression schemes prevented the attack: the attacker fails to guess the secret token within the HTTP header.

Compression Side-Channel Attack on Lempel-Ziv with Weak Cipher. The weak cipher that the plain-text goes through before being compressed increases the entropy of the message. Since the plain-text changed, some original repetitions did not happen. So the forged token might not match the real token. The length of the compressed text depends on how many repetitions that were kept. Thus, the attack does not succeed since this increase in entropy hides the exact length of the compressed plain-text.

Compression Side-Channel Attack on LZWC. By varying the output, the real length of the plain-text is also hidden. After the plain-text has been compressed, some of its output pairs are duplicated. This duplication is random and the plain-text with a correct forged token might have more duplicates than a plain-text with an incorrect forged token; thus, the incorrect guess will result in more outputs after the compression algorithm. This way, the attack will make a wrong guess, and won't be able to decode the secret.

Compression Side-Channel Attack on LZWCF. Similar to the previous scheme, this also prevents the compression side-channel attack. This scheme adds more randomization by feeding the output back into the compression algorithm, making the length of the compressed text even more random. Hence, this also prevents the attack.

4   Strong Compression Side-Channel Attack

The existing compression side-channel attack can be easily prevented if the victim employs one of the three aforementioned schemes. The randomness of the algorithm masks the length of the compressed files, which would be deterministic without any randomness involved. This way, the attacker cannot determine for certain that the shortest encrypted message has the correct guess. However, the methods cannot provide complete immunity against this strong compression side-channel attack described in this section.

4.1   Model and Analysis of Strong Compression Side-Channel Attack

A modified compression side-channel attack can still recover the token. We call this Strong Compression Side-Channel Attack (SCSCA), shown in Algorithm 3. The strong compression side-channel attack is similar to the normal one, Algorithm 2, but with a few differences listed below:

1. After compressing and encrypting the message, instead of sending only one single request for each character ζ_j, the adversary makes the victim send K requests per character, line 11. The adversary then collects the lengths of all K encrypted requests, and saves all of them in a new list T, shown in lines 14–15.

Algorithm 3. STRONG CSCA(*http_request*)

```
 1:  header ← HTTP header from http_request
 2:  known_prefix ← secret's prefix from adversary
 3:  guess_secret ← empty string of length  L  set by adversary
 4:  for i = 0 to i = secret_length  do
 5:      L ← empty list
 6:      for each ζ ∈ Σ do
 7:          guess_secret[i] ← ζ
 8:          g_ζ ← known_prefix||guess_secret
 9:          M_ζ ← header||g_ζ
10:          T ← empty list
11:          for j = 0 to j = K  do
12:              C_ζ ← Enc(LZ77(M_ζ))
13:              C_ζ gets sent over network
14:              l_ζ ← length(C_ζ)
15:              T.insert(l_ζ)
16:          end for
17:          L.insert(avg(T))
18:      end for
19:      guess_secret[i] ← {ζ|ζ = argmin_ζ{l_ζ ∈ L}}
20:  end for
21:  return  guess_secret
```

2. Then the adversary computes the average of all K messages that has the same guessing character ζ, and saves that average in the list L, shown in line 17.

   The last part is the same as the normal attack: the adversary chooses the character that gives the lowest average to be the guess character, shown in line 19.

4.2   Results from Simulation of Strong Compression Side-Channel Attack on Randomized LZ Models

The same testing environment, which was described above, was used to simulate a strong compression side-channel attack on our three randomized LZ models.

Strong Compression Side-Channel Attack on Randomized LZ Models. The modified LZ77 with randomization can successfully prevent a normal compression side-channel attack. In this section, we will see how they do against a strong compression side-channel attack.

Strong Compression Side-Channel Attack on LZ77 with Weak Cipher. In Fig. 4, the red line indicates the length of the compressed plain-text with a forged token with correct guess, and blue lines indicates the ones with incorrect guesses. We see that for most of the cases, the attack can hardly recover one character after 2000 requests. Thus, this scheme is capable of resisting against a strong compression side-channel attack.

Strong Compression Side-Channel Attack on LZWC. Unlike the previous scheme, this one does not resist the strong compression side-channel attack very well. From Fig. 5, 300 requests were enough to decode one character in most cases.

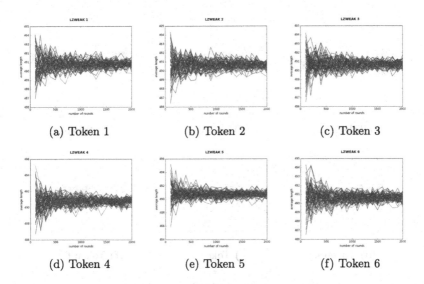

Fig. 4. Results of SCSCA on LZ with weak cipher

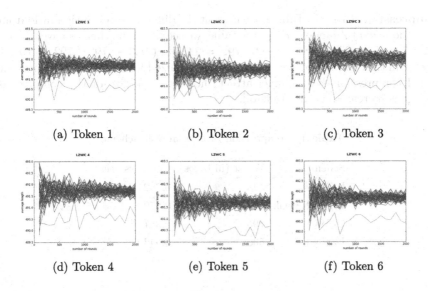

Fig. 5. Results of SCSCA on LZWC

Strong Compression Side-Channel Attack on LZWCF. The testing results of LZWCF are displayed in Fig. 6. As shown in the graphs, LZWCF does better than LZWC, but still cannot prevent the strong compression side-channel attack. To guess one correct character, 500 requests is usually enough.

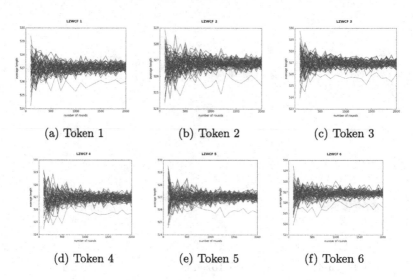

(a) Token 1   (b) Token 2   (c) Token 3

(d) Token 4   (e) Token 5   (f) Token 6

Fig. 6. Results of SCSCA on LZWCF

Compression Rate. In Table 1, we present the different compression ratio from our randomized LZ models. From the table, we see that our schemes have $(.879 - .792)/.792 = 11.0\%$, $(.881 - .792)/.792 = 11.2\%$, $(.943 - .792)/.792 = 19.1\%$ increase in the compressed size. Our three randomized LZ model schemes prevent normal compression side-channel attack, however, the size of the compressed message is increased as the trade-off.

Table 1. Compression ratio from each scheme

Scheme	Worst (in bytes)	Comp vs orig
LZ	445	0.792
LZ with weak	494	0.879
LZWC	495	0.881
LZWCF	530	0.943

Timing. The downside of strong compression side-channel attack is that it requires a long time to execute. In this section, we investigate the time it take to resolve one secret of length 228. During testing, the time to guess one character using iterations is also recorded. The Fig. 7 shows the average time it takes to append the forged token and to compress. The graphs explain the relative time across all three schemes. The scheme LZWC has the fastest time: 482 s for the attack with 2000 iterations. The two other schemes, LZWeak and LZWCF, are twice as slow: 837 and 949 s respectively for the same number of iterations.

Previously, we have seen that LZWeak requires more than 2000 requests, so to decode one secret, the attack needs $837 \times 228 = 190836\,\text{s} \approx 53\,\text{h}$ to decode one secret. For LZWC, 300 iterations take 72 s to execute, so the total time it takes is $72 \times 228 = 16416\,\text{s} \approx 5\,\text{h}$. For LZWCF, 500 iterations take 237 s to execute, so the total time taken would be $237 \times 228 = 54036\,\text{s} \approx 15\,\text{h}$. These hours are only the time it takes to compress, more hours will be added for encryption and transmission.

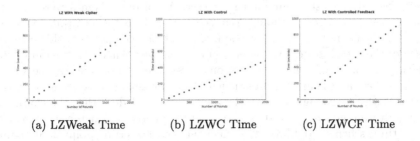

| (a) LZWeak Time | (b) LZWC Time | (c) LZWCF Time |

Fig. 7. Timing Graphs of SCSCA on Randomized LZ Models

4.3   Number of Requests

When performing the strong compression side-channel attack, we assumed that we can send an unlimited number of HTTP headers to the oracle, the server in this case. However, in practice, sending that many requests is easily detectable by the server. If the server sets a limit on the rate of requests a client can make, then it would nullify this strong compression side-channel attack. Thus, strong compression side-channel attack is only possible if the oracle allows an unlimited number of requests.

5   Summary, Conclusion and Future Work

An attacker can impersonate a client by using compression side-channel attack to retrieve the client's authentication token that is shared between the victim and the server. The authentication token is hidden inside the HTTP header, but when the header is compressed then encrypted, the attacker could retrieve this token. To respond to this type of attack, TLS/SSL will disable compression in its most recent version. We analysed the compression side-channel attack that brought the disabling of compression in SSL 1.3 protocol.

With the implementation of Lempel-Ziv77 compression algorithm and our own TLS/SSL, we simulated compression side-channel attack and successfully retrieved the secret inside an encrypted HTTP header.

We proposed three schemes to counter compression side-channel attack by adding randomization to Lempel-Ziv77 compression algorithm. Each of the three schemes adds randomization in different ways: the first scheme, Lempel-Ziv with weak cipher, changes few characters of the plaintext and then pass it to the Lempel-Ziv77 compression; the second scheme, Lempel-Ziv with Control, repeats some the outputs according to a random control bit stream; and finally, the third scheme, Lempel-Ziv with Control and Feedback, repeats some the outputs like the previous scheme, then decompress the outputs into a file then compressed the file again.

After implementing the three schemes, we tested them against compression side-channel attack using our internal server. All of our schemes were able to resist to the attack, even though our schemes reduce the compression rate. We also implemented a stronger version, called strong compression side-channel attack, of the attack to test robustness of our schemes. This attack requires the adversary to make multiple queries for one guess. From those queries, the adversary can collect all the indeterministic lengths and calculates the mean of all the lengths. With the average lengths, the adversary can deduce that the character with lowest average length must correspond to the actual character of the secret.

Our three schemes could resist to the attack until a certain point. Eventually, all our schemes fail to resist to the attack when the amount of requests is high. If an attacker launches this attack, then the Lempel-Ziv with Weak Cipher scheme requires more than 2000 requests to be sent per character, and this would require more than 53 h. For the Lempel-Ziv with Control, the secret would be safe for 5 h, and for Lempel-Ziv with Controlled Feedback, the secret couldn't be retrieved within less than 15 h.

The compression ratios of the three models did not decrease significantly: Lempel-Ziv with Weak Cipher model ratio increased by 11%; Lempel-Ziv with Control model increased by 11.2%; and Lempel-Ziv with Controlled Feedback increased by 19.1%. So, our models provides more security, but with a compression rate loss.

To conclude, TLS has disabled compression to prevent compression side-channel attacks for now. Our three models encourage TLS/SSL to re-enable compression to increase the flow of network traffic. These models can be implemented without much effort in the server and client: only an additional key is required to synchronize the randomization. Also, the required overhead time of our schemes is not as much compared to Lempel-Ziv77. It is relatively difficult to prevent the attack by preventing users from downloading malwares, but the application of our schemes will ensure that compression side-channel attack malwares remain ineffective. More focused work could be done in the future, which are summarized as follows.

A. Entropy Analysis. We fixed our bit-stream generator to generate 1's ten percent of the time, and 0 ninety percent of the time. We could analyse the ratio of our bit-stream generator in depth with other file types, since all HTTP headers have similar entropy. For instance, XML files have less entropy and could be better compressed than HTTP header by Lempel-Ziv77. By simulating the attack on our models with different file types, we can determine the best ratio for each file type. If we could establish relationships between file entropy and randomness required to prevent compression side-channel attack, then we could maximizing security while minimizing compression loss.

B. PermuLZ Implementation. We expect PermuLZ to resist the compression side-channel attack. When the file is being fragmented into blocks, the secret token is fragmented and the secret fragments are rearranged. Even if the adversary could retrieve all the secret fragments, to figure out the correct chronological fragment order has the same time complexity as a permutation of n elements, $O(n!)$. We also expect to reach a better compression ratio as our first scheme, Lempel-Ziv with weak cipher. The entropy of the plaintext may not vary as much. Shorter repeated strings could be found unchanged, but in different fragments, so file would still be compressed. However, longer repeated strings cannot be compressed as well as shorter strings, because they are fragmented, where as these would compress less. Overall, PermuLZ provides compression and security. It could be used as a possible solution in the future as a compression algorithm used prior to encryption.

Acknowledgements. The work was supported by NSERC SPG grants.

References

1. Rescorla, E.: The Transport Layer Security (TLS) protocol version 1.3 (draft). RFC TBD, RFC Editor, July 2017
2. Kelsey, J.: Compression and information leakage of plaintext. In: Daemen, J., Rijmen, V. (eds.) FSE 2002. LNCS, vol. 2365, pp. 263–276. Springer, Heidelberg (2002). https://doi.org/10.1007/3-540-45661-9_21
3. Duong, T., Rizzo, J.: The CRIME attack. In: Presentation at ekoparty Security Conference (2012)
4. Gluck, Y., Harris, N., Prado, A.: BREACH: reviving the CRIME attack. Unpublished manuscript (2013)
5. SSL Pulse: TLS Compression/CRIME, June 2019. https://www.ssllabs.com/ssl-pulse/
6. Ziv, J., Lempel, A.: Compression of individual sequences via variable-rate coding. IEEE Trans. Inf. Theory **24**(5), 530–536 (1978)
7. Rescorla, E.: HTTP over TLS. RFC 2818, RFC Editor, May 2000
8. Deutsch, P.: DEFLATE compressed data format specification version 1.3. RFC 1951, RFC Editor, May 1996
9. Deutsch, P.: GZIP file format specification version 4.3. RFC 1952, RFC Editor, May 1996
10. Golomb, S.W.: Shift register sequences: secure and limited-access code generators. Efficiency Code Generators, Prescribed Property Generators, Mathematical Models. World Scientific (2017)
11. Fan, X., Mandal, K., Gong, G.: WG-8: a lightweight stream cipher for resource-constrained smart devices. In: Singh, K., Awasthi, A.K. (eds.) QShine 2013. LNICST, vol. 115, pp. 617–632. Springer, Heidelberg (2013). https://doi.org/10.1007/978-3-642-37949-9_54

12. Matsumoto, M., Nishimura, T.: Mersenne twister: a 623-dimensionally equidistributed uniform pseudo-random number generator. ACM Trans. Model. Comput. Simul. (TOMACS) **8**(1), 3–30 (1998)
13. Rijmen, V., Daemen, J.: Advanced encryption standard. In: Proceedings of Federal Information Processing Standards Publications, pp. 19–22. National Institute of Standards and Technology (2001)
14. Chen, L., Gong, G.: Communication System Security. CRC Press, Boca Raton (2012)
15. Gong, G., Youssef, A.M.: Cryptographic properties of the Welch-Gong transformation sequence generators. IEEE Trans. Inf. Theory **48**(11), 2837–2846 (2002)
16. Diffie, W., Hellman, M.: New directions in cryptography. IEEE Trans. Inf. Theory **22**(6), 644–654 (1976)
17. Cover, T.M., Thomas, J.A.: Elements of Information Theory. Wiley, Hoboken (2012)
18. Hollenbeck, S.: Transport layer security protocol compression methods. RFC 3749, RFC Editor, May 2004
19. Ziv, J., Lempel, A.: A universal algorithm for sequential data compression. IEEE Trans. Inf. Theory **23**(3), 337–343 (1977)

Secure Logging with Security Against Adaptive Crash Attack

Sepideh Avizheh[✉], Reihaneh Safavi-Naini, and Shuai Li

University of Calgary, Calgary, AB, Canada
`sepideh.avizheh1@ucalgary.ca`

Abstract. Logging systems are an essential component of security systems and their security has been widely studied. Recently (2017) it was shown that existing secure logging protocols are vulnerable to *crash attack* in which the adversary modifies the log file and then crashes the system to make it indistinguishable from a normal system crash. The attacker was assumed to be non-adaptive and not be able to see the file content before modifying and crashing it (which will be immediately after modifying the file). The authors also proposed a system called SLiC that protects against this attacker. In this paper, we consider an (insider) adaptive adversary who can see the file content as new log operations are performed. This is a powerful adversary who can attempt to rewind the system to a past state. We formalize security against this adversary and introduce a scheme with provable security. We show that security against this attacker requires some (small) protected memory that can become accessible to the attacker after the system compromise. We show that existing secure logging schemes are insecure in this setting, even if the system provides some protected memory as above. We propose a novel mechanism that, in its basic form, uses a pair of keys that evolve at different rates, and employ this mechanism in an existing logging scheme that has forward integrity to obtain a system with provable security against adaptive (and hence non-adaptive) crash attack. We implemented our scheme on a desktop computer and a Raspberry Pi, and showed in addition to higher security, a significant efficiency gain over SLiC.

Keywords: Secure logging · Crash attack · Adaptive attack · Forward security

1 Introduction

Computer systems use logging function to store and keep track of important events in the system. Log files are used for a variety of purposes including trouble shooting, intrusion detection and forensics [1, 7, 9]. In many cases, adversaries want to stay covert and be able to modify the log files without being detected. Thus, integrity of log data is essential, and protecting the log files against tampering and modification has been an active area of research. The simplest form

© Springer Nature Switzerland AG 2020
A. Benzekri et al. (Eds.): FPS 2019, LNCS 12056, pp. 137–155, 2020.
https://doi.org/10.1007/978-3-030-45371-8_9

of protection is to store each log entry with the corresponding message authentication code (MAC), and with a key that is unique to the entry to ensure the entries cannot be permuted [3]. One cannot expect any protection after the time of system compromise: the attacker is assumed to have access to the system, algorithms, and the keys at the compromise time (full state of the system) and can add any log that they desire afterwards. Thus the goal of protection is maintaining integrity of the past logs. This is called *forward security* or *forward integrity* [3] and is achieved by evolving forward (using a one-way function) the key that is used for generating integrity information of log entries. In [13], authors used forward integrity based on MAC and hash chains and proposed a secure audit log for a local untrusted logging device that has infrequent communication with the verifier. LogCrypt [8] made some improvement to [13] such as the ability to use public key cryptography as well as aggregating multiple log entries to reduce latency and computational load. Forward integrity, however, does not protect against truncating of the log file: the adversary can remove entries at the end without being detected. This attack can be protected against by including an aggregate MAC (signature) to the file, proposed in [10,11], through the notion of forward-secure sequential aggregate authentication. The authentication data (tag) per log entry is sequentially aggregated and the individual tag is removed.

When a system crash happens, the data that are stored in caches (temporary memories) will be erased or become unreliable. Caches may include new log entries and updates to the stored log entries, so a crash would result in the loss of new entries, that have not been stored yet, and inconsistency of existing ones. This provides a window of opportunity for attackers to modify the log file and remain undetected by crashing the system. Crash attack was introduced by Blass and Noubir [6]. They showed that all existing secure log systems are vulnerable to this attack. Blass and Noubir formalized the security notion of crash integrity using a game between the adversary and a challenger, and proposed a system, SLiC, that provides protection in this model. SLiC encrypts and permutes the log entries so that they are unknown to a non-adaptive adversary who gets only one time read and tampering access to the system.

Our Work: We consider a secure logging system that uses an initial key (that is shared with the verifier) to generate authenticated log entries that are stored in the log file. We assume an (insider) *adaptive crash adversary* who can adaptively choose the messages that will be logged and can see the log file after each logging operation. The goal of the adversary is to remove and/or tamper with the logged elements. We show that without other assumptions and by the verifier only using their secret key, it is impossible to provide security against adaptive crash attack (please see full version of the paper[1] for details). We thus assume the system stores (and evolves) its keys in a small protected memory, that will become accessible to the adversary after the system is compromised. Such a memory can be implemented using trusted hardware modules whose content will not be observable during the normal operation of the system, but can become accessible

---

[1] Available online at https://arxiv.org/abs/1910.14169.

if the system crashes. We formalize security and show that SLiC is insecure in this model and an adversary who can see the intermediate states of the log file can successfully *rewind* the system to a previous state.

Adaptive Crash Resistance: We introduce a *double evolving key mechanism* which, in the nutshell, uses two keys, one evolving with each log event and one evolving at random intervals, that reduces the success chance of crash attack even if the adversary is adaptive. The keys become available after the system compromise but the random interval evolution limits the success probability of the adversary to successfully rewind the system to a previous state. We analyze this system in our proposed model and prove its security against an adaptive attacker. This mechanism can be extended to multiple independent keys evolving at different rates to enhance the security guarantee of the system. We implemented double evolving key mechanism on a windows PC and Raspberry PI and compared the results with those reported for SLiC [6], showing significantly improved time-efficiency.

Discussion: The double evolving key mechanism keeps the logged events in plaintext and provides an elegant and very efficient solution against non-adaptive crash attack. SLiC, the only secure logging system with security against (non-adaptive) crash attack, provides security by encrypting and permuting elements of the log file. This makes access to logged data extremely inefficient: one needs to reverse the encryption and permutation to access the required element. For functionalities such as searching for a pattern or keyword, this means recovering the whole log file which is impractical. The comparison of the two systems is further discussed in Sect. 5.

Organization: Section 2 gives the background; Sect. 3, describes adaptive crash model and its relation to non-adaptive case. Section 4 proposes the double evolving key mechanism and Sect. 5 is on the security and complexity analysis of our scheme. Section 6 explains the implementation, and Sect. 7 concludes the paper.

2   Preliminaries

We use the system model of Blass et al. [6] which models many systems that are used in practice, and focus on the settings where the verifier is mostly offline and checks the log file once in a while (infrequently).

An *event* m_i is a bit string that is stored in the log file together with an authentication tag h_i, such as $h_i = HMAC_{k_i}(m_i)$. The key k_i is for authentication of the ith log entry and is generated from an initial seed. The key k_i is evolved to k_{i+1} for $(i+1)^{th}$ entry and k_i is removed. Using a different key for each element protects not only against reordering, but also ensures that if the key is leaked, past keys cannot be obtained and past entries cannot be changed. A common way of evolving a key is by using a *pseudorandom function family* $PRF_k(.)$ indexed by a set of keys [3], that is, $k_{i+1} = PRF_{k_i}(\chi)$, where χ is a constant. The security guarantee of a PRF family, informally, stated as follows: a function that is chosen randomly from the PRF family cannot be distinguished from a random oracle (a function whose outputs are chosen at random), using an efficient algorithm, with significant advantage. To protect against *truncation attack* where the adversary removes the last t elements of the log file, one can add an aggregate hash $h_{i+1} = HMAC_{k_{i+1}}(m_{i+1}, h_i)$ and delete h_i, or use an *aggregate signature* where signatures generated by a single signer are sequentially combined. If verification of aggregate signature is successful, all the single signatures are valid; otherwise, at least one single signature is invalid.

In all these schemes, the event sequence order in the log file remains the same as the original event sequence, and the verification requires only an original seed from which the key for the rest of the system can be reconstructed. Crash attack uses this property and the fact that a crash will remove all the new events and a number of the stored events that must be updated, so it makes parts of the log file, including the stored keys, inconsistent. This possibility in a crash can be exploited by the adversary to launch a successful truncation attack. Blass et al. system, called SLiC [6], protects against crash attack by encrypting each stored log entry (so makes them indistinguishable from random), and uses a randomized mapping that permutes the order of the log entries on the log file using a pseudorandom number generator (PRG). Informally, a PRG uses a seed to generate a sequence of numbers that is indistinguishable from a random sequence. Using the PRG, the order of stored events in the log file will appear "random" to the adversary who does not know the PRG seed and so truncation attack is prevented. This protection however will not work against an adaptive attacker who will be able to see the result of storing a new event, and by comparing the new re-ordered log file with the previous one learn the places that can be tampered with (see Sect. 3.3 for details of the attack).

As outlined above, storing a new event and its authentication data will result in the update of some existing entries in the log file. In particular, to update a stored value x to x', the following steps will happen: (i) read x and compute x', (ii) store x', and (iii) delete x. However the last two steps may be re-ordered by the operating system, so when a crash happens, the state of the update will become unknown: that is x has been deleted and x' has not been written yet. This reordering would result in inconsistency during the log verification. When a crash happens, the data in the cache becomes unreliable and the verification of the log file requires not only the initial seed, but also an estimate of the part of the log file that is verifiable. Similar situation can happen in the update of keys, resulting in both k_{i-1} and k_i to become unavailable for the system recovery. The goal of the verifier is to recover the largest verifiable log sequence from the crashed system.

3   System and Adversary Model

We first give an overview of our system and the adversary model. There are three entities: (1) a logging device $\mathcal{L}$, (2) a verifier $\mathcal{V}$, and (3) an adversary $\mathcal{A}$.

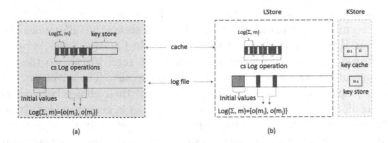

Fig. 1. (a) Non-adaptive adversary, (b) Adaptive adversary. The shadowed parts are invisible to adversary before compromising the system.

Logging device $\mathcal{L}$, stores the event sequence and current keys using the following types of storages: (i) LStore is a disk (long term storage) that stores log events. This disk can be read by the attacker when the system is compromised. (ii) Log cache is a temporary memory that is used for the update of the LStore. (iii) KStore is the key disk that is used to store current keys of the system. This is a non-volatile memory that will become available to the adversary when the system crashes. KStore uses a protected cache for its update. The state of the logging device after m_i is logged, is specified by $\Sigma_i = [\Sigma_i^K, \Sigma_i^L, Cache_i]$, where Σ_i^L, Σ_i^K and $Cache_i = \{cache_i^L, cache_i^K\}$ are the states of the LStore, the KStore and their caches, respectively, after m_i is logged.

The *log operation* $Log(\Sigma_{i-1}, m_i)$ takes the state Σ_{i-1}, and the log event m_i, uses the cache as a temporary storage, and updates LStore for the storage of the (processed) log event. This operation uses KStore cache to update the keys in the KStore. We assume this cache only holds the required data for updating k_{i-1} to k_i that is used in $Log(\Sigma_{i-1}, m_i)$. This assumption is used to estimate the amount of key information that will be unreliable after a crash. We also assume that KStore has enough size to hold the current key k_i. The $Log(\Sigma_{i-1}, m_i)$ operation, (i) generates a set of write operations $\{o(m_u) \cdots o(m_v)\}$, which we denote with $\mathcal{O}^{Log}(\Sigma_{i-1}, m_i)$, on the LStore (i.e. Σ_i^L and its associated cache are updated), and (ii) updates KStore (i.e. Σ_i^K and its cache are updated). A disk write operation $o(m_i)$ (we call it a log file entry) writes m_i together with its authentication data to the disk. The initial states of LStore and KStore are denoted by Σ_0^K and Σ_0^L, respectively. Σ_0^L contains an initial event that is used to detect complete deletion of the disk. Σ_0^K contains the initial keys of the system. As log events are processed, the states of the two storage systems will be updated in concert: after n log operations, the length of Σ_0^L is n, and the length of Σ_0^K is unchanged, but the content has been updated to the new values. The initial state of the system Σ_0 will be securely stored and later used for verification.

Adversary, $\mathcal{A}$, (i) adaptively generates events that will be processed by the $Log(\cdot, \cdot)$ operation of $\mathcal{L}$; $\mathcal{A}$ can see LStore and its cache after each $Log(\cdot, \cdot)$ operation; (ii) compromises $\mathcal{L}$ and accesses KStore and its cache, and modifies the state of $\mathcal{L}$, and finally crashes the system. The goal of the crash adversary is to modify the LStore and KStore such that a verifier who uses the initial state of the system, and the crashed state cannot detect the attack. In Sect. 3.3, we define our security game using this model. Figure 1 shows the differences between our adversarial model and that of Blass et al. [6]. In Fig. 1(a) $Log(\cdot, \cdot)$ operation generates disk writes in the cache first, which are then written to the log file. The system current key resides in the system cache also. The adversary can use the $Log(\cdot, \cdot)$ operation on the message sequence of their choice but cannot see the intermediate results of logging until the system is compromised. It is easy to see that in this model it is impossible to provide security if the adversary is given access to the system after each $Log(\cdot, \cdot)$ operation: the adversary observes the current key and can simply use it to generate any arbitrary log event and later write it in the log file without being detected. Figure 1(b) shows our model.

We will not consider the case that the adversary adds new entries to LStore: this can always be done undetectably because the adversary knows the content of the KStore after the compromise. We however require that the log events that have been stored "before the time of the compromise (crash)", remain untouched.

Verifier, $\mathcal{V}$, uses $Recover(\cdot, \cdot)$ algorithm that takes the current state of the logging system, and the initial state Σ_0, and outputs either the list of consistently stored events, or $\perp$ which indicates untrusted log.

3.1   Logging Protocols

A logging protocol Π consists of three algorithms:

1. $Gen(1^\lambda)$: Gen takes a security parameter λ and outputs the initial state, $\Sigma_0 = [\Sigma_0^L, \Sigma_0^K, Cache_0 = \emptyset]$, and will be stored securely for future use by the verifier $\mathcal{V}$. The initial state includes: (i) Σ_0^L which is initialized securely to protect against complete removal of the log file, (ii) Σ_0^K stores the initial seed keys, and (iii) $Cache_0 = \{cache_0^L, cache_0^K\}$ are initially empty.
2. $Log(\Sigma_{i-1}, m_i)$: Let $\Sigma_{i-1} = [\Sigma_{i-1}^K, \Sigma_{i-1}^L, Cache]$ be the current state after $i - 1$ sequence of events are logged. For an event $m_i \in \{0, 1\}^*$, and the current state Σ_{i-1}, the operation $Log(\cdot, \cdot)$ outputs, either a new state Σ_i, or a special state Σ_i^{cr}, called a *crashed state*. A non-crashed state is a *valid state* that is the result of using $Log(\cdot, \cdot)$ consecutively on a sequence of log events. If $Log(\cdot, \cdot)$ outputs a crashed state, the device $\mathcal{L}$ has been crashed and needs to be initialized.
3. $Recover(\Sigma, \Sigma_0)$: Receives an initial state Σ_0 and a (possibly crashed) state Σ, and verifies if it is an untampered state that has resulted from Σ_0 through consecutive invocation of $Log(\cdot, \cdot)$. $Recover(\Sigma, \Sigma_0)$ reconstructs the longest sequence of events in the LStore that pass the system integrity checks, or outputs $\perp$ which indicates an untrusted log. If Σ had been obtained from Σ_0 by consecutive applications of n $Log(\cdot, \cdot)$, then $Recover(\Sigma, \Sigma_0)$ will output the n logged events. Otherwise the set, $\mathcal{R}$, of recovered events consists of $n' < n$ pairs $\mathcal{R} = \{(\rho_1, m_1'), ..., (\rho_{n'}, m_{n'}')\}$. If one of $m_j' \neq m_{\rho_j}$, the adversary has been able to successfully modify a log entry. For example the correct pair with $\rho_i = 4$ will have $m_i' = m_4$. We use n and n' to denote the length of the logged sequence before crash, and the highest index of the log file seen by

$Recover(\cdot, \cdot)$. The input state Σ to $Recover(\cdot, \cdot)$ can be: (i) a valid state of the form $(Log(Log(...Log(\Sigma_0, m_1)...), m_n)$, so $Recover(\cdot, \cdot)$ outputs, $\{(1, m_1), ..., (n, m_n)\}$; (ii) a state which is the result of a normal crash, so $Recover(\cdot, \cdot)$ outputs, $(\rho_1, m_1'), \cdots (\rho_{n'}, m_{n'}')$ where $n' < n$; (iii) a state which is neither of the above, so $Recover(\cdot, \cdot)$ outputs $\bot$, and a modified (forged) or missing event is detected.

Efficiency: To support high frequency logging and resource constrained hardware, $Log(., .)$ is required to be an efficient algorithm.

3.2 Cache

We use (a parameter) cache size cs, first introduced in [6], to estimate the effect of crash when recovering the log file. cs is the maximum number of log events that will be lost during a normal crash. This number can be estimated for a particular implementation (e.g., taking into account the caches of operating system, file system, hard disk, ...), and allows us to estimate the maximum length of unreliable log events.

Logging the event m_i will generate a set of disk write operations, $\mathcal{O}^{Log}(\Sigma_{i-1}, m_i) = \{o(m_u), ..., o(m_v)\}$, that will add a new entry to the LStore and may update a number of other entries. If $\mathcal{L}$ crashes before $Log(\Sigma_{i-1}, m_i)$ completes, all $o(m_j) \in \mathcal{O}^{Log}(\Sigma_{i-1}, m_i)$ will be lost. This is because all these operations are in cache. For simplicity, we assume the KStore stores the key k_j which is used in constructing $o(m_j)$ only. To perform $Log(\Sigma_{i-1}, m_i)$, each $o(m_j) \in \mathcal{O}^{Log}(\Sigma_{i-1}, m_i)$ will be processed once at a time (the argument can be extended to the case that KStore is larger). If crash happens, the k_j that is being updated will also become unreliable. The notion of expendable set, first introduced in [6], captures the *LStore* entries that are considered unreliable when a crash happens.

Definition 1 (Expendable set). Let Σ_n be a valid state comprising events $\{m_1, ..., m_n\}$, and $Cache_n = \emptyset$. Let $Cache_{n'}$ be the content of cache after $\mathcal{L}$ adds events $(m_{n+1}, ..., m_{n'})$ using the $Log(\cdot, \cdot)$ operation. An event m_i is expendable in state $\Sigma_{n'}$, iff $(o(m_i) \in \{O^{Log}(\Sigma_n, m_{n+1}) \cup \cdots \cup O^{Log}(\Sigma_{n'-1}, m_{n'})\}) \wedge (o(m_i) \in Cache_{n'})$. The set of all expendable log entries is denoted by $ExpSet$.

The definition identifies $o(m_i)$s that are in the expendable set assuming the first and the last state of the cache are known. In practice however, the verifier receives a log file of size n' (events) and without knowing the final state of the system must decide on the length of the file that has reliable data. If the cache can hold cs events, then we consider $2cs$ events (the interval $[n - cs + 1, n + cs]$) as expendable set. This is the set of events who could have resided in the cache when crash occurs. Note that logging an event may generate more that one disk write operation that could be the update of the earlier entries in the log file. The following proposition summarizes the discussion above.

Proposition 1. *(Determining expendable set).* *Let $\Sigma_{n'}$ be the state of the system after logging $m_1, \cdots, m_{n'}$. An event m_i is expendable in a state $\Sigma_{n'}$, where n' is the highest index of a log entry in the LStore[2],*
if $o(m_i) \in \{O^{Log}(\Sigma_{n'-cs}, m_{n'-cs+1}) \cup \cdots \cup O^{Log}(\Sigma_{n'+cs-1}, m_{n'+cs})\}$ and possibly $o(m_i) \in Cache_{n'}$. The set of all expendable log entries in the recovered state $\Sigma_{n'}$ is: $ExpSet = \{m_i : m_i$ is expendable in $\Sigma_{n'}\}$.

Proof. We assume cache can hold up to cs log events. These events, (i) may all be events after n'; that is, from $Log(\Sigma_{n'}, m_{n'+1}) \cup \cdots \cup Log(\Sigma_{n'+cs-1}, m_{n'+cs})$, events $[(n'+1, o(m_{n'+1})), \ldots, (n'+cs, o(m_{n'+cs}))]$ may have been lost, and other disk write events may not have been completed, or (ii) the writing is incomplete, so the logging of up to cs events before n' will have incomplete disk write and $Log(\Sigma_{n'-cs}, m_{n'-cs+1}) \cup \cdots \cup Log(\Sigma_{n'-1}, m_{n'})$ have been damaged, or (iii) a random set of cs events in $Log(\Sigma_{n'-cs}, m_{n'-cs+1}) \cup \cdots \cup Log(\Sigma_{n'+cs-1}, m_{n'+cs})$ have been lost. Therefore, all the log events in the range $[n' - cs + 1, n' + cs]$ is considered to be expendable set.

3.3   Security Definition

The effect of crash on the system in general depends on the hardware, and is abstracted by the cache size parameter cs. Our new security definition for adaptive crash attack is given in Algorithm 1. We define a security game between the challenger and an adversary $\mathcal{A}$ that has access to the following oracles.

Gen oracle: $GEN_Q()$ allows the adversary $\mathcal{A}$ to initialize a log on $\mathcal{L}$. $\mathcal{C}$ runs $Gen(1^\lambda)$ and returns the initial state of LStore $\Sigma_0^{\prime L}$ and its associated cache $cache_0^{\prime L}$. The state Σ_0' is stored in the set Q that records the log queries made by the adversary.

Log oracle: $LOG_{\Sigma, Q}()$, is a stateful function, which allows the adversary $\mathcal{A}$ to adaptively log events on $\mathcal{L}$: the adversary chooses a message m to be logged, $\mathcal{C}$ runs $Log(\cdot, \cdot)$, and returns, $\Sigma^{\prime L}$ (state of the LStore) and the $cache^{\prime L}$ (state of the cache) to $\mathcal{A}$. The state Σ' is stored in the set Q.

Recover oracle: $REC_\Sigma()$, is a stateful function, that can be called in any state by $\mathcal{A}$. To respond, $\mathcal{C}$ runs $Recover(\Sigma, \Sigma_0)$ and returns the recovered set $\mathcal{R}$ which can be either $\perp$ or $\{(\rho_1, m_1'), \cdots, (\rho_{n'}, m_{n'}')\}$.

Crash oracle: $CRASH_\Sigma()$, is a stateful function, that can be called by $\mathcal{A}$ on any state Σ and allows $\mathcal{A}$ to learn the effect of crash on the system by accessing the complete state Σ of the system including the KStore. $CRASH_\Sigma()$ returns Σ^{cr} as the state of the logging device $\mathcal{L}$.

---

[2] Note that this LStore may be the result of normal logging operation, or after a crash.

In Algorithm 1, the first stage is for adversary to learn. $\mathcal{A}$ gets oracle access to all the functions mentioned above and chooses n messages to log. Challenger $\mathcal{C}$, generates the initial keys and initializes the $KStore$, $LStore$, and the $Cache$. At this stage, adversary has oracle access to $GEN_Q()$, $LOG_{\Sigma,Q}()$ and $CRASH_\Sigma()$. $\mathcal{A}$ adaptively issues n log queries, $m_1 \ldots m_n$, to $LOG_{\Sigma,Q}()$ oracle. The oracle executes $Log(\Sigma, m)$ for each message and returns the LStore and $cache'^L$ of the resulting state Σ' to adversary. Σ' is stored in the queried set Q. After n calls to $Log(\cdot, \cdot)$, $\mathcal{A}$ calls $CRASH_\Sigma()$, gets full access to the LStore, KStore and Cache, which all will be tampered as desired, and then crashes the system. Adversary outputs a sequence of ℓ positions α_i, where $\alpha_i \in [1, n]$, none of which correspond to the index of an element in the expendable set, assuming n is the highest index in LStore seen by the verifier. The algorithm $Recover(\cdot, \cdot)$ outputs a sequence of $n' < n$ index-event pairs $\{(\rho_i, m'_i)\}$. Intuitively, the adversary wins if, (i) one of their outputted indexes appear in $\mathcal{R}$ with a value different from the original logged sequence (i.e. changed by the adversary), (ii) one of the outputted indexes does not appear in $\mathcal{R}$ (i.e. deleted by the adversary), or (ii) the recovered list $\mathcal{R}$ matches the LStore of one of the queried states.

Definition 2 (Crash Integrity). A logging protocol $\Pi = (Gen, Log, Recover)$ provides $f(\lambda)$-crash integrity against adaptive adversary $\mathcal{A}$, iff for all PPT[3] adversaries there exist a negligible function $f(\cdot)$ such that:

$$Pr[Exp_{A,\Pi}^{AdapCr}(1^\lambda, cs)] \leq f(\lambda).$$

3.4   Impossibility Result

Existing secure log schemes, i.e. [3,8,11,13], consider an ordered log where a new log entry is appended to the end of LStore. These schemes use key evolution but do not use secure hardware or platforms to store the latest secret key that captures the state of the log file. Nor do they rely on a trusted third party to safeguard this information. These protocols are vulnerable to non-adaptive crash attack [6] because adversary knows the order of log entries, can truncate the log file and delete the keys, leaving the system in a stateless situation, which makes it impossible to distinguish a crash attack from a normal crash. SLiC, is the only known crash tolerant scheme [6] which masks the order of elements in the log file by encrypting them and applying a random permutation on the location of log entries in the LStore. However, it cannot protect against rewinding in an adaptive adversarial model. All existing schemes, including SLiC, are vulnerable to adaptive crash attack even considering a protected KStore according to our model. This is because the KStore can be undetectably removed or modified when the system is compromised and this will again put the logging system in a state that is indistinguishable from a normal crash.

---

[3] Probabilistic Polynomial Time.

In another words, a logging system that cannot *reliably* protect its state information during logging operation, and assuming an adaptive adversary who can see the LStore, is subject to rewinding. We note that $Exp_{\mathcal{A},\Pi}^{AdapCr}()$ is stronger than $Exp_{\mathcal{A},\Pi,Crash}^{CrInt}()$ game [6]. This can be proved by showing two claims. Claim 1: if a non-adaptive adversary $\mathcal{A}_{na}$ is successful in breaking a scheme, an adaptive adversary $\mathcal{A}_a$ will also succeed with at least the same probability. This implies that all existing schemes [3,8,11,13] are vulnerable to adaptive crash. Claim 2: SLiC that is secure against a non-adaptive adversary cannot protect against rewinding. These two arguments are formalized in the full version of the paper.

4   An Adaptive Crash Recovery Scheme

The above impossibility result shows that if no key information can be trusted after the crash, it will not be possible to distinguish between an accidental crash and a crash attack. One may use an external reliable storage such as blockchain [2,14]. In such an approach, the blockchain stores data that will allow the recovery algorithm to detect a crash state. Such a solution has challenges including the need for a high rate of access to blockchain. Our goal is to design a solution without using an external point of trust.

4.1   The Proposed Scheme

We build the basis of our protocol close to the PRF-chain FI-MAC protocol of Bellare and Yee [3]. We assume that each log event is appended to the end of the log with an authentication tag, a HMAC. We use PRF to evolve the keys needed for HMAC. Multiple keys can be used in our scheme to prevent rewinding, but for simplicity, we describe the mechanism with a pair of keys as below:

Double Evolving Key Mechanism. To prevent rewinding, we generate two key sequences that are evolved with different rates. One of the keys evolves per log entry to prevent re-ordering and log modification, and guarantees forward security. We call this key as sequential key. The second key, which is called state-controlled key, is updated slower relative to the first key at random points of time. This key is used to reduce the probability that key is removed from the disk after a normal crash. For each log entry, we use a choice function $CF()$ which receives the index of the new log entry and the current state-controlled key $CF(k'_{j-1}, i)$ and outputs 0 or 1. If the output is 0 we use the sequential evolving key and if it is 1 we use state-controlled key to compute the HMAC.

We require that state-controlled key evolves randomly, so attacker cannot guess or estimate the positions that KStore is updated. For this, we use a choice function $CF()$ which gets a random input and outputs 0 or 1. Thus, $CF()$ has the following properties: (i) by observing the input/output of $CF()$, adversary

Algorithm 1. $Exp_{\mathcal{A},\Pi}^{AdapCr}(1^\lambda, cs)$:

1: $(m_1, m_2, \ldots, m_n) \leftarrow \mathcal{A}(1^\lambda, GEN_Q(), LOG_{\Sigma,Q}(), REC_\Sigma(), CRASH_\Sigma())$
2: $\Sigma_0 \leftarrow Gen(1^\lambda)$
    $// \Sigma_0 = [\Sigma_0^K, \Sigma_0^L, Cache_0]$
3: $(\Sigma^{cr}, \alpha_1, \ldots, \alpha_\ell) \leftarrow \mathcal{A}^{GEN_Q(), LOG_{\Sigma,Q}(), CRASH_\Sigma()}(\Sigma_0^L, m_1, \ldots, m_n)$
    $// \Sigma^{cr} = [\Sigma^{cr,L}, \Sigma^{cr,K}, Cache^{cr}], \alpha_i \in [1, n]$
4: $\mathcal{R} \leftarrow Recover(\Sigma^{cr}, \Sigma_0)$
    $// \mathcal{R} = \bot$ or $\mathcal{R} = (\rho_1, m_1'), \ldots, (\rho_{n'}, m_{n'}')$
5: **if** $\mathcal{R} = \bot$ **then**
6:    Output $\bot$
7: **else if**
    $[\exists (\alpha_i, \rho_j) : (\alpha_i = \rho_j) \wedge (m_{\alpha_i} \neq m_j')] \vee$ $//Modify$
    $[\exists \alpha_i \notin ExpSet : \rho_j \neq \alpha_i, \forall j = 1, \ldots, n'] \vee$ $//Delete$
    $[\mathcal{R} = \Sigma'^L, \Sigma' \in Q]$ $//Rewind$
8:    Output $Success$ **then**
9: **end**

$//GEN$ runs $Gen(\cdot)$, returns Σ_0
$GEN_Q()$:
  $\Sigma_0' \leftarrow Gen(1^\lambda)$
  $Q \leftarrow Q \cup \Sigma_0'$
  Return $(\Sigma_0'^L, cache_0'^L)$

$//LOG$ runs $Log(\cdot, \cdot)$ on m,
returns the state of LStore and Cache
$LOG_{\Sigma,Q}(m)$:
  $\Sigma' \leftarrow Log(\Sigma, m)$
  $// \Sigma' = [\Sigma'^L, \Sigma'^K, Cache']$
  $Q \leftarrow Q \cup \Sigma'$
  Return $(\Sigma'^L, cache'^L)$

$//REC$ runs $Recover(\cdot, \cdot)$, returns $\mathcal{R}$
$REC_\Sigma()$:
  $\mathcal{R} \leftarrow Recover(\Sigma, \Sigma_0)$
  Return $\mathcal{R}$

$//CRASH$ crashes the $\mathcal{L}$, returns Σ^{cr}
$CRASH_\Sigma()$:
  Return (Σ^{cr})

cannot predict the previous outputs; (ii) $CF()$ outputs 1 with probability $\frac{1}{m}$. With this setting, we can say the state-controlled key is "ϵ_stable" *relative to* the sequential evolving key.

Definition 3. A key mechanism is called "ϵ_stable" if the probability that the key is removed by a normal crash is ϵ.

We use $H(k_{j-1}', i) < T$ as our choice function $CF()$, where H is a cryptographic hash function like SHA-256, k_{j-1}' is the current state-controlled key, i is the index of the log entry that is going to be stored in LStore, and T is a target value. T is chosen such that the above equation holds with rate $\frac{1}{m}$ on average, that is the state-controlled key is evolved with probability $\frac{1}{m}$ at each log entry. We show in Sect. 6, how to determine T for a given m and prove the security of our scheme using this choice function in Theorem 1. A similar choice function has been used in Bitcoin [12]. Note that even by choosing a random choice function, adversary can find the index of the event corresponding to the last usage of state-controlled key. This can be done by exhaustive search in the tail end of the log file, using the HMAC on every event with the state-controlled key seen in the KStore. To prevent this attack we require that when using state-controlled key to compute the HMAC, another source of randomness is also needed. We use the previous state-controlled key (before updating) as this randomness and concatenate it with the event m_i, i.e. $h_i = HMAC_{k'_j}(m_i, k'_{j-1})$. Remember that KStore contains this key during the evolving process and removes it later on, so attacker cannot find it after compromise. It is also worth mentioning that adversary can only succeed in rewinding $\mathcal{L}$ to an old state if it forges the state-controlled key associated with that state. By using PRF to generate the key sequences this probability is negligible.

Details. Log file consists of a list of events $S = \{s_1, s_2, \dots\}$, where each element s_i corresponds to one event. Each new event, m_i, is concatenated with a HMAC, h_i, and appended to $S = S||s_i$, and $s_i = (m_i, h_i)$, where , denotes the concatenation and $||$ represents appending. The system algorithms are described in Algorithms 2, 3, 4.

$Gen(1^\lambda)$: We use a PRF to generate the required keys. Let $PRF : \mathcal{K} \times \mathcal{Y} \to \mathcal{Z}$ be a function where $\mathcal{K}$ is the key space, $\mathcal{Y}$ is the domain and $\mathcal{Z}$ is the range, all are determined by security parameter λ. $PRF(k, \cdot)$ is often denoted by $PRF_k(\cdot)$. There are two initial keys, one for computing sequential keys, denote it with k_0, and one for computing state-controlled keys, denote it with k'_0. All the secrets are shared with the verifier at the beginning of the log file and they are removed from the system after updating it to the next key. Note that PRF also takes a second input which does not need to be secret and it is stored at the logging device and also shared with the verifier (we represent these inputs with χ and χ'). PRF evolves as follows: $k_i = PRF_{k_{i-1}}(\chi)$ (similarly $k'_i = PRF_{k'_{i-1}}(\chi')$). State-controlled key is initially k'_0. S is initialized with a message containing the information of log initialization such as the date, size, device id and etc; this is to prevent total deletion attack. We use $Log(.,.)$ algorithm that is described next to log the initial event, $init\_message$. We assume that cache is initially empty, and the state of the $\mathcal{L}$ is $\Sigma_0 = (\Sigma_0^K, \Sigma_0^L, Cache_0)$, where the state of the KStore is $\Sigma_0^K = (k_0, k'_0)$ and the state of the LStore is $\Sigma_0^L = (S)$.

$Log(\Sigma_{i-1}, m_i)$: Each log entry is of the form $s_i = (m_i, h_i)$ and it is appended to the dynamic array $S = S||s_i$, where h_i is the HMAC of m_i using either k_i or $X = k'_j$. For each log entry at index i, $CF(k'_{j-1}, i)$ is calculated; if the output is 1 then k'_{j-1} is updated to k'_j and HMAC of m_i is computed using k'_j and k'_{j-1}, $h_i = HMAC_{k'_j}(m_i, k'_{j-1})$, otherwise k_i is used for computing the HMAC, $h_i = HMAC_{k_i}(m_i)$. Figure 2 shows how Log algorithm works. When $CF()$ outputs 1, the corresponding log entry uses the state-controlled key.

Algorithm 2. Gen(1^λ)

Input: Security parameter λ
Output: Initial state Σ_0
1: $k_0, k_0' \leftarrow \{0,1\}^\lambda$
2: $\chi, \chi' \leftarrow \{0,1\}^\lambda$
3: Let $S \leftarrow init\_message$ //S is a dynamic array
4: **Output** $\Sigma_0 = (\Sigma_0^K, \Sigma_0^L, Cache_0)$
   // where $\Sigma_0^K = (k_0, k_0')$, $\Sigma_0^L = (S)$, and $Cache_0 = \emptyset$;

Algorithm 3. Log(Σ_{i-1}, m_i)

Input: old state Σ_{i-1}, **log event** m_i
Output: updated state Σ_i
$\Sigma_{i-1} = [\Sigma_{i-1}^K, \Sigma_{i-1}^L, Cache_{i-1}]$,
$\Sigma_{i-1}^K = (k_{i-1}, k_{j-1}')$ and $\Sigma_{i-1}^L = (S)$, $|S| = i - 1$;
//new log event m_i arrives
1: $k_i = PRF_{k_{i-1}}(\chi)$
   //Compute the choice function
2: **if** $CF(k_{j-1}', i) = 1$ **then**
3:    $k_j' = PRF_{k_{j-1}'}(\chi')$
4:    $h_i = HMAC_{k_j'}(m_i, k_{j-1}')$
5: **else**
6:    $h_i = HMAC_{k_i}(m_i)$
7: $s_i = (m_i, h_i)$
8: $S = S||s_i$
9: **Output** $\Sigma_i = [\Sigma_i^K, \Sigma_i^L, Cache_i]$
   //where $\Sigma_i^K = (k_i, k_i')$ and $\Sigma_i^L = (S)$

Algorithm 4. Recover(Σ, Σ_0)

Input: State Σ **to check, initial state** Σ_0
Output: Recovered log events $\{(\rho_i, m_i'), 1 \le i \le n'\}$
//Let $s_i = (m_i, h_i)$
1: $\mathcal{R} = \emptyset$ (recover set), $ExpSet = \emptyset$ (expendable set)
   //compute keys
2: **for** $i = 1$ to $n' + cs$ **do**
3:    $k_i = PRF_{k_{i-1}}(\chi)$
4:    $\mathbb{KS} \cup (i, k_i, \bot)$
5:    **if** $CF(k_{j-1}', i) = 1$ **then**
6:       **if** $i > n'$ **then**
7:          $K' \cup k_{j-1}'$
8:       $k_j' = PRF_{k_{j-1}'}(\chi')$
9:       $\mathbb{KS} \cup (i, k_j', k_{j-1}')$
10:      Remove $(i, k_i, \bot)$ from $\mathbb{KS}$
11: $K' \cup k_j'$
   //verify HMACs using the key set $\mathbb{KS}$ which is of form (i, k_i, κ_i) where κ_i is $\bot$ or k_{j-1}'
12: **for** $i = 1$ to n' **do**
13:    **if** $HMAC_{k_i}(m_i, \kappa_i) = h_i, k_i, \kappa_i \in \mathbb{KS}$ **then**
14:       Update $\mathcal{R} \cup (i, m_i)$
   //compute expendable logs
15: **for** $i = n' - cs + 1$ to $n' + cs$ **do**
16:    $ExpSet \cup i$
   //Plausibility check
17: **if** $X \notin K'$ **then**
18:    Outputs $\bot$
19: **else if** $|R| < 1 \vee \exists i \in \{1, \ldots, n'\} : \{(i, .) \notin \mathcal{R} \wedge i \notin ExpSet\}$ **then**
20:    Outputs $\bot$
21: **else**
22:    Outputs $\mathcal{R}$

Recover(Σ, Σ_0): Verifier $\mathcal{V}$ receives the state Σ consisting of n' log events (possibly crashed) in LStore. $\mathcal{V}$ knows the size of each log entry and can parse the LStore to n' log entries. $\mathcal{V}$ also knows the initial state of the $\mathcal{L}$, so re-computes all the random coins and the keys and stores the keys in the set $\mathbb{KS}$. $\mathcal{V}$ can verify the HMAC of each log entry using either the sequential key or the state-controlled key depending on the output of the choice function $CF()$. The indexes between $n' - cs + 1$ to $n' + cs$ are considered as expendable set. $\mathcal{V}$ also finds the set of possible state-controlled keys that may be in the KStore at the time of the crash. After the crash one such key will be in KStore (lines 6–11). If the size of the log file is n', the last key that has been updated before n' will be in the KStore (because logging is immediately after key update). Since it is possible to have a situation where the cache contains a new event and KStore contains the updated state-controlled key, but the corresponding event has not been written to the log file, we will have the following. For a log file of length n' the key set K' consists of (i) state-controlled keys that are generated between index n' and

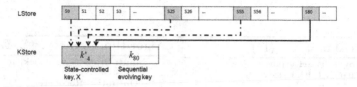

Fig. 2. The logging operation using double evolving keys; log entry s_{55} uses k'_3 and then k'_3 evolves to k'_4 which is used for s_{80}.

Fig. 3. Estimating the set of possible key mechanism. Blue cells are the locations that state-controlled key has been updated and the red rectangular shows the Expset. $K' = \{k'_3, k'_4\}$, k'_3 is related to the last update, and k'_4 is related to an unwritten event. (Color figure online)

$n' + cs$ (future keys), and (ii) the last state-controlled key generated before the event n'. Figure 3 shows how to find this key set.

Plausibility Check. If the state-controlled key, X, is not in the key set K' then we output $\perp$ meaning untrusted log. If the number of recovered events are less than 1 there is a total deletion attack. If there is an index which is neither in the expendable set nor in the recovered set, then there is a deletion/modification attack. Otherwise, $Recover(.,.)$ outputs index-message pairs.

5   Security and Efficiency

In the following, Lemma 1 shows the stability of our mechanism and Lemma 2 shows the relation between $\frac{1}{m}$, and the number of log entries that adversary can truncate from the end of log, denote with ℓ.

Lemma 1. *The double evolving key mechanism is $\frac{\alpha^2}{m}$-stable if the choice function $CF()$ outputs 1 with probability $\frac{1}{m}$.*

Let α denotes the probability that a key is deleted from KStore (because of re-ordering procedure in the system). If state-controlled key evolves with probability $\frac{1}{m}$ at each event, the probability that both sequential and state-controlled keys, are removed during a normal crash will be $\alpha \times \frac{\alpha}{m}$. Note that by choosing large values for m, this probability becomes negligible. If we use two independent state-controlled keys, using different PRFs and evolving at different rates ($\frac{1}{m_1}$ and $\frac{1}{m_2}$, respectively), then the probability that after a normal crash, the sequential key and both state-controlled keys are missing will be reduced to $\alpha \times \frac{\alpha}{m_1} \times \frac{\alpha}{m_2}$. This method can be used to dramatically decrease the chance of key removal key in a normal crash if we do not want to increase the value of m directly.

Note that we cannot unlimitedly increase m. If m is chosen to be so large, attacker may want to keep the state-controlled key untouched and truncate the log file for a number of events, $cs + \ell$, such that the key is still valid in the truncated state. Consider that attacker compromises the logging device at state n where the set of possible keys is K'_n and then cuts off $cs + \ell$ log events from the end which results in the malicious state n'; the set of possible state-controlled keys is denoted by $K'_{n'}$ at state n'. If K'_n and $K'_{n'}$ have intersection and the key in the KStore is one of the keys in the intersection of the two key sets then verifier cannot distinguish the crash attack from the accidental crash and hence crash attack ends up successfully. The value of ℓ is important for the security of our system and our goal is to reduce ℓ.

Lemma 2. *Assuming that the evolving probability of state-controlled key is $\frac{1}{m}$, and attacker compromises the device at sate Σ_n, truncates $cs + \ell$ events from the log file, results in malicious state $\Sigma_{n'}$, and keeps the key in KStore untouched. The success probability of such attacker is bounded to $P_s = (1 - \frac{1}{m})^\ell \times \frac{1}{\lfloor \frac{cs}{m} \rfloor + 1}$.*

Theorem 1. *Our scheme provides $[\epsilon_{PRF}(\lambda), \epsilon_{PRF}(\lambda), f(n, n', \ell, cs, \lambda)]$ - Crash Integrity against an adaptive attacker $\mathcal{A}$, where PRF-HMAC is $\epsilon_{PRF}(\lambda)$_secure, ℓ is the number of events adversary wants to delete, cs is the cache size, n is the size of log file at state Σ_n, n' is the number of log entries returned by adversary in the malicious state $\Sigma_{n'}$, λ is the security parameter, and $f()$ is as follows:*

$$f = \begin{cases} 0, & \text{if } n' < 1 \\ max\{\epsilon_{PRF}(\lambda), (1 - \frac{1}{m})^\ell \times \frac{1}{\lfloor \frac{cs}{m} \rfloor + 1}\}, & \text{otherwise} \end{cases} \tag{1}$$

Theorem 1 shows that m can be chosen to make the success probability of truncating the log to be negligible. This choice however will result in small value of m (bigger than 1). Achieving ϵ_stability requires large values of m, while crash integrity suggests small m. By using multiple evolving keys we can keep m small while achieving ϵ_stability guarantee of the mechanism. This is because each key has a small evolving probability, so the probability that all keys are removed at the same time will be negligible. If attacker truncates the file by more than cs events, there is at least one key that will be affected and this will reveal the attack. The number of keys, n_{sc}, depend on the probabilities $\{\frac{1}{m_1}, \frac{1}{m_2}, ..., \frac{1}{m_{n_{sc}}}\}$. One can also choose a different distribution for the choice function. By using uniform distribution for double evolving key mechanism, adversary can truncate the file by at most m log entries, with success probability $\frac{m-\ell}{m+cs}$ for $\ell < m^4$. Finding the best probability distribution for $CF()$ to minimizes the attacker's success probability is an interesting future research direction.

5.1   Complexity Analysis

According to $Log(\cdot, \cdot)$ (Algorithm 3), the complexity of adding one event is $O(1)$ since it needs (i) evolving the keys and (ii) computing the HMAC. Although in

---

[4] Details of this analysis are given in the full version of the paper.

Table 1. Comparison between computation complexity of our scheme and SLiC

Algorithm	Our scheme	SLiC [6]	SLiC^{Opt} [6]
$Log(\cdot,\cdot)$	$O(1)$	$O(1)$	$O(1)$
$Recover(\cdot,\cdot)$	$O(n')$	$O(n'log(n'))$	$O(n')$

Table 2. The total time (in seconds) to log 2^{20} events

Hardware	Scheme	Exp1	Exp2	Exp3	Exp4	Exp5
Windows PC	Our scheme	40.2	40.2	40.4	40.7	40.5
	SLiC	95.2	96.0	95.2	95.4	96.0
	Plain	2.0	2.0	2.0	2.0	2.0
Raspberry Pi	Our scheme	330.5	325.4	319.0	324.5	319.6
	SLiC	790.2	792.0	777.9	789.2	796.8
	Plain	18.8	18.7	18.8	19.0	18.9

SLiC [6] the computational complexity of logging is $O(1)$, our proposed system is faster: the required computation in SLiC consists of (i) updating the keys, (ii) encrypting the log event, and (iii) performing a local permutation on the log file. Additionally, each log operation in our scheme requires one write operation on disk whereas in SLiC each log operation requires two write operations. Moreover, in our system the order of events is preserved in the log file, so that searching a specific event is efficient. The complexity of $Recover(\cdot,\cdot)$ in our scheme (Algorithm 4) for verifying the total number of n' events is equal to $O(n')$; the first and the second loop in Algorithm 4 takes $O(n')$ computations, the third loop has complexity of $O(1)$ and the plausibility check has $O(n')$. In SLiC [6], the complexity of recover algorithm is $O(n'log(n'))$ since it needs running sort algorithm for verification. The complexity of our scheme is less than SLiC, but it is the same as SLiC^{Opt} [6] (please see Table 1).

6   Implementation and Evaluation

We have implemented and evaluated the double evolving key mechanism in Python. The experiments have been performed on two hardware platforms: a windows computer with 3.6 GHz Intel(R) Core(TM) i7-7700 CPU; a Raspberry Pi 3, Model B with 600 MHz ARM CPU running Raspbian.

Logging Performance: We measure the logging performance on a prepared text file as the source of system events. The text file contains 2^{20} random strings, each with 160 characters. To implement our log scheme, we used ChaCha20 [4] for PRFs and SHA-256 as hash function in HMACs. We found the cache size of our machine using the same approach explained in [6]; the maximum UDP packet sending rate is 500 event/s (please see the full version of the paper for the result of our experiment). Accordingly, the cache size, cs is $15000 \approx 2^{14}$ events considering the page eviction time of 30 s. We set $m = cs$, and T value in the $CF()$ is determined to be $2^{242} = 2^{256}/2^{14}$ which outputs 1 with probability $1/2^{14}$ [5] (please see the full version of the paper for the related experiments). The length of both keys is 256 bits. We implemented two logging schemes to compare with our logging scheme: (i) *Plain scheme:* each event is stored in the log file as plaintext. (ii) *SLiC:* the logging algorithm proposed in [6] is used. For SLiC, we initialized the system with $\lambda = 2^{15}$ randomly ordered dummy events, the same as the experiment in [6]. For encryption, we used AES-CTR-256[5].

By comparing our scheme with the plain scheme we can find the extra cost to provide crash integrity. We also compare our scheme with SLiC to find the extra cost of protecting against an adaptive adversary. Table 2 shows the total runtime to log 2^{20} system events using three aforementioned logging schemes on Windows PC and Raspberry Pi. We repeat the experiments for 5 times, each time with a new file containing 2^{20} events (the other settings remain same). For the same hardware and the same logging schemes, but with different files, the runtime remains same. This is aligned with our expectation: logging performance is independent of file content. On the windows PC, our scheme takes $\approx$40 s ($\approx$26K events/s) on average. This represents a multiplicative overhead of 20, compared to the plain scheme, while SLiC takes $\approx$95 s, with an overhead of 47. Compared to our log scheme, SLiC has a multiplicative overhead of 2, while our scheme provides extra security protection. However, in [6], they observed a slowdown factor of 20 for logging rate. The PRF they chose or the difference between their hardware and ours may cause the discrepancy of the result.

The runtime on the Pi is roughly 8 times the runtime on the desktop, because of the computational limit of Raspberry Pi. The results show that our logging scheme is still lightweight for the resource-constrained devices. It takes $\approx$324 s ($\approx$3.2K events/s) on average to log 2^{20} events. The overhead of our scheme compared to plain scheme is 17. SLiC has a multiplicative overhead of 2 compared to our scheme, and an overhead of 42 compared to plain scheme.

Recovery Performance: Normally, we consider that the logging results are written to a file in the OS, and if crash happens, the verifier can always get the number of events (n') based on the size of the file. In our implementation, the value of n' is 2^{20}. We run our *Recover(., .)* algorithm on the five log files generated earlier before. Table 3 shows the total runtime to recover log files on two platforms. It takes $\approx$37.4 s on average to recover all the system events on the desktop and $\approx$308.4 s on the Pi. We can observe that it takes slightly more time for logging than recovery, maybe because of the poor I/O handling of Python. In our implementation of log algorithm, the key is evolved per new line from the I/O, while in the implementation of recovery algorithm, all the keys are reconstructed before any reading from the I/O.

---

[5] The size of the key is 256 bits.

Table 3. The total runtime (in seconds) to recover a log file of size 2^{20} events

Hardware	Exp 1	Exp 2	Exp 3	Exp 4	Exp 5
Windows PC	37.1	37.6	37.5	37.3	37.3
Raspberry Pi	311.0	303.1	302.0	303.4	303.3

7 Conclusion

We proposed adaptive crash attack where adversary can see intermediate states of the logging operation. By compromising the logging device, adversary can rewind the system back to one of the past states and then crash it to appear as a normal crash. We showed that this attack is strictly stronger than non-adaptive crash attack and all existing schemes are subject to this attack. We also proposed double evolving key mechanism as a protection against rewinding. The security of scheme is proved and the performance of our approach is evaluated on both a desktop and Raspberry Pi. Ensuring crash integrity against an adaptive attacker without considering a protected memory for keys is left as future work.

Acknowledgments. This work is in part supported by a research grant from Alberta Innovates in the Province of Alberta in Canada.

References

1. Andrews, J.H.: Testing using log file analysis: tools, methods, and issues. In: 13th IEEE International Conference on Automated Software Engineering, pp. 157–166. IEEE (1998)
2. Avizheh, S., Doan, T.T., Liu, X., Safavi-Naini, R.: A secure event logging system for smart homes. In: 2017 Workshop on Internet of Things Security and Privacy, pp. 37–42. ACM (2017)
3. Bellare, M., Yee, B.: Forward integrity for secure audit logs. Technical report, Computer Science and Engineering Department, University of California at San Diego (1997)
4. Bernstein, D.J.: ChaCha, a variant of Salsa20. In: Workshop Record of SASC, vol. 8, pp. 3–5 (2008)
5. Bitcoinwiki: Difficulty in mining (2018). https://en.bitcoinwiki.org/wiki/Difficulty_in_Mining. Accessed January 2019
6. Blass, E.O., Noubir, G.: Secure logging with crash tolerance. In: IEEE Conference on Communications and Network Security (CNS), pp. 1–10. IEEE (2017)
7. Butin, D., Le Métayer, D.: Log analysis for data protection accountability. In: Jones, C., Pihlajasaari, P., Sun, J. (eds.) FM 2014. LNCS, vol. 8442, pp. 163–178. Springer, Cham (2014). https://doi.org/10.1007/978-3-319-06410-9_12
8. Holt, J.E.: Logcrypt: forward security and public verification for secure audit logs. In: Australasian Workshops on Grid Computing and E-research, vol. 54, pp. 203–211. Australian Computer Society, Inc. (2006)

9. Lalla, H., Flowerday, S., Sanyamahwe, T., Tarwireyi, P.: A log file digital forensic model. In: Peterson, G., Shenoi, S. (eds.) DigitalForensics 2012. IAICT, vol. 383, pp. 247–259. Springer, Heidelberg (2012). https://doi.org/10.1007/978-3-642-33962-2_17

10. Ma, D., Tsudik, G.: Forward-secure sequential aggregate authentication. In: IEEE Symposium on Security and Privacy, pp. 86–91. IEEE (2007)

11. Ma, D., Tsudik, G.: A new approach to secure logging. ACM Trans. Storage (TOS) 5(1), 2 (2009)

12. Nakamoto, S.: Bitcoin: a peer-to-peer electronic cash system (2008)

13. Schneier, B., Kelsey, J.: Secure audit logs to support computer forensics. ACM Trans. Inf. Syst. Secur. (TISSEC) 2(2), 159–176 (1999)

14. Tomescu, A., Devadas, S.: Catena: efficient non-equivocation via bitcoin. In: 2017 IEEE Symposium on Security and Privacy (SP), pp. 393–409. IEEE (2017)

Enroll, and Authentication Will Follow
eID-Based Enrollment for a Customized, Secure, and Frictionless Authentication Experience

Silvio Ranise⍟, Giada Sciarretta(✉)⍟, and Alessandro Tomasi⍟

Security and Trust, Fondazione Bruno Kessler, Via Sommarive 18, 38123 Trento, Italy
{ranise,giada.sciarretta,altomasi}@fbk.eu
https://stfbk.github.io/

Abstract. High-assurance user identification and credentials provisioning are crucial for accessing digital services. Usability, service customization, and security should be carefully balanced to offer an appropriate user experience. We propose an eID-based enrollment approach for tailoring authentication to the particular needs of the service provider and strike a good trade-off between usability and security via the registration of authenticators, artifacts providing identity proofs. We demonstrate the practicality of our approach in the case of patient access to Electronic Health Records (EHR) through an Android application: enrollment is done by using the Italian national eID card to register the mobile authenticator, unlocked by the user's fingerprint, customized to interact with the identity and access management system of the EHR.

Keywords: eID · eIDAS · FIDO · Hyperledger fabric · Android

1 Introduction

As digital services are growing and the Internet of Things is getting larger, individuals need to be in control of their digital identities to manage their interactions with increasingly complex services. Failing to design and deploy usable and secure solutions for Identity Management (IdM) may result in a lack of trust in digital ecosystems with negative impact on the economy (e.g., higher fees on financial transactions) and society (e.g., limitation of electronic healthcare solutions). For instance, it is well-known (see, e.g., [12]) that passwords are the root cause of over 80% of data-breaches. This is so because of several factors including the use of easily guessable passwords and the re-use of the same password for several services because of the difficulty in remembering it (more than 51% of the passwords turns out to be re-used [12]). To mitigate these problems, Multi Factor Authentication (MFA) and Single-Sign-On (SSO) solutions have been introduced. The former requires additional identification factors (e.g. a fingerprint) to successfully conclude an authentication process; the latter allow users to enter just one set of credentials to access multiple services and applications.

© Springer Nature Switzerland AG 2020
A. Benzekri et al. (Eds.): FPS 2019, LNCS 12056, pp. 156–171, 2020.
https://doi.org/10.1007/978-3-030-45371-8_10

While MFA and SSO contribute to the hardening of IdM solutions, they are not easy to deploy securely (see, e.g., [4,15]) and they assume enrollment as a prerequisite so that users have been identified (identity proofing) and provisioned with suitable credentials. In case enrollment is flawed or performed without an appropriate level of assurance (e.g., digital identities of most social login solutions are self-asserted), then fake digital identities can be forged with the result of greatly weakening authentication. This becomes critical when users access sensitive services including those to perform financial transactions (e.g., payments) or for interacting with the public administration to, e.g., obtain certificates and documents with legal validity. Market and regulatory pressures add requirements to enrollment processes as paradigmatically illustrated by financial services (see, e.g., [1] where the enrollment is part of the client on-boarding process performed by the financial institution to start a customer relationship).

Although client on-boarding sets the tone for the entire relationship between a financial institution and a customer (as it represents their first interaction), it is characterized by multiple friction points such as being re-routed to different channels and the need to provide physical identification. Improving client on-boarding, and therefore the enrollment process, becomes more and more urgent as new players (e.g., fintechs) enter the market and new regulations (such as the revised Payment Directive, PSD2 [10]) promise to significantly enlarge the offerings of financial services and simplify their change.

To alleviate these problems and strike a good trade-off between the desired level of assurance in enrollment and a frictionless but secure authentication experience (especially for accessing sensitive services), private organizations and governments have proposed standards. For the former, the FIDO Alliance [12] is an industry association whose goal is to develop standards that reduce the reliance on passwords while improving identification and credential provision. For governments, the European Union stimulated the development of national electronic identification (eID) schemes (many of which are based on smartcards) with the ultimate goal of helping public administrations (and private service providers) to extend the use of their online services to citizens from any European country as mandated by the eIDAS regulation [11] with the ultimate goal of building the so-called Digital Single Market. Needless to say, these standards are major stepping stones for advancing the state-of-the-art of digital identity solutions; however, they show complementary weaknesses and strengths. On the one hand, the FIDO proposal focuses on secure and frictionless authentication procedures while leaving unspecified the identity proofing process. On the other hand, eID schemes provide a high level of assurance for identification and credential provision with less friendly user experiences, especially in some authentication scenarios (e.g., accessing services via mobile devices).

The complementarity of FIDO and eID seems to suggest the possibility to combine them into an approach that hopefully inherits the best of both worlds while reducing as much as possible their drawbacks. In the rest of the paper, we explore this opportunity and propose an eID-based enrollment process that is capable of (1) simplifying enrollment by authentication of users via eID schemes;

thereby providing a high level of assurance typically offered by such schemes that provision digital identity to citizens following rigorous and well-established procedures; and (2) tailoring authentication to the particular needs of the service provider to obtain the desired balance between usability and security (e.g., strong branding with MFA for financial services) via the activation of suitably configured *authenticators*, i.e. software or hardware artifacts providing identity proofs, that can be seen as a generalization of the FIDO authentication standards based on public key cryptography.

Our approach also supports the situation in which users already have accounts with a service provider but are willing to link them with the digital identities provisioned by an eID scheme to simplify their user experience and reduce password fatigue. To show the practical applicability of our approach, we consider the case of patient access to Electronic Health Records (EHR) through their smartphones: enrollment is done by using the Italian national eID card (featuring encryption and Near Field Communication capabilities) whereas authentication uses the fingerprint scanning capabilities available on many smartphones to enable an authenticator implementing a cryptographic challenge-response protocol.

Plan of the Paper. Section 2 gives a brief overview of eID and FIDO. Section 3 discusses the advantages and limitations of using both eID and FIDO for enrollment and authentication, recall some basic definitions from NIST approach to IdM, and then precisely describe our proposal to overcome the limitations and inherit the benefits of both eID and FIDO for enrollment. Section 4 describes a use case scenario and an implementation of our approach to enrollment. Section 5 concludes and gives some pointers to future work.

2   State of the Art on Digital Identity

We provide a brief overview of eID schemes and FIDO specifications.

2.1   Electronic Identity Schemes

To establish an European Union (EU) framework for cross-border trust services in the EU digital single market, the EU Commission introduced eIDAS (electronic IDentification and Authentication Services) – Regulation (910/2014 [11]), expanding the previous Directive (1999/93/EC [9]) on digital signatures. eIDAS stands as a legal and technical basis for interoperability and portability of digital identities issued by EU Member States.

An important aspect, introduced in Article 8, is the Level of Assurance (LoA), which defines the degree of confidence – *low*, *substantial* or *high* – in establishing the real identity of a person through electronic identification. According to the LoA required by a specific online service, the processes leading up to and including the authentication process itself, must be performed with the appropriate degree of confidence. For instance, when registering to a social network, the required LoA can be low whereas to use a public service (e.g., one issuing birth certificates) the LoA should be high.

When an eID scheme is correctly notified and has the appropriate LoA (i.e. its LoA is equal to or higher than the LoA required to access the service), the scheme shall be recognized by all Member States. Note that the eIDAS Regulation does not intrude in the definition of the different national eID schemes, but it provides a legal framework for the mutual recognition of the digital identity among Member States. This is the basis of the portability of national identities, i.e., citizens of a Member State can use their own national eID to access services provided by another Member State without barriers and in a secure way.

The complete list of notified eID schemes under eIDAS is available at [2]. Being released by national institutions, all the notified eID schemes require a rigorous user identification procedure that provides a high LoA for identity proofing. The LoA for authentication varies based on the scheme. Many of these are eID cards; e.g., the German eID card (Personalausweis) [5] and the Italian Carta d'Identità Elettronica [6]. Such cards are equipped with a microchip featuring communication (e.g., NFC) and cryptographic capabilities; they are intended to provide both personal identity verification following the ICAO Machine Readable Travel Documents (MRTD) standard [18], and online authentication functionalities following the Identification Authentication Signature European Citizen Card (IAS ECC) specification [13].

2.2 FIDO Alliance

The FIDO (Fast IDentity Online) Alliance [12] has the mission of developing an open ecosystem for standard-based and interoperable authentication solutions for both ensuring strong authentication and reducing the use of passwords. FIDO specifications are based on standard public key cryptography and challenge-response authentication. Authentication presumes a phase during which the authenticator is registered, which involves the creation of a key pair on a local keystore—be it a trusted execution environment or a hardware secure element—such that the private key is only ever generated and stored locally, while the service provider can associate the public key with a specific account. When attempting to authenticate, users will be requested to sign a challenge by using their private key; the server will thus be able to check the signature by using the corresponding known public key.

FIDO Alliance provides three specs: Universal Authentication Framework (UAF) enabling passwordless authentication, Universal Second Factor (U2F) enabling second-factor authentication, and the Client to Authenticator Protocol (CTAP) that is part of the FIDO2 project, together with the W3C Web Authentication specification, also known as WebAuthn [27]. While WebAuthn defines a standard web API so that online services are able to use FIDO authentication, CTAP specifies how external devices take part in the authentication protocols as authenticators. WebAuthn has recently been natively implemented in the major web browsers. Since authentication secrets never leave users' devices and are not stored in any server, this protocol prevents threats such as phishing, password theft and replay attack. Furthermore, it allows both passwordless and second-factor scenarios; in every case, authenticators could be either embedded (as biometric readers) or external (over BLE, NFC or USB).

3   eIDs as Enabler of Digital Services

We discuss the current limitations and open challenges of integrating eID schemes in existing digital services (Sect. 3.1), provide a brief overview of the basic notions on which our approach is based (Sect. 3.2), and present our approach for tackling them by providing secure and frictionless user authentication through eID-based enrollment (Sect. 3.3).

3.1   eID Scheme: Open Challenges

eIDs have been proposed and promoted as a key enabling technology for digital services in the EU single market, as for instance recognized in eIDAS, which provides both a regulatory framework and an infrastructure for authentication that service providers can leverage (as discussed in Sect. 2.1).

The integration of eID schemes in online services has several benefits: eIDs can be used to increase the number of end-users of an online service, providing a high LoA on citizens' identity for both enrollment and authentication, including cross-border authentication. For example, an eID scheme could be used to perform online enrollment, instead of requiring a citizen to physically go to an office to perform in-person identification.

However, while eID schemes are recognized as an essential means for establishing trust in citizen identification and authentication processes, their integration into existing digital services is subject to constraints of different nature including usability, regulations, and integration in service providers.

For usability, one of the main problems of using eID schemes – especially cards and schemes that provide a high LoA – is that the authentication procedure is usually long and complex. Many services require a daily use, so understandably users are unlikely to favor a complex procedure each time they want to read or update their data, especially on mobile devices. For example, if the eID scheme requires the use of an authenticator (such as mobile application) generating an OTP, the user may be forced to move back and forth between the authentication and the service provider's mobile application with the risk of getting lost and not being able to complete the authentication process correctly, or in the time frame of the validity of the OTP code.

For these reasons, in Italy only few service providers of the public administration support a high LoA in the case of native mobile applications. In addition, legal constraints may complicate the situation as is the case of the Italian SPID scheme [25] ("Allegato 3") that specifies that when a high LoA authentication is performed, it is not possible in any way to keep the access active; therefore, requiring an authentication for each access. In case of mobile applications, this could become burdensome for the user. It is therefore necessary to carry out further analyses in order to have solutions that are sufficiently safe and usable.

Another integration constraint is that to properly protect their data, many services define their own access control policies and require the validation of attributes specific to the service (e.g., the roles involved) that are usually not provided by eID schemes; thus requiring an extra step in the enrollment process.

Even if in European Member States there are several services currently using eID schemes, mainly from the public sector, to the best of our knowledge, a clear and comprehensive approach that clarifies how to integrate eID schemes in existing digital services, and identifies the potential trade-offs among security, usability and interoperability is currently missing. To bridge this gap, we propose an eID-based enrollment that retains the high assurance and security of eID authentication but enables service providers to deliver a frictionless experience, tailored to their standards and best practices.

3.2 Digital Identity: NIST Definitions

The National Institute of Standards and Technology (NIST) recently released Special Publication 800-63 [14], which provides several technical guidelines for federal agencies implementing digital identity services. Below, we summarize the notions that are relevant to our work; all citations below are taken from [14].

In a digital identity lifecycle, we can distinguish two main phases: *enrollment* and *authentication*.

Enrollment is the process through which a user applies to receive a credential or authenticator from a *Credential Service Provider (CSP)*. A *credential* is "an object or data structure that authoritatively binds an identity—via an identifier or identifiers—and (optionally) additional attributes, to at least one authenticator possessed and controlled by a user." An *authenticator* is something the user possesses and controls (such as a cryptographic module) that is used to authenticate the user. During enrollment, the *CSP* collects, validates, and verifies information about a person (*Identity Proofing*). A *CSP* may issue credentials for its own use or be an independent third party whose authenticators are used by a *Relying Party (RP)*; in both cases, we say that the authenticator is trusted by the *RP*. When a new credential is issued based on proof of possession of an authenticator associated with a previously issued credential, the identity proofing is not necessary and the new credential is called *derived credential*.

Authentication is the process of demonstrating to a *verifier* that a user (called *claimant*) has possession and control of at least one authenticator, in order to verify his/her identity. Each authenticator can attest one or more *authentication factors*, which are divided into three categories: knowledge (e.g. passwords), possession (e.g. SIM cards), and inherence (e.g. fingerprints). Authenticators may generate an output, intended to prove that the claimant possesses and controls the authenticator. When an authentication process requires more than one authentication factor, it is referred to as *multi-factor authentication*.

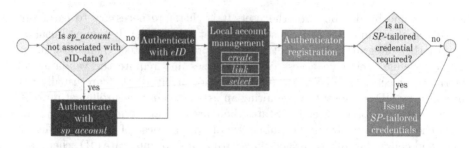

Case	sp_account?	sp_account linked with eID-data?	User authentication	Local account management	Registration & credentials
1	no	no	*eid_auth*	*create;link*	*reg;vc*^opt
2	yes	yes	*eid_auth*	*select*	*reg;vc*^opt
3	yes	no	*sp_account; eid_auth*	*select;link*	*reg;vc*^opt

Fig. 1. eID-based enrollment phases.

3.3   Our eID-Based Approach

To provide the best tradeoff between security and usability, our approach is based on the idea of establishing trust in the enrollment, for each service provider (SP), of a frictionless authenticator through the use of an eID scheme.

The proposed eID-based enrollment is applicable whenever an SP wishes to issue a derived credential that binds the user's identity—via an eID-data identifier—and (optionally) additional SP-tailored attributes, to a frictionless authenticator possessed and controlled by the user.

Similarly to the FIDO authenticator registration (cf. Sect. 2.2), the user may or may not already be in possession of an SP account. However, the authentication performed is outside the scope of FIDO specs. Our approach details this phase adding a trust layer though the use of an eID scheme.

Even if the idea of using eID scheme to derive credentials is not new, to the best of our knowledge, there are currently only draft and not detailed proposals to do this; see, e.g., [22]. In addition, to provide a better interoperability with the technologies and architecture of an SP we also specify how to link existing accounts with the new authentication method and how to optionally associate an access control mechanism.

Formally, let u be a user with: *(a)* an identity (eID) obtained from a national eID scheme, *(b)* (optionally) an account ($sp\_account$) obtained from an SP, and *(c)* an authenticator ($authr$) trusted by the SP. The derived credential issuance through an eID-based enrollment for u wrt SP consists of three main phases (shown in Fig. 1): user authentication with eID (and $sp\_account$), local account management, and $authr$ registration with issuance of SP-tailored credentials (if required).

After the establishment of a new, trusted and frictionless authentication method, subsequent authentication is done with the registered authenticator.

Using NIST terminology, during the enrollment process the *SP* plays the role of a *CSP* as well as a *RP* towards the eID provider. In the subsequent authentication, the *SP* plays the role of *RP* towards itself, due to the previously issued credentials.

We discuss each phase of our eID-based enrollment approach and the different cases enumerated in the table of Fig. 1 in more detail below.

User Authentication. To retain a high assurance level in the derived credential, we require authentication with an eID (*eid_auth*). Based on the selected eID, the *eid_auth* could be directly implemented by the *SP* (e.g., using eID cards) or require a federation with national identity providers managing the eID scheme (e.g., SPID in Italy [25]). In some cases, the eID can be used in both scenarios and the final choice is up to the *SP*. Given that application developers are not usually security experts and they mainly focus on implementing new features, we advise the federation with national identity management infrastructure.

While *eid_auth* is a mandatory step, as shown in the "User authentication" column of Fig. 1, in Case 3 an additional authentication with the *SP* (*sp_auth*) is required. Indeed, if an *SP* has existing user accounts not linked with eID-data, then to avoid the creation of multiple users and provide an undesired user experience, an *sp_auth* is required to recover the existing account and link it with a unique eID identifier. In addition, we assume that when an *sp_account* is linked with eID-data, this is an entry in the account management database.

In our approach, we do not consider the case of user data linked with eID-data without an *sp_account*. We assume that if an *SP* has collected user data, then it should provide the user with an authentication method to access them. We do consider the opposite, Case 3, in which an *SP* manages an account that is not yet tied to eID data, but the establishment of this link is required. This could happen for different reasons: an *SP* could decide to offer an account recovery procedure to *sp_account* tied to the eID data, or the *SP* may need to comply with new legal obligations requiring a high LoA (e.g., to manage payments).

Example (Case 3). Let us consider for concreteness a *u* with: *(a)* the Italian electronic identity card (CIE 3.0) as *eID*, *(b)* an *sp_account* based on username and password that is not linked with eID-data, and *(c)* a key pair managed by the Android keystore and unlocked by fingerprint as *authr*. Figure 2 shows a user-experience mockup of the user authentication phase.

For users not already in possession of an *sp_account* (Case 1) or with an *sp_account* linked with eID-data (Case 2), only the *eid_auth* with the eID will be performed.

Local Account Management. As summarized in the "Local Account Management" column of Fig. 1, based on the *sp_account* a user has, different actions are performed during the local account management phase:

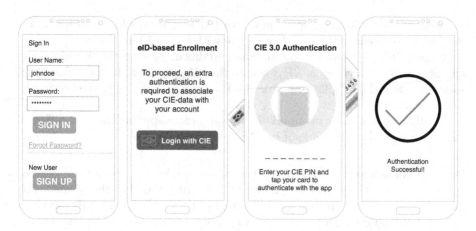

Fig. 2. User authentication with existing accounts not linked with eID-data.

Case 1. If users do not have an *sp_account*, they authenticate with eID and a new *sp_account* will be created (*create*) and linked with eID-data (*link*).

Case 2. If users do have an *sp_account* associated with an eID-data, they authenticate with eID and the corresponding *sp_account* will be selected (*select*).

Case 3. If users do have an *sp_account* but it is not associated with an eID-data, they will authenticate with the *SP* (*sp_auth*) and the corresponding *sp_account* will be selected (*select*), then with eID (*eid_auth*) and the *sp_account* will be linked with an eID-data (*link*).

We are non-specific in our approach to which eID-data the procedure requires to link an *sp_account* as there are differences between eID issued by different states. For example, Italian eIDs include a unique identifier – "codice fiscale" (*CF*) – which is associated with the data subject, generally assigned shortly after birth, and persists regardless of the specific document. The *CF* is an encoding of the subject's personal information with error correction, and is designed to disambiguate persons with the same birth information. In the case of an eIDAS-notified eID scheme, together with security, another inherited benefit of federating with the national identity management is the cross-border support.

Example (Case 3). After the authentication with *SP* (*sp_auth*) and CIE 3.0 (*eid_auth*), the local account manager selects the *sp_account* and links it with the Italian *CF*. This process is completely transparent to the user.

Authenticator Registration and Credentials. The last phase of our approach consists in the registration of a new frictionless authenticator. We suggest to exploit existing standards and solutions for registering a new authenticator, such as the use of QR codes or FIDO 2. To offer the best tradeoff between security and usability, the choice of the registration method and authenticator type (e.g., a hardware token or a software token protected by a biometric factor) must

Fig. 3. Authenticator registration using fingerprint.

be evaluated based on the scenario. In Sect. 4, we will provide a concrete example for an e-Health mobile application that integrates modern phishing-resistant protocols to associate a public key-based authenticator with a user account based on proof of identity through an eID.

In some cases, services will wish to issue their own tailored credentials. These could be traditional X.509 certificates issued for purposes within the service only, or they might be more general credentials in the sense of the W3C model [26].

Example (Case 3). In our running example, *authr* is a key pair managed by the Android keystore and unlocked by fingerprint. After authentication with *eID*, *u* is asked to register *authr* by providing her fingerprint. Figure 3 shows a user-experience mockup of the authenticator registration phase. The *SP*-tailored credential issuance is transparent to *u*.

Once the enrollment procedure is completed, subsequent authentication is done with the registered *authr* without requiring further *eID* authentication.

3.4 A Comparison with eID-Card Solutions

Although several eID schemes have been developed, most use cards (cf. Sect. 2.1). Our approach offers several advantages over constantly using an eID card.

Privacy. The eID card is used only once, and the link between eID-data and *sp_account* is stored by the *SP*. No eID-data need be involved in future authentication sessions, thereby minimizing the number of times it is transmitted. In addition, if the *eid_auth* is performed with a national eID infrastructure, our approach provides better privacy, avoiding the involvement of the national eID infrastructure in every future authentication session.

Security. Reduced chance of unwanted eID PIN disclosure due to phishing attacks, shoulder-surfing, keyloggers.

Extensions. After the authenticator registration, additional credentials can be issued to accommodate other access control methods (e.g. ABAC [17]) or cryptographic standards (e.g. elliptic curve cryptography).

UX. The mobile-fingerprint combination offers an improved user experience over smartcard-PIN: higher familiarity, quicker interaction and hence shorter login times, biometric authentication factor does not require memorization.

Availability. eID cards frequently lock after a small number of mistaken PIN entries. Unlocking the card requires an unlock code (PUK) that users typically do not carry with them.

On the con side, eID cards may be considered tamper-proof and impossible to duplicate, while using a software keystore is thought to carry greater risks. Serious side-channel attacks on smart cards are known – see e.g. [21] for a review of known techniques – but most would be difficult to execute on a reader controlled by the user; in most common scenarios, smart cards offer a higher LoA compared with a software keystore. Nevertheless, our approach is non-specific as to the nature of the authenticator and could encompass a software keystore or hardware secure module built into the device (e.g. for the Google Pixel phones).

4   Use Case

As a concrete demonstration of our proposed approach, we consider the case of patient access to Electronic Health Records (EHR) through their smartphone. Of the many possible deployment models, we consider a centralized EHR system in which patients interact with one or more Health Service Providers (HSP) – e.g. hospitals, laboratories, or local health authorities – using a custom application to store and retrieve EHR, and for each interaction with the HSPs, a centralized Health Authority (HA) is obliged to authenticate the involved parties and authorize the interaction based on their credentials. The HA is considered the data controller for the purposes of the GDPR [8] and is responsible for writing the policies for all HSP under its authority. In an effort to comply with the principles of GDPR, secure remote access to EHR is to be granted to users, and since this should be as frictionless as possible we consider the use of their mobile phone.

This is a very realistic use case scenario in many EU countries – for instance Italy, where eID cards are issued at the national level but health services are administered by local health authorities, with each service enabling access to EHR with its own infrastructure and protocols. A common way to authenticate patients would improve nation-wide accessibility to data, as well as enable interoperability of services, such as doctors in one region issuing electronic prescriptions redeemable in another. Additionally, if an eIDAS-compliant eID scheme is used, this could facilitate union-wide cross-border healthcare provision.

This scenario falls under Case 2 in Fig. 1: patients have an account with every HA by default, and this account is always linked with eID data. We make use of the Italian eID card, CIE 3.0 (see Sect. 2.1), which contains an X.509 certificate with the unique identifier "codice fiscale", which health services associate with each patient; the eID is therefore the only authentication token required.

Concretely, our newly registered authenticator is a key pair managed by the Android keystore and unlocked by fingerprint authentication to the OS. We assume users to be in possession of an eID card and a smartphone with a fingerprint sensor and NFC capability; additionally, we assume they are enrolled with a local account on their mobile device OS through fingerprint authentication. The HA runs a back-end service through which users can authenticate with eID and register new authenticators. Additionally, we issue users with an *SP*-tailored credential signed by the *SP*'s certificate authority, as we discuss in Sect. 4.1.

4.1   Implementation

We proposed in [23] an access control back-end layer designed to increase accountability and mitigate against insider attacks. Our access control layer uses attribute-based access control (ABAC) [17] and is implemented in nodejs and Hyperledger Fabric (HF) [16], a private and permissioned distributed ledger technology (DLT). To authenticate and authorize users, HF uses Public Key Infrastructure (PKI): users are issued with an X.509 certificate [19] containing subject attributes. HF is packaged with its own built-in certificate authority (CA): the CA and its registration procedures are an essential part of the HF service because every principal transacting on the network must digitally sign every transaction, and their certificates contain attributes for ABAC policy decisions.

While we mainly addressed issues of authorization, we did not detail a procedure by which these certificates were to be issued, or how the corresponding private keys were to be stored and provisioned. A key security requirement is to devise a robust procedure by which the *SP* can decide whether to issue *SP*-tailored credentials – or in our case, whether to sign a Certificate Signing Request (CSR) made by an alleged user from a new mobile device.

We used CIE 3.0, to enable users to authenticate to the HA and to enable the HA to set up an automated procedure for the registration of a new authenticator and the issuance of an *SP*-tailored credential. Our native mobile client is written for Android API level 28 and communicates with CIE 3.0 over NFC.

We developed our proof-of-concept as part of a Joint Lab with IPZS [20], of which we use the eID infrastructure. Our goal was to design an authentication procedure to be as streamlined as possible. The certificate within the CIE is read directly by the client app, and the CIE is used to authenticate the user via the client directly to the HA; it is the HA's responsibility to verify the certificate.

The proposed steps are shown in Fig. 4. With respect to the entities defined in Sect. 3.3, we have the following mapping: *(i)* the HA is considered the service provider (*SP*); *(ii)* the Android keystore is the authenticator (*authr*); *(iii)* the eID is CIE 3.0, containing a certificate signed by the national eID CA; *(iv)* the certificate signed by the HA's CA is our SP-tailored credential.

We summarize the enrollment steps as follows:

1. The mobile app requests a challenge (32-byte random nonce) from the HA.

2. The user enters their CIE PIN number and places the CIE in proximity of the mobile's NFC sensor. The mobile app reads the CIE certificate and requests a signature of the challenge from the CIE.
3. The app forwards the CIE certificate and the CIE-signed challenge to the HA. The HA verifies the certificate with the CA, verifies the signature, and replies with OK/KO. This completes the authentication phase.
4. The mobile app requests a challenge (32-byte random nonce) from the HA.
5. The mobile app requests a key pair from the keystore, unlocked with OS fingerprint authentication (see Android docs [3]). We call this the service key pair to distinguish it from the CIE key pair. The app generates a Certificate Signing Request (CSR), and obtains a signature with the service key.
6. The app forwards the keystore-signed CSR to the HA. The HA checks the validity of the CSR. If all checks are passed, the HA signs the CSR and returns a signed certificate to the app.

Note that the HF service is only designed to support elliptic curve cryptography-based signatures (ECDSA), while CIE 3.0 only contains RSA keys. This is a concrete example of the Extensions advantage in Sect. 3.4, allowing us to bootstrap proofs of identity to different protocols from the original. Additionally, in the context of DLT it would be difficult to justify direct use of the eID certificate for all transactions, of which an immutable record is kept.

4.2 Security Remarks

A detailed security assessment of the approach in Sect. 3.3 is subject to the specific protocols and technology employed in practice. We use our proof-of-concept implementation, as described in Sect. 4.1, to highlight some important security issues, but leave a thorough security assessment until other future work has been carried out – in particular, integration with eIDAS and FIDO APIs. We make the following assumptions.

Firstly, OS integrity is required for the NFC channel to be secure: the mobile OS only gives access to the channel to the active app, and that app can establish a secure channel with the card. This allows one to limit a security assessment to the channel between mobile client and server. OS integrity is also necessary to guarantee that the keystore is secure.

Secondly, a genuine app is required in order to prevent PIN stealing and user impersonation. This is an intrinsic risk in any mobile application involving eID operations with PIN. Additionally, a genuine and honest app is required to allow users to express an informed consent as to the nature of the data contained in the eID certificate they are sharing, and the entities it will be shared with, in compliance with applicable regulation. Our proof-of-concept implementation is more permissive than some eID schemes, e.g. in Germany, where service providers are required to undergo a process of certification of their data requests, and eID data is provided indirectly by the IDP, with SPs never having direct access to user data from the card.

Thirdly, we assume the client-server channel is protected by TLS. The client establishes the channel, and may resort to certificate pinning in the genuine app.

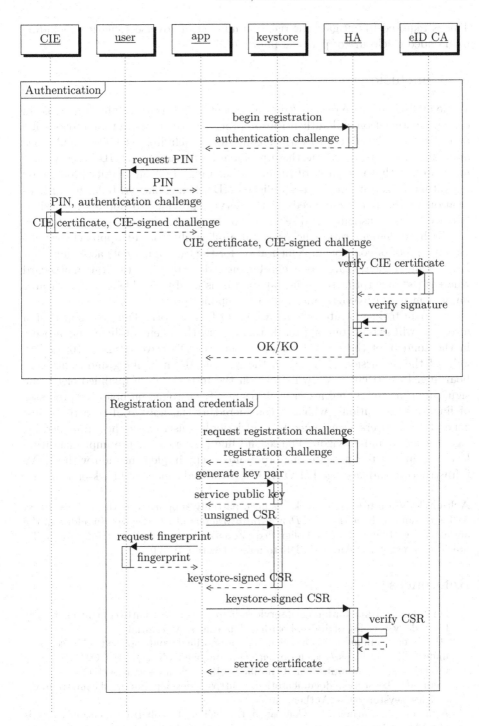

Fig. 4. Instance of the approach.

This is required to mitigate the risk of a number of adverse scenarios, including unintended disclosure of personal information.

5   Conclusions

While eID schemes are recognized as an essential means for establishing trust in citizen identification and authentication processes, their integration into existing digital services is subject to various constraints including usability, regulations and extensions. To overcome these problems, we propose an eID-based enrollment process that is capable of *(a)* providing a high LoA on identity proofing by exploiting a rigorous and well-established eID scheme; and *(b)* tailoring authentication to the particular needs of the service provider to obtain the desired balance between usability and security via the registration of authenticators.

We have demonstrated the practical applicability of our approach by providing a proof-of-concept implementation for the case of patients accessing their EHR through their smartphone: enrollment is done by using the Italian eID card whereas the fingerprint scanning capabilities is used to enable an authenticator implementing a cryptographic challenge-response protocol.

We plan to investigate two main lines of future work. The first is at design level: we will extend our approach to support the client on-boarding process in the context of the revised Payment Services Directive (PSD2) [10] and in light of the discussion in [7,24] on the role of eID in banking and digital on-boarding. In particular, we will focus on the integration of qualified electronic signature procedures that are crucial to simplify customer on-boarding processes of financial institutions, which is considered as the holy grail to attract new generations of users accustomed to the frictionless user experiences provided by, e.g., Facebook and Amazon. The second line of work is at the implementation level: we intend to integrate our proof-of-concept implementation with eIDAS infrastructure and leverage FIDO APIs for Android clients and back-end servers.

Acknowledgements. This work has been partially supported by the activity 19184 API Assistant of the action line *Digital Infrastructure* of EIT Digital. In addition, the authors are grateful to Istituto Poligrafico e Zecca dello Stato Italiano (IPZS) for kindly providing a prototype Android SDK to interact with CIE 3.0.

References

1. Digital onboarding for financial services. https://www2.deloitte.com/lu/en/pages/technology/articles/digital-onboarding-financial-services.html
2. eID User Community: Overview of pre-notified and notified eID schemes under eIDAS. https://ec.europa.eu/cefdigital/wiki/display/EIDCOMMUNITY/Overview+of+pre-notified+and+notified+eID+schemes+under+eIDAS
3. Android keystore documentation. https://developer.android.com/training/articles/keystore#UserAuthentication
4. Armando, A., Carbone, R., Compagna, L., Cuéllar, J., Tobarra, L.: Formal analysis of SAML 2.0 web browser single sign-on: breaking the SAML-based single sign-on for Google apps, pp. 1–10 (2008). https://doi.org/10.1145/1456396.1456397

5. BSI: Advanced security mechanisms for machine readable travel documents and eIDAS token (2015). https://www.bsi.bund.de/EN/Publications/TechnicalGuidelines/TR03110/BSITR03110
6. Carta d'Identità Elettronica. https://www.cartaidentita.interno.gov.it/
7. Deloitte: Value proposition of eIDAS-based eID - banking sector, July 2018. https://ec.europa.eu/cefdigital/wiki/display/EIDCOMMUNITY/Study+on+the+opportunities+and+challenges+of+eID+for+Banking
8. EU: General data protection regulation (GDPR), May 2016. http://data.europa.eu/eli/reg/2016/679/2016-05-04
9. European Parliament and Council: Directive 1999/93/EC on a community framework for electronic signatures. http://eur-lex.europa.eu/legal-content/EN/TXT/PDF/?uri=CELEX:31999L0093&from=EN
10. European Parliament and Council: Directive 2015/2366 on payment services in the internal market. http://data.europa.eu/eli/dir/2015/2366/2015-12-23
11. European Parliament and Council: Electronic identification, authentication and trust services (eIDAS). http://data.europa.eu/eli/reg/2014/910/oj
12. FIDO. https://fidoalliance.org/what-is-fido/
13. GIXEL: IAS ECC - Identification authentication signature European citizen card, European card for e-Services and National e-ID applications, February 2009
14. Grassi, P.A., Garcia, M.E., Fenton, J.L.: Digital identity guidelines. NIST, June 2017. https://doi.org/10.6028/NIST.SP.800-63-3
15. Grimes, R.: 12 ways to hack MFA, March 2019. https://www.rsaconference.com/industry-topics/presentation/12-ways-to-hack-2fa
16. Hyperledger fabric docs. https://hyperledger-fabric.readthedocs.io/
17. Hu, V., et al.: Guide to attribute based access control (ABAC) definition and considerations. NIST, January 2014. https://doi.org/10.6028/NIST.SP.800-162
18. Machine Readable Travel Documents (2015). https://www.icao.int/publications/pages/publication.aspx?docnum=9303
19. IETF RFC 5280: Internet X.509 public key infrastructure certificate and certificate revocation list (CRL) profile. https://tools.ietf.org/html/rfc5280
20. Istituto poligrafico e zecca dello stato (IPZS). https://www.ipzs.it/
21. Koeune, F., Standaert, F.-X.: A tutorial on physical security and side-channel attacks. In: Aldini, A., Gorrieri, R., Martinelli, F. (eds.) FOSAD 2004-2005. LNCS, vol. 3655, pp. 78–108. Springer, Heidelberg (2005). https://doi.org/10.1007/11554578_3
22. Kowalksi, B.: FIDO, strong authentication and eID in Germany. https://www.slideshare.net/FIDOAlliance/keynote-fido-strong-authentication-and-eid-in-germany
23. Morelli, U., Ranise, S., Sartori, D., Sciarretta, G., Tomasi, A.: Audit-based access control with a distributed ledger: applications to healthcare organizations. In: Mauw, S., Conti, M. (eds.) STM 2019. LNCS, vol. 11738, pp. 19–35. Springer, Cham (2019). https://doi.org/10.1007/978-3-030-31511-5_2
24. PWC: Study on eID and digital on-boarding. https://doi.org/10.2759/94773
25. Sistema Pubblico per la gestione dell'Identità Digitale (SPID). http://www.agid.gov.it/agenda-digitale/infrastrutture-architetture/spid
26. W3C: Verifiable credentials data model. https://www.w3.org/TR/verifiable-claims-data-model/
27. W3C: Web authentication: an API for accessing public key credentials level 2. https://www.w3.org/TR/webauthn-2/

TATIS: Trustworthy APIs for Threat Intelligence Sharing with UMA and CP-ABE

Davy Preuveneers[✉] and Wouter Joosen

imec-DistriNet, KU Leuven, Celestijnenlaan 200A, 3001 Heverlee, Belgium
{davy.preuveneers,wouter.joosen}@cs.kuleuven.be
https://distrinet.cs.kuleuven.be

Abstract. Threat intelligence platforms offer cyber emergency teams and security stakeholders access to sightings of cyberthreats and indicators of compromise. Given the sensitivity of the information, access may be restricted to certain members within an organization, offered to the general public, or anything in between. Service providers that host such platforms typically expose APIs for threat event producers and consumers, and to enable interoperability with other threat intelligence platforms. Not only is API security a growing concern, the implied trust by threat event producers and consumers in the platform provider remains a non-trivial challenge. This paper addresses these challenges by offering protection against honest but curious platform providers, and putting the access control back into the hands of the owner or producer of the threat events. We present TATIS, a solution for fine-grained access control to protect threat intelligence APIs using User Managed Access (UMA) and Ciphertext-Policy Attribute-Based Encryption (CP-ABE). We test the feasibility of our solution using the Malware Information Sharing Platform (MISP). We validate our contribution from a security and privacy point of view. Experimental evaluation on a real-world OSINT threat intelligence dataset illustrates our solution imposes an acceptable performance overhead on the latency of API requests.

Keywords: Threat intelligence · API security · User Managed Access · Ciphertext-Policy Attribute-Based Encryption

1 Introduction

Nowadays, organizations collaborate to define defensive actions against complex attack vectors by sharing information and knowledge about threats, sightings, indicators of compromise (IoC), and mitigation strategies. Threat Intelligence Platforms (TIP) have therefore become a critical security component within the enterprise to deal with the increasing volume and sophistication of cyber attacks [12]. These software platforms are cloud or on-premise systems that facilitate the aggregation and correlation of threat events from different parties

© Springer Nature Switzerland AG 2020
A. Benzekri et al. (Eds.): FPS 2019, LNCS 12056, pp. 172–188, 2020.
https://doi.org/10.1007/978-3-030-45371-8_11

and multiple sources [8], including security monitoring and data analytics tools. To simplify the sharing of threat information between different TIPs, they often rely on standardized data exchange formats, such as STIX 2.0[1].

Due to the sensitive nature of the threat events that TIPs collect, the way the information is shared with cyber emergency teams and other security stakeholders is subject to access rules that designate who is authorized to receive certain information. The Traffic Light Protocol (TLP)[2] is a well-known scheme developed to facilitate and encourage the exchange of threat events. The user sending a threat event with various attributes to the platform (i.e. the producer), tags these attributes with a color that indicates the appropriate audience with whom it may be further disseminated (i.e. the consumer). Information within a threat event may be intended:

- TLP:RED: Only for the direct addressees (e.g. those present at a meeting)
- TLP:AMBER: For (certain people within) an organization
- TLP:GREEN: For a community (e.g. peers and partner organizations)
- TLP:WHITE: To be freely disseminated (but subject to copyright rules)

The TLP marking of an attribute serves as an information exchange policy enforced within the TIP. The TLP scheme is only a labeling scheme. It therefore requires a certain level of trust in the system in that all parties (TIP provider, interlinked TIPs, threat event producers and consumers, etc.) are assumed to adhere to the protocol, as any event consumer is in principle able to disseminate events through out-of-bound channels beyond control of the TIP.

TIPs protect a treasure trove of sensitive and confidential information, and expose data exchange, search and analytics capabilities not only through web-based user interfaces, but also through RESTful APIs. The security of these API endpoints becomes a critical concern. Indeed, many of such enabling technologies that are used to improve the security of enterprise systems and networks, are also being targeted. Adversaries may abuse sensitive information within the TIP to attack organizations, use the information to evade detection, or poison the data to harm communities. In their report [3], ENISA confirmed TIPs do not only offer opportunities, but also have trust limitations:

1. The event producer trusts the platform provider to not expose confidential data to unauthorized recipients.
2. The event producer trusts the event consumers that they handle shared information according a predefined protocol (e.g. TLP).
3. The platform provider and event consumers trust the event producer that the information shared is reliable and credible.

In our work, we mainly address the first challenge for an honest but curious platform provider. We present TATIS, a solution for fine-grained access control to protect threat intelligence APIs using User Managed Access (UMA) and

---

[1] http://docs.oasis-open.org/cti/stix/v2.0/stix-v2.0-part2-stix-objects.html.
[2] https://www.us-cert.gov/tlp.

Ciphertext-Policy Attribute-Based Encryption (CP-ABE). The main contributions are (1) protection against honest but curious threat intelligence platform providers and data leakage through vulnerabilities in the TIP itself, and (2) more fine-grained access management by the producer of threat events when offered through APIs under the control of a potentially curious platform provider.

The remainder of this paper is structured as follows. In Sect. 2, we describe relevant related work on threat intelligence platforms. Section 3 describes how UMA and CP-ABE are used to fortify the threat intelligence platform. In Sect. 4 we provide a qualitative evaluation on security and privacy, and measure the performance impact of our solution in terms increased REST request latencies. We conclude in Sect. 5 summarizing the main insights and offering suggestions for further work.

2   Related Work

This section reviews relevant related work on threat intelligence platforms, and the cybersecurity threats they expose themselves.

Wagner et al. [13] presented MISP[3], an open source threat intelligence sharing platform, initially focusing on malware information, but now also used for other threat vectors, such as financial indicators for fraud detection and prevention. MISP operates on events and attributes. Events typically encapsulate tags to link events with one another (e.g. the TLP labels), objects from other information sharing tools, and attributes with various system or network related indicators. The *category* of an attribute puts it in a certain context, whereas the *type* of an attribute describes the indicator. Given the widespread use of the technology, we use MISP as the base TIP for our experimentation. More details about MISP and event examples will be provided in the next section.

Sauerwein et al. [11] conducted a systematic study of 22 threat intelligence sharing platforms, including MISP. A comparison of these platforms resulted in eight key findings, including (1) the lack of a common definition of threat intelligence sharing platforms, (2) STIX being the de-facto standard for threat information, (3) the sharing of indicators of compromise as main goal, (4) the closed source nature of most platforms, (5) the focus on data collection rather than analysis, (6) neglected trust issues, (7) an increasing interest in academia and industry, and (8) manual tasks making the user a bottleneck. Our work aims to address the 6th observation.

Indicators of compromise (IoC) and threat sightings may carry sensitive confidential information, and affected parties may be reluctant to share this threat information with other security stakeholders. Without appropriate measures, parties may only be willing to share intelligence with those parties with whom they already established a trust relationship. This concern was explored by van de Kamp et al. [5]. The authors propose cryptographic approaches to hide details of an indicator or sighting while still enable sharing, hereby limiting the possibility of information misuse. The proposed method implemented on top of MISP

---

[3] https://www.misp-project.org/.

relies on hashing with non-secret salts chosen at random for each IoC such that precomputation of the hashes is not possible. While technically feasible, it limits the data analysis and correlation of related events. Furthermore, the values of certain typed attributes may not meet certain formatting criteria (e.g. a hostname or IP address), which may limit the practical feasibility of the hashing method as a privacy enhancing technology.

Iklody et al. [4] explored the steady increase and volatility of IoCs. When attack strategies evolve − e.g. IP addresses changes or domain names are being deleted − certain IoCs may become outdated or invalid. The authors therefore propose a generic scoring model for decaying IoCs that are shared among MISP communities. The proposed scoring model leverages a.o. a base score for an attribute, the elapsed time between when an attribute was first and last seen, the end-time of an attribute (when the overall score should be 0), and a decay rate at which the overall score should decrease over time. The base score itself is constructed from various other parameters. From a trust perspective, the authors argue that organizations may consume information of multiple hops away, and they may not know the producers. Fake information may harm an organization or disrupt the sharing between communities. Related research by the same authors was presented in recent follow-up work by Mokaddem et al. [7].

The gap we aim to bridge is not just to conceal sensitive information, but put the owner of the back in control of who can access his threat data in the TIP. To that extent, we specifically target the protection of the RESTful APIs with a reusable solution that is not tailored to any specific TIP, such as MISP.

3   Enhanced API Security for Threat Intelligence Platforms

In this section, we will present the basic building blocks of TATIS and illustrate how it is deployed to protect the REST APIs of a MISP instance. As with many commercial threat intelligence platforms, each user in MISP belongs to an organization, and is granted a specific role (admin, organization admin, publisher, user, etc.) that is associated with certain permissions to manage users, or to read, modify, and publish events, etc. MISP provides a RESTful API as part of its automation capabilities. We will first exemplify the basic functionality, before we explain how our TATIS solution strengthened the security of these APIs with User Managed Access (UMA) 2.0 and Ciphertext-Policy Attribute-Based Encryption (CP-ABE).

3.1   Background on MISP Automation APIs

The automation capabilities of MISP[4] are exposed as RESTful APIs. The way users authenticate and gain access is with an authorization header and a user-specific key, as illustrated in Fig. 1.

---

[4] https://www.circl.lu/doc/misp/automation/.

```
1   misp@work:~$ curl --header "Authorization: LLOkALJsBlPhUjGhFi..." \
2     --header "Accept: application/json" \
3     --header "Content-Type: application/json" \
4     https://localhost:8443/events/2
5
6   {
7       "Event": {
8           "id": "2",
9           "orgc_id": "5",
10          "org_id": "1",
11          "date": "2014-10-03",
12          "threat_level_id": "2",
13          "info": "OSINT New Indicators of Compromise for APT Group ...",
14          "published": true,
15          "uuid": "54323f2c-e50c-4268-896c-4867950d210b",
16          "attribute_count": "29", ...
17          "Attribute": [
18              {
19                  "id": "1068",
20                  "type": "link",
21                  "category": "External analysis", ...
22              }, ...
23          ], ...
24          "Tag": [
25              {
26                  "id": "1",
27                  "name": "type:OSINT", ...
28              }, {
29                  "id": "2",
30                  "name": "tlp:green", ...
31              }
32          ]
33      }
34  }
```

Fig. 1. Retrieving a specific event with given identifier from MISP

The `LLOkALJsBlPhUjGhFi...` authentication key is passed along in the HTTP GET request to obtain the event (and associated tags, objects and attributes) with identifier 2. Adding and deleting events occur in a similar manner using the HTTP POST and DELETE methods. Each user has his own authentication key whose lifetime is in principle unlimited, and which can be manually reset from within MISP's administrative web interface. Contrary to state-of-practice access token-based security solutions, such as OAuth 2.0, this is a rather crude form of API authorization and access control.

3.2 User Managed Access

The OWASP API Security Top 10 of 2019[5] identifies important API security threats. According to these guidelines, the security of the MISP RESTful APIs can be improved with more fine-grained object level access control and with resource usage and request rate limiting. Additionally, the user submitting the events should have more flexibility to manage access control to his own events.

To address these challenges, TATIS's goal is to protect individual events and attributes with the User Managed Access (UMA) protocol. Rather than

---

[5] https://github.com/OWASP/API-Security/raw/develop/2019/en/dist/owasp-api-security-top-10.pdf.

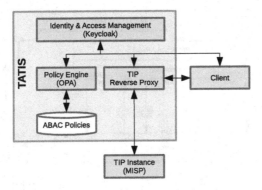

Fig. 2. TATIS offering UMA and ABAC based API security through a reverse proxy.

modifying the existing MISP code base, we developed a TIP reverse proxy, as depicted in Fig. 2. The *TIP Reverse Proxy* is implemented as a Spring Cloud Greenwich.SR2 microservice acting as an API gateway to the actual TIP instance and as the *resource server* for the threat events. The solution was designed as a reserve proxy (rather than modifying an existing TIP code base) to also transparently serve other types of TIPs or platform providers with critical APIs. This design is ideally suited for organizations that externalize the hosting of the TIP itself to a third party while only hosting the reverse proxy at their premises.

For the authentication and authorization framework, we rely on RedHat's Keycloak 6.0.1 open source Identity and Access Management platform[6]. The access control rules and conditions under which authorization is granted are declared in an attribute-based access policy language. The definition of the authorization policies are beyond the scope of the UMA specification as the policy evaluation is done out-of-band. This allows TATIS to use access control solutions, such as the eXtensible Access Control Markup Language (XACML) [9] or the Open Policy Agent (OPA) [10]. Our proof-of-concept implementation uses the declarative OPA policy language. As the authorization policy framework of Keycloak does not support this language out-of-the-box, a JavaScript policy from within Keycloak acts as a bridge by externalizing the policy evaluation. The JavaScript policy invokes the OPA policy engine to obtain an authorization decision. This way, threat event producers can host their own OPA policy engine and define their own OPA policies. More details about why we chose this policy language will be provided in the next subsection on CP-ABE.

From a policy management point of view, our approach completely decouples the authorization logic for invoking APIs from the information exchange policy imposed by the TLP marking of an event. Our policy-based authorization can also enforce the TLP constraints, and seemingly make the authorization within the TIP redundant. However, our solution only targets a TIP's APIs and not its web-based user interface. Hence, both authorization mechanisms are needed.

---

[6] https://www.keycloak.org/.

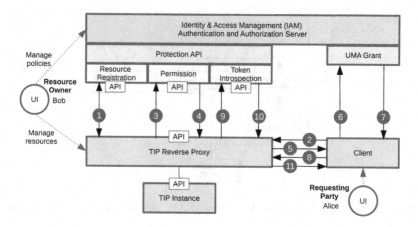

Fig. 3. User-Managed Access (UMA) 2.0 for granting access to threat events

Using Keycloak, the APIs of the *TIP Reverse Proxy* are protected with the UMA 2.0 specification, i.e. the UMA 2.0 Grant for OAuth 2.0 Authorization[7]. Threat events are represented as resources that are exposed through APIs protected by the reverse proxy. Event producers and consumers can only invoke these APIs through the reverse proxy, not by contacting the TIP instance directly. The way access is granted to a single or a set of events is illustrated in Fig. 3. These are the different steps in the UMA protocol that Bob (i.e. the threat event producer) and Alice (i.e. the threat event consumer) should follow:

1. Bob − being the *resource owner* − registers one or more events at the *Resource Registration Endpoint* of the *authorization server*, and configures who can access which resources under which permission scopes.
2. The *client* of Alice − the *requesting party* − makes an access request to the protected event, but without a valid *Requesting Party Token* (RPT).
3. The resource server requests the permissions (i.e. the *scopes*) bounded to the event from the *Permission Endpoint* of the authorization server.
4. The *Permission Endpoint* returns a permission ticket.
5. The resource server returns the URI of the authorization server and the permission ticket to Alice's client.
6. The client submits the permission ticket as well as any necessary claims to the UMA Grant endpoint to retrieve an access token.
7. The UMA Grant endpoint of the authorization server issues an RPT token to Alice's client after evaluating associated authorization policies.
8. The client again requests access to the protected event resource, but now with a valid RPT token.
9. The resource server introspects the RPT token at the *Token Introspection Endpoint* of the authorization server.
10. The authorization server returns the status of the token introspection.
11. The resource server grants access to the protected event resource.

---

[7] https://docs.kantarainitiative.org/uma/wg/rec-oauth-uma-grant-2.0.html.

This scenario assumes that Alice can authenticate against the same authorization server that protects the resources so that relevant identity claims can be gathered for evaluation of the access control policies at the authorization server.

```
1    package httpapi.authz.cs4e
2
3    default allow = false
4
5    allow {
6         input.role[_] = "admin"
7    }
8
9    allow {
10        input.role[_] = "owner"
11   }
12
13   allow {
14        input.subject = "alice"
15        input.location = "work"
16   }
```

Fig. 4. Example of a declarative OPA policy to grant access to a threat event

The declarative OPA policy example in Fig. 4 is merely a simple illustration of how different attributes can be used to decide on granting or denying access to event resources. This way, TATIS combines the strengths of UMA 2.0 and an attribute-based access control (ABAC) model implemented with externalized OPA policies. It is much more flexible and granular compared to the role-based access control (RBAC) model typically offered in TIPs, including MISP:

1. More sophisticated policies incorporate dynamic attributes, such as time, location or usage statistics for more fine grained access control decisions.
2. The owner of the data can define different privileges per API method for each user, even disabling certain methods in response to an attack.
3. When the policy denies access to a requester, the owner can still grant access, hereby bypassing the policy. This consent can be revoked by the owner.

However, the above does not guarantee trust in the platform provider hosting the threat intelligence sharing platform. A malicious platform provider or administrator is still able to directly access the underlying database (i.e. MariaDB in the case of MISP) and gain access to all the sensitive and confidential information. A vulnerability in the software stack may lead to similar concerns. These concerns are addressed with our following contribution.

3.3   Ciphertext-Policy Attributed-Based Encryption

To further protect the threat events stored within the database, we consider an *honest-but-curious* adversary model, i.e. parties that are curious and try to find out as much as possible about the sensitive threat events despite following the protocol. The TIP provider or cloud infrastructure operator can be considered as such candidate adversaries. Additionally, a vulnerability in the TIP itself may grant unauthorized subjects access to sensitive information. Later on, we will discuss the limitations for a *malicious user* adversary model.

To address this challenge, we pursue a defense-in-depth strategy that not only protects the API endpoints with UMA but also the underlying data exposed by these APIs. Database encryption is not a sufficient solution as the encryption key is typically stored server-side. Also, deterministic encryption, order-preserving encryption, or order-revealing encryption schemes that were suggested to support database querying capabilities, have been shown to leak information [6] if an attacker can observe queries and the associated responses. Fully-homomorphic encryption and oblivious RAM − while adequate from a security point of view − are known to be computationally expensive techniques.

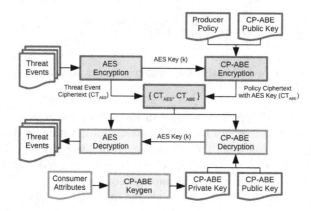

Fig. 5. CP-ABE based encryption and decryption of threat events

Our solution aims to encrypt events and attributes so that the confidentiality is guaranteed w.r.t. unauthorized subjects, but at the same time the event producer still wants to grant access to event consumers based on his own authorization policies. Obviously, the event producer cannot use a common encryption key for all event consumers. For scalability reasons, the event producer cannot encrypt the same information multiple times with the different public keys belonging to the event consumers.

The *TIP Reverse Proxy* component of TATIS solves this through Ciphertext-Policy Attribute-Based Encryption (CP-ABE) [2], as illustrated in Fig. 5. Bob encrypts the threat events with an AES symmetric key k into a ciphertext CT_{AES}, and uses a policy (i.e. a boolean access structure resembling a decision tree based on user attributes) and CP-ABE to encrypt the AES symmetric key k into a ciphertext CT_{ABE}. A user's private decryption key is linked to a set of user attributes that represent this user's permissions to decrypt. So, Alice can only decrypt the event ciphertext CT_{AES} if she can obtain the AES key k. To do so, she must decrypt CT_{ABE} with a CP-ABE private key generated from her set of user attributes. The decryption will fail if Alice's attributes do not match the access structure defined by Bob's policy.

Referring back to the declarative OPA policy example in Fig. 4, the boolean access structure with which the plaintext is encrypted, corresponds with:

$$\text{role:admin} \lor \text{role:owner} \lor (\text{subject:alice} \land \text{location:work}) \qquad (1)$$

The ability to easily translate declarative OPA policies into a boolean access structure is the main reason to use OPA rather than XACML for our attribute-based access control policy language (discussed in the previous subsection).

For the actual implementation, our *MISP Reverse Proxy* as well as Alice's client application use the Java-based CP-ABE implementation by Wang [14]. This means that the above policy is translated into a policy post-fix notation and syntax that this Java-based implementation understands:

$$\text{role\#admin role\#owner subject\#alice location\#work 2of2 1of3} \qquad (2)$$

Obviously, Alice should not be able to define her own attributes and create a multitude of private decryption keys with which she can attempt to decrypt the data. The *TIP Reverse Proxy* returns a private decryption key to Alice, and the user attributes upon which the key is based, should originate from a trustworthy source. We leverage the UMA 2.0 protocol to obtain trustworthy user attributes from the RPT token that is passed along with each REST request. The RPT access token is a JSON Web Token (JWT), and the attributes in the RPT token are digitally signed by the IAM, and hence trusted. A subset of the attributes in this RPT token are used for the private key generation in the CP-ABE scheme.

Even if a local MISP instance pulls events from a remote one or multiple TIPs synchronize event feeds with one another, the encryption is preserved. The policy-based decryption of attributes will continue to work as long as the identity management systems operate in a federated manner, and share identity claims about subjects so that decryption keys can be generated based on these claims.

In summary, TATIS protects the APIs and underlying MISP events, and stores the encrypted threat events in the same MariaDB database as before. We do not encrypt the event and linked attributes as a whole, but only those attributes that are considered sensitive. Given the type of an attribute, MISP imposes a particular format for the value (e.g. a valid IP address or hostname). As the AES cryptographic algorithm does not support format-preserving encryption [1], we encrypt an attribute as a whole − not just the type, category or value of the attribute. To customize TATIS towards other threat intelligence platforms, the corresponding REST APIs and JSON objects that are being intercepted and secured by the reverse proxy, need to be adapted.

4 Evaluation

In this section we provide a qualitative security and privacy evaluation, and measure the performance impact of our TATIS solution in terms of increased REST request latencies against a baseline of a TIP instance without our enhancements.

4.1   Qualitative Evaluation

Revisiting the three trust related challenges as identified in the ENISA report [3], our solution addresses the first by enforcing API access control at the REST endpoints and encrypting sensitive confidential data while leaving the controls in the hands of the data owner rather than the platform provider hosting the TIP instance. In an *honest-but-curious* adversary model, the above building blocks prohibit disclosure to unauthorized parties. In a *malicious user* adversary model, our solution does not prevent a malicious consumer of threat data − let's call her Eve − to share her private decryption key (or the decrypted threat events) out-of-band with other adversaries to leak data to unauthorized parties. We also cannot guarantee that the threat information provided by malicious producers is reliable, but the logging features of the *TIP Reverse Proxy* can detect and hold less reputable sources of incredible information accountable with a post-factum machine learning based audit analysis.

Our solution builds upon both the UMA 2.0 protocol and CP-ABE. Under the assumption that the OPA policy can be translated into an equivalent policy that the CP-ABE can handle, one may ask what is the benefit of using both security measures to protect the API of the threat intelligence platform. The reasons are performance related and three-fold:

- The CP-ABE encryption and decryption are executed by the client applications of the producer and consumer of the threat information − not by the TIP instance − to protect against a curious but honest TIP administrator.
- The OPA policies prevent access to encrypted data that consumers cannot decrypt anyway if their user attributes do not match the CP-ABE policy.
- The private decryption key can be returned at the same time as the RPT access token of the UMA-protocol. Consumers do not have to explicitly request a CP-ABE private decryption key, and the attributes are digitally signed.

In practice, the OPA policies are responsible for other security measures compared to the CP-ABE ciphertext policies. TATIS uses the OPA policies to implement resource usage control and request rate limiting.

We put the owner of the data − or the threat event producer − back in control by letting him specify under which rules and conditions a requesting party or threat event consumer is granted an RPT access token. These rules and conditions are externally defined in access control policies and evaluated by the owner's OPA policy engine. In fact, rather than specifying authorization conditions in such an OPA access control policy, the event producer can decide to not share at all by default (equivalent to a single deny policy), but individually grant access in a consent-based manner. This UMA-based consent can later on be revoked by the owner through the Identity and Access Management platform.

There are still some practical concerns that are not addressed with TATIS. For example, our solution limits the event correlation capabilities of the TIP instance to only the unencrypted event fields and attributes. However, this concern is easily addressed by having consumers set up their own private TIP instance in which data is stored unencrypted. We in fact recommend such an approach for privacy reasons, as queries launched against this private instance cannot be abused as a side channel by a curious TIP administrator to reveal sensitive information regarding the requesting party (i.e. the event consumer).

4.2 Quantitative Evaluation

We set up a TIP instance (version 2.4.111) in a Docker 19.03 environment running on a Dell PowerEdge R620 server with an Intel Xeon CPU E5-2650 16-core processor running at 2.00 GHz (with hyper-threading enabled resulting in 32 virtual CPUs) and 64 GB of memory.

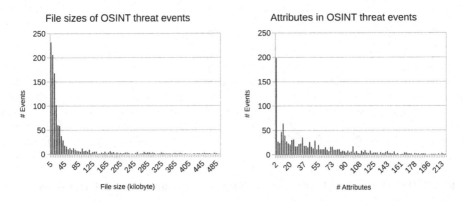

Fig. 6. File sizes and number of attributes for the OSINT threat events

As a baseline benchmark, we feed a plain MISP instance with the CIRCL OSINT Feed available at https://www.circl.lu/doc/misp/feed-osint/. At the time of writing (July 2019), this feed contains 1292 events in indented JSON format. The histograms in Fig. 6 illustrate the number of events with a certain file size and number of attributes. 50% of the events has a file size of less than 20 kilobytes and less than 40 attributes. One event with unique identifier 5c5be78a-3908-47c4-bf7c-4487950d210f has a filesize of 317 megabytes (containing several attributes with binary attachments), another one with identifier 544f8aa7-9224-46ad-a73f-30f9950d210b has 20970 attributes. These events were submitted by a client to a remote MISP instance over a wired Gigabit link using HTTP POST requests over a secure SSL network connection. Figure 7 shows the distribution of the HTTP POST request latencies in seconds, as well as the correlation with the number of attributes in an event. These graphs illustrate that the request latency has a strong correlation with the number of attributes, which we suspect is due to the way threat information is stored in the MariaDB database. In general, 50% of the HTTP POST requests were handled in less than 3 s.

To measure the impact of the UMA 2.0 protocol and the CP-ABE encryption (using AES encryption of the event attributes), we benchmark the amount of

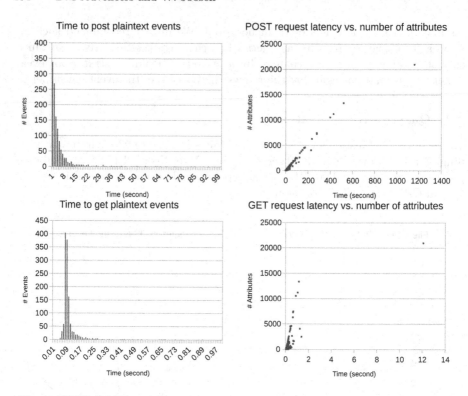

Fig. 7. HTTP POST and GET request latencies for plaintext OSINT threat events

time required to AES encrypt the JSON representation of the event attributes and the latency of the corresponding HTTP POST requests. Note, we only encrypt attributes that are directly associated with the event, excluding those attributes that are associated with objects embedded in the event. For example, the event with identifier 544f8aa7-9224-46ad-a73f-30f9950d210b has 20970 attributes in total. However, the event has 4724 embedded objects having 14172 attributes which were not encrypted. For this event, we hence encrypted only the remaining 6798 attributes. For a fair and realistic performance comparison, we compute for each event a new CP-ABE ciphertext policy using the same boolean access structure, as exemplified in (2). The results and performance impact of TATIS are shown in Fig. 8. There is no significant difference in terms of latency for submitting plaintext threat events versus AES encrypted threat events. The reason for this is that the AES encryption of each attribute does not increase the size of the payload (beyond some padding).

Table 1 depicts the mean and standard deviation performance overhead on the latency of CP-ABE encryption and decryption relative to respectively the HTTP POST and GET requests for all 1292 threat events.

These results illustrate that the impact for HTTP POST requests is minimal, i.e. less than 2%. The small performance impact can be explained by the fact

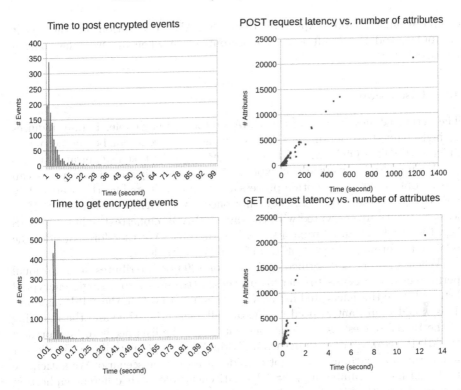

Fig. 8. HTTP POST and GET request latencies for encrypted OSINT threat events

Table 1. Performance impact of CP-ABE encryption and decryption

Measure	Mean (seconds)	Standard dev
HTTP POST Plaintext	9.152	43.582
HTTP POST Encrypted	9.023	44.076
CP-ABE Encrypt	0.157	0.016
HTTP GET Plaintext	0.112	0.346
HTTP GET Encrypted	0.069	1.110
CP-ABE Decrypt	0.027	0.012

that the amount of time required to complete the POST request for uploading a threat event in plaintext is already quite large. For HTTP GET requests, again, there is no significant difference between the operation retrieving plaintext threat events and encrypted threat events. However, the time required to decrypt the attributes in the encrypted threat events is relatively larger compared to the latency of the HTTP GET request itself. The request latency increased with up to 40%. Further analysis pointed out that the largest part of the extra time is spent on the CP-ABE decryption of the AES key. CP-ABE decryption is computationally more expensive than the AES decryption of the event attributes, and the result is even more outspoken when an event has only a few attributes.

4.3 Discussion

The actual latency impact of the UMA protocol is negligible. It only requires a single request to obtain an RPT token, as this token can be reused across different HTTP POST and GET requests up until the token's expiration time.

When multiple events are encrypted with the same ciphertext policy, one can further optimize the decryption process and significantly reduce the overhead by CP-ABE decrypting the AES key only once rather than for each event. If at least 10 events are encrypted with the same CP-ABE ciphertext policy and AES key, the overhead drops from 40% to less than 5%. We therefore consider the relative performance impact of TATIS to be acceptable.

When an event is described with 100s or 1000 s of attributes, an additional performance strategy is to encrypt all these attributes into a single encrypted list, and store this encrypted list as a single attribute within the MISP instance. This would significantly speed up the overall encryption time and the handling of the POST request as now only one entry (i.e. the list) needs to be stored in the MISP instance rather than each individually encrypted attribute. We did not follow this approach, as we do not consider it a realistic scenario. We anticipate that multiple attributes may be CP-ABE encrypted with different ciphertext policies, hence the need for storing each encrypted attribute individually.

We only AES encrypted individual attributes within a threat event. As mentioned before, a threat event may also have objects embedded in its description, and these objects can in turn be described by attributes. These and other fields of an event (such as the TLP tag associated with an attribute) were not encrypted. The main reason for this decision is to allow the MISP instance to carry out an event correlation analysis on the unencrypted fields. However, if need be, these fields can be encrypted too in a similar way.

5 Conclusions

In this work, we presented TATIS, a solution to protect the APIs of threat intelligence sharing platforms. TATIS is based on the User Managed Access 2.0 protocol Ciphertext-Policy Attribute-Based Encryption to protect the threat events in the database from honest but curious platform providers. Compared to the typical role-based access control, our solution enables attribute-based access control through OPA policies in order to offer more fine-grained object level access control. Furthermore, threat event producers can define their own authorization policies, which brings access control back into the hands of the data owners. TATIS was designed as a reverse proxy solution in order to be easily reused and adapted towards other threat intelligence platforms, and its API monitoring and logging capabilities allow for post-factum auditing. We evaluated

TATIS on top of an open source threat intelligence data set, and measured the impact on the latency of HTTP POST and GET requests towards the MISP platform. Although the impact for GET requests is more outspoken, we identified optimization strategies that bring the overhead of our solution down to 5%.

As future work, we will evaluate CP-ABE schemes with a more expressive policy syntax, explore the interoperability with other threat intelligence platforms, and augment TATIS with machine learning based auditing capabilities.

Acknowledgments. This research is partially funded by the Research Fund KU Leuven. Work for this paper was supported by the European Commission through the H2020 project CyberSec4Europe (https://www.cybersec4europe.eu/) under grant No. 830929.

References

1. Bellare, M., Ristenpart, T., Rogaway, P., Stegers, T.: Format-preserving encryption. In: Jacobson, M.J., Rijmen, V., Safavi-Naini, R. (eds.) SAC 2009. LNCS, vol. 5867, pp. 295–312. Springer, Heidelberg (2009). https://doi.org/10.1007/978-3-642-05445-7_19
2. Bethencourt, J., Sahai, A., Waters, B.: Ciphertext-policy attribute-based encryption. In: 2007 IEEE Symposium on Security and Privacy (SP 2007), pp. 321–334, May 2007
3. ENISA: Exploring the opportunities and limitations of current threat intelligence platforms. Technical report, December 2017. https://www.enisa.europa.eu/publications/exploring-the-opportunities-and-limitations-of-current-threat-intelligence-platforms
4. Iklody, A., Wagener, G., Dulaunoy, A., Mokaddem, S., Wagner, C.: Decaying indicators of compromise. CoRR abs/1803.11052 (2018)
5. van de Kamp, T., Peter, A., Everts, M.H., Jonker, W.: Private sharing of IOCs and sightings. In: Proceedings of the 2016 ACM on Workshop on Information Sharing and Collaborative Security, WISCS 2016, pp. 35–38. ACM, New York (2016)
6. Kellaris, G., Kollios, G., Nissim, K., O'Neill, A.: Generic attacks on secure outsourced databases. In: Proceedings of the 2016 ACM SIGSAC Conference on Computer and Communications Security, CCS 2016, pp. 1329–1340. ACM, New York (2016)
7. Mokaddem, S., Wagener, G., Dulaunoy, A., Iklody, A.: Taxonomy driven indicator scoring in MISP threat intelligence platforms. CoRR abs/1902.03914 (2019)
8. Qamar, S., Anwar, Z., Rahman, M.A., Al-Shaer, E., Chu, B.T.: Data-driven analytics for cyber-threat intelligence and information sharing. Comput. Secur. **67**(C), 35–58 (2017)
9. Rissanen, E.: eXtensible Access Control Markup Language (XACML) Version 3.0. OASIS Standard, January 2013. http://docs.oasis-open.org/xacml/3.0/xacml-3.0-core-spec-os-en.html
10. Sandall, T.: Open policy agent (2019). https://www.openpolicyagent.org/
11. Sauerwein, C., Sillaber, C., Mussmann, A., Breu, R.: Threat intelligence sharing platforms: an exploratory study of software vendors and research perspectives. In: Leimeister, J.M., Brenner, W. (eds.) Towards Thought Leadership in Digital Transformation: 13. Internationale Tagung Wirtschaftsinformatik, WI 2017, St. Gallen, Switzerland, 12–15 February 2017 (2017)

12. Tounsi, W., Rais, H.: A survey on technical threat intelligence in the age of sophisticated cyber attacks. Comput. Secur. **72**, 212–233 (2018)
13. Wagner, C., Dulaunoy, A., Wagener, G., Iklody, A.: MISP: the design and implementation of a collaborative threat intelligence sharing platform. In: Proceedings of the 2016 ACM on Workshop on Information Sharing and Collaborative Security, WISCS 2016, pp. 49–56. ACM, New York (2016)
14. Wang, J.: Java realization for ciphertext-policy attribute-based encryption (2012). https://github.com/junwei-wang/cpabe/

Protecting Android Apps
from Repackaging Using Native Code

Simon Tanner$^{(\boxtimes)}$, Ilian Vogels, and Roger Wattenhofer

ETH Zurich, Zürich, Switzerland
{simtanner,ivogels,wattenhofer}@ethz.ch

Abstract. Android app repacking allows malicious actors to modify apps, bundle them with malware or steal revenue. Current detection mechanisms of app distribution services are questionable in their effectiveness, and other proposed repackaging protection schemes do not have the necessary protection against circumvention. We propose a repackaging protection architecture that verifies the app's integrity at runtime. We make use of encrypted sections of bytecode that can be decrypted with a key derived at runtime. The method partially relies on native code, and as such is difficult to circumvent. We show that our implementation provides a practical integration in the workflow of an app developer.

Keywords: Repackaging protection · Android · App security

1 Introduction

Android is the most common mobile operating system. Due to its popularity, Android also attracts malware developers. Apps submitted to Google Play are screened before they are published[1] and Android's Google Play Protect regularly scans apps that are installed on devices, regardless from which source the apps originate.[2] Even though these security mechanisms are in place, their effectiveness is debatable as they do not detect every malicious app submitted to the service. Several malicious apps were published on Google Play in 2017 and 2018, impacting millions of users.[3,4] Additionally, many third party app stores have weaker security checks. In China, the majority of Android users do not have access to Google Play and have to use third-party app stores, many of which are not trustworthy and distribute modified versions of popular apps [9].

---

[1] https://source.android.com/security/reports/Android_WhitePaper_Final_02092016.pdf.

[2] https://source.android.com/security/reports/Google_Android_Security_2017_Report_Final.pdf.

[3] https://blog.checkpoint.com/2017/04/24/falaseguide-misleads-users-googleplay/.

[4] https://blog.cloudflare.com/the-wirex-botnet/.

The authors of this paper are alphabetically ordered.

© Springer Nature Switzerland AG 2020
A. Benzekri et al. (Eds.): FPS 2019, LNCS 12056, pp. 189–204, 2020.
https://doi.org/10.1007/978-3-030-45371-8_12

Attackers can unpack apps contained in APK files, modify their content and then repackage and distribute them. It is common that malware is hidden within copies of existing popular apps. Attackers may also repackage popular apps to divert ad revenue. Therefore, making repackaging of Android apps harder or even impossible is of interest to both users and developers of apps.

In this work we propose and implement[5] a mechanism to protect apps from being repackaged by transforming them after compilation, before they are distributed to the public. The app is transformed without any impact on the user experience, except for a small slowdown. However, the transformation prevents normal execution if the app has been tampered with. To make the protection difficult to circumvent, it relies on encrypted integrity checks in native code. This protection prevents an attacker from modifying the app, and potentially bundling malware with it.

2   Related Work

Several solutions have been proposed to prevent the distribution of repackaged Android applications. The methods can be divided into centralized and decentralized approaches.

Centralized Approaches. The centralized approaches typically analyze features from the collection of apps hosted by a central distribution platform; they identify similar features between apps, such as the instruction sequence patterns [3,20], their call graphs [4], the trace of system calls [15], the layout of the Android Activities [12,13,18], or the presence of software watermarks [19]. In this scenario, the application distribution service monitors the apps submitted by developers and removes suspected repackaged apps. This requires removing the infringing apps in a timely manner, before the offending apps are distributed to a significant amount of users.

Decentralized Approaches. With a decentralized approach, the repackaged app is detected at runtime on the user's device. This way, the app verifies its own integrity during runtime. This has the advantage that it distributes the repackaging detection workload. As soon as tampering has been detected, an appropriate response mechanism can be executed during which the app may abruptly stop executing and inform the user about the tampering.

Several works about software protections that assert the software's integrity at runtime have been proposed by the research community. For instance, [2] proposes a generic integrity checking and tamper prevention scheme which involves inserting multiple pieces of code, called *guards*, that protect a specified region of code. These pieces of code typically compute a checksum over the region of machine code instructions. Droidmarking [10] proposes a non-stealthy repackaging detection approach which sends watermarking information to a separate

---

[5] The source code is provided at https://github.com/ilian/repackaging-protection.

standalone app that is responsible for validating the integrity of protected apps. However, Droidmarking also relies on the distribution platform to statically scan the apps for tampering.

The Stochastic Stealthy Network (SSN) [6] is another dynamic repackaging protection method. It validates the public key of the developer by comparing substrings of the public key obtained at runtime with obfuscated hard-coded substrings. The public key of the developer is obtained at runtime using Java reflection. The different function names that are called using reflection are obfuscated to make static analysis more difficult for an attacker trying to circumvent the applied protections. Zeng et al. [17] propose *BombDroid*, a repackaging protection scheme based on logic bombs and encrypted code blocks. A logic bomb is a piece of code that executes when specified conditions are met. The code responsible for detecting tampering is stored within an encrypted code block. The proposed approach is designed in such a way that the decryption key is unknown to the attacker without running the application.

Issues with SSN and BombDroid. While the authors of SSN consider different dynamic attacks, a much simpler and more practical attack can be performed instead: as reflection is used to invoke a method to obtain the developer's public key, an attacker can rewrite the method invocations to invocations of a method that is injected by the attacker. The attacker can pass the instance and arguments of the original reflective method invocation to the newly injected method. This injected method can then return the original public key. This attack scenario can be performed without any dynamic analysis and can disable the repackaging detection for all apps protected with SSN. As most method calls in typical Java applications are not invoked using reflection, there is not a lot of runtime overhead when performing such an attack.

There are also some potential issues with BombDroid. We consider an attacker who can inject code that allows the modified app to perform code analysis and modification at runtime. Such a dynamic attacker can modify the decrypted instructions before they are executed. Similar to the previously discussed problem, the attacker can modify the instructions that obtain information from the environment, which is being relied on for the repackaging detection such as the public key of the developer and file descriptors to the original APK. An attacker can divert invocations of methods that provide environment information to injected methods that return simulated information to spoof the environment. When such an attack is performed, the repackaging detection mechanism is circumvented. Such attacks can be performed in practice by modifying and generating Dalvik bytecode at runtime.

3   Design Overview

We propose a resilient repackaging protection scheme that is based on encrypting code blocks. It partially relies on native code to address the attacks possible on previous work as discussed in Sect. 2. The system modifies the application provided by the app developer and adds integrity checking in a robust manner. If repackaging is detected, an appropriate response mechanism is invoked.

The app to protect can be provided as an APK containing compiled bytecode and native code. After compiling the Android app to Dalvik bytecode and native code, the binary files are bundled together with resources and assets (images, audio, video, raw files, etc.) into an APK file. Our proposed repackaging protection scheme can be applied to this APK file to generate the protected app. The repackaging protection can thus be easily integrated into the workflow of app developers as an additional step in the compilation pipeline. As the protection is embedded within the application itself, we can distribute the protected APK to many users and distribution platforms regardless of their enforcement of repackaging protection. The transformation could also be performed by an app store to protect all apps it serves.

We aim to insert integrity checks that take action whenever repackaging has been detected. These code snippets are inserted in many locations in the app, such that the integrity is asserted at different locations throughout the execution. The challenge is to make the applied protection tamper-resistant such that it is difficult for an attacker to bypass or remove the added protection measures. Once the repackaging has been detected, response code can be executed. Many different responses are possible such as informing the user, informing the developer or crashing the app. Our repackaging protection scheme is not only robust against static analysis, but also against attackers that perform dynamic analysis.

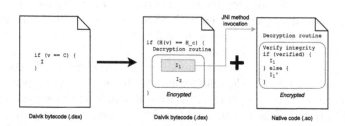

Fig. 1. Transformation of candidate code blocks (Color figure online)

Static Analysis. The proposed system adds code to the apps to perform the repackaging detection and countermeasures. This added code has to be protected from static analysis to make removal by the attacker difficult. We make use of a technique called *conditional code obfuscation* [11] to prevent static analysis of code blocks. The condition v == C for a variable v and constant C is transformed to the semantically equivalent (assuming no hash collisions) H(v) == H_c where H is a one-way hash function and H_c is a constant equivalent to H(C). We can exploit the fact that the value of the variable v is not known to an attacker, unless a brute force attack is performed. A key k is derived from the constant value C to encrypt all the bytecode within the true branch of such if-bodies during the transformation phase. The protection scheme is depicted in Fig. 1 in which these encrypted blocks in the bytecode are represented by the instructions surrounded by a red border.

Dynamic Analysis. Repackaging detection and response code is not inserted in Dalvik bytecode because it is not difficult for an attacker to replay any environment information as if the original application is running instead of a repackaged one, as discussed in Sect. 2. Instead, we perform the checks in native code, which is also encrypted to prevent static analysis. Using native code makes dynamic analysis more difficult since it has to be performed on a machine-instruction level instead of the much simpler bytecode-instruction level. A native method is called from within an encrypted bytecode block using the Java Native Interface (JNI). A key is passed to it to decrypt a native code block. At runtime, the native code is decrypted and the integrity of the application is verified. The use of both bytecode and native code encryption thus increases the difficulty of inspecting the behavior that is performed at runtime.

Code Removal. An attacker could still remove or bypass the native code and the integrity checks contained in the native code would not get executed. To prevent this, we enforce that the native code has to be executed to preserve the functionality of the app. We therefore move a sequence of bytecode instructions, $I_1 \subseteq I$, to the native code as can be seen in Fig. 1. These instructions are rewritten to equivalent JNI function calls, which have the same effect as executing the bytecode instructions directly. The attacker cannot remove the native method invocation because the normal application behavior depends on it.

Detection of Repackaging. To detect repackaging, we compare parts of files within the APK using a one-way hash function. These are typically the Dalvik Executable files, but our protection mechanism can also be configured to protect assets such as images and audio files. Integrity validation is performed in the native code when an encrypted block is encountered. Each encrypted block computes the hash of a different part of the files to reduce the impact on the performance when reading the files from storage. Alternatively, a digest of the developer's public key (located under the META-INF directory) can be validated to further increase performance. These computed hash values are compared to known hash values of the original app. Once the application has verified that it has not been repackaged, the instructions that have been moved to the native code (I_1) are executed. Otherwise, the response behavior is executed (I'_1).

4   Implementation

The protection system transforms the bytecode of the app to an intermediate representation, without having access to the source code, and then performs the analysis to find suitable locations for bytecode encryption. The native method invocations are added such that the integrity checks are called at runtime. These checks must depend on a reference state of all files. Therefore, the native code is generated after the Dalvik bytecode has been transformed.

Performing static analysis and modifications directly on Dalvik bytecode can be error-prone and cumbersome. In our implementation, we use the Jimple [14] intermediate representation for analysis and modifications. We use the Java API of the Soot framework[6] to perform modifications on the Jimple intermediate representation. After performing the necessary modifications for the repackaging protection in the Jimple code of the app, the Soot framework allows us to transform the Jimple code back to Dalvik bytecode and a new APK file can be generated.

Finding Candidate Blocks. Our goal is to find a list of statements I, also referred to as a block, that is executed after a condition of the form

```
if (v == C) {
    I
}
```

has been evaluated to be true, where v is a variable and C is a constant. We iterate through all if-statements within each method body. A key to encrypt the code block can then be derived from C. In our implementation SHA-1 is used to transform the if condition. We must ensure that all statements within the if-body are only executed after the condition has been evaluated to true. Unconditional jump statements could jump to any statement in I without having satisfied the condition of the if-statement. In this case we could not compute the encryption key that is derived from the constant C. Therefore, if such a jump statement is encountered the code block does not get transformed and encrypted.

Transformation of a Block. We derive the decryption key for a block from v when the true branch has been taken, and want to decrypt the bytecode corresponding to the statements within the if-body. Thus, we need a facility to decrypt and execute bytecode at runtime. Unfortunately, redefining classes containing the encrypted bytecode with ones that contain the decrypted bytecode is not possible with the Android Runtime (ART), as the instrumentation package java.lang.instrument that provides the redefineClasses method is not available on Android. We instead load a *new* class for each encountered encrypted block by making use of the dalvik.system.InMemoryDexClassLoader class (present since the release of Android 8.0) which can load classes in the form of Dalvik bytecode from memory. This new class has a method containing the extracted code block. The bytecode of this class gets encrypted in the transformation phase. This method is then invoked at runtime after loading the class

---

[6] https://github.com/Sable/soot.

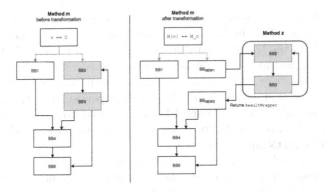

Fig. 2. Comparison of an example of a control flow graph before and after transformation. Basic blocks (BB) with a red background represent the basic blocks whose instructions can be extracted to a separate class and encrypted. (Color figure online)

containing the decrypted bytecode. We invoke this method containing the original statements to preserve the semantics of the app. Because we have extracted statements from within the if-body to a separate class, we hereafter call the newly generated class, the *extracted class*. Since the statements are executed in the context of a different class and method than in the original if-body, workarounds need to be put in place in order to preserve semantic equivalence between the original and transformed app.

A method z is added to the new class with the sequence of statements I, local variables, and trap handlers of the original block. For every local variable used in a statement in I, a parameter is added to the method signature of z. We refer to the method that originally contains I as m. The original method m is transformed to remove the sequence of instructions I and add a call to z passing the corresponding local variables. The condition before executing I is replaced in m by the hashed comparison. The original constant C is therefore not present anymore. When the local variables get modified in method z, these changes are not visible outside of z. To preserve semantic equivalence between the original and transformed method m, z returns a list of the modified primitives and references to m, allowing these changes to be reflected in the context of m.

Jump targets in Dalvik bytecode, for both conditional and unconditional goto statements, must be contained within the same method as the jump statement. As we have copied the jump statements from the original method to the extracted class, the jump target is potentially not contained within the same method anymore. To resolve this, an identifier for the jump target is returned to the caller of z whenever a jump to a statement outside of z needs to be performed. The jump is subsequently performed in the transformed method m, after z has returned.

To pass all the discussed information from z back to m, a helper class `ResultWrapper` is used.

Figure 2 shows an example of the transformation of the control flow graph. The nodes BB2 and BB3 in the figure are the basic blocks corresponding to the instructions I. In the transformed method, BB_{NEW1} is responsible for decryption and calling method z. The inserted instructions responsible for restoring the modified primitives and handling return values are omitted in this illustration. We can see that jumps from BB3 to BB2 persist after transformation, whereas jumps from BB3 to BB4 and BB5 are removed from BB3 after transformation, and instead return the corresponding jump identifier to BB_{NEW2} using the returned `ResultWrapper` instance.

Some class members that were accessible in the original method are not accessible anymore when called from the method z outside of the original class. Java access modifiers are not only enforced during compile time, but also during runtime. In the Dalvik Executable format, access modifier bit fields are stored for classes, inner-classes, fields and methods in the `access_flags` bit field.[7] As we are potentially accessing or modifying a field, or calling a method that the newly generated class does not have access to, we need to statically set the access modifier of the relevant classes and class members to public.

Adding Native Integrity Checks. Integrity checking is performed in native code which is called via the Java Native Interface (JNI). More precisely, the extracted method z will call a native method to perform integrity checking. Our implementation generates C++ code to be compiled to a shared object file. For every native method added to the Jimple intermediate representation, we write its corresponding method signature to the generated C++ source file. To prevent an attacker from ignoring method calls to the shared library, we move a statement from the extracted block I to the native code by emulating the execution of the statement using the C++ JNI. The native program code is then encrypted with a randomly chosen symmetric key stored in the encrypted bytecode of z.

A statement w from the extracted block is chosen to be woven into the native code. A static native method signature is added to a new Java class that contains all the added native methods. Note that this Java class only contains a list of method names, return type and parameters it accepts without providing any direct implementation. This injected class is responsible for loading the compiled shared object file that contains the native code for all blocks in its class initialization method. The parameters of the native methods are set such that all local variables needed to execute statement w in the native code and a decryption key to decrypt the native code can be passed down from z to the native method. The statement w is then removed from the extracted block, and is instead substituted by a static invocation of the native method, passing the local variables referenced by w and a randomly chosen decryption key k used to decrypt the native code. This key gets decrypted at runtime together with the bytecode of the extracted class. The generated native code consists of code

---

[7] https://source.android.com/devices/tech/dalvik/dex-format.

that asserts the integrity of the running app and the JNI method calls needed
to emulate the effect of the woven code w.

The execution of the generated native methods consist of three parts:

1. Decryption of the native code using the supplied key, passed as an argument
   to the native method.
2. Validating the integrity of the installed Android application.
3. Executing statement w using JNI to preserve semantic equivalence between
   the transformed and original application.

We write the code to be encrypted (all but the decryption procedure) to
a dedicated function that will be decrypted at runtime. We can use a function
pointer to obtain the memory location of the function that needs to be decrypted
in the context of the decryption routine with the supplied key that is passed as
an argument. Before decrypting the instructions that are located within the text
segment, we must ensure that the memory pages where the decrypted instructions will be written to are marked as writable. Note that as the decryption of
the instructions are performed in-place, the memory locations of the encrypted
and decrypted instructions are the same. As specified by the p_flags field in the
ELF header of the compiled shared object file, the text segment is by default
marked as readable and executable. Thus, the memory pages that contain the
encrypted instructions are first marked as writable using the mprotect system
call. We mark the relevant memory pages as writable in preparation for decrypting the instructions in-place. Encryption and decryption is performed with a
stream cipher, as we want to preserve the length of instructions in the ELF
binary so we can statically encrypt during the transformation phase in-place,
and decrypt during runtime in-place. We decided to use AES-128 in CTR mode,
which turns the block cipher into a usable stream cipher for our purpose. Each
byte to be decrypted is XORed with the byte generated by the stream cipher
based on the chosen key.

After decrypting the instructions, the permissions of the memory pages can
be restored to readable and executable for security reasons. A static boolean
within each generated method is set to indicate that the code has already been
decrypted such that the instructions are only decrypted once.

After the native code has been decrypted, the instruction pointer enters the
instructions that were previously encrypted. We validate the integrity of the
running application by obtaining the path to the APK file that contains the
code of the currently running app. We can obtain this path by invoking the
Android PackageManager binary, located at /system/bin/pm when supplying it
with the package name of the currently running application. We compute hashes
of parts of the files within the APK archive to verify its integrity.

Each generated native method computes and compares the hash of a section
of a file with the precomputed hash that was determined statically during the
transformation procedure. At this point in the transformation process, we are
generating C/C++ code for the native library. This implies that we can statically compute the hash of every file that will be bundled with the APK, except
for the shared library file itself and files added after compilation such as the

developer's code signature. Note that we can also assert integrity of the developer's certificate file, which might be a good choice when all applications signed by this certificate are trusted by the developer. If the hashes match, the woven statement w is executed to ensure correctness of the transformed application. If the hashes do not match, we execute our response mechanism. In the current implementation a null-pointer is dereferenced, such that a segmentation fault is raised. An alternative to this would be to also execute a JNI call, but instead of emulating the same effect as w, we could randomly invoke a Java method with random parameters or launch a new activity that is not supposed to be launched under normal circumstances in order to interrupt the normal behavior of the application.

As the symmetric key used to encrypt and decrypt the native code is known during the transformation phase, we statically encrypt the relevant code sections after compilation using the offsets of the functions to be encrypted. Non-static functions have external linkage, and are contained in the symbol table. The symbol table contains a mapping between the symbolic names and their offsets within the compiled binary. We encode and store the symmetric key in the name of the function before compilation (with C linkage to prevent function name mangling) such that both the offset to start encrypting at and key to encrypt are known when reading the symbol table of the compiled binary. After compilation, we can thus easily encrypt the relevant sections by reading the keys and offsets in the ELF header with the nm utility. After encrypting the instructions, we strip the keys from the symbol table with the strip utility so we do not leak the key used to encrypt the native code to the attacker.

5   Security Analysis

The goal of the system is to make it as difficult as possible for the attacker to circumvent the added repackaging protection. In general, removing all encrypted blocks and restoring the woven code or bypassing the detection code is sufficient to thwart the protection scheme. We aim to make it harder for an attacker to circumvent this scheme than to reimplement the app from scratch.

Static Attacks. An attacker may try to remove the protection by statically examining and modifying the code of the protected Android app. The encrypted blocks in the bytecode and native code can easily be detected. However, removal of these sections would lead to an inconsistent state at runtime, and most likely crash the app. The attacker is forced to decrypt the encrypted code. For each block, the decryption key can be derived from the replaced if-condition if(H(v) == H_c) {...} by inverting the one-way hash function.

When a brute force approach is used, the attacker has to try each value from the domain of the variable v. For primitives in Dalvik bytecode, the domain can be as large as 2^{64} in the case for long or double variables. Therefore, 2^{63} hash operations and comparisons have to be computed on average to obtain the correct key. Note that in practice, the distribution of such constant values are not uniformly random (see Fig. 3), which can be advantageous for the attacker.

Dynamic Attacks. The attacker can not only analyze the protected application statically, but can also transform the protected application. This enables the attacker to perform more complex attacks. Code can be injected that can perform code analysis or change the behavior of the application at runtime.

The challenge of finding the correct encryption key can be solved without a lot of effort when considering a dynamic attack in which the virtual method invocation that passes the decrypted contents to the class loader is hooked: the method invocation can be modified by an attacker such that its arguments are passed to an arbitrary method. In this newly injected method, the attacker can tamper with the decrypted Dalvik bytecode at runtime. Additionally, the attacker can determine the decryption key for the current encrypted block. Since these encrypted blocks are present in different locations in the bytecode, the attacker has to find enough execution traces to decrypt all code blocks to completely remove the applied protections.

As discussed in Sect. 3, the repackaging protection code is inserted into the native shared libraries, woven together with parts of the original code of the application. The proposed protection is specifically designed in such a way that bytecode analysis is not sufficient to bypass the protections. Combining application code and integrity checks in the native code requires the attacker to also analyze native code at runtime. Dalvik bytecode allows the attacker to deduce a lot of semantic information due to the verbosity of the Dalvik instructions. Useful information such as variable types or which type of method invocation is performed (private method invocation, interface invocation, class initializer invocation, ...) can be extracted. Machine code, on the other hand, is more difficult to analyze. The usage of pointer arithmetic, self-modifying machine code [7], complex machine instructions or even undocumented instructions[8] can significantly increase the complexity of the analysis. With our approach of forcing attackers to analyze native code dynamically, code obfuscation frameworks operating on native code [5] can be used instead of being limited to bytecode-level transformations.

The integrity of the running application is verified by making use of the C standard library to obtain a file handle of the APK file that corresponds to the running application. The methods that provide the file handle and read its content are provided by Bionic, Android's C library. An attacker might try to hook these library functions by statically overwriting pointers in the Global Offset Table (GOT) or Procedure Linkage Table (PLT) of the ELF binary, which are tables filled by the dynamic linker that contains offsets to procedures of shared libraries. Modifying the relocation information for dynamically linked Bionic functions gives the attacker control over the libraries that are loaded by the dynamic linker. In this way, fopen() and read() calls can be hooked. This attack could easily be mitigated by not relying on any shared library, but instead only on system calls by passing interrupt vectors to the kernel using an interrupt signal.

---

[8] https://github.com/xoreaxeaxeax/sandsifter/blob/master/references/
domas_breaking_the_x86_isa_wp.pdf.

Another possible attack scenario involves sandboxing of the protected app in a host app, where the attacker can potentially modify the behavior of the sandboxed application by modifying its memory at runtime, or by running malicious code in a separate thread unbeknownst to the sandboxed app. To be resilient against such attacks, the repackaging protection scheme should detect whether the application is being executed with sandboxing or debugging. This can often be achieved by comparing the result of system calls at runtime with expected values. Another work [1] achieves sandboxing by making use of the `ptrace` system call, often used by debugging tools. The application that is being sandboxed can detect that it is being traced using several techniques such as spawning a subprocess that traces itself, preventing itself from being traced by other processes because a process may only be traced by a single process.

These countermeasures raise the difficulty of the attack, but are no permanent solution. This problem can be reduced to solving the anti-debugging or anti-sandboxing problem. Solving this problem lies outside of the scope of this work, but is actively being researched [8].

6   Evaluation

We evaluate the proposed repackaging protection system using a collection of free apps downloaded from Google Play and F-Droid.[9]

As mentioned in Sect. 5, the distribution of the constant values in the transformed conditions is important for the resilience of the system against brute-force attacks. Figure 3 shows the observed distribution of the constants. This serves as an indication of how much effort an attacker needs to invest to statically attack the protection scheme. We can observe that some apps have the same constant values as others, which might help an attacker guess the encryption

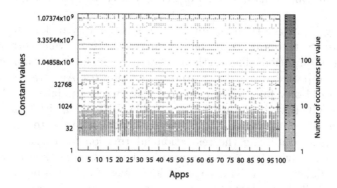

Fig. 3. Distribution of 32-bit constant values encountered during transformation. Apps are taken from the list of most popular applications on Google Play. Constants within the interval $[-9, 9]$ are ignored.

---

[9] https://f-droid.org/en/.

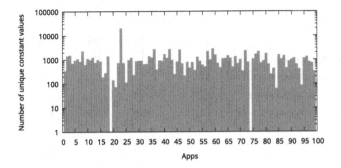

Fig. 4. Number of unique constant values encountered during transformation. Apps are taken from the same sample of apps as Fig. 3.

keys. Note that if a library is being utilized by an app, the constants appearing in the bytecode of that library will be shared amongst all apps which include it.

The unique number of constants within an app is shown in Fig. 4. This figure shows how many blocks can be utilized for transformation. We also observe that for a few apps, no constants have been found. This might be due to Android packers interfering with the static analysis process of finding candidate blocks because the original bytecode has been compressed or encrypted [16]. Additionally, some code obfuscators might artificially increase the number of constants in if-statements which we suspect to be the case for Facebook Messenger (com.facebook.orca, app number 23 in Figs. 3 and 4).

We have measured the runtime overhead when executing a transformed block as opposed to executing the original code block. This overhead was measured on an LG Nexus 5X running the factory image of Android 8.1.0. For each encrypted block, we observed an overhead of approximately 27 ms upon first execution and approximately 3 ms for subsequent executions as shown in Fig. 5. Most of the overhead occurs when an encrypted code block is executed for the first time which involves decrypting the Dalvik bytecode, invoking the class loader to load the decrypted class and decrypting the native code.

The overhead of a sample of apps is shown in Table 1. Each of the apps were given random input for 2 min using Monkey.[10] The number of blocks encountered and executed at runtime for the first time are referred to as block misses. Blocks that are executed subsequently, are called block hits. The total overhead per app is computed by multiplying block misses and block hits by the average measured overhead of that type in Fig. 5. The overhead noticed by the user in practice may be lower since multiple threads may execute different blocks at the same time.

Figure 6 shows how over time, different code paths for an app are taken when providing random input, and thus encountering new transformed blocks which need to be decrypted at runtime. We observe that initially the rate of unique blocks encountered is high, but declines over time as more blocks are already decrypted and loaded into memory.

---

[10] https://developer.android.com/studio/test/monkey.

Table 1. Performance overhead after transformation

	# misses	# hits	Total (s)	Total (%)
com.aappstech.flpmaps	17	415	1.704	1.42
com.takeaway.android	34	1232	3.939	3.28
org.mozilla.firefox	33	3874	12.513	10.42
com.whatsapp	12	698	2.418	2.01

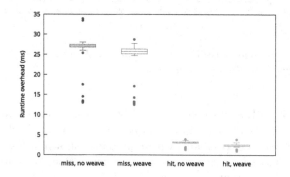

Fig. 5. Boxplot of runtime overhead per encountered encrypted block. The first two boxes illustrate the overhead when a block is first encountered. When a code block is reached that already has been decrypted (referred to as a hit), the overhead is much smaller, as shown in the last two boxes.

We have encountered some issues with the transformation of a portion of apps. An Android APK can contain native libraries for a set of ABIs. Some of the APKs are only provided with native libraries of an ABI that is deprecated in the current NDK toolchain. Some of those are not available in the current NDK version. These apps can therefore not be transformed with our implementation. The developer has to provide a set of shared object files whose ABIs are not deprecated.

We are using the third-party library Soot to perform our transformation on the Jimple intermediate representation, which has some issues[11] when transforming some of the applications from the collection.

We have built a testing workflow which compares the execution of a Java source file before and after transformation. This helped us to discover issues with the implementation and resolve them fairly quickly. Many apps on Google Play are obfuscated with ProGuard, which makes debugging issues with our implementation and Soot's time consuming.

We have evaluated how many apps from our collection are successfully transformed and do not experience unwanted side-effects such as app crashes or thrown exceptions: We have randomly selected 200 apps as a sample from the F-Droid marketplace. 2% of the sample could not be transformed (e.g. when

---

[11] https://github.com/Sable/soot/issues/969.

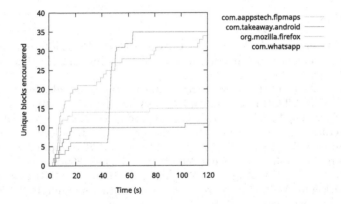

Fig. 6. Unique blocks encountered while running a few apps from Google Play while providing a random input every 100 ms for 2 min using Monkey.

the original APK only contains native code with deprecated ABIs). 7.5% of the sample introduced new exceptions at runtime after transformation. We also evaluated the 100 most popular apps from Google Play. 12% of the sample could not be transformed, and 41% of the sample introduced new exceptions at runtime after transformation. We compared the exceptions thrown by the original app to those thrown by the app after transformation. We made use of Monkey to send a pseudo-random stream of input events to each original and transformed app.

7 Conclusion

In this work, we discussed the limitations of recent work on repackaging protection embedded in apps. We proposed a complete architecture to protect an app from being repackaged by unauthorized actors based on native code. The evaluation shows that the proposed approach only has a limited impact on the performance of the protected apps.

The strength of the system against brute-force attacks depends on the distribution of constants in the candidate blocks. Approaches to insert artificial constants which are compared at runtime to a variable could be inserted to increase the number of encrypted blocks.

This work has focused on a repackaging detection architecture, and shifted the integrity problem from the bytecode level down to the machine-code level. Integrity of the compiled native code in our implementation is important because it is responsible for triggering the response behavior upon detecting an integrity mismatch. As discussed in Sect. 2, integrity protection of native code has been discussed by the research community in depth. Because of the complexity and difficulty to analyze machine code, circumventing the proposed protection is more difficult than protection based on bytecode. The attacker can either brute-force all the encryption keys and then analyze the machine code or the analysis has to be performed at runtime.

References

1. Bianchi, A., Fratantonio, Y., Kruegel, C., Vigna, G.: NJAS: sandboxing unmodified applications in non-rooted devices running stock Android. In: SPSM 2015, Denver, CO, USA, pp. 27–38 (2015)
2. Chang, H., Atallah, M.J.: Protecting software code by guards. In: ACM CCS-8 Workshop DRM 2001, Philadelphia, PA, USA, pp. 160–175 (2001)
3. Hanna, S., Huang, L., Wu, E., Li, S., Chen, C., Song, D.: Juxtapp: a scalable system for detecting code reuse among Android applications. In: Flegel, U., Markatos, E., Robertson, W. (eds.) DIMVA 2012. LNCS, vol. 7591, pp. 62–81. Springer, Heidelberg (2013). https://doi.org/10.1007/978-3-642-37300-8_4
4. Hu, W., Tao, J., Ma, X., Zhou, W., Zhao, S., Han, T.: MIGDroid: detecting app-repackaging Android malware via method invocation graph. In: ICCCN 2014, Shanghai, China, pp. 1–7 (2014)
5. Junod, P., Rinaldini, J., Wehrli, J., Michielin, J.: Obfuscator-LLVM - software protection for the masses. In: SPRO 2015, Florence, Italy, pp. 3–9 (2015)
6. Luo, L., Fu, Y., Wu, D., Zhu, S., Liu, P.: Repackage-proofing Android apps. In: DSN 2016, Toulouse, France, pp. 550–561 (2016)
7. Mavrogiannopoulos, N., Kisserli, N., Preneel, B.: A taxonomy of self-modifying code for obfuscation. Comput. Secur. **30**(8), 679–691 (2011)
8. Nevolin, I.: Advanced techniques for anti-debugging. Master's dissertation, Ghent University (2017)
9. Ng, Y., Zhou, H., Ji, Z., Luo, H., Dong, Y.: Which Android app store can be trusted in China? In: COMPSAC 2014, Vasteras, Sweden, pp. 509–518 (2014)
10. Ren, C., Chen, K., Liu, P.: Droidmarking: resilient software watermarking for impeding Android application repackaging. In: ASE 2014, Vasteras, Sweden, pp. 635–646 (2014)
11. Sharif, M.I., Lanzi, A., Giffin, J.T., Lee, W.: Impeding malware analysis using conditional code obfuscation. In: NDSS 2008, San Diego, CA, USA (2008)
12. Soh, C., Tan, H.B.K., Arnatovich, Y.L., Wang, L.: Detecting clones in Android applications through analyzing user interfaces. In: ICPC 2015, Florence/Firenze, Italy, pp. 163–173 (2015)
13. Sun, M., Li, M., Lui, J.C.S.: Droideagle: seamless detection of visually similar android apps. In: Proceedings of the 8th ACM Conference on Security & Privacy in Wireless and Mobile Networks, New York, NY, USA, pp. 9:1–9:12 (2015)
14. Vallee-Rai, R., Hendren, L.J.: Jimple: simplifying Java bytecode for analyses and transformations. Technical report (1998)
15. Wang, X., Jhi, Y., Zhu, S., Liu, P.: Detecting software theft via system call based birthmarks. In: ACSAC 2009, Honolulu, Hawaii, USA, pp. 149–158 (2009)
16. Yu, R.: Android packers: facing the challenges, building solutions. In: Proceedings of the 24th Virus Bulletin International Conference (2014)
17. Zeng, Q., Luo, L., Qian, Z., Du, X., Li, Z.: Resilient decentralized android application repackaging detection using logic bombs. In: CGO 2018, Vösendorf/Vienna, Austria, pp. 50–61 (2018)
18. Zhang, F., Huang, H., Zhu, S., Wu, D., Liu, P.: Viewdroid: towards obfuscation-resilient mobile application repackaging detection. In: WiSec 2014, Oxford, United Kingdom, pp. 25–36 (2014)
19. Zhou, W., Zhang, X., Jiang, X.: Appink: watermarking android apps for repackaging deterrence. In: ASIA CCS 2013, Hangzhou, China, pp. 1–12 (2013)
20. Zhou, W., Zhou, Y., Jiang, X., Ning, P.: Detecting repackaged smartphone applications in third-party android marketplaces. In: CODASPY 2012, San Antonio, TX, USA, pp. 317–326 (2012)

Access Control Models
and Cryptography

Command Dependencies in Heuristic Safety Analysis of Access Control Models

Peter Amthor$^{(\boxtimes)}$ and Martin Rabe

Technische Universität Ilmenau, P.O. Box 100565, 98684 Ilmenau, Germany
{peter.amthor,martin.rabe}@tu-ilmenau.de

Abstract. The principle merits of access control models lie in the ability to precisely reason about their security properties in lineage of the *safety* problem. It formalizes the question if future changes in a model's protection state may eventually violate a security requirement, thereby falsifying model correctness. One fundamental problem of safety analysis is that, as proven in the seminal HRU model calculus, this property is undecidable for the most expressive class of models. To tackle this problem in practical security engineering, a heuristic approach has proven useful that exploits the fact that model commands share dependencies, which are assumed to be (1) one-dimensional and (2) static. In complex models for modern application domains, such as type enforcement in operating systems, both assumptions cannot be made. This paper studies both problems and provides a heuristic solution approach for the problem of dynamic dependencies. Based on our heuristic, we demonstrate the practical impact of this analysis problem and discuss the general implications on model design and analysis strategies.

Keywords: Security policy · Security model · Access control · Model safety · Heuristic analysis · Operating systems security · Security engineering

1 Introduction

Satisfying security properties of critical software systems relies on a correct security policy. A security policy precisely describes strategies that realize these properties, which makes it an extremely critical engineering artifact. To this end security models are used to guarantee policy correctness.

For decades, such guarantees are based on formal analyses of security models [5,8,10,11,13–16] (model-based security engineering). Model analysis aims at confirming formal policy properties, some of which are tractable by static methods, while others require to reason about the dynamic evolution of a system. In the domain of access control (AC) models, such dynamic properties concern the authorization to execute security-critical operations (*commands* in model terms). Analyzing these properties has been termed *security analysis* [16], which can be subdivided in two classes of questions: Given some AC model at a given

© Springer Nature Switzerland AG 2020
A. Benzekri et al. (Eds.): FPS 2019, LNCS 12056, pp. 207–224, 2020.
https://doi.org/10.1007/978-3-030-45371-8_13

moment in time (in model terms, a *protection state* to analyze), is it possible
(1) that some (desired) property will ever become false; or (2) that some (undesired) property will ever become true? While the first question mainly deals
with availability, the intention of the second question is to validate restrictions
on authorized commands which are, for example, demanded by confidentiality
or integrity goals of the security policy. For historical reasons, this second family
of questions is called *safety* properties.

As has been proven in the seminal HRU model [8], safety properties are
generally undecidable for models of unrestricted computational power. To nevertheless take advantage of the high expressiveness of such models, simulative
analysis approaches are used, which leverage the semi-decidability of the problem [2,5,6]: The dynamic model behavior is implemented, simulated and every
protection state change is tested for a possible safety violation. Once any such
violation has been found, it can be demonstrated that the given model is *unsafe*
for the given protection state. The practical value of such results for security
engineers is to provide hints at possible errors in the security policy, by repro-
ducing a sequence of legitimate operations in the underlying system (*command
sequence* in the model) which ultimately leads to a safety violation.

In order to efficiently find such errors, simulative analysis is controlled by a
heuristic algorithms. It makes assumptions about critical command sequences
such that chances of a safety violation as an effect of one of these commands are
maximal. For a promising class of heuristics used to date, called DEPSEARCH
[2,5], these assumptions are quite restrictive: they demand a model to be specified in such a manner that only certain classes of causal dependencies between
commands may occur. This makes the analysis approach inflexible and, as a
consequence, impractical to use for more complex model semantics. Examples
for such models are the SELX model for the SELinux operating system [1] or the
RePM$_G$ model for an online social network [11]: to cover the complexity of these
AC policies, some amount of errors is introduced by rewriting them as a model
that is heuristically analyzable. These errors must be balanced against those
errors potentially eliminated through formal analysis. Even worse, the interpretation of simulative analysis results – a command sequence in the rewritten
model – is hampered by semantical gaps, making it even more burdensome to
identify the source of errors in the first place. Hence the goal of this paper is
to study the idea of DEPSEARCH heuristics for models in which possible dependencies between commands are less restricted. As a first step we will address the
subproblem of dynamic dependencies. We study the costs introduced in terms
of runtime overhead and demonstrate their practical impact.

The contributions of this work are (1) a formal generalization of command dependency, including a classification in static/dynamic and one-/multi-
dimensional; (2) a formalism to represent dynamic dependencies for general
access control models; (3) a heuristic strategy and the specification of an
extended heuristic algorithm to analyze models with dynamic dependencies; (4)
a study of heuristic runtime properties and generalizable model properties that

follow from dynamic dependencies, based on a study of both a synthetic and a practical model.

Paper Organization: After discussing related work in the next section, Sect. 3 introduces formalisms and presents the DEPSEARCH heuristic. In Sect. 4, we theoretically define the generalization of command dependencies and adapt the idea of DEPSEARCH to handle the class of dynamic dependencies. Section 5 then discusses the practical impact of this approach on analysis performance, including implications on model design. We conclude with a summary of our findings and resulting goals of ongoing and future work in Sect. 6.

2   Related Work

This work is closely related to both model calculi for safety analysis as well as analysis approaches for tackling the potential undecidability of this problem. Both fields are tightly coupled, as is expressed in the literature: A large body of work related to safety analysis focuses on restricting the computational power of AC models in a non-harmful way w. r. t. some application domains, e. g. fixed-operations Take-Grant models [10], acyclic, ternary MTAM models [14], finite attribute domains in the $PreUCON_A^{finite}$ model [13], or trusted administration in the RePM$_G$ model [11]. All these restrictions lead to models with a less-than-Turing-complete computational power, yet retaining the expressive power sufficient to being useful in their respective application domain.

A fundamentally different, approximative approach is followed by [2,5,6,15]. Here, the goal is to reason about safety without restricting the computational power of a model, thus merely strengthening assumptions about the correctness of policies based on the absence of errors found, while accepting possible non-termination of analysis algorithms. In [2,4–7], the motivation behind this approach is to deliberately avoid restricting model semantics (and thus analysis strategies) to some application domain, but to provide a pattern for naturally expressing and analyzing arbitrary security policies – including different paradigms for authorization semantics (such as access control, information flow, and non-interference) as well as for model abstractions (such as identity-based, roles-based, attribute-based, or relationship-based access control). Since this motivation aims at a less application-dependent model engineering method, an according formal calculus is needed such as core-based modeling [6,9,12] or aspect-oriented modeling [1–3]. Consequently, this model calculus must not assume any restrictions in expressive nor computational power, and so must any safety analysis approach general enough to tackle such models.

This paper describes a semi-decision approach for this which is based on the idea of trading precision for tractability. We build on previous work in the area of heuristic safety analysis by model simulation [2,5,6] which aims at falsifying some definition of safety for a given model of a security policy. More precisely, we scrutinize the DEPSEARCH heuristic algorithm introduced there based on a more precise definition of "dependency" and point out its limitations w. r. t. certain properties of a security policy. Our notation for generic access control models is roughly based on similar, conventional notations from [3,8,16].

3   Heuristic Safety Analysis

Before discussing dependency-based heuristic safety analysis, we agree upon a formalism for representing both AC models and their analysis questions in the first part of this section. After this, our existing approach for simulative analysis of HRU safety, called DEPSEARCH, is sketched on a principal level.

Models and Queries. To formally express AC policies, a set of formal model components is defined. These typically are either sets of atomic identifiers, or mappings/relations[1] that associate them with each other in a meaningful way (e. g. to specify authorization rules). We will refer to such components as $A_1 \ldots A_n$. An HRU model [8] e. g. contains the components $A_1 = S$ (subjects set), $A_2 = O$ (objects set), $A_3 = R$ (access rights set), and $A_4 = acm : S \times O \to 2^R$ (access control matrix). As a more complex example, a SELX model [1] contains components such as $A_1 = E$ (entities set), $A_2 = T$ (types set), $A_3 = cl$ (entity classification function), $A_4 = con$ (security context function), $A_5 = \hookrightarrow_r$ (role transition relation), or $A_6 = \hookrightarrow_t$ (type transition relation).

For reasoning about dynamic model properties, the definition of components is not sufficient. Instead, we consider these components as a specific view on model engineering, tailored to find the most appropriate and natural formal definitions for the semantics used in an AC policy. Another view, more tailored towards dynamic analysis, has been introduced by [6,9,12] and treats an AC system as a deterministic state machine, based on the original idea of [8].

Definition 1 (Dynamic AC Model). *A dynamic access control model is a state machine defined by a tuple* $\langle \Gamma, \Sigma, \Delta \rangle$, *where*

- *the* state space Γ *is a set of protection states;*
- *the* input set $\Sigma = \Sigma_C \times \Sigma_Y^*$ *defines possible inputs that may trigger state transitions, where* Σ_C *is a set of* command *identifiers used to represent operations a policy may authorize and* Σ_Y *is a set of* values *that may be used as actual parameters of commands;*[2]
- *the* state transition scheme (STS) $\Delta \subseteq \Sigma_C \times \Sigma_X^* \times \Phi \times \Phi$ *defines state transition pre- and post-conditions for any input of a command and formal parameters, where* Σ_X *denotes a set of* variables *to identify such parameters.*

We use Φ to represent the set of boolean expressions in first-order logic (without implying any specific language) and $\top$ as a shortcut for boolean *true*.

For defining each $\langle cmd, x, \phi, \phi' \rangle \in \Delta$, a notation borrowed from the classical HRU authorization scheme is used: $cmd(x) ::= \mathsf{PRE} : \phi; \mathsf{POST} : \phi'$. We call the boolean term ϕ the pre-condition (abbreviated $cmd.\mathsf{PRE}$) and ϕ' the post-condition (abbreviated $cmd.\mathsf{POST}$) of any state transition to be authorized via

---

[1] To formally comply with set algebra, we treat mappings equally to relations.

[2] We use the Kleene operator to indicate that multiple parameters may be passed.

▶ **delegateRead**$(s_{\text{caller}}, s_{\text{deleg}}, o_{\text{rec}})$ ::=
  PRE: $\text{own} \in acm_\gamma(s_{\text{caller}}, o_{\text{rec}})$
    $\wedge \text{ read} \in acm_\gamma(s_{\text{caller}}, o_{\text{rec}})$;
  POST: $acm_{\gamma'} = acm_\gamma[\langle s_{\text{deleg}}, o_{\text{rec}}\rangle$
    $\mapsto acm_\gamma(s_{\text{deleg}}, o_{\text{rec}}) \cup \{\text{read}\}]$

(a) *delegateRead* in HRU

▶ **relabel**(e, r', t') ::=
  PRE: $e \in E_\gamma \wedge cl_\gamma(e) = \text{process}$
    $\wedge\ con_\gamma(e) = \langle u, r, t\rangle$
    $\wedge\ r \hookrightarrow_r r' \wedge t \hookrightarrow_t t'$;
  POST: $con_{\gamma'} = con_\gamma[e \mapsto \langle u, r', t'\rangle]$

(b) *relabel* in SELX

Fig. 1. Exemplary command definitions.

cmd. On a state machine level, this means that *cmd*.PRE restricts which states γ to legally transition from, while *cmd*.POST defines any differences between γ and the state γ' reachable by any input word $\langle cmd, x\rangle$. This matches the intention of the conditions part (indicated by the *if* keyword) and the body (indicated by *then*) of a command in the HRU authorization scheme. Since our goal is to reason about possible state transitions, we adopt the principle of only modeling commands *cmd* that modify γ, expressed by *cmd*.POST $\neq \top$.

To distinguish between the value domains of individual variables in x, we use a refined definition of Σ_X to reflect distinct namespaces of variable identifiers for each model component. These are denoted by sets X_{A_i} so that $\bigcup_{1 \leq i \leq n} X_{A_i} = \Sigma_X$ for a model with n components. For example, an HRU model for an exemplary information system policy may be defined as follows: $\Gamma = 2^S \times 2^O \times ACM$, where $\gamma = \langle S_\gamma, O_\gamma, acm_\gamma\rangle \in \Gamma$ is a single protection state; $\Sigma_C = \{\text{createRecord}, \text{delegateRead}, \ldots\}$; $\Sigma_Y = S \cup O$; $\Sigma_X = X_S \cup X_O$; Δ is defined by a set of definitions as illustrated in Fig. 1a by the example of *delegateRead*.

To define our analysis goal, we express a safety question related to a dynamic AC model as a safety analysis query (or just query):

Definition 2 (Safety Analysis Query). *A safety analysis query q for a given dynamic AC model $\langle \Gamma, \Sigma, \Delta\rangle$ is a tuple $\langle \gamma_0, \tau\rangle$, where $\gamma_0 \in \Gamma$ is a model state and $\tau \in A_i$ is a value of some component A_i.*

The goal of heuristic analysis is to detect a leakage of τ. We define this as a necessary condition for reaching a state γ' that falsifies safety: Any input leading to a successful state transition from γ to γ' as defined by Δ is called *leaking* τ if τ appears in some model component in γ', where it not also appears in γ. In case such state transition exists, we say γ' contains a *leakage* of τ. In contrast to a mere leakage, our definition of safety adheres to the widespread interpretation that any state γ_τ reachable from γ_0 renders the former unsafe iff τ was entered into a set, matrix, relation etc., which did not already have this value in γ_0 (also called *simple-safety* [2,17]). In particular, if an input sequence re-enters τ into the same component that already contained τ in γ_0, safety is not violated. The reason why we nevertheless aim at a *leakage* in heuristic analysis is that it can be easily detected (by comparing γ' with γ after any state transition), though we still need to subsequently falsify safety with respect to γ_0.

Heuristic Strategies. The objective of a heuristic safety analysis strategy is to demonstrate the occurrence of a leakage. When the strategy finds an input sequence that eventually leaks τ in a state γ_τ, we may prove γ_0 to be unsafe with respect to τ; as long as no γ_τ is found, the search continues. Therefore, the chances of any single input to contribute to such a sequence must be maximized.

When simulating model behavior, test inputs are generated and the states reached via them are tested for a leakage of τ. For generating each input, a heuristic has to choose a command to execute and value assignments for its variables. In our previous work, we have identified command dependencies as a promising model property to maximize chances for a successful input sequence. This is the basis of the DEPSEARCH strategy for HRU safety analysis [5].

DEPSEARCH was developed based on the insight that in the hardest case, right leakages appear only after long state transition sequences where each command executed depends exactly on the execution of its predecessor. Essentially, the algorithm consists of two phases: In the first phase, a static analysis of the STS is performed. It yields a formal description of command dependencies, constituted by entering (as a part of POST) and requiring (part of PRE) the same right in two different commands. These dependencies are encoded in a *command dependency graph* (CDG) whose nodes are commands, and any edge from c to c' denotes that c' depends on the execution c:

Definition 3 (HRU CDG). *A command dependency graph (CDG) of an HRU model $\langle \Gamma, \Sigma, \Delta \rangle$ is an edge-weighted, directed multigraph $\langle V, E \rangle$, $E \subseteq V \times V \times R$, such that $V \subset \Sigma_C$ is the set of command identifiers and $\langle c, c', r \rangle \in E$ if a term in c.POST enters r in $acm_{\gamma'}$ and a term in c'.PRE requires r in acm_γ.*

The CDG is assembled such that all paths from nodes without incoming edges to nodes without outgoing edges indicate input sequences for reaching γ_τ from γ_0. To achieve this, two virtual commands c_0 and c_τ are generated: c_0 is the source of all paths in the CDG, since it mimics the state γ_0 to analyze, represented by a virtual command specification in Δ such that c_0.POST requires all subjects in S_{γ_0}, all objects in O_{γ_0}, and all rights in acm_{γ_0}. In a similar manner, c_τ is the destination of all paths, which represents all possible states γ_τ; c_τ.PRE hence requires the presence of the target right τ in some matrix cell of acm_γ:

▶ $c_0()$ ::=   ▶ $c_\tau(s, o)$ ::=
  PRE: $\top$;   PRE: $\tau \in acm_\gamma(s, o)$;
  POST: $S_{\gamma'} = S_{\gamma_0} \wedge O_{\gamma'} = O_{\gamma_0} \wedge acm_{\gamma'} = acm_{\gamma_0}$ POST: $\top$

In the second, simulative analysis phase, the CDG is used to generate input sequences. The commands in each sequence correspond to different paths from c_0 to c_τ, which we expect to leak τ once completely executed. In case a sequence fails because of an unsatisfiable PRE, another path is selected based on the last successfully reached state. This strategy is based on the assumption that even a partially executed command sequence contributes to pre-conditions of any next sequence generated. Each effected state transition is simulated by the algorithm, and once a CDG path is completed, the falsification of safety is checked.

4   Command Dependencies

To heuristically analyze more complex model semantics such as for the SELinux AC model SELX [1], rewriting the STS to HRU syntax is impractical, error-prone, and the results of the analysis may not be interpretable w. r. t. the underlying system. To this end, we generalize the definition of command dependency beyond entering and requiring access rights in an ACM cell. We then adapt the DEPSEARCH idea to handle the more general class of dynamic dependencies.

4.1   Problem Analysis

HRU has two distinct properties that enable the static pre-analysis of STS commands in DEPSEARCH: (1) dependencies are created solely by entering or requiring a right, (2) all rights are fixed by command definitions, i. e. static values during model simulation. Both properties enable DEPSEARCH to create the CDG (Definition 3) as a representation of static command dependencies. Assume a model where dependencies between commands originate from multiple model components, represented in the STS by variables whose values are dynamically assigned during runtime. Since this model violates above properties, the static dependency analysis in DEPSEARCH does no longer produce significant results.

To clarify these differences consider our exemplary HRU command *delegateRead* (Fig. 1a) and the command *relabel* of a SELX model (Fig. 1b): As becomes evident in *delegateRead*, PRE depends only on the presence of the right values "own" and "read" in some matrix cell, since a conjunction of such conditions is the only allowed PRE in HRU. In *relabel* however, a conjunction of more heterogeneous conditions relate to different components of a SELX model: first, a set E_γ and a mapping cl_γ are checked for the presence of a process, second, a mapping con_γ is used to lookup security attributes, third, two relations $\hookrightarrow_r$ and $\hookrightarrow_t$ are checked to validate the requested relabeling.[3] The fact that values from a total of five different model components (entities, classes, three attributes) are checked violates property 1, the fact that all these values but one are represented by variables violates property 2.

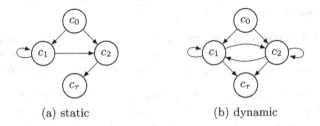

(a) static   (b) dynamic

Fig. 2. Graphs for different types of dependencies.

---

[3] For the sake of a more concise discussion, we ignore the SELinux-concept of *entry-points*.

Intuitively, applying a dependency analysis approach such as DEPSEARCH to a model such as SELX raises both formal and semantical issues, notably related to how dependencies are formalized through a CDG. We will discuss these issues in the following based on an exemplary HRU STS:

▶ $c_1(s_1, s_2, o) ::=$ ▶ $c_2(s_1, s_2, o) ::=$
 PRE: read $\in acm_\gamma(s_1, o)$;   PRE: read $\in acm_\gamma(s_1, o)$;
 POST: $acm_{\gamma'} = acm_\gamma[\langle s_2, o\rangle$ POST: $acm_{\gamma'} = acm_\gamma[\langle s_2, o\rangle$
   $\mapsto acm_\gamma(s_2, o) \cup \{read\}]$ $\mapsto acm_\gamma(s_2, o) \cup \{write\}]$

If DEPSEARCH would use this STS to create a CDG with the target right "write", the result would be a CDG as shown in Fig. 2a. In case the STS violates property 2, e.g. it contains only right variables, this would result in the graph in Fig. 2b. It is important to note that, despite showing dependencies in both cases, these graphs differ in edge semantics: the edges of the CDG in Fig. 2a represent actual dependencies, the edges in the graph in Fig. 2b represent potential dependencies. This explains why the graph in Fig. 2b contains more edges and thus more potential paths from c_0 to c_τ.

Assume an STS that violates property 1 as follows: It contains a command that creates a certain subject in POST but does not enter any rights. Assume further that the only command that leaks our target right requires (aside from certain rights) the existence of the aforementioned subject in PRE. A CDG created by DEPSEARCH would not contain the first command since DEPSEARCH only checks dependencies regarding rights. The result would be that the command leaking our target right could never be executed since the command that would create the needed subject is not part of the CDG and thus also never part of any path generated.

4.2   Classes of Dependencies

We now generalize our observations regarding HRU made in the previous examples. On a more formal level, both properties mentioned there may be used in a heuristic to recognize different types of dependency. This intention is reflected in the following definitions, which express *necessary* conditions for one command to require a previous execution of another command. We assume that any single value or variable used in a PRE or POST term is significant for its boolean value, as e.g. achieved by canonical CNF.

Definition 4 (Static Dependency). *Let $c_1, c_2 \in \Sigma_C$ be two commands in a dynamic AC model. If c_2 statically depends on c_1, then there is a model component A_i such that a value $y \in A_i$ occurs in both $c_1.POST$ and $c_2.PRE$.*

This type of dependency is attributed *static* since actual values must be matched to identify a dependency relationship. Likewise, we may also observe *dynamic dependency* based on variables that *potentially* match, depending on their dynamically assigned values:

Definition 5 (Dynamic Dependency). *Let $c_1, c_2 \in \Sigma_C$ be two commands in a dynamic AC model. If c_2 dynamically depends on c_1, then there is a model* component A_i such that a variable $x_1 \in X_{A_i}$ occurs in $c_1.POST$ and a variable $x_2 \in X_{A_i}$ occurs in $c_2.PRE$.

If more than one distinct model component A_i satisfies Definitions 4 or 5, we speak of *multi-dimensional* dependencies (*one-dimensional* otherwise).

These definitions basically yield four classes of possible models, each with different implications on a correct and efficient representation of dependencies as a heuristic criterion for safety analysis: such where (1) only static and one-dimensional, (2) only static but both one- and multi-dimensional, (3) static and dynamic, but only one-dimensional, and (4) all types of dependencies may occur.

It should be highlighted that HRU is already a model from the last class: the presence of a subject $s \in S_\gamma$ is a necessary condition for satisfying a PRE expression $r \in acm_\gamma(s, o)$. As a simple example, consider a special case of HRU whose STS features solely static values for subjects. In this case, executing any command that requires a right r assigned to a subject s depends both on any command that enters r and on any command that creates s. We hence observe multi-dimensional dependencies, which are – in case of general HRU models – also partially dynamic. However, DEPSEARCH makes implicit assumptions about model semantics that allow the CDG to ignore both dynamic and multi-dimensional dependencies: PRE terms in HRU do not allow to directly check for the presence of subjects or objects, but only indirectly as having some rights assigned via *acm*. Based on this observation, DEPSEARCH interprets the matrix as a more fine-grained rights set, which is therefore considered the only dependency-relevant model component. Only subject and object variables are allowed, while rights are always static in an HRU STS.

To this end, our existing heuristic algorithm is only capable to correctly handle static, one-dimensional command dependencies. To get a first understanding of the implications of these classes for models where they cannot be neglected, we focus on dynamic dependencies in the following, which are commonly found in todays AC policies (cf. Sect. 5.2).

4.3   Dealing with Dynamic Dependencies

To isolate the problem of dynamic dependencies, we start with a more concise model notation: we modify the original HRU syntax in a way that only dynamic, one-dimensional dependencies can be expressed. Based on this model we address dependencies with a generalized CDG, termed pCDG, which is an overapproximation of any possible CDG. A CDG created from this graph, which we call a pCDG instance, may then be analyzed using DEPSEARCH [2, 7].

As discussed in the last section, dynamic dependencies are observable in HRU. To make them more explicit however, we define a very simple calculus for dynamic AC models, which is used to isolate the relevant phenomena of one-dimensional, yet dynamic dependencies. The goal here is to have this type of dependency, as defined in Sect. 4.2, directly reflected in command definitions, while eliminating any syntax and semantics beyond it (e. g. the ACM).

Despite the discussion is based on HRU terminology, we are only interested in the impact of rights on establishing dynamic dependencies. This leads to the class of HRU* models defined as follows:

Definition 6 (HRU*). *An HRU* model is a dynamic AC model* $\langle \Gamma, \Sigma, \Delta \rangle$ *with a single component* $A_1 = R$ *and* $\Gamma = 2^R$, $\Sigma_Y = R$, $\Sigma_X = X_R$.

Note that HRU* may be expressed by an access control matrix consisting of a single cell, but not in an HRU model due to the difference in Σ_X. In the following we use HRU* models for different sets Σ_C. Consequently, for the sake of readability, we abbreviate the notation of Δ by only listing right values and right variables in PRE and POST, respectively:

Example 1. For an HRU* model with $R = \{\text{spam}, \text{ham}, \text{eggs}, \text{beans}\}$ and $\Sigma_C = \{c_1, c_2, c_3\}$, Δ is defined as

  ▶ $c_1(r_1, r_2) ::=$ ▶ $c_2(r_1, r_2) ::=$ ▶ $c_3(r_1, r_2) ::=$

    PRE: r_1, r_2 ;   PRE: r_1 ;   PRE: r_1 ;

    POST: spam   POST: r_1, r_2 POST: r_2

For globally unique variable identifies, we will write $c_1.r_1$ for variable r_1 in command c_1. We then write $c_1.X_{\text{PRE}} = \{c_1.r_1, c_1.r_2\}$ for the set of all variables in pre-conditions of c_1 and likewise $c_1.X_{\text{POST}} = \emptyset$ for its post-conditions.[4] The global set of right variable identifiers is denoted by $X_R = \{c_1.r_1, c_1.r_2, c_2.r_1, c_2.r_2, c_3.r_1, c_3.r_2\}$.

Based on the DEPSEARCH idea, dynamic dependencies are encoded in a graph. For this we introduce the abstraction of dependency variables:

Definition 7 (pCDG). *A potential command dependency graph (*PCDG*) of a dynamic AC model* $\langle \Gamma, \Sigma, \Delta \rangle$ *is an edge-weighted, directed multigraph* $\langle V_p, E_p \rangle$, $E_p \subseteq V_p \times V_p \times VAR$, *such that* $V_p = \Sigma_C$ *is the set of command identifiers and VAR is a set of dependency variables based on* Σ_X.

A PCDG is constructed just as an HRU CDG, with the only difference that the original dependency condition (cf. Definition 3) is modified according to Definition 5: Any edge $\langle u, v, x_{uv} = \langle x_u, x_v \rangle \rangle$ now means that assigning some value to variable $x_u \in u.X_{\text{POST}}$ implies that command v potentially satisfies its pre-condition based on some value assigned to variable $x_v \in v.X_{\text{PRE}}$. This means that for any CDG containing this edge, both values must be the same. We call the tuple x_{uv} a *dependency variable* (an alias for two variable identifiers, i.e. $VAR \subseteq X_R \times X_R$).

Due to the abstraction of *potential* dependency represented in a PCDG, static dependencies according to Definition 4 cannot be captured by its edges. However, our approach is to first model potential dependency in the PCDG, which are mapped to actual dependencies in a CDG in the next step. To this end, static dependencies have to be considered in PCDG creation as if it were potential dependencies: By substituting each value used in command definitions

---

[4] Note that "spam" is a right value, not a variable.

by a unique synthetic variable, such as r_{spam} for "spam" in the example. When later assigning values to variables, we require that those synthetically introduced may only be assigned one fixed value (we henceforth call them *fixed-value variables*). This approach enables us to deal with an STS containing mixed dynamic and static dependencies. For the above Example 1, this leads to $VAR = \{x_{11}^1 = \langle c_1.r_{\text{spam}}, c_1.r_1 \rangle, x_{11}^2 = \langle c_1.r_{\text{spam}}, c_1.r_2 \rangle, x_{12}^1 = \langle c_1.r_{\text{spam}}, c_2.r_1 \rangle, x_{13}^1 = \langle c_1.r_{\text{spam}}, c_3.r_1 \rangle, x_{21}^1 = \langle c_2.r_1, c_1.r_1 \rangle, x_{21}^2 = \langle c_2.r_2, c_1.r_1 \rangle, \dots \}$.

The resulting graph is designed to contain every possible edge of any CDG that may be built from the STS, hence the attribute "potential". This implies that a PCDG is always a complete graph, additionally including all possible self-loops. Figure 3 shows the PCDG resulting from the STS in Example 1.

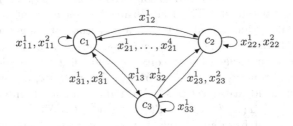

Fig. 3. PCDG for Example 1. Multi-edges are denoted by the union of their dependency variables.

By Definition 7, PCDG creation is independent from any analysis query $q = \langle \gamma_0, \tau \rangle$. However, for answering such queries, we first need to break down its semantics to solely represent *actual* dependencies which we are able to heuristically analyze. This step is called *instantiation*. The goal of PCDG instantiation is to enable heuristic search strategies to infer command sequences (paths in this graph) just as with a regular CDG. As a consequence, the resulting graph needs to satisfy necessary properties of a CDG. From these requirements, we derive the approach of instantiation: first, nodes for c_0 and c_τ are added and connected to ensure the presence of paths significant for q; second, a variable assignment function is found that substitutes dependency variables by specific values; third, validity rules for a CDG are applied to restrict E_p based on this assignment. The result is called an *instance* of a PCDG:

Definition 8 (pCDG Instance). *A* PCDG *instance is an edge-weighted, directed multigraph* $\langle V, E \rangle, E \subseteq V \times V \times R$ *created from a* PCDG $\langle V_p, E_p \rangle$ *via a query* $\langle \gamma_0, \tau \rangle$ *and an assignment function* $\mathcal{I} : VAR \rightarrow R$, *where* $V = V_p \cup \{c_0, c_\tau\}$.

To meet the base assumption of our heuristics, that traversing certain paths in a CDG subsequently establishes necessary conditions for a right leakage, we define the nodes c_0 and c_τ as source and destination of any such path. This is done based on γ_0 and τ, in a similar manner as with an HRU CDG (cf. Definition 3).

Example 2. Given the STS in Example 1, a state $\gamma_0 = \{\text{ham}, \text{beans}\}$ and a target $\tau = \text{eggs}$. We then need to add two commands c_0 and c_τ defined as:

▶ $c_0()$ ::= PRE: $\top$; POST: ham, beans   ▶ $c_\tau()$ ::= PRE: eggs; POST: $\top$

Note that, before performing the variable assignment, fixed-value variables ($c_0.r_{\text{ham}}, c_0.r_{\text{beans}}, c_\tau.r_{\text{eggs}}$ in the example) have to be introduced as already done for those commands in Σ_C. Because of its significance in terminating any CDG path, we will refer to the single variable in $c_\tau.X_{\text{PRE}}$ as r_τ. We eventually connect both additional nodes with those in V_p using the same dependency condition as during PCDG construction: By introducing edges and dependency variables for $c_0.X_{\text{POST}}$ and any $c.X_{\text{PRE}}$, and any $c.X_{\text{POST}}$ and $c_\tau.X_{\text{PRE}}$, respectively.

Then, for assigning values to dependency variables, an $\mathcal{I}$ is defined such that any variable $x_{uv} = \langle x_u, x_v \rangle$ mapped to some right value $\mathcal{I}(x_{uv}) = y$ implies that both x_u and x_v are assigned y. This leads to an edges set E annotated with rights instead of variables. Since for any PCDG, a multitude of assignment functions may produce different instances, care must be taken in handling fixed-value variables. Since their assignment is constant over all $\mathcal{I}$, we model it through an auxiliary alias function: Any $\mathcal{I}$ is from a function space; any fixed-value variable is from an identifier set Σ_X^{syn}. We require for all $\mathcal{I}$ and $x^{syn} \in \Sigma_X^{syn}$ that $\mathcal{I}(\langle x_u, x^{syn} \rangle) = \mathcal{I}(\langle x^{syn}, x_v \rangle) = \mathcal{C}(x^{syn})$ where $\mathcal{C} : \Sigma_X^{syn} \to R$ is the alias function, independent from any $\mathcal{I}$, which assigns constant values to fixed-value variable identifiers. To ensure variable assigment validity, $\mathcal{I}$ must satisfy three validation rules:

$$\langle u, c_\tau, \mathcal{I}(x_{u\tau}) \rangle \in E \Rightarrow \mathcal{I}(x_{u\tau}) = \tau \tag{1}$$

$$\langle c_0, v, \mathcal{I}(\langle x_0, x_v \rangle) \rangle \in E \Rightarrow \mathcal{I}(\langle x_0, x_v \rangle) = \mathcal{C}(x_0) \tag{2}$$

$$\begin{gathered} \langle u, v, \mathcal{I}(x_{uv}) \rangle, \langle u', v', \mathcal{I}(x'_{uv}) \rangle \in E, \\ \langle u, v, x_{uv} \rangle \approx_n \langle u', v', x'_{uv} \rangle \Rightarrow \mathcal{I}(x_{uv}) = \mathcal{I}(x'_{uv}) \end{gathered} \tag{3}$$

where $\approx_n \subseteq E_p \times E_p$ is the edge neighborship relation. Two PCDG edges are neighbors iff they represent the same variable of an incident node:

$$\langle u, v, \langle x_u, x_v \rangle \rangle \approx_n \langle u', v', \langle x'_u, x'_v \rangle \rangle \Leftrightarrow (u = u' \wedge x_u = x'_u) \vee (u = v' \wedge x_u = x'_v)$$
$$\vee (v = u' \wedge x_v = x'_u) \vee (v = v' \wedge x_v = x'_v).$$

Validation rule 1 ensures that the target value is leaked after executing a path from c_0 to c_τ; rule 2 ensures that pre-conditions of commands on any such path can be satisfied by values already present in γ_0. Note that by design of the instantiation approach – through the definitions of c_0, c_τ and $\mathcal{C}$ – we have already satisfied both rules. Rule 3 ensures that any two different dependency variables representing the same variable in the STS are assigned the same value.

Example 3. In the PCDG in Fig. 3, the dependency variable x_{12}^1 is an alias for $c_1.r_{\text{spam}}$ and $c_2.r_1$. Likewise, x_{23}^1 is an alias for $c_2.r_1$ and $c_3.r_1$. Let $\mathcal{I}$ be an assignment function that instantiates this PCDG, then $\mathcal{I}(x_{12}^1) = \mathcal{C}(c_1.r_{\text{spam}}) =$

spam since $c_1.r_{\text{spam}}$ is a synthetic variable for the static right "spam". Assume that $\mathcal{I}(x^1_{23})$ = beans: from rule 3, we now infer that not both edges $\langle c_1, c_2, x^1_{12} \rangle$ and $\langle c_2, c_3, x^1_{23} \rangle$ must be present in E since otherwise, $\mathcal{I}$ is contradictory w.r.t. the value assigned to $c_2.r_1$.

Any edge that violates assignment validity must be removed from E. In case there are multiple candidates for removal, such as in Example 3, this offers room for heuristically optimizing CDG properties that are more prospective for efficiently producing a leak; this problem is subject to ongoing work.

After removing invalid edges, the resulting graph may become partitioned – in the worst case with c_0 and c_τ in separate partitions. To exclude such cases from the analysis, any PCDG instance must be validated against a connectivity rule in order to be analyzable in the same manner as a traditional CDG: A PCDG instance $\langle V, E \rangle$ is a CDG iff

$$v \in V \setminus \{c_0, c_\tau\} \Rightarrow v \text{ is on a path from } c_0 \text{ to } c_\tau. \tag{4}$$

After the CDG is validated, any further pre-processing may be performed before running DEPSEARCH. Especially, efficiency optimizations through statically analyzable leakage properties as we have described in [2] may be applied after this step.

4.4   Path Search

The original idea of DEPSEARCH is to simulate a sequence of commands where each command creates a necessary condition for the execution of the next, to ultimately cause a right leakage. This sequence is created by searching a path from c_0 to c_τ in the CDG.

The PCDG introduced in Definition 7 represents potential dependencies. The approach described above is to instantiate it in a manner that results in a CDG, which may then be analyzed using DEPSEARCH. This approach has the drawback that paths used for the analysis always stem from the same CDG, which can be mitigated by creating different CDGs and switching between them during simulation. As already mentioned, a criterion for comparing CDGs to decide which is more prospective for leaking the target right is subject to ongoing work.

We therefore decided to perform a path search directly in the PCDG. For this, c_0 and c_τ are added to the graph (the result is referred to as PCDG$^+$). Then all dependency variables of this path are assigned in such a way that assignment

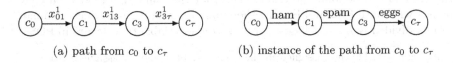

(a) path from c_0 to c_τ (b) instance of the path from c_0 to c_τ

Fig. 4. Path instantiation examples.

validity is satisfied.[5] Afterwards the corresponding command sequence can be used to analyze the model for a right leakage. This approach allows to evaluate the path in terms of its prospects of success during the runtime of the analysis. Figure 4a shows a possible path of the PCDG$^+$ created from the PCDG in Fig. 3.

The dependency variables of this path are now assigned in such a way that the assignment validity is satisfied, e. g. $\mathcal{I}(x_{01}^1) = \text{ham}, \mathcal{I}(x_{13}^1) = \text{spam}$ and $\mathcal{I}(x_{3\tau}^1) =$ eggs. With this assignment, the path shown in Fig. 4a can be instantiated which results in the path shown in Fig. 4b. This path can then be used by existing analysis tools [6]. If no right leakage is found using this path, we may either change the assignment function or search a new path in the PCDG$^+$.

5   Impact on Safety Analysis

In this section we study the implications of dynamic dependencies on the efficiency of safety analyses. To this end, in Sect. 5.1, we discuss both properties of the heuristic algorithm and representative model properties of HRU*. In Sect. 5.2 we then show that the latter are indeed properties of practical models, which supports their significance. This will be done in the context of SELX, a model designed to enable safety analyses of SELinux operation systems.

5.1   HRU*

This section determines model properties relevant for analysis efficiency. Based on the runtime complexity of the algorithms and the influence of command definitions a worst-case STS is specified, which we then use to demonstrate the actual impact on analysis runtime.

Runtime Complexity. The generation of the PCDG$^+$ has a runtime complexity of $\mathcal{O}(n^2)$, where $n = |\Sigma_C|$.[6] The path search runs in $\mathcal{O}(m)$, where m is the number of edges in the PCDG$^+$. Since m depends on $|\Sigma_C|^2$, the runtime complexity is $\mathcal{O}(n^2)$. The edge neighborship check has a runtime complexity of $\mathcal{O}(m^2) = \mathcal{O}(n^4)$ and the creation of the assignment function has a runtime complexity of $\mathcal{O}(m) = \mathcal{O}(n^2)$. This confirms that the number of commands $|\Sigma_C|$ has the greatest impact on analysis runtime.

STS Specification. We now discuss how the definition of commands affects analysis efficiency. To this end we examine relevant types of commands in HRU*. First of all, consider an STS without static dependencies. From this STS, commands that only have $\top$ in PRE can be ignored, since they always lead to a right leakage and can be found statically. Thus, for the evaluation model, only commands with both PRE and POST other than $\top$ are of interest. Such commands can be divided into two classes: (1) every right variable that occurs in POST is

---

[5] All right variables not assigned in this step may be randomly assigned with values.

[6] The runtime is also influenced by the number of right variables ($|X_{\text{PRE}} \cup X_{\text{POST}}|$). However for a static set R this means that: $\forall c \in \Sigma_c : |c.X_{\text{PRE}}| \leq |R|$ (analogous for $c.X_{\text{POST}}$). Therefore this impact can be assumed as constant.

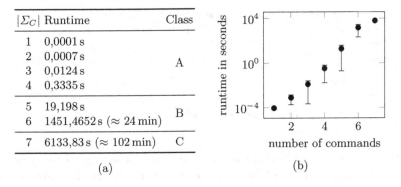

$|\Sigma_C|$	Runtime	Class
1	0,0001 s	
2	0,0007 s	A
3	0,0124 s	
4	0,3335 s	
5	19,198 s	B
6	1451,4652 s ($\approx$ 24 min)	
7	6133,83 s ($\approx$ 102 min)	C

(a)

(b)

Fig. 5. Evaluation results (error bars: standard deviation).

also checked in PRE, and (2) at least one right variable in POST does not occur in PRE. Examples for both classes are the following c (class 1) and c' (class 2):

▶ $c(r)::=$ PRE: r ; POST: r ▶ $c'(r_1, r_2)::=$ PRE: r_1 ; POST: r_2

Commands of class 1 cannot cause a right leakage, since they always enter the same rights in POST that were checked in PRE. Thus, if the variable r is assigned with τ, the target right must already exist in the current state for this command to be executable. This in turn means that another command must already have entered τ which terminates the analysis.[7] Consequently, these commands can be ignored for this evaluation. Commands of class 2 however may immediately lead to a right leakage, since all variables are freely assignable: a variable in POST can be assigned with τ and all variables in PRE can be assigned with rights that exist in the current state. In this respect, commands of class 2 resemble commands that have only $\top$ in PRE. This illustrates a property of models which have a command of class 2 that makes it possible to circumvent the simulative analysis, since these commands can be found with a static pre-analysis. Because of this we use a model with both static and dynamic dependencies for the runtime measurements:

▶ $c_1()::=$ ▶ $c_2()::=$ ▶ $c_3()::=$ ▶ $c_8(r)::=$
PRE: 1;   PRE: 2;   PRE: 3;   ...   PRE: 8;
POST: 2   POST: 3   POST: 4   POST: r_2

To perform the simulative analysis the definition of the component R and the query $\langle \gamma_0, \tau \rangle$ are required: $R = \{1, 2, 3, 4, 5, 6, 7, 8, 42\}$, $\gamma_0 = \{1\}$ and $\tau = 42$.

Model Simulation. This model was analyzed for right leakages. In order to be able to represent the runtime behavior with increasing number of commands, we performed analyses of models with one through eight commands. These models fulfill the same assumptions as the one specified above, i. e. they have both static and dynamic dependencies. Figure 5a shows the runtime measurements of these analyses. For models with $|\Sigma_C| \leq 5$ the specified values are averaged from 100 runs, for $|\Sigma_C| = 6$ from 10 runs, and for $|\Sigma_C| = 7$ one run was performed. The models were divided into runtime classes (class A for < 1 s, class B for < 1 h and

---

[7] Note that this implication of the command classification holds for HRU* only.

	sh	usr_t	admin_t
sh	usr_t		
usr_t			$\top$
admin_t		$\top$	

(a) acm_γ

▶ $relabel(p_1, t_1, t_2) ::=$
  PRE: $t_1 \in acm_\gamma(p_1, p_1)$
    $\wedge \top \in acm_\gamma(t_1, t_2)$;
  POST: $acm_{\gamma'} = acm_\gamma[\langle p_1, p_1 \rangle \mapsto \{t_2\}]$

(b) $relabel$ basic command

Fig. 6. SELX* model specifications.

class C for $\geq 1\,$h). Figure 5b illustrates these results. The runtime was measured from the generation of the PCDG$^+$ to the successful finding of a right leakage.[8]

Discussion of Results. As becomes evident from Fig. 5, analyzing models with both dynamic and static dependencies drastically increases the runtime. While for classes A and B a sensible runtime may be achieved, the time required for class C exceeds one hour, already at $|\Sigma_C| = 7$. This demands an alternative approach for such models e. g. via the static classification introduced above.

5.2   SELX

In this section, a practical system will be used to demonstrate that the model property discussed above, i. e. the existence of commands with no static dependencies and different variables in PRE and POST, is in fact a property of practical models. To this end we specify a model SELX* which mimics the behavior of a type transition in a SELX model. In SELX the safety property is not focused on whether a right is leaked, but whether a type is leaked ((t)-simple-unsafety [3, Def. 5.5]). This is due to the fact that e. g. processes have no rights, but types directly assigned while access rights are assigned to these types. Processes are represented in the entities set E and the types in the types set T. The association of entities to types is the so called security context, which is modeled via the function $con : E \to T$. We define the SELX* model as follows:

Definition 9 (SELX*). *A SELX* model is a dynamic AC model $\langle \Gamma, \Sigma, \Delta \rangle$ with the components $A_1 = E$, $A_2 = T$ and $A_3 = acm : E \times E \to T$. It is defined as follows: $\Gamma = 2^E \times ACM$, where for any $\gamma = \langle E_\gamma, acm_\gamma \rangle \in \Gamma$, $acm_\gamma : E_\gamma \times E_\gamma \to T$, $\Sigma_Y = E \cup T$ and $\Sigma_X = X_E \cup X_T$.*

E and T are encoded in acm_γ as follows: $p_1 \in E_\gamma, t_1 \in T : acm_\gamma(p_1, p_1) = \{t_1\} \Leftrightarrow con_\gamma(p_1) = t_1$ specifies which type is the active type of a process and $t_1, t_2 \in T : acm_\gamma(t_1, t_2) = \{\top\} \Leftrightarrow t_1 \hookrightarrow_t t_2$ specifies which type transitions are allowed. Figure 6a shows an example matrix containing the entity sh $\in E_\gamma$ with usr_t $\in T$ assigned as the active type. There is another type admin_t $\in T$ and a transition is allowed from usr_t to admin_t, but not from each type to itself.

There are fixed basic commands in the SELX model for describing protection state changes. When adapted to SELX*, only the basic command *relabel* (Fig. 6b)

---

[8] A machine with an Intel i5 CPU at 2.90 GHz and 8 GB RAM was used.

may fulfill (t)-simple-unsafety, since it allows a process to transition to a new type. As becomes evident, this command has a right variable in POST that does not occur in PRE, so it has the same properties as commands of class 2 in HRU*. As established in the last section, such a definition always leads to a right leakage, or in this context to the model being (t)-simple-unsafe and can be found statically. The conclusion is that practical models may indeed have commands that have the same properties as class 2 commands of HRU*.

6   Conclusions and Future Work

We studied command dependencies in AC models, focused on the class of dynamic dependencies, for which we presented a safety analysis algorithm. The definition of dependency was generalized and formalized, resulting in a graph abstraction which enables a heuristic search to steer a simulation.

This heuristic serves as a basis to study the practical impact of dynamic dependencies. Our findings show that (1) the runtime complexity mainly depends on the number of commands in the STS, (2) the generalized dependency definition increases runtime complexity of the simulation to $\mathcal{O}(n^4)$ compare to $\mathcal{O}(n)$ in DepSearch. The severe increase demonstrates that dynamic dependencies are a serious obstacle to heuristic safety analysis. To mitigate this conclusion in practice, we have identified model properties that circumvent the need for simulation, since they can be found statically. While this result in principle strengthens the semi-decision approach, it might as well indicate that traditional safety properties to describe an undesired model state are too unspecific. As a consequence, general queries like "leaking of a certain right" might not be significant in models featuring dynamic dependencies. In models where dependency based analysis turns out to be fundamentally inefficient due to dynamic dependencies, we may now at least identify such cases based on a formal criterion.

Our immediate ongoing work extends this study to multi-dimensional dependencies, as well as to explore more fine-grained safety queries and additional heuristic information that allow for efficient analyses of well-defined cases of command dependencies.

References

1. Amthor, P.: The entity labeling pattern for modeling operating systems access control. In: Obaidat, M.S., Lorenz, P. (eds.) ICETE 2015. CCIS, vol. 585, pp. 270–292. Springer, Cham (2016). https://doi.org/10.1007/978-3-319-30222-5_13
2. Amthor, P.: Efficient heuristic safety analysis of core-based security policies. In: Proceedings of the 14th International Conference on Security and Cryptography. SECRYPT 2017, pp. 384–392 (2017). https://doi.org/10.5220/0006477103840392
3. Amthor, P.: Aspect-Oriented Security Engineering. Cuvillier Verlag, Göttingen (2019), ISBN 978-3-7369-9980-0
4. Amthor, P., Kühnhauser, W.E., Pölck, A.: Model-based safety analysis of SELinux security policies. In: Samarati, P., Foresti, S., Hu, J., Livraga, G. (eds.) Proceedings of 5th International Conference on Network and System Security, pp. 208–215. IEEE (2011)

5. Amthor, P., Kühnhauser, W.E., Pölck, A.: Heuristic safety analysis of access control models. In: Proceedings of the 18th ACM Symposium on Access Control Models and Technologies, SACMAT 2013, pp. 137–148. ACM, New York (2013). http://doi.acm.org/10.1145/2462410.2462413

6. Amthor, P., Kühnhauser, W.E., Pölck, A.: WorSE: a workbench for model-based security engineering. Comput. Secur. **42**, 40–55 (2014). https://doi.org/10.1016/j.cose.2014.01.002. http://www.sciencedirect.com/science/article/pii/S0167404814000066

7. Fischer, A., Kühnhauser, W.E.: Efficient algorithmic safety analysis of HRU security models. In: Katsikas, S., Samarati, P. (eds.) Proceedings of the International Conference on Security and Cryptography (SECRYPT 2010), pp. 49–58. SciTePress (2010)

8. Harrison, M.A., Ruzzo, W.L., Ullman, J.D.: Protection in operating systems. Commun. ACM **19**(8), 461–471 (1976). http://doi.acm.org/10.1145/360303.360333

9. Kühnhauser, W.E., Pölck, A.: Towards access control model engineering. In: Jajodia, S., Mazumdar, C. (eds.) ICISS 2011. LNCS, vol. 7093, pp. 379–382. Springer, Heidelberg (2011). https://doi.org/10.1007/978-3-642-25560-1_27

10. Lipton, R.J., Snyder, L.: A linear time algorithm for deciding subject security. J. ACM **24**(3), 455–464 (1977)

11. Masoumzadeh, A.: Security analysis of relationship-based access control policies. In: Proceedings of the 8th ACM Conference on Data and Application Security and Privacy, CODASPY 2018, pp. 186–195. ACM, New York (2018). http://doi.acm.org/10.1145/3176258.3176323

12. Pölck, A.: Small TCBs of policy-controlled operating systems. Universitätsverlag Ilmenau, May 2014

13. Rajkumar, P.V., Sandhu, R.: Safety decidability for pre-authorization usage control with finite attribute domains. IEEE Trans. Dependable Secure Comput. **13**(5), 582–590 (2016). https://doi.org/10.1109/TDSC.2015.2427834

14. Sandhu, R.S.: The typed access matrix model. In: Proceedings of the 1992 IEEE Symposium on Security and Privacy, SP 1992, pp. 122–136. IEEE Computer Society, Washington, DC (1992). http://dl.acm.org/citation.cfm?id=882488.884182

15. Stoller, S.D., Yang, P., Gofman, M., Ramakrishnan, C.R.: Symbolic reachability analysis for parameterized administrative role based access control. Comput. Secur. **30**(2–3), 148–164 (2011)

16. Tripunitara, M.V., Li, N.: A theory for comparing the expressive power of access control models. J. Comput. Secur. **15**(2), 231–272 (2007). http://dl.acm.org/citation.cfm?id=1370659.1370662

17. Tripunitara, M.V., Li, N.: The foundational work of Harrison-Ruzzo-Ullman revisited. IEEE Trans. Dependable Secur. Comput. **10**(1), 28–39 (2013). https://doi.org/10.1109/TDSC.2012.77

On Attribute Retrieval in ABAC

Charles Morisset[1], Sowmya Ravidas[2(✉)], and Nicola Zannone[2]

[1] Newcastle University, Newcastle upon Tyne, UK
charles.morisset@newcastle.ac.uk
[2] Eindhoven University of Technology, Eindhoven, The Netherlands
{s.ravidas,n.zannone}@tue.nl

Abstract. Despite the growing interest in Attribute-Based Access Control (ABAC) and the large amount of research devoted to the specification and evaluation of ABAC policies, to date only little work has addressed the issue of attribute management and retrieval. In many modern systems, the attributes needed for policy evaluation are often retrieved from external sources (*e.g.*, sensors, access points). This poses concerns on the correctness of policy evaluation as the policy decision point can be provided with incorrect attribute values, which can potentially yield incorrect decisions. In this paper, we investigate the problem of selecting mechanisms for attribute retrieval and its relation with the accuracy of policy evaluation. We first introduce the notion of policy evaluation under error rate and use this notion to compute the evaluation accuracy of a policy. We formulate the Attribute Retrieval Mechanism Selection Problem (ARMSP) in terms of evaluation accuracy and show that ARMSP is exponential in the number of attribute values. To overcome this computation limitation, we investigate approaches to estimate the evaluation accuracy of a policy while maintaining the computation feasible.

1 Introduction

Attribute-Based Access Control (ABAC) is becoming the predominant access control paradigm due to its expressiveness, flexibility and scalability. While several efforts have been devoted to the definition of languages and models for the specification and evaluation of ABAC policies [2,6,8,11], to date very little attention have been given to attribute management and retrieval. We argue that these are key concerns that have to be addressed in order to design effective ABAC mechanisms.

Existing ABAC models typically assume a centralized view where all relevant attributes are stored in a policy information point and available to the policy decision point during policy evaluation [1,5]. This assumption, however, does not hold in modern IT systems like Internet of Things and building automation. In these systems, the authorization mechanism increasingly relies on external sources for retrieving the attributes needed for policy evaluation, for example, by employing occupancy detection sensors or other sensors to gather environment attributes.

© Springer Nature Switzerland AG 2020
A. Benzekri et al. (Eds.): FPS 2019, LNCS 12056, pp. 225–241, 2020.
https://doi.org/10.1007/978-3-030-45371-8_14

The use of external sources for attribute retrieval poses concerns on the reliability of the retrieved attribute values and, consequently, on the correctness of policy evaluation. For instance, those sources might not be available at the time of policy evaluation or might provide incorrect values due to intrinsic limitations of the mechanism used for their retrieval. This can lead to incorrect decisions, thus compromising the system's security and business continuity. While the problem of missing information has been largely studied in ABAC [2, 12, 13] and existing ABAC mechanisms are often equipped with mechanisms to handle missing information [8, 11], to the best of our knowledge, no prior work has investigated the effect of incorrect attribute values on policy evaluation.

Different mechanisms can be used to gather a given attribute and each mechanism can have a different cost and provide information at a different level of accuracy. For example, identity information can be collected using a pre-issued access card or a biometric identification system. While biometric systems usually provide information at a higher accuracy, they have higher costs compared to the use of access cards. Therefore, the selection of an appropriate mechanism for retrieving a certain attribute requires a trade-off between accuracy, cost and other properties of the candidate mechanisms.

This work makes a first step towards the definition of an approach to guide the selection of mechanisms for attribute retrieval. In particular, we investigate to what extent errors affecting the retrieval of attributes affect the accuracy of policy evaluation. In this respect, the problem of selecting mechanisms for attribute retrieval can be formulated as the problem of finding the set of mechanisms that maximize the accuracy of policy evaluation.

In practice, it is unlikely that all attributes have the same importance on policy evaluation, as certain attributes can be more critical to reach a reliable decision. To this end, we devise metrics that account for *both* the error rate of mechanisms and the impact of attributes on policy evaluation to assess the evaluation accuracy of a policy. The underlying intuition is that, for the retrieval of attributes with high impact, one might prefer mechanisms that provide high accuracy while relaxing other constraints such as their cost.

Our contributions can be summarized as follows:

- We introduce the notions of *policy evaluation under error rate* and *policy evaluation accuracy* to illustrate the challenges in attribute retrieval and its impact on policy evaluation using an example in the domain of smart buildings.
- We formulate the Attribute Retrieval Mechanism Selection Problem (ARMSP) in terms of policy evaluation accuracy, and show it is exponential in the number of attribute values, making it possibly intractable for large policies.
- We propose a metric that estimates the evaluation accuracy of a policy while maintaining the computation feasible.

The remainder of the paper is organized as follows. The next section presents background on ABAC. Section 3 introduces our problem statement using an example in the context of smart buildings. Section 4 introduces the notion of policy evaluation under error rate. Section 5 presents a metric to assess the evaluation accuracy of a policy and formalizes the attribute retrieval mechanism selection problem. Section 6 provides a feasible approach to compute an approximation of the evaluation accuracy of a policy. Finally, Sect. 7 discusses related work and provides conclusions and directions for future work.

2   Preliminaries

For the specification of ABAC policies, we employ PTaCL [2], a policy language that provides an abstraction of the XACML standard [11]. First, we present the PTaCL language and, then, we explain the extended policy evaluation in PTaCL [3,8].

ABAC Syntax. Let $\mathcal{A} = \{a_1, \ldots, a_n\}$ be a finite set of attributes and, given an attribute $a \in \mathcal{A}$, $\mathcal{V}_a$ denote the domain of a. A query $q = \{(a_1, v_1), \ldots, (a_k, v_k)\}$ is a set of attribute name-value pairs (a_i, v_i) such that $a_i \in \mathcal{A}$ and $v_i \in \mathcal{V}_{a_i}$. We represent a query space as a directed acyclic graph $(Q_\mathcal{A}, \rightarrow)$, where $Q_\mathcal{A} = \wp(\bigcup_{i=1}^{n} a_i \times \mathcal{V}_{a_i})$ is a set of queries and $\rightarrow \subseteq Q_\mathcal{A} \times Q_\mathcal{A}$ is a relation such that, given two queries $q, q' \in Q_\mathcal{A}$, $q \rightarrow q'$ if and only if $q' = q \cup \{(a, v)\}$ for some attribute a and value $v \in \mathcal{V}_a$.

PTaCL provides two languages: $\mathcal{T}_\mathcal{A}$ for targets and $\mathcal{P}_\mathcal{A}$ for policies. A target $t \in \mathcal{T}_\mathcal{A}$ defines the applicability of policies. Targets can be constructed using the following grammar:

$$t = (a, v) \mid \mathsf{op}(t_1, \ldots, t_n)$$

where (a, v) is an attribute name-value pair and $\mathsf{op}(t_1, \ldots, t_n)$ represents a composite target with op an n-ary operator defined over the set $\mathcal{D}_3 = \{1, 0, \bot\}$. Here, 1 indicates that the target matches the query, 0 that it does not match the query and $\bot$ indicates indeterminate (*i.e.*, that an error occurred in the evaluation). The two operators we use here are $\triangledown$ and $\triangle$, which roughly correspond to the XACML operator *permit-overrides* and *deny-overrides* respectively [9], and which are defined as follows. $x \triangledown y = \bot$ when both x and y are equal to $\bot$, $x \triangledown y = 1$ when either x or y is equal to 1, and $x \triangledown y = 0$ otherwise. Conversely, $x \triangle y = \bot$ when both x and y are equal to $\bot$, $x \triangle y = 0$ when either x or y is equal to 0, and $x \triangle y = 1$ otherwise. For the sake of exposition, we do not define other operators and refer to [4] for further work on the canonical completeness of PTaCL.

A policy $p \in \mathcal{P}_\mathcal{A}$ is then defined as:

$$p = 1 \mid 0 \mid (t, p) \mid \mathsf{op}(p_1, \ldots, p_n)$$

where a policy can be a single decision, either *permit* (1) or *deny* (0), a target policy (t, p) or a composite policy $\mathsf{op}(p_1, \ldots, p_n)$ with op an n-ary operator defined on the set $\{1, 0, \bot\}$, where $\bot$ represents the *not-applicable* decision. It is worth emphasizing that, even though the evaluation of both targets and policies uses the set $\{1, 0, \perp\}$, these values have a different interpretation. The interpretation should be always clear from the context.

Morisset et al. [8] observed that some combinations of attribute name-value pairs may not represent a plausible view of the world. For example, a citizen of India cannot have other nationalities. Thus, a query stating that the requester is both Indian and, for instance, Dutch, is not possible. To capture the set of valid queries (*i.e.*, plausible views of the world), Morisset and colleagues have introduced the notion of *query constraints* to encode domain specific requirements into policy evaluation. For the sake of exposition, we do not introduce the formal language for query constraints here. Instead, we simply use $Q_{A|C}$ to denote the set of queries that satisfy the set of constraints C (i.e., $Q_{A|C}$ is the set of all *valid queries*), and we refer to [8] for further details.

Policy Evaluation. Given the set of policies $\mathcal{P}_A$, the set of valid queries $Q_{A|C}$ and the decision set $\mathcal{D}$, an evaluation function is a function $[\![\cdot]\!] : \mathcal{P}_A \times Q_{A|C} \rightarrow \mathcal{D}$ such that, given a query q and a policy p, $[\![p]\!](q)$ represents the decision of evaluating p against q. Different evaluation functions have been defined for PTaCL. Here, we present the extended evaluation function introduced in [8], which provides an approach to evaluate ABAC policies that is robust to missing attributes. Note that this approach is different from the one used in XACML as the latter can lead to misleading decisions when not all relevant attributes are provided [3]. Next, we provide an overview of the extended evaluation function and refer to [8] for further details.

The evaluation of a policy requires evaluating the target (if present) to determine the applicability of the policy to a query. The semantics of a target t for a query q is defined as follows:

$$[\![\cdot]\!]_T : \mathcal{T}_A \times Q_{A|C} \rightarrow \mathcal{D}_3$$

$$[\![(a, v)]\!]_T(q) = \begin{cases} 1 & \text{if } (a, v) \in q \\ 0 & \text{otherwise} \end{cases}$$

$$[\![op(t_1, \ldots, t_n)]\!]_T(q) = op([\![t_1]\!]_T(q), \ldots, [\![t_n]\!]_T(q))$$

The extended evaluation of a policy uses two evaluation functions: the simplified evaluation function $[\![\cdot]\!]_B$ and the extended evaluation function $[\![\cdot]\!]_E$. The simplified evaluation function ignores missing attributes and always returns singleton decisions within $\mathcal{D}_3$. Its semantics is defined as follows:

$$[\![\cdot]\!]_B : \mathcal{P}_A \times Q_{A|C} \rightarrow \mathcal{D}_3$$
$$[\![1]\!]_B(q) = 1$$
$$[\![0]\!]_B(q) = 0$$

$$[\![(t, p)]\!]_B(q) = \begin{cases} [\![p]\!]_B(q) & \text{if } [\![t]\!]_T(q) = 1 \\ \perp & \text{otherwise} \end{cases}$$

$$[\![op(p_1, \ldots, p_n)]\!]_B(q) = op([\![p_1]\!]_B(q), \ldots, [\![p_n]\!]_B(q))$$

The extended evaluation function $\llbracket \cdot \rrbracket_E$ evaluates a query to all possible decisions that can be obtained by adding possible missing attributes.

$$\llbracket \cdot \rrbracket_E : \mathcal{P}_A \times Q_{A|C} \to \mathcal{D}_7 = \wp(\{1, 0, \bot\}) \setminus \emptyset$$

$$\llbracket p \rrbracket_E(q) = \{\llbracket p \rrbracket_B(q') \mid q \to^* q' \wedge q' \in Q_{A|C}\}$$

where $\to^*$ denotes the transitive closure of relation $\to$. For the sake of exposition, and when no confusion arises, we omit the brackets for singleton decisions $\{1\}$, $\{0\}$ and $\{\bot\}$, and we write $\llbracket p \rrbracket_E(q) = d$ whenever $\llbracket p \rrbracket_E(q) = \{d\}$.

3   Motivations

A key aspect for the evaluation of ABAC policies is the ability of the policy decision point to retrieve the attribute values necessary for policy evaluation. In this work, we aim to understand and quantify the impact of incorrect attribute values on the accuracy of policy evaluation. In this section, we present an illustrative example and provide our problem statement.

As an illustrative example, consider a smart building hosting a company. The smart building comprises public and restricted areas; restricted areas include workplaces, meeting rooms and conference halls. The company is divided into three departments, namely production, research and business units. The company's personnel are assigned to a role based on their job function (*e.g.*, administrator, employees). Employees can be affiliated with only one department. Persons entering the building can also be visitors (*e.g.*, vendors, consultants). Office hours are between 7am and 6pm on working days.

The areas personnel can access depend on their role and the department in which they work. Administrators have access to all areas. Employees have access to public areas and to the restricted areas of the department in which they work. In addition, employees of the production and research units can access each other's restricted areas, whereas access to restricted areas in the business unit is restricted to employees of that unit. For safety reasons, personnel can access the building outside office hours only if the building is not empty.[1] Visitors can access restricted areas only if they are accompanied by an employee of the respective department and within office hours.

We now show how the access requirements above can be formalized in PTaCL. First, we define the attributes needed for policy specification along their domain:

$$role : \mathcal{V}_{role} = \{admin, employee, visitor\}$$
$$dept : \mathcal{V}_{dept} = \{prod, res, bus\}$$
$$otime : \mathcal{V}_{otime} = \{true, false\}$$
$$pres : \mathcal{V}_{pres} = \{true, false\}$$
$$hprox : \mathcal{V}_{hprox} = \{true, false\}$$
$$area : \mathcal{V}_{area} = \{public, rprod, rres, rbus\}$$

---

[1] For the sake of simplicity, we do not consider the scenario when an employee is alone and is already inside the building (*i.e.*, if she remains in the building after office hours).

Attributes *role* and *dept* specify the role and department of personnel, respectively. Attribute *otime* indicates whether the current time is within office hours, *pres* indicates whether someone is in the building and *hprox* indicates whether the host is in proximity of her visitor. Attribute *area* indicates whether an area is public or restricted (in which case it specifies to which department it belongs). Based on the domain requirements above, all attributes can assume only one value in a query. This can be represented by imposing a query constraint on each attribute.

Based on these attributes, the policies encoding the access requirements for our scenario can be specified in PTaCL as follows. For the sake of space, we only provide the policy for the restricted areas of the production unit.

$$p = ((area, rprod), p_0 \vartriangle p_2 \vartriangle p_4)$$
$$p_0 = ((role, admin), p_1 \vartriangle 1)$$
$$p_1 = ((otime, false) \vartriangle (pres, false), 0)$$
$$p_2 = ((role, visitor), p_3 \triangledown 0)$$
$$p_3 = (((otime, true) \vartriangle (dept, prod)) \vartriangle (hprox, true), 1)$$
$$p_4 = ((role, employee), p_5 \triangledown 0)$$
$$p_5 = ((dept, prod) \triangledown (dept, res), p_6 \triangledown p_7)$$
$$p_6 = ((otime, true), 1)$$
$$p_7 = ((otime, false) \vartriangle (pres, true), 1)$$

Policy p is a target policy that applies to requests for accessing restricted areas of the production unit. Access to these areas is determined by policies p_0, p_2 and p_4. These policies specify the permissions for each role and are combined using the *deny-overrides* operator ($\vartriangle$). Policy p_0 indicates that administrators have full access to restricted areas during office hours and when the building is not empty (represented by p_1). Policy p_2 defines the permissions of visitors. Specifically, this policy allows visitor to access restricted areas during working time and only if her host is in the proximity (represented by p_3); otherwise, access is denied (represented by default policy 0). Here, p_3 and the default policy are combined using the *permit-overrides* operator ($\triangledown$). Policy p_4 defines the permissions of employees. This policy specifies that employees can access the restricted areas of the production unit only if they work in the production or research unit (represented by policy p_5) and access is within office time (represented by p_6). Employees in the production and research units can also access restricted areas outside office time but the building should not be empty (represented by p_7).

For the evaluation of policy p, the policy decision point requires information on the current state of the systems and the surrounding environment, represented by the values of the attributes used in the policy. Attribute values can be retrieved from different sources, depending on the nature of the attribute. For instance, values for attributes *role*, *dept*, *area* and *otime* can be retrieved from the organization's database (*e.g.*, the system records the entrance of employees in the building). On the other hand, different mechanisms can be conceived to retrieve values for attributes *pres* and *hprox*.

Attribute values attesting the presence of employees in the building can be obtained *(i)* through occupancy detection sensors, *(ii)* by requiring employees to swipe their access card when they enter and exit the building or *(iii)* by employing a guard that physically checks for the presence of people in the building. Although, the accuracy of occupancy detection sensors varies depending on the quality of the sensors, commonly used sensors often have a low accuracy. For example, Newsham et al. [10] show that the use of ceiling-based passive infrared sensors to detect the presence in a room has a high false negative rate. The use of access cards provides information on the presence of personnel in the building that is more accurate compared to the one obtained using occupancy detection sensors. However, this mechanism is not free from errors because employees might forget to swipe their card. Presence information can also be gathered by a guard that manually checks the presence of people in a building. This solution, however, might not provide reliable attribute values.

To retrieve attribute *hprox*, the organization can use *(i)* distance sensors or *(ii)* geo-location information from mobile phones to estimate the proximity between the visitor and her host. Distance sensors usually calculate the distance by measuring the delay between sending a request from a sensor and receiving a response from another. Such sensors, however, are not very accurate. On the other hand, the use of geo-location information can determine the proximity with high accuracy by tracking the position of both the host and visitor using a geo-location mobile app and, then, computing their proximity from their position.

As illustrated above, the retrieval of attribute values from external sources can be subject to errors due to inherent limitations of the mechanism used for their retrieval. This can have a significant impact on policy evaluation. Consider, for instance, an employee of the research department who want to enter a restricted area of the production department after office hours for a project meeting with a colleague already in the building. This state of the system can be captured by the following query:

$$q = \{(role, employee), (dept, res), (otime, false), (pres, true), (area, rprod)\}$$

Evaluating this query against policy p gives *permit*, i.e. $[\![p]\!]_E(q) = 1$, indicating that access should be granted to the employee. Suppose now that attribute *pres* is retrieved using occupancy detection sensors and that the sensors fail to detect the presence of persons in the building. In this case, the query evaluated by the policy decision point is:

$$q' = \{(role, employee), (dept, res), (otime, false), (pres, false), (area, rprod)\}$$

It is easy to verify that $[\![p]\!]_E(q') = 0$ and, thus, access is denied.

The example above clearly shows that retrieving incorrect attribute values can have a significant impact on the accuracy of policy evaluation. In this work, we assume that the mechanisms in charge of gathering attribute values can be affected by an *error rate* and, thus, can provide the policy decision point with incorrect attribute values. Note that the notion of error rate is fundamentally different from that of missing attribute, studied in previous literature [2,12,13]: in the former case, the decision point is provided with a value that might be wrong, while in the latter case no value is provided to the decision point.

To guide the selection of mechanisms for attribute retrieval, we investigate how to quantify the impact of the use of incorrect attribute values on the accuracy of policy evaluation by taking into account *both* the error rate of mechanisms for attribute retrieval and the impact of attributes on policy evaluation. In particular:

- We introduce the notion of *policy evaluation under error rate* to determine the probability of obtaining a certain decision when the retrieval of attributes is affected by a given error rate (Sect. 4).
- Based on this notion, we devise a metric to assess the *evaluation accuracy* of a policy and use this metric to formalize the *attribute retrieval mechanism selection problem*. We also discuss the computational complexity of this problem (Sect. 5).
- Computational results show that solving the attribute retrieval mechanism selection problem can be intractable in the general case. To this end, we propose a metric that provides an approximation of evaluation by sampling the query space (Sect. 6).

4   Policy Evaluation Under Error Rate

In this section, we introduce a novel policy evaluation function that takes into account the error rate of the mechanisms used for attribute retrieval. Intuitively, this function computes the probability of obtaining a certain decision knowing that the retrieval of attributes is affected by a given error rate. For the sake of simplicity, we consider the attributes affected by an error rate to be Boolean.[2]

Let $\mathcal{A}_E \subseteq \mathcal{A}$ be a subset of Boolean attributes and $\rho : \mathcal{A}_E \times \mathbb{B} \to [0,1]$ an error rate function, such that each $a \in \mathcal{A}_E$ is associated with an error rate $\rho(a, true)$ when a is true and $\rho(a, false)$ when a is false. In other words, if a query contains attribute name-value pair $(a, true)$, then there is a probability $\rho(a, true)$ that *false* is the actual value for a, and conversely if the query contains $(a, false)$. Note that $\rho(a, true)$ is not necessarily equal to $\rho(a, false)$. For instance, the probability that an occupancy sensor is wrong when detecting someone might be different than the probability the same occupancy sensor is wrong when detecting no-one.

Given two queries q and q', we now define the notion of closeness $\delta(q', q \mid \rho)$ between q and q' knowing the error rate function ρ. Intuitively, given a query q describing the environment as observed by the system, $\delta(q', q \mid \rho)$ represents the likelihood that the actual environment (represented by query q') corresponds to q.

To define δ, we first introduce the function δ_a, such that $\delta_a(q', q \mid \rho)$ corresponds to the notion of closeness between q and q' with respect to an attribute

---

[2] An attribute a associated with n values $v_1, \ldots, v_n$ can be modeled as n Boolean attributes $a_{v_1}, \ldots, a_{v_n}$, one for each attribute value.

Table 1. Definition of the closeness between queries q and q' with respect to attribute a knowing the error rate ρ.

$$
\delta_a(q', q \mid \rho) = \begin{cases}
1 - \rho(a, true) & \text{if } a \in \mathcal{A}_E, (a, true) \in q \text{ and } (a, true) \in q' \\
\rho(a, true) & \text{if } a \in \mathcal{A}_E, (a, false) \in q \text{ and } (a, true) \in q' \\
1 - \rho(a, false) & \text{if } a \in \mathcal{A}_E, (a, false) \in q \text{ and } (a, false) \in q' \\
\rho(a, false) & \text{if } a \in \mathcal{A}_E, (a, true) \in q \text{ and } (a, false) \in q' \\
1 & \text{if } a \notin \mathcal{A}_E, \{v \mid (a, v) \in q\} = \{v \mid (a, v) \in q'\} \\
0 & \text{otherwise.}
\end{cases}
$$

a. This function simply looks at the corresponding error rate if the attribute is in $\mathcal{A}_E$ and requires all values to be identical if the attribute is not in $\mathcal{A}_E$. The formal definition is given in Table 1. Interestingly, we can observe that the closeness is the same when the attribute is in $\mathcal{A}_E$ with a null error rate, and when the attribute is Boolean and not in $\mathcal{A}_E$.

We are now in the position to define the closeness between two queries w.r.t. all attributes. Under the assumption that attributes are independent, the probability for a query to be obtained given the actual system's state can be computed as the product of the probabilities for each attribute forming the query. Accordingly, given two queries q and q', the closeness over all attributes is defined as:

$$
\delta(q', q \mid \rho) = \prod_{a \in \mathcal{A}} \delta_a(q', q \mid \rho)
$$

As an example, let us consider the following query:

$$
q_1 = \{(pres, true), (hprox, true), (role, visitor), (area, rprod)\}
$$

Suppose that values for attributes $pres$ and $hprox$ are retrieved using access cards and distance sensors, respectively. The error rates of these mechanisms are defined by error rate function ρ_1 such that

$$
\rho_1(pres, true) = \rho_1(pres, false) = 0.1
$$
$$
\rho_1(hprox, true) = \rho_1(hprox, false) = 0.25
$$

We consider here that the retrieval of attributes $role$ and $area$ is not affected by an error rate. We can derive the following closeness:

$\delta(\{(pres, true),(hprox, true),(role, visitor),(area, rprod)\}, q_1 \mid \rho_1) = 0.9 \times 0.75 = 0.675$
$\delta(\{(pres, false),(hprox, true),(role, visitor),(area, rprod)\}, q_1 \mid \rho_1) = 0.1 \times 0.75 = 0.075$
$\delta(\{(pres, true),(hprox, false),(role, visitor),(area, rprod)\}, q_1 \mid \rho_1) = 0.9 \times 0.25 = 0.225$
$\delta(\{(pres, false),(hprox, false),(role, visitor),(area, rprod)\}, q_1 \mid \rho_1) = 0.1 \times 0.25 = 0.025$
For any other query q', we have $\delta(q', q_1 \mid \rho_1) = 0$.

The notion of closeness allows us to introduce the notion of policy evaluation under error rate, which associates each query and each decision with a probability to return that decision, taking into account a specific error rate.

Definition 1 (Policy evaluation under error rate). *Given a query q, a decision d and an error rate function ρ, we define the probabilistic evaluation of q w.r.t. a policy p as:*

$$\llbracket p \rrbracket_{\mathrm{P}}(q, d \mid \rho) = \sum_{\{q' \in Q_{\mathcal{A}|C} \mid \llbracket p \rrbracket_{\mathrm{E}}(q')=d\}} \delta(q', q \mid \rho)$$

Note that this definition resembles the definition of probabilistic evaluation introduced by Crampton et al. in [3]; however, the latter focuses on the problem of missing information, while here we focus on the notion of error rate.

Given policy p defined in Sect. 3 and error rate function ρ_1 in the example above, we can compute the evaluation under error rate for query q_1:

$$\llbracket p \rrbracket_{\mathrm{P}}(q_1, 1 \mid \rho_1) = 0.75$$
$$\llbracket p \rrbracket_{\mathrm{P}}(q_1, 0 \mid \rho_1) = 0.25$$

For any other decision $d \in \mathcal{D}_7 \setminus \{\{1\}, \{0\}\}$, we have $\llbracket p \rrbracket_{\mathrm{P}}(q_1, d \mid \rho_1) = 0$.

5   Attribute Retrieval Mechanism Selection Problem

The notion of policy evaluation under error rate allows us to quantify the impact of error rates on the accuracy of policy evaluation, thus providing a means to guide the selection of mechanisms for attribute retrieval. In this section, we first introduce the notion of accuracy for the evaluation of a policy and, then, we use this notion to formalize the *attribute retrieval mechanism selection problem*.

We measure the accuracy of policy evaluation as the probability of making the correct decision under error rates.

Definition 2 (Evaluation accuracy). *The evaluation accuracy for a query q w.r.t. a policy p under an error rate function ρ can be defined as the probability of obtaining the correct decision.*

$$\overline{EA}(p, q \mid \rho) = \llbracket p \rrbracket_{\mathrm{P}}(q, \llbracket p \rrbracket_{\mathrm{E}}(q) \mid \rho)$$

The evaluation accuracy for the policy is the aggregation of the evaluation accuracy over all queries:

$$EA(p \mid \rho) = \sum_{q \in Q_{\mathcal{A}|C}} \overline{EA}(p, q \mid \rho) \cdot |Q_{\mathcal{A}|C}|^{-1}$$

We can easily show that the policy evaluation accuracy increases when the error rate over attributes decreases.

Lemma 1. *Given a policy p, a set of attribute $\mathcal{A}_E$ and two error rate functions ρ and ρ' such that, for any attribute a in $\mathcal{A}_E$ and any Boolean b, $\rho(a, b) \leq \rho'(a, b)$, we have: $EA(p \mid \rho) \geq EA(p \mid \rho')$.*

Proof: The proof follows easily from the observation that given such ρ and ρ', we have $\delta(q, q \mid \rho) \geq \delta(q, q \mid \rho')$, for any query q.

Given a set of attributes $\mathcal{A}_E$, we call a set of mechanisms for attribute retrieval a *configuration* c if, for any attribute $a_i \in \mathcal{A}_E$, c contains exactly one mechanism for the retrieval of a_i[3]. Any configuration c is associated with an error rate function ρ, which allows us to define the attribute retrieval mechanism selection problem.

Definition 3 (Attribute Retrieval Mechanism Selection Problem).
Given a policy p and a non-empty set of configurations for attribute retrieval C, such that each configuration $c_i \in C$ is associated with an error rate function ρ_i, the attribute retrieval mechanism selection problem consists in finding the configuration $c_\top \in C$ such that, for any $c_i \in C$, $EA(p \mid \rho_i) \leq EA(p \mid \rho_\top)$. Hereafter, we write $\mathsf{ARMSP}(p, C)$ for such a problem.

Clearly, $\mathsf{ARMSP}(p, C)$ is trivial when there exists only one configuration, i.e., $|C| = 1$, or only one attribute is affected by an error rate, i.e., $|\mathcal{A}_E| = 1$. Following usual algebraic definitions, we say that a configuration c is *minimal* if there exists no other configuration c' such that, for any attribute $a \in \mathcal{A}_E$ and Boolean b, the error rate of c' is lower than that of c. Using Lemma 1, it is easy to see that $\mathsf{ARMSP}(p, C)$ can be reduced to $\mathsf{ARMSP}(p, \min(C))$, where $\min(C)$ consists of the set of minimal elements of C. We can then conclude that $\mathsf{ARMSP}(p, C)$ is trivial when C has a single minimal element (i.e., when there exists a configuration c with an error rate lower than that of any other configuration c').

Consider, for instance, the configurations that can be obtained by employing the mechanisms for the retrieval of attributes *pres* and *hprox* presented in Sect. 3.[4] These configurations are presented in the table on the right along with the error rate associated with each mechanism forming the configuration and the corresponding evaluation accuracy (EA). It is easy to see that the configuration consisting of the use of access cards and

Configuration	Error rate	EA
Access card	0.10	96.7%
Geo-location information	0.10	
Occupancy detection sensors	0.15	95.3%
Geo-location information	0.10	
Manual check	0.40	88.3%
Geo-location information	0.10	
Access card	0.10	95.8%
Distance sensors	0.25	
Occupancy detection sensors	0.15	94.4%
Distance sensors	0.25	
Manual check	0.40	87.5%
Distance sensors	0.25	

geo-location information is the one that provides the highest accuracy as it is the minimal configuration. Along the same line, we can conclude that the configuration consisting of manual check and distance sensors is the least preferable configuration.

In the following, we focus our attention to the case where there are at least two distinct minimal elements in C, and we say that the set of configurations C is *open* in such a case. This situation can occur, for instance, when the company

---

[3] We leave for future work the case where multiple mechanisms cover the same attribute.

[4] We assume $\rho(a_i, true) = \rho(a_i, false)$ for any attribute $a_i \in \mathcal{A}_E$.

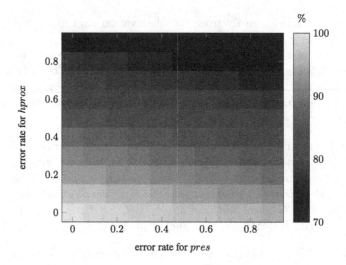

Fig. 1. Evaluation accuracy for the example policy, with variations of the error rates for attributes *hprox* and *pres*

would consider choosing between occupancy detection sensors and geo-location information (configuration c_1, 0.15 and 0.10 error rates), or access cards and distance sensors (configuration c_2, 0.10 and 0.25 error rates). Using the error rates presented in the table above, it is clear that both c_1 and c_2 are minimal, since their respective error rates are not comparable.

Intuitively, one might want to consider c_1 as "better" than c_2, since the aggregated error rate for c_1 is 0.25, compared to 0.35 for c_2. However, we can see that the evaluation accuracy of c_2 (95.8%) is actually better than that of c_1 (95.3%). Of course, these values depend on the policy, and with a different policy, c_1 might have actually have a better evaluation accuracy than c_2.

This simple example shows that the ARMSP can be particularly challenging to solve in general, due to the different impact that different attributes might have on the evaluation accuracy of the policy. Figure 1 presents a heat map of the evaluation accuracy of policy p while varying the error rates for attributes *hprox* and *pres*. We can observe an accuracy of 100% when the error rate for both attributes is 0 and decreases as the error rate of any of them increases. However, the impact on evaluation accuracy differs for the *hprox* and *pres* attributes. The figure indicates that attribute *hprox* has more impact on policy evaluation as, when the error rate for this attribute increases, the accuracy of policy evaluation shows a more accentuated decrease.

Solving ARMSP, however, is computationally expensive. In particular, the complexity of solving this problem is exponential in the number of attribute values. This follows from the fact that, in non-trivial cases, solving the ARMSP requires computing the evaluation accuracy (EA) of the policy, which is

---

Algorithm 1. Computing the Empirical Evaluation Accuracy

Require: A policy p, an error rate function ρ, and a sample size k. **Note:** We write $q[a]$ for the value associated with the attribute a in the query q.

1: **function** EEA(p, ρ, k)
2:      $T \leftarrow 0$
3:      **for** $i \leftarrow 1$ to k **do**
4:          $q \leftarrow$ random query from $Q_{A|C}$
5:          $q' \leftarrow q$
6:          **for** a in $\mathcal{A}_E$ **do**
7:              $r \leftarrow$ random number in $[0, 1]$
8:              **if** $r \leq \rho(a, q[a])$ **then**
9:                  $q'[a] \leftarrow \neg q[a]$
10:            **end if**
11:        **end for**
12:        **if** $[\![p]\!]_E(q') = [\![p]\!]_E(q)$ **then**
13:            $T \leftarrow T + 1$
14:        **end if**
15:    **end for**
16:    **return** T/k
17: **end function**

---

quadratic in the number of queries, and the size of the query space is exponential in the number of attribute values.

6 Empirical Evaluation Accuracy

The computational results presented in the previous section indicate that solving the ARMSP in non-trivial cases can be intractable: as shown in [7], the constrained query space for relatively large policies can comprise hundreds of millions of queries. Therefore, we introduce a metric, called *empirical evaluation accuracy*, which provides an approximation of evaluation accuracy given in Definition 2.

The idea underlying the empirical evaluation accuracy is to compare the differences in evaluation between queries in which attribute values reflect the actual state of the system and environment and queries in which attribute values are affected by an error rate, over a sampling of the constrained query space. Intuitively, the former queries represent the ideal situation in which no error occurs, thus resulting in the correct access decision. On the other hand, the latter queries may contain attribute values subject to an error, which can potentially lead to an incorrect access decision.

To compute the empirical evaluation accuracy of a policy, we follow Algorithm 1. Intuitively, we generate valid queries capturing the actual state of the system and the corresponding queries that could have been obtained from the attribute values provided by attribute retrieval mechanisms (lines 3–11), and check if both queries evaluate to same decision (line 12). Note that we assume here that, given a valid query q (i.e., satisfying the given query constraints), the query q' generated by the for-loop starting on line 6 is also valid. This assumption is trivial for Boolean attributes, which can usually have only one value in the query (which is the case in the example policy), and therefore swapping that value has no effect on the validity of the query. It is also worth noting that we encode the valid query space as a BDD (following [7]), and sampling random valid queries is therefore relatively straightforward.

To demonstrate the feasibility of computing the empirical evaluation accuracy of a policy, we have computed this metrics for a variant of our example policy p, varying the sampling size of the constrained query space (k in Algorithm 1). The constrained query space of the policy considered in the previous section consists of 72 queries. While this makes the computation of evaluation accuracy feasible, real policies usually have a much larger query space [7]. To study the computation of the (empirical) evaluation accuracy in a more realistic setting, we have considered six additional departments besides research, production and business, and removed the restriction on the number of departments an employee can affiliated with (i.e., an employee can be affiliated with an arbitrary number of departments). The constrained query space of the modified policies consists of 12264 queries. It is worth noting that, due to the difference in the size of the constrained query space, the values of EA reported in the previous section might differ from the ones reported here.

Table 2 reports the empirical evaluation accuracy (EEA) for the different configurations of mechanisms for attribute retrieval considered in the previous section. Specifically, we computed the empirical evaluation accuracy for varying sizes of (random) sampling of the constrained query space (i.e., 50, 100, 200, 500, 1000). For each sampling size, we repeated the computation 10 times. In the table, we report the mean empirical evaluation accuracy along with the standard deviation (in parentheses) and the evaluation accuracy (EA) for each configuration. From the table, we can observe that the value of the empirical evaluation accuracy is close to the actual evaluation accuracy already for a sampling of size 50. Moreover, the empirical evaluation accuracy tends to converge towards the evaluation accuracy when increasing the sampling size. At the same time, the standard deviation decreases, thus providing more stable values of empirical evaluation accuracy.

The computation time is of course much faster for the empirical evaluation accuracy, ranging from 1.9 s on average for 50 queries, to 38 s on average for 1000 queries (the computation time is simply linear in the number of queries), with no particular variation between the different configurations. In comparison, the computation time for EA in Table 2 took on average 6848 s (all computations have been performed on a Intel(R) Xeon(R) CPU E5-2630 0 2.30 GHz with 15 GB of RAM). Therefore, we can conclude that the empirical evaluation accuracy provides a good estimation of the evaluation accuracy while maintaining the computation feasible.

Table 2. Mean (in percentage) and standard deviation (in parentheses) for the empirical evaluation accuracy for (a variant of) the example policy for different configurations and different sample query set sizes.

Configuration		EEA(50)	EEA(100)	EEA(200)	EEA(500)	EEA(1000)	EA
Mechanism	Error rate						
Access card	0.10	94.7 (1.1)	94.7 (2.4)	94.2 (1.6)	95.1 (1.3)	95.2 (0.6)	95.0
Geo-location information	0.10						
Occupancy detection sensors	0.15	93.1 (3.1)	92.9 (2.0)	92.6 (2.0)	93.6 (0.8)	93.2 (1.0)	93.3
Geo-location information	0.10						
Manual check	0.40	84.1 (4.7)	84.2 (3.2)	84.8 (2.2)	84.0 (1.3)	84.8 (1.2)	85.0
Geo-location information	0.10						
Access card	0.10	91.8 (3.5)	91.5 (2.2)	92.8 (1.8)	92.4 (1.7)	92.7 (1.0)	92.5
Distance sensors	0.25						
Occupancy detection sensors	0.15	90.0 (3.5)	91.8 (2.6)	91.3 (1.7)	90.9 (0.9)	91.0 (0.6)	90.8
Distance sensors	0.25						
Manual check	0.40	84.7 (5.4)	81.7 (3.4)	82.4 (3.1)	82.7 (2.2)	82.3 (0.8)	82.5
Distance sensors	0.25						

7   Related Work and Conclusions

In this work, we investigated the problem of attribute retrieval in ABAC and its relation with the accuracy of policy evaluation. Mechanisms for attribute retrieval can be affected by an error rate, thus providing the policy decision point with incorrect attribute values. This is a critical issue in ABAC since the use of incorrect attribute values for policy evaluation can yield incorrect access decisions, resulting in data breaches or affecting business continuity.

A large body of research has studied the problem of missing information in ABAC [2,3,12,13] and a number of mechanisms have been proposed to handle missing attributes in the evaluation of ABAC policies [2,8,11]. Our work complements this body of research by focusing on policy evaluation when the attribute values used for policy evaluation can be incorrect. To the best of our knowledge, this is the first work that provides a comprehensive solution for policy evaluation under error rate.

In this paper, we introduced the notion of probabilistic evaluation under error rate and used this notion to assess the impact of the error rate affecting mechanisms for attribute retrieval on the accuracy of policy evaluation. We formalized the Attribute Retrieval Mechanism Selection Problem in terms of evaluation accuracy and showed that solving this problem can be intractable in the general case. To this end, we proposed a metric to estimate the evaluation accuracy of a policy while maintaining the computation feasible. By providing an effective way of quantifying the impact of error rates on the accuracy of policy evaluation, our approach allows unveiling and quantifying the inherent risks of obtaining incorrect decision.

To the best of our knowledge, the only other work that aims to quantify the impact of attributes on policy evaluation is [7], which uses the Banzhaf

Power Index to measure the number of times the addition of an attribute value is responsible for swinging the access decision across all possible configurations. However, the metric in [7] requires strict assumptions on the monotonicity/anti-monotoniticy of query constraints. Moreover, it is tailored to analyze the impact of missing information rather than the effect of incorrect attribute values on policy evaluation.

Attributes can be gathered using different mechanisms, each mechanism characterized by different properties. In this work, we focused on the accuracy of policy evaluation but other properties of mechanisms for attribute retrieval (e.g., cost, privacy level offered) might be considered for their selection. In future work, we will investigate how to evaluate mechanisms for attribute retrieval with respect to different dimensions and devise methods for trade-off analysis over these dimensions.

The notion of probabilistic evaluation introduced in this work can pave the way for other new research directions. In future work, we will extend this notion to design resolution mechanisms that help a decision maker in taking a final decision when policy evaluation is performed under uncertainty. Although a probabilistic evaluation of access control policies offers new opportunities, its computation is expensive since it requires exploring the whole query space. Handling such a complexity is important for large-scale access control systems. Therefore, further research should be conducted to design efficient methods for computing the probabilistic evaluation of a policy.

Acknowledgements. This work is partially funded by the ITEA3 project APPSTA-CLE (15017).

References

1. Byun, J.W., Li, N.: Purpose based access control for privacy protection in relational database systems. VLDB J. **17**(4), 603–619 (2008)
2. Crampton, J., Morisset, C.: PTaCL: a language for attribute-based access control in open systems. In: Degano, P., Guttman, J.D. (eds.) POST 2012. LNCS, vol. 7215, pp. 390–409. Springer, Heidelberg (2012). https://doi.org/10.1007/978-3-642-28641-4_21
3. Crampton, J., Morisset, C., Zannone, N.: On missing attributes in access control: non-deterministic and probabilistic attribute retrieval. In: Proceedings of Symposium on Access Control Models and Technologies, pp. 99–109. ACM (2015)
4. Crampton, J., Williams, C.: On completeness in languages for attribute-based access control. In: Proceedings of the 21st ACM on Symposium on Access Control Models and Technologies, pp. 149–160. ACM (2016)
5. den Hartog, J., Zannone, N.: A policy framework for data fusion and derived data control. In: Proceedings of International Workshop on Attribute Based Access Control, pp. 47–57. ACM (2016)
6. Ferraiolo, D.F., Chandramouli, R., Hu, V.C.: Extensible access control markup language (XACML) and next generation access control (NGAC). In: Proceedings of International Workshop on Attribute Based Access Control, pp. 13–24. ACM (2016)

7. Morisset, C., Willemse, T.A.C., Zannone, N.: A framework for the extended evaluation of ABAC policies. Cybersecurity **2**(1), 1–21 (2019). https://doi.org/10.1186/s42400-019-0024-0

8. Morisset, C., Willemse, T.A.C., Zannone, N.: Efficient extended ABAC evaluation. In: Proceedings of Symposium on Access Control Models and Technologies, pp. 149–160. ACM (2018)

9. Morisset, C., Zannone, N.: Reduction of access control decisions. In: Proceeding of Symposium on Access Control Models and Technologies, pp. 53–62. ACM (2014)

10. Newsham, G.R., et al.: Testing the accuracy of low-cost data streams for determining single-person office occupancy and their use for energy reduction of building services. Energy Build. **135**, 137–147 (2017)

11. OASIS: eXtensible Access Control Markup Language (XACML) Version 3.0. OASIS Standard (2013)

12. Tschantz, M., Krishnamurthi, S.: Towards reasonability properties for access-control policy languages. In: Proceedings of Symposium on Access Control Models and Technologies, pp. 160–169. ACM (2006)

13. Turkmen, F., den Hartog, J., Ranise, S., Zannone, N.: Formal analysis of XACML policies using SMT. Comput. Secur. **66**, 185–203 (2017)

Incorporating Off-Line Attribute Delegation into Hierarchical Group and Attribute-Based Access Control

Daniel Servos$^{(\boxtimes)}$ and Michael Bauer

Department of Computer Science, Western University, London, ON, Canada
{dservos5,bauer}@uwo.ca

Abstract. Efforts towards incorporating user-to-user delegation into Attribute-Based Access Control (ABAC) is an emerging new direction in ABAC research. A number of potential strategies for integrating delegation have been proposed in recent literature but few have been realized as full ABAC delegation models. This work formalizes one such strategy, entitled User-To-User Attribute Delegation, into a working delegation model by extending the Hierarchical Group and Attribute-Based Access Control (HGABAC) model to support dynamic and *"off-line"* attribute delegation. A framework to support the proposed delegation model is also presented and gives implementation details including an updated Attribute Certificate format and service protocol based on the Hierarchical Group Attribute Architecture (HGAA).

Keywords: Delegation · Attribute-Based Access Control · ABAC · HGABAC

1 Introduction

Attribute-Based Access Control (ABAC) is an access control model in which users are granted access rights based on the attributes of users, objects, and the environment rather than a user's identity or predetermined roles. The increased flexibility offered by such attribute-based policies combined with the identityless nature of ABAC have made it an ideal candidate for the next generation of access control models. The beginnings of ABAC in academic literature date back as early as 2004 with Wang et al.'s Logic-Based Framework for Attribute Based Access Control [9] and even earlier in industry with the creation of the eXtensible Access Control Markup Language (XACML) [1] in 2003. However, it is only in recent years that ABAC has seen significant attention [7]. This renewed interest has lead to the development of dozens of ABAC models, frameworks and implementations, but to date, few works have touched on the subject of delegation or how it might be supported in attribute-based models.

Delegation is a key component of comprehensive access control models, enabling users to temporarily and dynamically delegate their access control rights

© Springer Nature Switzerland AG 2020
A. Benzekri et al. (Eds.): FPS 2019, LNCS 12056, pp. 242–260, 2020.
https://doi.org/10.1007/978-3-030-45371-8_15

to another entity after policies have been set in place by an administrator. This ability allows users to adapt to the realities of everyday circumstances that are not possible to foresee during policy creation and is critical in domains such as healthcare [3]. ABAC brings new problems and complications when incorporating delegation that are not present in the traditional models (RBAC, DAC, MAC etc.) [6]. In the traditional models, delegation is relatively straightforward, a set of permissions or role memberships (as in RBAC) is delegated directly by a delegator to a delegatee under set conditions (e.g. an expiry date or "depth" of delegation). In ABAC, this is complicated by identityless nature of ABAC (i.e. access control decisions being made on the basis of attributes rather then the user's identity) and the flexibility of attribute-based policies that may include dynamic attributes such as the current time, physical location of the user, or other attributes of the system's environment.

In a previous work [6], we offered a preliminarily investigation into the possible strategies for incorporating delegation into ABAC and the benefits and drawbacks of each method. A number of these proposed strategies have been further developed into working models by others, such as the work by Sabathein, et al. [4] towards creating a model of delegation for the Hierarchical Group and Attribute-Based Access Control (HGABAC) [5] model using our User-to-Attribute Group Membership Delegation Strategy [6]. In this paper, we seek to explore and put forth a novel attribute-based delegation model based on an unutilized delegation strategy, User-to-User Attribute Delegation [6]. We offer both an extension to the HGABAC model to provide a theoretical blueprint for incorporating delegation as well as an extension to Hierarchical Group Attribute Architecture (HGAA) [8] to provide a practical means of implementing it. Unlike current efforts, a particular emphasis is placed on maintaining the identityless nature of ABAC as well as the ability to delegate attributes in an "off-line" manner (i.e. without the user having to connect to a third party to perform delegation).

The remainder of this paper is organized as follows; Sect. 2 introduces the potential delegation strategies developed in our previous work and gives background on the HGAA and HGABAC model. Sect. 3 details our model of User-to-User Attribute Delegation and how it is incorporated into the HGABAC model. Sect. 4 provides a framework for supporting our delegation model and details modifications to the HGAA architecture to support it, including new extensions to the Attribute Certificate format to include delegation concepts. Finally, Sect. 5 gives concluding remarks and directions for future work.

2   Background

2.1   The HGABAC Model

HGABAC [5] offered a novel model of ABAC that introduced the concept of hierarchical user and object groups. Attributes are assigned both directly to access control entities (e.g. users and objects) and indirectly assigned through groups. Users then have a *direct* set of attributes, directly assigned by an administrator, as well as an *inherited* set of attributes, indirectly assigned to them via their

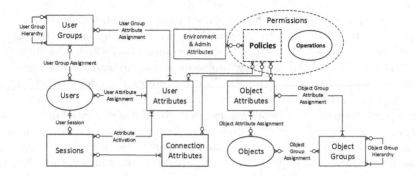

Fig. 1. HGABAC relations and components denoted in Crow's Foot Notation. Primitive components are shown in ovals.

membership in one or more user groups. The set of attributes used for policy evaluations is the user's *effective* attribute set, that is, the set that is the result of merging their *direct* and *inherited* attribute sets. This style of group membership and attribute inheritance is also used to assign attributes indirectly to objects via objects membership in object groups. These relations and the basic elements of HGABAC are shown in Fig. 1 and a brief description of the basic HGABAC entities, relations and functions are as follows:

- **Attributes:** attributes are defined as attribute name, type pairs, that is $att = (name, type)$, where *name* is a unique name for the attribute and *type* is a data type (e.g. string, integer, boolean, etc.). When assigned to entities via direct assignment (e.g. User Attribute Assignment) or groups (e.g. User Group Attribute Assignment) they are associated with a set of values being assigned for that attribute.
- **Users (U):** entities that may request access on system resources through sessions.
- **Objects (O):** resources (files, devices, etc.) for which access may be limited.
- **Operations (Op):** operations that may be applied to an object (read, write, etc.).
- **Policies (P):** policy strings following the HGPL policy language.
- **Groups (G):** a hierarchical collection of users or objects to which attributes may be assigned. Group members inherit all attributes assigned to the group and the groups parents in the hierarchy. Defined as $g = (name, m \subseteq M, p \subseteq G)$ where *name* is the name of the group, m is the set of members, M is either the set of all Users or all Objects, p is the groups parents and G is the set of all groups.
- **Sessions:** sessions allow users to activate a subset of their effective attributes. This subset is used as the user attributes for policy evaluations. Sessions are represented as a tuple s in the form $s = (u \in U, a \subseteq effective(u \in U), con\_atts)$ where u is the user who owns the session, con_atts is the set of connection attributes for the session and a is the set of attributes the user is activating.

```
P1: /user/age >= 18 AND /object/title = "Adult Book"
P2: /user/id = /object/author
P3: /policy/P1 OR /policy/P2
P4: /user/role IN "doctor", "intern", "staff" AND /user/id != /object/patient
```

P1 describes a policy requiring the user to be 18 or older and the title of the object to be "Adult Book". P2 requires the user to be the author of the document. P3 combines policies P1 and P2, such that the policy is satisfied if either policy (P1 or P2) is satisfied. Finally, P4, requires a user's role to be one of "doctor", "intern", or "staff" and that they are not listed as the patient.

Fig. 2. Example HGABAC HGPLv2 [8] policies.

- **Permissions:** a pairing of a policy string and an operation in the form $perm = (p \in P, op \in Op)$. A user may perform an operation, op, on an object if there exists a permission that contains a policy, p, that is satisfied by the set of attributes in the user's session, the object being accessed and the current state of the environment.
- **inherited(x):** mapping of a group or user, x, to the set of all attributes inherited from their group memberships and the group hierarchy.
- **effective(x):** mapping of a group or user, x, to the attribute set resulting from merging the entities directly assigned and inherited attribute sets.

The largest advantage of attribute groups is simplifying administration of ABAC systems, allowing administrators to create user or object groups whose membership indirectly assigns sets of attribute/value pairs to its members. The hierarchical nature of the groups, in which child groups inherit all attributes from their parent groups, allow for more flexible policies, administration and even emulation of traditional models such as RBAC, MAC and DAC when combined with the HGABAC policy language.

Permissions in HGABAC take the form of operation/policy pairs, in which an operation is allowed to be performed if the policy is satisfied by the requesting user's active attribute set, attributes of the object being affected, the current state of the environment and a number of other attribute sources. Policies are defined in the HGABAC Policy Language (HGPL), a C style language using ternary logic to define statements that result in *TRUE, FALSE* or *UNDEF*. Example HGPLv2 policies are given in Fig. 2 and the full language is defined in [8]. These policies would be combined with an operation to form a permission. For example the permission $Perm_1 = (P1, read)$ would allow any user who is at least 18 years of age to read the object titled "Adult Book" based on the permission P1 from Fig. 2. Similarly, the permission $Perm_2 = (P2, write)$ would allow any author of an object to write to that object.

2.2 Hierarchical Group Attribute Architecture (HGAA)

While HGABAC provides an underlying model for ABAC, a supporting architecture is still required to provide a complete system and facilitate use in real-world distributed environments. HGAA [8] provides a system architecture and implementation details for HGABAC that answer questions such as *"who assigns the*

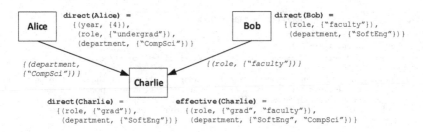

Fig. 3. Example of User-to-User Attribute Delegation. Arrows denote direction of delegation (arrow points to delegatee), boxes represent users of the system.

attributes?", "how are attributes shared with each party?", "how does the user provide proof of attribute ownership?". and *"where and how are policies evaluated?"* that are often left unanswered by ABAC models alone. HGAA accomplishes this by adding five key components:

- **Attribute Authority (AA):** A service responsible for managing, storing and providing user attributes by issuing attribute certificates.
- **Attribute Certificate (AC):** A cryptographically secured certificate listing a user's active attributes for an HGABAC session as well as revocation information.
- **HGABAC Namespace:** A URI-based namespace for uniquely identifying attributes and HGABAC elements across multiple federated domains and authorities.
- **Policy Authority:** A service which manages and evaluates HGABAC policies on behalf of a user service provider.
- **User Service Provider:** A provider of a service to end users that has restricted access on the basis of one or more HGABAC policies (i.e. the service on which access control is being provided).

In a system following HGAA, users request Attribute Certificates (AC) from their home domain's Attribute Authority (AA) containing a list of their attributes for a session. Users may then use this AC to make requests on protected user services (both in their home domain or run by external organizations). These protected services verify the user's AC and check that the user has permission to access the service using their local domains Policy Authority. A key feature of the architecture is the separation of the AA from the other services. Once users are issued an AC, there is no longer a need for the user or other parties to contact the AA for the duration of the session. Separating services in this way simplifies the problem of user's using their attribute based credentials across independent organizational boundaries. Services run by external organizations need not communicate with the user's home organization to verify their attributes beyond trusting the home organization's public key used to sign ACs.

The framework presented in Sect. 4 extends the AC format to add delegation related features. ACs are ideal for this purpose as room has been left for future

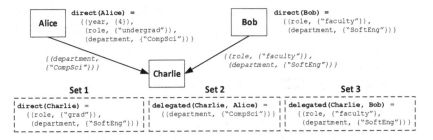

Fig. 4. Example of Isolated Attribute Delegation. Arrows denote delegation direction and solid boxes users. Charlie may activate one set shown in dashed boxes at a time.

extensions including space for delegation extensions that were not part of the original work. Sect. 4 also presents a modification to the HGAA protocol to add an optional delegation step in which users may delegate part of their certificate to another user.

2.3 Potential Delegation Strategies

In our previous work [6], we explored possible strategies for integrating delegation into ABAC and propose several potential methods primarily based on the access control element being delegated (e.g. attributes, group memberships, permissions, etc.). Each family of strategies results in unique proprieties and complications to overcome. The delegation model and architecture presented in the subsequent sections (Sects. 3 and 4) of this paper are based on the User-to-User Attribute Delegation strategy in which users acting as a delegator, delegate a subset of their user attributes to another user acting as the delegatee. The delegated attributes are merged with the delegatee's directly assigned attributes (i.e. assigned through any means but delegation) to form the delegatee's set of user attributes used in policy evaluations.

An example of this style of delegation is shown in Fig. 3, in which Alice (the delegator) delegates a subset of their directly assigned attributes to the user Charlie (the delegatee) such that Charlie may satisfy the policy requiring the user to be in the Computer Science department (e.g. `user.department = "CompSci"`). At the same time, the user Bob (a second delegator) also delegates a subset of their attributes to Charlie such that Charlie may satisfy a policy requiring him to be a faculty member in the Software Engineering department (e.g. `user.role = "faculty" AND user.department = "SoftEng"`). In this example, both the attributes delegated by Alice (a *department* attribute with the value *"CompSci"*) and the attributes delegated by Bob (a *role* attribute with the value *"faculty"*) are combined with Charlie's directly assigned attributes to form their effective attribute set. Note that Bob only needed to delegate the *role* attribute as Charlie already had a *department* attribute with the value *"SoftEng"*.

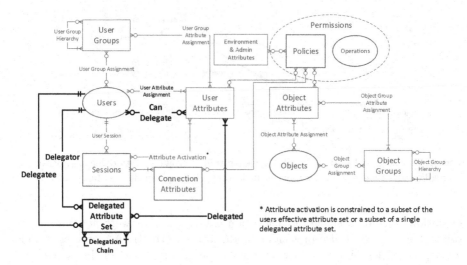

Fig. 5. User-to-User Attribute Delegation extension to the HGABAC model. Added components are bold and black, original components are greyed out.

While this style of attribute delegation may seem straightforward, our previous investigation [6] identified a number of potential issues regarding Attribute Delegation:

Conflicting Policy Evaluations: Merging attribute sets can lead to multiple values for an attribute. While this is an intended feature of HGABAC, it can lead to unintended conflicts when the values are a result of delegation as opposed to careful design. For example, the policy user.department $\neq$ "SoftEng" results in two different results for Charlie in Fig. 3 depending on the value of *department* used.

User Collusion: Merging attribute sets allows users to combine their attributes such that they may satisfy policies they could not individually. In Fig. 3, Alice and Charlie may collude to satisfy the policy user.department = "CompSci" and user.role = "grad", if Alice delegates her *department* attribute such that Charlie satisfies the policy.

Loss of Attribute Meaning: A key ABAC feature is that attributes are descriptive of their subjects and policies are created with this in mind. Merging attribute sets leads to an effective set that is no longer descriptive of the user. In Fig. 3, it is not clear what Charlie's role or department is based solely on their effective attribute set. While this makes delegation possible, it increases the difficulty of policy creation as all allowable delegations and combinations of attributes would need to be taken into account.

To resolve these issues, the delegation model and architecture described in this paper takes a modified approach to User-To-User Attribute Delegation in which the attributes delegated to a delegatee from delegators are isolated and not merged with the delegatee's directly assigned attribute set. A delegatee may then choose to activate either their own directly assigned attributes or their delegated attributes in a given session but never both at the same time. An example of this approach is shown in Fig. 4. In this example, Alice still wishes to delegate their attributes such that Charlie may satisfy the policy user.department = "CompSci" and Bob still wishes Charlie to satisfy the policy user.role = "faculty" AND user.department = "SoftEng". In Alice's case, they still only delegate their *department* attribute, however, now Charlie must choose between activating the directly assigned attribute set, *Set 1*, or the set delegated by Alice, *Set 2*. Charlie is unable to combine their own directly assigned attributes with those delegated by Alice and must activate the delegated attributes *(Set 2)* to satisfy the policy user.department = "CompSci". Note that in this case Alice was only required to delegate a subset of their attributes to satisfy this policy.

In the case of Bob, it is now required that both Bob's *role* and *department* attributes are delegated to Charlie. In the previous example (Fig. 3), Bob only needed to delegate their *role* attribute as Charlie was already assigned a *department* attribute with the value *"SoftEng"* and it was merged with the attributes delegated by Bob. With the attributes sets isolated, both attributes are required as Charlie may not merge them with his own. The policy user.role = "faculty" AND user.department = "SoftEng" will only be satisfied when the set delegated by Bob *(Set 3)* is activated.

Isolation of delegated attributes avoids conflicting policy evaluations (at least those caused by delegation) and user collusion as attributes sets are not merged. Attribute meaning is maintained to the extent that the active attribute set will be descriptive of either the delegatee or delegator. Issues with user comprehension, while still an open ABAC problem [7], are abated as the delegator can be ensured that regardless of the attributes delegated, the delegatee will not be able to satisfy any extra policy that they themselves are not able to. It is important to note that negative policies such as role $\neq$ "undergrad" are still problematic as a user could simply not delegate an attribute with a restricted value. This is however a problem with negative policies in all ABAC models that allow users to activate a subset of their attributes (such as HGABAC) and not simply one limited to attribute delegation.

3 Delegation Model

3.1 Delegated Attribute Set

Several extensions to HGABAC model are required to support User-to-User attribute style delegation. The most critical is the addition of the *Delegated Attribute Set* component (shown in Fig. 5 with the other extensions), which contains the set of attributes delegated to a user in addition to the rules under which the delegation is permitted. This component is defined as follows where *DAS* is the set of all *Delegated Attribute Set*s in the system:

$$\forall das \in DAS :$$
$$das = (delegatee \in U, delegator \in U, att\_set, depth \in \mathbb{N}_{\leq 0}, rule\_set \subseteq P, parent \in DAS) \quad (1)$$

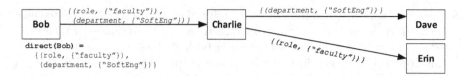

Fig. 6. Example delegation chain. Bob delegates a *role* and *department* attribute to Charlie, who delegates the *department* attribute on to Dave and *role* attribute to Erin.

where *delegatee* is the unique ID of the user who is the recipient of the delegation, and *delegator* is the unique ID of the user who initiated the delegation. *att_set* is the set of attributes being delegated and their corresponding values (defined the same as attribute sets in the HGABAC model). The *att_set* is constrained to only containing attributes listed in *delegatable(delegator)* function (as defined in Sect. 3.2). *depth* is a positive integer selected by the delegator that describes how many more levels of delegation are permitted (e.g. if the user can further delegate these attributes on to another user). *rule_set* is the set of policies in the HGPL policy language selected by the delegator that must all evaluate to TRUE for the delegation to be maintained. Finally, *parent* is a reference to another *Delegated Attribute Set* in the case of subsequent delegations (see Sect. 3.3) or ∅ if this is the root of the delegation chain.

For example, the following *Delegated Attribute Set* would be created by the user Bob to delegate their role and department attribute to Charlie as shown in Fig. 4.

$$
\begin{aligned}
del\_att\_set = (\quad & Charlie, \\
& Bob, \\
& \{ \quad (role, \{"faculty"\}), \\
& \quad (department, \{"SoftEng"\}) \quad \}, \\
& 0, \\
& \{ \quad "/environment/date < 2020 - 04 - 12", \\
& \quad "/connection/ip = 129.100.16.66" \quad \} \\
& \emptyset \\
)
\end{aligned} \tag{2}
$$

In this case, the delegation is constrained with two policies; /environment/date < 2020-04-12 revokes the delegation if the current date is past April 12th, 2020 and /connection/ip = 129.100.16.66 only makes this delegation valid if the delegatee is connecting from the IP address 129.100.18.66. A depth value of 0 limits the delegatee from further delegating these attributes onto other users. A null parent (∅) indicates that this is the first level of delegation and that Bob is first delegator in the chain.

3.2   Constraints on Delegatable Attributes

The set of attributes that may be assigned via delegation is not unlimited. There are two major constraints placed on the attributes and values a delegator may pass on to a delegatee. The first constraint is that delegator must have the delegated attribute and corresponding values in their effective attribute set (i.e. the set of attributes directly assigned to the delegator combined with those the delegator inherited from group membership). The second constraint placed on delegatable attributes comes from the new *Can Delegate (CD)* relation added to the HGABAC model (as shown in Fig. 5). The *CD* relation allows a system administrator to directly constrain the set of attributes a user may delegate to a finite list and is defined as follows:

$$\forall cd \in CD : \\ cd = (delegator \in U, att\_name \subseteq \{name|(name, type) \in UA\}, max\_depth \in \mathbb{N}_{\leq 0}) \quad (3)$$

where *delegator* is the unique ID of the user who is permitted to delegate the set of user attributes listed in *att_name*, a list of unique user attribute names from the set of all user attributes (*UA*). *max_depth* is a positive integer value that limits the value of *deph* used in the *Delegated Attribute Set* such that *depth* $\leq$ *max_depth*. A delegator may not select a *depth* larger than *max_depth* when delegating an attribute in the set *att_name*. A *max_depth* of 0 would limit the attributes from being further delegated.

The attributes a delegator may delegate is defined by the *delegatable* function which combines both constraints and maps a user to the set of attributes they may delegate:

$$delegatable(u) = \{att\_name|(att\_name, values) \in effective(u) \\ \wedge att\_name \in att\_set \\ \wedge (u, att\_set, depth) \in CD\} \quad (4)$$

where *u* is the ID of the delegator and *effective(u)* is the delegator's effective attributes set as defined by HGABAC. The result is an attribute only being delegatable if it is both assigned to the delegator normally (through User *Attribute Assignment* or *User Group Attribute Assignment*) and explicitly permitted via the *Can Delegate* relation.

3.3 Subsequent Delegations and Delegation Chains

In addition to the attributes listed in *delegatable(u)*, users may also further delegate attribute sets they have been delegated so long as the maximum depth has not been reached. If a user, *u*, wishes to delegate a set of attributes they have been delegated, $das_{old} \in DAS$, they create a new *Delegated Attribute Set*, das_{new}, such that:

$$das_{new} = (\quad delegatee \in U, \\ u, \\ att\_set_{new} \subseteq das_{old}.att\_set, \\ depth < das_{old}.depth, \\ rule\_set_{new} \supseteq das_{old}.rule\_set, \\ das_{old} \\ ) \quad (5)$$

That is das_{new} must contain the same or a subset of the attributes of das_{old}, must have a depth less than the depth listed in das_{old}, must have a rule set that is more restrictive than das_{old} (i.e. must contain the same rules plus optionally any additional rules) and must list das_{old} as the parent. These conditions ensure that subsequent delegations in a delegation chain are always more restrictive than their parents, the maximum depth is maintained and that attribute sets remain isolated.

An example delegation chain is shown in Fig. 6. In this case, the user Bob is delegating his *role* attribute with the value *"faculty"* and *department* attribute with the value *"SoftEng"* to the user Charlie. This is the same delegation as discussed in Sect. 3.1 and Bob creates the same DAS as shown in Eq. 2 but with a *depth* of at least 1. This DAS is referred to as das_C. The key difference is that Charlie now further delegates a subset of these attributes on to Dave and Erin. In the case of Dave, Charlie delegates just the *department* attribute and in the case of Erin, only the *role* attribute. To accomplish this, the following DASs are created, das_D for Dave and das_E for Erin:

$$
\begin{aligned}
das_D = (\\
&Dave, \\
&Charlie, \\
&\{(department, \{\text{``SoftEng''}\})\}, \\
&0, \\
&\{\text{``}/environment/date < 2020-04-12\text{''}, \\
&\text{``}/connection/ip = 129.100.16.66\text{''} \\
&\text{``}/user/age >= 18\text{''}\}, \\
&das_C \\
)
\end{aligned}
\tag{6}
$$

$$
\begin{aligned}
das_E = (\\
&Erin, \\
&Charlie, \\
&\{(role, \{\text{``Faculty''}\})\}, \\
&0, \\
&\{\text{``}/environment/date < 2020-04-12\text{''}, \\
&\text{``}/connection/ip = 129.100.16.66\text{''} \\
&\text{``}/environment/date < 2020-04-01\text{''}\}, \\
&das_C \\
)
\end{aligned}
\tag{7}
$$

das_D delegates the *department* attribute to Dave, but also adds in a new constraint on the delegation, /user/age >= 18, which requires that the user of this attribute set must have an *age* attribute in their effective attribute set (*effective(u)*) with a value equal to or greater than 18 for this delegation to be valid. All other constrains from das_C are present in das_D as required by Eq. 5. If the *depth* in das_C was greater than 0, and Dave further delegated this attribute set on to another user, the /user/age >= 18 constraint would have to be maintained, requiring all future delegatees in the chain to also be 18 years or older to use the delegated attributes.

The das_E set delegates the *role* attribute to Erin, but also adds an additional constraint of /environment/date < 2020-04-01 which invalidates the delegation after April 1st, 2020. It is important to note that this does **not** conflict with the existing rule, /environment/date < 2020-04-12, from the parent set, das_C, but further constrains it as all policy rules must evaluate to TRUE for the delegation to be valid. In this way, subsequent delegators may tighten constrains on delegations but not loosen them.

Cycles in the delegation chain are permitted but not useful as each child in the chain must have the same or stricter constraints. The impact of such cycles is negligible as delegated attributes are isolated from each other and the user's

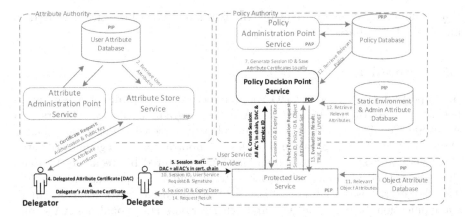

Fig. 7. Updated HGAA protocol to support delegation step. New and modified components shown in bold dark black, pre-existing HGAA components shown in light grey.

effective attribute set as only one such set may be activated in a given session as discussed in Sect. 3.4. Cycles are prevented from being infinite in length as the *depth* of each set in the chain must be less than that of the parent and eventually reach 0, preventing further delegation.

3.4 Sessions and Attribute Activation

An important feature of the proposed User-to-User Attribute Delegation model is the isolation of delegated attributes from the user's effective set of attributes as well from other delegated attribute sets. This is accomplished through a modification of HGABAC's session definition. In the original HGABAC model, sessions are defined as a tuple of the form $s = (u \in U, att\_set \subseteq effective(u), con\_atts)$ where u is the user the session belongs to, att_set is the subset of the user's effective attributes being activated for this session and con_atts is the set of connection attributes that describe this session (e.g. IP address, time the session was started, etc.). To support delegation, we update the definition of a session to the following:

$$
\begin{aligned}
s = (\ & u \in U, \\
& att\_set_{effective} \subseteq effective(u) \vee att\_set_{delegated} \in \{\ del\_att\_set \mid \\
& \quad das \in DAS \wedge das = (u,\ delegator,\ del\_att\_set,\ depth, rule\_set,\ parent)\}, \\
& con\_atts\ )
\end{aligned}
\tag{8}
$$

Or more simply put, the activated attribute set in a session may now be one of $att\_set_{effective}$ or $att\_set_{delegated}$ where $att\_set_{effective}$ is any subset of the user's effective attribute set (as per the original HGABAC session definition) and $att\_set_{delegated}$ is one of the delegated attribute sets delegated to the user via the new *Delegated Attribute Set* component. This limits users to either using their normally assigned attributes or **one** of their delegated attributes sets at a time, eliminating or vastly reducing the issues discussed in Sect. 2.2 related to merging delegated attribute sets.

3.5   Revocation

An important feature of the HGAA architecture is maintaining a separation between the Attribute Authorities (AA) which grant attributes to users (via Attribute Certificates (AC)), and the Policy Enforcement Points and Policy Decision Points. This separation provides an important advantage in distributed and federated systems as no communication is required between the AAs and the services their attributes grant access to beyond a user passing on their AC. This, however, raises a number of issues when it comes to revocation. As direct communication between the AAs and other services is optional, an AA's (and by extension it's user's) ability to revoke delegated attributes is limited to the predefined delegation rules in the *rule_set* component of the *DAS*. As is shown in the example *DAS*s (in Eqs. 2, 6 and 7) these rules may be any valid HGPL policy. If all policies evaluate to *TRUE* the delegation is valid, if the result is *FALSE* or *UNDEF* it is considered to be revoked.

In cases of delegation chains (as shown in Fig. 6), if any policy in a *rule_set* is invalidated all subsequent delegations in the chain are also revoked. This is in part a consequence of all *rule_set*s in subsequent delegations being required to be a superset of the parent *rule_set* as is stated in Eq. 5 (i.e. they must contain at least all policies in the parent rule set), but it is further required that each user in the chain satisfies the policies in their own *rule_set*. For example, if the policy */user/age >= 18* is made a condition of a delegation from Bob to Charlie and Charlie subsequently delegates the attributes on to Dave, both Charlie and Dave must have their own **age** attribute that has a value of 18 or greater. The value of environment and administrator attributes are determined based on their current value at the Policy Decision Point. As the value of connection attributes for parents in the delegation chain may be unknown or undefined, how they are evaluated is left as an implementation decision (i.e. conditions involving connection attributes of parent users can be assumed to be *TRUE*, *UNDEF*, based on the last known values, or based on their values at the time of delegation).

Formally, we define the recursive function *active* which takes a Delegatable Attribute Set, *das*, and returns *TRUE* if the delegation is active (not revoked) and *FALSE* if the delegation is considered to be revoked.

$$
active(das) = \begin{cases} active(das_{parent}) & \text{if } das.parent \neq \emptyset \\ \quad \wedge \ das.depth < das.parent.depth \\ \quad \wedge \ das.depth \geq 0 \\ \quad \wedge \ das.att\_set \subseteq delegatable(das.delegator) \\ \quad \wedge \ das.rule\_set \supseteq das.parent.rule\_set \\ \quad \wedge \ \forall rule \in das.rule\_set : valid(rule, das.delegatee) = TRUE \\[1em] das_{att\_set} \subseteq delegatable(das.delegator) & \text{if } das.parent = \emptyset \\ \quad \wedge \ \forall rule \in das.rule\_set : valid(rule, das.delegatee) = TRUE \end{cases}
$$

$$(9)$$

where *valid* is a HGABAC function which takes an HGPL policy and a user and returns *TRUE* if the user satisfies that policy for the current value of that user's attributes (including connection attributes) and the current state of the system (environment attributes and administrator attributes), *FALSE* if the policy is violated and *UNDEF* if the policy cannot currently be evaluated.

A secondary means of revocation is possible through HGAA's optional AC revocation lists. In HGAA, each AA may publish a revocation list that includes the serial number of any revoked AC issued by the authority. Policy Decision Points may optionally request this list either on demand or periodically depending on the nature of their service and if communication with the AA is possible. In the delegation framework detailed in the next section (Sect. 4), DAS are represented as special Delegated Attribute Certificates (DAC). These DACs may be revoked by the same mechanism. If a revoked DAC is part of a delegation chain, all subsequent delegations are also revoked.

4   Delegation Framework

The proceeding section (Sect. 3) laid out the theoretical delegation model and extensions to HGABAC to incorporate User-To-User Attribute Delegation. This section seeks to provide more practical details for how this delegation model may be implemented by extending HGAA to create a supporting delegation framework. Two key aspects of HGAA need to be expanded; the Attribute Certificate (AC) format to include delegation extensions and rules (detailed in Sect. 4.2), and the communication steps between users and services to provide a full certificate chain (detailed in Sect. 4.1).

4.1   Protocol Additions

In HGAA, users are issued an AC from an AA's Attribute Store Service. This document provides proof of a user's attributes in a cryptographically signed document as well as providing a mechanism for single sign-on and authentication with remote services. The AC format includes a listing of the user's attributes, details of the issuing authority, a public key assigned to the user, a range of dates for which the certificate is valid and a number of areas reserved for future extensions. User's prove ownership of an AC via a private key corresponding to the public key embedded in the AC. As the certificate is signed and contains all information about the user to base policy decision on, direct communication between the service being accessed and the AA is not required.

In the original architecture, after being issued an AC, users use the certificate to make requests on services. To support delegation, an additional delegation step is needed (as shown in Fig. 7 as step 4). Rather than directly querying services, a user may now delegate all or a subset of the attributes in their AC to a third party by issuing a new AC called a Delegated Attribute Certificate (DAC). The DAC is identical to an AC issued by an AA but lists the delegator as the issuer and signer (rather than an AA), and the delegatee as the holder. The extensions to the AC format to support DACs and delegation, detailed in Sect. 4.2, enable the delegator to include delegation rules to trigger revocation (as discussed in Sect. 3.5), set a maximum delegation depth for subsequent delegations and select what subset of the attributes in their AC will be contained in the DAC (and delegated to the delegatee).

To complete the delegation, the delegator sends their AC and the new DAC to the delegatee. The delegatee validates both by checking the following:

1. The original components of the AC are valid as described in [5] (i.e. correctly signed by the AA, that the AC has not expired, etc.)
2. The *ACHolder* from the AC is the *ACIssuer* in the DAC (same UID, key, etc.).
3. The *ACHolder* given in the DAC is the delegatee (correct UID, public key, etc.).
4. All attributes listed in the DAC are also found in the AC and have a *maxDepth* greater than zero in the AC.
5. All attributes in the DAC have the delegator listed as the delegator and a *maxDepth* less than or equal to the *maxDepth* in the DAC for that attribute.
6. The *ACRevocationRules* in the DAC are the same or stricter than in the AC.
7. The *ACDelegationRules* in the DAC are the same or stricter than in the AC.
8. The overall delegation *depth* in the DAC is less than the delegation *depth* in the AC and greater than or equal to 0.
9. That the delegation has not been revoked (i.e. all delegation rules return *TRUE*).
10. The DAC is signed by the delegator with the public key listed in the *ACHolder* sequence of the AC and the *ACIssuer* sequence of the DAC.

These checks enforce the rules on DASs described in Sect. 3.1 and ensure the delegation has not been revoked (as per Sect. 3.5). If the AC and DAC are valid, the delegatee may make requests upon services by sending both the AC and DAC with their request. The remainder of the HGAA protocol remains the same, but with the DAC being sent with the AC in steps 5 and 6 (Fig. 7). The Policy Decision Point also makes the same checks (as listed above) on the DAC when validating the deletagee's attributes.

Subsequent delegations by the delegatee, to further delegatees, are supported. In such cases, the delegatee becomes the delegator and issues a new DAC using the processes previously described (their existing DAC becoming the AC and they become the issuer of the new DAC). This creates a chain of certificates leading back to the AA, each certificate being signed by the parent delegator. This process is shown in the Low Level Certificate Chain Diagram found in Appendix A. To allow services and the Policy Decision Point to verify subsequent delegations, each certificate in the chain is included with the first request upon a service and each certificate is validated.

Listing 1.1. Updates to the AC format to support Atrtibute Delegation writen in ASN.1 notation. Bold text indicate addtions. Only updated sequences are shown.

```
Attribute  ::= SEQUENCE {
    attributeID OBJECT IDENTIFIER,
    attributeType    OBJECT IDENTIFIER,
    attributeValue   ANY DEFINED BY attributeType OPTIONAL,
    attributeName    VisibleString OPTIONAL,
    maxDepth INTEGER(0..255),
    delegatorUniqueIdentifier OBJECT IDENTIFIER OPTIONAL,
}

ACDelegationRules  ::= SEQUENCE {
    SEQUENCE OF DACDelegationRule
}

DACDelegationRule ::= SEQUENCE {
    HGPLv2Policy VisibleString
}

- One instance of ACExtension with the following values
UToUAttDelv1 ACExtension ::= SEQUENCE {
    extensionID "ext:UToUAttDelv1",
    depth INTEGER(0..254),
    rootAuthorityUniqueIdentifier OBJECT IDENTIFIER,
    SEQUENCE OF DACCertificateSerial
}

DACCertificateSerial ::= SEQUENCE {
    certificateSerial INTEGER
}
```

4.2   Attribute Certificate Delegation Extensions

To incorporate our delegation model and updated HGAA protocol, several extensions to the AC format are required (described in Listing 1.1). The *Attribute* sequence is extended to include a *maxDepth* and *delegatorUniqueIdentifier* value for each attribute in the certificate. *delegatorUniqueIdentifier* states the ID of the original delegator (first in the chain) of the attribute or no value if not delegated. *maxDepth* corresponds to the *Can Delegate* relation (defined in Sect. 3.2) and has a value equal to 0 if this attribute cannot be delegated, 255 if there is no limit on the delegation depth or some value between 1 and 254 equal to the maximum depth allowed for this specific attribute.

Delegation rules from the DAS (defined in Sect. 3.1) are encoded in a new *DACDelegationRule* sequence which contains a HGPLv2 policy for each rule. The *depth* value from the DAS is included in a new instance of the *ACExtension* sequence in addition to a record of the original AA and the serial number of each certificate in the chain.

The extended AC is kept backwards compatible with the original AC format by only updating sections marked for future extension. The changes have a minimal impact on the certificate size, adding at worst $3 + U$ bytes per attribute (where U is the size of the largest delegator ID), $2 * P$ bytes per delegation rule (where P is the maximum length of a HGPL policy), and $1 + S$ bytes per certificate in the chain (where S is the serial number size in bytes). A byte level representation of the new AC is found in Appendix B.

5   Conclusions and Future Work

We have introduced the first model of User-to-User Attribute Delegation as well as a supporting architecture to aid implementation. Extensions to the HGABAC model (Sect. 3) add relations for authorizing what attributes can be delegated (*Can Delegate*) and to what depth. A new access control element, the *Delegated Attribute Set*, is added for representing current delegations in the system and the restrictions placed on them. Delegated attributes are kept isolated to prevent issues with Attribute Delegation, including user collusion and unexpected side effects on policy evaluations.

Updates to the HGAA protocol and AC format have been made (Sect. 4) to support the extended HGABAC model. These changes to the AC format are minimal in size, scaling with the number of attributes, delegation rules, and certificates in the chain. As changes have only been made to sequences marked for future expansion, the extended AC format remains backwards compatible with the original HGAA AC. Care has been given to ensure that delegation is preformed in an *"off-line"* manner, without the need to contact a third party, to maintain the distributed nature of HGABAC and HGAA. However, support for *"off-line"* delegation comes at the cost of revocation flexibility and limits the possibility for real time revocation invoked by the delegator. To combat this, HGPL policies are used to embed delegation rules that trigger revocation.

This work is part of an ongoing effort towards introducing delegation to ABAC and directions for future work will follow this path. To date, models for User-To-User Attribute and User-to-Attribute Group Membership [4] Delegation have been completed. The next steps will involve creating models for and implementing the remaining strategies so they can be fully explored, validated, evaluated and compared. Directions for the User-To-User Attribute Delegation model include exploring the use of a *"Can Receive"* relation for users in place of *"Can Delegate"* for attributes and experimenting with adding constraints that prevent specified users form being delegated a restricted attribute (e.g. to prevent certain users from stratifying a policy via delegation). Such *"Can Receive"* relations have been used in RBAC models [2] and were shown to add flexibility. Work is needed to see if the same will hold true for ABAC. Finally, a more thorough evaluation of our delegation model is planned that will involve both formal validation (safety analysis) and experimental evaluation (reference implementation).

A   Low Level Certificate Chain Diagram

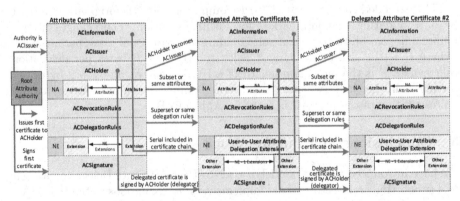

B   Low Level Extended Attribute Certificate Diagram

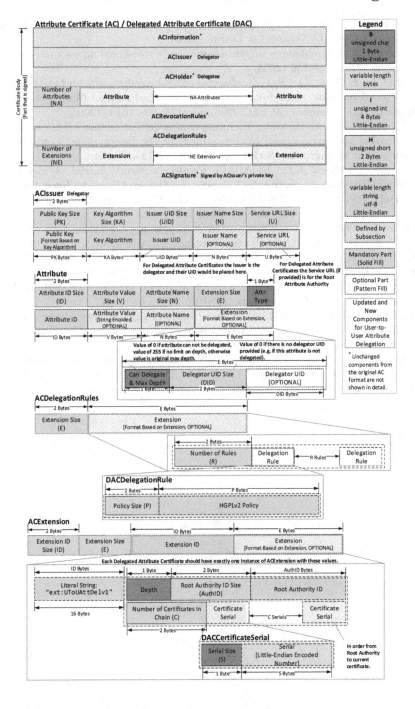

References

1. Anderson, A., Nadalin, A., Parducci, B., et al.: eXtensible Access Control Markup Language (XACML) Version 1.0. OASIS (2003)
2. Crampton, J., Khambhammettu, H.: Delegation in role-based access control. Int. J. Inf. Secur. **7**(2), 123–136 (2008)
3. Rostad, L., Edsberg, O.: A study of access control requirements for healthcare systems based on audit trails from access logs. In: 22nd Annual Computer Security Applications Conference (ACSAC 2006), pp. 175–186. IEEE (2006)
4. Sabahein, K., Reithel, B., Wang, F.: Incorporating delegation into ABAC: healthcare information system use case. In: Proceedings of the International Conference on Security and Management (SAM), pp. 291–297 (2018)
5. Servos, D., Osborn, S.L.: HGABAC: towards a formal model of hierarchical attribute-based access control. In: Cuppens, F., Garcia-Alfaro, J., Zincir Heywood, N., Fong, P.W.L. (eds.) FPS 2014. LNCS, vol. 8930, pp. 187–204. Springer, Cham (2015). https://doi.org/10.1007/978-3-319-17040-4_12
6. Servos, D., Osborn, S.L.: Strategies for incorporating delegation into Attribute-Based Access Control (ABAC). In: Cuppens, F., Wang, L., Cuppens-Boulahia, N., Tawbi, N., Garcia-Alfaro, J. (eds.) FPS 2016. LNCS, vol. 10128, pp. 320–328. Springer, Cham (2017). https://doi.org/10.1007/978-3-319-51966-1_21
7. Servos, D., Osborn, S.L.: Current research and open problems in attribute-based access control. ACM Comput. Surv. (CSUR) **49**(4), 65 (2017)
8. Servos, D., Osborn, S.L.: HGAA: an architecture to support hierarchical group and attribute-based access control. In: Proceedings of the Third ACM Workshop on Attribute-Based Access Control, pp. 1–12 (2018)
9. Wang, L., Wijesekera, D., Jajodia, S.: A logic-based framework for attribute based access control. In: Proceedings of the 2004 ACM Workshop on Formal Methods in Security Engineering, pp. 45–55 (2004)

U-EPS: An Ultra-small and Efficient Post-quantum Signature Scheme

Guang Gong, Morgan He, Raghvendra Rohit, and Yunjie Yi[✉]

Department of Electrical and Computer Engineering, University of Waterloo,
Waterloo, ON N2L 3G1, Canada
{ggong,myhe,rsrohit,yunjie.yi}@uwaterloo.ca

Abstract. Lamport and Winternitz signature schemes are well known one-time quantum resistant digital signature schemes. Along this line, several new one-time signature schemes are proposed. However, their private key and signature sizes are of $\mathcal{O}(n^2)$ for $k < n$-bit security. Considering the applications in Internet of Things (IoT) and blockchains, $\mathcal{O}(n^2)$ size is notably high. In this paper, we introduce a new one-time post-quantum signature scheme called U-EPS which achieve $k = 112$-bit security with private key size $2n$ and signature sizes $3n$ bits (for $n = 256$), respectively. Our scheme only requires two calls of hash function and a single call of encryption/decryption algorithm for signature generation and verification procedures. We provide a concrete instantiation and implementation of U-EPS using SPIX-256 which is a NIST Lightweight Cryptographic Project Round 2 candidate. Finally, we give the comparison results with existing schemes.

Keywords: Digital signature · Internet-of-Things (IoT) · Lightweight cryptography

1 Introduction

With the advent of overwhelming research towards building quantum computers and their after-effects on currently deployed non-quantum resistant cryptographic primitives, there has been a surge in the design of cryptographic primitives which are quantum resistant [1]. One of such primitive is Digital Signature Scheme (DSS) which generates the electronic fingerprint of a given message. Currently, there are three well known types of one-time[1] digital signature schemes which are quantum resistant. These are (1) Hash-based DSS: Lamport [2,26] and Winternitz signature schemes along with their variants [12,13,17,19,23,29,32], (2) Lattice-based DSS: qTelsa [9] and NTRU [6], and (3) Code-based DSS: McEliece [28] and Niederreiter [30] signature schemes.

---

[1] For signing multiple messages, a Merkle tree based approach is typically used.

Supported by NSERC.

© Springer Nature Switzerland AG 2020
A. Benzekri et al. (Eds.): FPS 2019, LNCS 12056, pp. 261–272, 2020.
https://doi.org/10.1007/978-3-030-45371-8_16

Among the aforementioned schemes, hash based signatures are becoming popular because of their simple constructions and straightforward implementations [14]. Moreover, such schemes are the core of most of the cryptocurrencies such as Bitcoin and Ethereum. The enormous growth of cryptocurrencies along with Internet of Things (IoT) has paved a way to boom the eco-environment of IoT devices. A few examples include IoT cryptocurrencies such as IOTA [34], IOTW [27] and IoTex [35].

An interplay between IoT and cryptocurrency seems a good choice theoretically, however, it is not straightforward practically. For instance, not all IoT devices have unintelligible power supplies and some of them operate on low power batteries or operate by harvesting power from receiving signal (such as radio frequency identification systems). Additionally, their memory space is much smaller than that of general personal computers and servers, and it could be even smaller if they do not support external storage because of the design limitations. Thus, the underlying cryptographic primitives (e.g., hash function) of both IoT devices and blockchain has to be as small as possible. Currently, Lamport and Winternitz One Time Signature (WOTS) are the most efficient hash-based digital signature schemes [16]. They provide n-bit security with key and signature sizes of $\mathcal{O}(n^2)$ bits, respectively. Hence, for IoT devices which typically operate in resource constrained environment, such large key and signature sizes are not justified.

In this paper, we introduce an ultra-small and efficient one-time quantum resistant signature scheme called U-EPS for IoT and blockchain based applications. Thus, our contributions are summarized as follows.

- We propose a one-time quantum resistant signature scheme that provides n-bit security with sizes of public key, private key and signature being n, $2n$ and $3n$ bits, respectively. Our scheme is based on the concept of delayed signatures, i.e., first we use an n-bit secret value r to encrypt the XOR value of two distinct n-bit components of private key. The encrypted value is then used as a part of signature. However, the value, called the auxiliary key, used to obtain r is released after a specific interval of time (based on communication bandwidth) which is then used for verification. Security analysis is also provided.
- Our scheme is ultra-small and efficient as it can be instantiated with any lightweight hash function and encryption (decryption) algorithm while requiring only two calls of hash function and a single call of encryption (decryption) algorithm for signature generation and verification procedures.
- We provide a concrete instantiation and performance results of U-EPS in hardware using SPIX-256 [3]. For software performance, we compare U-EPS instantiated with SPIX-256 and AES-256. Overall, our scheme achieves 112 bit security with state size 256 bits. The auxiliary key can be released at the same time as transmitting message with its signature component by employing a sequential memory-hard encryption scheme, which is also implemented by SPIX-256 and AES-256 in the sponge structure [8] with rate 1.

Outline of the Paper. The rest of the paper is organized as follows. In Sects. 2 and 3, we provide the formal description of U-EPS along with its correctness and security analysis, respectively. Section 4 presents the implementation details of U-EPS and the comparison results. Finally, the paper is concluded in Sect. 5.

2   U-EPS: A New LWC Based Digital Signature Scheme

2.1   Notations

We use the following notation throughout the paper.

- n is a positive integer
- $\mathbb{Z}_2 = \{0,1\}$, $\mathbb{Z}_2^p = \{x = (x_0, \cdots, x_{p-1}) \mid x_i \in \{0,1\}\}$, the binary vector space of dimension p.
- The addition $+$ means either XOR or pairwise XOR depends on the context.
- $\{0,1\}^*$ is the set consisting of all bit streams.
- For $a, b \in \mathbb{Z}_2^n$, $a\|b$ is the concatenation of two bit streams of a and b.
- $\mathcal{H}$ is a family of collision resistant hash functions from $\{0,1\}^*$ to $\mathbb{Z}_2^n$.
- $\mathcal{F}$ is a family of symmetric encryption algorithms $c = Enc_k(m)$ which is secure under chosen plaintext attack (CPA) where the key k, message m, and ciphertext c are all n-bit. The corresponding decryption algorithm is denoted by $m = Dec_k(c)$.
- $\mathcal{G}$ is a family of sequential memory-hard symmetric encryption algorithms $g(k, m)$ where the key space, message space, and ciphertext space are n-bit vectors, and the ciphertext is denoted as $c = MemEnc_k(m)$. Similarly, we denote $m = MemDec_k(c)$.
- Here sequential memory-hard means that parallel algorithms cannot asymptotically achieve efficiency advantage than non-parallel ones. This method is introduced in [31] for design of the password-based key derivation function scrypt in order to thwart parallel brute-force attacks using GPUs, FPGAs or ASIC chips on passwords, and has been widely used by cryptocurrencies, e.g., Litecoin, Dogecoin and Mastercoin.

2.2   A U-EPS One-Time Signature Scheme

Our U-EPS one-time digital signature scheme consists of three algorithms (**Gen, Sig, Ver**) where the first two are probabilistic polynomial-time algorithms, and *Ver* is a deterministic algorithm, defined as follows.

Gen Algorithm. The key-generation algorithm **Gen** takes as input a security parameter 1^n where n is the security parameter and output the private and public key pair (sk, pk) which are generated as follows. Uniformly take $a, b \in \mathbb{Z}_2^n$, and set the private key $sk = (a, b)$. The corresponding public-key, pk is the hash value of sk, i.e., uniformly pick $h \in \mathcal{H}$ and compute $pk = h(a\|b)$.

Sig Algorithm. The signing algorithm **Sig** takes as input a private key sk and a message m from a message space. It outputs a signature, and we write this as $Sig_{sk}(m)$ which is computed as follows.

1. For signing message $m \in \{0,1\}^*$, **Sig** algorithm uniformly picks $h \in \mathcal{H}$ and computes $t = h(m) \in \mathbb{Z}_2^n$. We denote $t = (t_0, t_1, \ldots, t_{n-1})$.
2. It computes $s = (s_0, \cdots, s_{n-1}) \in \mathbb{Z}_2^n$ and c by uniformly selecting $u \in \mathbb{Z}_2^n$:

$$s_i = \begin{cases} a_i & \text{if } t_i = 0 \\ b_i & \text{if } t_i = 1, \end{cases} \qquad c = Enc_r(a+b) \text{ where } r = h(t||u). \tag{1}$$

3. The signature consists of two components s and c, i.e., $Sig_{sk}(m) = (s,c)$. The random number u will be released after $\delta_t > 0$ time after $(m, Sig_{sk}(m))$ is released. We call (s,c), a *signature component*, and u an *auxiliary key* with δ_t time delayed transmission.

Ver Algorithm. The deterministic verification algorithm **Ver** takes as input a public key pk, a message m, and a signature. It outputs a bit σ, with $\sigma = 1$ meaning valid and $\sigma = 0$ meaning invalid, for which σ is determined as follows.

1. Recovering the sum of the private-key sk: A verifier receives (m, s, c) first, and then computes $t = h(m) = (t_0, \cdots, t_{n-1}) \in \mathbb{Z}_2^n$. After δ_t time interval, it receives u. Upon receiving u, it computes $r = h(t||u)$, and decrypts c to get $a+b$, i.e.,
$$a+b = Dec_r(c), \text{ where } r = h(t||u). \tag{2}$$

2. sk recovering process: Using the signature component s of the signature, t, and $a+b$, the private-key a and b can be recovered as follows. For $i = 0, 1, \cdots, n-1$,

$$\begin{aligned} &\text{if } t_i = 0, \text{ then } s_i = a_i, \text{ computes } b_i = s_i + (a_i + b_i) \\ &\text{if } t_i = 1, \text{ then } s_i = b_i, \text{ computes } a_i = s_i + (a_i + b_i). \end{aligned} \tag{3}$$

3. The value of σ is determined by

$$\sigma = \begin{cases} 0 & \text{if } pk \neq h(a||b) \\ 1 & \text{if } pk = h(a||b). \end{cases} \tag{4}$$

We write this as $\sigma = Ver_{pk}(m, Sig)$. In other words, $\sigma = 1$, then the verification is successful, otherwise it fails.

3 Security Analysis

3.1 Correctness

We first show that except with negligible probability over (pk, sk) output by $Gen(1^n)$, it holds that $Ver_{pk}(m, Sig_{sk}(m)) = 1$ for every (legal) message m. Once the verifier receives u, he recovers $a+b$ as follows. If $t_i = 0$, from (1), he knows that $s_i = a_i$. Together with the value of $a_i + b_i$, he can recover b_i by computing $s_i + (a_i + b_i) = a_i + (a_i + b_i) = b_i$. Similarly, if $t_i = 1$, he knows that $s_i = b_i$, then a_i can be recovered. Thus for each i, both a_i and b_i are recovered. If both a and b are recovered, the verification of the equality $pk = h(a||b)$ will be successful for every message m.

3.2 Impossibility of Forgery Without Knowing the Auxiliary Key

Next we look at whether an adversary can forge a valid signature by only knowing the signature component. Given the signature component (s, c), from s, the adversary can obtain half of bits in a and half of bits in b in average, but no more than that. So, for a new message m', first the adversary may attempt to make $h(m') = h(m)$, then (s, c) can be used as a signature component as m'. However, h is collision resistant, the probability to be successful is negligible. The second way for the adversary is to attempt to recover the private key $sk = (a, b)$. However, the exhaustive search for the remaining half bits of a and b each is 2^n on average. As long as n is greater than the security parameter, this is not possible. Thirdly, the adversary may try to find another pair of a' and b' such that $pk = h(a'\|b')$. But this is prevented by the collision resistant property of h. Thus, the probability is negligible if the adversary tries to forge a signature on a new message without knowing sk.

3.3 The Role of Auxiliary Key

However, once u is released, the adversary can recover sk together with the signature component. So this is a one-time signature scheme. If the adversary receives u prior to receiving the first transmitted data, i.e., the message and its signature component, the adversary still cannot make a forgery. This is because to recover the private key a and b, he needs the data sent in the first transmission. In other words, he needs to do: (1) decrypt c which needs $t = h(m)$ (see (2)), (2) once $a + b$ is recovered, he needs s together with $a + b$ to recover the other half bits of a and b (see (3)). Thus using only data u without receiving the first data, the adversary cannot forge a valid signature. Note that the order of releasing the signature component (s, c) and the auxiliary key u, and the time delay δ_t are important. This is a similar case as TESLA [33] for the delayed message authentication, i.e., it releases authentication tag first, then after δ_t time, it releases the key which is used to generate the tag.

3.4 The Mismatched Order by Transmission Traffic and Jamming Attacks

Due to some extreme communication congestion problems, it may happen that an adversary receives both data (m, s, c) and u at a very short time difference. In this case, the adversary can recover sk and forges a valid signature (s', c') on a new message m' by selecting different u' from u (note since c is message-dependent and h is collision resistant, the adversary cannot use the same u for message m'). Thus in this case, the adversary has to retransmit two forged data, (m', s', c') and u'. However, this is a one-time signature scheme. A verifier will reject the later received signature in most of applications (e.g., peer-to-peer systems). Thus, this cannot cause a treat. However, if this is a wireless channel, then the adversary may first jam the channel for the valid two transmissions (i.e., first transmitting data (m, s, c), then the auxiliary key u). When the time it releases the forged signature on m' and then the auxiliary key u', the time interval is much greater than δ_t. In order to defeat this threat from jamming attacks, we may add one more condition in the verification algorithm, i.e., if the timing that a verifier receives the signature is much greater than δ_t from the notifying signal, then it will directly reject the signature.

3.5   The Case of Sending the Auxiliary Key Without Delay

For blockchain applications, since a blockchain does not allow multiple transmissions for each transaction, so we could not send the auxiliary key u in a delayed manner. In other words, we need to send the entire signature components (m, s, c, u) as one transmission. From the above analysis, we only need to prevent the adversary to recover $a + b$ from c, so it cannot recover a and b in order to forge a signature.

We can achieve this by employing a sequential memory-hard encryption algorithm. In this case, δ_t is provided by computational time for recovering $a + b$ instead by delayed transmission. In order to distinguish these two cases, we refer to the first as *delayed transmission*, and the second case as *non-delayed transmission* in our implementation in the following section.

Remark 1. A formal security proof under the security model of existential unforgeability will be given in a full version of this work. For the concept of existential unforgeable secure, the reader is referring to [25] (Sect. 4.2) and XMSS paper [11] for which, their scheme is proved to be existential unforgeable under this security model.

Remark 2. The scheme can be made to generate multiple signature using a common public-key using the same methods introduced in [11,15].

4   Implementation

In this section, we provide the instantiation of the U-EPS one-time signature scheme with delayed and non-delayed versions using SPIX and AES permutation (with state size 256 bits) in the sponge structure. We first give a brief overview of significance of time interval δ_t and then provide the performance results.

4.1   Time Interval δ_t

In our scheme, δ_t denotes the amount of time for signature generation (except key generation phase) and verification procedure. Thus, to achieve the security requirements of the protocol design with the auxilary key u, we need to ensure that δ_t satisfies the following condition

$$\delta_t > \frac{Q}{R} \tag{5}$$

and

$$R > \frac{Q}{\delta_t} = R', \tag{6}$$

where Q is data transmitted in megabits per transaction and R is the transmission rate, and we denote $\frac{Q}{\delta_t}$ as R'. Note that for non-delayed version, it denotes the sequential memory-hard computation time.

Relation of δ_t to Blockchain Transactions. The current transmission rates for WiFi, 3G, 4G-LTE and 5G are 50–320 Mbps (for approx. 100 m distance), 2.4 Mbps (5–70 km), 75 Mbps (up-link 2–103 km) and 1 Gbps (2–150 km), respectively [21]. For blockchain, the current known Bitcoin Core protocol limits the block size to 1 MB, and each block contains around 4,000 transactions atmost [22]. Therefore, Q equals $\frac{8}{4000} = 0.002$ megabits per transaction. Accordingly, it will be secure once the transmission rate R is greater than $\frac{0.002}{\delta_t}$.

4.2 Instantiation of U-EPS

In order to evaluate the performance of the new signature scheme, the implementation includes three phases which are key generation phase, signing phase and verification phase. The three phases use the sponge structure of 256-bit SPIX [3,4] to perform hash, encryption and decryption. Similarly, we use the exact same sponge structure for comparison with AES except that the 256-bit SPIX is replaced by 256-bit AES permutation [18]. The sequential memory-hard encryption scheme is implemented by setting the rate for encryption to execute the permutation once to encrypt one bit plaintext, referred to as non-delayed cases in the implementation.

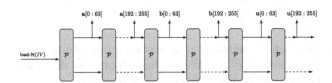

Fig. 1. The function to generate **a**, **b** and **u**

To generate the vectors a, b and u, we use the sponge structure illustrated in Fig. 1 where $\mathcal{P}$ is either SPIX or AES. The state is first loaded with a random IV and then 64-bits of state are extracted each time to obtain a, b and u.

For generating pk and c, we use the hash mode depicted in Fig. 2. The state is first loaded with a constant initialization vector. Then the message ($m \in \{a\|b, t\|u\}$) is absorbed into the state 64 bit at a time. After the absorbing phase, 256 bit message digest $H_0\|H_1\|H_2\|H_3$ is taken as the output.

For the signing phase, we use the Encryption algorithm as shown in Fig. 3. The initial state is first loaded with the secret value r and then the permutation

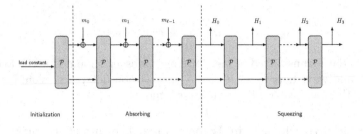

Fig. 2. Hash algorithm in a sponge mode

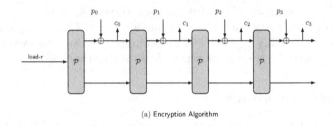

(a) Encryption Algorithm

Fig. 3. Encryption algorithm in a sponge mode

Table 1. Performance of U-EPS using AES and SPIX

Scheme (256-bit perm)	KeyGen (ms)	Sign (ms)	Verify (ms)
SPIX_Delayed	2.36	0.75	1.63
SPIX_Non_Delayed	2.31	9.61	10.47
AES_Delayed	1.81	0.50	1.12
AES_Non_Delayed	1.81	2.59	2.74

is applied. Then, each 64 plaintext p_i is absorbed into the state and the corresponding 64 bit ciphertext c_i is taken as the output. The decryption algorithm is similar to encryption and hence the details are omitted.

4.3   Implementation Results and Analysis

In Tables 1 and 2, we present the performance results of U-EPS and the corresponding values of δ_t and R', respectively.

Table 3 shows the comparison with existing other schemes. The latency for our signature scheme is much smaller than others. The second smallest one ECC on 2^{131} is 18 times more than U-EPS. Note that the data of first three rows in Table 3 is taken from [20].

Table 4 presents the key sizes comparison with other existing chemes. By setting the same public key size and achieving the same security level, U-EPS has much smaller private key and signature sizes compared to Winternitz, XMSS

Table 2. The parameters δ_t and R'

Scheme (256-bit perm)	δ_t (ms)	R' (Mbps)
SPIX_Delayed	2.38	0.840
SPIX_Non_Delayed	20.08	0.0996
AES_Delayed	1.62	1.235
AES_Non_Delayed	5.33	0.375

Table 3. Cost and latency comparison with existing solutions

Scheme	Latency [clock cycles]	Resources
ECC on 2^{131} [5]	75 000	15 K Gates
NIST p-256 SW [24]	15 584 000	34 KB code + HW Multiplier
NIST p-256 HW-SW [10]	6 000 000	11.7 K gates
PQ-Secure XMSS [20]	4 814 160	13.5 K Gates + 5.22 KB code
Our U-EPS (SPIX-256)[3]	4 032	2742 (130 nm ASIC) or 2611 (65 nm ASIC)

Table 4. The sizes of signatures, public and private keys in bits

	Public key	Private key	signature	Comments
U-EPS	256	$2n = 2 \times 256$	$3n = 3 \times 256$	This paper
Winternitz [29] XMSS [11] SPHINCS [7]	256	$\frac{n}{w}n = 32 \times 256$	$\frac{n}{w}n = 32 \times 256$	$w = 8$

and SPHINCS. Note that from [11], the public-key size for all those schemes (in Table 4) can make into the size n using a hash chain, but the verification is much more expensive compared with our scheme, since we only have one call for the hash function to generate the public-key.

5 Conclusion

We have proposed a new post-quantum signature scheme U-EPS which achieve 112-bit security and has private key, public key and signature size of 256, 2×256, and 3×256 bits, respectively. Compared to the existing schemes, our scheme has much smaller key and signature sizes. Moreover, it is highly efficient as the number of calls of cryptographic primitive (hash and encryption/decryption algorithm) is at most 2. We have also provided the performance results using SPIX and AES. Our results show that our post-quantum signature scheme U-EPS is suitable for building quantum resistance blockchain systems for IoT applications. In our future work, we will consider the formal security proof for our scheme and analysis for resistant to side channel attacks.

Acknowledgment. The work is supported by NSERC SPG Grant.

References

1. NIST Post Quantum Standardization Project (2017). https://csrc.nist.gov/Projects/Post-Quantum-Cryptography/Post-Quantum-Cryptography-Standardization
2. Alboaie, S., Cosovan, D., Chiorean, L., Vaida, M.F.: Lamport n-time signature scheme. In: 2018 IEEE International Conference on Automation, Quality and Testing, Robotics (AQTR), pp. 1–6 (May 2018)
3. AlTawy, R., Gong, G., He, M., Mandal, K., Rohit, R.: SPIX: an authenticated cipher round 2 candidate to the NIST LWC competition (2019)
4. Altawy, R., Rohit, R., He, M., Mandal, K., Yang, G., Gong, G.: SLISCP-light: towards hardware optimized sponge-specific cryptographic permutations. ACM Trans. Embed. Comput. Syst. **17**(4), 81:1–81:26 (2018)
5. Batina, L., Guajardo, J., Kerins, T., Mentens, N., Tuyls, P., Verbauwhede, I.: An elliptic curve processor suitable for RFID-tags. Cryptology ePrint Archive, Report 2006/227 (2006). https://eprint.iacr.org/2006/227
6. Bernstein, D.J., Chuengsatiansup, C., Lange, T., van Vredendaal, C.: NTRU prime: reducing attack surface at low cost. Cryptology ePrint Archive, Report 2016/461 (2016). https://eprint.iacr.org/2016/461
7. Bernstein, D.J., et al.: SPHINCS: practical stateless hash-based signatures. In: Oswald, E., Fischlin, M. (eds.) EUROCRYPT 2015. LNCS, vol. 9056, pp. 368–397. Springer, Heidelberg (2015). https://doi.org/10.1007/978-3-662-46800-5_15
8. Bertoni, G., Daemen, J., Peeters, M., Van Assche, G.: Sponge functions. In: ECRYPT Hash Workshop, vol. 2007. Citeseer (2007)
9. Bindel, N., et al.: Submission to NIST's post-quantum project: lattice-based digital signature scheme qTESLA (2018)
10. Bosmans, J., Roy, S.S., Jarvinen, K., Verbauwhede, I.: A tiny coprocessor for elliptic curve cryptography over the 256-bit NIST prime field. In: 2016 29th International Conference on VLSI Design and 2016 15th International Conference on Embedded Systems (VLSID), pp. 523–528 (January 2016)
11. Buchmann, J., Dahmen, E., Hülsing, A.: XMSS - a practical forward secure signature scheme based on minimal security assumptions. In: Yang, B.-Y. (ed.) PQCrypto 2011. LNCS, vol. 7071, pp. 117–129. Springer, Heidelberg (2011). https://doi.org/10.1007/978-3-642-25405-5_8
12. Buchmann, J., Dahmen, E., Klintsevich, E., Okeya, K., Vuillaume, C.: Merkle signatures with virtually unlimited signature capacity. In: Katz, J., Yung, M. (eds.) ACNS 2007. LNCS, vol. 4521, pp. 31–45. Springer, Heidelberg (2007). https://doi.org/10.1007/978-3-540-72738-5_3

13. Buchmann, J., García, L.C.C., Dahmen, E., Döring, M., Klintsevich, E.: CMSS – an improved merkle signature scheme. In: Barua, R., Lange, T. (eds.) INDOCRYPT 2006. LNCS, vol. 4329, pp. 349–363. Springer, Heidelberg (2006). https://doi.org/10.1007/11941378_25

14. Butin, D.: Hash-based signatures: state of play. IEEE Secur. Priv. **15**(4), 37–43 (2017)

15. Chalkias, K., Brown, J., Hearn, M., Lillehagen, T., Nitto, I., Schroeter, T.: Blockchained post-quantum signatures. In: 2018 IEEE International Conference on Internet of Things (iThings) and IEEE Green Computing and Communications (GreenCom) and IEEE Cyber, Physical and Social Computing (CPSCom) and IEEE Smart Data (SmartData), pp. 1196–1203 (July 2018)

16. Chalkias, K., Brown, J., Hearn, M., Lillehagen, T., Nitto, I., Schroeter, T.: Blockchained post-quantum signatures. IACR Cryptol. ePrint Arch. **2018**, 658 (2018)

17. Cruz, J.P., Yatani, Y., Kaji, Y.: Constant-sum fingerprinting for Winternitz one-time signature. In: 2016 International Symposium on Information Theory and its Applications (ISITA), pp. 703–707 (October 2016)

18. Daemen, J., Rijmen, V.: The Design of Rijndael: AES-The Advanced Encryption Standard. Springer, Berlin (2013). https://doi.org/10.1007/978-3-662-04722-4

19. Dods, C., Smart, N.P., Stam, M.: Hash based digital signature schemes. In: Smart, N.P. (ed.) Cryptography and Coding 2005. LNCS, vol. 3796, pp. 96–115. Springer, Heidelberg (2005). https://doi.org/10.1007/11586821_8

20. Ghosh, S., Misoczki, R., Sastry, M.R.: Lightweight post-quantum-secure digital signature approach for IoT motes. Cryptology ePrint Archive, Report 2019/122 (2019). https://eprint.iacr.org/2019/122

21. Gong, G.: Securing Internet-of-Things. In: Zincir-Heywood, N., Bonfante, G., Debbabi, M., Garcia-Alfaro, J. (eds.) Foundations and Practice of Security, pp. 3–16. Springer, Cham (2019). https://doi.org/10.1007/978-3-030-18419-3

22. Göbel, J., Krzesinski, A.E.: Increased block size and bitcoin blockchain dynamics. In: 2017 27th International Telecommunication Networks and Applications Conference (ITNAC), pp. 1–6 (November 2017)

23. Hülsing, A.: W-OTS+ – shorter signatures for hash-based signature schemes. In: Youssef, A., Nitaj, A., Hassanien, A.E. (eds.) AFRICACRYPT 2013. LNCS, vol. 7918, pp. 173–188. Springer, Heidelberg (2013). https://doi.org/10.1007/978-3-642-38553-7_10

24. Hutter, M., Schmidt, J.-M.: Radio frequency identification. In: Security and Privacy Issues 9th International Workshop, RFIDsec 2013, Graz, Austria, July 9–11, 2013, Revised Selected Papers, pp. 147–160. Springer (2013). https://doi.org/10.1007/978-3-642-41332-2

25. Katz, J., Lindell, Y.: Introduction to Modern Cryptography. Chapman and Hall/CRC, Boca Raton (2014)

26. Lamport, L.: Constructing digital signatures from a one-way function. Technical report, Technical Report CSL-98, SRI International Palo Alto (1979)

27. Leung, F., Chan, T., Mehrotra, K., Chan, P.: IoTW: IoT blockchain infrastructure using proof of assignment whitepaper (2018)

28. McEliece, R.J.: A public-key cryptosystem based on algebraic. Coding Thv. **4244**, 114–116 (1978)

29. Merkle, R.C.: A certified digital signature. In: Brassard, G. (ed.) CRYPTO 1989. LNCS, vol. 435, pp. 218–238. Springer, New York (1990). https://doi.org/10.1007/0-387-34805-0_21

G. Gong et al.

30. Niederreiter, H.: Knapsack-type cryptosystems and algebraic coding theory. Prob. Control Inf. Theory **15**(2), 159–166 (1986)
31. Percival, C.: Stronger key derivation via sequential memory-hard functions (2009)
32. Perin, L.P., Zambonin, G., Martins, D.M.B., Custódio, R., Martina, J.E.: Tuning the Winternitz hash-based digital signature scheme. In: 2018 IEEE Symposium on Computers and Communications (ISCC), pp. 00537–00542 (June 2018)
33. Perrig, A., Canetti, R., Tygar, J.D., Song, D.: Efficient authentication and signing of multicast streams over lossy channels. In: Proceedings of IEEE Symposium on Security and Privacy, vol. 2000, pp. 56–73 (2000)
34. Popov, S.: The Tangle, IOTA whitepaper (2018)
35. The IoTeX Team: IoTeX: a decentralized network for Internet of Things powered by a privacy-centric blockchain (2018)

An Efficient Identification Scheme Based on Rank Metric

Edoukou Berenger Ayebie$^{(\boxtimes)}$, Hafsa Assidi, and El Mamoun Souidi

Faculty of Sciences, Laboratory of Mathematics, Computer Science,
Applications and Information Security, Mohammed V University in Rabat,
BP 1014 RP, 10000 Rabat, Morocco
berenger.ayebie@gmail.com, assidihafsa@gmail.com, emsouidi@gmail.com

Abstract. Using random double circulant codes, we design a rank metric version of Aguilar, Gaborit and Schrek (AGS) identification scheme which is resistant to attacks using quantum computers. We achieve optimum results in different scales comparing public key size, secret key size and communication cost with known identification schemes. Moreover, our protocol is more efficient and practical for different resource constrained devices such as smart cards or Radio Frequency Identification (RFID) tags. Furthermore, using the Fiat-Shamir paradigm, we design an efficient signature scheme.

Keywords: Identification scheme · Zero-knowledge protocols · AGS · Coding theory · Rank metric code · Random double circulant codes

1 Introduction

In 1994, assuming the existence of a quantum computer, Shor has proved in [19] that the discrete logarithm and the factorization problems can be solved in polynomial time. This paper has enabled the emergence of post-quantum cryptography. The security of the most important post-quantum primitives relies on the difficulty of solving decoding problems in specific metrics (Hamming metric for codes, Euclidean metric for lattices for example). The security of an identification scheme is based on the security of the difficult problem to which it is linked.

Identification protocols are very useful in the electronic communications area. For example, identification protocols are used in ticketing, e-passport, e-health, control access systems, etc. The choice of code-based cryptography for identification schemes is mainly motivated by the capacity of future quantum computer. An identification scheme is said to be Zero-knowledge if it is an interactive protocol where one proves the knowledge of something, without revealing any information on this knowledge. This implies that the verifier cannot learn the secret, also he or she cannot replay the protocol and especially he or she cannot convince another person that the prover was aware of the secret.

© Springer Nature Switzerland AG 2020
A. Benzekri et al. (Eds.): FPS 2019, LNCS 12056, pp. 273–289, 2020.
https://doi.org/10.1007/978-3-030-45371-8_17

Over the years, many Zero-knowledge identification schemes have been proposed using Hamming metric [1,7,20,22]. Based on the instances of Syndrome Decoding problem, Stern presented in [20] a pioneering work that is the first code-based Zero-knowledge identification scheme whose cheating probability is $\frac{2}{3}$. In this scheme, the prover has to convince the verifier that he or she knows a word e of small weight such that $He^\top = y$ where the matrix $H \in \mathcal{M}_{(n-k)\times n}(GF(2))$ which is a parity check matrix of a linear binary code of length n and dimension k and the vector $y \in GF(2)^{(n-k)}$ are public parameters. Thereafter, to decrease the cheating probability to $\frac{1}{2}$, Stern proposed in [20] an extended version of his first protocol that consists on five pass rather than three pass. This improvement impacts a reduction of the signature size. But on the other hand, it increases the communication cost. The second advanced work was presented in [22] by Veron where he proposed a different formulation of secret key using the General Decoding (GD) problem (see below). In this case the prover has to prove his knowledge of a couple of vectors (f, e) that verifies $x = fG \oplus e \in GF(2)^{(n-k)}$ where the matrix $G \in \mathcal{M}_{n\times k}(GF(2))$ and x are public parameters. This new formulation decreases the communication cost but increases the key size. In [12], Gaborit and Giraut proposed to use a double circulant matrices to represent the public matrix. This proposition enables to decrease dramatically the public key size. In [7] using a q-ary codes, Cayrel et al. proposed another protocol with cheating probability of $\frac{1}{2}$. The last and the most efficient protocol in Hamming metric has been presented by Aguilar et al. in [1] which is based on the Veron's scheme and achieves a cheating probability of $\frac{1}{2}$ while preserving a low communications cost.

Chen in [9] proposed a new code-based Zero-knowledge identification scheme using another metric called rank metric. This new three pass identification scheme differs from Stern protocol [20] on the following points:

- The lack of hash function; the first version of Chen identification scheme [9] did not use hash function but matrix multiplication. This property has been very useful since the use of hash function increases the complexity of the identification scheme.
- The choice of another family of error correcting codes; Stern has used a family of error correcting codes using Hamming metric but Chen protocol [9] has used codes in rank metric. This choice can provide smaller key size than Hamming metric.

A few month after the publication of Chen's identification scheme [9], Chabaud and Stern have presented in [8] the first attack on the syndrome decoding problem in rank metric. Thus, to keep Chen's protocol safe, Chabaud and Stern [8] proposed to recalibrate the security parameters. However, the second attack presented by Gaborit et al. in [13] that is based on the lack of a hash function allows a passive attacker to quickly recover the user secret. To repair the Chen's protocol, Gaborit et al. [13] proposed a new version with hash function. This new protocol can be seen as the rank version of Stern's protocol. Recently the research in rank metric codes applied to the cryptography area is quite active with the publication of many paper like [13,16].

In this paper we present a five pass Zero-knowledge code-based identification scheme in metric rank with a cheating probability of $\frac{1}{2}$. Like in AGS protocol [1], our protocol uses double-circulant matrices to represent public generator matrix. Moreover the matrices used to mask user secrets in the protocol running are also circulant. This technique combined with rank metric instead of Hamming metric provide an efficient identification scheme with small key size and low communications cost. In practice, our scheme is more efficient since the public data are 276 bits rather than 350 bits in AGS protocol for 80 bits security level which implies a reduction of 21%. Moreover, for a security level of 128 bits, we get 434 bits as public data size that is better than 550 bits in the AGS protocol, which implies a gain of 21%. Also, for a security of 2^{80}, we get a signature size of 83160 bits whitch is better than AGS [1] case where the signature size is about 93000 bits. By applying the Fiat-Shamir paradigm [11] to a Zero-knowledge identification scheme it is easy to obtain a signature scheme.

The reminder of this paper is organized as follows: in Sect. 2 we present some mandatory preliminaries and definitions for the well understanding of the paper. Section 3 is devoted to our Zero-knowledge identification scheme. We present the security analysis of our protocol in Sect. 4 and give some practical results in Sect. 5. Then we conclude in Sect. 6.

2   Backgrounds and Definitions

In this section we give some necessary notions in code-based cryptography to make the understanding of our paper easier and set some notations.

Let q be a power of a prime p, m an integer and let $V(n)$ be an n dimensional vector space over the finite field $GF(q^m)$. We denote by $GL_m(GF(q))$ the group of invertible $(m \times m)$ matrices over $GF(q)$. Let $\beta = (\beta_1, \cdots, \beta_m)$ be a basis of $GF(q^m)$ over $GF(q)$. Let $\mathcal{F}_i$ be the map from $GF(q^m)$ to $GF(q)$ where $\mathcal{F}_i(x)$ is the i-th coordinate of x in the basis β. To any $v = (v_1, \cdots, v_n)$ in $V(n)$ we associate the matrix $\overline{v} \in \mathcal{M}_{m,n}(GF(q))$ where

$$\overline{v} = (\overline{v}_{i,j})_{i=1,\cdots,m; j=1,\cdots,n} = \mathcal{F}_i(v_j) \tag{1}$$

The rank weight of a vector v noted $rank(v)$ is defined as the rank of the associated matrix $\overline{v}$. For a given basis β, we denote by Φ_β the invert of the map

$$V(n) \to \mathcal{M}_{m,n}(GF(q)) : v \mapsto \overline{v} \tag{2}$$

computed in the basis β. let S be a finite set and a be an element of S we write $a \xleftarrow{\$} S$ if a is chosen uniformly at random in the finite set S. We denote by $\oplus$ the bitwise XOR operator. We define $P(A = a)$ as being the probability to have the event $A = a$. We denote by h a hash function.

2.1   Rank Metric

A code C of length n and dimension k over $GF(q^m)$ is a subspace of dimension k of $GF(q^m)$. Like in Hamming metric, the minimum rank distance of a code C is the minimum rank weight of non null vectors of the code C. Loidreau showed in [17] that these codes satisfy a Gilbert-Varshamov-like bound and that random codes can easily reach this bound.

Let $S(n, m, q, t)$ be the sphere of center 0 and radius t in $GF(q^m)^n$ and $B(n, m, q, t)$ be the ball of center 0 and radius t in $GF(q^m)^n$. The number of elements of $S(n, m, q, t)$ is given in [17] by:

$$\#S(n, m, q, t) = \prod_{j=0}^{t-1} \frac{(q^n - q^j)(q^m - q^j)}{q^t - q^j} \tag{3}$$

From (3), the volume of $B(n, m, q, t)$ is given by:

$$\#B(n, m, q, t) = \sum_{i=0}^{t} \#S(n, m, q, i) \tag{4}$$

Now let us focus on the crypto-systems security in rank metric. This security is relied to the rank version of the NP-Hard Syndrome decoding problem [6].

Problem 1 (Syndrome Decoding Problem (SD) [6]). Let n, k and ω be non negative integers, given a uniformly random matrix $H \in \mathcal{M}_{n-k \times n}(GF(q^m))$ and a uniformly random syndrome $y \in GF(q^m)^{(n-k)}$, find a vector $s \in GF(q^m)^n$ such that $wt(s) = \omega$ and $H \cdot s^\top = y^\top$ where wt denotes the Hamming weight and $s^\top$ the transpose of s.

The Syndrome Decoding Problem in Hamming metric (Problem 1) can be extended to the rank metric :

Problem 2 (Rank Syndrome Decoding Problem (RSD) [8]). Let n, k and r be non negative integers, given a uniformly random matrix $H \in \mathcal{M}_{n-k \times n}(GF(q^m))$ and a uniformly random syndrome $y \in GF(q^m)^{(n-k)}$, find a vector $s \in GF(q^m)^n$ such that $rank(s) = r$ and $H \cdot s^\top = y^\top$.

Problem 3 (Rank General Decoding Problem (RGD) [8]). Let n, k and r be non negative integers, given a uniformly random matrix $G \in \mathcal{M}_{k \times n}(GF(q^m))$ and a uniformly random vector $x \in GF(q^m)^n$, find vectors $e \in GF(q^m)^n$ and $f \in GF(q^m)^k$ such that $rank(e) = r$ and $fG \oplus e = x$.

In [2], Aguilar *et al.* proved that the Rank syndrome Decoding Problem (Problem 2) is difficult.

We say that a matrix H is double circulant if $H = [B|A]$ where B and A are circulant matrices of length k, *i.e.* a $k \times k$ matrix generated from its first row $a = (a_0, \cdots, a_{k-1})$

$$A = \begin{pmatrix} a_0 & a_1 & \cdots & a_{k-1} \\ a_{k-1} & a_0 & \cdots & a_{k-2} \\ & & \vdots & \\ a_1 & a_2 & \cdots & a_0 \end{pmatrix} \tag{5}$$

We adapt the rank syndrome decoding problem to the case of random double circulant codes instead of random codes. The Decisional Rank s-Quasi Cyclic Syndrome Decoding Problem defined in [2] is the general case of the decisional version of the rank syndrome decoding problem using random double circulant codes. As far as we know there is so far no reduction from the RSD problem to its decisional version. But, the best know attack on the decisional version of RSD problem is the exhaustive attack on the RSD problem.

2.2 Properties of the Asterisk Product

In [5], Berger computed the isometry group for the rank distance using right multiplication by an invertible matrix over $GF(q)$ and multiplication of columns by a non-zero element of $GF(q^m)$. These families give the possibility to transform a word with fixed rank to any other word with the same rank. In Hamming metric to transform a word with given weight to any other word with the same weight we use a permutation. We now recall from [14] the definition of asterisk product "$*$".

Definition 1 (Asterisk Product "$*$"). *Let $Q \in \mathcal{M}_{m,n}(GF(q))$, $v \in V(n)$ and β a basis of $GF(q^m)$ over $GF(q)$. We define the product $Q * v$ by*

$$Q * v = \Phi_\beta(Q\overline{v}),$$

where $\overline{v}$ is constructed from the basis β as in (1) and Φ_β as in (2).

Proposition 1 ([14]). *The asterisk product has the important following properties :*

1. *For all $x \in V(n)$ and $Q \in GL_m(GF(q))$, $rank(Q * x) = rank(x)$.*
2. *For all $x \in V(n)$, $P \in \mathcal{M}_{n,n}(GF(q))$ and $Q \in \mathcal{M}_{m,m}(GF(q))$, we have $(Q * x)P = Q * (xP)$.*
3. *For all $x, y \in V(n)$ and $rank(x) = rank(y)$, it is possible to find $P \in \mathcal{M}_{n,n}(GF(q))$ and $Q \in \mathcal{M}_{m,m}(GF(q))$ such that $x = Q * yP$.*

2.3 AGS Zero-Knowledge Identification Protocol

Based on the Veron's Protocol [22], Aguilar, Gaborit and Shreck presented an efficient Zero-knowledge identification protocol in [1]. Their scheme presented two improvements, the first one is about using double-circulant codes to increase the number of possible challenges, and the second one consists in a better use of commitments by compressing them. We recall this protocol in Algorithm 1. Let r be an integer such that $0 \leq r \leq k$, we denote by Rot_r the left shift rotation of r positions applied to vectors of $GF(2)^k$, this map is applied by block of size k.

Private key: (e, f) with $e \in GF(2)^n$ of Hamming weight w and f a random element of $GF(2)^k$.

Public key: (G, x, w) with G a random matrix of size $k \times n$ and $x = e \oplus fG$.

Algorithm 1. The AGS protocol

1. A prover $\mathcal{P}$ randomly chooses $u \in GF(2)^k$ and a permutation σ of $\mathcal{S}_n$. Then $\mathcal{P}$ sends to a verifier $\mathcal{V}$ the commitments c_1 and c_2 such that: $c_1 = h(\sigma)$ and $c_2 = h(\sigma(uG))$ where h is a hash function.
2. The verifier $\mathcal{V}$ sends $0 \leq r \leq k - 1$ (the number of shifted positions) to $\mathcal{P}$.
3. The prover $\mathcal{P}$ builds $e_r = Rot_r(e)$, $f_r = Rot_r(f)$ and sends the last part of the commitments: $c_3 = h(\sigma(uG \oplus e_r))$.
4. The verifier $\mathcal{V}$ sends $g \in \{0, 1\}$ to $\mathcal{P}$:
5. Two possibilities:
   - if $g = 0$: $\mathcal{P}$ reveals $(u \oplus f_r)$ and σ.
   - if $g = 1$: $\mathcal{P}$ reveals $\sigma(uG)$ and $\sigma(e_r)$.
6. Verification Step, two possibilities:
   - if $g = 0$: $\mathcal{V}$ verifies that c_1, c_3 have been honestly computed;
   - if $g = 1$: $\mathcal{V}$ verifies that c_2, c_3 have been honestly computed and that $wt(\sigma(e_r)) = w$.

3 The Proposed Zero-Knowledge Identification Protocol

In this section we describe our proposed Zero-knowledge identification protocol that we call RankId. The Zero-knowledge protocols such as Shamir's Permuted-Kernel-Problem-based protocol [18], Chen's scheme [10], Stern's Constrained-Linear-Equations-based scheme [21], Cayrel-Véron-ElYousfi protocol [7] and Aguilar-Gaborit-Shreck protocol [1] are all of them a five pass protocol and their security is not based on number theory. Beside having a cheating probability close to $\frac{1}{2}$, they all have one more thing in common: after a prover has sent the commitments, a verifier $\mathcal{V}$ chooses a random element in the base field that it sent to a prover $\mathcal{P}$. Then using this element combined with its secret and all masked using various techniques, the prover sends a last commitment to the verifier. In this paper we propose to adapt these techniques to the syndrome decoding problem in rank metric. Our technique is mainly based on the well exploiting of the double circulant structure of the public matrix. We first introduce a special multiplication law that we will use in our protocol.

Let r be an integer such that $r > 1$, to any $\alpha \in GF(q^m)^*$ we associate the symmetric matrix $\tilde{\alpha}_r \in \mathcal{M}_{r,r}(GF(q^m))$ such that:

$$\tilde{\alpha}_r = \begin{pmatrix} \alpha & & & \\ & \alpha^2 & & \\ & & \ddots & \\ & & & \alpha^r \end{pmatrix} \tag{6}$$

Definition 2 (Bullet Product "•"). *Let α be an element of $GF(q^m)^*$, r be an integer such that $r > 1$ and $v = v_1 \parallel v_2$ (where $\parallel$ is the concatenation symbol) be a vector of $GF(q^m)$ such that v_1, $v_2 \in V(r)$. We define the product $v \bullet \alpha$ as follow:*

$$v \bullet \alpha = v_1 \tilde{\alpha}_r \parallel v_2 \tilde{\alpha}_r \tag{7}$$

Proposition 2. *For any integer $r > 1$, $\alpha \in GF(q^m)^*$ and v a vector of $GF(q^m)$.*

$$rank(v \bullet \alpha) = rank(v) \tag{8}$$

Proof. Let A be an $(m \times n)$-matrix over $GF(q^m)$. In this proof we denote by $\mathcal{C}(A)$ the subspace of $GF(q^m)^n$ generated by the vectors column of A. Since $v = (v_1 \parallel v_2)$ where v_1, v_2 are in $V(k)$ we have:

$$\begin{aligned} rank(v) &= rank(\overline{v}_1 \parallel \overline{v}_2) \\ &= Dim(\mathcal{C}(\overline{v}_1) + \mathcal{C}(\overline{v}_2)) \end{aligned} \tag{9}$$

Then we have:

$$\begin{aligned} rank(v \bullet \alpha) &= rank(v_1 \tilde{\alpha}_r \parallel v_2 \tilde{\alpha}_r) \\ &= rank(\overline{v}_1 \tilde{\alpha}_r \parallel \overline{v}_1 \tilde{\alpha}_r) \\ &= Dim(\mathcal{C}(\overline{v}_1 \tilde{\alpha}_r) + \mathcal{C}(\overline{v}_2 \tilde{\alpha}_r)) \end{aligned} \tag{10}$$

Because $\tilde{\alpha}_r$ is symmetric and invertible ($\alpha \neq 0$) we get the following equation:

$$\mathcal{C}(\overline{v}_1 \tilde{\alpha}_r) = \mathcal{C}(\tilde{\alpha}_r \overline{v}_1^\top) = \mathcal{C}(\overline{v}_1) \tag{11}$$

and

$$\mathcal{C}(\overline{v}_2 \tilde{\alpha}_r) = \mathcal{C}(\tilde{\alpha}_r \overline{v}_2^\top) = \mathcal{C}(\overline{v}_2) \tag{12}$$

by (9), (10), (11) and (12) we deduce that:

$$\begin{aligned} rank(v \bullet \alpha) &= Dim(\mathcal{C}(\overline{v}_1) + \mathcal{C}(\overline{v}_2)) \\ &= rank(v) \end{aligned} \tag{13}$$

∎

3.1 Key Generation

Our Zero-knowledge protocol uses a public $k \times n$ (with $n = 2k$) random double circulant matrix G over $GF(q^m)$. This matrix G can be considered as a generator matrix of an $[n, k]$ rank-metric code over $GF(q^m)$. To get a very compact public key we can consider the matrices of type $G = (I_k, G_1)$ where G_1 is a $k \times k$ matrix

---

Algorithm 2. Key generation algorithm

Input: κ
Output: pk, sk, (k, m, q, r)

Choose k, m, q and r such that $W(k, m, q, r) \geq 2^\kappa$
$G \overset{\$}{\leftarrow} \mathcal{M}_{k,2k}(GF(q^m))$
$e \overset{\$}{\leftarrow} V(2k)$ such that $rank(e) = r$
$f \overset{\$}{\leftarrow} V(k)$
$x \leftarrow fG \oplus e$
$pk \leftarrow (G, r, x)$, $sk \leftarrow (e, f)$

---

over $GF(q^m)$ and I_k is the $k \times k$ identity matrix. Let κ be a security level. The key generation process which is described in Algorithm 2 takes as input κ and outputs the public parameters (k, m, q, r), the user public key pk and the user secret key sk. Let W denotes the workfactor of the best known attacks on Rank Syndrome Decoding Problem.

3.2 Identification Protocol

In our Zero-knowledge protocol (RankId) described in Algorithm 3, to prove its identity, a prover has to prove the knowledge of the secret key (e, f) by using two blinding techniques. The first one is to Xor a random vector to the secret key f and unlike the case of Hamming metric where it is common to use a permutation, the second blinding technique is to use the "$\bullet$" and "$*$" products to multiply the secret e to random values. Moreover the security of our protocol relies on the hardness of the rank general decoding problem, that is on the difficulty of finding a couple (e, f) such that $x = fG \oplus e$ where x and G are public.

Algorithm 3. The proposed identification protocol (RankId)

---

1. A prover $\mathcal{P}$ randomly chooses $u \in V(k)$, $P \in Gl_{2k}(GF(q))$ and $Q \in Gl_m(GF(q))$. Then $\mathcal{P}$ sends to a verifier $\mathcal{V}$ the commitments c_1 and c_2 such that: $c_1 = h(P \parallel Q \parallel (uG_1 \oplus f))$ and $c_2 = h(Q * (uG)P)$. Where h is a hash function.
2. A verifier $\mathcal{V}$ sends $\alpha \xleftarrow{\$} GF(q^m)$ to $\mathcal{P}$.
3. A prover $\mathcal{P}$ builds $c_3 = h(Q * (uG \oplus (e \bullet \alpha))P)$.
4. A verifier $\mathcal{V}$ sends $g \in \{0, 1\}$ to $\mathcal{P}$:
5. Two possibilities:
   - if $g = 0$: $\mathcal{P}$ reveals $(u \oplus f\bar{\alpha}_k)$, $(uG_1 \oplus f)$ and $(P \parallel Q)$.
   - if $g = 1$: $\mathcal{P}$ reveals $Q * ((uG))P$ and $Q * (e \bullet \alpha)P$.
6. Verification Step, two possibilities:
   - if $g = 0$: $\mathcal{V}$ verifies that c_1, c_3 have been honestly computed;
   - if $g = 1$: $\mathcal{V}$ verifies that c_2, c_3 have been honestly computed and $rank(Q * (e \bullet \alpha)P) = r$.

---

4 Properties and Security of the Scheme RankId

In this section we study the completeness and soundness of our identification scheme presented in Algorithm 3. We also show that this protocol is Zero-knowledge with cheating probability around $\frac{1}{2}$.

Completeness. We obtain the completeness of RankId described in Algorithm 3 by showing that if an honest prover $\mathcal{P}$ and an honest verifier $\mathcal{V}$ execute our protocol it always succeeds.

Theorem 1. *If a prover $\mathcal{P}$ and a verifier $\mathcal{V}$ honestly execute RankId, we have for any round*

$$Pr[RankId_{\mathcal{P},\mathcal{V}} = Accept] = 1.$$

Proof. The completeness proof is natural since a prover $\mathcal{P}$ and a verifier $\mathcal{V}$ are supposed to be honest. We just notice that to verify c_3 in the case $g = 0$ the verifier $\mathcal{V}$ can compute

$$
\begin{aligned}
(u \oplus f\tilde{\alpha}_k)G \oplus x \bullet \alpha &= uG \oplus f\tilde{\alpha}_k G \oplus (fG \oplus e) \bullet \alpha \\
&= uG \oplus f\tilde{\alpha}_k G \oplus fG \bullet \alpha \oplus e \bullet \alpha \\
&= uG \oplus f\tilde{\alpha}_k G \oplus (f\tilde{\alpha}_k \parallel fG_1\tilde{\alpha}_k) \oplus e \bullet \alpha \\
&= uG \oplus f\tilde{\alpha}_k G \oplus (f\tilde{\alpha}_k \parallel f\tilde{\alpha}_k G_1) \oplus e \bullet \alpha \\
&= uG \oplus f\tilde{\alpha}_k G \oplus f\tilde{\alpha}_k G \oplus e \bullet \alpha \\
&= uG \oplus e \bullet \alpha
\end{aligned}
$$

And in the case $g = 1$ by applying Propositions 1 and 2 we can check that

$$rank(Q * (e \bullet \alpha)P) = r.$$

∎

Zero-Knowledge. To ensure the Zero-knowledge, we use the classical idea of resettable simulation presented in [15].

Theorem 2. *The protocol defined in Algorithm 3 is a prover-verifier Zero-knowledge protocol in random oracle model.*

Proof. Let $\mathcal{S}$ and δ be respectively a simulator using a dishonest verifier and the number of rounds that take an honest identification process execution. Given two interactions with the prover, we assume that the dishonest verifier could construct the two following strategies: the first one $St_1(c_1, c_2)$ takes as input the prover's commitments and outputs a value $\alpha \in GF(q^m)$. The last one $St_2(c_1, c_2, c_3)$ takes as input the prover's commitments and the answer c_3 and outputs the challenge $b \in \{1, 2\}$. The simulator $\mathcal{S}$ will generate a communication transcript representing the interaction between a prover and a verifier. The goal is to generate an indistinguishable communication transcript from a real communication transcript generated by a honest interaction. The simulator $\mathcal{S}$ is defined in three steps:

Step 1. The simulator $\mathcal{S}$ chooses randomly $b \in \{0, 1\}$.
- If $b = 0$, $\mathcal{S}$ chooses randomly $u \in V(k)$, $P \in Gl_{2k}(GF(q))$ and $Q \in Gl_m(GF(q))$ and solves the equation $x = fG \oplus e$ without necessary satisfying the condition $rank(e) = r$. Then he computes $c_1 = h(P \parallel Q \parallel (uG_1 \oplus f))$ and c_2 is taken as random value. $\mathcal{S}$ simulates the verifier by applying $St_1(c_1, c_2)$ to get $\alpha \in GF(q^m)$ and then $\mathcal{S}$ can computes $c_3 = h(Q*(uG \oplus (e \bullet \alpha))P)$. Now $\mathcal{S}$ has the needed information to generate a simulated communication data between a prover and a verifier. Therefore the elements to be written in the communication transcript consist

of components $C = (c_1, c_2)$, c_3 and $R = (P \parallel Q, (u \oplus f\tilde{\alpha}_k), (uG_1 \oplus f))$. Given the variables used to compute C, c_3 and R were chosen randomly, it follows that the distribution of these elements is indistinguishable from the resulting from a honest interaction.

- If $b = 1$, $\mathcal{S}$ chooses randomly $u \in V(k)$, $P \in Gl_{2k}(GF(q))$ and $Q \in Gl_m(GF(q))$. This time he randomly choses $f \in V(k)$ and $e \in V(2k)$ such that $rank(e) = r$. Then he computes $c_2 = h(Q * (uG)P)$ and c_1 is taken as random value. $\mathcal{S}$ simulates the verifier by applying $St_1(c_1, c_2)$ to get $\alpha \in GF(q^m)$ and then $\mathcal{S}$ can compute $c_3 = h(Q*(uG \oplus (e \bullet \alpha))P)$. Now $\mathcal{S}$ have the needed information to generate a simulated communication data between a prover and a verifier. Therefore the elements to be written in the communication transcript consist of components: $C = (c_1, c_2)$, c_3 and $R = (Q * (uG)P, Q * (e \bullet \alpha)P)$. Given that the variables used to compute C, c_3 and R were chosen randomly, it follows that the distribution of these elements is indistinguishable from the resulting from an honest interaction.

Step 2. The simulator $\mathcal{S}$ uses the verifier's strategy $St_2(c_1, c_2, c_3)$ to get as result b'.

Step 3. If $b = b'$, the simulator $\mathcal{S}$ writes on its communication transcript the values of C, α, c_3, b and R. Else, nothing is written and the simulator returns to Step 1.

Therefore, in 2δ rounds on average, $\mathcal{S}$ generates a communication transcript indistinguishable from another communication transcript that corresponds to a honest identification process execution.   ∎

Soundness. Let $GF(q^m)$ the used finite field. To prove the soundness of our scheme we start to show that for each round a dishonest prover can cheat with a probability that does not exceed $\frac{q^m}{2(q^m-1)}$.

We assume that a dishonest prover can use the following strategies to deal with the challenge that the verifier should send. The first strategy St_0 corresponds to the actions taken by the dishonest prover when he or she hopes to receive 0 as challenge. He or she randomly choses u, P and Q and solves the equation $x = f'G \oplus e'$ without necessary satisfying the condition $rank(e') = r$ where $f' \in V(k)$ and $e' \in V(2k)$. Then he or she computes $c_1 = h(P \parallel Q \parallel (uG_1 \oplus f))$ and set c_2 at random data. Thus the dishonest prover will be able to answer the challenge $b = 0$ regardless the value of α chosen by the verifier. The second strategy St_1 corresponds to the case where the dishonest prover hopes to receive 1 as challenge. He or she randomly choses u, P and Q and then randomly generates the couple (f', e') such that $rank(e') = r$. In this case he or she can compute $c_2 = h(Q * (uG)P)$ and set c_1 at random data. In this case the $rank$ of e' is valid. Thus the dishonest prover can correctly answer the challenge $b = 1$ regardless the value of α.

By trying to guess α, the two strategies can be improved. Let v' the guessed value of α. Thus the dishonest prover can compute $h(v)$ where $v = Q * (uG \oplus e \bullet v')P$.

In St_0, instead of randomly generating c_2, the dishonest prover computes $c_2 = h(v \oplus v")$ where $v"$ is a random vector of *rank* r which will be sent as an answer if $b = 1$ instead of $Q * (e' \bullet v')P$. With this strategy, the dishonest prover can answer to $b = 0$ regardless the value of α chosen by the verifier and to $b = 1$ if $\alpha = v'$.

Let B be a vector in $V(m)$ and n an integer with $m \geq n$, $B_{[n]}$ represents the n last components of B. In St_1, instead of randomly generating c_1, the dishonest prover computes

$$c_1 = h(P \parallel Q \parallel (((Q^{-1} * vP^{-1}) \oplus (e' \bullet v'))_{[k]} \oplus f')).$$

With this strategy, the dishonest prover can answer to $b = 1$ regardless the value of α chosen by the verifier and to $b = 0$ if $\alpha = v'$.

Therefore, the success probability of a strategy St for one round is given by:

$$P = \sum_{i=0}^{1} P(St = St_i)P(b = i) + P(St = St_i)P(b = 1 - i)P(\alpha = v') \tag{14}$$
$$= \frac{q^m}{2(q^m - 1)}$$

We now show that if a dishonest prover successes to cheat with a probability higher than $\left(\frac{q^m}{2(q^m - 1)}\right)^\delta$ where δ is the number of rounds then he or she can solve the Rank Syndrome Decoding Problem (Problem 2).

Theorem 3. *Let ϵ be a real number > 0, if $\mathcal{V}$ is an honest verifier who accepts a cheating prover $\mathcal{C}$ proof with probability $\left(\frac{q^m}{2(q^m-1)}\right)^\delta + \epsilon$, then there exists a polynomial time probabilistic algorithm $\mathcal{A}$ which, with a big probability, either computes a valid secret (f, e) or finds a collision for the hash function h. Where h is used to hash the commitments.*

Proof. Let Γ be the interaction tree between a cheating prover $\mathcal{C}$ and a verifier $\mathcal{V}$ corresponding to all challenges sended by $\mathcal{V}$ when the adversary has a random transcript τ. The verifier $\mathcal{V}$ has to ask $2(q^m - 1)$ challenges at each round. Each challenge is a couple (α, b) where $\alpha \in GF(q^m)$ and $b \in \{0, 1\}$. In the following, we will show that a secret key (f, e) can be found from a vertex of $q^m + 1$ children. So we will show that $\mathcal{A}$ can find a such vertex in Γ with a big probability.

Let Λ be a vertex with $q^m + 1$ children. We are in the case where $\mathcal{C}$ is able to answer to $q^m + 1$ queries. It means that for a fixed commitments c_1 and c_2 there exist α such that the cheater answered correctly to the challenges $(\alpha, 0)$, $(\alpha, 1)$. Thus the cheater sends the following answers:

- (v, p, q) for the challenge $(\alpha, 0)$,
- (y, z) for the challenge $(\alpha, 1)$.

where $v = (u \oplus f\tilde{\alpha}_k)$, $p = (uG_1 \oplus f)$, $q = (P \parallel Q)$, $y = Q * (uG)P$ and $z = Q * (e \bullet \alpha)P$ and G_1 is a $k \times k$ matrix over $GF(q^m)$ such that $G = (I_k, G_1)$.

Thus we have either that the cheater can find a collision in hash function h or get the following equations:

$$Q * (vG \oplus (e \bullet \alpha))P = z \oplus y \qquad (15)$$

$$rank(z) = r \qquad (16)$$

from the above equation we get:

$$vG \oplus (Q^{-1} * zP^{-1}) = (Q^{-1} * yP^{-1}) \oplus (x \bullet \alpha) \text{ and } rank(z) = rank(Q^{-1} * zP^{-1}) = r.$$

Therefore the values $(Q^{-1} * yP^{-1}) \oplus (x \bullet \alpha)$ and $(v, (Q^{-1} * zP^{-1}))$ can be respectively used as public and private keys to impersonate a legitimate prover.

Now we focus on the probability for Γ to get such vertex of $q^m + 1$ sons. Let τ and Y be respectively a random transcript where $\mathcal{C}$ chooses randomly its values and a non empty set in $GF(q^m)^* \times \{0, 1\}$. We notice that the sets τ and Y are considered as probability space with uniform distribution. Now let (c, α, b) be the communication data between $\mathcal{C}$ and $\mathcal{V}$ for a complete identification process where c, α and b are a set of commitments and responses, the set of first challenge and the set of second challenge respectively. We say that (c, α, b) is valid if the identification of $\mathcal{C}$ by $\mathcal{V}$ is a success.

Let us consider Λ a subset of $(\tau \times Y)^\delta$, the set of all possible communication transcript data between $\mathcal{C}$ and $\mathcal{V}$ for a complete identification process, composed by all valid triple (c, α, b) (by $\#E$ we mean the cardinal of the set E). By Theorem 3 assumption we have:

$$\frac{\#\Lambda}{\#((\tau \times Y)^\delta)} \geq \left(\frac{q^m}{2(q^m - 1)} \right)^\delta + \epsilon \qquad (17)$$

Let Ω_δ be a subset of τ^δ such that:

- if $c \in \Omega_\delta$, then $(q^m)^\delta + 1 \leq \#\{(\alpha, b) \text{ such that } (c, \alpha, b) \text{ be valid }\} \leq (2(q^m - 1))^\delta$;
- if $c \in \tau^\delta \setminus \Omega_\delta$, then $0 \leq \#\{(\alpha, b) \text{ such that } (c, \alpha, b) \text{ be valid }\} \leq (q^m)^\delta$.

Then $\Lambda = \{$valid (c, α, b) such that $c \in \Omega_\delta\} \cup \{$valid (c, α, b) such that $c \in \tau^\delta \setminus \Omega_\delta\}$, therefore

$$\#\Lambda \leq \#\Omega_\delta (2(q^m - 1))^\delta + (\#(\tau^\delta) - \#\Omega_\delta)(q^m)^\delta. \qquad (18)$$

Thus

$$\frac{\#\Lambda}{\#((\tau \times Y)^\delta)} \leq \frac{\#\Omega_\delta}{\#((\tau)^\delta)} + (q^m)^\delta \left((2(q^m - 1))^{-\delta} - \frac{\#\Omega_\delta}{\#((\tau \times Y)^\delta)} \right)$$

$$\leq \frac{\#\Omega_\delta}{\#((\tau)^\delta)} + \left(\frac{q^m}{2(q^m - 1)} \right)^\delta.$$

It follows that

$$\frac{\#\Omega_\delta}{\#((\tau)^\delta)} \geq \epsilon. \tag{19}$$

By (19) we have the probability that a cheater prover can answer to at least $(q^m)^\delta + 1$ challenges, by choosing random values, is greater than ϵ. Whereas, if a cheater prover can answer to more than $(q^m)^\delta + 1$ challenges then we can find at least a vertex with $q^m + 1$ sons at an interaction tree between $\mathcal{C}$ and Λ. Thus it is possible to find an interaction tree with a vertex with $q^m + 1$ sons with a probability close to 1, by reseting and repeating $[\frac{1}{\epsilon}]$ times the cheater $\mathcal{C}$. Therefore, it is clear that our protocol has a cheating probability too close to $\frac{1}{2}$. ∎

5 Parameters and Results

In this section we present sets of parameters for our identification scheme. Let k, m, q, n and r be integers with $n = 2k$. Our scheme uses as public matrix a random double circulant matrix $G = (I_k | G_1)$ where G_1 is $k \times k$ circulant matrix over $GF(q^m)$. Then to stock a public matrix G we just need $\log_2(q) \times k \times m$-bits. For each user, we use as private key the couple (f, e) where $f \in V(k)$ and $e \in V(2k)$ such that $rank(e) = r$ and as public key we use $x \in V(2k)$ such that $x = fG \oplus e$. Thus to stock a public key we need $2 \times k \times \log_2(q)$-bits and to stock private key we need $3 \times k \times \log_2(q)$-bits. All sets of parameters proposed lie on the

Table 1. Comparison between different code-based Zero-knowledge schemes for a 2^{-16} cheating probability with a security of 2^{80}

	Rounds	Public matrix (bit)	Public key (bit)	Secret key (bit)	Communication (bit)
Stern [20]	28	122500	350	750	42019
Veron [22]	28	122500	700	1050	35486
CVE [7]	16	32768	512	1024	31888
AGS [1]	18	350	700	700	20080
Stern Rank version [14]	28	1980	180	400	22400
RankId	16	276	552	552	16888

Table 2. Comparison between different code-based Zero-knowledge schemes for a 2^{-16} cheating probability with a security of 2^{128}

	Rounds	Public matrix (bit)	Public key (bit)	Secret key (bit)	Communication (bit)
CVE [7]	16	86528	832	1664	47248
AGS [1]	18	550	1100	1100	32304
RankId	16	434	868	868	26064

Gilbert-Varshamov bound for rank metric codes [17]. Also the proposed sets of parameters deal with the complexity of the best known attack on Rank Syndrome Decoding problem [4] and the complexity of the attack proposed in [13], because in the case of double circulant code we have always $\lceil \frac{(k+1)(r+1)-(n+1)}{r} \rceil \leq k$, which is about

$$min(\mathcal{O}\left((n-k)^3 m^3 q^{r\lceil \frac{(k+1)m}{n}\rceil - m}\right), \mathcal{O}\left(k^3 r^3 q^{r\lceil \frac{(k+1)(r+1)-(n+1)}{r}\rceil}\right)).$$

The first one is to get a security of 2^{80} for a standard using. The second set of parameters is to get a security of 2^{128}. We propose these latest parameters to prevent the fast evolution of computer processors.

Now let l_h be the length of the hash function h and δ be the number of rounds of our protocol. To authenticate the prover in δ rounds, the prover and the verifier have to exchange:

$$\delta \times \left(1 + l_h + \log_2(q) \times m + \frac{(6 \times m \times k + 2 \times k + m) \times \log_2(q)}{2}\right) + 2 \times l_h\text{-bits}$$

To have a cheating probability of 2^{-16} with a security of 80 bits we propose the following parameters:

$$q = 2, \ m = 23, \ k = 12, \ r = 7, \ \delta = 16 \text{ and } l_h = 160. \tag{20}$$

In this case the known attacks on Rank Syndrome Decoding problem lead to a complexity of at least 2^{92} operations and we get:

- The needed space to store the public matrix is 276 bits,
- the needed space to store the public or private key is 552 bits,
- and the total data exchanged to authenticate a prover is 16888 bits.

We also propose the following parameters to get a cheating probability of 2^{-16} with a security of 128 bits:

$$q = 2, \ m = 31, \ k = 14, \ r = 8, \ \delta = 16 \text{ and } l_h = 236. \tag{21}$$

In this case the known attacks on Rank Syndrome Decoding problem lead to a complexity of at least 2^{131} operations and we get:

- The needed space to store the public matrix is 434 bits,
- the needed space to store the public or the private key is 868 bits,
- and the total data exchanged to authenticate a prover is 26064 bits.

To end this section we show in Tables 1 and 2 the performances of our scheme compared to existing code-based Zero-knowledge identification protocols.

Through the practical results presented in Tables 1 and 2, it is easy to see that our Zero-knowledge identification protocol is the most efficient from code-based ones. Indeed, in the case of the parameters for a cheat probability of 2^{-16} with a security of 2^{80} (Table 1), the storage of the public matrix, the public key and the secret key requires 1380 bits in our protocol and 1750 bits in the best Zero-knowledge code-based authentication protocol [1], which represents a gain of 21%. Then, the size of the communication data needed to authenticate a prover is 16888 bits in our protocol and 20080 bits in the best code-based Zero-knowledge identification protocol [1], which represents a gain of 16%. In addition, in the case of parameters for a cheat probability of 2^{-16} with a security of 2^{128} (Table 2), the storage of the public matrix, the public key and the secret key requires 2170 bits in our protocol and 2750 bits in the best Zero-knowledge code-based authentication protocol [1], which represents a gain of 21%. Next, the size of the communication data needed to authenticate a prover is 26064 bits in our protocol and 32304 bits in the best code-based Zero-knowledge protocol [1], which represents a 19% gain.

Computational Cost. We divided the computational cost in two parts. the first part is the verifier's computation which is about $2^{11.5}$ operations in $GF(q)$. The second part is the prover's computation witch is about $2^{14.9}$ operations in $GF(q)$ while in AGS identification scheme [1] the prover's computation is about 2^{21} in $GF(2)$.

Signature. Let n be an integer ≥ 1. In [3] Dagdelen *et al.* gave a generic methodology to prove the security of signature scheme obtained by applying the Fiat-Shamir paradigm [11] to $(2n + 1)$-pass identification scheme. Then we can apply in safe the Fiat-Shamir paradigm to our five-pass Zero-knowledge identification scheme to obtain a signature scheme. In our case to generate a signature for a security of 2^{80}, we use parameters presented by expression (20) and we perform 80 rounds to keep a cheating probability of 2^{-80}. Thus we get a signature size of 83160 bits which is better than AGS [1] case where the signature size is about 93000 bits.

6   Conclusion

In this paper, we have proposed an efficient Zero-knowledge identification scheme based on coding theory assumptions which is supposed to be resistant to quantum computers. We have used rank metric rather than the classical Hamming metric. This choice implies a significant reduction in public data size and in communication cost. For instance, we achieve a gain of 47% in our protocol if compared to AGS identification scheme [1] for a 80 bits security. Our scheme presents optimal results in comparison with all code based identification schemes. It is also possible to turn it into a signature scheme by applying the Fiat-Schamir Transformation described in [11].

References

1. Aguilar Melchor, C., Gaborit, P., Schrek, J.: A new Zero-Knowledge code based identification scheme with reduced communication. In: 2011 IEEE Information Theory Workshop, pp. 648–652. IEEE Press, Paraty (2011)

2. Aguilar Melchor, C., Blazy, O., Deneuville, J.C., Gaborit, P., Zémor, G.: Efficient encryption from random quasi-cyclic codes. IEEE Trans. Inf. Theor. **64**(5), 3927–3943 (2018)
3. Dagdelen, Ö., Galindo, D., Véron, P., Alaoui, S.M.E.Y., Cayrel, P.L.: Extended security arguments for signature schemes. Des. Codes Crypt. **78**(2), 441–461 (2016)
4. Aragon, N., Gaborit, P., Hauteville, A., Tillich, J.P.: A new algorithm for solving the rank syndrome decoding problem. In: ISIT, no. 8437464, pp. 2421–2425. IEEE (2018)
5. Berger, T.: Isometries for rank distance and permutation group of Gabidulin codes. IEEE Trans. Inf. Theor. **49**(11), 3016–3019 (2003)
6. Berlekamp, E.R., McEliece, R.J., Van Tilborg, H.C.: On the inherent intractability of certain coding problems. IEEE Trans. Inf. Theor. **24**, 384–386 (1978)
7. Cayrel, P.-L., Véron, P., El Yousfi Alaoui, S.M.: A zero-knowledge identification scheme based on the q-ary syndrome decoding problem. In: Biryukov, A., Gong, G., Stinson, D.R. (eds.) SAC 2010. LNCS, vol. 6544, pp. 171–186. Springer, Heidelberg (2011). https://doi.org/10.1007/978-3-642-19574-7_12
8. Chabaud, F., Stern, J.: The cryptographic security of the syndrome decoding problem for rank distance codes. In: Kim, K., Matsumoto, T. (eds.) ASIACRYPT 1996. LNCS, vol. 1163, pp. 368–381. Springer, Heidelberg (1996). https://doi.org/10.1007/BFb0034862
9. Chen, K.: A new identification algorithm. In: Dawson, E., Golić, J. (eds.) CPA 1995. LNCS, vol. 1029, pp. 244–249. Springer, Heidelberg (1996). https://doi.org/10.1007/BFb0032363
10. Chen, M.: Improved girault identification scheme. Electron. Lett. **30**(19), 1590–1591 (1994)
11. Fiat, A., Shamir, A.: How to prove yourself: practical solutions to identification and signature problems. In: Odlyzko, A.M. (ed.) CRYPTO 1986. LNCS, vol. 263, pp. 186–194. Springer, Heidelberg (1987). https://doi.org/10.1007/3-540-47721-7_12
12. Gaborit, P., Girault, M.: Lightweight code-based identification and signature. In: 2007 IEEE International Symposium on Information Theory, ISIT 2007, Nice, France, pp. 191–195 (2007)
13. Gaborit, P., Ruatta, O., Schreck, J.: On the complexity of the rank syndrome decoding problem. IEEE Trans. Inf. Theor. **62**(2), 1006–1019 (2016)
14. Gaborit, P., Schrek, J., Zémor, G.: Full cryptanalysis of the chen identification protocol. In: Yang, B.-Y. (ed.) PQCrypto 2011. LNCS, vol. 7071, pp. 35–50. Springer, Heidelberg (2011). https://doi.org/10.1007/978-3-642-25405-5_3
15. Goldreich, O.: Zero-Knowledge twenty years after its invention. In: Electronic Colloquium on Computational Complexity, no. 063 (2002). http://eccc.hpi-web.de/eccc-reports/2002/TR02-063/index.html
16. Hauteville, A., Tillich, J.P.: New algorithms for decoding in the rank metric and an attack on the LRPC cryptosystem. In: Information Theory (ISIT), pp. 2747–2751. IEEE (2015)
17. Loidreau, P.: Properties of codes in rank metric. CoRR, abs/cs/0610057 (2006)
18. Shamir, A.: An efficient identification scheme based on permuted kernels (extended abstract). In: Brassard, G. (ed.) CRYPTO 1989. LNCS, vol. 435, pp. 606–609. Springer, New York (1990). https://doi.org/10.1007/0-387-34805-0_54
19. Shor, P.W.: Algorithms for quantum computation: discrete logarithms and factoring. In: 1994 Proceeding of Foundations of Computer Science, pp. 124–134. IEEE, Santa Fe (1994)

20. Stern, J.: A method for finding codewords of small weight. In: Cohen, G., Wolf-mann, J. (eds.) Coding Theory 1988. LNCS, vol. 388, pp. 106–113. Springer, Heidelberg (1989). https://doi.org/10.1007/BFb0019850
21. Stern, J.: Designing identification schemes with keys of short size. In: Desmedt, Y.G. (ed.) CRYPTO 1994. LNCS, vol. 839, pp. 164–173. Springer, Heidelberg (1994). https://doi.org/10.1007/3-540-48658-5_18
22. Véron, P.: Improved identification schemes based on error-correcting codes. Appl. Algebra Eng. Commun. Comput. 8(1), 57–69 (1997)

Security Analysis of Auctionity: A Blockchain Based E-Auction

Pascal Lafourcade[1(✉)], Mike Nopere[2], Jérémy Picot[2(✉)], Daniela Pizzuti[2], and Etienne Roudeix[2]

[1] LIMOS, Université Clermont Auvergne, Clermont-Ferrand, France
pascal.lafourcade@uca.fr
[2] Domraider, Clermont-Ferrand, France
jeremy_p@auctionity.com

Abstract. Auctions are widely used to sell products between different users. In this paper, we present *Auctionity*, an English e-auction based on blockchain. We describe the different protocols used in Auctionity. We also define the security models and the associated properties. We formally prove some security properties of this protocol using ProVerif.

Keywords: Blockchain · Security · E-auction · ProVerif

1 Introduction

An auction is a method to sell products in which a seller proposes goods or services for sale, and bidders present the amount they are willing to pay for it. Auctions have been used since Antiquity, reportedly starting in Babylon as early as 500 BC [13]. Over the years, several kinds of auctions have been invented. The most well-known is *English auction*, in which the bidder who offers the highest price wins the auction. *Dutch auction* is a mechanism where the seller sets up an initial price and the price is lowered until a bidder accepts the current price. *Sealed Bid auction* is a form of auction where bids are not public. All bidders simultaneously submit sealed bids and the highest bid wins the auction. *Vickery auction* is a sealed bid auction where the highest bid wins, but the winner only pays the second-highest bid value.

The easy access to the Internet and the birth of modern cryptography in the 80's made the use of digital systems to buy or sell products a common practice. Following this trend, auctions began to take place online, known as *e-auctions*. The e-auctions market is huge, as demonstrated by websites like eBay, which had more than *170* million active buyers in *2018* [10]. E-auction systems often apply cryptographic mechanisms to be secure, but they use a centralized authority to manage transactions between sellers and bidders.

With Bitcoin [16] and Ethereum [21], the blockchain technologies are nowadays a key component of the modern digital world. Essentially, a blockchain is a distributed and decentralized ledger that does not allow the modification of data

© Springer Nature Switzerland AG 2020
A. Benzekri et al. (Eds.): FPS 2019, LNCS 12056, pp. 290–307, 2020.
https://doi.org/10.1007/978-3-030-45371-8_18

stored in it without the consensus of the peers. This property is generally called *immutability* and it clearly is a key feature for auctions based on the blockchain technology. Moreover, several blockchain platforms support smart contracts that can be defined as secure and unstoppable computer programs that represent an agreement to be automatically executed and enforced [1]. Our goal is to design a secure e-auction protocol based on a blockchain.

Contributions: Our main contributions are:

- Design of *Auctionity*, our e-auction system based on the Ethereum blockchain.
- Definition of the relevant security properties for Auctionity.
- Formal analysis of Auctionity security properties.
- Proof of concept of Auctionity implemented using Ethereum.

Auctionity relies on the main Ethereum network (also called mainchain or ELNET) and a private blockchain (also called sidechain or ACNET). We use a sidechain in order to reduce both energy and gas costs of the system. Indeed, ACNET is a Proof Of Authority (POA) blockchain which has 0 gas cost. When interacting with ACENET, user will not have to pay any gas fees and transactions will be validated without consuming as much energy power as ELNET.

The main properties achieved by Auctionity are: *Highest Price Wins*: the bidder who submitted the highest valid bid is the one who wins the auction. *Non-cancellation*: all bids count to the result and the winning amount is the highest. *Non-repudiation*: a bidder who submitted a bid is not able to argue that she did not submit it. *Individual Verifiability*: a bidder can be sure her bid counts correctly for the result. *Universal Verifiability*: any observer may verify that the result of an auction is fair. *Auction End Voucher Validity*: the winner and the amount of its winning bid on the mainchain corresponds to an existing bid submitted by the winner to the sidechain. *Withdrawal Voucher Validity*: a withdrawal request on the mainchain corresponds to a withdrawal request submitted by the same user, with the same amount, on the sidechain.

Related Work: The closest work to Auctionity is STRAIN (Secure aucTions foR blockchAINs) presented in [3]. In this paper, the authors introduce a sealed bid auction system based on blockchain and cryptographic primitives like Multi-Party Computation (MPC) and Zero-Knowledge Proofs (ZKP). They provide security proofs to guarantee bid confidentiality against fully-malicious parties. The aim of Auctionity is different, since its design is of an English auction system where the bids are public. It leads Auctionity to a different paradigm.

Another work that can be considered to have some similarities with Auctionity is the protocol presented by Omote and Miyaji [18]. This work presents an English auction protocol where bids are registered on a bulletin board, which can be compared to the registration of bids done by Auctionity in its private blockchain. The protocol uses two authorities, one that registers bidders (registration manager) and the other that records the bids of each auction (auction manager). At the end of an auction, the auction manager publishes the winning value and the registration key used by the bidder, that corresponds to the bidder's identity stored by the registration manager. As for Auctionity, the bidders signature is always verified and the bids are publicly available. The main differences consist in the fact that this protocol aims to provide privacy for bidders and the protocol does not use blockchain.

Opensea offers a blockchain based auction system. Bids are public. Bidders can bid with any amount, not necessarily higher than the highest bid. Sellers can end the auction at anytime, accepting a bid, not necessarily the highest one. Bidders can cancel their bids at any time. Unlike Auctionity, this system does not guarantee non-cancellation of bids, neither that the highest price wins.

Portio offers a blockchain based auction system. Bidding amounts are deposited on a Portio Ethereum address that is not a smart contract. Therefore, bidders need to fully trust Portio. Unlike Auctionity, this system does not guarantee payment.

There exist several other e-auction protocols among [4,6,7,12,17,19,20]. However, none of them uses blockchain and they aim at providing anonymity mechanisms for the bids. Here again, the aim of Auctionity is clearly different.

Concerning the analysis of e-auction systems security properties, Dreier et al. [9] used the applied pi calculus to generically define auction protocols and the properties of fairness, authentication and privacy. They used ProVerif to analyze the auction protocols by Brandt [4], and by Curtis et al. [6]. In [8] they also defined the property of verifiability and analyzed the same protocols cited above. Our formal analysis of Auctionity follows these works. We also use Proverif in order to analyse the security of Auctionity.

Outline: In the next section, we describe Auctionity. In Sect. 3, we present the security model of Auctionity and its formal model made with ProVerif to analyse the security of the protocol. In Sect. 4, we discuss the performance of our proof of concept of Auctionity deployed during 6 months.

2   Description of Auctionity

Auctionity uses Ethereum and is composed of the following principals:

- **Ethereum Live Net (ELNET or Γ)** is the Ethereum public blockchain, where the smart contract (SC) Deposit[1] (D) is running. It is responsible for holding bidder's deposit, processing withdrawal and payment demands on ELNET.
- **Auctionity Network (ACNET or Ω)** is the private blockchain owned by Auctionity, where the following smart contracts are running:
  - **Treasurer (T)** is responsible for holding bidders deposit and processing withdrawal demands on ACNET.
  - **Auction (A)** is responsible for processing auctions. However, while the previous smart contracts are instantiated only once, for each auction there is an Auction instance, created by the seller.

---

[1] Smart contract names are written in true type.

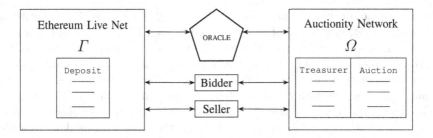

Fig. 1. General structure of auctionity.

Table 1. Notations, where u is a user.

Notation	Description	Notation	Description
ACNET or Ω	Auctionity Network	AEV_u	Auction End Voucher
ELNET or Γ	Ethereum Live Network	P_u	Parameters sent by u to Ω and Γ
B	Bidder	WV_u	Withdraw Voucher
O	Oracle	S	Seller
ad_u	Address of u	L	Current leader of an auction
am_u	Amount of u	W	Winner of an auction
co_u	Counter of u	EVM	Ethereum Virtual Machine
de_u	Deposit balance of u	SC	Smart Contract
in_u	Information of u	H	Hash function
m	Message	Sig	Signature function
pk_u	Public key of u	SIG	Message and the signature of its hash
sk_u	Secret key of u	A	Auction Smart Contract
ts_u	Timestamp of a message sent by u	D	Deposit Smart Contract
		T	Treasurer Smart Contract

- **Oracle (O)** is the Auctionity server that transfers information between ELNET and ACNET. Unlike blockchain, Oracle is not decentralized. However it does not compromise the security properties we want for Auctionity. Oracle has no responsibility in trusting information, it is just a relay between the two blockchains which can themselves do their own security checks since they share the same cryptographic mechanisms.
- **Bidder (B)** is a user that participates in an auction on ACNET.
- **Seller (S)** is the user that auctions a product on ACNET.

In Fig. 1, the exchanges between these principals in Auctionity are shown. It is important to notice that bidders and sellers directly interact with ELNET and ACNET, while ELNET and ACNET communicate between themselves via the Oracle, that, by allowing their communication, plays the role of a trusted third party.

Notations: A user is denoted by u. It can be a seller, a bidder or the Oracle. Each user has a pair of ECDSA (Elliptic Curve Digital Signature Algorithm) [11] keys, denoted by pk_u for the public key, and, sk_u for the secret key. Each

Smart Contract or user has an address (ad_{SC} or ad_u), which is their identity on the system, that, in the case of users is based in their ECDSA public key and in the case of SCs is based in the address of the SC's creator and the value of her internal counter, denoted by co_u, at the moment of the contract creation. A hash function, denoted by $H(m)$, and a signature algorithm, denoted by $\text{Sig}_{sk_u}(m)$ for signing a message m with the secret key sk_u are also considered. The notation SIG_u represents that a message is sent with its signature, as shown bellow: $\text{SIG}_u(m) = (m\|\text{Sig}_{sk_u}(H(m)))$. In Table 1, all the notations used to describe Auctionity are listed.

In order to communicate with ELNET and ACNET, a user should respect the SC formalism. It is why the messages sent by u to ELNET and ACNET carry the following Ethereum parameters:

- co_u: it denotes the number of transactions sent by the sender. We notice that in [21], this counter is called *nonce*.
- $gasPrice_u$: the price to be paid by u per gas^2 unit.
- $gasLimit_u$: the limit of gas to be used for the transaction execution.
- $value_u$: the number of Wei^3 to be sent from u's account to the recipient or new contract.
- to_u: it is the recipient of the message sent by u. It corresponds to an address ad_v of a SC or another user v.
- $\text{Sig}_{sk_u}(H(m))$: the transaction signature, where m contains the previous parameters in addition to specific content of each message.

The notation P_u is used to represent the following set of parameters, sent by users in their messages to ACNET and ELNET:

$$P_u = (co_u\|gasPrice_u\|gasLimit_u\|value_u\|to_u).$$

Interacting with Γ and Ω a user can bid, withdraw her deposit (amount the bidder has on Ω used as *Payment Guarantee*[4]) and create an auction or end it (to obtain the payment locked on the Ω **Treasurer**. We have four protocols, one for each of those actions.

Create Auction Protocol: it allows a seller to create a new instance of an **Auction**. To create an auction, a seller S sends a signed message to ACNET, with the **Auction** binary code, denoted by "EVMCode$_{SC}$" and the auction information, denoted by *in*:

- *title*: bit string chosen by S to be the title of her auction.
- *startAmount*: value chosen by S to be the minimum bid of her auction.

---

[2] Gas is the pricing value required to execute operations on the Ethereum Virtual Machine (EVM).

[3] Wei is the smallest money unit of Ethereum, which is equal to 10^{-18} Ether.

[4] Payment Guarantee is a functionality offered by the system that ensures sellers that they will receive the winning amount of their auctions. It is done thanks to the deposit made by bidders, that is blocked when they bid until another bid is accepted.

Fig. 2. Create auction protocol.

- *startTime*: date chosen by S to be start time of her auction.
- *endTime*: date chosen by S to be the end time of her auction.
- *bidIncrement*: value chosen by S to be the minimum bid increment a bidder will be able to make to her auction.
- *antiSnippingTriggerPeriod*: time value chosen by S as the period of time before *endTime* during which the anti snipping is triggered. Its maximum value is 194 days, 4 h, 20 min and 16 s, which corresponds to the maximum value of the type *uint24*, in seconds.
- *antiSnippingDuration*: time value chosen by S to be the duration of the anti snipping. Its maximum value is 18 h, 12 min and 16 s, which corresponds to the maximum value of the type *uint16*, in seconds.

The parameter *endTime* is stored as *originalEndTime*. We consider *bidTime* as the time when a bid is accepted. The *endTime* is updated only if *bidTime* is greater than the difference between *antiSnippingTriggerPeriod* and *endTime*, which triggers the update of *endTime* to *bidTime* plus *antiSnippingDuration*.

The Create Auction Protocol is described in Fig. 2 and works as follows:

1. S $\rightarrow$ Ω: SIG$_S$(P_S ∥ EVMCode$_{SC}$ ∥ *in*). A seller S signs with her secret key the following parameters: P_S, EVMCode$_{SC}$ and *in*. Then, S sends it to ACNET. Finally, ACNET creates an `Auction` with these parameters.
2. Ω $\rightarrow$ S: ad_{SC}. ACNET sends to S, through ACNET's WebSocket[5], the address of her `Auction` as a confirmation that it has been created. At this point, with the `Auction` instance written on the blockchain, it is not possible to cancel the auction.

Close Auction Protocol: it allows a seller to receive the winning amount of her auction. Anyone can request to close an auction. As ACNET cannot emit an event by itself when the auction end time is reached, S is expected to call the function that closes her auction. However, as in the case if only S could do it, S could "freeze" an auction by never ending it, this action can be taken by anybody. If the original end time, plus the triggered anti snipping period, is not reached, the end auction request cannot be performed.

---

[5] WebSocket is a protocol for the connection between a *http* client and a server. It is used by Auctionity because it allows Ethereum nodes to broadcast information to anyone who listens to it, so the users do not need to constantly interrogate the network.

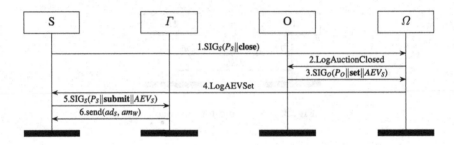

Fig. 3. Close auction protocol.

When an end auction request is received by the `Auction` instance, an Auction End Voucher (AEV), which is a bit string issued by the Oracle with the auction results, as the winner's address and winning amount, is added to the `Auction`. It is then submitted by the seller to ELNET in order to withdraw her auction winning amount, denoted by am_W where W is the bidder who won the auction.

The Close Auction Protocol is described in Fig. 3 and works as follows:

1. $S \rightarrow \Omega$: $SIG_S(P_S \parallel$ **close**). Anyone can call the `Auction` function[6] **close** to close an auction, but this call is considered to be made by a seller S who created this auction. S signs with her secret key the following parameters: P_S and **close**. Then, S sends it to ACNET. Finally, as a result of the call of the `Auction` function **close**, ACNET emits the Ethereum event[7], LogAuctionClosed, which indicates that this `Auction` instance received a valid close auction request.

2. $\Omega \rightarrow O$: LogAuctionClosed. The Oracle O, listening to ACNET's WebSocket, gets the information of the Ethereum event, LogAuctionClosed, triggered by the `Auction` function **close**, of the `Auction` instance created by S on ACNET.

3. $O \rightarrow \Omega$: $SIG_O(P_O \parallel$ **set** $\parallel AEV_S)$. O signs with its secret key the following parameters: P_O, **set** and AEV_S. Then, O sends it to ACNET. Finally, as a result of the call of the `Auction` function **set** with the parameter AEV_S, ACNET emits the Ethereum event LogAEVSet, which indicates that AEV_S was set to S's `Auction` instance.

4. $\Omega \rightarrow S$: LogAEVSet. S, listening to ACNET's WebSocket, gets the information of the Ethereum event, LogAEVSet, triggered by the `Auction` function **set**, of her `Auction` instance. Then, S gets her AEV_S.

5. $S \rightarrow \Gamma$: $SIG_S(P_S \parallel$ **submit** $\parallel AEV_S)$. S, provided with her AEV_S, signs with her secret key the following parameters: P_S, **submit** and AEV_S. Then, S sends it to ELNET. Finally, as a result of the call of the Deposit SC function **submit**, with the parameter AEV_S, ELNET emits the Ethereum event LogAEVSubmitted, which indicates that ELNET received a valid AEV_S from S.

---

[6] SC function names are written in bold.

[7] An Ethereum event is an event emitted as result of a function computation. Every event is broadcasted through WebSockets.

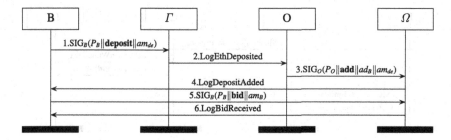

Fig. 4. Bid protocol.

6. $\Gamma \to$ S: send(ad_S, am_W). The ELNET Deposit SC, provided with a valid AEV_S, uses the Solidity[8] function **send** to send the winning amount am_W, to S's address, denoted by ad_S.

Bid Protocol: Acting as a bidder, a user makes deposits on ELNET that are valid on ACNET thanks to the Oracle. The bidder is able to bid an amount am_B if it is smaller or equal her current deposit balance de_B. This is required by the Payment Guarantee feature in order to secure the payment to the seller.

The Bid Protocol is described in Fig. 4 and is composed of depositing (1 to 4) and bidding (5 and 6). It works as follows:

1. B $\to$ Γ: $SIG_B(P_B \parallel$ **deposit** $\parallel am_{de})$. A bidder B signs with her secret key the following parameters: P_B, **deposit** and am_{de}. Then, B sends it to ELNET. Finally, as a result of the call of the Deposit SC function **deposit**, with the parameter am_{de}, ELNET emits the Ethereum event LogEthDeposited, which indicates that a deposit of amount am_{de} was made by B and added to B's deposit balance, denoted by de_B.
2. $\Gamma \to$ O: LogEthDeposited. The Oracle O, listening to ACNET's WebSocket, gets the information of the Ethereum event, LogEthDeposited, triggered by the Deposit SC function **deposit**.
3. O $\to$ Ω: $SIG_O(P_O \parallel$ **add** $\parallel ad_B \parallel am_{de})$. O signs with its secret key the following parameters: P_O, **add**, ad_B and am_{de}. Then, O sends it to ACNET. Finally, as a result of the call of the **Treasurer** function **add**, with the parameters ad_B and am_{de}, ACNET emits the event, LogDepositAdded, which indicates that the amount am_{de} was added to B's deposit balance on the **Treasurer**.
4. $\Omega \to$ B: LogDepositAdded. B, listening to ACNET's WebSocket, gets the information of the Ethereum event, LogDepositAdded, triggered by the **Treasurer** function **add**. Then, B gets the current balance of her deposit.
5. B $\to$ Ω: $SIG_B(P_B \parallel$ **bid** $\parallel am_B)$. B signs with her secret key the following parameters: P_B, **bid** and am_B. Then, B sends it to ACNET. Finally, as a result of the call of the **Auction** function **bid**, with the parameter am_B, ACNET emits the Ethereum event, LogBidReceived, which indicates that

---

[8] Solidity is a programming language for writing Ethereum smart contracts.

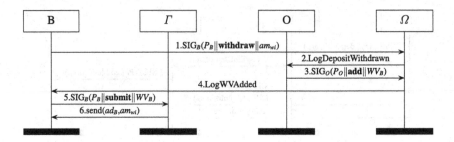

Fig. 5. Withdrawal deposit protocol.

B's bid of amount am_B on an `Auction` instance ad_{SC} (the recipient of the message) was received by ACNET.

6. $\Omega \to$ B: LogBidReceived. B, listening to ACNET's WebSocket, gets the information of the Ethereum event, LogBidReceived, triggered by the function **bid** of the `Auction` instance ad_{SC}. Then, B gets the status of her bid (accepted or rejected).

Each `Auction` instance stores the address of the leader, denoted by ad_L, as leader is denoted by L, and its bid amount. The `Auction` is also responsible for checking the validity of each bid. In order to be valid, a bid must respect the following criteria:

– Sig_{sk_B} matches ad_B: the transaction is signed with a secret key that corresponds to the bidder's address (ad_B).
– $ts_{start} \leq ts_{cur} \leq ts_{end}$: the block timestamp ($ts_{block}$) is bigger or equal to the *startTime* (ts_{start}) of the auction and smaller or equal to the *endTime* (ts_{end}) of the auction.
– $ad_B \neq ad_S$: the bidder's address (ad_B) is different from the sellers (ad_S).
– $am_B > am_{min}$: the *bid amount* (am_B) is higher than the *minimumAmount* (am_{min}) or than the *leaderAmount* (am_L) and is it a multiple of the *bidIncrement* (am_{inc}) set by the seller.
– $de_B \geq am_B$: the bidder's deposit (de_B) on ACNET is higher or equal the payment guarantee, which is equal to the bid amount, required by the auction.

At the end of the auction, the bidder's address stored in the `Auction` variable ad_L is the winner, and the variable am_L is the winning amount.

Withdraw Deposit Protocol: it allows a bidder to get her deposit back to her account on ELNET. Another action made by a user as a bidder is to withdraw her deposit, which corresponds to having the Ether that she previously deposited but did not use, sent back to her address on ELNET. When a bidder wants to get her money back, she communicates with ACNET to request a Withdrawal Voucher (WV_B), which is a bit string issued by the Oracle after getting the information of a new valid withdrawal request, which means, of an amount smaller or equal to B's current balance, made to the Treasurer SC. It is then submitted by the bidder to ELNET in order to withdraw the amount denoted am_{wi}.

The Withdrawal Protocol is described in Fig. 5 and works as follows:

1. $B \to \Omega$: $SIG_B(P_B \parallel \textbf{withdraw} \parallel am_{wi})$. A bidder B signs with her secret key the following parameters: P_B, **withdraw** and am_{wi}. Then, B sends it to ACNET. Finally, as a result of the call of the `Treasurer` function **withdraw**, with the parameter am_{wi}, ACNET emits the event, LogDepositWithdrawn, which indicates that the `Treasurer` received a withdrawal request of amount am_{wi} from B.

2. $\Omega \to O$: LogDepositWithdrawn. The Oracle O, listening to ACNET's Web-Socket, gets the information of the Ethereum event, LogDepositWithdrawn, triggered by the `Treasurer` function **withdraw**.

3. $O \to \Omega$: $SIG_O(P_O \parallel \textbf{add} \parallel WV_B)$. O signs with its secret key the following parameters: P_O, **add** and WV_B. Then, O sends it to ACNET. Finally, as a result of the call of the `Treasurer` function **add**, with the parameter WV_B, ACNET emits the event LogWVAdded, which indicates that a Withdrawal Voucher was added for B.

4. $\Omega \to B$: LogWVAdded. B, listening to ACNET's WebSocket, gets the information of the Ethereum Event, LogWVAdded, triggered by the `Treasurer` function **add**. Then, B gets her WV_B.

5. $B \to \Gamma$: $SIG_B(P_B \parallel \textbf{submit} \parallel WV_B)$. B signs with her secret key the following parameters: P_B, **submit** and WV_B. Then B sends it to ELNET. Finally, as a result of the call of the `Deposit` function **submit**, with the parameter WV_B, ELNET emits the Ethereum event LogWVSubmitted, which indicates that ELNET received a valid WV_B from B.

6. $\Gamma \to B$: $send(ad_B, am_{wi})$. The ELNET `Deposit`, provided with a valid WV_B, uses the SC function **send** to send the withdrawal amount am_{wi}, to B's address, denoted by ad_B.

3   Security Analysis

We model Auctionity in applied pi calculus in order to use the ProVerif [2] tool to analyze its security properties. ProVerif provides automatic analysis of cryptographic protocols in the symbolic Dolev-Yao model for unbounded number of sessions. The tool can handle many different cryptographic primitives, including encryption, signatures and hash functions. We start by formally defining an Auction End Voucher (AEV).

Definition 1. *An* Auction End Voucher *is a tuple (pk$_W$, am$_W$, creationProof$_S$, bidProof$_W$, σ) where pk$_W$ is the public key of the auction winning bidder, am$_W$ is the value of the winning bid, creationProof$_S$ is the creation transaction submitted by S to ACNET, bidProof$_W$ is the bid transaction submitted by the bidder W to ACNET and σ is the Oracle's signature of the AEV.*

An Auction End Voucher is requested by a seller to her `Auction` after the auction end time is reached. Next, the `Auction` verifies if pk_L has am_L blocked on the `Treasurer` for the auction ad_A. If so, an Ethereum event is emitted by the `Auction`, informing that the public key of the leader pk_L is the winner pk_W of the auction. The Oracle gets this event, verifies the validity of the request and sends a signed AEV_S to the Auction SC. The seller retrieves the AEV_S and submits it to the `Deposit` on ELNET, that verifies its validity, sends am_W to the seller's public key and update the balance of pk_W on ELNET. We now define a Withdrawal Voucher (WV).

Definition 2. *A* Withdrawal Voucher *is defined by a tuple (pk_B, am_B, withdrawalProof$_B$, σ) where pk_B is the public key of the user who requested the withdrawal, am_B is the value the user requested to withdraw, withdrawalProof$_B$ is the withdrawal request transaction submitted by B, and σ is the Oracle's signature of the other components of the WV.*

A Withdrawal Voucher is requested by a bidder to the `Treasurer` to get her money back on ELNET. Next, the `Treasurer` verifies if pk_B has am_B as balance. If so, an event is emitted by the `Treasurer`, informing that the public key of the bidder pk_B requested to withdraw the amount am_B. The Oracle verifies the validity of the request and sends a signed WV_B to the `Treasurer`. The bidder retrieves the WV_B and submits it to the `Deposit` on ELNET, which verifies its validity, sends am_B to the bidder's public key and updates the balance of pk_B on ELNET.

For each security property, we prove either manually or with ProVerif the corresponding theorems[9].

3.1   Highest Price Wins

This property presented in [9] establishes that the bidder who submitted the highest valid bid is the one who wins the auction. As Auctionity is based on blockchain, this property can be accomplished under the statement that the bidder who submitted the highest **accepted** bid is the one who wins the auction. So, in the model, when a bid is accepted, the address of the `Auction` to which it was submitted, the public key of the bidder and her bid amount are inserted in the table called *auction*. When ACNET receives a bid, it verifies if there is an entry on the ProVerif table of a bid with an amount greater or equal than the received bid. If there is not, the bid is accepted, if there is, the bid is rejected and the event bidRejected is emitted.

Theorem 1. *Auctionity ensures the property* Highest Price Wins (HPW) *if there exists a trace where all accepted bids are lower or equal than an highest accepted bid.*

3.2   Authentication

We consider two authentication properties defined in [9]: Non-cancellation and Non-repudiation.

---

[9] The detailed proofs are available in [14] and the Proverif code in [15].

Non-cancellation. In an English auction each valid bid must be greater than the current latest bid, therefore, the bidder who submitted the last accepted bid must win the auction. The Non-cancellation property aims at preventing the annulment of bids. To model this in ProVerif, we introduce the event bidAccepted(*ad, pk,am*) that corresponds to the acceptance of a bid. All the accepted bids are stored as events and update the variables that store the current leader and current winning amount, modeled by the event won(*ad, pk, am*). This leads us to the following formal property of Non-cancellation.

Theorem 2. *Auctionity ensures* Non-cancellation (NC) *if for any auction which contains a bidder $B(\sigma_{ad_p}\sigma_{am_p})$ who submits the highest accepted bid, i.e., $\forall u_p \neq u_q$: $am_{u_p} > am_{u_q}$, there is no trace containing the events bidAccepted(ad, pk, am) and won(ad, pk, am) for another bid with $am \neq am_p$.*

Non-repudiation. If it is possible that a bidder would win without submitting the winning bid, she could try to claim that she did not submit the winning bid even in a case where she rightfully won. To ensure Non-repudiation, a bidder who submitted a bid must not be able to argue that she did not submit it.

Theorem 3. *Auctionity ensures* Non-repudiation (NR) *if for every auction on every possible execution trace the event won(ad, pk, am) is preceded by a corresponding event bid(ad, pk, am).*

3.3   Verifiability

Verifiability is one of the key properties for Auctionity, as each participant needs to trust that the system operates correctly. Verifiability can be Individual or Universal.

Individual Verifiability: This property establishes that, for any received bid, the bidder needs to be able to verify the correctness of her bid outcome to rejection or acceptance. In short, any bidder needs to be able to verify that the bid she sent counts correctly for the result.

Theorem 4. *Auctionity ensures* Individual Verifiability *if for any bidReceived (pk_B, am_B), the bidder B can verify the correctness of her bid outcome to bidRejected(pk_B, am_B) or bidAccepted(pk_B, am_B).*

Universal Verifiability: This property defined in [9] establishes that any observer may verify that the result of an auction is correct, with the public information available. The property can be divided into Integrity Verifiability and Outcome Verifiability.

To ensure Integrity Verifiability, anyone needs to be able to verify that all the accepted bids satisfied the validation criteria by the time the transaction containing it was mined and that the winning bid is one of the accepted bids.

Outcome Verifiability depends on the different participants:

- For a loosing bidder, she needs to verify that her bid was inferior to the winning bid, and that the winning bid was sent by another bidder.
- For the winner, she needs to verify that she actually submitted the winning bid, that the winning amount is correctly computed, that all other bids originated from bidders, and that no bid was modified.
- For the seller, she needs to verify that the winning amount is actually the highest submitted bid and the announced winner is correct.

Theorem 5. *Auctionity ensures* Universal Verifiability *if there exist Verification Tests* IV_b, IV_w, OV_l, OV_w, OV_s *respecting the following soundness conditions:*

1. *Integrity Verifiability (IV):*
   - *Anyone can verify that all the accepted bids are valid.*
   $IV_b = true \Rightarrow \forall accBids(pk_B, am_B):$
   - Sig_{sk_B} *matches* ad_B,
   - $ts_{start} \leq ts_{cur} \leq ts_{end}$,
   - $pk_B \neq pk_S$,
   - $am_B > am_{min}$ *OR* $am_B >$ *previous* am_L,
   - $de_B \geq am_B$,
   $IV_w = true \Rightarrow winBid \in bidAccepted(L)$
2. *Outcome Verifiability (OV):*
   - *A loosing bidder can verify that her bid was not the winning bid:*
   $OV_l = true \Rightarrow myBid \neq win(getAmount(L))$.
   - *A winning bidder can verify that her bid was the winning bid:*
   $OV_w = true \Rightarrow myBid = win(getAmount(L))$.
   - *The seller can verify that the winning bid is actually the highest submitted bid:*
   $OV_s = true \Rightarrow winBid = win(getAmount(L))$.

   as well as the following completeness condition:

- *If all participants follow the protocol correctly, the above tests succeed (i.e., the implications hold in the opposite direction,* $(\Leftarrow$, *as well).*
  where - with abuse of notation - getAmount(L) is written for getAmount(L[1]), ..., getAmount(L[n]).

Informally, we have that:

- Any bidder can verify that her bid was accepted by checking the event emitted by Auction to which the bid was made. An accepted bid triggers an event *bidAccepted* and updates the pk_L and the am_L variables.
- Loosing bidders: any loosing bidder can verify that the winning bid is superior to her bid, as both bids are publicly available on the blockchain. Also, she can be convinced that the winning bid was submitted by another bidder due to the message signature registered as part of the bid transaction on the blockchain.

- Winning bidder: the winner can check that she submitted the winning bid, as well as the bid amount correctness, by verifying if the signature of the bid transaction hash was signed with her secret key. Besides, she can verify that all the other bids were originated by real users, by checking their signature and that they lost, by checking their amount. It is also possible to verify that the seller did not bid, or at least, that her public key is not linked to any bid because if it is, the `Auction` rejects the bid and registers it as an event.
- A seller can create another public key in order to bid in her own auction and it can not be prevented, which is the same for any online auction protocol where the seller can create different accounts or even to physical auctions, to which the seller can send someone else to bid on her behalf aiming to raise the final amount. To prevent this, the payment guarantee discourages the seller to apply this tactic. Even if the money will come back to her public key in the case she wins, she will still have her money blocked for some time plus the cost on ELNET for deposit and withdraw operations.
- Seller: the seller is interested in verifying that the winner's public key and the final amount are correct. In order to do that, she can see all the history of bids made to her `Auction` to check that the highest amount is the final amount and that the winner is the public key linked to this highest amount bid.

3.4   Validity

Auctionity is based in two blockchain networks: ACNET and ELNET. They do not have a direct communication channel and use the Oracle to exchange information. Validity proofs of the content issued by the Oracle are covered by the two following properties.

Auction End Voucher Validity. As ELNET is not aware of the transactions processed on ACNET, the AEV_S is used to carry relevant information of the auctions to ELNET. So, to ensure that this information is valid, the property of Auction End Voucher Validity establishes that, for any AEV_S submitted on ELNET, the contents of the AEV_S need to be enough to prove to the Deposit SC that the winner pk_W and the amount of her winning bid am_W correspond to a bid signed by W to the `Auction` instance to which the AEV_S was issued.

Theorem 6. *Auctionity ensures* Auction End Voucher Validity *if for any Auction End Voucher submitted on ELNET:*

- *The issuance of the AEV was made after the end time of the corresponding auction:* $(ev_t) = true \Rightarrow ts_{end} < ts_{AEV}$.
- *The seller's public key corresponds to the public key that created the auction:* $(ev_a) = true \Rightarrow pk_S =$ *creator of* $AEV(ad_{SC})$.
- *The winner's public key and the amount of its winning bid are equal to the ones on the* `Auction` : $(ev_w) = true \Rightarrow won(pk, am) = AEV(won(pk, am))$.

Table 2. Transaction cost of SC function calls in gas.

Protocol	Net	Function and Caller	Payer		
			ACNET	ELNET	
			Auctionity	Bidder	Seller
Create auction	Ω	Deploy A by S	2,870,670	0	0
Close auction	Ω	**close** by O	55,950	0	0
	Ω	**set** by O	196,777	0	0
	Γ	**submit** by S	0	0	112,921
Bid	Γ	**deposit** by B	0	85,476	0
	Γ	another **deposit** by same B	0	30,421	0
	Ω	**add** by O	107,839	0	0
	Ω	1st **bid** by 1st B	167,672	0	0
	Ω	1st **bid** by another B	136,081	0	0
	Ω	another **bid** by 1st B	80,464	0	0
	Ω	another **bid** by another B	67,994	0	0
Withdrawal	Ω	**withdraw** by any B	30,160	0	0
	Ω	**add** by O	247,071	0	0
	Γ	**submit** by any B	0	111,736	0

Withdrawal Voucher Validity. As ELNET is not aware of the transactions processed on ACNET, the WV_B is also used to carry information to ELNET, in this case, the withdrawal requests. So, to ensure that this information is valid, the property of Withdrawal Voucher Validity establishes that for any Withdrawal Voucher submitted on ELNET, the contents of the WV_B are enough to prove to the Deposit that the bidder's public key corresponds to the public key that signed the Withdrawal Voucher request and this request is of the same amount as the one contained in the WV_B.

Theorem 7. *Auctionity ensures* Withdrawal Voucher Authenticity *if for any Withdrawal Voucher submitted on ELNET:*

- *The bidder's public key corresponds to the public key that signed the Withdrawal Voucher request.* $(wv_a) = true \Rightarrow pk_B = pk_{(withdrawal\|z\|Sig_B)}$
- *The bidder public key has the same value withdrawn in both ELNET and ACNET after the application of the Withdrawal Voucher.* $(wv_v) = true \Rightarrow (\Gamma\ deposits.am_B - am_{WV}) = \Omega\ deposits.am_B$

4   Experimental Results

The four protocols of Auctionity were tested over a period of 6 months. We describe how the gas is used in Auctionity, what is the block time duration and some statistics of this experiment.

Table 3. Protocols and properties (properties in bold proven with ProVerif).

Protocol	Properties
Create auction	–
Bid	**HPW, NC, NR**, IV, UV
End auction	AEV validity
Withdraw deposit	WV validity

Gas cost: Gas is a term used in Ethereum network to denote a fee for computations on the EVM. Its complete usage and calculation is presented in the Ethereum Yellow Paper [21]. The cost of each action, measured with the Geth function eth_estimateGas, is shown in Table 2. B_1 is the first bidder to bid on an auction and B_n is any other bidder.

In the Auctionity system, users only pay for actions that take place on ELNET, which means, deposits and withdrawals. The *gasPrice* depends of the usage of ELNET. *transactionCost = gasUsed * (gasPrice * 1 Gwei)*[10].

Also, in order to accept a large number of transactions on each block, the ACNET block gas limit is 4,503,599,627,370,496 while the ELNET block gas limit is about 8,000,000.

Block Time: The time period between 2 blocks is 1 s on ACNET and 14 s on ELNET. The Oracle waits 10 blocks to confirm a deposit made on ELNET, following the proof made by Buterin [5]. Therefore, a deposit takes place in 140 s after being included in a block. A user can bid as many times as she wants, as long as she has a sufficient deposit amount for the bids she wants to submit. Considering that the deposit can be withdrawn at any time, and in order to avoid having to wait the deposit validation time before bidding, it is expected of bidders to deposit a sufficient amount for the auctions they intend to participate in and withdraw it whenever needed.

Statistics: Firstly, we have tested, with some automated scripts, all protocols and their chronological auction sequence: Create Auction Protocol, Bid Protocols and Close Auction Protocol. These scripts were also used to estimate the growing load of Auctionity blockchain. The following data includes the different script tests, and some real human behaviours using the Auctionity website. This represents a total of 462 users for all auctions. The users sent 38,000 deposits on ELNET and got back 35,000 withdraws on ACNET. The difference can be explained by the fact that a user can deposit 4 ETH and after 6 ETH, which makes two deposits, and later withdraw 10 ETH at once, which makes only one withdraw. They have also created 23,000 auctions, and the same number of closed auctions. The average auction duration was of 5 days and the maximum auction duration was of 21 days. The total number of bids was equal to 144,000 and the number of auctions with no bids was equal to 377.

---

[10] GWei is equal to 10^9 Wei and 10^{-9} Ether.

5   Conclusion

In this paper we presented Auctionity, our English auction protocol based on the blockchain. We presented the details of the protocols used, defined security models and properties that Auctionity should satisfy and provide a formal analysis and experimental results. The protocols and their properties are summerized in Table 3.

Further developments will be made to improve decentralization of the Oracle and sidechain while keeping or improving throughput, and allowing usage of tokens from other blockchains than Ethereum.

References

1. Bashir, I.: Mastering Blockchain: Distributed Ledger Technology, Decentralization, and Smart Contracts Explained. Packt Publishing Ltd., Birmingham (2018)
2. Blanchet, B., Smyth, B., Cheval, V., Sylvestre, M.: ProVerif 2.00: automatic cryptographic protocol verifier, user manual and tutorial (2018)
3. Blass, E.-O., Kerschbaum, F.: Strain: a secure auction for blockchains. In: Lopez, J., Zhou, J., Soriano, M. (eds.) ESORICS 2018. LNCS, vol. 11098, pp. 87–110. Springer, Cham (2018). https://doi.org/10.1007/978-3-319-99073-6_5
4. Brandt, F.: How to obtain full privacy in auctions. Int. J. Inf. Secur. **5**, 201–216 (2006). https://doi.org/10.1007/s10207-006-0001-y
5. Buterin, V.: On slow and fast block times, July 2015
6. Curtis, B., Pieprzyk, J., Seruga, J.: An efficient eAuction protocol. In: ARES, pp. 417–421. IEEE Computer Society (2007)
7. Dreier, J., Dumas, J., Lafourcade, P.: Brandt's fully private auction protocol revisited. J. Comput. Secur. **23**(5), 587–610 (2015)
8. Dreier, J., Jonker, H., Lafourcade, P.: Defining verifiability in e-auction protocols. In: Proceedings of the 8th ACM SIGSAC Symposium on Information, Computer and Communications Security (ASIA CCS 2013) (2013)
9. Dreier, J., Lafourcade, P., Lakhnech, Y.: Formal verification of e-Auction protocols. In: Basin, D., Mitchell, J.C. (eds.) POST 2013. LNCS, vol. 7796, pp. 247–266. Springer, Heidelberg (2013). https://doi.org/10.1007/978-3-642-36830-1_13
10. eBay: Our company webpage, July 2018
11. Johnson, D., Menezes, A., Vanstone, S.: The elliptic curve digital signature algorithm (ECDSA). Int. J. Inf. Secur. **1**(1), 36–63 (2001). https://doi.org/10.1007/s102070100002
12. Juels, A., Szydlo, M.: A two-server, sealed-bid auction protocol. In: Blaze, M. (ed.) FC 2002. LNCS, vol. 2357, pp. 72–86. Springer, Heidelberg (2003). https://doi.org/10.1007/3-540-36504-4_6
13. Krishna, V.: Auction Theory. Academic Press, Cambridge (2009)
14. Lafourcade, P., Picot, J., Pizzuti, D., Nopere, M., Roudeix, E.: Formal definition of the auctionity protocol and its security properties. Technical report, LIMOS (2018). http://sancy.univ-bpclermont.fr/~lafourcade/technical.pdf
15. Lafourcade, P., Picot, J., Pizzuti, D., Nopere, M., Roudeix, E.: http://sancy.univ-bpclermont.fr/~lafourcade/auctionity.tar (2019)
16. Nakamoto, S.: Bitcoin: A Peer-to-Peer Electronic Cash System (2009)
17. Naor, M., Pinkas, B., Sumner, R.: Privacy preserving auctions and mechanism design. In: ACM Conference on Electronic Commerce, pp. 129–139 (1999)

18. Omote, K., Miyaji, A.: A practical english auction with one-time registration. In: Varadharajan, V., Mu, Y. (eds.) ACISP 2001. LNCS, vol. 2119, pp. 221–234. Springer, Heidelberg (2001). https://doi.org/10.1007/3-540-47719-5_19
19. Peng, K., Boyd, C., Dawson, E., Viswanathan, K.: Robust, privacy protecting and publicly verifiable sealed-bid auction. In: Deng, R., Bao, F., Zhou, J., Qing, S. (eds.) ICICS 2002. LNCS, vol. 2513, pp. 147–159. Springer, Heidelberg (2002). https://doi.org/10.1007/3-540-36159-6_13
20. Sako, K.: An auction protocol which hides bids of losers. In: Imai, H., Zheng, Y. (eds.) PKC 2000. LNCS, vol. 1751, pp. 422–432. Springer, Heidelberg (2000). https://doi.org/10.1007/978-3-540-46588-1_28
21. Wood, G.: Ethereum: a secure decentralised genereralised transaction ledger (2018)

Dynamic Searchable Encryption with Access Control

Johannes Blömer and Nils Löken[✉]

Paderborn University, Paderborn, Germany
{johannes.bloemer,nils.loeken}@uni-paderborn.de

Abstract. We present a searchable encryption scheme for dynamic document collections in a multi-user scenario. Our scheme features fine-grained access control to search results, as well as access control to operations such as adding documents to the document collection, or changing individual documents. The scheme features verifiability of search results. Our scheme also satisfies the forward privacy notion crucial for the security of dynamic searchable encryption schemes.

1 Introduction

Searchable encryption [16] allows users to remotely store their data in an encrypted fashion without losing the ability to search their data efficiently. Particularly, the data can be searched while it resides in the cloud without revealing plaintexts to the cloud. Many searchable encryption schemes with various properties have been proposed. There are single-user schemes, as well as those that allow multiple users, either on the data creation or on the data usage side, or both. Some schemes allow updates to the searchable document collection, or allow for users to verify the correctness of search results. Some multi-user schemes feature access control, so users can only find documents in search results that they are allowed to access. Other multi-user schemes include all relevant documents in a search result, ignoring access restrictions to documents.

Despite the many proposed features, searchable encryption schemes rarely implement more than one or two features. Due to specialized constructions, it is also hard to combine features into a single scheme in a straightforward and provably secure manner.

We construct a searchable encryption scheme that allows for many users with a multitude of different access rights to jointly maintain and update a remotely stored document collection. The collection is searched remotely, and users can verify the correctness of search results. Both, the search and the update processes, respect users' access rights. The server that stores the document collection neither learns the documents it stores, nor what users search for.

This work was supported by the Ministry of Culture and Science of the German State of North Rhine-Westphalia within the research program "Digital Future."
The full version of this paper is available from the IACR e-print archive [4].

© Springer Nature Switzerland AG 2020
A. Benzekri et al. (Eds.): FPS 2019, LNCS 12056, pp. 308–324, 2020.
https://doi.org/10.1007/978-3-030-45371-8_19

Related Work. Research on searchable encryption started with the seminal paper of Song et al. [16]. Since then, various flavors of searchable encryption have emerged; see the survey encryption by Bösch et al. [6] for an overview.

One focus of research is on searchable symmetric symmetric (SSE), heavily influenced by Curtmola et al. [9]. SSE mainly addresses the single-user setting, although multi-user SSE has been constructed from single-user SSE by replacing symmetric encryption by broadcast encryption [9] or attribute-based encryption [11]. The main advantage of SSE is its efficiency, which stems from the use of symmetric primitives, as well as elaborate index data structures.

An alternative to SSE is public key encryption with keyword search (PEKS), introduced by Boneh et al. [5], which allows multiple sources to produce ciphertexts that only a designated user can search. In the multi-source setting, maintaining efficient search structures is hard. Therefore, typical PEKS schemes create tags for each keyword that a document contains and append these tags to the document ciphertext. For search, each tag is checked against the search query. The simplicity of this approach allows for easy additions of documents to the searchable document collection at the cost of an inefficient search procedure (in comparison to SSE schemes). Variants of PEKS include attribute-based encryption with keyword search [18,21]. In [21], the tag-based approach is made verifiable, but the necessary data structures make the document collection static.

Dynamics in document collections have been identified as a threat in searchable encryption [20], with file injection attacks being the main concern. Such attacks exploit the possibility to apply old search queries to new documents. Forward privacy prevents new documents from being found via old queries [17], and forward private SSE schemes have been proposed in the literature [7,10].

In the multi-user setting, searchable encryption schemes enforce varying degrees of fine-grained access control to data and search results. This is achieved through data structures [1] or attribute-based encryption (see above). Typically, only read access to data is considered, whereas write access is ignored [3].

Our Contribution. We propose *dynamic multi-user* searchable encryption with *verifiable search results.* Our scheme provides *fine-grained* read and write access, and the remotely stored searchable documents can be updated in a *forward private* way. The nevoelty of our research lies in the *combination of properties into a single scheme.* Our scheme is secure in the random oracle model.

Paper Organization. In Sect. 2, we discuss our model and techniques for dynamic searchable encryption with access control. In Sect. 3, we define dynamic searchable encryption with access control, its security, and building blocks. In Sect. 4, we present our searchable encryption scheme; we focus on verifiability of search results, and outline how to achieve the other properties.

2   Our Approach to Searchable Encryption

Here, we describe our model for searchable encryption, explain some of the primitive's functional properties, and give ideas on how to implement them.

2.1   Our Scenario

We construct a searchable encryption scheme in a multi-user setting, so users can search a common document collection for arbitrary keywords, or rather, the parts of the collection the respective users have access to. Our construction also allows users to add to the searchable document collection, and s with read access, write access must obey fine-grained access control, which comes in two flavors: write access to documents and ownership, i.e. write access to write access policies. Our construction prevents the removal of documents from the document collection, including overriding documents through modification, so malicious users are unable to permanently damage the collection by deleting documents.

We illustrate the above points in an example that we use throughout this paper. This includes a shorthand notation for access rights. An entry of an (unprocessed) document collection is a 5-tuple $(d{:}v, \mathrm{r{:}A_{read}}, \mathrm{w{:}A_{write}}, \mathrm{o{:}A_{own}}, KW)$, meaning that the tuple represents the v-th version of document d, the document has read, write, and access policies $\mathrm{A_{read}}, \mathrm{A_{write}}, \mathrm{A_{own}}$, respectively, and contains keywords KW. We have users Alice, Bob, and Charly with access rights $\{a\}$, $\{b\}$, and $\{b,c\}$, respectively. Our document collection is $\{(d_1{:}1, \mathrm{r{:}}\{b\}, \mathrm{w{:}}\{a\}, \mathrm{o{:}}\{b\}, \{w_1, w_2\}), (d_2{:}1, \mathrm{r{:}}\{b\}, \mathrm{w{:}}\{b\}, \mathrm{o{:}}\{c\}, \{w_1\})\}$. Here, access policies are given as sets of attributes that users need to hold in order to gain access to the data.

Suppose Alice's search for keyword w_2 results in document d_1, despite Alice being disallowed from accessing d_1, so Alice would have learnt some of the document's contents. Such information gain must be prevented by considering access rights during search. Next, consider Alice updating the existing document collection by adding tuple $(d_1{:}2, \mathrm{r{:}}\{c\}, \mathrm{w{:}}\{a\}, \mathrm{o{:}}\{b\}, \{w_1, w_3\})$, i.e. a new version of document d_1. Alice is capable of adding this tuple, because her access rights satisfy the write policy of the document's previous version. Due to a lack of access rights, Bob and Charly are incapable of performing this particular update. However, while Alice can change the document's read policy, she cannot change its write or ownership policies, because her access rights do not satisfy the document's ownership policy. Charly's access rights allow him to change the document's write policy; this, however, cannot be exploited to obtain read access, because the modified write policy only affects future document versions. Since we keep old documents after updates, document version $d_1{:}1$ is still present in the document collection after Alice has performed her update.

Alongside access control, we make search results verifiable, so users can check that the server that stores the document collection and performs search on user's behalf has performed search properly. This necessitates users to keep a state.

Our scheme considers the effects of malicious users, particularly, their ability to cause a protocol abiding server to observe malformed data that the server cannot handle. We tackle this issue by introducing conflict resolution, a means by which the server can use to blame a user's malicious actions on the user. A trusted party, called judge, checks the server's claims of a user's wrongdoing, issuing notifications that enable users to distinguish whether the server was unwilling or unable to perform the operation properly. Users need to enroll in our system, so the judge can distinguish the server's actions from users' actions.

Many of these aspects are captured by Löken's security model [12]. However, we need to adapt this model to the dynamic setting. The model allows for attacks that no adversary can reasonably perform if it only controls either the server or corrupt users, because the adversary lacks the option to combine knowledge.

For notational purposes, we group together all data stored by the server, i.e. the searchable document collection and auxiliary data structures, and denote it as the server's state, which needs to be initialized by an enrolled user. For updates to the document collection, we adopt the notion of batch updates, i.e. users submit new and updated documents in batches, rather than individually.

2.2   Our Techniques

Our construction of dynamic searchable encryption with access control relies on Löken's SEAC scheme [12], which provides searchable encryption with access control for static document collections. That is, SEAC does not permit updates to the document collection and, thus, does not handle versions and write access. Instead, the searchable collection is set up once and for all by an honest party, so SEAC does not provide means of conflict resolution. It also lacks verifiability of search results. We, thus, improve upon SEAC by achieving multi-writer document collection dynamics, forward privacy, verifiability, and fine-grained write access.

We achieve document collection dynamics by maintaining multiple SEAC collections, one for each batch update. Since these collections are static, users, during the update procedure, sign all (pre-computed) search results from the update, as there is one pre-computed result per keyword–(read) access policy pair from the batch. During search, some of the pre-computed results are recovered to form the overall search result. Signatures on pre-computed results are used in conflict resolution to blame malicious updates on the respective user, but also allow (other) users to verify the correctness of search results on a per-batch basis.

We use authenticated dictionaries to enable users to check that they have received all batch-specific results for the keyword they search for. These checks are performed relative to a digest of the data structure that is stored as part of the users' states. Additional authenticated dictionaries are used for managing document versions and fine-grained write access in a verifiable manner.

3   Formalism and Building Blocks

In this section, we discuss dynamic searchable encryption with access control and the primitives we use to construct it.

3.1   Dynamic Searchable Encryption with Access Control

Our searchable encryption primitive features two main operations: searching and updating a document collection. Additionally, we have some helper operations: system setup, user enrollment, server initialization, and conflict resolution.

Definition 1. *A dynamic searchable encryption scheme with access control consists of six (interactive) protocols that involve five types of parties: users, a server, a key issuer, a judge, and a party for system setup.*

Setup   *takes in security parameter* 1^Λ *and outputs public key PK, secret key MSK for the key issuer, and secret key JSK for the judge. This algorithm is executed by a* trusted party.

UserJoin   *involves a* prospective user *and the* key issuer. *Both parties take in PK; the user also takes in her desired attribute set U; the key issuer also takes in MSK and set CL of all user certificates. The key issuer outputs an updated set of user certificates; the user outputs state* st_{uid} *and secret key* usk_{uid}.

Init   *involves an enrolled user uid and the* server. *Both parties take in PK and CL; the user additionally takes in* usk_{uid} *and* st_{uid}; *the server additionally takes in its state* st_{server}. *Both parties outputs their updated states.*

Update   *involves a user uid and the* server. *Both parties take in PK and CL; the user additionally takes in* usk_{uid}, st_{uid} *and a batch B of documents;[1] the server additionally takes in state* st_{server}. *The server may reject the update. Both parties output their updated states.*

Search   *involves a user uid and the* server. *Both parties take in PK and CL; the user also takes in* usk_{uid}, st_{uid} *and a keyword kw; the server also takes in* st_{server}. *The server may reject the search request. Both parties output their updated states; the user also outputs search result X.*

Resolve   *involves the* server *and the* judge. *Both parties take in PK and CL; the server additionally takes in* st_{server}; *the judge takes in JSK. The server outputs an updated state; the judge may output one or more notifications.*

For every properly set up system, joined user uid, and initialized server, for every document doc from a document batch B used in any **Update** *not rejected by the server, for every keyword kw: upon executing non-rejected* **Search** *for kw on behalf of uid resulting in output X, (1) kw* $\notin$ *doc, or (2) kw* $\in$ *doc, but doc's read policy is not satisfied by uid's attributes, or (3) doc* $\in$ *X, or (4) there is a notification from an execution of the* **Resolve** *protocol on doc's document batch.*

Correctness requires search results to contain all documents that contain the searched keyword, unless the document is inaccessible to the user on whose behalf search is performed, or stems from a certifiably malicious update.

For security, we consider the notions of *verifiability, fork-consistency, forward privacy,* and *data confidentiality*. Verifiability ensures that correctness holds in the presence of malicious entities; the notion assumes a linear history of updates, captured by fork consistency. Intuitively [8], fork consistency means that if a fork occurs, honest users can only ever observe updates that occur on one of the forks, which implies that forks cannot be merged using reasonable amounts of resources. Forward privacy means that the server is unable to determine whether a new document (batch) contains any given keyword, even if that keyword has

---

[1] A set of tuples as in Sect. 2.1.

Real$_{\Pi,\mathcal{A}}(\Lambda)$:

Setup: run $(PK, MSK, JSK) \leftarrow \mathsf{Setup}(1^\Lambda)$ and give PK to adversary $\mathcal{A}$.

Queries: adversary $\mathcal{A}$ adaptively queries oracles $\mathcal{O}_{HJ}(U)$, $\mathcal{O}_{CJ}()$, $\mathcal{O}_{UC}(uid)$, $\mathcal{O}_{Ini}(uid)$, $\mathcal{O}_{Upd}(uid,B)$, $\mathcal{O}_{Sea}(uid,kw)$, and $\mathcal{O}_{Res}()$, where U is a set of attributes, uid is a user identifier, B is a batch of documents, and kw is a keyword. $\mathcal{A}$ can only use user identifiers uid that are part of results to previous calls to either oracle $\mathcal{O}_{HJ}$ or oracle $\mathcal{O}_{CJ}$. A user identifier uid output as part of a result to a call to oracle $\mathcal{O}_{CJ}$ or used as input to oracle $\mathcal{O}_{UC}$ is marked as corrupt; a corrupt uid cannot be used as input to any oracle call. Oracle $\mathcal{O}_{Ini}$ can be called at most once.

Responses: Upon query

$\mathcal{O}_{HJ}(U)$, run protocol UserJoin, playing both the user and the key issuer, with inputs (PK,U) and (PK,MSK), respectively; remember the user's outputs usk_{uid} and st_{uid} for future use, where uid is as in the certificate (uid,uvk_{uid}) published by the key issuer.

$\mathcal{O}_{CJ}()$, play the key issuer's part of UserJoin with input (PK,MSK).

$\mathcal{O}_{UC}(uid)$, output previously generated user key usk_{uid} and user state st_{uid}.

$\mathcal{O}_{Ini}(uid)$, play the user's part of Init on input

$(PK,CL,usk_{uid},st_{uid})$; store user state st'_{uid}.

$\mathcal{O}_{Upd}(uid,B)$, on input $(PK, CL, usk_{uid}, st_{uid}, B)$, play the user's part of protocol Update; store user state st'_{uid}.

$\mathcal{O}_{Sea}(uid,kw)$, on input $(PK, CL, usk_{uid}, st_{uid}, kw)$, play the user's part of protocol Search; store user state st'_{uid}.

$\mathcal{O}_{Res}()$, play the judge's part of protocol Resolve with input (PK,CL,JSK).

Whenever applicable, $\mathcal{A}$ plays server's or corrupt user's part in oracle interactions. Oracle queries that take a user identifier as input are ignored, if the respective identifier has not been output by a prior oracle query, or is marked as corrupt.

Guess: $\mathcal{A}$ outputs a bit that is output by the experiment.

Sim$_{\Pi,\mathcal{A},\mathcal{S}}(\Lambda)$:

Setup: run simulator $PK \leftarrow \mathcal{S}(1^\Lambda)$ and give PK to adversary $\mathcal{A}$.

Queries: $\mathcal{A}$ gets oracle access as before, and with the same restrictions on user identifiers.

Responses: Upon query $\mathcal{O}_{op}(arg)$, give leakage $\mathcal{L}_{op}(arg)$ to $\mathcal{S}$, where $op \in \{HJ,CJ,UC,Ini,Upd, Sea,Res\}$. $\mathcal{S}$ can interact with $\mathcal{A}$.

Guess: $\mathcal{A}$ outputs a bit that is output by the experiment.

Fig. 1. The data confidentiality experiment for dynamic searchable encryption

been searched for before. We maintain an informal view on verifiability, fork consistency and forward privacy in searchable encryption due to space constraints.

We take a more formal approach towards data confidentiality, i.e. what adversaries can learn from participating in searchable encryption, particularly, adversaries that fully control the server and can adaptively corrupt users We capture data confidentiality in a simulation-based experiment adapted from Löken [12]: an adversary tries to distinguish a "real world" setup from a simulated setup. If the simulator, given only leakage of the real data, is capable of simulating the system such that the adversary cannot distinguish the setups, then the adversary in the real world cannot learn more than the leakage given to the simulator.

Leakage is computed from stateful leakage functions with a shared state, i.e. the every function evaluation depends on inputs and outputs of all previous evaluations of all leakage functions. We have one leakage function for each operation observable by the adversary, as well as for user corruption. Hence, there are leakage functions for operations Init, Update, Search, and Resolve, for the enrollment of honest and corrupt users, and for the corruption of a once honest user.

In our security experiment, the adversary interacts with the system via oracles, one oracle for each of the above actions (and corresponding leakage functions). In the "real world," the experiment plays the part of all parties and has access to all arguments passed to the oracles. In the simulation, arguments of

---

Experiment Exp$_{\Pi,\mathcal{A}}^{\text{hide}}(\Lambda)$:

Setup: run $(sk,vk) \leftarrow \text{Setup}(1^\Lambda)$ and give vk to $\mathcal{A}$.

Phase I: $\mathcal{A}$ adaptively queries oracle $\text{Sign}(msg)$. Answer oracle queries by computing $(\sigma,o) \leftarrow \text{Sign}(sk,msg)$ and give σ to $\mathcal{A}$.

Challenge: $\mathcal{A}$ outputs two messages msg_0, msg_1 of equal length. Pick bit $b \leftarrow_\$ \{0,1\}$, run $(\sigma^*, o^*) \leftarrow \text{Sign}(sk, msg_b)$, and give σ^* to $\mathcal{A}$.

Phase II: same as Phase I.

Guess: $\mathcal{A}$ outputs a bit b'. Output 1 iff $b=b'$.

Fig. 2. Hiding experiment for hiding signature schemes

oracle calls are passed to the respective leakage functions and the leakage is given to the simulator. The experiment is shown in Fig. 1.

Definition 2. *A dynamic searchable encryption scheme* Pi *with access control provides data confidentiality relative to leakage functions* $\mathcal{L}_{\text{HJ}}, \mathcal{L}_{\text{CJ}}, \mathcal{L}_{\text{UC}}, \mathcal{L}_{\text{Ini}}, \mathcal{L}_{\text{Upd}}, \mathcal{L}_{\text{Sea}},$ *and* $\mathcal{L}_{\text{Res}}$ *if for every ppt adversary* $\mathcal{A}$ *there is a ppt simulator* $\mathcal{S}$ *such that* $|\Pr[\mathbf{Real}_{\text{Pi},\mathcal{A}}(\Lambda) = 1] - \Pr[\mathbf{Sim}_{\text{Pi},\mathcal{A},\mathcal{S}}(\Lambda) = 1]| \leq \text{negl}(\Lambda)$, *where the probabilities are over the random bits of* $\mathcal{A}, \mathcal{S},$ *and the experiments.*

3.2 Building Blocks

We now present the main building blocks for our construction of dynamic searchable encryption with access control.

Signatures. Our discussion of building blocks starts with signature schemes and a natural, yet unusual, security property. We want some signatures to hide the signed message until the signer decides to reveal the message by publishing an open value. At the same time, the origin of the signature should be verifiable even before the open value is published. Hence, there are two verification algorithms.

Definition 3. *A signature scheme with delayed verifiability features four algorithms* $\textsf{Setup}(1^\Lambda) \to (sk, vk)$, $\textsf{Sign}(sk, msg) \to (\sigma, o)$, $\textsf{VSig}(vk, msg, \sigma, o) \to \{0,1\}$, *and* $\textsf{VOrig}(vk, \sigma) \to \{0,1\}$, *where* σ *is the signature and* o *is the corresponding open value. We require for all messages* msg: *if* $(sk, vk) \leftarrow \textsf{Setup}(1^\Lambda)$ *and* $(\sigma, o) \leftarrow \textsf{Sign}(sk, msg)$, *then* $\textsf{VSig}(vk, msg, \sigma, o) = 1 = \textsf{VOrig}(vk, \sigma)$.

For security, we adopt the standard unforgeability notion that must hold relative to both verification algorithms. Additionally, the hiding property must hold; for the relevant experiment, see Fig. 2.

Definition 4. *A signature scheme* Pi $= (\textsf{Setup}, \textsf{Sign}, \textsf{VSig}, \textsf{VOrig})$ *with delayed verifiability is* hiding, *if for all ppt adversaries* $\mathcal{A}$ $|\Pr[\mathbf{Exp}_{\text{Pi},\mathcal{A}}^{\text{hide}}(\Lambda) - 1/2| \leq \text{negl}(\Lambda)$, *where the probability is over the random bits of* $\mathcal{A}$ *and the experiment.*

Hiding signatures with delayed verifiability can be obtained from combining standard signature schemes and commitment schemes in a commit-then-sign fashion. Signatures then consists of a commitment on the signed message and a signature (of the original scheme) on the commitment, while the open value is the commitment's decommit value.

Append-Only Authenticated Dictionaries. We commence our discussion of building blocks by reviewing append-only authenticated dictionaries (AADs). An AAD is a data structure that is stored at a server, and users can append data to the dictionary. A dictionary maps a label ℓ to a (multi-)set of values $\mathbf{v}$.[2] Initially all labels are mapped to the empty set. A user's append operation for a given label extends the (multi-)set that the label maps to. The server that stores an AAD can prove whether or not the dictionary maps any given label to a non-empty set of values. Tomescu et al. [19] propose authenticated append–only dictionaries that work as follows.

Definition 5. *An* AAD *features six ppt algorithms:*

Setup *takes in security parameter 1^Λ and capacity β. The algorithm outputs public parameters pp and verification key VK.*

Append *takes in pp, dictionary D, digest $\overline{D}$, and a label–value pair (ℓ, v). The operation fails if the data structure has reached its capacity β. Otherwise, the operation outputs an updated dictionary and corresponding digest.*

ProveMemb *takes in pp, dictionary D and label ℓ. The algorithm outputs the set $\mathbf{v} = D[\ell]$ and (non-)membership proof $\pi_{\ell,\mathbf{v}}$.*

ProveAppend *takes in pp and two versions D_i, D_j of a dictionary with version numbers $i < j$. The algorithm outputs a proof $\pi_{i,j}$ for the statement that version D_j was created from version D_i by $j - i$ many* Append *operations.*

VrfyMemb *takes in VK, digest $\overline{D_i}$ (associated with version D_i of the dictionary), label-values pair $\ell, \mathbf{v}$ and proof $\pi_{\ell,\mathbf{v}}$. The algorithm outputs a bit.*

VrfyAppend *takes in VK, two digests $\overline{D_i}, \overline{D_j}$ (associated with versions D_i, D_j of the dictionary, respectively), corresponding version numbers i, j and proof $\pi_{i,j}$. The algorithm outputs a bit.*

Servers execute the Append *and* Prove *operations, while clients execute the* Verify *operations. The* Setup *operation is performed by a trusted party. We require AADs to provide* membership correctness *(mc) and* append-only correctness *(aoc), i.e. in all correctly set up systems,*

mc: *for any non-empty sequence of* Append *operations that results in dictionary D with digest $\overline{D}$, given $\pi \leftarrow$ ProveMemb(pp, D, ℓ), we have* VrfyMemb$(VK, \overline{D}, (\ell, \mathbf{v}), \pi) = 1$.

aoc: *for any sequence of $m \geq 1$* Append *operations that results in dictionary D_m with digest $\overline{D_m}$ and any sequence of $n - m \geq 1$* Append *operations that, applied to D_m, results in dictionary D_n with digest $\overline{D_n}$, given proof $\pi \leftarrow$ ProveAppend(pp, D_m, D_n), we have* VrfyAppend$(VK, \overline{D_m}, \overline{D_n}, m, n, \pi) = 1$.

Membership correctness means that, upon call ProveMemb, the server outputs a membership proof and all values associated with a given label, and VrfyMemb accepts the proof. Append-only correctness means that for any sequence of Append operations, the server can produce a proof relating the dictionary digest from before the Append operation to the dictionary digest after

---

[2] In the data structures literature, labels are typically called keys. We prefer the term "label" as to avoid confusion with cryptographic keys.

these operations, and VrfyAppend accepts the proof. Note that this notion of authenticated dictionaries *does not use secret keys*.

For security, Tomescu et al. [19] put forth the following security notions.

Definition 6. *An AAD is* membership secure *(ms),* append-only secure *(aos), and* fork consistent *(fc), respectively, if in a properly set up system, no ppt adversary can, with probability non-negligible in Λ,*

ms: *compute* $(\overline{D}, \ell, \mathbf{v}, \mathbf{v}', \pi, \pi')$, $\mathbf{v} \neq \mathbf{v}'$, *s.t.* VrfyMemb$(VK, \overline{D}, \ell, \mathbf{v}, \pi) = 1 =$ VrfyMemb$(VK, \overline{D}, \ell, \mathbf{v}', \pi')$.

aos: *compute* $(\overline{D}_i, \overline{D}_j, i, j, \pi_a, \ell, \mathbf{v}, \mathbf{v}', \pi, \pi')$, $i < j$, $\mathbf{v} \not\subseteq \mathbf{v}'$, *s.t.* VrfyAppend$(VK, \overline{D}_i, \overline{D}_j, i, j, \pi_a) =$ VrfyMemb$(VK, \overline{D}_i, \ell, \mathbf{v}, \pi) =$ VrfyMemb $(VK, \overline{D}_j, \ell, \mathbf{v}', \pi') = 1$.

fc: *compute* $(\overline{D}_i, \overline{D}'_i, \overline{D}_j, i, j, \pi_i, \pi'_i)$, $\overline{D}_i \neq \overline{D}'_i$, *s.t.* VrfyAppend$(VK, \overline{D}_i, \overline{D}_j, i, j, \pi_i) = 1 =$ VrfyAppend$(VK, \overline{D}'_i, \overline{D}_j, i, j, \pi'_i)$.

Membership security means that it is hard to find membership proofs for distinct result sets, but the same label and dictionary digest. Append-only security means that it is hard to produce membership proofs that associate a value with a label at some point, but not at a later point. Fork-consistency means that the adversary cannot compute append-only proofs that certify a digest to be a successor digest to two distinct older digests for the same time stamp.

Attribute-Based Encryption. Ciphertext-policy [2] attribute-based [14] encryption (ABE) can be used to cryptographically enforce access control. In ABE, users hold a set of attributes, access rights, in the form of secret keys, ciphertexts are associated with access policies, and a user can decrypt a ciphertext only if her attributes satisfy the policy. Colluding users are unable to decrypt ciphertexts that neither colluding user can decrypt on her own.

Definition 7. *Formally, ABE features four ppt algorithms:*

Setup *takes in security parameter 1^Λ, and outputs public parameters pp and master secret msk.*
KeyGen *takes in pp, msk and a set U of attributes, and outputs a user key usk.*
Enc *takes in pp, access policy $\mathbb{A}$, and message msg, and outputs a ciphertext ct.*
Dec *takes in pp, usk and ct, and outputs a message msg.*

For correctness, we require in every properly set up system, for all messages msg, if the attribute set U used to generate a user key usk satisfies an access policy $\mathbb{A}$ then Dec(pp, usk, Enc(pp, $\mathbb{A}$, msg)) = msg.

For security, we adopt the standard cpa security notion for ABE; see Fig. 3 for the cpa security experiment.

Definition 8. *A ABE scheme Pi is cpa secure if for every ppt adversary $\mathcal{A}$, $|\Pr[\boldsymbol{Exp}^{\mathrm{cpa}}_{\mathrm{Pi}, \mathcal{A}}(\Lambda) = 1] - 1/2| \leq \mathsf{negl}(\Lambda)$, where the probability is over the random bits of $\mathcal{A}$ and the experiment.*

Experiment $\mathbf{Exp}^{cpa}_{\Pi,\mathcal{A}}(\Lambda)$:	two messages msg_0, msg_1 of equal length. Pick bit $b \leftarrow_\$ \{0,1\}$, run $ct^* \leftarrow Enc(pp, \mathbb{A}^*, msg_b)$ and give ct^* to $\mathcal{A}$.

Setup: run $(pp, msk) \leftarrow Setup(1^\Lambda)$ and give pp to $\mathcal{A}$.

Phase I: $\mathcal{A}$ adaptively queries oracle KeyGen$(\cdot)$. Upon query KeyGen(U): compute $usk \leftarrow$ KeyGen(pp, msk, uid, U), and give it to $\mathcal{A}$.

Challenge: $\mathcal{A}$ outputs an access policy $\mathbb{A}^*$ and

Phase II: same as Phase I.

Guess: $\mathcal{A}$ outputs a bit b'. The experiment outputs 1 if and only if (1) $b = b'$, and (2) for no query to oracle KeyGen(U), U satisfies $\mathbb{A}^*$. Otherwise, the experiment outputs 0.

Fig. 3. The cpa security experiment for ABE

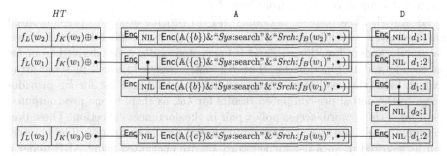

Fig. 4. An example of SEAC's search structure, using our (post-update) example document collection from Sect. 2.1, ignoring for now that SEAC does not allow for updates. We write $\mathbb{A}(\{b\})$ and $\mathbb{A}(\{c\})$ to denote an access policy that is satisfied by attribute sets $\{b\}$ and $\{c\}$, respectively; these policies are used as the D lists being pointed to group together documents with these access policies.

We also make use of the ability to derive sub-keys from user keys, i.e. keys for a subset of the attribute set used to generate the original user key. This property holds for many of the ABE schemes in the literature, e.g. [2] and [13].

SEAC. Our construction relies on SEAC [12], which we briefly review here.

Definition 9. *SEAC provides six ppt algorithms and involves three types of parties: a party for system setup and key generation, a data owner, and users. The algorithms are* $Setup(1^\Lambda) \rightarrow (pp, msk, ok)$, $KeyGen(pp, msk, uid, U_{uid}) \rightarrow usk_{uid}$, $BuildIndex(pp, ok, B) \rightarrow (Index, CT)$, $Query(pp, usk_{uid}, kw) \rightarrow t_{uid,kw}$, $Search(pp, (Index, CT), t_{uid,kw}) \rightarrow X \subseteq CT$, *and* $Dec(pp, usk_{uid}, ct) \rightarrow doc$.

SEAC ensures, in every properly set up system, that for $X \leftarrow Search(pp, Index, t_{uid,kw})$ *and all* $doc \in B$, *we have (1)* $kw \notin doc$, *(2)* U_{uid} *does not satisfy doc's access policy, or (3) there is* $ct \in X$ *such that* $Dec(pp, usk_{uid}, ct) = doc$.

Correctness of SEAC requires that the search result for keyword kw contains ciphertexts of all documents from B that are accessible to the user and contain kw. Security-wise, SEAC provides semantic security against malicious servers that collude with corrupt users. However, the security of SEAC does not translate to security of our construction, so we do not discuss SEAC's security any further.

SEAC employs access control such that only a user who can access a document may find that document in a search result. Technically, SEAC pre-computes search results, stores results in encrypted linked lists,[3] and provides access to relevant lists through a dictionary that holds an entry for each keyword from the document collection. Hence, SEAC uses a search structure similar to the one by Curtmola et al. [9]; however, SEAC's data structure incorporates access control by means of ABE. See Fig. 4 for an example index structure computed from our example document collection from Sect. 2.1.

As stated, SEAC uses a dictionary HT to provide access to pre-computed search results for each keyword. HT's entry for kw uses a label derived from kw via pseudorandom function f_L, and is encrypted under a key derived from kw via pseudorandom function f_K. The HT entry points to a cell in some array A which holds the head of an encrypted linked lists. The A list for kw provides access to the actual pre-computed results for kw, as there is one pre-computed result for each keyword–access policy pair in the document collection. These pre-computed results are stored as encrypted linked lists in an array D. The pointers to D lists stored in an A list for keyword kw are encrypted using ABE under a policy that depends on the policy shared by all documents from the D list being pointed to, the fact that the policy is used in an A list, and a term derived from the kw via pseudorandom function f_B. D lists point to document ciphertexts, that are stored in a separate data structure CT not shown in Fig. 4.

As can be seen from the above access policy for pointers to D lists, SEAC uses three classes of attributes Usr, $Srch$, and Sys. The class names are prefixes to the names of attributes from the respective class. Class Usr is used for "normal" attributes of users (e.g. role-specific attributes), $Srch$ prefixes names of keyword dependent attributes, and Sys prefixes names of attributes used to distinguish ciphertexts of pointers to D lists from document ciphertexts via attributes "Sys:search" and "Sys:read", respectively.

SEAC's user keys consist of ABE keys that represent the user's access rights (attributes of class Usr), keyword dependent attributes (from class $Srch$, derived from keywords via function f_B), attributes "Sys:search" and "Sys:read", and keys to pseudorandom functions f_L, f_K, f_B. These keys enable users to make search queries containing keyword dependent labels and decryption keys for HT, and subsets of the users' attribute-specific keys used for decrypting ABE ciphertexts from A lists. Particularly, search queries never contain attribute "Sys:read", as that attribute does not occur in A lists, but is used exclusively in document ciphertexts' policies as to prevent the server from using queries' attributes to decrypt document ciphertexts. Keyword dependent attributes in A lists prevent the server from using a query's attributes to decrypt the policies from other keywords' A lists. Pseudorandom functions hide keywords from the server.

---

[3] A linked list, symmetrically encrypted node by node with a node's decryption key being stored as part of the pointer to that node.

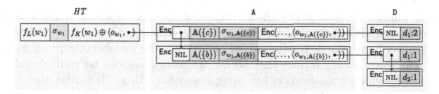

Fig. 5. Data structure changes due to verifiability, applied to the entry for keyword w_1 from Fig. 4. List authenticators on A lists and the data they authenticate are marked light gray; list authenticators on D lists and the data they authenticate are marked dark gray. As before, we write $\mathbb{A}(\{b\})$ and $\mathbb{A}(\{c\})$ to denote an access policy that is satisfied by attribute sets $\{b\}$ and $\{c\}$, respectively; these are the policies shared among documents from the two D lists being pointed to from the A list.

4   Construction

We now present our dSEAC scheme for dynamic searchable encryption with access control, implementing the ideas from Sect. 2.

4.1   Extending SEAC

We extend SEAC in four dimensions, each providing progress towards one of our goals. Our first extension provides verifiability of per-SEAC-instance search results. Creation time awareness helps in achieving forward privacy. Document and version management enables document updates and fine-grained control of (write) access to data. Conflict resolution allows recovery from malicious user's actions, admitting our construction to be used in a multi-writer setting. In dSEAC, all writers hold signing keys, and the corresponding verification keys are part of the user's certificate from certificate list *CL*.

Verifiability. For verifiability of search results, we rely on hiding signatures and AADs. We retain the search structure from SEAC (c.f. Fig. 4), and enhance it by list authenticators. As shown in Fig. 5, list authenticators authenticate data stored in lists, but ignore administrative data required for maintaining the list structure. List authenticators on D lists are hiding signatures on the set of pointers to documents from the lists, i.e. documents that share a keyword and an access policy. List authenticators on A lists are hiding signatures on the sets of lists authenticators on and access policies of D lists an A list points to. List authenticators are stored alongside pointers to the respective lists, with the corresponding open values being encrypted as part of the pointers.

With our changes, search results include (1) a membership proof for the *HT* label generated from the searched keyword, (2) the list authenticator on the A list that the keyword's *HT* entry points to (including the authenticator's open value), (3) list authenticators on and access policies of D lists that the A list points to, and (4) sets of documents being pointed to from those D lists whose access policies are satisfied by the attributes of the user on whose behalf search is performed, including open values for the list authenticators on these D lists.

For verifying search results, a user (1) verifies the membership proof from the search result, (2) verifies that all list authenticators can be verified under the same signature verification key using algorithm VOrig, (3) verifies that the list authenticator on the A list can be verified using algorithm VSig and the open value, list authenticators on and access policies of D lists, and (4) verifies that, for every access policy satisfied by the user's access rights, an open value and set of documents are contained in the search results, such that the list authenticator on the respective list can be verified using algorithm VSig.

List authenticators satisfying the hiding notion prevent adversaries from guessing the lists, and using the authenticators to confirm their guesses. The above verification steps are establish verifiability of per-SEAC-instance search results, because the AAD prevents adversaries from tampering with list authenticators on A lists, which in turn prevent adversaries from tampering with list authenticators on, and access policies and contents of D lists.

Time Awareness. In order to achieve forward privacy, labels and decryption keys for the same keyword must differ between SEAC instances; otherwise, it is easy to determine that two instances share a keyword. We also need to prevent adversaries from combining time dependent bits from one search query with time independent bits from another search query. Therefore we need to make *HT* entries *and* access policies in A lists creation time dependent. We use a combination of Bost's technique [7] and a dedicated class *Time* of attributes (c.f. SEAC's attribute classes *Usr*, *Srch*, and *Sys*) to achieve time awareness; Bost's technique applies to *HT* entries, while *Time* attributes are in employed in access policies in A list nodes. We provide a detailed discussion of time awareness, and the techniques we use to achieve it, in the full version of this paper.

Document and Version Management. We enhance SEAC by a data structure for storing documents, such that the data structure allows for fine-grained control over write access and ownership, while also keeping track of document updates. We achieve this by employing two AADs *Man* and *Dat* that hold information on documents and their access rights. AAD *Man* holds management tuples that contain information on documents' ownership and write policies. AAD *Dat* holds data tuples that contain information on documents read policies and contents.

The tuples enforce fine grained access rights through a combination of ABE and signatures; a combination inspired by the Sharoes system [15]. Since the tuples are stored in AADs, we also ensure that documents cannot be remove from the searchable document collection. We extend our discussion of document management in the full version of this paper.

Conflict Resolution. Malicious users may create SEAC instances that do not adhere to the prescribed structure, e.g. by containing pointers to non-existent

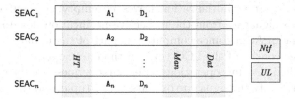

Fig. 6. Data structures when combining multiple SEAC instances into dSEAC.

data. The deviation may result in the server getting stuck during search operations. An honest server then needs a mechanism to blame the malicious action on the user responsible. Conflict resolution provides that mechanism.

Whenever the server sees a need for conflict resolution, it submits the potentially flawed SEAC instance and a description of how the flaw was found, e.g. a search query, to a judge for review. Once an investigation is over, the judge again certifies its findings. We call the judge's certificates *notifications*. Notifications certify a SEAC instances' maliciousness for the purpose of correctness of dSEAC.

In order for notifications to serve their purpose, they must state their purpose, i.e. what SEAC instance is affected; the notification must also be verifiable. Hence, notifications consist of the issuance time, the affected time (SEAC instance), and a signature on the tuple under the judge's signing key. The judge advances time by performing an update with an empty document collection once it has concluded its investigation.

4.2 Combining the Extensions: dSEAC

We now present dSEAC, our dynamic searchable encryption scheme with access control. The scheme implements the ideas laid out in Sect. 2, and combines the changes and extensions to SEAC proposed in Sect. 4.1.

Integration of SEAC Instances. Figure 6 displays the integration of SEAC instances on the data structure level. Every SEAC instance retains its separate A and D data structures, but a single dictionary HT is shared among the instances. Similarly, the SEAC instances share dictionaries Man and Dat. While the dictionaries could be static for single SEAC instances before, they now need to allow for additions of data. Since data is only ever added to these dictionaries, we implement them as AADs. dSEAC uses two more data structures UL and Ntf. The update log UL contains, for each operation that has been performed, a summary of the post-operation system state, called "last completed operation." The notification collection Ntf simply stores all notifications issued by the judge.

The last completed operation (LCO) has been adopted from Cachin and Geisler [8] and represents a post-operation system state. For that purpose, the LCO contains a time stamp t, digests dig of AADs, a summary ch of changes, a signature verification key vk, and a signature σ on the tuple. The verification key belongs to the party that performed the operation. The summary ch depends on the operation: server initialization leaves ch empty; for conflict resolution, ch is the judge's signature from the respective notification; for updates, ch is a signature on the SEAC instance computed as part of the update.

Users' states consist of the LCO tuple of the latest operation they have performed or verified. During operations, users first request the latest LCO tuple from the server, verify the signature on the server's tuple, and then ask the server to provide append–only proofs for the digests contained in the users' and the server's LCO tuples. If the server's append–only proofs can be verified successfully, users adopt the server's tuple as their own. When performing updates, users compute their new LCO tuples from information obtained during the operation.

Protocols of dSEAC. We now give an overview of dSEAC's protocols.

Setup The setup party computes SEAC and AAD keys, and signing keys for the judge and the key issuer, publishes all public and verification keys, and hands over secret keys to the key issuer and the judge.

UserJoin The user picks her signing key and gets it certified by the key issuer. The key issuer computes the user's SEAC key and gives it to the user.

Init The user creates an initial LCO tuple and stores it alongside empty data structures at the server. The user stores the LCO tuple as her state.

Update The user obtains and verifies the current LCO tuple from the server as outlined above, computes a new SEAC instance, and computes a new LCO tuple. She adopts the LCO tuple as her new state and sends the computed data to the server, which adopts the received data into its state.

Search The user obtains and verifies the current LCO tuple from the server as outlined above, computes a SEAC search query, and sends it to the server. The server applies the query to each SEAC instance and sends the per-instance results, including necessary proofs, to the user. The user verifies the response relative to her LCO tuple and relevant public keys, and finally outputs document plaintexts computed from the received results.

Resolve The server sends the flawed SEAC instance, the search query that lead to the flaw's detection, and the current LCO tuple to the judge. The judge investigates the received data and issues notifications as outlined above, and finally computes a new LCO tuple that is sent to the server. The server adopts received notifications and the LCO tuple into its state.

Correctness, Efficiency, and Security. The outlined protocols can be realized in ways similar to other constructions of searchable encryption schemes that use encrypted linked lists, e.g. [9,12]. Due to these similarities and our use of notifications, it is clear that dSEAC can be realized so it satisfies the correctness notion for dynamic searchable encryption with access control.

The efficiency of dSEAC heavily depends on the number of keyword–(read) policy pairs, both in terms of storage and computation. If the number of such pairs is high, the number of ABE decryptions during search is high on the server's side, and users need to perform a high number of signature verifications on precomputed search results. Likewise, during updates, those ABE ciphertexts and list authenticators need to be computed.

Theorem 1 (informal). *dSEAC provides data confidentiality (in the random oracle model), and is fork consistent, verifiable, and forward private.*

The proofs can be found in the full version of this paper [4].

References

1. Alderman, J., Martin, K.M., Renwick, S.L.: Multi-level access in searchable symmetric encryption. In: Brenner, M., et al. (eds.) FC 2017. LNCS, vol. 10323, pp. 35–52. Springer, Cham (2017). https://doi.org/10.1007/978-3-319-70278-0_3
2. Bethencourt, J., Sahai, A., Waters, B.: Ciphertext-policy attribute-based encryption. In: S&P 2007, pp. 321–334. IEEE (2007)
3. Blömer, J., Löken, N.: Cloud architectures for searchable encryption. In: ARES 2018, pp. 25:1–25:10. ACM (2018)
4. Blömer, J., Löken, N.: Dynamic searchable encryption with access control. IACR Cryptology ePrint Archive 2019/1038 (2019)
5. Boneh, D., Di Crescenzo, G., Ostrovsky, R., Persiano, G.: Public key encryption with keyword search. In: Cachin, C., Camenisch, J.L. (eds.) EUROCRYPT 2004. LNCS, vol. 3027, pp. 506–522. Springer, Heidelberg (2004). https://doi.org/10.1007/978-3-540-24676-3_30
6. Bösch, C., Hartel, P.H., Jonker, W., Peter, A.: A survey of provably secure searchable encryption. ACM Comput. Surv. **47**(2), 18:1–18:51 (2014)
7. Bost, R.: $\Sigma o\phi o\varsigma$: forward secure searchable encryption. In: CCS 2016, pp. 1143–1154. ACM (2016)
8. Cachin, C., Geisler, M.: Integrity protection for revision control. In: Abdalla, M., Pointcheval, D., Fouque, P.-A., Vergnaud, D. (eds.) ACNS 2009. LNCS, vol. 5536, pp. 382–399. Springer, Heidelberg (2009). https://doi.org/10.1007/978-3-642-01957-9_24
9. Curtmola, R., Garay, J.A., Kamara, S., Ostrovsky, R.: Searchable symmetric encryption: improved definitions and efficient constructions. J. Comput. Secur. **19**(5), 895–934 (2011)
10. Etemad, M., Küpçü, A., Papamanthou, C., Evans, D.: Efficient dynamic searchable encryption with forward privacy. PoPETs **2018**(1), 5–20 (2018)
11. Kaci, A., Bouabana-Tebibel, T.: Access control reinforcement over searchable encryption. In: IRI 2014, pp. 130–137. IEEE (2014)
12. Löken, N.: Searchable encryption with access control. In: ARES 2017, pp. 24:1–24:6. ACM (2017)
13. Rouselakis, Y., Waters, B.: Practical constructions and new proof methods for large universe attribute-based encryption. In: CCS 2013, pp. 463–474. ACM (2013)
14. Sahai, A., Waters, B.: Fuzzy identity-based encryption. In: Cramer, R. (ed.) EUROCRYPT 2005. LNCS, vol. 3494, pp. 457–473. Springer, Heidelberg (2005). https://doi.org/10.1007/11426639_27
15. Singh, A., Liu, L.: Sharoes: a data sharing platform for outsourced enterprise storage environments. In: ICDE 2008, pp. 993–1002. IEEE (2008)
16. Song, D.X., Wagner, D.A., Perrig, A.: Practical techniques for searches on encrypted data. In: S&P 2000, pp. 44–55. IEEE (2000)
17. Stefanov, E., Papamanthou, C., Shi, E.: Practical dynamic searchable encryption with small leakage. In: NDSS 2014. The Internet Society (2014)

18. Sun, W., Yu, S., Lou, W., Hou, Y.T., Li, H.: Protecting your right: verifiable attribute-based keyword search with fine-grained owner-enforced search authorization in the cloud. IEEE Trans. Parallel Distrib. Syst. **27**(4), 1187–1198 (2016)

19. Tomescu, A., Bhupatiraju, V., Papadopoulos, D., Papamanthou, C., Triandopoulos, N., Devadas, S.: Transparency logs via append-only authenticated dictionaries. IACR Cryptology ePrint Archive 2018/721 (2018)

20. Zhang, Y., Katz, J., Papamanthou, C.: All your queries are belong to us: the power of file-injection attacks on searchable encryption. In: USENIX 2016, pp. 707–720. USENIX Association (2016)

21. Zheng, Q., Xu, S., Ateniese, G.: VABKS: verifiable attribute-based keyword search over outsourced encrypted data. In: INFOCOM 2014, pp. 522–530. IEEE (2014)

Short Papers

Short Papers

Get-your-ID: Decentralized Proof of Identity

Pascal Lafourcade[1] and Marius Lombard-Platet[2,3(✉)]

[1] Université Clermont-Auvergne, LIMOS CNRS UMR 6158, Aubière, France
pascal.lafourcade@uca.fr
[2] Be-Studys, Geneva, Switzerland
[3] Département d'informatique de l'ENS,
École normale supérieure, CNRS, PSL Research University, Paris, France
marius.lombard-platet@ens.fr

Abstract. In most systems without a centralised authority, users are free to create as many accounts as they please, without any harmful effect on the system. However, in the case of e-voting, for instance, proof of identity is crucial, as sybil identities can be used to breach the intended role of the system. We explore the conditions under which a decentralised proof of identity system can exist. We also propose such a scheme, called Get-your-ID (GYID), and prove its security. Our system allows a user to generate and revoke keys, via an endorsement mechanism, and we prove that under some conditions which we discuss, no user can have more than one active key. We then show how voting protocols can be adapted on top of our system, thus ensuring that no user is able to cast a valid vote more than once.

Keywords: Identity system · Decentralized ledger · Protocol security · E-voting

1 Introduction

User account management is a long-time subject of research in computer science. In most cases, the effort is made on account security rather than account unicity: it does not matter that a user has several accounts, as long as no one else can use these accounts. However, in some applications, it is instead required that a user cannot own more than one account. Such applications include e-voting protocols, where a physical person can only vote once (or a definite number of times), and universal income protocols, such as Duniter [5].

Preventing these duplicate accounts (also called Sybil accounts) is usually done by referring to a central authority. For instance, by checking a user's ID card, issued by a central government. However, the central authority may deny people's right to get an ID card, sometimes for political or simply technical reasons. Such events have already occurred in 2017 in the Philippines[1], and in

---

[1] https://www.asiatimes.com/2017/11/article/chinese-filipina-denied-identity-card-tells-struggle/.

© Springer Nature Switzerland AG 2020
A. Benzekri et al. (Eds.): FPS 2019, LNCS 12056, pp. 327–336, 2020.
https://doi.org/10.1007/978-3-030-45371-8_20

2018 in the United States[2], for instance. In any case, the failure of the central authority to reliably deliver ID to any citizen complying with the rules means that no one, organizing an online vote (or any other application relying on unique accounts), can have perfect faith in the central authority. With a decentralised system, one can trust the honesty of the network, rather than necessarily trusting the honesty of the central user.

As a matter of fact, blockchain-based votes have already been used in real elections, in Issy-les-Moulineaux[3] (France) in August 2018, and Tsukuba[4] (Japan) in September 2018. However, details about these implementations are very sparse and do not allow for security audit. Furthermore in both cases the city hall was in charge of establishing the voters list, which is paradoxical considering that the blockchain is supposed to enhance decentralised applications: the system still relies on the trust of the city hall. As such we introduce the concept of proof of identity: a guarantee that a user only owns at most one valid identity.

Related Work: A first draft for proofs of identity has been proposed in [6], but the paper lacks any practical protocol description. A notable work is the Web of Trust, a network of peer certification that has been introduced for PGP. The concept of Web of Trust is the main idea on which relies the blockchain Duniter. However, it is possible (and easy) to obtain several distinct identities in this blockchain.

Despite these caveats, a protocol of proof of personhood has been described in [3], in which the physical existence of a user is verified. The certification process is filmed and published online for public verification. However, proof of personhood does not equate proof of identity, as one user can register several times at different parties.

Finally, the idea of storing cryptographic keys on a blockchain is by no means new, as a matter of fact, blockchain PKI has already been proposed in [1], but simply as a decentralized ledger rather than a new opportunity of building a network of trust and managing identities.

Our Approach: We propose a new way of managing identities, in which no user can own more than one non-revoked public key. For auditability reasons, the transactions are public and stored in a blockchain. In order to avoid relying on an authority for deciding who is eligible to the system, we provide a protocol in which a user must be co-opted by several other users, thus allowing a user to bypass possible censorship by a central authority. Hence we propose Get-your-ID, our novel identity management protocol. Proofs and further discussions have been removed from this technical report, and appear on the full paper version.

---

[2] https://www.aclu-nm.org/en/press-releases/groups-seek-immediate-order-stop-states-illegal-denial-non-real-id-licenses-and.

[3] http://issy.com/taxonomy/term/817/issy-les-moulineaux-va-tester-le-vote-electronique-avec-la-blockchain (in French).

[4] https://www.japantimes.co.jp/news/2018/09/02/national/politics-diplomacy/new-online-voting-system-introduced-city-tsukuba/.

Contributions: In this paper, we present several results. First, we offer a formalisation of the problem, giving a clear definition of the tools we use and a formal description of the real-life hypotheses we make. Under these hypotheses, we show that it is impossible to have a proof of identity system without members having more power than others.

Then, we place ourselves in the context where trusted members are allowed, allowing us to build a proof of identity system, in which a user can get at most one valid identity at all times. Any user can obtain a validity through an endorsement process, and for privacy, all endorsements are secret until the user decides to reveal them. In our model, each user can have the same role, i.e. no user has any privilege. We give a full description of our protocol.

Outline: In Sect. 2, we define the terms we use in the rest of the paper. We then prove that under reasonable assumptions, no verifiable decentralized proof of identity can exist. Furthermore, we exhibit a decentralized protocol of proof of identity, where as much as possible data is publicly verifiable, and we provide a security proof of the protocol. Finally, we discuss about compatibility of our protocol with voting protocols and further improvements.

2 Preliminaries

2.1 Biometric Authentication

The topic of biometric authentication has been an active field of research in the last decade. Notably, several different biometrics methods have been surveyed in [4]. From various biometric methods, we can cite DNA, iris and retina patterns, palm and fingerprints, but also more exotic methods such as facial thermogram, gait analysis or body odor.

Authors of [4] also insist on the fact that no method is perfect, and that one should choose a system with several biometric methods, in order to compensate for the deficiencies of each method. For instance, DNA authentication has a very high distinctiveness rate (only twins can reasonably produce duplicates), but its extraction is currently still costly and time-consuming. Faster methods may be, for instance, iris recognition or face recognition.

2.2 Proof of Identity Concepts

We now introduce the concept of proof of identity. The underlying idea is that any physical person is uniquely identified by a set of properties, most likely biometric properties, that is unforgeable and unique to the user. We argue in the next sections that these properties are the only ones that can be used for an identity system, and we explore the limitations around them. Proof of identity system is not an application that is designed to run for itself; rather is it designed to be the support of many other applications. We intend to build an identity repository, that other applications can use for their own purposes. Such other applications can be for instance an e-voting application, a universal income scheme, both or anything else.

Definition 1 (Essential properties). *A set of properties that uniquely define any user is called a set of essential properties. The set of essential properties of the user U is noted P_U.*

For instance, it is most probable that the DNA and fingerprints of a user uniquely define them. We call this set the **essential properties**.

Definition 2 (Digital Fingerprint). *If a user U has for essential properties P_U, then its digital fingerprint F_U is defined as $F_U = F(P_U)$ where F is a hash function[5].*

For both security and efficiency, we use the digital fingerprint rather than the essential properties. For instance, in case of DNA authentication, the data can be several gigabytes big, and also sensitive data. Moreover, errors can occur during the acquisition of biometric data. This inherent fuzziness can be lessened with several techniques described in [7]. Put together, these techniques can be incorporated in F.

For these reasons, the raw use of biometrics is neither practical nor secure. On the other hand, a hash of these data is short and does not leak any information since it is preimage resistant. Finally, users are still uniquely defined by their digital fingerprint because the hash function is collision resistant, so it is extremely unlikely that two user's essential fingerprint hashes shall collide.

3   Impossibility Theorem

We assume the following hypotheses to be true. Discussion about these hypotheses is made in the longer version of this paper:

Hypothesis 1. *The essential properties rely on physical properties that the system stores in digital memory. These physical properties can be considered as PUFs.*

Hypothesis 2. *In order to be sure that a digital fingerprint maps to a physical person, a user must compute the digital fingerprint by herself. Notably, she must acquire the biometric data herself, with a device she trusts (home made or from a trusted manufacturer). We further assume that the user must be physically next to the person in order to obtain their essential properties.*

Hypothesis 3. *The current state of the art does not allow for an acquisition of fewer than $10\,s$ on average, travel time included.*

Hypothesis 4. *A system with N users requiring at least $N \cdot t$ amount of time from each user individually is not scalable.*

---

[5] We require that it is hard to find a collision on F. In the random oracle model, this is an immediate consequence, but in more general models, we say that F is collision-resistant (see [8]).

From these hypotheses, we get the following result:

Theorem 1 (Impossibility Result). *There exists no system in which each user can verify by herself the validity of all the digital fingerprints.*

Proof. If we want the system to be fully verifiable, then any user is able to verify every other user's digital fingerprint. Given that the essential properties are physical (hypothesis 1) and that the verifying user must acquire the data by themselves (hypothesis 2). For this reason, each user will require $O(N)$ of their time for verifying each other user. Even worse, a user can be solicited for verification $O(N)$ times.

As a conclusion, in such a system, a user must dedicate $O(N)$ of their own time for being verified by other users. If the user also wants to verify other users, they must dedicate another $O(N)$ amount of time. Given hypothesis 3, this is not scalable as this amount of time grows unrealistic with N. □

For instance, assuming a system of 1,000,000 users, a verification process (according to hypothesis 4) requires 16 months of 40-h weeks purely dedicated to the verification process. The 1,000,000 value is arbitrary but represents well the number of inhabitants in a country, according to 2017 UN censuses[6,7], and as such is a relevant threshold for any nationwide system. Even though this result was quite straightforward, it leads to the following conclusion:

Corollary 1. *Scalable, decentralized and verifiable proof of identity systems do not exist.*

The next conclusion is that in a (scalable) identity system, a user must trust at least one person, which we call an authority, to operate at least some of the verifications. A system in which all users trust one person is very close to the current governmental system, where all citizen trust the government (although many people in the government have the power to issue identities). However, such a system is not perfect, as the trust is centralized: a user needs to be sure the authority will never turn malicious.

4   Get-your-ID Protocol

Even though a 'fully verifiable' solution (in which each user has a proof of the validity of the system) cannot exist, we propose a solution, that we call Get-your-ID, in which a user does not need to trust a central authority, but that allows any user to become an authority, and as importantly, in which no authority can craft a malicious identity without collusion. Moreover, as authorities may want to preserve some kind of monopoly, we provide a system in which a user may keep their endorsements secret until they decide to unveil them. Thus, no authority can prevent a user to become an authority as well.

---

[6] https://population.un.org/wpp/Download/Standard/Population/.

[7] In 2017, 158 countries out of the 195 (81%) UN member or observer countries have more than 1 million inhabitants.

Note that our protocol requires some participants to gather at the same place at a given time (for signing parties). Even though some might find this solution impractical, we remark that because a system only allowing for a single identity per user must somehow rely on the physical properties of said user, and because there is no clear possibility of securely obtaining these physical properties in an other way than a physical meeting. Hence, we argue that the signing parties are a necessary part of our protocol.

4.1   Intuition of the Protocol

A user is able to get endorsements on their identity. The endorsements are secret until disclosed by the user. After some number of endorsements, the user reveals said endorsements, which are verified by the network before being accepted as such. If they are valid, the user is granted an active identity on the system. Endorsements can only be delivered by special users, which we call authorities. An authority verifies that the user is who she claims to be (by verifying their essential properties) before handing them an endorsement. Any user can become an authority, simply by gathering some number of endorsements (this threshold being higher than the threshold to get an identity)[8]. Because authorities may want to keep their monopoly, endorsements are made secret until a user decides to reveal them. Thus, authorities have no way of knowing who is close to become an authority (thus having no incentive to deviate from the protocol).

For security reasons, endorsements are only valid when they are carried during what we call a signing party: several authorities announce they will host a party at a given place and date. A user then has to get endorsements from all (or at least some fraction f, with $f > 0.5$) of the present authorities. We require a majority of endorsements, so that dishonest authorities cannot influence the signing party, as long as they are in minority. Endorsements are recorded in public blockchain. The blockchain behaves like a list of publications. Each publication is given a unique ID by the blockchain, that can be considered as an index.

Each transaction written on the blockchain carries some new data; for simplicity, we assume that our ledger is composed of five registries. One stores announcements, another stores endorsements, another one the *active keys* of users with a valid identity, the last registry stores the *revoked keys*, the identities that have been revoked (compromise, loss...). The fifth registry stores the authority keys.

Note that the authority keys are, in our protocol, user keys with enough endorsements. Therefore, the fifth registry only contains keys that are also stored in the user registry, and is used for performance reasons: without this registry, each user would need to verify that a key is indeed an authority by checking, from the endorsement registry, if there are enough endorsements.

---

[8] This definition leads to an initialization problem: at the beginning, how can we endorse a user if there is no authority? We suppose that a given number of authorities are named as such when the blockchain is first created, in the genesis block.

4.2   Description of Get-your-ID

We use a hash function H that we consider inside the random oracle model and an existential-forgery resistant signing function Sign. Each user U possess a key-pair (sk_U, pk_U). We also use two distinct messages ENDORSE, REVOKE, and the existence of a uniform random number generator, whose outputs are more than 120 bits long, in accordance to current NIST's security recommendations [2].

The blockchain ledger is consisting of five registries[9]: an authority key registry, an active key registry, a revoked key registry, an announcement registry and an endorsement registry. Depending on the nature of the message, a user will write on either of these registries. In each of these registries, one entry will automatically be assigned a unique integer id.

Definition 3 (Authority). *An authority is a user who has been designated as an authority in the genesis block, or whose public key has been validly endorsed by at least S distinct authorities.*

As mentioned earlier, given that a user must gather some endorsements by an authority before becoming an authority themselves, some authorities must be generated during the initialisation of the blockchain (in the genesis block). When several authorities decide to gather in the same physical place at a given date and time, the event is called a **signing party**. In this signing parties, any user can receive endorsements on their public key.

Definition 4 (Endorsement). *An endorsement of a user U by an authority A_i is a claim made from A_i that they have verified U's essential properties. An endorsement of U is valid if at least a fraction f of the authorities present at the signing party has endorsed U.*

Definition 5 (Active key, Revoked key). *A public key pk is considered as active when there is an entry $(F, pk, proof)$ in the active key registry, with F a digital fingerprint, but no entry pk in the revoked key registry.[10] If pk is present in the revoked key registry, then the key is considered revoked. The key pk is linked to a user U of digital fingerprint F_U if (F_U, pk) is in the active key registry.*

Our proof of identity protocol has three main steps, namely the endorsement step, the registration step, and the revocation step.

Endorsement Step. In order to receive endorsements, a user must present herself to signing parties, where authorities will endorse the user's key.

---

[9] Registries are an abstraction that helps to separate data. It can be implemented by a 3-bits prefix on each transaction message.

[10] *proof* is a proof that the user with digital fingerprint F_U has indeed received enough endorsements on their public key pk_U. We give more details about this proof later on.

Announcement. First, any group of authorities $A_1, \ldots, A_n$ can decide to host a signing party at the place of their convenience. They broadcast their intent in the form of a message Event $= ([\mathsf{pk}_{A_1}, \ldots, \mathsf{pk}_{A_n}], place, date)$, signed by all authorities. $[\mathsf{pk}_{A_1}, \ldots, \mathsf{pk}_{A_n}]$ is the list of the authorities $A_1, \ldots, A_n$'s public keys, and *place* and *date* are indications about where and when the event will be held. The announcement, being stored in the blockchain, is assigned an id *party_id*.

Individual Endorsement. Any user can join the signing party. If a user wants to have the public part pk_U of her keypair $(\mathsf{sk}_U, \mathsf{pk}_U)$ endorsed, she proceeds as follows, for each authority A_i. Given that U and A_i are physically at the same place, we assume the existence of a confidential channel between both entities, i.e. a channel that cannot be eavesdropped or altered. Which is immediate to achieve as the user can directly interact with the authority's measurement tools.

1. U generates a random number r and sends $\mathsf{Sign}(\mathsf{sk}_U, \mathsf{pk}_U \| r)$ to A_i.
2. A_i receives $\mathsf{Sign}(\mathsf{sk}_U, \mathsf{pk}_U \| r)$, checks the validity of the signature and collects U's essential properties P_U. If the signature is incorrect, then emit an error and stop. Otherwise, A_i transforms P_U into U's fingerprint F_U.
3. A_i sends U her digital fingerprint F.
4. A_i broadcasts the endorsement $\mathsf{Sign}(\mathsf{sk}_{A_i}, party\_id \| \mathsf{ENDORSE} \| H(F_U \| \mathsf{pk}_U \| r))$.

An emitted endorsement is only accepted by the blockchain if it is emitted by an authority, and if the endorsement comes on the day of the related signing party, by one of the authorities who signed the party announcement.

Key Activation. Once a user has gathered the required number of endorsements for her key pk_U, she broadcasts her intention of activating her key. For activating her key, both following conditions must be met:

- U discloses at least T valid endorsements by at least T distinct authorities. In order for the network to determine whether the endorsements are valid or not, U must provide at least $f \cdot N$ endorsements for each signing party with N authorities.
- No active key is currently linked to U.

Disclosing an endorsement is made by announcing F_U, pk_U, r and the id of the endorsement on the blockchain. For instance, if an endorsement $E = \mathsf{Sign}(\mathsf{sk}, party\_id \| \mathsf{ENDORSE} \| H(F_U \| \mathsf{pk}_U \| r))$ for some private key sk has been broadcast during a signing party, the blockchain automatically assigns an id to the endorsement. Then U claims ownership of the endorsement by publishing $id, F_u, \mathsf{pk}_U, r$. Given that an endorsement is valid only if at least $f \cdot N$ of the N authorities hosting the signing party have indeed endorsed the same user, U has to prove ownership of at least $f \cdot N$ endorsements for each signing party-related endorsement she wishes to use.

Even though U can own several endorsed keys, only one of them can be considered valid at a given time. For this reason, before adding a new key to the valid keys registry, the network checks that no other active key is linked to F_U.

Authority Activation. Similarly, in order to become an authority, a user discloses at least T endorsements. An authority being a user, the endorsed key must be an active key.

Key Revocation. Key revocation is critical for most systems. Due to this, a user must be able to revoke their current active public key, even if they have lost the matching private key. Classical key revocation mechanisms require knowledge of the private key, as is the case in GPG, for instance. We argue that such a protocol is not suited for a wide public adoption, as most users will not generate their revocation message until too late. Given that Get-your-ID does not allow several accounts to be owned by the same user, such a mistake would be permanent. Therefore, we propose another key revocation protocol, in which the user does not need to store anything for revocation purposes.

During a signing party held by authorities $A_1, \ldots, A_n$, a user U wanting to revoke her active key pk_U will proceed as follows:

1. U computes a random number r and sends $\mathsf{REVOKE}, \mathsf{pk}_U, r$ to A_i.
2. A_i receives $\mathsf{REVOKE}, \mathsf{pk}_U, r$ and collects U's essential properties P_U, and transforms it into U's fingerprint F_U.
3. A_i publishes an endorsement of the revocation $\mathsf{Sign}(\mathsf{sk}_{A_i}, party\_id \| H(F_U \| \mathsf{pk}_U) \| \mathsf{REVOKE} \| r))$.

When U has more than R revocation endorsements, she can send a new entry to the revocation registry, consisting of their active public key, F_U, the revocation endorsement ids and the random numbers used in each endorsement, similarly as what she did for the key endorsement.

Before accepting the revocation the network checks that the key pk_U is indeed an active key, mapped to F_U and that the revocation endorsements provided by the user are valid, i.e., that these were emitted during a signing party by the organizing authorities, and that for each party at least a fraction f of the authorities have emitted a similar statement.

5 Conclusion

In this paper, we showed that even though a fully verifiable decentralized proof of identity is impossible for all practical applications, we can still achieve a proof of identity with a maximum amount of decentralization and verifiability, if we defer some of the verification to what we called authorities. We thus described Get-your-ID, a protocol in which no user can have more than one account (one active key), and we proved that voting protocols are immediately pluggable on top of our system, thus allowing an effective decentralized voting protocol.

Even though perfect prevention against sybil identities is unlikely to exist, we point several improvements that can be made on our protocol, that could be investigated in some future work.

References

1. Axon, L., Goldsmith, M.: PB-PKI: a privacy-aware blockchain-based PKI. In: SECRYPT (2017)
2. Barker, E.B., Barker, W.C., Burr, W.E., Polk, W.T., Smid, M.E.: Sp 800–57. recommendation for key management, part 1: General (revised). Technical report, Gaithersburg, MD, United States (2007)
3. Borge, M., Kokoris-Kogias, E., Jovanovic, P., Gasser, L., Gailly, N., Ford, B.: Proof-of-personhood: redemocratizing permissionless cryptocurrencies. In: 2017 IEEE European Symposium on Security and Privacy Workshops (EuroS PW), pp. 23–26, April 2017. https://doi.org/10.1109/EuroSPW.2017.46
4. Delac, K., Grgic, M.: A survey of biometric recognition methods. In: Proceedings Elmar-2004 46th International Symposium on Electronics in Marine, pp. 184–193, June 2004
5. Duniter Consortium: Duniter (2016). https://duniter.org/en/
6. Ford, B.: Pseudonym parties: an offline foundation for online accountability (preliminary draft), March 2012
7. Kanade, S., Petrovska-Delacretaz, D., Dorizzi, B.: Cancelable iris biometrics and using error correcting codes to reduce variability in biometric data. In: 2009 IEEE Conference on Computer Vision and Pattern Recognition, pp. 120–127, June 2009. https://doi.org/10.1109/CVPR.2009.5206646
8. Rogaway, P., Shrimpton, T.: Cryptographic hash-function basics: definitions, implications, and separations for preimage resistance, second-preimage resistance, and collision resistance. In: Roy, B., Meier, W. (eds.) FSE 2004. LNCS, vol. 3017, pp. 371–388. Springer, Heidelberg (2004). https://doi.org/10.1007/978-3-540-25937-4_24

Towards Secure TMIS Protocols

David Gerault[1]($\boxtimes$) and Pascal Lafourcade[2]

[1] Nanyang Technological University, Singapore, Singapore
david@gerault.net
[2] LIMOS, Universite Clermont Auvergne, Clermont-Ferrand, France

Abstract. Telecare Medicine Information Systems (TMIS) protocols aim at authenticating a patient in a telecare context, and permitting information exchange between the patient and a distant server through a verifier. In 2019, Safkhani and Vasilakos [10] showed that several protocols of the literature were insecure, and proposed a new protocol. In this paper, we show that their proposal is insecure, mainly due to incorrect use of distance bounding countermeasures, and propose a secure version, resistant to distance bounding related threats.

1 Introduction

RFID technologies can be used in a wide range of applications, from access management to tracking of people and goods or contactless payments. An RFID interaction is performed between a reader (also called verifier) and a tag (also called prover), typically withing a close distance from each other, without contact. Over a few years, the use of RFID technologies has become prominent in medical technologies [8], helping to solve various problem. The most notorious one is baby theft or misplacement [5,9], which have dramatic consequences on families when they occur. Other application include drugs tracking, or patient identification. In this paper, we focus on Telecare Medicine Information Systems (TMIS) in which a patient's RFID wristband or implant interacts with a distant server through an RFID reader. In these systems, the distant server sends data from the Electronic Medical Record (EMR) of the patients to the reader.

TMIS Protocols: Research for generic secure RFID protocols is very active: for instance, a recent survey compares 38 protocols [1]. As for protocols specifically designed for TMIS systems, Masdari et al. presented a complete classification in [8], and show that no protocol in the litterature satisfies all the security requirements. More recently, Safkhani et al. presented a cryptanalysis of four recent protocols (Li et al. [7], Zheng et al. [12], Zhou et al. [13], and Benssalah et al. [2]) in [10], and showed that they were insecure. They proposed a new protocol, SV, which they proved secure using the automated framework Scyther [4]. The SV protocol makes use of time measurements, a typical feature of distance bounding protocol.

© Springer Nature Switzerland AG 2020
A. Benzekri et al. (Eds.): FPS 2019, LNCS 12056, pp. 337–344, 2020.
https://doi.org/10.1007/978-3-030-45371-8_21

Distance Bounding Protocols: Distance bounding protocols were introduced by Brands and Chaum in [3] to counter relay attacks. In a distance bounding protocol, a verifier estimates an upper bound on the distance of a prover by measuring the time elapsed during challenge response rounds. Distance bounding protocols must be resistant to *mafia fraud*, in which a man-in-the-middle adversary attempts to impersonate a distant prover to the verifier, as well as attacks where a dishonest, distant prover tries to appear close to the verifier. These distance-related attacks can be declined in different forms: a single distant prover (distance fraud), a distant prover using the proximity of a honest prover near the verifier (distance hijacking), or a distant prover helped by an accomplice located near the verifier (terrorist fraud). Distance bounding protocols, as authentication mechanisms, have similarities with TMIS systems. They however differ, in that no authentication is performed between the verifier and the prover (they do not share keys) in TMIS, as the authentication is delegated to a distant server. Additionally, in TMIS schemes, the privacy of the prover is crucial, wheareas few distance bounding protocols consider it as a requirement. Moreover, in TMIS protocols that include time measurement, the prover typically replies to the challenge of the verifier with a hash. This practice was ruled out by the distance bounding community for years, because the time taken to compute a hash was deemed too long and unpredictable. Recently, Gerault [6] made arguments in favour of allowing complex responses during the timed exchanges, based on the general improvements of hardware, and the cryptography community effort to provide lightweight and zero-latency primitives. These differences between distance bounding and RMIS protocols make using off-the-shelf distance bounding protocols for TMIS non trivial.

Relay attacks are a very serious concern for TMIS: an adversary impersonating a distant patient potentially gains access to prescription drugs, and sensitive medical information about that patient. Attacks by distant dishonest provers are also relevant: for instance, some systems use RFID to prevent baby theft. A reader periodically checks whether the rfid tag of the baby is within range. If the used protocol is vulnerable to a distance fraud, a criminal can walk away with the baby, and pass the checks from a distance, so that he is far away by the time someone notices the baby is missing. Distance hijacking attacks can also be harmful: a distant dishonest prover making the authentication of a honest patient appear as his own could cause serious damage, as the honest patient may then receive treatment based on the identity of the adversary, which could lead to severe complications in case of allergy.

To address distant prover authentication issues, we make the following contributions:

1. We show that the time measurement performed in the SV protocol are not sufficient to counter relay attacks.
2. We propose a new TMIS protocol similar to SV, that is secure against distance bounding related attacks.

2   Protocol of Safkhani and Vasilakos

2.1   The Protocol

In [10], Safkhani and Vasilakos show that previous RMIS protocols are insecure, and propose the SV protocol (Fig. 1).

The authors do not include time measurements on the verifier side, in order to resist adversaries that can control the verifier's clock.

Server S		Verifier V		Prover P
K_{SV}, K_{SP}		K_{SV}		K_{SP}
$N_S \xleftarrow{\$} \{0,1\}^n$		$N_V \xleftarrow{\$} \{0,1\}^n$		$N_P \xleftarrow{\$} \{0,1\}^n$
	$\xleftarrow{Query, N_V}$			
$T1 \leftarrow$ timestamp	$\xrightarrow{T1, N_S}$		$\xrightarrow{T1, N_S, N_V}$	$N1 \leftarrow h(K_{SP} \oplus N_V, T1, N_P, N_S)$
$T2 \leftarrow$ timestamp	$\xleftarrow{N1, N2, N_P}$	$N2 \leftarrow h(K_{SV} \oplus N_V, N1 \oplus N_S)$	$\xleftarrow{N1, N_P}$	
Retrieve K_{SP} from $N1$				
Retrieve K_{SV} from $N2$				
If $T2 - T1 > \Delta t$ or				
$N1$ or $N2$ incorrect				
then abort; else				
$N3 \leftarrow h(K_{SV} \oplus N_V, N_S)$				
$N4 \leftarrow h(K_{SP} \oplus N_P, N_S)$	$\xrightarrow{N3, N4}$	If $N3$ incorrect		
		then abort; else		
			$\xrightarrow{N4}$	Check $N4$

Fig. 1. The TMIS protocol proposed by Safkhani and Vasilakos [10]. Comas denote concatenation, and h is a hash function.

In the next section, we show that the SV protocol is actually not resistant to relay attacks, and exhibit other limitations on its design.

2.2   Flaws in the Protocol of Safkhani and Vasilakos

The SV protocol [10], presented in the previous section, does not grant resistance to relay attacks.

The SV protocol performs a time check to prevent relay attacks, but this check is done by the distant server, over an internet access. This time measurement is therefore highly unreliable: depending on the network traffic, the bandwidth, and the location of the verifier, combined to the possible use of a wireless network by the verifier, the measured time can vary significantly. In a communication over the internet, a message passes through several routers, which essentially perform a relay between the server and the verifier: therefore, relay attack resistance over the internet is by essence vain.

Under the assumption that the provers do not have an internal clock, and that only a prover, a verifier and a server are involved, over a classical TCP/IP connection, reliable relay attack protection can only be done by the verifier. This, in turn, would expose to attacks in which the time of the verifier is altered, as mentioned in [10]. In this paper, we make the common assumption that verifiers are honest, so that their clock can be trusted. If, on the other hand, a stronger guarantee is needed, one can include the methods of [11] to enforce reliable time measurement on the verifier side.

3 Our Protocol

The SV protocol successfully fixes security issues of previous protocols, but remains insecure, due to its lack of relay attack resistance. We therefore propose a fixed protocol. Our protocol is very similar to SV, the main differences being that the verifier performs the time checks, and N1, N2, N3, N4 do not contain XORs of messages anymore. Additionally, the timestamps are not sent to the prover anymore (as the unicity of nonces makes them redundant, and we assume honest verifiers) Finally, to account for distance cheating attacks, the verifier's nonce is not sent to the server beforehand: otherwise, a dishonest prover could compute $N1$ in advance after eavesdropping N_S and N_V over the channel.

Assumptions. We make the following assumptions:

1. The verifiers and servers are honest
2. The verifier's clock cannot be manipulated
3. The prover does not have a reliable clock
4. The computation time for the hash function is small compared to the RTT of messages

Our protocol is depicted on Fig. 2. It starts with the verifier sending a query to the server, as well as its identifier ID_V, and the server replying with his nonce N_S. The verifier sends his nonce N_V, ID_V and N_S to the prover, and starts a timer. The prover replies with his nonce N_P, as well as $N1 = h(K_{SP}, ID_V, N_V, N_P, N_S)$. The verifier stops its timer and compares the time elapsed with a predefined bound Δt. If the time taken is greater than Δt, it aborts the protocol. Otherwise, it computes $N2 = h(K_{SV}, N_V, N_P, N_S, N1)$ and sends $N1, N2, N_P, N_V$ to the server. The server retrieves K_{SP} by computing $h(K'_{SP}, ID_V, N_V, N_P, N_S))$ with the prover keys K'_{SP} of its database, until it finds the one that matches $N1$. If no match is found for $N1$, or if $N2$ is incorrect, then it aborts the protocol. Otherwise, it sends $N3 = SE_{K_{SV}}(N1, N2, Data)$ and $N4 = h(K_{SP}, N1)$ to the verifier, who checks the correctness of $N3$. It deciphers $N3$ as $(N1', N2', Data')$. If $N1' \neq N1$ or $N2' \neq N2$, it aborts. Otherwise, it retrieves $Data$ and sends $N4$ to the prover. Finally, the prover checks the correctness of $N4$, and aborts if it is incorrect.

4 Security Analysis

Notations: We consider that a TMIS protocol has a *security parameter* λ, such that the nonce and key sizes are polynomial in λ. The adversaries we consider are polynomially bounded in λ, and we denote by *negligible* any function that is negligible in λ. In this section, we respectively denote a prover, a verifier, a server and an adversary by $P, V, S, \mathcal{A}$. A *dishonest prover* $\mathcal{A}^*$ refers to an adversary who legitimately registered his secret key into the system. We sometimes write *party*

Server S	Verifier V	Prover P
$K_{SV}, K_{SP}, SK_S, Data$	$ID_V, K_{SV}, \Delta t$	K_{SP}
$N_S \xleftarrow{\$} \{0,1\}^n$	$\xleftarrow{Query, ID_V}$ $N_V \xleftarrow{\$} \{0,1\}^n$	$N_P \xleftarrow{\$} \{0,1\}^n$
	$\xrightarrow{N_S}$	
	$T1 \leftarrow$ timestamp $\xrightarrow{N_S, N_V, ID_V}$	
	$T2 \leftarrow$ timestamp $\xleftarrow{N1, N_P}$ $N1 \leftarrow h(K_{SP}, ID_V, N_V, N_P, N_S)$
	If $T2 - T1 > \Delta t$	
	then abort; else	
Retrieve K_{SP} from $N1$	$\xleftarrow{N1, N2, N_P, N_V}$ $N2 \leftarrow h(K_{SV}, N_V, N_P, N_S, N1)$	
If $N1$ or $N2$ incorrect		
then abort; else		
$N3 \leftarrow SE_{K_{SV}}(N1, N2, Data)$		
$N4 \leftarrow h(K_{SP}, N1)$	$\xrightarrow{N3, N4}$ If $N3$ incorrect	
	then abort; else	
	retrieve $Data$ from $N3$ $\xrightarrow{N4}$ Check $N4$

Fig. 2. Our TMIS protocol. Comas denote concatenation, h a cryptographic hash function, and SE a symmetric key encryption algorithm.

to denote a honest party, either prover, verifier or server. We denote by *session* the three-party execution of a TMIS protocol, involving a prover, a verifier, and a server. The *transcript* of such a session contains all the messages sent by the 3 involved parties. Finally, we say that a prover is *distant* if he is at a distance grater than the maximum distance allowed in the protocol, defined by Δt. Otherwise, the prover is said to be *close*.

Security Properties: Our protocol has similar security goals to the SV protocol, additionally considering distance fraud and distance hijacking attacks. We do, however, not consider adversaries who can control the clock of the verifier. Our protocol is resistant to: impersonation and replay attacks, traceability attacks, relay attacks, and distance fraud and distance hijacking.

Definition 1. *Resistance against impersonation attacks Let Π be a TMIS protocol. Π is resistant against impersonnation attacks if no polynomially bounded adversary $\mathcal{A}$, given oracle access to provers, verifiers and servers, can be successfully authenticated with a non-negligible probability either:*

- *as a legitimate prover to a verifier or a server; or*
- *as a legitimate verifier to a server or a prover; or*
- *as a legitimate server to a verifier or a prover*

For the attack to be valid, at least one of the protocol messages must be produced by the adversary: otherwise, this would constitute a relay attack, which are treated separately.

The next property is relay attacks: here, we only consider relay between a prover and a verifier, as relay between servers and other parties over a TCP/IP connection hardly makes sense.

Definition 2. *Resistance against relay attacks Let Π be a TMIS protocol. Π is resistant against relay attacks if no polynomially bounded adversary $\mathcal{A}$, given oracle access to provers, verifiers and servers, can be successfully authenticated with a non-negligible probability as a legitimate prover which is not in range of the verifier.*

Traceability deals with the ability of an adversary to link two sessions by a prover.

Definition 3. *Resistance against traceability attacks Let Π be a TMIS protocol with $n_P > 1$ different provers. Consider the following security game: the adversary $\mathcal{A}$ is given the transcripts of two different sessions, and must determine whether the two sessions were ran by the same prover or not. Let $p_\mathcal{A}$ denote the success probability of $\mathcal{A}$ in this game, and $adv(\mathcal{A})$ denote the advantage of the adversary $\mathcal{A}$, computed as $|\frac{1}{2} - p_\mathcal{A}|$. Π is resistant against traceability attacks if, for all polynomially bounded $\mathcal{A}$, $adv(\mathcal{A})$ is negligible.*

Finally, distance attacks are attacks in which a distant dishonest prover, holding a valid secret key, is authenticated by a verifier. The difference with impersonnation attacks where a prover is impersonated is that, in distance attacks, the adversary knows the the secret key of the distant prover he is authenticating as.

Definition 4. *Resistance to distance attacks Let Π be a TMIS protocol. Π is distance attack resistant if no polynomially bounded dishonest prover $\mathcal{A}^*$, given oracle access to servers, verifiers, and honest provers (both close and distant) can be successfully authenticated with a non-negligible probability.*

Security Statement: Our security claims hold in the Random Oracle Model (ROM), where hash functions are modeled as random oracles, returning a truely random bitstring $O(x)$ when called on any bitstring x, such that later queries to O on the same x return the same value $O(x)$.

Resistance Against Impersonnation Attack: In the following, we assume that the symmetric encryption scheme SE is a secure Pseudo-Random Permutation (PRP). This implies that no polynomial adversary can, with non-negligible probability, recover the secret key used to encrypt a message, nor guess the encryption of a message of his choice.

Impersonnation of the Server: In our protocol, the verifier authenticates the server based on the message N_3, and the prover authenticates the server based on the message N_4. First, under the assumption that h is a random oracle, and that SE is a secure PRP, $\mathcal{A}$ cannot extract the secret keys of the server from these messages, nor generate a valid N_3 or N_4 for valid ones on his own. Moreover, the probability for N_3 or N_4 from a previous session to be valid in a new session is negligible: it would require either the same nonces being used twice, or a collision in the hash function. Therefore, our protocol is secure against server impersonnation attacks.

Impersonnation of the Verifier: Using a similar argument with N_2, our protocol is secure against impersonnation of verifiers to servers. The authentication of the verifier to the prover is indirect: the prover accepts the verifier as legitimate if it receives a valid N_4 from the server, meaning that the server authenticated a verifier with identity ID_V. As shown in the server impersonnation sketch of proof, no polynomial adversary can forge a legitimate fresh N_4: hence, our protocol is secure against impersonnation of verifiers to provers.

Resistance Against Relay Attacks: The time measurement prevents the adversary from sending the correct nonces to a distant prover, receiving the response, and forwarding it to the verifier in time to be accepted. Furthermore, the probability of the adversary to guess the either the correct nonces to send to the prover or the response of the prover in advance is negligible. Hence, our protocol is secure against relay attacks.

Resistance Against Traceability Attacks: In our protocol, the key identifying the prover only appears within hashes, in the random oracle model: it is therefore completely hidden to the adversary. Therefore, it may only leak if the same N_1 appears, in two different sessions, which occurs with negligible probability, due to N_P being chosen by the prover. Therefore, our protocol is resistant against traceability attacks.

Resistance Against Distance Attacks: For a prover to be accepted by the verifier, it needs to send its response within the time bound during the timed exchange. Let $\mathcal{A}^*$ be a dishonest, distant prover. If $\mathcal{A}^*$ waits to receive the nonces from the verifier to send his response, it will arrive too late, by definition of Δt. Hence, for $\mathcal{A}^*$ to be accepted, the verifier must receive a valid response by the server within the time bound. This occurs if either (a) $\mathcal{A}$ sends a response in advance by guessing correct nonce values, or (b) a honest prover near V sends a response correct for $\mathcal{A}^*$, and both occur only with negligible probability. Finally, $\mathcal{A}^*$ may send an incorrect response, and attempt to replace it with a valid one in the message sent by the verifier to the server. This strategy would however fail, since the initial N_1 and N_P values are authenticated by the verifier through a hash that is not falsifiable by $\mathcal{A}^*$, as it contains the shared key between V and S.

5 Conclusions and Discussion

In this paper, we exhibit a flaw in the relay attack resistance of the protocol of Safkhani and Vasilakos, and propose a new secure protocol. To the best of our knowledge, our protocol is the first TMIS protocol to be secure against distance bounding related attacks, as well as the classical threats. It does, however, not provide forward security, which is an interesting property left for future work.

References

1. Baashirah, R., Abuzneid, A.: Survey on prominent RFID authentication protocols for passive tags. Sensors **18**, 3584 (2018)

2. Benssalah, M., Djeddou, M., Drouiche, K.: Security analysis and enhancement of the most recent RFID authentication protocol for telecare medicine information system. Wirel. Pers. Commun. **96**(4), 6221–6238 (2017). https://doi.org/10.1007/s11277-017-4474-y

3. Brands, S., Chaum, D.: Distance-bounding protocols. In: Helleseth, T. (ed.) EURO-CRYPT 1993. LNCS, vol. 765, pp. 344–359. Springer, Heidelberg (1994). https://doi.org/10.1007/3-540-48285-7_30

4. Cremers, C.J.F.: The Scyther tool: verification, falsification, and analysis of security protocols. In: Gupta, A., Malik, S. (eds.) CAV 2008. LNCS, vol. 5123, pp. 414–418. Springer, Heidelberg (2008). https://doi.org/10.1007/978-3-540-70545-1_38

5. Dunbar, P.: 300,000 babies stolen from their parents-and sold for adoption: haunting bbc documentary exposes 50-year scandal of baby trafficking by the catholic church in spain. Daily Mail (2011)

6. Gerault, D., Boureanu, I.: Distance bounding under different assumptions: opinion. In: Proceedings of the 12th Conference on Security and Privacy in Wireless and Mobile Networks (WiSec 2019), pp. 245–248. ACM, New York (2019). https://doi.org/10.1145/3317549.3319729

7. Li, C.T., Weng, C.Y., Lee, C.C.: A secure RFID tag authentication protocol with privacy preserving in telecare medicine information system. J. Med. Syst. **39**(8), 1–8 (2015). https://doi.org/10.1007/s10916-015-0260-0

8. Masdari, M., Ahmadzadeh, S.: A survey and taxonomy of the authentication schemes in telecare medicine information systems. J. Netw. Comput. Appl. **87**, 1–19 (2017). https://doi.org/10.1016/j.jnca.2017.03.003. http://www.sciencedirect.com/science/article/pii/S1084804517300978

9. Osaimi, A.A.A., Kadi, K.A., Saddik, B.: Role of radio frequency identification in improving infant safety and the extent of nursing staff acceptance of RFID at King Abdulaziz Medical City in Riyadh. In: 2017 International Conference on Informatics, Health and Technology (ICIHT), pp. 1–7 (2017)

10. Safkhani, M., Vasilakos, A.: A new secure authentication protocol for telecare medicine information system and smart campus. IEEE Access, 1 (2019) https://doi.org/10.1109/ACCESS.2019.2896641

11. Chothia, L.C.T., Boureanu, I.: Making contactless EMV payments robust against rogue readers colluding with relay attackers. In: the 23rd International Conference on Financial Cryptography and Data Security (Financial Crypto 2019) (2019, to appear)

12. Zheng, L., et al.: A new mutual authentication protocol in mobile RFID for smart campus. IEEE Access, 1 (2018). https://doi.org/10.1109/ACCESS.2018.2875973

13. Zhou, Z., Wang, P., Li, Z.: A quadratic residue-based RFID authentication protocol with enhanced security for TMIS. J. Ambient Intell. Humaniz. Comput. **10**(9), 3603–3615 (2018). https://doi.org/10.1007/s12652-018-1088-5

Detecting Ransomware in Encrypted Web Traffic

Jaimin Modi[1], Issa Traore[1(✉)], Asem Ghaleb[1], Karim Ganame[2], and Sherif Ahmed[3]

[1] ECE Department, University of Victoria, Victoria, BC, Canada
jaiminmodi@uvic.ca, itraore@ece.uvic.ca, aalmekhlafy@gmail.com
[2] StreamScan, 2300 Rue Sherbrooke E, Montreal, QC, Canada
ganame@streamscan.io
[3] Computer Science Department, University of Windsor, Victoria, Canada
Sherif.SaadAhmed@uwindsor.ca

Abstract. To date, only a small amount of research has focused on detecting ransomware at the network level, and none of the published proposals have addressed the challenges raised by the fact that an increasing number of ransomware are using encrypted channels for communication with the command and control (C&C) server, mainly, over the HTTPS protocol. Despite the limited amount of ransomware-specific data available in network traffic, network-level detection represents a valuable extension of system-level detection as this could provide early indication of ransomware activities and allow disrupting such activities before serious damage can take place. To address the aforementioned gap, we propose, in the current paper, a new approach for detecting ransomware in encrypted network traffic that leverages network connections, certificate information and machine learning. We leverage an existing feature model developed for general malware and develop a robust network flow behavior analysis model using machine learning that separates effectively ransomware traffic from normal traffic. We study three different classifiers: random forest, SVM and logistic regression. Experimental evaluation on a diversified dataset yields a detection rate of 99.9% and a false positive rate of 0% for random forest, the best performing of the three classifiers.

Keywords: Ransomware detection · Encrypted web traffic · Machine learning · Network traffic

1 Introduction

Maintaining adequate communication channel between an infected device and the command and control server (C&C) is an essential characteristic of modern malware. Increasingly, such communications are taking place using web protocols, such as HTTPS. According to a report by Cyren, a leading enterprise cybersecurity service provider, 37% of malware now utilize HTTPS [4]. The same report also stated that every major ransomware family since 2016 has used HTTPS communication [4]. Although several approaches have been published in the literature for ransomware detection, the current

© Springer Nature Switzerland AG 2020
A. Benzekri et al. (Eds.): FPS 2019, LNCS 12056, pp. 345–353, 2020.
https://doi.org/10.1007/978-3-030-45371-8_22

approaches overwhelmingly focus on analyzing system data available on the endpoint with limited or no consideration for the C&C communications. Network level detection is made more complicated because, as aforementioned, malware communications are increasingly carried over HTTPS encrypted channels. Only a limited amount of research have been published on detecting malware in encrypted traffic [5, 7, 9]. To the best of our knowledge, all the existing works have focused on general malware, while none of them has addressed the challenges pertaining to ransomware specifically.

We propose, in the current paper, a new model for detecting ransomware from encrypted network traffic. We use a feature model introduced in a previous work on general malware detection from encrypted traffic by Strasak [9] and develop a robust network flow behavior analysis model using machine learning. The approach consists of generating initially log files from network captures using the BRO intrusion detection system (IDS). We construct the flows by aggregating network packets from the log files and calculate the feature values. We utilize a wide variety of ransomware families and normal traffic data for constructing a diversified dataset to evaluate our approach. Experimental evaluation results are presented for balanced and imbalanced datasets. The remainder of the paper is structured as follows. Section 2 summarizes and discusses related works. Section 3 presents our datasets. Section 4 describes our feature model. Section 5 presents the experimental evaluation of our proposed approach. Section 6 makes some concluding remarks.

2   Related Work

Ransomware detection has been studied extensively in recent years. The existing works can be divided into three major categories: static, dynamic and hybrid. Dynamic approaches can be divided into system level and network level approaches. The majority of the dynamic approaches work at the system level. Examples of such proposals include ShieldFS by Continella et al. [3] and ELDERAN by Sgandurra et al. [8]. A much smaller number of proposals have been published on network-based dynamic analysis, including works by Cabaj et al. [2] and Almashhadani et al. [1]. Most of the current work on network-based dynamic analysis were based only on a small number of ransomware families. For instance, the experiment in [2] was based only on 2 ransomware families, while in [1] only a single ransomware family (i.e. locky) was considered.

3   Evaluation Datasets

To the best of our knowledge, there is no publicly available ransomware detection dataset. It has been decided at the ISOT lab to fill this gap by collecting a new dataset to be shared with the research community. The collected dataset includes both network and file activities generated from ransomware as well as benign applications. The binaries collected in the ISOT dataset consist of 666 different samples from 20 different ransomware families. Table 1 provides a detailed breakdown of the ransomware samples from each family.

Table 1. Ransomware dataset breakdown

Family	Samp	%	Family	Samp	%
TeslaCrypt	348	52.3	Mole	4	0.597
Cerber	122	18.236	Satan	2	0.299
Locky	129	19.28	CTBLocker	2	0.299
CryptoShield	4	0.597	Win32.Blocker	18	2.69
Unlock26	3	0.448	Spora	5	0.747
WannaCry	1	0.149	Jaff	3	0.448
CryptoMix	2	0.299	Zeta	2	0.149
Sage	5	0.747	Striked	1	0.149
Petya	2	0.299	GlobeImposter	4	0.598
Crysis	8	1.196	Xorist	2	0.299
Flawed	1	0.149			
Total	**666**				

The normal (i.e., benign) dataset was collected in 2 different ways - manual data collection and network files from the Stratosphere project [10]. The manual data collection was done while keeping Wireshark on capture mode and browsing through the websites on Alexa top 100 list. The duration for each capture was 30 min and 30 total samples were collected. More details on the dataset can be found in [6].

4 Feature Model

In this section, we present our feature model, and explain the creation of our flow dataset. More details on feature definitions and extraction can found in [6].

4.1 Creating Flows

After collecting the log files through Bro IDS, the next step is to preprocess the data and calculate the feature values. Before calculating the feature values, it is important to build the flows from the log files. The three major log files that are used for building flows in the current work are – ssl.log, conn.log and x509.log. Since the traffic is encrypted, we start by building our flow from the ssl.log file. An overview of the connection information provided by the ssl.log, conn.log and x509.log files is provided in Fig. 1.

The important point while building the flows is to connect all the log files. As it can be seen from Fig. 1, ssl.log and conn.log files can be connected through the Unique ID of connection (UID) column. Similarly, the ssl.log and x509.log files can be connected using the certificate identifier (cert_id) column from ssl.log file. The 'cert_chain_uid' column in the ssl.log file is a vector of strings such that each string value is present in the 'id' column of x509.log file. If the 'cert_id' column is empty, then the corresponding

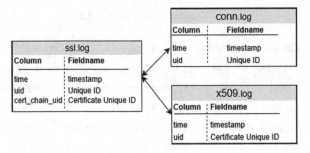

Fig. 1. Bro log files connection information

packet does not contain any certificate related information. Ultimately for a given flow, three different types of values will be added to it as the key: ssl values, connection values and certificate values. The basic algorithm for building a flow can be found in [6].

4.2 Feature Definitions

Our feature model which is based on the work of Strasák [9] consists of 3 groups of features carved out from each of the log files. In total, the model consists of 28 features as follows:

Conn.log features

- Number of flows
- Average duration of flows
- Standard deviation of flows duration
- Percent of standard deviation of flows
- Originator payload size
- Responder payload size
- Ratio of responder to originator payload size
- Percentage of established connections
- Inbound packets
- Outbound packets
- Periodicity average
- Periodicity standard deviation

Ssl.log features

- SSL flow ratio
- SSL-TLS ratio
- SNI-SSL ratio
- SNI as IP
- Certificate path average
- Self-signed certificate ratio

X509.log features

- Public key average
- Average certificate validity
- Standard deviation of certificate validity
- Certificate validity during capture
- Average certificate age
- Number of certificates
- Average number of domains in SAN
- Certificate-ssl logs ratio
- SNI in SAN DNS
- CN in SAN DNS

5 Classification and Evaluation Experiments

In the current paper, we use and compare three different classification algorithms, including logistic regression (LR), random forest (RF) and support vector machine (SVM). We use the current dataset as it is and a balanced dataset analysis using the smote oversampling technique. Table 2 shows the accuracy results for all classifiers with and without smote for the '*train_test_split*' set (80% training and 20% testing). Similarly, Table 3 shows the accuracy for the 10-fold cross validation. We present and discuss the performance results for each of the separate classifiers in the following.

Table 2. Accuracy score for the classifiers for 'train_test_split' set

Classifier	Accuracy (%)	
	Without SMOTE	With SMOTE
Logistic regression	94	94
Random forest	100	100
Support vector machine	95	94

Table 3. Accuracy score for the classifiers for 10-fold cross validation set

Classifier	(Average) Accuracy (%)	
	Without SMOTE	With SMOTE
Logistic regression	91	96
Random forest	98	100
Support vector machine	91	96

Table 4. Classification report for the logistic regression classifier

Classification report				
Metrics	SMOTE		Without SMOTE	
	Normal	Ransomware	Normal	Ransomware
Precision (%)	100	72	97	79
Recall (%)	93	100	96	83
f1 - score (%)	96	84	97	81
Support	2640	465	2640	465

Logistics Regression: Table 2 shows that smote has no effect on accuracy for *'train_test_split'* method. Table 4 shows the classification report for the logistic regression classifier.

Since applying smote on the dataset gives better output, we perform hyper-parameter tuning only for that dataset. The following model parameters were utilized for tuning:

a. *C* (Inverse of regularization strength) is varied from 0.0001 to 1000.
b. *Penalty* – We explore two possibilities in our work called L1 and L2 regularizations as follows: L1 regularization (also known as Lasso regression.) and L2 regularization (also called Ridge regression).

After doing a grid search through the parameters, the logistic regression gives best accuracy at 96% for the following parameter values: *C = 1* and *Penalty = L1*. This means that accuracy does not change, however, by looking at the confusion matrix shown in Fig. 2 it can be observed that there is a decrease in false positive as well as false negative rates.

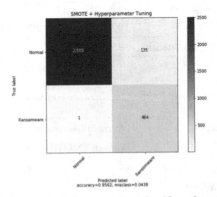

Fig. 2. Confusion matrix for the logistic regression classifier after applying hyper-parameter tuning

Random Forest: Random forest gives the best accuracy amongst all the three classifiers.

Table 5 show the classification results for the random forest classifier. The random forest classifier achieves an accuracy of 100% and a detection rate of almost 100% with an FPR of 0%. We obtain a FPR of 0% since we have no false positives. The only reason for applying hyper-parameter tuning is to check if this can reduce the false negatives to 0. That way we can achieve perfect detection rate. The parameters considered for tuning were as follows:

Table 5. Classification report for the random forest classifier

Classification report				
Metrics	SMOTE		Without SMOTE	
	Normal	Ransomware	Normal	Ransomware
Precision (%)	100	100	100	100
Recall (%)	1.00	1.00	1.00	99
f1 - score (%)	100	100	100	100
Support	2640	465	2640	465

a. *n_estimators* – the number of trees to be used in the classifier, varied from 1 to 200.
b. *max_features* – the number of features to be considered while splitting the treed, varied from 1 to 28.
c. *max_depth* – the depth of each tree in the classifier, varied from 1 to 32.

After conducting a grid search, the random forest classifier gives an accuracy of 100%. The number of false positives and false negatives also remain the same. Hence, there is no change in the detection rate.

SVM: Table 2 shows that SVM does not perform best in terms of cross validation accuracy. Again, smote does well in reducing the number of false negatives. Table 6 show the classification results for the SVM classifier.

Table 6. Classification report for the SVM classifier

Classification report				
Metrics	SMOTE		Without SMOTE	
	Normal	Ransomware	Normal	Ransomware
Precision (%)	97	81	1.00	73
Recall (%)	96	85	93	1.00
f1 - score (%)	97	83	97	84
Support	2640	465	2640	465

The parameters considered for hyper-parameter tuning is C – the area of hyperplane created by misclassified training samples around the hyperplane. We vary the value of C from 1 to 100. The SVM classifier achieves an accuracy of 96% with value of '$C = 15$'. Also, hyper-parameter tuning SVM improves the detection rate slightly.

6 Conclusion

In the current paper, we proposed a new system for detecting ransomware in encrypted web traffic. Our approach consists of extracting meaningful information from network connections and certificates, and utilizing machine learning for detecting ransomware packets in network data. We explored a feature space in three broad domains of network characteristics: connection based, encryption based, and certificate based. We implemented and studied 3 different classifiers for our model, namely, logistic regression, SVM and random forest. Our experimental evaluation yields for random forest, the best performing classifier, a detection rate of 99.9% and a false positive rate of 0%. The obtained results are very encouraging and an indicator of the feasibility of effective ransomware detection from encrypted network traffic.

Although detecting ransomware in network traffic data is our main focus, identifying the family to which the ransomware belong would be beneficial. Our future work will explore how to extend our model to detect specific ransomware families, in addition to detecting individual ransomware samples.

References

1. Almashhadani, A.O., Kaiiali, M., Sezer, S., O'Kane, P.: A multi-classifier network-based crypto ransomware detection system: a case study of locky ransomware. IEEE Access **7**, 47053–47067 (2019)
2. Cabaj, K., Gregorczyk, M., Mazurczyk, W.: Software-defined networking-based crypto ransomware detection using HTTP traffic characteristics. Comput. Electr. Eng. **66**, 353–368 (2018)
3. Continella, A., et al.: ShieldFS: a self-healing, ransomware-aware filesystem. In: Proceedings of the 32nd Annual Conference on Computer Security Applications, pp. 336–347. ACM (2016)
4. Cyren - SSL Traffic Growth - Malware is Moving Heavily to HTTPS. https://www.cyren.com/blog/articles/over-one-third-of-malware-uses-https
5. Prasse, P., Machlica, L., Pevný, T., Havelka, J., Scheffer, T.: Malware detection by analysing encrypted network traffic with neural networks. In: Ceci, M., Hollmén, J., Todorovski, L., Vens, C., Džeroski, S. (eds.) ECML PKDD 2017. LNCS (LNAI), vol. 10535, pp. 73–88. Springer, Cham (2017). https://doi.org/10.1007/978-3-319-71246-8_5
6. Modi, J., Traore, I., Ghaleb, A., Ganame, K., Ahmed, S.S.: Detecting ransomware in encrypted web traffic. Technical report ECE-2019-10-1, University of Victoria, ECE Department, 5 October 2019. http://www.uvic.ca/engineering/ece/isot/publications/index.php
7. Niu, W., Zhuo, Z., Zhang, X., Du, X., Yang, G., Guizani, M.: A heuristic statistical testing based approach for encrypted network traffic identification. IEEE Trans. Veh. Technol. **68**(4), 3843–3853 (2019)

8. Sgandurra, D., Muñoz-González, L., Mohsen, R., Lupu, E.C.: Automated dynamic analysis of ransomware: benefits, limitations and use for detection, arXiv preprint arXiv:1609.03020 (2016)
9. Strasák, F.: Detection of HTTPS malware traffic. Bachelor's thesis, Czech Technical University in Prague, May 2017
10. Normal Captures—Stratosphere IPS. https://www.stratosphereips.org/datasets-normal. Accessed 19 July 2019

Digital Forensics in Vessel Transportation Systems

Alessandro Cantelli-Forti[1,2](✉) and Michele Colajanni[3]

[1] RaSS National Laboratory, CNIT, Pisa, Italy
alessandro.cantelli.forti@cnit.it
[2] University of Pisa, Pisa, Italy
[3] University of Modena and Reggio Emila, Modena, Italy
michele.colajanni@unimore.it

Abstract. Large vessels are safety-critical systems where operations, performance and component availability are continuously monitored by means of multiple sensors producing large amount of data. Relevant information is preserved in *Event Data Recorders* that are fundamental for the reconstruction of scenarios related to serious malfunctions and incidents in technical and legal terms. By considering the state-of-the-art and two important naval accidents we evidence some issues related to the exploitation of recorded data in reconstructing the events timeline and the semantics of the scenarios. These studies motivate our proposal that aims to guarantee strong data integrity and availability of all information registered in Event Data Recorders. Our results are fundamental for the precise identification of the sequences of events and for the correct attribution of human and/or machine responsibilities.

Keywords: Transportation systems · Event data recorder · Forensics · Responsibility · Data integrity and availability

1 Introduction

Critical transportation systems, such as air and naval vectors, may cause people's death and injury, severe damage to equipment or environmental harm in case of failure or malfunction. Both US (since 1996 and then the Patriot Act in 2001) and Europe (EPCIP program) have adopted a critical infrastructure protection program for transportation [1]. Any modern transportation system is controlled by some software components where process engineering and management are essential features. Often, the hardware and software components are subject to standards and certifications [2] requiring precise procedures for coding, inspection, documentation, test, verification and analysis [3]. Unfortunately, some safety improvements in transport systems are still implemented through the "learning the hard way" from incidents [6, 11]. In modern systems, multiple sensors continuously monitor systems performance and operations and produce a large amount of data that is used for real-time monitoring of proper operations. The most relevant data is registered in an *Event Data Recorder* (EDR) that should allow the technical and legal reconstruction of the scenario when serious malfunctions and incidents occur.

© Springer Nature Switzerland AG 2020
A. Benzekri et al. (Eds.): FPS 2019, LNCS 12056, pp. 354–362, 2020.
https://doi.org/10.1007/978-3-030-45371-8_23

For these reasons, data integrity and availability of EDR are essential features for a solid attribution of human and/or machine responsibilities even in legal and insurance terms [8].

Typical EDR are specifically designed and embedded devices that are controlled by a software that is not considered life critical and is not subject to the typical directives for critical infrastructures. Specific legal and regulatory rules about data collection and preservation are defined by "minimum requirements" for each transport system that are then transposed into national and international rules. For example, aviation is regulated by FAA and EU (e.g., EUROCAE ED-112); navigation by the International Convention for the Safety of Life at Sea (IMO Res.A.861/20); automotive in US by the NHTSA (49 CFR Part 563); railway transport system by US regulations (CFR 49 Ch II 229.5), and by UK and Ireland GM/RT 2472. Typically, these requirements are less stringent than those related to life critical system and do not indicate formal methods for the software production nor standard verification systems. We think that a similar choice is a serious mistake because the exploitation of recorded data is fundamental for the legal reconstruction of the scenario in the case of serious malfunctions and incidents, hence regulations should take into account technological advancement. Up to now, the EDR producers have large margins of interpreting the characteristics as required by regulations [5–7], so most EDRs do not consider how the internal logic of the programs determines the format and semantics of the information produced by the sensors. Some architectural choices, trade-offs and limitations are common in the design of any event recorders of every transportation system. The drawbacks of this situation are highlighted by the Concordia and Norman Atlantic accidents, where the forensics analysis for the precise reconstruction of the scenario was restricted by the limited possibility of exploiting recorded data from EDR [5–7, 13]. Other problems are represented by the fragmentation of written data and by the lack of time synchronization protocols that are necessary when the sensors detect bursts of anomalous events at the same time that are typical of serious incidents. In this paper, we propose practicable solutions to guarantee data integrity and availability of EDR in the naval systems. This paper is organized as follows. Section 2 contains technical background. Section 3 highlights the practical limitations of current event recording systems. Section 4 describes operations of different naval "Voyage Data Recorder" technologies; lessons learned from case studies are also included. The section also presents our proposals for improving data integrity and availability of EDRs. Section 5 concludes the paper with some final remarks and suggestions for future work.

2 Technical Background and Limitations

The reconstruction of events occurred to a critical transport system is typically recorded by on board devices that are called *Event Data Recorder* (EDR); the "Voyage Data Recorder" (VDR), used in naval transportations is the main focus of this paper. The minimum registration time required by the regulations must be sufficient for a timely reconstruction of the event that are recorded through a circular memory paradigm. Safety standards indicate the minimum time that should be recorded [2]. It is possible to avoid overwriting of specific events through a manual command.

The analyses of the most important technical reports about naval, aviation, and rail investigation of serious incidents, such as Accident Investigation, *Tri-Branch data recorder group of UK, Transport Accident Investigation Commission of New Zealand*, have evidenced twenty-one cases in which the EDR failed to provide some or all of the information necessary for investigation of aircraft, train or naval accidents. This number is the result of reading all the reports produced by the aforementioned institutional investigative bodies following the investigations. All this documentation is available online in a persistent cloud storage [12]. These cases evidence that the investigative limits related to EDR failures is not epistemic: the drawbacks are mentioned but not deeply studied. Incident reports related to the Costa Concordia and Norman Atlantic cases are unique because they devote relevant sections to fault analysis. They also evidence that adopted VDRs are less reliable than data recorders adopted in trains and airplanes. This is confirmed by Marine Accident Investigation Branch of the UK Marine Casualties Investigative Body that analyzed 230 VDRs. About 90% of the stored data sets evidenced issues related to content exploiting [11]. Besides an excessive number of malfunctioning VDRs, that is the focus of this paper, the maritime field has specific needs. One key feature is related to the periods useful for investigations that are longer than those related to airplane incidents. While in an air or rail disaster a violent impact defines the final moment of the accident, it may represent an initial event in the naval case. If a ship is damaged, its sensors keep generating huge quantities of data likely for a long time. These data sets are essential to identify and attribute human and/or machine responsibilities [4–8]. In the case of an accident, a physical damage to a means of transport, as well as to the sensors connected to an VDR, will also increase the density of data sent per unit of time by several orders of magnitude [4, 7]. This constraint is not always considered as the reconstruction of the two most serious accidents to passenger ships in Europe (since the mandatory introduction of the VDRs) has been more complex or less successful than expected. In the case of the Costa Concordia cruise ship (capsized and partially sank in 2012), the valuable data of the Safety Management System required the rewriting of part of the raw data parsing software that did not provide for this such a great number of events per minute [4]. In the case of the passenger ferry Norman Atlantic (destroyed by fire in 2014 in the Strait of Otranto), the VDR, the Ship Automation System and the Fire System have completely failed in providing useful data to the investigators. The main reason was due to the overwriting of the data concerning the origin of the fire [7]. A concomitant reason for these shortcomings was the granularity of the type of circular memory of the fire alarm system: no less than a quarter of the oldest memory could be erased during standard operations. The solid-state memory of the fire alarm critical system was divided into few partitions; without a real file system, the minimum erase unit was an entire partition.

The choice of the subset of data to be sent to the VDR is described in [4] and [6]. Before being saved in a hardened capsule, that is resistant to catastrophic events, the data can go through *Data Concentration* systems and optional *Replay Systems* enabling the on-board review of events. The data concentrators are used to contain the largest quantity of data chosen by the sensors and to decimate them in time sampling. In the Costa Concordia investigation, the capsule was damaged due to a bad block in the solid-state memory containing the Real-Time Operating System [4, 6]. The data were taken from the Replay System that luckily remained on the emerged side of the ship. For similar reasons of overwriting, data was unavailable in the Norman Atlantic investigation. The data copy of the Norman Atlantic's VDR was too general and did not indicate the specific fire sensors but only the general alarms. The most complete source of information was sent to a small printer connected to the Fire System Panel which reported the data about the intense fire on thermal paper.

3 Data Recorder Operations

The proposal of possible solutions to the VDR drawbacks requires a detailed analysis of the typical operations of the data recorded systems.

Data are generated by the multiple sensors installed in a naval system. Every received event is contained in a line of text, called *sentence* or *telegram*, following the NMEA 0183 data standard [10]. The header declares the beginning of an event, the sensor(s) that originated it, and the type of content. For instance, a data coming from a satellite-based radio navigation system receiver can be flagged in terms of time or position type and can embed details such as type or reception quality as in GPS, GLONASS, GALILEO, Standard or Augmented.

After the header or the identification tag, each line of text contains the payload consisting of strings separated from each other. The payload is composed by a specific apparatus that receives sampled sensors' data. Accident investigation experiences have shown that a timestamp should be attached as soon as the data is collected, before storing a telegram. After being generated, the telegram is sent to a data concentrator. If it is relevant, it is also sent to the hardened capsule. Just a receipt timestamp (not required by the regulations) is generated and recorded by the data concentrator in a first-come-first-served order. Reception timestamp can be a prefix or suffix to each line; the creation timestamp, when provided, would be part of the payload.

Data from sensors is received simultaneously from different transmission channels (by a point-to-point link or network), and an indication of the channel number is part of the telegram structure. In order to verify the correct operation of the sentence generator and its subsequent re-transmissions, an errors detection algorithm adds a XOR checksum control characters at the end of each sentence [10]. The final exploitation of this data could be an easily readable graphic system (Replay System) that can be used to retrospectively reconstruct the events of interest. In none of the analyzed case studies it was possible to use these replay systems as they were inconsistent when trying to reproduce the same event. Some data was not reproduced at all.

3.1 Integration of Subsystems

Ships are a peculiar critical transport infrastructure as they are not mass produced. The biggest ones, like the Costa Concordia, resemble floating cities hosting thousands of people. All the subsystems, starting from the most important ones, like the engines, to the critical ones, like the automation systems, are not the result of a holistic design approach of the whole ship, but it is an assemblage of independent parts [6] where different data paradigms are adopted.

When a transport system is an integration of subsystems, a proper documentation regarding every single data recorded by the VDR becomes of primary importance. In addition to the significance of the physical recorded value, it is necessary to be sure of its location in the payload area which contains several measurements referred to the same identification tag. In addition, the range, the metric system and the possible non-linearity of a digitized analog value (for instance, the aerodynamic shipping surfaces of an aircraft or a rudder of a ship) need to be documented. This is a complicated task if we consider the project dimensions and the number of involved suppliers and systems integrators.

3.2 Data Sentences Fragmentation

Existing solutions suffer from fragmentation problems that are internal and external to the sentences. The industrial sub-systems generate sentences starting from their internal logs that are not intended for data integration. In addition to the semantic limits, a lack of documentation causes problems of format size. For example, NMEA messages have a maximum length of 82 characters on one line including the "$" and the "!" characters and the ending Line Feed character. Minimum time resolution is one second. Hence more lines may be necessary to represent some critical data such as alarms. The position within the sentence defines the type of data. Fragmentation can cause wrong positioning in the payload space at critical moments when many alarms are received [6]. Moreover, the raw logs of some subsystems are often transposed in NMEA format by specific modules. When the module detects too much information in the same second, then it acts to divide logs in more sentences. The combination of these two fragmentation behaviors might requires complex reverse engineering process and writing of specific parsers for each analyzed case.

3.3 Clock Synchronization

Every sentence is an atomic and independent information that indicates one sensor read, such as the temperature of a component or the wind direction. Understanding more complex data describing an event requires more than one sentence and the integration of data coming from multiple sensors. In this case, it is important to know the exact order of events with a precision that should be defined a priori. Accordingly, a synchronization system needs to be provided, such as Network Time Protocol or IEEE standard 1588v2 [9] since every real-time clock will shift.

3.4 Push and Pull Architectures

When the alarms condition or other measurements are distinguished only by high and low states, it is fundamental to decide whether to use a push or pull architecture on data. In the former case, all status changes are recorded while they are occurring; in the latter case they are retrieved at regular intervals. In a push architecture, the time accuracy of the status change detection can be defined in the project, whereas in the pull cases the refresh time generates an interval of uncertainty.

In the survey of Costa Concordia disaster, it was understood that the watertight doors were monitored by a system that sent the data directly to the VDR system and to an emergency system called the Safety Management System (SMS) that redirected it to the VDR [6]. These systems were generating data with pull technologies in the first case and with push architecture when processed a priori by the SMS system. The data received in near real-time in push mode did not consider the actual state of the fully open sensor, but they expressed only the positions of complete or incomplete shutting given from the fully closed sensor. The data received in pull mode was aware of booth sensors and could distinguish complete closing, partial opening which meant movement, full open with a delay of up to 16 s [4, 5]. Some events in the latter case could be missed when status changes were short.

As a further complication, it is important to evidence that the two ways of receiving data were recorded independently by the VDR based on the time they were received. They were not received with a fixed delay that depends on the type of transmission medium: serial link for push, Ethernet LAN for the pull. After the incident, because of the water flood and damages, data traffic increased uncontrollably and serial multiplexers generated delays due to congestion, different delays were from the data transmitted over LANs. As a consequence of the lack of the telegram generation timestamp, the only way to align "push" and "pull" based data was to find shared patterns for alignment. This alignment required that short status changes were not recorded via pull and the alarms were only detailed in the pull data. Indeed, in the push cases, there was only an indication of general alarm and not related to specific doors.

The alarms related to the Hydraulic Power Pack, representing the hydraulic energy reserves indispensable in the event of a blackout for the running of the watertight doors, are not detected in the event of a power outage. Such alarms, such as low oil, low oil pressure, blackouts, obviously trigger off only in the absence of electricity. This design limit is present in many ships and it is an evident result of the regulations interpretations that do not support the connection of the weathertight doors to the Emergency Diesel Generator, as the doors are too power hungry [4]. These regulations do not even account the use of UPS which in that position, under the main deck, would be flooded. For these reasons, during the criminal investigation, it was very difficult to decipher both the state of the doors at the time of the accident and their actual closure during the capsize.

One of the aspects of the Norman Atlantic investigation referred to the Fire System that similarly sent data to the Event Logger with two distinct paths. Even though they were both push, they suffered from different and unpredictable delays to the extent that alignment was necessary through the comparison between the recorded alarms [7]. Other problems regarded data semantics: one of the two paths considered the manual reset of the command and control panel of the general error to be sent whereas the other didn't.

4 Solutions

From the previous analyses we can conclude that the analyzed VDRs fail their primary purpose because they are not designed to detect anomalies related to an emergency. The choice of the most relevant data to be preserved in hardened memories should be evaluated carefully. When this is not well designed, it becomes of primary importance to decide when to suspend the circular registration [5]. The present solution is to trigger a timeout that nowadays is forced by regulations in the case of blackout events. Any

VDR can recognize a lack of tension because a UPS can operate as a buffer supply and communicate the lack of main power to the recording system through a serial link. Critical transport systems are provided with an Emergency Electric Generator that feeds the utilities required by the regulations for a certain period of time in the event of a blackout. In ships and trains this is called the Emergency Diesel Generator, while the planes are equipped with a small wind turbine called RAT (Ram Air Turbine) which in some analyzed cases was not expected to power the data recorders. Their activation indicates an emergency and the loss of propulsion and services. Therefore, every Event Recorder should have an independent continual power system and should monitor the main power line and not the emergency line. Other serious shortcomings are due to a lack of documentation and of an integrated approach to the configuration of the Event Data Recorders components and sources of information. The absence of attention to synchronization problems, to effective timestamping, to protection against data fragmentation and an effective paradigm for managing the data sampling and representation are other common sources of problems that can cause a sensor data recorder to be ineffective in the case of incidents. Most issues are caused by the lack of proper documentation and by the difficulty of integrating subsystems that are designed for generic purposes and not for specific incidents. Other drawbacks could be solved by the adoption of information security technologies.

4.1 Understanding and Exploitation of Data

Future regulations should include a qualitative approach that can evaluate the type of data recorded on the basis of a data taxonomy. This solution would facilitate a cognitive decimation, thus mitigating the problem of data bursts during emergencies. All system clocks should be synchronized to avoid ambiguities. The documentation of how the information should be exploited has to consider complex dynamics of synchronization, integration, semantics and worst-case throughput. A one message per event approach generates the least possible overhead, but it is dependent on a correct documentation. A markup language could allow each piece of information to carry its semantics, but it has not been pursued because of the slowness for updating and applying rules [2].

4.2 Data Integrity and Availability

From an event data recorder technology prospective, we can suggest that the use of Copy-On-Write cryptographic system allows us to verify the data integrity, to enforce anti-tampering and to digitally sign the maintenance operations performed and give redundancy to critical equipment such as recording medium. OpenZFS (as btrfs) is designed for long term storage of data by means of hierarchical check-summing of data and metadata, in order to ensure that the entire storage system can be verified on use, and confirmed to be correctly stored, or remedied if corrupt. With the send/receive operations, by means of Copy-On-Write technology, a forensically sound approach could be ensured without further technical complications. The cryptographic file system' primitives, such as snapshotting and cloning, could preserve useful recorded intervals, that are identified by anomaly detection algorithms.

4.3 Forensics-Oriented Procedures

Any forensics approach to an investigation requires repeatable data extraction procedures. For this reason, we propose that the internal memories of crash survival modules should enforce a specific forensic procedure that is not implemented yet. Producers go out of market, the know-how is dispersed, and the retrofits imposed by the regulations complicate the readings which currently take place with custom procedures. On the other hand, specific read only mode could allow a forensic and bit-by-bit copy that is guaranteed by cryptographic hash functions. A standardization based on open formats would further benefit the entire critical transport infrastructure industry [13].

5 Conclusions

The contents of Voyage Data Recorders are fundamental for legal and technical reconstruction related to malfunctions and incidents. We evidence main issues related to the recorders currently adopted by the maritime industry and then we propose some solutions that can leverage recent technological advancements. Due to the high percentage of VDR failures, we can expect that manufacturers will make a joint effort to harmonize their improvements for the definition of future standards and certified implementations.

References

1. US Department of Homeland Security: Critical Infrastructure Security (2018). https://www.dhs.gov/critical-infrastructure-sectors. Accessed 30 July 2019
2. International Maritime Organization, Maritime Knowledge Centre (MKC), 1974–2018. www.imo.org. Accessed 30 July 2019
3. Bowen, J., Stavridou, P.: Safety-critical systems, formal methods and standards. Softw. Eng. J. **8**(4), 189–209 (1993)
4. Cavo-Dragone, G., Dalle-Mese, E., Maestro, M., Carpinteri, F.: Technical report for the Court of Grosseto, Italy (2012)
5. Cantelli-Forti, A.: Evidence recovery and analysis from the Costa Concordia's digital data by means of forensic techniques: turning data into information. In: European Maritime Safety Agency Seminar on Voyage Data Recorders and Electronic Evidence. Cranfield University, UK (2016)
6. Marine Casualties Investigative Body: Cruise Ship Costa Concordia Marine casualty on January 13th, 2012 Report on the safety technical investigation. Ministry of Infrastructure and Transport, Rome (2013)
7. Carpinteri, F., et al.: Norman Atlantic shipwreck, 28 December 2014. Technical report for the Court of Bari, Italy (2017)
8. Kean, T.: Event Data Recorder, An Overview. Virginia State Police, Virginia (2014)
9. Serrano, J., et al.: The White Rabbit project. In: Proceedings of the 2nd International Beam Instrumentation Conference, Oxford, UK (2013)
10. National Marine Electronics Association: The NMEA 0183 V 4.10 Standard. Severna Park, Maryland, USA (2012)

11. Clinch, S.: VDRs the most important tool? In: European Marine Accident Investigators International Forum, Santa Margherita Ligure, Italy (2013)
12. RaSS-Cloud public archive on EDRs failures during accident investigations. https://rass. cloud/index.php/s/XxGww8iRY8e3mtz. Accessed 30 July 2019
13. Cantelli-Forti, A.: Forensic analysis of industrial critical systems: the Costa Concordia's voyage data recorder case. In: Proceedings of 2018 IEEE International Conference on Smart Computing (2018)

A Privacy Protection Layer for Wearable Devices

Muhammad Mohzary[3,4], Srikanth Tadisetty[1], and Kambiz Ghazinour[1,2](✉)

[1] Department of Computer Science, Kent State University, Kent, OH 44240, USA
Stadiset@kent.edu
[2] Center for Criminal Justice, Intelligence and Cybersecurity,
State University of New York, Canton, NY 13617, USA
ghazinourk@canton.edu
[3] School of Computing and Engineering, University of Missouri-Kansas City,
Kansas City, MO 64110, USA
mm3qz@mail.umkc.edu
[4] College of Computer Science and Information Technology, Jazan University,
Jazan 45142, Saudi Arabia

Abstract. The use of wearable devices is growing exceptionally which helps the individuals to track their daily activities, habits, health status, etc. They are be-coming so powerful and affordable that in some cases replace the use of mobile devices. Users are not aware of the extent and quality of the data being collected by these devices and the inherent risk of data security and privacy violation. This research introduces a privacy aware layer built over a sample smartwatch OS to limit user data access through enforcement of user set privacy settings. Since the nature of wearable devices leaves little space for interaction between the device and users, we develop a interface to capture user's privacy preference. Two user studies, one using the Tizen platform and one with the privacy protection layer, are performed to compare its effectiveness.

Keywords: Privacy · Wearables · User Interface · Framework

1 Introduction

Wearable devices with sensory features have shown their capability in improving the quality of life of their users and also in various big data initiatives. Gadgets such as fitness trackers and smartwatches are growing in popularity. Their ability to track and transform a user's health information in real time is perhaps one of the reasons for their increased popularity despite their privacy concerns. They continuously collect, transmit and store data. Their collected data are shared which can result in surveillance of individuals [15]. An activity tracker that synchronizes data (i.e. location and photos) and communicates this data in an authenticated friend network impacts privacy. The people belonging to the network of the user are not necessarily aware of the data collected and for what

© Springer Nature Switzerland AG 2020
A. Benzekri et al. (Eds.): FPS 2019, LNCS 12056, pp. 363–370, 2020.
https://doi.org/10.1007/978-3-030-45371-8_24

purpose or what degree it is being used for. According to a HP study [3] on top 10 popular Smartwatches in the market, 100% of the tested smartwatches contain significant vulnerabilities – poor authentication, lack of encryption and privacy issues. A report from Pricewater-houseCoopers' Health Research Initiative (HRI) in 2014 notes that nearly a third of smartwatch owners use them on a daily basis and that privacy is their main concern [14]. Three issues should be considered: The availability of user privacy preference settings; the option to selectively agree or disagree to parts of the terms of agreement, while still maintain basic operation of the application; and third, a proper framework to support the flexibility to run applications based on privacy policies as defined by wearable devices' users. This research introduces a privacy-aware layer (built over the Tizen OS). The purpose is to educate and protect user's personal data. The Graphic User Interface (GUI) enables users to select privacy preferences for each application based on the design principles suggested by [1,2]. The model motivates the user to interact with the system and understand the application's data access requests. The effectiveness of this proposed layer is examined through user studies, surveys and statistics collected from users' interactions with the developed apps: the spyware-app and privacy-protector-app. The rest of this paper is organized as follows: Sect. 2 discusses some related work. Section 3, introduced the proposed model. Section 4 presents our user studies and results. Section 5 concludes the paper.

2   Related Work

Barker et al. [7] define a data provider to be an individual or organization that provides data that is to be collected, while the data owner has ownership of the data. A third-party is defined through having obtained data from the data collector. Barker et al. [7] argue that the original data provider is the only one who should have the ownership of data regardless of how many transactions it may undergo. Four elements of data privacy are proposed: Purpose, visibility, granularity, and retention that every privacy-aware model should address. Ghazinour and Barker [10] proposed a privacy-aware access control model that uses lattice structure to facilitate the negotiation phase between data provider and data collector on the above four privacy elements. Wearable devices currently use two methods to handle user permissions – AOI (ask-on-install) or AOFU (ask-on-first-use). Research has shown that users do not pay attention to application permissions being presented at install time [8]. Tizen uses a simplified mandatory access control kernel (SMACK) [4,13] to grant access. If developers want access to pedometer, heart rate or sleep monitor sensor data, then they must also include health information privilege as a prerequisite [9]. Privacy policies are generally hard to understand. Ghazinour et al. [12] proposed a visualization model called PPVM to help users better understand the policies. Policy frameworks such as P3P only assist in demonstrating their policies to customers, but do not help to enforce them. P3P was originally built for web browser to enable websites or applications to display their privacy practices in a standard format for human comprehension. An issue is that there is no negotiation among data collector and user if the request does not match the user's preferences [11]. EPAL (enterprise privacy authorization language) is a tool to write enterprise privacy policies however it does not define how users are authenticated, nor how policies are associated with collected data [5]. To address the shortfalls of EPAL and P3P, Ghazinour et al. [11] proposed a lattice-based model that enforces privacy policies as defined by the data collector and provider through negotiation. Through a lattice structure, both the user and data collector are able to select a range of preferences rather than fixed permissions. XML documents hold the practices of data collectors are parsed according to the taxonomy elements in [6] through which a lattice is built. Users are presented with the practices and allowed to make selections, which are stored as their privacy preferences and the access control model evaluates each access request based on the customized privacy preferences. We use this lattice-base structure as the backbone of our privacy negotiation phase between the wearable device user and data collectors [11].

3   Proposed Work

In the proposed model, the user controls what, who, to what degree, and how long the data collected by the wearable device can be used or disclosed [7].

3.1   Privacy-Aware Layer

The layer handles both the user application preferences and application access (Fig. 1).

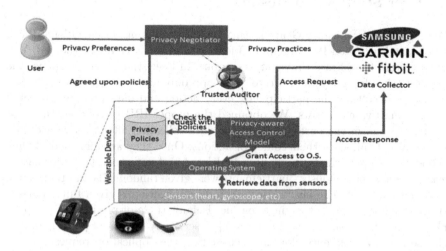

Fig. 1. Privacy-aware layer framework

Each application must have a JSON file consists of privacy practices for each sensor request represented in JSON format. In turn, the user may not define preferences. We define four key elements in privacy policy: purpose, visibility, granularity, and retention. Each policy has multiple options set by the data collector. Upon data collection, users can select privacy preferences within a given range. The privacy catalogue stores the preferences with the data so that when a data collector submits an access request of a particular user, the data catalogue is cross-references so the appropriate response is given back to the requester. The data collector and user negotiate over a lattice structure with possible nodes. For example, Visibility set V = {only me, my lab, Public}, the purpose set P = {None, Personal Record, research, any}, the granularity set G = {Existential, Partial, Specific}, and the retention set R = {Forever, 03/01/2019, 01/09/2018}.

Fig. 2. Privacy protection layer UI

4   User Studies and Results

We use several Samsung Gear S2 smartwatches running Tizen OS for the 2 studies and recruited 19 males and 13 females and ran a survey at the end. Volunteers from Kent State University's campus. In User study 1, the users use the smartwatches for 2 days and are told the app only accesses heart rate whereas in reality it collects the participants' every action and data possibly collected by the smartwatch sensors. We obtained the proper IRB to conduct this case study. We inform the participants about data collection after they're acquired so we do not influence their course of actions. Once they are informed, if they choose not to participate, their data is deleted and not used. The information was collected anonymously - participants were given random IDs and their name were not collected. The heart rate (spyware) application is given full privileges storing all the usage history in a log file. Default tuple of privilege is {v, p, g, r} = {our lab, research, specific, forever}. User study 2 allowed participants to choose privacy preferences for each sensor that the application requests access for (Fig. 2). Tables 1, 2, 3 and 4 show sample data from Participant 7 to show interested readers what data has been collected. After 2 days we showed the participants how much information could potentially collected from them and they were shocked! In user study 2, we gave the same participants the option to use our privacy protector app installed on the smartwatches. They are asked to select their application privacy preferences in the privacy protector application. They then continue to use the spyware application for another 2 days. The number of collected records in the two user studies are shown in Table 5.

Table 1. Participant 7 sleep date

Day 1	Day 2
Start: 6:15 a.m	Start: 3:35 a.m
Wake-up: 2:55 p.m	Wake-up: 11:16 a.m

Table 2. Participant 7 heart rate data

Participant	Heart rate	Date & Time
7	112	Sun May 27 2018 01:16:24 GMT-0400 (EDT)

Table 3. Participant 7 pedometer data

Measurement	Value
Speed	4.30
Walk frequency	1.7000
Distance	11.720
Calories	5.4400
Step count	174
Walk step count	161
Run step count	0

Table 4. Participant 7 GPS data

Participant	Latitude	Longitude	Date & Time
7	41.18922	-81.43522	Sun May 27 2018 01:16:24 GMT-0400 (EDT)

After the user studies, we asked participants how important {very important (VI), somewhat important (SI), Neutral (N), somewhat unimportant (SUI), unimportant (UI)} a need for consent is for gathering location, vitals, application usage, calendar, contact, video/audio data {Loc, Vitals, App, Cal, Cont, Rec} data (Fig. 3). Individuals felt their privacy was being compromised when have

Table 5. Collected records for user studies (sample)

Participant	User study 1	User study 2
1	52K records	84 records
2	21K records	657 records
3	26K records	–
4	35K records	–
5	43K records	187 records
6	27K records	236 records
7	18K records	194 records
8	16K records	–

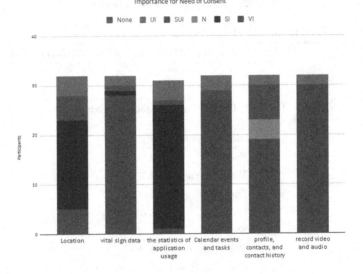

Fig. 3. Concern statistics for watch data collection

to share any vital sign, calendar, user profile and video/audio data. Location and application usage statistics were of less importance. We gathered that 100% of participants felt that they have no control over their data. They also felt that applications were not giving notifications for sensors accesses. The participants also revealed for what purpose the use their smartwatches (see Fig. 4).

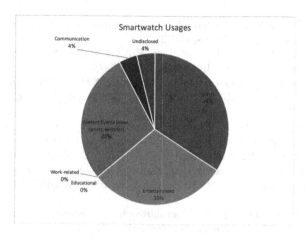

Fig. 4. Usage statics of smartwatches

5   Discussion

The user studies help individuals to understand how much can be known about their lives given that data collectors have full access without restriction (Tables 1, 2, 3 and 4). Based on user preferences, the privacy protector effectively diminishes the amount of data being collected by the spyware application. With the unique ability to select from a hierarchical lattice, the application is not completely deterred from functioning even if the user chooses to be more restrictive for purpose, visibility, granularity, and retention categories. However, it is the responsibility of the data collector to provide such flexible options. Our survey indicates that individuals want consent when it comes to data such as vital sign, calendar, user profile and video/audio data; more so with video/audio data. 25 participants were concerned about sharing data due to being asked for sensitive information, while 20 were concerned because they did not know the company enough. Smartwatches are primarily used for entertainment, sports, current events and communication (Fig. 4). Our privacy aware access control model provides users a protection layer through a lattice-based negotiation framework. In this respect, it adheres to common privacy principles and requirements. We believe this is a good first step and more research will be done to develop usable security and privacy tools.

References

1. Design for Wear OS [Internet]. https://developer.android.com/design/wear/. Accessed 26 Nov 2018
2. Design Principles—Tizen Developers [Internet]. https://developer.tizen.org/design/wearable/design-principles. Accessed 26 Nov 2018
3. HP Study [Internet]. https://www8.hp.com/us/en/hp-news/press-release.html?id=2037386#.Vi18G7crLIU. Accessed 19 Feb 2019

4. Aciicmez, O., Blaich, A.: Understanding the permissions and access control model for tizen application sandboxing (2012)
5. Anderson, A.: A Comparison of Two Privacy Policy Languages: EPAL and XACML. Sun Microsystems Inc., Santa Clara (2005)
6. Barker, K.: A data privacy taxonomy. In: Sexton, A.P. (ed.) BNCOD 2009. LNCS, vol. 5588, pp. 42–54. Springer, Heidelberg (2009). https://doi.org/10.1007/978-3-642-02843-4_7
7. Ching, K.W., Singh, M.M.: Wearable technology devices security privacy vulnerability analysis. Int. J. Netw. Secur. Appl. 8(3), 19–26 (2016)
8. Felt, A. P., Ha, E., Egelman, S., Haney, A., Chin, E., Wagner, D.: Android permissions: user attention, comprehension, and behavior. In: Proceeedings of the Eighth Symposium on Usable Privacy and Security (SOUPS 2012). ACM, New York (2012)
9. Gadyatskaya, O., Massacci, F., Zhauniarovich, Y.: Security in the firefox OS and Tizen mobile platforms. Computer 47(6), 57–63 (2014)
10. Ghazinour, K., Barker, K.: A privacy preserving model bridging data provider and collector preferences. In: Proceedings of the Joint EDBT/ICDT 2013 Workshops, Genoa, Italy, pp. 174–178, 18–22 March 2013
11. Ghazinour, K., Barker, K.: Capturing P3P semantics using an enforceable lattice-based structure. In: Proceedings of the 4th International Workshop on Privacy and Anonymity in the Information Society, Uppsala, Sweden, pp. 1–6, 25 March 2011
12. Ghazinour, K., Majedi, M., Barker, K.: A model for privacy policy visualization. In: 2009 33rd Annual IEEE International Computer Software and Applications Conference, vol. 2, pp. 335–340 (2009)
13. Im, B., Ware, R.: Tizen security overview. In: Tizen Developer Conference, May 2012. http://download.tizen.org/misc/media/conference2012/tuesday/ballroom-c/2012-05-08-1600-1640-tizen_security_framework_overview.pdf. Accessed 25 May 2018
14. Li, H., et al.: Examining individuals adoption' of healthcare wearable devices: an empirical study from privacy calculus perspective. Int. J. Med. Inform. 88, 8–16 (2016)
15. Motti, V.G., Caine, K.: Users' privacy concerns about wearables. In: Brenner, M., Christin, N., Johnson, B., Rohloff, K. (eds.) FC 2015. LNCS, vol. 8976, pp. 231–244. Springer, Heidelberg (2015). https://doi.org/10.1007/978-3-662-48051-9_17

Validating the DFA Attack Resistance of AES (Short Paper)

Hakuei Sugimoto$^{(\boxtimes)}$, Ryota Hatano$^{(\boxtimes)}$, Natsu Shoji$^{(\boxtimes)}$,
and Kazuo Sakiyama$^{(\boxtimes)}$

The University of Electro-Communications, 1-5-1 Chofugaoka,
Chofu, Tokyo 182-8585, Japan
{hakueisugimoto,r.hatano,n.shoji,sakiyama}@uec.ac.jp

Abstract. Physical attacks are a serious threat to the Internet of Things devices. Differential power analysis attacks are the most well-known physical attacks that exploit physical information leaked from hardware devices to retrieve secret information. Fault analysis attacks, a type of physical attack, are often considered more powerful than side-channel attacks if an attacker can inject the attacker's intended faults. In fact, a few times of fault injections have enabled the attacker to retrieve the secret key. In this study, we propose a new model to validate the resistance of block ciphers to Differential Fault Analysis (DFA) attacks by assuming an ideal block cipher in which the differential probability is the same for all input and output differences. We show that Advanced Encryption Standard (AES) is near ideal for DFA attack resistance according to the experimental results.

Keywords: AES · Physical attack · Attack resistance · Abstraction model · Differential Fault Analysis · Survival probability · Key identification

1 Introduction

Many practical attacks have been reported against cryptosystems [1,2]. Among them, physical attacks combined with cryptanalysis have received considerable attention as one of the most powerful attack methods. Commonly used block ciphers such as Advanced Encryption Standard (AES) [3] are considered secure enough against theoretical cryptanalysis. However, in reality, physical attacks enable attackers to bypass theoretical protection. Probing attacks and Differential Fault Analysis (DFA) attacks are well-known examples of physical attacks. The probing attack directly obtains one or multiple bit(s) of internal value from the hardware on which the ciphers are implemented, and it deduces a secret key [4,5]. On the contrary, the DFA attack injects a fault to limit the possible difference in the intermediate value, and it retrieves the secret key from the output difference in the ciphertext [2].

This work was supported by JSPS KAKENHI Grant Number JP18H05289.

© Springer Nature Switzerland AG 2020
A. Benzekri et al. (Eds.): FPS 2019, LNCS 12056, pp. 371–378, 2020.
https://doi.org/10.1007/978-3-030-45371-8_25

It is possible to evaluate the resistance to physical attacks with heuristic observations of the attack, e.g., the number of fault trials necessary to identify the secret key from the experiments. However, there are two main issues. First, simulations using a low-level abstraction model, i.e., full description of the cipher behavior, require an enormous amount of time, because the attack efficiency follows some distribution; thus, Monte Carlo simulations have to be performed using random numbers. Note that a hardware-based simulation will accelerate the evaluation time, but the effects are limited. Second, even if the probability distribution is obtained for the attack efficiency, there is no reference to validate the results. Motivated by these issues, [6,7] propose high-level abstraction models for physical attacks on block ciphers. The physical attack model can offer an efficient simulation and an ideal metric of attack resistance, which means that the above-mentioned issues can be solved. More precisely, for the first issue, a simulation with high-level abstraction modeling enables us to perform a deterministic simulation for the physical attack, which reduces the cost and time required for the simulation. For the second issue, the model can be idealized for each physical attack to validate the attack resistance of existing ciphers.

1.1 Our Contribution

In this study, we extend the proposal of [7], in which the authors modeled the probing attack on block ciphers, to the DFA attack based on the assumption that the differential probability of an S-box is uniform in an ideal cipher. Then, we show that AES is near ideal for the DFA attacks using several well-known fault models [8,9]. The proposed model quantitatively offers a metric of the physical attack resistance, and it helps us validate the experimental results of low-level abstraction simulations with several fault models in the 8th, 9th, and 10th rounds of AES.

1.2 Previous Work

The DFA attack was proposed in 1997 as a type of physical attack [2]. In [8], the 8th-round DFA attack was performed on a 128-bit AES, and the authors could identify the secret key experimentally after about two fault trials. In [9], the 9th-round DFA attack on AES was performed based on two fault models, and the authors checked the attack efficiency using actual experiments. However, the experimental results' validity is not strictly discussed in either work. In [6], the DFA attack on a block cipher is modeled under the assumption that the amount of leaked information is constant for each DFA trial. The authors could successfully check the optimality of several existing DFA attack results; however, the due to simplicity of the assumption, the DFA attack results with some fault models, such as [9], are not properly validated in their model.

Another new model is proposed in [7]. The authors assumed that each false key in a key-candidate list is withdrawn with the same probability, called survival probability, for each probing trial. In other words, the key-reduction sequence in

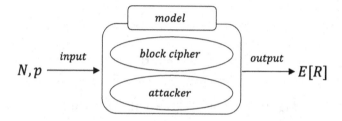

Fig. 1. Overview of the proposed model in [7].

the probing attack on an ideal cipher is regarded as a Markov chain. Then, the attack efficiency of the 1-bit probing attack is validated on several existing block ciphers. Let R be a random variable whose values are the number of probing trials necessary to identify the secret key, let p be the survival probability of the false key, and let N be the total number of false keys.

The overview of the proposed model is shown in Fig. 1. Abstracting many inputs in actual situation, the inputs of the model are only N and p. Notice that this model does not need to consider the plaintext, the details of key identification algorithm, the parameters for an experiment environment and so on. Only with the information of N and p, the expected number of probing trials can be obtained as

$$E[R] = \sum_{r=1}^{\infty} r \Pr[R = r], \tag{1}$$

where

$$\Pr[R = r] = (1 - p^r)^N - (1 - p^{r-1})^N. \tag{2}$$

In [7], the model value of the attack trials is only for probing attacks, and one for the DFA attack has not been proposed.

2 Proposed Model for DFA Attacks

The DFA attack and the probing attack both share the same characteristic wherein the attacker extracts possible key candidates using information about the intermediate and public values. Therefore, Eqs. (1) and (2) can be applied to the DFA attack as well by only changing the survival probability appropriately and considering an ideal property of the block ciphers against the DFA attack. As discussed in [7], we assume that the ideal cipher has a property such that all false keys have equal survival probabilities for each DFA trial.

The target block cipher of the DFA attack is shown in Fig. 2. Let x be input value of an n-bit bijective function f. Let Δx be the input difference, and let $\mathcal{X}$ be a set of $\Delta x (\neq 0)$. The possible values for Δx are determined by the fault model. The attacker injects a fault into the input of the function f and obtains output

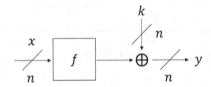

Fig. 2. Target block cipher of the DFA attack.

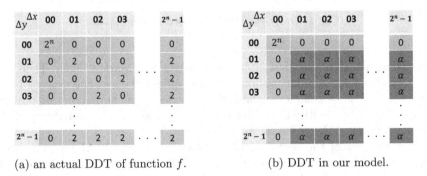

Δy \ Δx	00	01	02	03		2^n-1
00	2^n	0	0	0		0
01	0	2	0	0		2
02	0	0	0	2	$\cdots$	2
03	0	0	2	0		2
2^n-1	0	2	2	2	$\cdots$	2

Δy \ Δx	00	01	02	03		2^n-1
00	2^n	0	0	0		0
01	0	α	α	α		α
02	0	α	α	α	$\cdots$	α
03	0	α	α	α		α
2^n-1	0	α	α	α	$\cdots$	α

(a) an actual DDT of function f.   (b) DDT in our model.

Fig. 3. Modeling difference distribution table (DDT) of function f.

value y and output difference Δy. Here, we consider the survival probability of a key k, considering the above-mentioned ideal block cipher property. If k is the correct key, the survival probability is one. On the other hand, the survival probability of the false keys is determined using the fault model and the function f. We will explain the details. The attacker creates a key candidate set $\mathcal{K}$ as

$$\mathcal{K} = \left\{ k \mid f^{-1}(y \oplus k) \oplus f^{-1}(y \oplus \Delta y \oplus k) \in \mathcal{X} \right\}. \tag{3}$$

For existing block ciphers, the size of $\mathcal{K}$ follows the difference distribution table (DDT), as shown in Fig. 3(a). In the proposed model, we use DDT as shown in Fig. 3(b). The values in DDT are averaged values except for $\Delta x = 0$ and $\Delta y = 0$; this is to make the target as resistant as possible to differential analysis. Namely, we assume that the ideal block cipher has a property wherein the differential probability of f is uniformly distributed for any Δx and Δy, w.r.t. the DFA attacks.

We present the detailed DDT in our model here. Then, the sum of the values in DDT, i.e., the total count of keys satisfying Eq. (3) for any Δx and Δy, is equal to

$$\sum_{\Delta x} \sum_{\Delta y} \# \left\{ k \mid f^{-1}(y \oplus k) \oplus f^{-1}(y \oplus \Delta y \oplus k) = \Delta x \right\} = (2^n)^2. \tag{4}$$

As we can exclude the cases for $\Delta x = 0$ and $\Delta y = 0$ from the DFA attack, for a given $(\Delta x, \Delta y)$, let N be the total number of false keys. The averaged value α is derived as

$$\alpha = \frac{(2^n)^2 - 2^n}{(2^n - 1)^2} = \frac{2^n}{2^n - 1} \doteq 1 + \frac{1}{N}. \tag{5}$$

That is, for the attacker who obtains $\mathcal{X}$ and Δy, the number of key candidates becomes $\alpha|\mathcal{X}|$ by counting the number of α in DDT after a DFA trial. Therefore, we use the following as the survival probability of the false keys in the proposed model.

$$p = \frac{\alpha|\mathcal{X}| - 1}{N}. \tag{6}$$

3   Validating DFA Attack Resistance on AES

3.1   Case for the 10th-Round DFA Attack

First, we used our model to validate the experimental results of simulations with several fault models at the 10th round of AES. We considered the 10th round of AES as function f, as shown in Fig. 2, and we obtained the model value of the number of DFA trials, i.e., the attack resistance against the DFA attack. A comparison of the model and experimental values is shown in Table 1.

Table 1 shows that the DFA attack resistance of AES is slightly higher than that of the ideal cipher of our model.

For example, on the 1-bit fault model, there are 8-bit positions to inject fault. Thus, $|\mathcal{X}| = 8$. The larger the number of $|\mathcal{X}|$, the smaller the difference between the number of key candidates of the actual DDT and those of our model's DDT. The same is true for 2-bit to 7-bit faults. Focusing on the 8-bit fault model in particular, the model value is about 1, while the experimental value is about 2. The reason for this result is the values in DDT. From Fig. 3, the values in an actual DDT of function f are 0, 2 or 4. However, the values in DDT in our model are all α. Namely, in the case of our model, we can identify the secret key in one attack. However, in the case of an actual DDT, we obtain 1 or 3 false key(s) other than the secret key. In this case, one more attack is required

Table 1. The model and experimental values for the 10th-round DFA ($n = 8$).

Fault model	p	$E[R]$	Experiments
1-bit random	2.757×10^{-2}	**2.181**	2.240
2-bit random	1.063×10^{-1}	**3.245**	3.286
3-bit random	2.165×10^{-1}	**4.503**	4.542
4-bit random	2.717×10^{-1}	**5.195**	5.235
5-bit random	2.165×10^{-1}	**4.503**	4.542
6-bit random	1.063×10^{-1}	**3.245**	3.285
7-bit random	2.757×10^{-2}	**2.181**	2.230
8-bit	1.538×10^{-5}	**1.004**	2.009

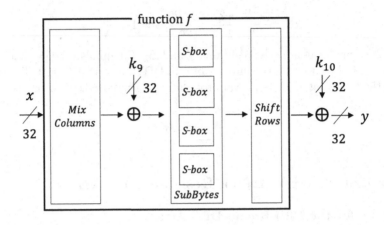

Fig. 4. Target of the 9th-round DFA attack on AES and function f

because the secret key cannot be identified. There is a difference in the amount of key information obtained in one attack of the ideal cipher and AES. This is one factor of the difference between the model value and experimental value.

3.2 Case for the 9th-Round DFA Attack

Next, we validated the experimental results of the case of a fault model that injects a 1-byte fault and one that injects a 4-byte fault at the 9th round in [9]. The target of the 9th-round DFA attack on AES and function f are shown in Fig. 4. At the 9th-round DFA attack on AES, the fault is injected before *MixColumns* processing. Since the active byte is 4 bytes, function f with ideal difference characteristics is set as shown in Fig. 4. In a fault model injecting a 1-byte fault into the 9th round, $|\mathcal{X}| = 2^8 - 1 = 255$. In the fault model by [9], the attacker injects a 4-byte fault in the 9th round, and $|\mathcal{X}| = (2^8 - 1)^4 = 255^4$. Moreover, the size of DDT of function f in Fig. 4 is $n = 32$.

The model value, experimental value, and survival probability p for the 9th round 1-byte fault model and the 9th round 4-byte fault model [9] are shown in Table 2. It shows that experimental values of the two fault models are higher than the model value.

Table 2. The model and experimental values for the 9th-round DFA ($n = 32$).

Fault model	p	$E[R]$	Experiments
1-byte fixed position	5.914×10^{-8}	**2.000**	2.017
4-byte fixed position [9]	9.845×10^{-1}	**1454**	1495

3.3   Case for the 8th-Round DFA Attack

Furthermore, we validated the experimental results of the case of a fault model that injects a 1-byte fault at the 8th round [8]. The target of the 8th-round DFA attack on AES and function f are shown in Fig. 5. It is assumed that the fault model of [8] injects a 1-byte fault into four locations, $|\mathcal{X}| = 255^4 \times 4$. Moreover, the size of DDT of function f in Fig. 5 is $n = 128$. The model value, experimental value, and survival probability p for the 8th-round 1-byte fault model [8] are shown in Table 3. The DFA attack resistance of AES can be considered close to the ideal cipher.

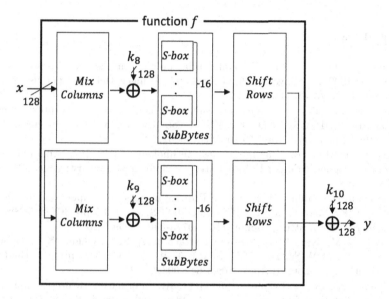

Fig. 5. Target of 8th-round DFA attack on AES and function f

Table 3. The model and experimental values for the 8th-round DFA ($n = 128$).

Fault model	p	$E[R]$	Experiments
1-byte random [8]	2.995×10^{-36}	**2.000**	$2.020^{\dagger}$

†From [8], we assume that 98% of the experiments identify the secret key with two DFA trials, and the remaining 2% need three trials.

4   Conclusion and Future Work

In this study, we presented a new model to validate the DFA attack resistance of block ciphers by assuming an ideal block cipher in which the differential probability of the S-box is uniform. In addition, we validated the experimental results of low-level abstraction simulations with several fault models at the 8th, 9th, and 10th rounds of AES. Under the assumption that the simulations to obtain the experimental values are properly performed, the results indicate that AES is near ideal for the DFA attack resistance. In the future, we will apply the proposed model to existing ciphers other than AES and validate their attack resistance. Furthermore, we will extend the model to other physical attacks.

References

1. Kocher, P., Jaffe, J., Jun, B.: Differential power analysis. In: Wiener, M. (ed.) CRYPTO 1999. LNCS, vol. 1666, pp. 388–397. Springer, Heidelberg (1999). https://doi.org/10.1007/3-540-48405-1_25
2. Biham, E., Shamir, A.: Differential fault analysis of secret key cryptosystems. In: Kaliski, B.S. (ed.) CRYPTO 1997. LNCS, vol. 1294, pp. 513–525. Springer, Heidelberg (1997). https://doi.org/10.1007/BFb0052259
3. National Institute of Standards and Technology. FIPS 197: Announcing the Advanced Ciphers Standard (AES). http://nvlpubs.nist.gov/nistpubs/FIPS/NIST.FIPS.197.pdf
4. Handschuh, H., Paillier, P., Stern, J.: Probing attacks on tamper-resistant devices. In: Koç, Ç.K., Paar, C. (eds.) CHES 1999. LNCS, vol. 1717, pp. 303–315. Springer, Heidelberg (1999). https://doi.org/10.1007/3-540-48059-5_26
5. Schmidt, J.-M., Kim, C.H.: A probing attack on AES. In: Chung, K.-I., Sohn, K., Yung, M. (eds.) WISA 2008. LNCS, vol. 5379, pp. 256–265. Springer, Heidelberg (2009). https://doi.org/10.1007/978-3-642-00306-6_19
6. Sakiyama, K., Li, Y., Iwamoto, M., Ohta, K.: Information-theoretic approach to optimal differential fault analysis. IEEE Trans. Inf. Forensic Secur. 7(1), 109–120 (2012)
7. Shoji, N., Sugawara, T., Iwamoto, M., Sakiyama, K.: An abstraction model for 1-bit probing attack on block ciphers. In: Proceedings of the International Conference on Computer and Communication Systems (ICCCS 2019), pp. 502–506. IEEE (2019)
8. Piret, G., Quisquater, J.-J.: A differential fault attack technique against SPN structures, with application to the AES and KHAZAD. In: Walter, C.D., Koç, Ç.K., Paar, C. (eds.) CHES 2003. LNCS, vol. 2779, pp. 77–88. Springer, Heidelberg (2003). https://doi.org/10.1007/978-3-540-45238-6_7
9. Moradi, A., Shalmani, M.T.M., Salmasizadeh, M.: A generalized method of differential fault attack against AES cryptosystem. In: Goubin, L., Matsui, M. (eds.) CHES 2006. LNCS, vol. 4249, pp. 91–100. Springer, Heidelberg (2006). https://doi.org/10.1007/11894063_8

A Rejection-Based Approach for Detecting SQL Injection Vulnerabilities in Web Applications

Lalia Saoudi[1(⊠)], Kamel Adi[2], and Younes Boudraa[1]

[1] Mohamed Boudiaf University, Msila, Algeria
Lalia.saoudi@univ-msila.dz, younesboudraa05@gmail.com
[2] Université du Québec en Outaouais, Gatineau, Canada
Kamel.Adi@uqo.ca

Abstract. According to OWASP top10 Application Security Risks [8,9] SQL injection (SQLi) remains the most dangerous and most commonly exploited vulnerability in web applications. Thus, a lot of attentions are devoted by the scientific community for the development of SQLi verification tools. In this paper we focus on the development of an efficient, black box, SQLi vulnerability scanner to achieve an accurate detection. Our new approach is based on the use of structural similarity between rejection pages and their corresponding injection pages. A software prototype has been implemented and showed promising results as compared to well-known web application scanners.

Keywords: SQL injection vulnerability detection · Web page structural similarity · Black box scanner

1 Introduction

A web application is a program implemented with different web technologies, stored on a remote server and executed over the HTTP protocol via a web browser. Unfortunately the highly heterogeneous nature of the web with its different technologies makes it difficult for web application developers to properly secure their applications, by doing a complete input validation and sanitization. Furthermore, the last two OWASP (Open Web Application Security Project) reports for the top 10 web application vulnerabilities show that SQL injection is ranked first among the other vulnerabilities [8,9].

To overcome this security problem, a variety of scanners have been developed to identify existing SQLi vulnerable Application Entry Points (AEPs) [1,10,11]. These scanners can be classified into two main categories: white_box and black_box scanners. In white_box scanners (static analysis), the source code of the web application is analyzed, with the full knowledge of the application, for potential vulnerabilities that could be exploited. While black_box scanners (dynamic analysis) take an outsider's attacker view; without any knowledge

© Springer Nature Switzerland AG 2020
A. Benzekri et al. (Eds.): FPS 2019, LNCS 12056, pp. 379–386, 2020.
https://doi.org/10.1007/978-3-030-45371-8_26

of the application's architecture; and analyze web applications while they are running. This type of scanners is widely used for identifying web applications vulnerabilities in an easy and automated fashion, however it suffers from false negative and false positive problems. Recent studies have shown that there is a need for improving the effectiveness and precision of existing SQLi vulnerability scanners [3]. To this end, we propose, in this work, a new approach for SQLi vulnerabilities detection, based on error matching and structural similarity between an injection page and its corresponding rejection page. The idea of our approach is based on the assumption that if the AEPs are filtered against SQLi requests, then their response pages have often the same structure as rejection pages, because the injected request are considered as random data. To prove the efficiency of our approach, we test it on different web applications, and compare its performance with famous web application scanners.

The rest of this paper is organized as follows. Section 2 provides general concepts about SQLi detection mechanisms and introduces our detection approach. Section 3 presents our proposed approach in details. Section 4 explains the experimental results. Finally, Sect. 5 contains a conclusion and some directions for future work.

2   General Concepts

To explain clearly our approach we need to define some technical concepts. Requests that can be sent through AEPs, can be classified into three main classes:

- random requests, noted RR.
- valid requests, noted VR.
- invalid requests, noted IR.

Class of Random Requests: requests in this class are generated from randomly selected words containing characters from [a–z, A–Z, 0–9]. Let's take an example of an authentication page containing the couple: *login/pass*:

$$login = aFged \quad pass = FRs0f$$

This generates the following SQL query:

$$SELECT * FROM users WHERE login =' afged' and pass =' FRs0f';$$

The response page for a random query is always a rejection page.

Class of Valid Requests: contains a set of syntactically valid SQL injection requests that are built for the purpose of generating execution pages. For example, the *login/ pass* pair that has the values: $'or'1' =' 1 - -$, *abcd*, generates the following SQL query:

$$SELECT * FROM users WHERE login =' 'or'1' =' 1 - -' and pass =' abcd';$$

This SQL query is syntactically valid and as a result, an execution page is returned to the client.

Class of Invalid Requests: contains a set of syntactically incorrect SQL injection requests sent to the web application to generate DBMS errors or rejection pages. For example, the request behind the URL:

http://www.example.com/page.php? login=' ' '&pass=' ' '

will generate a DBMS error.

3   The Principle of Our SQLi Vulnerability Detection Approach

The response pages of random queries on a specified AEP have a fixed structure, while the execution pages of valid queries on a specified AEP have a dynamic structure and it depends on the inputs values on that AEP. Therefore, it is easier to compare the response page of an injection query with a page of fixed structure than to compare with a page of dynamic structure. Furthermore, if we send a SQLi query to an AEP, we can be in one of the following cases:

- the application treats the query as random data. In this case, a rejection page for a random query or an execution page containing sub-strings of the injection query is returned and the AEP is considered as secure.
- the application treats the query as an SQL query and returns a valid response page or an error response page. In these two cases the AEP is considered as vulnerable.

The principle of our approach is to send different injection requests to each identified AEP in the Web application and extract the structure of the corresponding response page. If the response page contains any DBMS error, this means that the AEP is a vulnerable and the scanner stops injection and passes to the next identified AEP. If the response page does not contain any DBMS error, then we extract the response page for that AEP and compare its structural similarity with its corresponding rejection page using an adjusted structural similarity algorithm. If both pages are structurally similar, this means that the AEP is not vulnerable to this injection request. Furthermore if the AEP is a searchable input then we search for any word on the resulting page that contains a sub-string of the injection request. If that is not the case we conclude that this AEP is vulnerable.

3.1   Proposed SQLiVD Algorithm

We present our SQLi vulnerabilities detection approach on the Algorithm 1.1 below: The algorithm takes as input a set of extracted AEP's from a crawling phase, with two sets of invalid and valid requests and outputs the set of vulnerable AEP's. The first test is to check the resistance of this AEP against an error_based SQLi attack. The second test is to check the resistance of this AEP against valid requests, for this purpose the algorithm starts by extracting the sequence tags of the response page of random request (Seq_RR), then it iterates over each valid request in the given set to extract its response page (RPVR) after injection, with its sequence tags (Seq_VR). Next it passes the couple of sequences tags: (Seq_RR, Seq_VR) to the similarity function to calculate the similarity between the two sequences, if they are not similar then it means that the obtained response page is not a rejection page, in this case, the AEP is considered as vulnerable in two cases:

- if the AEP is in searchable form and if no substring of the valid request exists in the RPVR.
- if the AEP is not in searchable form.

Algorithm 1.1. SQLIV detection algorithm.

```
Inputs:
AEP: application entry points set
IR: invalid requests set
VR: valid requests set
RR: random request
Outputs:
VulnerableAEP: set of vulnerable AEPs
Begin
VulnerableAEP ← ∅;
for each X in AEP do (* for each entry point input *)
begin
  X.state ← Secure;
  RPRR ← Get_RP(RR); (* get a response page for a random request *)
  Seq_RR ← ExtractTags(RPRR);
  (* extract tags from a response page of the random request *)
  for each y in IR do (* for each invalid request *)
  begin
    RPIR ← Get_RP(y); (* get a response page for a invalid request *)
    If(error_found(RPIR)) then (* if the RPIR contains an error *)
    begin
    X.state ← Vulnerable; (* the entry point is vulnerable *)
    break;
    end
    else (* if no error is found *)
    begin
    Seq_IR ← ExtractTags(RPIR);
    (* extract tags from a response page of the invalid request *)
    Decision← Similarity(Seq_RR, Seq_IR);
    (* compute similarity between the two tag sequences *)
    If(Decision ≠ 1) then
    begin  X.state ← vulnerable;  break;  end
    end
  end
  for each Z in VR do (* for each valid request *)
  begin
    RPVR ← Get_RP(Z); (* get a response page for valid request *)
    Seq_VR ← ExtractTags(RPVR); (* extract tags from RPVR *)
    Decision ← Similarity(Seq_RR, Seq_VR);
    (* compute similarity between the two tag sequences *)
    If(Decision ≠ 1) then
    begin
      If(is_searchable(AEP)) then (* if the AEP is in searchable form *)
      begin
        Found ← SearchFor(RPVR, Z)
        (* searching for any substring of Z in RPVR *)
        If not_Found then (* if no substring of Z exists in the RPVR *)
          begin X.state ← Vulnerable; break; end
      end
      else (* the AEP is not a searchable input *)
        begin  X.state ← Vulnerable; break; end
    end
  end
  If X.state=vulnerable then
    begin VulnerableAEP ←VulnerableAEP ∪ X; end
end
```

3.2   HTML Page Similarity

As stated in [4], two HTML pages are structurally similar accrue when they have a similar layout observed in a browser. Based on that statement, our approach uses HTML tag sequences to represent the structure of pages under comparison, where tags of a web page are represented as a sequence of nodes. Our similarity detection algorithm has the following steps:

- first, it parses the pages under comparison and extracts their series of nodes using a Document Object Model (DOM) tree representation.
- second, it removes context-related tag attributes, such as href, src, alt, etc.
- third, it calculates the Longest Common Sub-sequence (LCS) between nodes of the two pages.
- the final step is to compute the similarity between the two HTML pages under comparison, using the following equation :

$$Sim(RP, VP) = \frac{2 * LCS(RP, VP)}{length(RP) + length(VP)}$$

where RP is a random page, VP is a valid page and both pages are represented by tag sequences. $LCS(RP, VP)$ is Longest Common Sub-sequence of the two pages and $length(X)$ is the number of tags in the sequence X. If $Sim(RP, VP) = 1$ then VP is a vulnerable page else VP is not vulnerable with this valid request.

4   Experimentation

There are many vulnerable applications designed as a support for teaching purposes and to be an aid for security professionals to test their tools in a legal environment. For our testing purposes, we have selected two online web applications:

- $Site_1$: is an online shop vulnerable application designed by Acunetix for testing purposes: http://testphp.vulnweb.com [2].
- $Site_2$: is an online shop application developed for training and testing purposes: https://www.hackthissite.org/missions/realistic [7].

These web applications can not cover all types of SQLi attacks. For this reason we decided to use three other vulnerable web applications: $site_3$ and $site_4$. We developed and coded them with the PHP languages and using MySQL as a backend data. Both applications are running on Apache Tocomat 7.0.27. $site_5$ is an academic vulnerable web application.

- $Site_3$: is a custom application of an online shop, containing two known SQLi vulnerabilities: one is error_based and the other is tautology_based.
- $Site_4$: is an online exam custom application, containing two known SQLi vulnerabilities: one is error_based and the other is blind_based.
- $Site_5$: known as "XVWA: Xtreme Vulnerable Web Application [6] and should be hosted in a local environment. It allows the learning of web application security.

Table 1 shows the types of vulnerabilities that exist in each tested site.

Table 1. Types of SQLi vulnerabilities in the tested sites

	$Site_1$	$Site_2$	$Site_3$	$Site_4$	$Site_5$
Error_based	1	0	1	0	1
Blind_based	1	1	0	1	1
Tautology_based	1	0	1	1	1

1 = vulnerable. 0 = not vulnerable.

4.1 The Scanners Used for Comparison Purposes

Experimentation will have more credibility if we involve scanners adopted by the scientific and professional community as a kind of reference to prove the power of our approach.

The scanners that we used are: our scanner SQLiVD [5], W3af [11], ZAP [10] and another commercial web vulnerability scanner named Acunetix [1].

4.2 Experimentation Results

This section shows the scan results of each tested application with the four scanners.

Results of Scanners for Each SQLi Type: The results of running the four scanners against the vulnerable applications are shown in Table 2. The three values in each cell represent the numbers of discovered vulnerabilities for each type of SQLi attacks (Error_based/blind_based/tautology_based).

Table 2. The results of running the four scanners against the vulnerable applications

	$Site_1$	$Site_2$	$Site_3$	$Site_4$	$Site_5$
W3af	1/0/0	0/0/0	1/0/0	0/0/0	0/0/0
ZAP	0/0/0	0/0/0	0/0/0	0/0/0	0/0/0
Acunetix	1/1/1	0/0/0	1/0/0	0/1/0	0/1/0
SQLiVD	1/1/1	0/1/0	1/0/1	0/1/1	1/1/1

The results show that Acunetix discovered two applications with blind_based SQLi vulnerability and one tautology_based SQLi vulnerability, while our SQLiVD scanner discovered all of them. SQLiVD is able to detect tautology_based SQLi vulnerability in $Site_3$, $Site_4$ and $Site_5$ and blind_based SQLi vulnerability in $Site_2$ and $Site_5$, as it is mentioned in Tables 3 and 4.

It is important to mention that SQLiVD is the only scanner that discovered a blind_based SQLiV in $Site_2$ thanks to our adopted approach. Furthermore, it is the only scanner that detects the error based vulnerabilities on $site_5$, because

Table 3. Successful authentication bypass and tautology-based SQLi detection by SQLiVD

	Input	Payload	Similarity
$Site_3$	loginId	' or username is not NULL or username = '	93.6
$Site_4$	password	1'AND 1=0 UNION ALL SELECT 'admin', '81dc9bdb52d04dc20036dbd8313ed055	0.21
$Site_5$	search	' order by 1#	61.73

Table 4. Successful detection of blind- based SQLi vulnerability by SQLiVD

	URL	Payload	Similarity
$Site_2$	https://www.hackthissite.org/ missions/realistic/4/products. php?category=	UNION ALL SELECT null, * , null, null FROM email;	0.99

the web application didn't generate any error key-words in it's error message as it is mentioned in Table 5. In this case, our scanner can detect it, because it is based on two mechanisms for error-based detection, first it checks the existence of any key-word of different HTTP or DBMS errors on the response page, then it verifies the structural similarity between the response page and its correspondent rejection page after an invalid request injection.

Table 5. Successful detection of error-based SQLi vulnerability by SQLiVD

	URL	Payload	Error	Similarity
$Site_5$	http://127.0.0.1/xvwa/ vulnerabilities/sqli/	'	Fatal error	Null
$Site_5$	http://127.0.0.1/xvwa/ vulnerabilities/sqli- blind/	'	Null	90.64

5   Conclusion

In this paper we described our SQLiVD scanner. The main idea behind our SQLi vulnerability detection approach is simple but efficient. It is based on the structural similarity between each valid SQLi's response page and its corresponding rejection page of a specific AEP. We tested our detection approach with three SQLi requests families: error-based, blind-based and tautology-based. An experimentation study allowed us to prove the performance and the efficiency of our approach in detecting SQLi vulnerabilities compared to the well-known scanners: ZAP, Acunetix, and W3af.

Future work will be focused on adopting an original approach for generating SQLi requests according to the input type and its applied SQLi filter, in order to inject the promising requests and try to bypass existing filters against a SQLi attack.

References

1. Acunetix: Acunetix scanner. https://www.acunetix.com/vulnerability-scanner. Accessed 21 June 2019
2. Acunetix-acuart: testphp. http://testphp.vulnweb.com. Accessed 21 June 2019
3. Aliero, M.S., Ghani, I., Qureshi, K.N., Rohani, M.F.: An algorithm for detecting SQL injection vulnerability using black-box testing. J. Ambient Intell. Humaniz. Comput. **11**(1), 249–266 (2019). https://doi.org/10.1007/s12652-019-01235-z
4. Djuric, Z.: A black-box testing tool for detecting SQL injection vulnerabilities. In: Second International Conference on Informatics Applications (ICIA), pp. 216–221, September 2013. https://doi.org/10.1109/ICoIA.2013.6650259
5. GitHub: SQLi scanner. https://github.com/lalia-dz/SQLiScanner. Accessed 22 Oct 2019
6. GitHub: XVWA. https://github.com/s4n7h0/xvwa. Accessed 26 Oct 2019
7. HackThisSite. https://www.hackthissite.org/missions/realistic. Accessed 21 June 2019
8. OWASP: OWASP_Top10_2017. https://www.owasp.org/index.php/Top_10-2017_Top_10. Accessed 21 June 2019
9. OWASP: Top_10_2013. https://www.owasp.org/index.php/Top_10_2013-Top_10. Accessed 21 June 2019
10. OWASP: ZAP scanner. https://www.zaproxy.org
11. W3af: w3af framework. http://w3af.org. Accessed 21 June 2019

Lightweight IoT Mutual Authentication Scheme Based on Transient Identities and Transactions History

Mohammed Alshahrani[1](✉), Issa Traore[1], and Sherif Saad[2]

[1] University of Victoria, Victoria, BC V8W 2Y2, Canada
{malshahr,itraore}@uvic.ca
[2] University of Windsor, Windsor, ON N9B 3P4, Canada
shsaad@uwindsor.ca

Abstract. Robust authentication of Internet of Things (IoT) is a difficult problem due to the fact that quite often IoT nodes are resource-constrained and lack the storage and compute capability required by conventional security mechanisms. We propose, in the current paper, a new lightweight multi-factor authentication scheme for IoT nodes that combines temporary identities and challenge/response based on transactions history. The approach allows IoT nodes to anonymously and mutually authenticate in an unlinkable manner. We evaluate the efficiency of the proposed scheme, and establish the security of our protocol through informal security analysis and formally by using the automated validation of Internet security protocols and applications (AVISPA) toolkit.

Keywords: IoT authentication · Multi-factor authentication · Cumulative hash chain · AVISPA · Transient identity

1 Introduction

The last few years have seen tremendous growth in the number of IoT nodes currently in operation around the world. It is forecasted that such number will grow exponentially in the near term. Security is one of the top issues besides interoperability and resource optimization in the design and operation of IoT infrastructure. In particular, authentication appears to be one of the Achilles heels of current IoT infrastructure. Many IoT nodes have very weak passwords or are still using manufacturer-issued default passwords, which make them vulnerable to botnets and exploit kits specially designed against IoT networks. At the same time hackers are able to connect rogue devices to IoT networks using fake or multiple identities without being caught. This is made possible because the landscape of IoT authentication is still at an early stage [4,6,7]. Existing authentication mechanisms involve heavy computations which cannot be afforded by IoT nodes which, quite often, are resource-constrained. Many IoT nodes do not have the required compute power, memory or storage to support

© Springer Nature Switzerland AG 2020
A. Benzekri et al. (Eds.): FPS 2019, LNCS 12056, pp. 387–397, 2020.
https://doi.org/10.1007/978-3-030-45371-8_27

the current authentication protocols, which rely on computationally intensive cryptographic algorithms, e.g., AES and RSA.

Additionally, these authentication mechanisms also require a degree of user-intervention in terms of configuration and provisioning. However, many IoT nodes will have limited access, thus requiring initial configuration to be protected from tampering, theft and other forms of compromise throughout their usable life, which in many cases could be years.

We propose a new approach for IoT nodes authentication using a multimodal platform which combines different methods based on a dynamic yet unique identity and proof of knowledge of transaction historical information. The dynamic identity uniquely determines the identity of an IoT device. Such identity involves both a stable and fixed component, and a slightly evolving time-dependent component. Transaction history-based authentication relies on the ability of the parties involved to show proof of knowledge of past transactions or activities. The approach involves using a cumulative keyed-hash chain model to track and store securely data related to the interaction over time between the IoT client and network controller.

The remaining sections are organized as follows. Section 2 gives an outline of the related works. Section 3 presents the protocol participants and interaction model, and the underlying threat model. Section 4 presents in detail the proposed protocol. Section 5 presents the protocol evaluation results in terms of performance and security. Finally, Sect. 6 makes some concluding remarks and outlines future work.

2   Related Work

Several proposals have been published on IoT authentication [4,6–8,12,13]. Recent progress in IoT authentication has focused on incorporating context information. Several contributions have been made in incorporating various types of context information, namely physical contexts, personal contexts, device contexts and historical information, among others.

Among these contributions, Kalamandeen et al. [11] presented a system called Ensemble that can offer proximity-based authentication that is based on a set of trusted personal devices in a ubiquitous environment. The authors utilized proximity-based context awareness to authenticate the device. Two proximity-based contexts were considered: time and GPS location.

Hayashi et al. [10] presented a context-aware scalable authentication (CASA) system based on the combination of passive and active authentication factors; they considered only the use of location as context information, representing a passive factor for authentication. However, PIN and password forms were utilized for the active authentication.

3   Authentication Roles and Threat Model

In this section, we present the participants and roles in our proposed authentication model, and discuss the underlying threat model.

3.1   Protocol Participants and Their Interaction Model

Our proposed authentication model relies on fog computing [5] to enhance efficiency and reduce the size of the data transmitted to the cloud for storage, processing and analysis. The proposed authentication protocol involves three different participants: IoT node (N), controller node (CRN) and manufacturer fog node (MFR).

A local IoT network is an interconnection of IoT nodes N, which are constrained devices, and controller nodes CRN which are regular unconstrained devices. While the nodes N can communicate directly with CRN, communication between nodes Ns is subject to CRNs permissions. The MFR, which can be within or outside the local IoT network, is a capable computing device (e.g. gateway, server, smartphone, etc.) that maintains a pre-trust relationship with the IoT nodes. The pre-trust relationship is initially established by the manufacturer by securely storing in the IoT node's memory a manufacturer fog node ID (ID_{MFR}) and master secret key (K_{MFR}). These parameters and other ones, as we are going to see in Sect. 4, are aimed at facilitating the IoT node membership validation process done by MFR.

3.2   Threat Model

Our attacker model is based on the Dolev-Yao threat model [9] and the following assumptions and considerations:

- Since the CRN is not a constrained device, we assume that it is secure and relies upon a set of strong conventional security mechanisms. We presume that an attacker could still compromise the CRN database, but the master secret key (K_{CRN}) is assumed completely beyond the reach of the attacker.
- The attacker can copy, intercept and tamper with the messages transmitted between the nodes.
- The attacker can take control of any IoT node N and access all secret information stored in memory. However, the takeover of N must not endanger the security of the other nodes in the network.

4   Protocol Framework

In this section, we describe our cumulative keyed-hash chain model, and the proposed authentication protocol which relies on it.

4.1   Transaction History Based on Cumulative Chained Hash

At the core of the proposed authentication scheme is a lightweight challenge response that relies on cumulative chained hash. Each node maintains a database containing hashes generated during previous authentication sessions. The authentication challenge will consist of requesting proof of knowledge of some previous entries from the database. Each authentication attempt will be based on a temporary secret key TK_N generated and sent by the node N being authenticated, and shared between N and the CRN.

Let x denote the authentication sequence number corresponding to the previous authentication record stored in the chained hash database for a given node N, and let ^xCH_F denote the corresponding cumulative hash value. To initiate a new request for authentication, the node N starts by generating the authentication message $H_F = h(H_0, TK_N, ^xCH_F)$, obtained by hashing the cumulative hash value (previously) stored in the hash-chain database, the shared secret key TK_N between N and CRN, and the hash of some authentication parameters sent by the node denoted H_0. Next, the node N will send to CRN, the authentication message consisting of the combination of H_F and the authentication parameters. Finally, the cumulative hash $^{x+1}CH_F = h(H_F, TK_N)$ is generated by hashing H_F and TK_N and stored in the database. Figure 1(a) summarizes the above cumulative chained-hash steps at the IoT node.

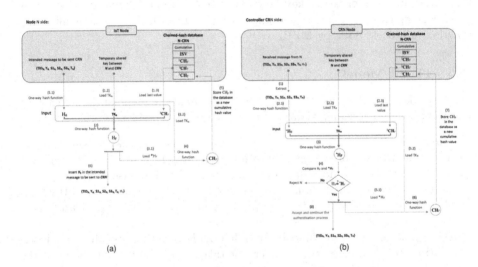

Fig. 1. Cumulative chained-hash process.

On the receiving side, the CRN applies the same technique to check the authenticity of the received message; Fig. 1(b) summarizes the steps involved in this process. The CRN extracts the received message parameters (i.e. without H_F) and generates a hash denoted H_0. Next, it generates the hash $^*H_F = h(H_0, TK_N, ^xCH_F)$, combining H_0, the cumulative hash previously stored in the CRN chained-hash database, and the shared secret key between itself and N. Then it compares $^*H_F$ and H_F, and if there is a match it will authenticate the sending node N, and it will generate a hash of the resultant value again with the shared secret key and store the obtained value in the hash-chain database, as $^{x+1}CH_F = h(H_F, TK_N)$. Otherwise, if the values do not match, the authentication of node N will fail.

An obvious threat to the above mentioned scheme is if the attacker can find out the database entries, in particular the first entry, then she would simply need knowledge of the shared secret key to compromise corresponding step in the protocol. However, such threat is mitigated by the fact that the secret key is temporary and changes. Even if the attacker was able to compromise the secret key of the first hash, such information will be useless due to the fact the key is valid only for one session.

4.2 Challenge-Response Mechanism Based on Transaction History

As aforementioned in the previous section, N and CRN store and keep all cumulative hash values ^xCH_F in their synchronized chained-hash database N-CRN. These values can be utilized to introduce a historical factor for authenticating IoT nodes as illustrated in Fig. 2. Authentication using history factor ensures mutual authentication through a challenge-response scheme and the mutual authentication is of high importance in IoT node-to-node authentication. This two-way challenge/response allows the controller to check the authenticity of the IoT node, and the IoT node to ensure that it is not communicating with a malicious controller. Cumulative hash history-based authentication counts on the ability of the IoT node and controller to show proof of knowledge of past cumulative hash values. The approach involves tracking and storing securely the cumulative hash values related to the interaction over time between the IoT node N and the controller CRN. In this process, when CRN receives an authentication request message from N, it starts the authentication process and triggers a challenge/response. CRN generates a challenge c (information about random cumulative hash value ^xCH_F stored previously), hashes the challenge c with the shared secret key and current timestamp $h(TK_N,c, T_{CRN})$, and sends it to N. N sends the response back using $h(TK_N,r, T_N)$, where r is the response (cumulative hash value ^xCH_F) and T_N is a new timestamp for when the response is sent ($T_{CRN} < T_N$). CRN verifies the correctness of the received ^xCH_F value by comparing it with the one stored in its chained-hash database N-CRN. If they are equal, CRN will accept N and resume the authentication process. Otherwise, N will be rejected.

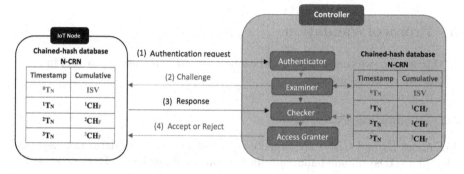

Fig. 2. Historical authentication process.

4.3   Authentication Protocol

Our proposed protocol framework consists of a registration phase and a protocol execution phase, which is broken into two other phases, namely, the initialization and the mutual authentication. During the initialization phase, the system administrator (SA) selects a random master secret key for the CRN denoted K_{CRN}. Initially, the CRN does not have knowledge of these information.

Our protocol framework ensures the enforcement of the security policy between nodes by setting up a virtual domain segregation and restricting nodes capabilities of sending and receiving instructions to or from other nodes. Simply put, our framework allows the IoT system administrators to virtually partition the IoT networks based on the IoT nodes capabilities of sending and receiving instructions, and the scope of interaction between these nodes into different domains during the registration phase. In addition, the capability assignment method complements the virtual domain segregation to strengthen the IoT network security. Device capability is one of the following capabilities: S denotes that the device is a sender, R denotes that the device is a receiver, and H denotes that the device is hybrid (sender and receiver). These two methods complement one another to ensure that if a hacker compromises one device, her/his power will not only be restricted by the virtual domain but also by the device capability. The phases of our framework are explained as follows.

Registration. The SA registers the IoT node N by selecting for it a virtual domain $(VD_N$ and a capability (Ca_N). Then, using the node unique identity (ID_N), the VD_N and the Ca_N, the SA generates three authentication parameters $S1_N = ID_N \oplus h(K_{\mathrm{CRN}}, ID_N)$, $S2_N = K_{\mathrm{CRN}} \oplus S1_N \oplus VD_N$, and $S3_N = Ca_N \oplus h(K_{\mathrm{CRN}}, S2_N)$.

Authentication. The authentication parameters provide a secure way to encapsulate and transmit the key parameters ID_N, Ca_N, VD_N, and TK_N during the authentication process between N and CRN. The use of one-way hash function makes it almost virtually impossible for an attacker to recover these parameters. Node N authenticates with the CRN anonymously by following a number of steps summarized in Fig. 3 and explained in more detail in [1].

5   Protocol Validation

In this section, we conduct the validation of our authentication protocol in terms of efficiency and security.

5.1   Evaluating Performance

IoT nodes (N and CRN) are expected to store two types of data: raw keys and identifiers (IDs) on one hand, and hashes, on the other hand. The raw keys/IDs are encoded over 16 bits, while hashes are 160 bits based on SHA-1 (as an example). Let n and m denote the number of ^xCH_F values and the number of IoT nodes N registered with CRN, respectively, the storage costs for N and CRN are summarized in Table 1.

Table 1. Storage cost for the different nodes

Nodes	Raw keys/IDs	Hashes	Hash-chain	Storage cost
N	ID_N, ID_{CRN}, ID_{MFR}, K_{MFR}	TID_N, $S1_N$, $S2_N$, $S3_N$, TK_N, ^xCH_F	160n bits	$160n + 864$ bits
CRN	ID_N, ID_{MFR}, ID_{CRN}, K_{CRN}, VD_N, Ca_N	TID_N, TK_N, ^xCH_F	160n bits	$80m + 160n + 320$ bits

Communication overheads can be measured based on the message transmitted. N and CRN exchange keys/IDs and hashes, which as indicated above are each 16 bits and 160 bits, respectively. In addition, N and CRN generate and send timestamps, which can be assumed to be 32 bits each.

N sends the tuple (TID_N, ID_{MFR}, PoF, Y_N, $S2_N$, $S3_N$, T_N, H_F). So, the message size for (N $\rightarrow$ CRN) is $6 \times 160 + 32 + 16 = 1008$ bits.

CRN sends to N the tuple (ID_{CRN}, G_{CRN}, T_{CRN}, H_F). So, the message size for (CRN $\rightarrow$ N) is $2 \times 160 + 32 + 16 = 368$ bits.

Our proposed authentication approach achieves low computation cost by using light cryptographic operations, specifically, XOR operation and one-way hash functions. Let T_h and T_{xor} denote the computation times for 1 XOR operation and 1 hash round, respectively. In the proposed scheme, N performs 8 hash invocations and 5 XOR operations, while CRN performs 9 hash invocations and 7 XOR operations.

Considering the triviality of XOR operations, the amount is negligible, so we can assume $T_{xor} \approx 0$. So, the computation costs for N and CRN are as follows, respectively,

$$CompCost(N) = 8 \times T_h + 5 \times T_{xor} \approx 8T_h \tag{1}$$

$$CompCost(CRN) = 9 \times T_h + 7 \times T_{xor} \approx 9 \times T_h \tag{2}$$

In Eq. 1, the IoT node N involves 8 hash and 5 XOR operations, which yield a total computation cost of $8 \times T_h + 5 \times T_{xor}$. In Eq. 2, on the other hand, the controller node CRN performs 9 hash and 7 XOR operations, which yield a total computation cost of $9 \times T_h + 7 \times T_{xor}$. Therefore, the total computation cost of N is $8 \times T_h + 5 \times T_{xor} \approx 8T_h$, while the computation cost of CRN corresponds to $9 \times T_h + 7 \times T_{xor} \approx 9 \times T_h$.

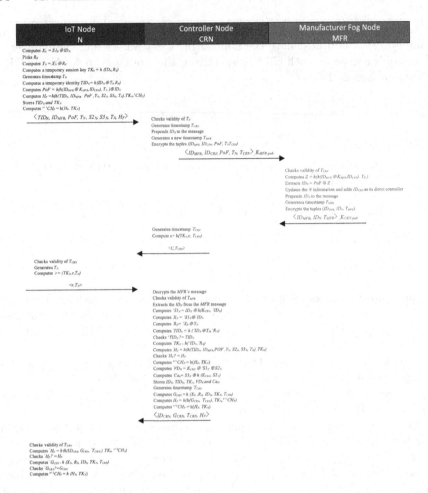

Fig. 3. The authentication and key exchange phase of our protocol for centralized smart home environment.

5.2   Evaluating Security

In this section, we discuss various known attacks and we elaborate how our protocol successfully resists and stops such attacks.

Replay Attack: The replay attack is defeated using timestamps and the temporary secret parameter R_N.

Eavesdropping Attack: This attack is defeated using temporary identity of IoT node TID_N, which changes in every session, and the Y_N, $S2_N$, $S3_N$ parameters, which are constituted of secure parameters that are out of the attacker reach.

Impersonation Attack: This attack is defeated using the TID_N and H_F, which is protected using the one-way hash function of the message parameters.

Man-in-the-middle Attack: Our scheme is protected against this attack using ID_N, R_N, TK_N and H_F.

Attack Against the Temporary Secret Key: This attack is defeated using the temporary secret key TK_N, which changes in every session.

Node Stolen Database Attack: If any IoT node is compromised, the other nodes will not be affected because the K_{CRN} is only used in the registration phase and then destroyed.

Forward/backward Security: Forward/backward security is achieved using the TK_N which dynamically changes with the sessions.

Session Key Guessing Attack: This attack is using the TK_N which dynamically changes in every the session.

5.3 Simulation Based on AVISPA Tool

We have evaluated the proposed authentication protocol using the Automated Validation of Internet Security Protocols and Applications (AVISPA) toolkit [2]. Figure 4 depicts the HLPSL code for role N.

```
%XXXXXXXXXXXXXXXXXXXXXXXXXXXXXXXXXXXXXXXXXXXXXXXXXXXXXXXXXXXXXXXXXXXXXXXXXXXXXXXXXXXXXXXXXXXXXXXXXXXXXXX%
role role_N
(SA:agent,N:agent,CRN:agent,MFR:agent,SK:symmetric_key,IDN,IDCRN,IDMFR,Kmfr:text,H:hash_func,Snd,Rcv:channel(dy))

played_by N

def=
        local
              State:nat,
              S1N,S2N,S3N,TN,XN,RN,YN,TCRN,CaN,VDN,KCRN:text,  TKN,TIDN:hash(text.text),GCRN:hash
(text.text.message.text),POF:message

const secKCRN,secKmfr,secIDN,secCaN,secVDN,secTKN,controller_node:protocol_id
        init
              State := 0
        transition
              2. State=0 /\ Rcv({S1N'.S2N'.S3N'}_SK) =|> State':=1 /\TN':=new()/\ XN':=xor(S1N',IDN)/\RN':=new
()/\YN':=xor(XN',RN')/\TKN' := H(IDN.RN')/\TIDN':= H(xor(IDN,TN').RN')/\POF':= xor(H(H(xor
(IDMFR,Kmfr).IDCRN).TN'),IDN) /\secret(IDN,secIDN,{SA,N,CRN,MFR}) /\ secret(KCRN,secKCRN,{SA,CRN}) /\ secret
(Kmfr,secKmfr,{N,MFR})/\secret (CaN,secCaN,{SA,CRN})/\secret (VDN,secVDN,{SA,CRN})/\ Snd
(IDCRN.IDMFR.POF'.TIDN'.S2N'.S3N'.YN'.TN')/\secret (TKN,secTKN,{N,CRN})
              6.State=1 /\ Rcv(GCRN'.TCRN')=|> State':=2 /\GCRN':=H(XN.IDN.TKN.TCRN')/\request
(N,CRN,controller_node,GCRN)/\secret(KCRN,secKCRN,{SA,CRN}) /\ secret (Kmfr,secKmfr,{N,MFR})/\secret (CaN,secCaN,
{SA,CRN})/\secret (VDN,secVDN,{SA,CRN})/\secret (TKN,secTKN,{N,CRN})/\secret(IDN,secIDN,{SA,N,CRN,MFR})

end role
%XXXXXXXXXXXXXXXXXXXXXXXXXXXXXXXXXXXXXXXXXXXXXXXXXXXXXXXXXXXXXXXXXXXXXXXXXXXXXXXXXXXXXXXXXXXXXXXXXXXXXXX%
```

Fig. 4. HLPSL code for role IoT Node played by N

We conducted the simulation using two widely-accepted back-end model checkers of AVISPA: the On-the-Fly Model-Checker (OFMC) and the Constraint-Logic-based Attack Searcher (CL-AtSe).

Figure 5 presents the CL-AtSe back-end checker report that assures that our scheme is SAFE and satisfies all the specified security goals.

Figure 6 presents the OFMC back-end checker report, which shows that our scheme is SAFE, thus meeting the specified security goals.

However, since we use the XOR operation, we were not able to use the TA4SP back-end checker owing to its limitation in supporting XOR operation, while The SATMC model checker has reported NOT SUPPORTED.

Fig. 5. CL-AtSe validation results.

Fig. 6. OFMC validation results.

6   Conclusion

We have proposed in the current paper a new secure lightweight authentication protocol for IoT nodes that uses temporary identities and secret session keys, which change every session and are exchanged in an unlinkable manner, and leverage cumulative hash-chain. The session key is used to encrypt and decrypt the data flow between the IoT nodes and the controller. The session key will be changed after every session, and this ensures that the data in transit will be safe every time. Performance and security analysis of the proposed scheme were conducted showing that it achieves relatively low footprint and is secure against known attack methods. Our future work will consist of extending the protocol to consider cases where the IoT node leaves one particular home network and joins another network. We will also implement the proposed scheme using Cooja contikia, which is an open source operating system for the IoT, and we will interface Cooja with an attack platform such as Kali to try various attacks against the system.

References

1. Alshahrani, M., Traore, I.: Secure mutual authentication and automated access control for IoT smart home using cumulative keyed-hash chain. J. Inf. Secur. Appl. **45**, 156–175 (2019). https://doi.org/10.1016/j.jisa.2019.02.003

2. Armando, A., et al.: The AVISPA tool for the automated validation of internet security protocols and applications. In: Etessami, K., Rajamani, S.K. (eds.) CAV 2005. LNCS, vol. 3576, pp. 281–285. Springer, Heidelberg (2005). https://doi.org/10.1007/11513988_27

3. Ashibani, Y., Kauling, D., Mahmoud, Q.H.: A context-aware authentication service for smart homes. In: 14th IEEE Annual Consumer Communications & Networking Conference (CCNC), pp. 588–589. IEEE, January 2017

4. Barbareschi, M., Bagnasco, P., Mazzeo, A.: Authenticating IOT devices with physically unclonable functions models. In: 10th International Conference on P2P, Parallel, Grid, Cloud and Internet Computing (3PGCIC), pp. 563–567. IEEE, November 2015

5. Bonomi, F., Milito, R., Zhu, J., Addepalli, S.: Fog computing and its role in the Internet of Things. In: Proceedings of the First Edition of the MCC Workshop on Mobile Cloud Computing, pp. 13–16. ACM, August 2012

6. Chu, F., Zhang, R., Ni, R., Dai, W.: An improved identity authentication scheme for Internet of Things in heterogeneous networking environments. In: 16th International Conference on Network-Based Information Systems (NBiS), pp. 589–593. IEEE, September 2013

7. Desai, D., Upadhyay, H.: Security and privacy consideration for Internet of Things in smart home environments. Int. J. Eng. Res. Dev. 10(11), 73–83 (2014)

8. Dorri, A., Kanhere, S.S., Jurdak, R., Gauravaram, P.: Blockchain for IoT security and privacy: the case study of a smart home. In: 2017 IEEE International Conference on Pervasive Computing and Communications Workshops (PerCom Workshops), pp. 618–623. IEEE, March 2017

9. Dolev, D., Yao, A.: On the security of public key protocols. IEEE Trans. Inf. Theory 29(2), 198–208 (1983)

10. Hayashi, E., Das, S., Amini, S., Hong, J., Oakley, I.: CASA: context-aware scalable authentication. In: Proceedings of the Ninth Symposium on Usable Privacy and Security, p. 3. ACM, July 2013

11. Kalamandeen, A., Scannell, A., de Lara, E., Sheth, A., LaMarca, A.: Ensemble: cooperative proximity-based authentication. In: Proceedings of the 8th International Conference on Mobile Systems, Applications, and Services, pp. 331–344. ACM, June 2010

12. Moosavi, S.R., et al.: SEA: a secure and efficient authentication and authorization architecture for IoT-based healthcare using smart gateways. Procedia Comput. Sci. 52, 452–459 (2015)

13. Park, G., Kim, B., Jun, M.: A design of secure authentication method using zero knowledge proof in smart-home environment. In: Park, J.J.J.H., Pan, Y., Yi, G., Loia, V. (eds.) CSA/CUTE/UCAWSN-2016. LNEE, vol. 421, pp. 215–220. Springer, Singapore (2017). https://doi.org/10.1007/978-981-10-3023-9_35

Towards Privacy-Aware Smart Surveillance

Emil Shirima[1] and Kambiz Ghazinour[1,2]([✉])

[1] Department of Computer Science, Kent State University, Kent 44240, USA
eshirima@kent.edu
[2] Center for Criminal Justice, Intelligence and Cybersecurity,
State University of New York, Canton 13617, USA
ghazinourk@canton.edu

Abstract. Cameras are rapidly becoming a daily part of our lives. Their constant streaming of information about people gives rise to different security and privacy concerns. Human analysis using cameras or surveillance footage has been an active field of research. Different methods have been introduced which showed success in both the detection and tracking of pedestrians. Once a human is detected and/or tracked, different motion analyses can be performed in order to better understand and model human behavior. A majority of these methods do not take user privacy or security into account, making security monitoring systems a significant threat to individuals' privacy. This threat becomes more serious and evident when the security cameras are installed in places where vulnerable people (e.g. elders, children) frequently spend time such as day-cares, schools, retirement homes, or violated to serve independent interests. This work presents a model that is able to understand human motion, and deploys an anonymization technique that facilitates the preservation of an individual's privacy and security.

Keywords: Privacy · Surveillance · Convolutional Neural Networks

1 Introduction

There have been significant concerns about the invasive nature of using digital technologies such as digital cameras, smart phones, and surveillance systems to our privacy. The recent widespread adoption of video surveillance systems is to ensure the general safety of both public and private areas of communities. These systems collect a massive amount of information which implies a direct threat to individuals' privacy and their right to preserve their personal information. In 2009, in the United States alone, there was an estimated 30 million surveillance cameras deployed, recording about 4 billion hours of video per week [12]. This massive amount of stored information can be used to create profiles of people. The power of the information held by video surveillance systems was exemplified in an experiment conducted by a BBC reporter in China [7] to determine how

© Springer Nature Switzerland AG 2020
A. Benzekri et al. (Eds.): FPS 2019, LNCS 12056, pp. 398–406, 2020.
https://doi.org/10.1007/978-3-030-45371-8_28

long it would take the system to identify him (reporter) in the crowded streets of Guiyang. It only took a mere 7 min for the system to pick him out and track his movements along the streets. At the time of the experiment, China had 170 million video surveillance systems, but plans were in place to add 400 million more by 2020. Most of these systems are put in place under the guise of "protecting the Public". In the cases where the systems actually assist in stopping a crime, or apprehending a criminal, it is a victory to the system. But what about the 99% of the time when they are just collecting information when no crime has been committed?

The major problem with the current surveillance systems is their design philosophy. Whatever the camera sees, it is simply displayed back to the operator as is without any form of anonymization applied. In turn, this leaves observed parties' privacy information exposed and at the mercy of the operator. In an attempt to change this, the European Union enforced the General Data Protection Regulation (GDPR) [11]. This work proposes a way of anonymizing video data in a manner that hides users privacy information such as face, body, gender, ethnicity, etc., and the video's utility is still preserved i.e. one can still infer the activities taking place.

2   Background

2.1   Action Recognition in Videos

A video is comprised of both spatial and temporal information. The spatial component provides a general description of the scene as a whole along with the illustrated objects. On the other hand, the temporal component relays motion information across frames. Current research attempts to better capture and represent spatio-temporal information from videos by extracting useful features that can be used to correctly understand the actions taking place.

Since video can be fragmented into spatial and temporal components, Simonyan, Zisserman proposed a *Two-stream convolutional networks for action recognition in videos* [8]. A spatial stream is responsible for capturing general scene information along with the objects while the temporal stream is responsible for motion representation. The spatial stream Convolutional Neural Network (CNN) operates on individual 224 × 224 frames while stacked optical flow displacement fields across several consecutive frames are fed as input into the temporal stream. Each stream works independent of the other with their results fused together to produce a final class score.

This notion of breaking a video into separate components and addressing each of them respectively was further extended by Wang et al. with the proposition of a *Three-stream CNN for action recognition* [13]. The proposed two-stream architecture [8] consisted of learned image CNN features along with temporal CNN features derived from locally computed optical flows. Wang et al. extended this architecture by including a separate third stream to compute the global temporal features of a video. Global motion features were accumulated in a template form called Motion Stacked Difference Image (MSDI). A soft Vector of Locally Aggregated Descriptors is used to represent the extracted features.

In spite the successes of the various stream networks, they are complex in nature, require a lot of pre-processing (calculating optical flow, motion history or energy images), and take a lot of time to train. Although the temporal stream(s) take in multiple frames as input, 2D convolutions were performed on them thus temporal information is lost after the first convolutional layer. Karpathy et al. proposed a *Slow Fusion* model [4] that attempted to preserve temporal information along convolutional layers of a network. Instead of using 2D convolutions at each layer, 3D convolutions were used to preserve the temporal information. Although 3D convolutions were only used on the first three layers of the network, it outperformed the other studied models.

Ji et al. proposed *3D Convolutional Neural Networks for Human Action Recognition* [3] capable of capturing spatial and temporal features simultaneously without decomposing the video into streams. The architecture consisted of one hard-wired layer, three convolution layers, two sub-sampling layers, and one full connected layer for classification. To evaluate the effectiveness of the model, it was compared to a frame-based 2D CNN, along with four other methods that build spatial pyramid matching features from local features. Overall, the 3D CNN model outperformed other methods consistently. The model was designed to recognize three actions namely *CellToEar*, *ObjectPut*, and *Pointing* from TRECVID [10].

2.2   Privacy Preservation in Videos

The rise in smart video surveillance systems poses a huge risk to the privacy of observed parties. The data collected by such systems can easily be misused if counter-measures are not put in place. When designed with care and privacy in mind, these systems can still be just as powerful. From a privacy protection standpoint, video data should only be accessed in an anonymized manner until a qualified operator determines it is necessary to access the unanonymized video. [14] proposed a clearance-based surveillance system. An RFID tag coupled with an XML-based policy engine is used to determine one's clearance. In the event of an authorized person, the foreground is extracted from each frame, compressed and encrypts the privacy information as a regular video bit-stream denoted as ρ_1. The background model then fills in the void left behind by the foreground and the resulting video is compressed into another bit-stream, ρ_2 with ρ_1 embedded as a watermark. Pramateftakis et al.'s method of surveillance video authentication [6] was adapted to authenticate ρ_2 against any form of tampering.

3   Proposed Framework

The reviewed state-of-the-art models are capable of recognizing human actions in videos but were trained without user privacy in mind. The data necessary to train these models comprised of unanonymized videos which consisted of users' privacy information. This information ranged from directly identifiable information such as face, gender, ethnicity, to derivable privacy information such as age. On the other hand, different anonymization techniques for video footage were reviewed but most of them either required extra hardware such as RFID sensors or were not able to find a good balance between anonymization and video utility. This section aims to explain the proposed solution to this challenge. It proposes an architecture capable of anonymizing the privacy information of users while retaining video utility. Next, it presents a model trained on the anonymized footage capable of recognizing actions taking place in the video. Section 3.1 reviews the anonymization technique adapted for the proposed action classification model in Sect. 3.2.

3.1   Human Pose Estimation

Human pose estimation (HPE) is the process of approximating the body's config-uration from an image. A skeleton is used to provide a graphical representation of the person's orientation. This skeleton is essentially a set of coordinates that can be connected to describe someone's pose. Each coordinate in the skeleton is referred to as a part, a key-point, or joint. A valid connection between two parts or key-points is known as a limb or pair.

The proposed work builds on the bottom-up approach proposed by Cao et al. where they proposed a *Real-time Multi-Person 2D Pose Estimation using Part Affinity Fields* [1]. The image is first normalized from $[0, 255]$ to $[-1, 1]$ and fed into the VGG-19 [9] network. The VGG-19 network outputs image features which are then passed into the two-branch Convolutional Pose Machine (CPM) that simultaneously predicts confidence maps and part affinity fields.

3.2   Classification Model

The proposed model takes in video feed consisting of human pose skeletons and produces a classification score of the actions taking place. Human pose skeletons have less textural information compared to standard images. As a result, a deep network architecture is not necessary. The proposed network consists of six 3D convolutional layers divided into three blocks, and two fully-connected layers as seen in Fig. 1. The network takes in 15 normalized RGB frames of size 120×120 as input. All convolution and pooling operations are performed in 3D with a stride of 1 and kernels of size $3 \times 3 \times 3$. Images are fully padded in both the convolutional and pooling layers in order to preserve the size.

The model is trained in 40 epochs with an initial learning rate of 0.002. With this initial value, the network is able to quickly make updates to its weights which allows it to rapidly learn new features. This is a desired phenomena initially since the model is trying to learn distinctive features of each category, but it can also lead to over-fitting or result into the network not learning at all as the training continues. To avoid this, the learning rate is reduced after every three epochs by a factor of 0.5 if the validation accuracy did not improve. Lowering the learning rate allows for the network weights to be updated less frequently

Privacy Aware Model

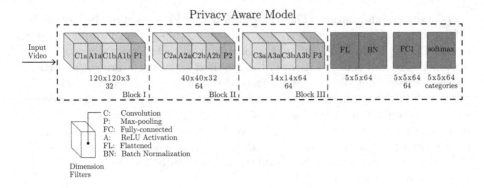

Fig. 1. Proposed privacy aware model for human action classification in videos.

which in turn leads to the network learning distinctive categorical features hence faster convergence. Lowering the learning rate leads to a slower learning process thus a minimum learning rate is set to 10^{-10}. Nadam [2] optimizer is used to calculate the model's error during training.

3.3   Dataset Preparation

The proposed model is trained on the HMDB51 [5] dataset.

HMDB51. This dataset comprises of more than 600 videos consisting of a different number of people performing 51 distinct actions. Five actions were chosen to train the model namely *climb stairs, hit, pick, run, shake hands*. The videos were first re-sized to 120×120 then fed as input to the CPM proposed by Cao et al. in [1] in order to extract human pose skeletons. For the purpose of preserving privacy, all human information (except for the pose) is removed from the video. Along with this, the video background is also removed in order to attain total anonymity. Upon completion, all categories consist of videos with only pose skeletons to represent actions taking place. Due to the nature of the video, some produced either poor or inadequate skeletons. For example some videos consisted of people performing actions with certain parts of their body obfuscated, such as being seated at a dinner table. In this scenario, the upper half of their bodies were visible but not the lower half. Some actions in videos were done in a mass setting thus resulting in mismatched body part pairings. Other videos consisted of multiple actions taking place in a single video. A few of the videos had poor lightning or the action was shot at a bad angle which resulted in no or poor skeletons produced. As a result, videos that exhibited such phenomena were either edited or completely deleted from the training set. With the pre-processing complete, the training set comprised of 157 videos. 31 videos were in the *climb stairs* category, 35 videos in *hit*, *pick* comprised of 33 videos, 35 videos in *run*, and 22 videos in *shake hands*.

4   Results

In order to evaluate the model, it was trained from scratch only on the HMDB51 dataset. This configuration provided a benchmark of the model's performance.

4.1   HMDB51

Since a small subset of the original HMDB51 dataset was used for this work, the initial network design was small in order to avoid over-fitting. The design of the convolutional blocks was preserved but the number of neurons in $FC1$ was halved to 32 neurons. The results of this model are shown in Fig. 2.

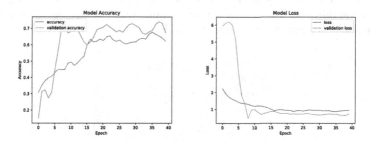

Fig. 2. Results of proposed model configured with $FC1 = 32$

From epoch 1 to 5, both the training and validation losses are decreasing. The validation loss drops more drastically during this stage compared to the training loss. From epoch 5 to 15, the train loss is still gradually decreasing but the validation loss has not changed as much. It spikes around the tenth epoch but evens out. Both losses experience minimal changes for the remainder of the training time. Due to the drastic fall in validation loss during the first five epochs, its accuracy experiences a short increment. Then it sharply increases until the tenth epoch. On the other hand, even though the training accuracy is rising, the gap between two is an early indication of the model under-fitting. The validation accuracy then experiences some fluctuations, but it stays above the training accuracy for the remainder of the training time. The initial model configuration i.e. $FC1 = 32$, under-fits the HMDB51 dataset. To solve this, the network was expanded to include the proposed 64 neurons and results are shown in Fig. 3.

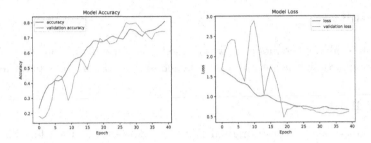

Fig. 3. Results of proposed model

With the increase in neurons, the model was able to attain a better generalization of the dataset. The model was tested on two separate batches of unseen video data and the results are presented in Fig. 4.

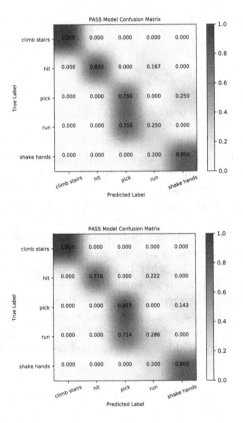

Fig. 4. HMDB51 confusion matrix

In both scenarios, the model was able to correctly predict the actions *climb stairs*, *hit*, *pick*, and *shake hands* with more than 75% confidence. The *run* action posed to be a challenge for the model. In both tests, more than 70% of the videos were wrongly classified into the *pick* category. This shows that the model was not able to fully learn the distinguishing features between the *run* and *pick* action category. A peek into the *pick* category videos revealed the presence of videos which consisted of persons running either before or after performing the action. Nevertheless, from these results, it is evident that the model struggles distinguishing correlated/overlapping actions.

5   Conclusion

This work proposes an initial first step towards privacy-aware surveillance. The proposed framework is capable of fully hiding people's privacy information in such a manner that the actions can still be inferred. A model that takes in human pose skeletons as input is proposed and evaluated. The model is tested on a subset of the HMDB51 dataset and performs rather well. In spite of this, several observations were made. Initially, the model suffered from both under-fitting and over-fitting and amendments had to be made to the original design. The model failed to distinguish activities which were closely related such as *pick* and *run*.

The proposed framework can be improvised by applying data augmentation during training. Different augmentations such as color inversion, Gaussian blur, rotate, re-size, center crop, translation, flips (vertical and horizontal), down-sample, up-sampling, can be applied to increase the dataset size during training thus assisting in learning distinguishing features between closely related actions. Transfer learning can be applied to boost the model's accuracy. The weights of a large model such as VGG-19 [9] can be used to instantiate the proposed model's weights. Motion-capturing methods such as optical flow can be incorporated into the training data to represent motion.

References

1. Cao, Z., Simon, T., Wei, S.-E., Yaser, S.: Realtime multi-person 2D pose estimation using part affinity fields. CoRR abs/1611.08050 (2016)
2. Dozat, T.: Incorporating Nesterov Momentum into Adam (2016)
3. Ji, S., Xu, W., Yang, M., Yu, K.: 3D Convolutional neural networks for human action recognition. IEEE Trans. Pattern Anal. Mach. Intell. **35**(1), 221–231 (2013)
4. Karpathy, A., Toderici, G., Shetty, S., Leung, T., Sukthankar, R., Fei-Fei, L.: Large-scale video classification with convolutional neural networks. In: 2014 IEEE Conference on Computer Vision and Pattern Recognition, June 2014, pp. 1725–1732 (2014)
5. Kuehne, H., Jhuang, H., Garrote, E., Poggio, T., Serre, T.: HMDB: a large video database for human motion recognition. In: Proceedings of the International Conference on Computer Vision (ICCV) (2011)

6. Pramateftakis, A., Oelbaum, T., Diepold, K.: Authentication of MPEG-4-based surveillance video. In: 2004 International Conference on Image Processing, ICIP 2004, October 2004, vol. 1, pp. 33–37 (2004)

7. Russell, J.: In Your Face: China's All-Seeing State, December 2017

8. Simonyan, K., Zisserman, A.: Two-stream convolutional networks for action recognition in videos. CoRR. 2014. abs/1406.2199

9. Simonyan, K., Zisserman, A.: Very deep convolutional networks for large-scale image recognition. arXiv:1409.1556 (2014)

10. Smeaton, A.F., Over, P., Kraaij, W.: Evaluation campaigns and TRECVid. In: MIR 2006: Proceedings of the 8th ACM International Workshop on Multimedia Information Retrieval, pp. 321–330. ACM Press, New York (2006)

11. Smith, J.: Data Protection, November 2016

12. Vlahos, J.: Surveillance Society: New High-Tech Cameras Are Watching You, November 2017

13. Wang, L., Ge, L., Li, R., Fang, Y.: Three-stream CNNs for action recognition. Pattern Recogn. Lett. VI. **92**(C), 33–40 (2017)

14. Zhang, W., Cheung, S.S., Chen, M.: Hiding privacy information in video surveillance system. In: IEEE International Conference on Image Processing, September 2005, vol. 3, pp. II-868 (2005)

Author Index

Printed in the United States
by Baker & Taylor Publisher Services

Printed in the United States
By Bookmasters